NCERT MATHEMATICS

REVISION WORK BOOK

Most Effective Revision
& Concept Zipper for >>>>

JEE & CUET

Vol 2 CLASS XII

NCERT MATHEMATICS

REVISION WORK BOOK

Most Effective Revision
& Concept Zipper for >>>>

JEE & CUET

Vol 2 CLASS XII

Authors
Naveen Kumar
Sandeep Singh

ARIHANT PRAKASHAN SERIES, MEERUT

卐 **Administrative & Production Offices**

Regd. Office
'Ramchhaya' 4577/15, Agarwal Road, Darya Ganj, New Delhi -110002
Tele: 011- 47630600, 43518550

卐 **Head Office**
Kalindi, TP Nagar, Meerut (UP) - 250002
Tel: 0121-7156203, 7156204

卐 **Sales & Support Offices**
Agra, Ahmedabad, Bengaluru, Bareilly, Chennai, Delhi, Guwahati, Hyderabad, Jaipur, Jhansi, Kolkata, Lucknow, Nagpur & Pune.

卐 **PRICE** ₹310.00

卐 **PO No :** TXT-59-T061769-11-24

Published by Arihant Publications (India) Ltd.

For further information about the books published by Arihant, log on to www.arihantbooks.com or e-mail at info@arihantbooks.com

Follow us on   

Super 6

ADVANTAGES OF REVISION WORK BOOKS

1. Learn with fun while practicing with Self Assessment.
2. Different question types are helpful in increasing the learning and understanding about **Core Concepts** and **Conceptual Applications**.
3. Small methodical question using real life situation also help in **enhancing visualisation**.
4. Innovative style of practice in Workbook manner helps in breaking the monotonicity of subject.
5. Complete sync with NCERT along with **Competition Connect** and **Competition Edge Up** helps in building the foundation for the preparation of competitions like JEE and CUET.
6. Questions with one word or maximum one sentence long answers are very helpful in **Faster Revision** and **Confidence Boost Up**.

FAB 4 *Features*

NCERT Tracker
Every topic is tagged with NCERT page numbers for better syncing with NCERT.

TOPIC 1
Types of Relations

1. Let A be the set of all students of a school, then the relation R in A given by $R = \{(a, b) : a \text{ is father of } b\}$ is the ______________________ relation.
2. Read the following statements and answer the question.
   Statement I A relation R in a set A is called empty relation, if no element of A is related to any element of A i.e. $R = \phi \subset A \times A$.
   Statement II A relation R in a set A is called universal relation, if each element of A is related to every element of A i.e. $R = A \times A$.

***12.** What should be included in the relation $R = \{(1, 1), (2, 2), (3, 3), (1, 2), (2, 3)\}$ from the set $\{1, 2, 3\}$ so that R is an equivalence relation?

____

***13.** The relation R in the set Z of integers given by $R = \{(x, y) : x + y \text{ is an even number}\}$ is not an equivalence relation.

True ☐ False ☐

Important Concept Tagging
Every question which is based on the important concept from JEE & CUET point of view is marked with *.

COMPETITION CONNECT

Competition Connect
Supplement Containing related portions of old NCERT which are present in JEE/CUET syllabus but removed from latest NCERT.

Properties of Inverse Trigonometric Functions [NCERT (Old) Pg. 42-54]

1. State True or False.

(i) $\sin^{-1}\dfrac{1}{x} = \operatorname{cosec}^{-1} x$, iff $x \le 1$ or $x \ge -1$

True ☐ False ☐

(ii) $\cos^{-1}\dfrac{1}{x} = \sec^{-1} x$, iff $x \ge 1$ or $x \le -1$

True ☐ False ☐

(iii) $\tan^{-1}\dfrac{1}{x} = \cot^{-1} x$ is true, iff $x > 0$

True ☐ False ☐

COMPETITION EDGE UP

1. Let $[t]$ be the greatest integer less than or equal to t. Let A be the set of all prime factors of 2310 and $f : A \to Z$ be the function $f(x) = \left[\log_2\left(x^2 + \left[\dfrac{x^3}{5}\right]\right)\right]$.
The number of one-to-one functions from A to the range of f is **[JEE Main 2024]**

(a) 20 ☐
(b) 25 ☐
(c) 24 ☐
(d) 120 ☐

3. Let a relation R on N × N be defined as: $(x_1, y_1) R (x_2, y_2)$ if and only if $x_1 \le x_2$ or $y_1 \le y_2$. **[JEE Main 2024]**
Consider the two statements :
I : R is reflexive but not symmetric.
II : R is transitive
Then, which one of the following is true?

(a) Only I is correct. ☐
(b) Only II is correct. ☐
(c) Neither I nor II is correct. ☐
(d) Both I and II are correct. ☐

Competition edge up
Selected PYQs in Sync with NCERT Chapter.

CONTENTS

Chapter 01

Relations and Functions

1. Let A be the set of all students of a school, then the relation R in A given by $R = \{(a, b) : a \text{ is father of } b\}$ is the ________________ relation.

2. Read the following statements and answer the question.

Statement I A relation R in a set A is called empty relation, if no element of A is related to any element of A i.e. $R = \phi \subset A \times A$.

Statement II A relation R in a set A is called universal relation, if each element of A is related to every element of A i.e. $R = A \times A$.

(a) Only Statement I is true
(b) Only Statement II is true
(c) Both statements are true
(d) Both statements are false

3. The number of set of elements of the relation $R = \{(a, b) :$ the product of a and b end with zero$\}$ in the set $A = \{x \in Z : 1 \le x \le 9\}$ is ________________

***4.** Determine whether each of the following relations are reflexive, symmetric and transitive.

(i) Let A be the set of all human beings in a town with R a relation in A given by $R = \{(x, y) : x$ is exactly five years younger than $y\}$.

(ii) Relation R in the set N of natural numbers defined as $R = \{(x, y) : y = 2x + 5 \text{ and } x < 4\}$.

(iii) The relation R in the set $\{1, 2, 3, 4\}$ given by $R = \{(1, 1), (2, 2), (3, 3), (4, 4), (1, 2), (2, 1), (2, 3), (3, 2)\}$.

(iv) Relation R in the set A of human beings in a town at a particular time given by $R = \{(x, y) : x \text{ is mother of } y\}$.

(v) Relation in set $A = \{1, 2, 3 \ldots 13, 14\}$ defined by $R = \{(x, y) : 9x - 3y = 0\}$.

*Concepts of all questions bearing * are important for JEE & CUET*

(vi) Relation in N defined as $R = \{(x, y) : y = x + 1, x \le 4\}$.

(vii) Relation in set $A = \{1, 2, 3, 4, 5, 6\}$ defined as $R = \{(x, y) : y$ is divisible by $x\}$.

***5.** If $A = \{1, 2, 3, 4\}$, then define relations on A, which have properties of being

(i) reflexive, transitive but not symmetric.

(ii) symmetric but neither reflexive nor transitive.

(iii) reflexive, symmetric and transitive.

***6.** Give an example of a relation, which is

(i) symmetric but neither reflexive nor transitive.

(ii) transitive but neither reflexive nor symmetric.

(iii) reflexive and symmetric but not transitive.

(iv) symmetric and transitive but not reflexive.

7. What type of relation is 'more than' in the set of real numbers?

(a) Only symmetric (b) Only transitive

(c) Only reflexive (d) Equivalence

8. Relation R in the set Z of all integers defined as $R = \{(x, y) : 2x + 3y$ is an integer$\}$.

Statement I The relation is symmetric.

Statement II The relation is reflexive.

Statement III The relation is transitive.

Statement IV The relation is equivalence.

(a) Only Statement I is correct (b) Statements I and II are correct

(c) Statements II and III are correct (d) Only Statement IV is correct

***9.** The relation R in the set R of real numbers defined by $R = \{(a, b) : a < b^2\}$ is an equivalence relation.

True ☐ False ☐

***10.** The relation R defined in the set A of all quadrilateral as $R = \{(Q_1, Q_2) :$ the diagonals of Q_1 and Q_2 are equal in length$\}$, is an equivalence relation.

True ☐ False ☐

***11.** Let L be the set of all lines, then the relation R in L defined as $R = \{(m, n) :$ the lines m and n lie on the same plane$\}$ is an

(a) only symmetric (b) only transitive

(c) only reflexive (d) equivalence

***12.** What should be included in the relation $R = \{(1, 1), (2, 2), (3, 3), (1, 2), (2, 3)\}$ from the set $\{1, 2, 3\}$ so that R is an equivalence relation?

***13.** The relation R in the set Z of integers given by $R = \{(x, y) : x + y$ is an even number$\}$ is not an equivalence relation.

True ☐ False ☐

***14.** S is a relation over the set R of all real numbers and it is given by $(a, b) \in S \Leftrightarrow ab \geq 0$. Then, S is

(a) symmetric and transitive only

(b) reflexive and symmetric only

(c) only symmetric relation

(d) an equivalence relation

***15.** The relation R on the set Z of all integers defined by $(x, y) \in R \Leftrightarrow (x - y)$ is multiple of 5 is an equivalence relation.

True ☐ False ☐

***16.** For integers x and y, we write $xRy \Leftrightarrow x - y + \sqrt{2}$ is an irrational number. Then, the relation R is not an equivalence relation.

True ☐ False ☐

***17.** Which one of the following relations on R is an equivalence relation?

(a) $aR_1 b \Leftrightarrow a$ is the son of b

(b) $aR_2 b \Leftrightarrow a$ is perpendicular to b

(c) $aR_3 b \Leftrightarrow a \geq b$

(d) $aR_4 b \Leftrightarrow |a| = |b|$

---

18. The number of equivalence relations defined in the set $S = \{a, b, c\}$ is ________

19. Let R_1 be a relation from $A = \{1, 3, 5, 7\}$ to $B = \{2, 4, 6, 8\}$ and R_2 be another relation from B to $C = \{1, 2, 3, 4\}$ as defined below

Statement I An element x in A is related to an element y in B (under R_1) if $x + y$ is divisible by 3.

Statement II An element x in B is related to an element y in C (under R_2) if $x + y$ is even but not divisible by 3.

Which is the composite relation $R_1 o R_2$ from A to C?

(a) $\{(1, 2), (1, 4), (3, 3), (5, 4), (7, 3)\}$ (b) $\{(1, 2), (1, 3), (3, 2), (5, 2), (7, 3)\}$

(c) $\{(1, 2), (3, 2), (3, 4), (5, 4), (7, 2)\}$ (d) $\{(3, 2), (3, 4), (5, 1), (5, 3), (7, 1)\}$

***20.** Let $A = \{1, 2, 3, 4, 5\}$ and R be the equivalence relation on $A \times A$ defined by $(a, b)\ R\ (c, d)$, if $ac = bd$. Find the equivalence class (1, 2).

TOPIC 2

Types of Functions

NCERT Pg 7-10

21. Which of the following figure is not a function?

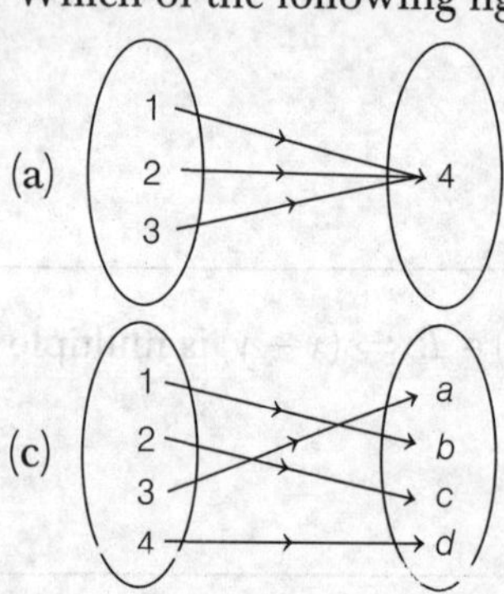

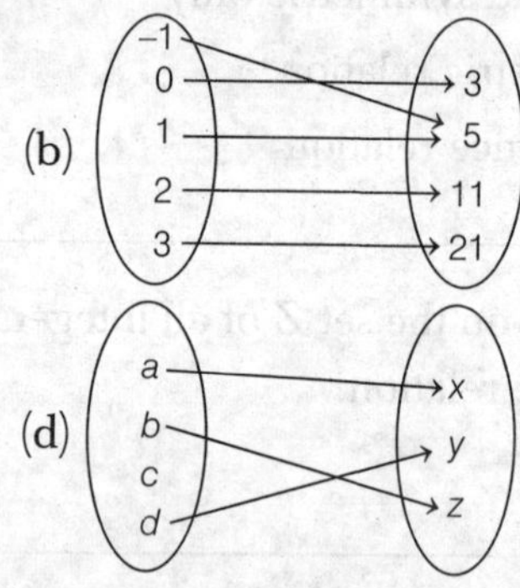

22. Let A and B are two non-empty sets and f is a function such that $f : A \times B \to B \times A$ such that $f(a, b) = (b, a)$ is a one-one function.

True ☐ False ☐

23. Let $A = \{1, 3, 4\}$ and $B = \{x, y, z\}$ and let $f = \{(1, y), (3, z), (M, x)\}$ be a function from A to B. For the function f to be one-one and onto, the value of M is ________

***24.** Check the injectivity and surjectivity of the following functions.

(i) $f : R \to R$ given by $f(x) = x^6$

(ii) $f : R \to R$ given by $f(x) = 3 - 4x$

(iii) $f : R \to R$ given by $f(x) = (x - 1)(x - 2)(x - 3)$

(iv) $f : N \to N$ given by $f(x) = n - (-1)^n, \forall n \in N$

25. The function $f: R \rightarrow R$ defined by $f(x) = \frac{1}{x^2}$ is one-one and onto.

True ☐ False ☐

26. For the function $f: R \rightarrow R$.

(i) The greatest integer function $f(x) = [x]$ is neither one-one nor onto.

True ☐ False ☐

(ii) The modulus function $f(x) = |x|$ is neither one-one nor onto.

True ☐ False ☐

(iii) The signum function is neither one-one nor onto.

True ☐ False ☐

27. Let $f: A \rightarrow B$ be a function defined such that $n(A) = n(B)$.

(i) A one-one function is always onto.

True ☐ False ☐

(ii) An onto function is always one-one.

True ☐ False ☐

***28.** Let $A = R - \{3\}$ and $B = R - \left\{\frac{2}{3}\right\}$, if $f: A \rightarrow B$ by $f(x) = \frac{2x-4}{3x-9}$, then the function f is a

(a) interjective (b) bijective

(c) surjective (d) Cannot be determined

***29.** Number of one-one functions from A to B, where $n(A) = 3$ and $n(B) = 4$.

***30.** Let $E = \{1, 2, 3, 4\}$ and $F = \{1, 2\}$. Then, the number of onto functions from E to F is

TOPIC 3

Composition of Functions and Invertible Functions

NCERT Pg 12-13

31. Let $f: \{3, 6, 7\} \rightarrow \{3, 2, 5\}$ and $g: \{3, 2, 5\} \rightarrow \{3, 6\}$ be given by $f = \{(3, 2), (6, 5), (7, 3)\}$ and $g = \{(3, 6), (2, 6), (5, 3)\}$, then find the value of

(i) $gof\ (3)$ ________

(ii) $gof\ (6)$ ________

(iii) $gof\ (7)$ ________

32. Let $f : \{1, 2, 3, 4\} \to \{7, 8, 9, 3\}$ and $g : \{7, 8, 9, 3\} \to \{10, 12, 13, 14\}$ be a function defined as $f(1) = 7, f(2) = 8, f(3) = 9, f(4) = 3, g(7) = 10, g(8) = 12, g(9) = 13$ and $g(3) = 14$. Find

(i) gof (1) ______

(ii) gof (2) ______

(iii) gof (3) ______

(iv) gof (4) ______

***33.** Find gof and fog, if

(i) $f(x) = \dfrac{2x-1}{2}$ and $g(x) = 4x + 2$

______

(ii) $f(x) = x^2 + x$ and $g(x) = \log x$

______

***34.** If $g(x) = x^2 + 7x + 9$ and $(gof)(x) = x^2 + 17x + 69$, then find the value of $f(x)$?

______

35. If $f : A \to B$ and $g : B \to C$ are bijective functions, then $gof : A \to C$ is also bijective function and *vice-versa.*

True ☐ False ☐

36. If $f : R - \left\{\frac{3}{4}\right\} \to R - \left\{\frac{5}{4}\right\}$ is defined by the function $f(x) = \dfrac{5x-9}{4x-3}$ and $g : R - \left\{\frac{5}{4}\right\} \to R - \left\{\frac{3}{4}\right\}$ is defined by the function $g(x) = \dfrac{3x-9}{4x-5}$, then fog and gof are the identity function.

True ☐ False ☐

37. Let f and g are real functions such that $f(x) = \dfrac{1}{x+5}$ and $g(x) = \dfrac{x+1}{2x+5}$, then

(i) find the value of $fog(x)$ ______

(ii) find the domain of $fog(x)$ ______

***38.** If $f(x) = \dfrac{ax-b}{bx-a}$, then $f\{f(x)\} = x, \forall\, x \in R - \left(\dfrac{a}{b}\right)$.

True ☐ False ☐

***39.** Find the value of $fof(x)$, if $f(x) = \sqrt[3]{3 - x^3}$.

______

40. If $f(x) = 2x + 3$, $g(y) = 4y + 3$ and $h(z) = \cos z$, then $ho(gof) \neq (hog)of$.

True ☐ False ☐

41. Let $f : R \to R$ be a function defined as $f(x) = 3x + 5$. If $fog = gof = I_R$, then the function $g(x)$ is ______

42. If $f : X \to Y$ and $g : Y \to Z$ be two invertible functions, then fog is also invertible with $(fog)^{-1} = f^{-1} og^{-1}$.

True ☐ False ☐

43. State with reason whether following functions have inverse.

(i) $f : \{1, 2, 3\} \to \{9, 10\}$ with $f = \{(1, 10), (2, 10), (3, 9)\}$

______

(ii) $g : \{1, 2, 8\} \to \{1, 5, 6, 4\}$ with $g = \{(1, 6), (2, 5), (8, 4)\}$

______

(iii) $h : \{1, 4, 5, 8\} \to \{7, 8, 10, 13\}$ with $h = \{(1, 7), (4, 8), (5, 10), (8, 13)\}$

______

44. Let $f : \{1, 2, 3\} \to \{a, b, c\}$ given by $f(1) = a$, $f(2) = b$ and $f(3) = c$, then the value of $\dfrac{f^{-1}(c) - f^{-1}(a)}{f^{-1}(b)}$ is

(a) 1 (b) 2 (c) 3 (d) 4

______

45. Let the function $f : R \to R$ be defined by $f(x) = x^2 + 7x + 9$, find $f^{-1}(-3)$.

______

46. Let $f : N \to Y$ be a function defined as $f(x) = 5x + 7$, where $Y = \{y \in N : y = 5x + 7$ for some $x \in N\}$. Find the inverse of the function.

______

47. Let $f : R - (-5) \to R - (2)$ be a function defined as $f(x) = \dfrac{2x}{x+5}$. Then, inverse of the function is

(a) $\dfrac{2x}{1-x}$ (b) $\dfrac{2x}{1+x}$ (c) $\dfrac{2x}{x-1}$ (d) None of these

______

48. If the function $f(x) = \dfrac{1}{2}(kx - 1)$, $k \neq 0$ is the inverse of itself, then the value of k is

______

49. Let $f : R \to R$ be the function defined by $f(x) = x^5 + 6$. Then, $f^{-1}(x)$ is

(a) $(x - 6)^{1/5}$ (b) $(x + 6)^{1/5}$ (c) $(6 - x)^{1/5}$ (d) None of these

______

Assertion-Reason Questions

The following questions consist of two statements – Assertion (A) and Reason (R). Answer these questions by selecting the appropriate option given below.
(a) Both A and R are true and R is the correct explanation of A.
(b) Both A and R are true, but R is not the correct explanation of A.
(c) A is true but R is false.
(d) A is false but R is true.

1. **Assertion** (A) $f : R \to R$ defined by $f(x) = \sin x$ is a bijection.

Reason (R) If f is both one-one and onto function, it is bijection.

(a) ☐ (b) ☐ (c) ☐ (d) ☐

2. **Assertion** (A) $f : R \to R$ is a function defined by $f(x) = \frac{2x+1}{3}$. Then, $f^{-1}(x) = \frac{3x-1}{2}$.

Reason (R) $f(x)$ is not a bijection.

(a) ☐ (b) ☐ (c) ☐ (d) ☐

3. **Assertion** (A) If f is even function, g is odd function, then $\frac{f}{g}$, $(g \neq 0)$ is an odd function.

Reason (R) If $f(-x) = -f(x)$ for every x of its domain, then $f(x)$ is called an odd function and if $f(-x) = f(x)$ for every x of its domain, then $f(x)$ is called an even function.

(a) ☐ (b) ☐ (c) ☐ (d) ☐

4. **Assertion** (A) Let $f : R \to R$ be defined by $f(x) = \frac{1}{x}$, then f is one-one and onto.

Reason (R) $x = 0$ does not belong to the domain of f.

(a) ☐ (b) ☐ (c) ☐ (d) ☐

5. **Assertion** (A) The function $f : R \to R$ given by $f(x) = x^3$ is injective.

Reason (R) The function $f : X \to Y$ is injective, if $f(x) = f(y) \Rightarrow x = y$ for all $x, y \in X$.

(a) ☐ (b) ☐ (c) ☐ (d) ☐

6. **Assertion** (A) If $f : R \to R$ and $g : R \to R$ be two mappings such that $f(x) = \sin x$ and $g(x) = x^2$, then $fog \neq gof$.

Reason (R) $fog(x) = f(x)\, g(x) = gof(x)$

(a) ☐ (b) ☐ (c) ☐ (d) ☐

7. **Assertion** (A) If the relation R defined in $A = \{1, 2, 3\}$ by aRb if $|a^2 - b^2| \leq 5$, then $R^{-1} = R$.

Reason (R) For above relation, domain of R^{+} = Range of R

(a) ☐ (b) ☐ (c) ☐ (d) ☐

8. **Assertion** (A) Let L be the set of all lines in a plane and R be the relations in L defined as $R = \{(L_1, L_2) : L_1$ is perpendicular to $L_2\}$. This relation is not equivalence relation.

Reason (R) A relation is said to be an equivalence relation if it is reflexive, symmetric and transitive.

(a) ☐ (b) ☐ (c) ☐ (d) ☐

9. **Assertion** (A) If f is an even function and g is an odd function, then the function fog is an even function.

Reason (R) $f(-x) = \begin{cases} f(x), & f(x) \text{ is even} \\ -f(x), & f(x) \text{ is odd} \end{cases}$

(a) ☐ (b) ☐ (c) ☐ (d) ☐

10. **Assertion** (A) A relation $R = \{(1, 1), (1, 2), (2, 2), (2, 3), (3, 3)\}$ defined on the set $A = \{1, 2, 3\}$ is reflexive.

Reason (R) A relation R on the set A is said to be reflexive if $(a, a) \in R \ \forall \ a \in A$.

(a) ☐ (b) ☐ (c) ☐ (d) ☐

Case Based Questions

Case 1 Sanju and Tanya are playing Ludo at home, during Covid-19. While rolling the dice, Sanju's sister Radha observed and noted the possible outcomes of the throw every time which belongs to the set {1, 2, 3, 4, 5, 6}. Let A be the set of players while B be the set of all possible outcomes i.e. $A = \{S, T\}$ and $B = \{1, 2, 3, 4, 5, 6\}$.

Based on the above information answer the following questions.

(i) Let $R : B \to B$ be defined by $R = \{(x, y) : y$ is divisble by $x\}$ is

(a) reflexive and transitive but not symmetric ☐

(b) reflexive and symmetric but not transitive ☐

(c) symmetric and transitive but not reflexive ☐

(d) equivalence ☐

(ii) Radha wants to know the number of functions from A to B. How many number of functions are possible?

(a) $6!$ ☐ (b) 2^6 ☐ (c) 6^2 ☐ (d) 2^{12} ☐

(iii) Let R be a relation on B defined by $R = \{(1, 2), (2, 2), (1, 3), (3, 4), (3, 1), (4, 3), (5, 5)\}$. Then, R is

(a) Symmetric ☐ (b) Transitive ☐

(c) Reflexive ☐ (d) None of these ☐

Case 2 Shiva visited the exhibition along with his family. The exhibition had a huge swing, which attracted many children. Shiva found that the swing traced the path of a parabola as given by $y = 2x^2$.

Based on the above information, answer the following questions.

(i) Let $f : R \to R$ be defined by $f(x) = 2x^2$ is

(a) neither one-one nor onto. ☐

(b) onto ☐

(c) one-one ☐

(d) both one-one and onto ☐

(ii) Let $f : N \to N$ be defined by $f(x) = 2x^2$ is

(a) onto but not one-one ☐

(b) onto ☐

(c) one-one ☐

(d) both one-one and onto ☐

(iii) Let $f : N \to R$ be defined by $f(x) = 2x^2$. Range of the function f is

(a) {1, 4, 9, 16, ...} ☐ (b) {2, 8, 18, 32, ...} ☐

(c) {1, 4, 8, 9, 10, ...} ☐ (d) {1, 4, 8, 16, ...} ☐

COMPETITION EDGE UP

1. Let $[t]$ be the greatest integer less than or equal to t. Let A be the set of all prime factors of 2310 and $f : A \to Z$ be the function $f(x) = \left[\log_2\left(x^2 + \left[\frac{x^3}{5}\right]\right)\right]$.

The number of one-to-one functions from A to the range of f is **[JEE Main 2024]**

(a) 20 ☐

(b) 25 ☐

(c) 24 ☐

(d) 120 ☐

2. Let $A = \{1, 3, 7, 9, 11\}$ and $B = \{2, 4, 5, 7, 8, 10, 12\}$. Then, the total number of one-one maps $f : A \to B$, such that $f(1) + f(3) = 14$, is

[JEE Main 2024]

(a) 180 ☐

(b) 120 ☐

(c) 480 ☐

(d) 240 ☐

3. Let a relation R on $N \times N$ be defined as: $(x_1, y_1) R (x_2, y_2)$ if and only if $x_1 \le x_2$ or $y_1 \le y_2$. **[JEE Main 2024]**

Consider the two statements :

I : R is reflexive but not symmetric.

II : R is transitive

Then, which one of the following is true?

(a) Only I is correct. ☐

(b) Only II is correct. ☐

(c) Neither I nor II is correct. ☐

(d) Both I and II are correct. ☐

4. If R is the smallest equivalence relation on the set {1, 2, 3, 4} such that $\{(1, 2), (1, 3)\} \subset R$, then the number of elements in R is **[JEE Main 2024]**

(a) 15 ☐

(b) 10 ☐

(c) 8 ☐

(d) 12 ☐

5. Let R be a relation on $Z \times Z$ defined by $(a, b)\ R\ (c, d)$ if and only if $ad - bc$ is divisible by 5. Then, R is **[JEE Main 2024]**

(a) Reflexive but neither symmetric nor transitive ☐

(b) Reflexive and transitive but not symmetric ☐

(c) Reflexive, symmetric and transitive ☐

(d) Reflexive and symmetric but not transitive ☐

6. The functionf $: N - \{1\} \to N$; defined by $f(n) =$ the highest prime factor of n, is **[JEE Main 2024]**

(a) neither one-one nor onto ☐

(b) both one-one and onto ☐

(c) onto only ☐

(d) one-one only ☐

7. Let $S = \{1, 2, 3, ..., 10\}$. Suppose M is the set of all the subsets of S, then the relation $R = \{(A, B) : A \cap B \neq \phi;\ A, B \in M\}$ is **[JEE Main 2024]**

(a) symmetric only ☐

(b) symmetric and reflexive only ☐

(c) reflexive only ☐

(d) symmetric and transitive only ☐

8. Let $A = \{2, 3, 6, 8, 9, 11\}$ and $B = \{1, 4, 5, 10, 15\}$. Let R be a relation on $A \times B$ defined by $(a, b)R(c, d)$ if and only if $3ad - 7bc$ is an even integer. Then, the relation R is **[JEE Main 2024]**

(a) an equivalence relation. ☐

(b) reflexive but not symmetric. ☐

(c) transitive but not symmetric. ☐

(d) reflexive and symmetric but not transitive. ☐

9. Let $A = \{(x, y) : 2x + 3y = 23,\ x, y \in N\}$ and $B = \{x : (x, y) \in A\}$. Then, the number of one-one functions from A to B is equal to .... **[JEE Main 2024]**

10. Let $A = \{1, 2, 3, ..., 100\}$. Let R be a relation on A defined by $(x, y) \in R$ if and only if $2x = 3y$. Let R_1 be a symmetric relation on A such that $R \subset R_1$ and the number of elements in R_1 is n. Then, the minimum value of n is .... **[JEE Main 2024]**

11. Let $A = \{1, 2, 3, 4\}$ and $R = \{(1, 2), (2, 3), (1, 4)\}$ be a relation on A. Let S be the equivalence relation on A such that $R \subset S$ and the number of elements in S is n. Then, the minimum value of n is .... **[JEE Main 2024]**

12. The number of symmetric relations defined on the set $\{1, 2, 3, 4\}$ which are not reflexive is .... **[JEE Main 2024]**

13. Let $f(x) = x^2 + 9$, $g(x) = \dfrac{x}{x - 9}$ and $a = fog(10)$, $b = gof(3)$. If e and l denote the eccentricity and the length of the latus rectum of the ellipse $\dfrac{x^2}{a} + \dfrac{y^2}{b} = 1$, then $8e^2 + l^2$ is equal to **[JEE Main 2024]**

(a) 6 ☐

(b) 12 ☐

(c) 8 ☐

(d) 16 ☐

14. If $f(x) = \dfrac{4x + 3}{6x - 4}$, $x \neq \dfrac{2}{3}$ and $(fof)(x) = g(x)$, where $g : R - \left\{\dfrac{2}{3}\right\} \to R - \left\{-\dfrac{2}{3}\right\}$, then $(gogog)(4)$ is equal to **[JEE Main 2024]**

(a) $\dfrac{19}{20}$ ☐

(b) -4 ☐

(c) $-\dfrac{19}{20}$ ☐

(d) 4 ☐

15. Let $f, g : R \to R$ be defined as $f(x) = |x - 1|$ and
$$g(x) = \begin{cases} e^x, & x \geq 0 \\ x + 1, & x \leq 0 \end{cases}$$
Then, the function $f(g(x))$ is **[JEE Main 2024]**

(a) one-one but not onto. ☐

(b) neither one-one nor onto. ☐

(c) onto but not one-one. ☐

(d) both one-one and onto. ☐

Scan this QR code from your mobile phone to get the solutions of **Competition Edge Up** of this chapter.

Chapter 02

Inverse Trigonometric Functions

Scan and take Chapter Test

TOPIC 1

Principal Value, Domain and Range

1. The inverse of a function f exists, if f is

(a) onto
(b) one-one
(c) one-one and onto
(d) None of these

2. Match the following columns.

	Column I (Function)	Column II (Domain → Range)
A.	Sine	1. $R-\{x : x = n\pi, n \in Z\} \to R-(-1,1)$
B.	Cosecant	2. $R \to [-1,1]$
C.	Tangent	3. $R-\{x : x = n\pi, n \in Z\} \to R$
D.	Cotangent	4. $R-\left\{x : x = (2n+1)\frac{\pi}{2}, n \in Z\right\} \to R$

Choose the correct option.

(a) A → 1, B → 2, C → 3, D → 4
(b) A → 2, B → 1, C → 4, D → 3
(c) A → 3, B → 4, C → 2, D → 1
(d) A → 4, B → 3, C → 1, D → 2

*Concepts of all questions bearing * are important for JEE & CUET*

3. If $f: X \to Y$ and $g: Y \to X$, where $x \in X$ and $y \in Y$ such that $g^{-1} = (f^{-1})^{-1} = f$, then the value of $(f^{-1} o f)(x)$ is equal to

(a) $-x$ (b) y (c) xy (d) x

---

4. State True or False.

(i) If the function sine is restricted with the domain $\left[-\frac{\pi}{2}, \frac{\pi}{2}\right]$, then its range is [0,1].

True ☐ False ☐

(ii) A branch with interval range $\left[-\frac{\pi}{2}, \frac{\pi}{2}\right]$ of the function $\sin^{-1}$ is called the principal value branch.

True ☐ False ☐

(iii) The graph of $\sin^{-1}$ function can be obtained from the graph of original function by interchanging X and Y-axes.

True ☐ False ☐

(iv) The range of the function $\sec^{-1} x$ is $[0, \pi]$.

True ☐ False ☐

(v) To define the inverse of the function $f(x) = \tan x$, any of the intervals $(-3\pi/2, -\pi/2)$, $(-\pi/2, \pi/2)$, $(\pi/2, 3\pi/2)$ etc. can be chosen.

True ☐ False ☐

5. If (a, b) is a point on the graph of sine function, then ________ becomes the corresponding point on the graph of inverse of sine function.

6. Two branches other than the principal value branch of $\sec^{-1} x$ is ________

***7.** Find the domain of the following functions.

(i) $\sin^{-1}(5x + 1)$ ________

(ii) $\cos^{-1}(\sqrt{x - 1})$ ________

(iii) $\sec^{-1}(3 - 2x)$ ________

8. State True or False.

(i) The inverse of $y = \sin x$ is $x = \sin^{-1} y \ \forall\ x \in \left[-\frac{\pi}{2}, \frac{\pi}{2}\right]$.

True ☐ False ☐

(ii) The inverse of $y = \cos x$ is $x = \cos^{-1} y \ \forall \ x \in [0, \pi]$.

True ☐ False ☐

(iii) The range of the function $\cot^{-1} x$ is $[-\pi, \pi] - \left\{\frac{\pi}{2}\right\}$.

True ☐ False ☐

***9.** Match the following function along with their domains and ranges.

Column I		Column II	
A.	$\sin^{-1}$	1.	$[-1, 1] \to [0, \pi]$
B.	$\cos^{-1}$	2.	$[-1, 1] \to \left[-\frac{\pi}{2}, \frac{\pi}{2}\right]$
C.	cosec^{-1}	3.	$R - (-1, 1) \to [0, \pi] - \left\{\frac{\pi}{2}\right\}$
D.	$\sec^{-1}$	4.	$R - (-1, 1) \to \left[-\frac{\pi}{2}, \frac{\pi}{2}\right] - \{0\}$
E.	$\tan^{-1}$	5.	$R \to (0, \pi)$
F.	$\cot^{-1}$	6.	$R \to \left(-\frac{\pi}{2}, \frac{\pi}{2}\right)$

Choose the correct option.

(a) A → 1, B → 3, C → 3, D → 1, E → 6, F → 5
(b) A → 2, B → 1, C → 4, D → 3, E → 6, F → 5
(c) A → 3, B → 2, C → 1, D → 2, E → 6, F → 5
(d) A → 4, B → 4, C → 2, D → 4, E → 6, F → 5

***10.** Find the principal value of the following functions.

(i) $\sin^{-1}\left(\frac{\sqrt{3}}{2}\right)$ ______

(ii) $\text{cosec}^{-1}\left(-\frac{2}{\sqrt{3}}\right)$ ______

(iii) $\sec^{-1}(-\sqrt{2})$ ______

11. State True or False.

(i) If $\sin\frac{5\pi}{6} = \frac{1}{2}$, then $\sin^{-1}\left(\frac{1}{2}\right) = \frac{5\pi}{6}$.

True ☐ False ☐

(ii) If $\tan\frac{4\pi}{3} = \sqrt{3}$, then $\tan^{-1}(\sqrt{3}) = \frac{4\pi}{3}$.

True ☐ False ☐

***12.** Find the value of the following functions.

(i) $\cos^{-1}\left(-\frac{1}{2}\right)+2\sin^{-1}\left(\frac{1}{2}\right)$ ____________

(ii) $\sin^{-1}\left(\frac{1}{2}\right)-\sec^{-1}(-2)$ ____________

(iii) $\cos^{-1}\left(-\frac{1}{\sqrt{2}}\right)+\tan^{-1}(-\sqrt{3})-\text{cosec}^{-1}(2)$ ____________

(iv) $\sin^{-1}\left(-\frac{\sqrt{3}}{2}\right)+\cos^{-1}\left(-\frac{\sqrt{2}}{2}\right)-\tan^{-1}\left(\frac{\sqrt{3}}{3}\right)+\cot^{-1}\left(-\frac{\sqrt{3}}{3}\right)$ ____________

TOPIC 2

Properties of Inverse Trigonometric Functions

13. State True or False.

(i) $\sin^{-1}(\sin\theta)=\theta$ provided that $\theta\in\left[-\frac{\pi}{2},\frac{\pi}{2}\right]$

True ☐ False ☐

(ii) $\tan^{-1}(\tan\theta)=\theta$ provided that $\theta\in\left(-\frac{\pi}{2},\frac{\pi}{2}\right)$

True ☐ False ☐

(iii) $\cot^{-1}(\cot\theta)=\theta$ provided that $\theta\in(0,\pi)$

True ☐ False ☐

(iv) $\text{cosec}^{-1}(\text{cosec}\,\theta)=\theta$ provided that $\theta\in[0,\pi]-\left\{\frac{\pi}{2}\right\}$

True ☐ False ☐

14. Simplify the following functions.

(i) $\sin[\tan^{-1}(-1)]$ ____________

(ii) $\cos^{-1}\left(\sin\frac{\pi}{2}\right)$ ____________

15. Find the value of the following functions.

(i) $\sin^{-1}\left\{\sin\left(\frac{3\pi}{4}\right)\right\}$ ____________

(ii) $\cot^{-1}\left[\cot\frac{3\pi}{4}\right]$ ____________

(iii) $\tan^{-1}\left\{\cot\left(\frac{37\pi}{6}\right)\right\}$ ____________

(iv) $\cos^{-1}\left[\sin\left[\cot^{-1}\left[\tan\left\{\cos^{-1}\left(\sin\frac{\pi}{3}\right)\right\}\right]\right]\right]$ ____________

(v) $\tan^{-1}[\cot\{\sin^{-1}(\cos\theta)\}]$ ____________

***16.** The value of $\sin^{-1}\left(\frac{\sin x + \cos x}{\sqrt{2}}\right)$, where $\frac{-\pi}{4} < x < \frac{\pi}{4}$, is

(a) $x + \frac{\pi}{4}$

(b) $x + \frac{\pi}{2}$

(c) $x - \frac{\pi}{4}$

(d) None of the above

***17.** Evaluate $\cos^{-1}(1 - 2x) - 2\sin^{-1}\sqrt{x}$.

18. Evaluate $\cot^{-1}\frac{\sqrt{a^2 - x^2}}{x} - \sec^{-1}\frac{a}{x}$ is ________

19. Express $\cos^{-1}\left(x^{\frac{3}{2}} - \sqrt{(1-x)(1-x^2)}\right)$ in the simplest form.

***20.** Find the domain of the following functions.

(i) $\tan^{-1}(-x) = -\tan^{-1} x$ is true, when $x \in$ ________

(ii) $\sec^{-1}(-x) = \pi - \sec^{-1}(x)$ is true, when $x \in$ ________

21. The value of $\cot^{-1}\frac{[(\sqrt{1-\cos x}) - (\sqrt{1+\cos x})]}{[(\sqrt{1-\cos x}) + (\sqrt{1+\cos x})]}$ is equal to

(a) $\frac{x}{2}$ ☐

(b) $\frac{3\pi}{2} - x$ ☐

(c) $\frac{\pi}{2} - x$ ☐

(d) $\frac{3\pi}{4} - \frac{x}{2}$ ☐

22. Value of $\cot^{-1}\left(\frac{\sqrt{1+\sin x}}{\sqrt{1-\sin x}}\right)$ is ________

Assertion-Reason Questions

The following questions consist of two statements – Assertion (A) and Reason (R). Answer these questions by selecting the appropriate options given below.
(a) Both A and R are true and R is the correct explanation of A.
(b) Both A and R are true, but R is not the correct explanation of A.
(c) A is true, but R is false.
(d) A is false, but R is true.

1. **Assertion** (A) The principal value of $\sin^{-1}\left(-\frac{1}{2}\right)$ is $-\frac{\pi}{6}$.

Reason (R) The principal value of $\sin^{-1}(-x)$ is $-\sin^{-1}x$, if $x \in [-1, 1]$.

(a) ☐ (b) ☐ (c) ☐ (d) ☐

2. **Assertion** (A) The principal value of $\cos^{-1}\left(-\frac{1}{\sqrt{2}}\right)$ is $-\frac{\pi}{4}$.

Reason (R) The principal value of $\cos^{-1}(-x)$ is $\pi - \cos^{-1}x$, if $x \in [-1, 1]$.

(a) ☐ (b) ☐ (c) ☐ (d) ☐

3. **Assertion** (A) The principal value of $\tan^{-1}\left(\tan\frac{3\pi}{4}\right)$ is $-\frac{\pi}{4}$.

Reason (R) The range of $\tan^{-1}x$ is $\left[\frac{-\pi}{2}, \frac{\pi}{2}\right]$

(a) ☐ (b) ☐ (c) ☐ (d) ☐

4. **Assertion** (A) The principal value of $\cos^{-1}\left(\cos\frac{5\pi}{3}\right) = \frac{\pi}{3}$.

Reason (R) The range of $\cos^{-1}x$ is $[0, \pi]$.

(a) ☐ (b) ☐ (c) ☐ (d) ☐

5. **Assertion** (A) $\tan^{-1}(-x) = -\tan^{-1}x, x \in R$.

Reason (R) $\sec^{-1}(-x) = \pi - \sec^{-1}x, x \in R$.

(a) ☐ (b) ☐ (c) ☐ (d) ☐

6. **Assertion** (A) The value of $\cos\left(\sec^{-1}\left(\frac{5}{3}\right)\right)$ is $\frac{3}{5}$.

Reason (R) The value of $\sec^{-1}x$ is $\cos^{-1}\frac{1}{x}$.

(a) ☐ (b) ☐ (c) ☐ (d) ☐

7. **Assertion** (A) The value of $\tan^{-1}\sqrt{3} - \sec^{-1}(-2)$ is $\frac{\pi}{3}$.

Reason (R) If $\cos^{-1}x = y$, then principal value of y is $0 \le y \le \pi$.

(a) ☐ (b) ☐ (c) ☐ (d) ☐

8. **Assertion** (A) The principal value of $\cos^{-1}\left(\cos\frac{13\pi}{6}\right)$ is $\frac{\pi}{6}$.

Reason (R) The principal value of $\tan^{-1}\left(\tan\frac{5\pi}{6}\right)$ is $\frac{5\pi}{6}$.

(a) ☐ (b) ☐ (c) ☐ (d) ☐

9. **Assertion** (A) The value of $\sin\left(\tan^{-1}\frac{a}{b}\right)$ is $\frac{a}{\sqrt{b^2-a^2}}$.

Reason (R) The value of $\tan\left(\cot^{-1}\frac{a}{b}\right)$ is $\frac{b}{a}$.

(a) ☐ (b) ☐ (c) ☐ (d) ☐

10. **Assertion** (A) The value of $\sin^{-1}\left(\cos\left(\sin^{-1}\frac{1}{2}\right)\right)$ is $\frac{\pi}{3}$.

Reason (R) The value of $\sin^{-1}(\cos x)$ is $\frac{\pi}{2}-x$.

(a) ☐ (b) ☐ (c) ☐ (d) ☐

Case Based Questions

Case 1 Read the following information and answer any four questions from (i) to (v).

Two men on either side of a 45m high tower observe its top at the angles of elevation α and β, respectively. (as shown in the figure below). The distance between the two men is $20\sqrt{3}$ m and the distance between the first person A and the tower is $15\sqrt{3}$ m.

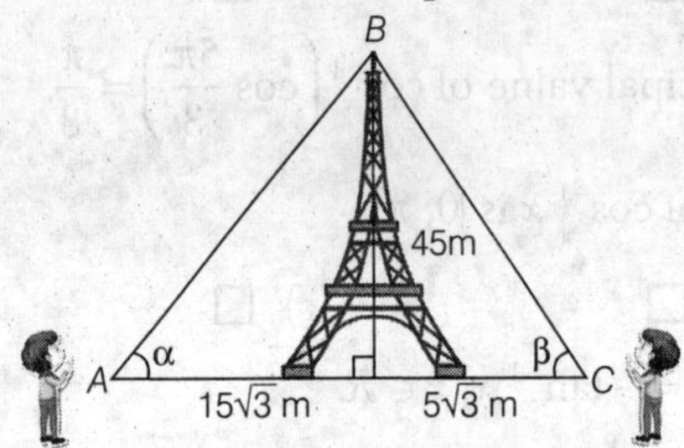

Based on the above information answer the following.

(i) $\angle CAB = \alpha =$

(a) $\sin^{-1}\left(\frac{2}{\sqrt{3}}\right)$ ☐ (b) $\sin^{-1}\left(\frac{1}{2}\right)$ ☐

(c) $\sin^{-1}(2)$ ☐ (d) $\sin^{-1}\left(\frac{\sqrt{3}}{2}\right)$ ☐

(ii) $\angle CAB = \alpha =$

(a) $\cos^{-1}\frac{1}{2}$ ☐ (b) $\cos^{-1}\left(\frac{2}{5}\right)$ ☐

(c) $\cos^{-1}\left(\frac{1}{2}\right)$ ☐ (d) $\cos^{-1}\left(\frac{4}{3}\right)$ ☐

(iii) $\angle BCA = \beta =$

(a) $\tan^{-1}\left(\frac{1}{2}\right)$ ☐ (b) $\tan^{-1}(2)$ ☐

(c) $\tan^{-1}\left(\frac{1}{\sqrt{3}}\right)$ ☐ (d) $\tan^{-1}(3\sqrt{3})$ ☐

(iv) $\angle ABC =$

(a) $\frac{\pi}{4} - \tan^{-1}\sqrt{3}$ ☐ (b) $\frac{\pi}{6}$ ☐

(c) $\cot^{-1}(3\sqrt{3})$ ☐ (d) $\frac{\pi}{3}$ ☐

(v) Domain and Range of $\cos^{-1} x$ are respectively

(a) $(-1, 1)$ $(0, \pi)$ ☐ (b) $[-1, 1]$ $(0, \pi)$ ☐

(c) $[-1, 1]$ $[0, \pi]$ ☐ (d) $(-1, 1)$, $\left[-\frac{\pi}{2}, \frac{\pi}{2}\right]$ ☐

Case 2 Read the following and answer any four questions from part (i) to part (v).

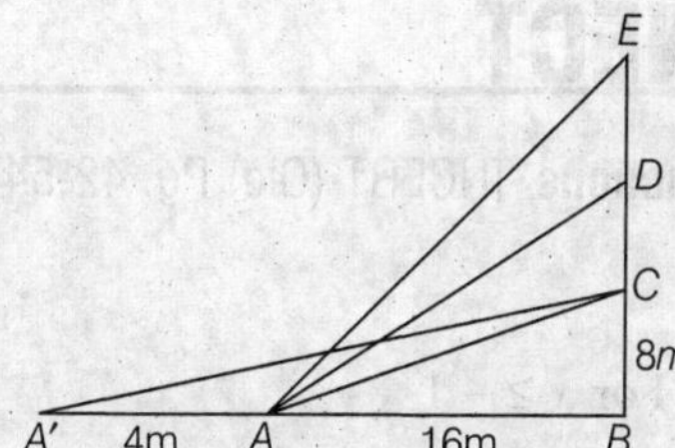

The Government of India is planning to fix a hoarding at the face of a building on the road of a busy market for awareness on COVID-19 protocol. Ramesh, Amit and Ravi are the three engineers who are working on this project. "*A*" is considered to be a person viewing the hoarding 16 m away from the building, standing at the edge of a pathway nearby. Ramesh, Amit and Ravi suggested to the firm to place the hoarding board at three different locations namely *C*, *D* and *E*. "*C*" is at the height of 8 m from the ground level. For the viewer *A*, the angle of elevation of "*D*" is double the angle of elevation of "*C*" The angle of elevation of "*E*" is triple the angle of elevation of "*C*" for the same viewer. Look at the figure given and based on the above information answer the following.

(i) Measure of $\angle CAB =$

(a) $\tan^{-1}(2)$ ☐ (b) $\tan^{-1}\left(\frac{1}{2}\right)$ ☐

(c) $\tan^{-1}(1)$ ☐ (d) $\tan^{-1}(3)$ ☐

(ii) Measure of $\angle DAB =$

(a) $\tan^{-1}\left(\frac{3}{4}\right)$ ☐ (b) $\tan^{-1}(3)$ ☐

(c) $\tan^{-1}\left(\frac{4}{3}\right)$ ☐ (d) $\tan^{-1}(4)$ ☐

(iii) Measure of $\angle EAB =$

(a) $\tan^{-1}(11)$ ☐ (b) $\tan^{-1}(3)$ ☐

(c) $\tan^{-1}\left(\frac{2}{11}\right)$ ☐ (d) $\tan^{-1}\left(\frac{11}{2}\right)$ ☐

(iv) 'A'' is another viewer standing on the same line of observation across the road. If the width of the road is 4 m, then the difference between $\angle CAB$ and $\angle CA'B$ is

(a) $\tan^{-1}\left(\frac{1}{12}\right)$ ☐ (b) $\tan^{-1}\left(\frac{1}{8}\right)$ ☐

(c) $\tan^{-1}\left(\frac{2}{5}\right)$ ☐ (d) $\tan^{-1}\left(\frac{11}{21}\right)$ ☐

(v) Domain and Range of $\tan^{-1} x$ are respectively

(a) $R^+, \left(-\frac{\pi}{2}, \frac{\pi}{2}\right)$ ☐ (b) $R^-, \left(-\frac{\pi}{2}, \frac{\pi}{2}\right)$ ☐

(c) $R, \left(-\frac{\pi}{2}, \frac{\pi}{2}\right)$ ☐ (d) $R, \left(0, \frac{\pi}{2}\right)$ ☐

COMPETITION CONNECT

Properties of Inverse Trigonometric Functions [NCERT (Old) Pg. 42-54]

1. State True or False.

(i) $\sin^{-1}\frac{1}{x} = \text{cosec}^{-1} x$, iff $x \le 1$ or $x \ge -1$

True ☐ False ☐

(ii) $\cos^{-1}\frac{1}{x} = \sec^{-1} x$, iff $x \ge 1$ or $x \le -1$

True ☐ False ☐

(iii) $\tan^{-1}\frac{1}{x} = \cot^{-1} x$ is true, iff $x > 0$

True ☐ False ☐

2. Find the value of the following functions.

(i) $\sin\left\{\frac{\pi}{3} - \sin^{-1}\left(-\frac{1}{2}\right)\right\}$ __________

(ii) $\cot[\pi - \cot^{-1}(-\sqrt{3})]$ __________

3. Choose the correct one in the following questions.

(i) The value of $\cos\left\{\cos^{-1}\left(-\frac{\sqrt{3}}{2}\right) + \frac{\pi}{6}\right\}$ is

(a) -1 (b) 2 (c) -2 (d) 1

(ii) The value of $\tan\{(\sin^{-1} m + \cos^{-1} m) - \cot^{-1}(1)\}$ is

(a) -1 (b) 1

(c) 2 (d) -2

(iii) If $\alpha \le 4\sin^{-1} x - 3\cos^{-1} x \le \beta$, then (α, β) is equal to

(a) $(-3\pi, 2\pi)$ (b) $(-5\pi, 2\pi)$

(c) $(-4\pi, \pi)$ (d) None of these

(iv) If $\sin^{-1} x > \cos^{-1} x$, then x is

(a) $x > \frac{1}{\sqrt{2}}$ (b) $x < \frac{1}{2}$

(c) $x > 1$ (d) $x < 1$

---

4. If $\cot^{-1} x + \cot^{-1} y = \frac{5\pi}{8}$, then find the value of $\tan^{-1} x + \tan^{-1} y$.

---

5. $\frac{7\pi}{30} - \frac{7}{15}\tan^{-1}\frac{21}{20} = \frac{7}{15}\sin^{-1}\frac{20}{29}$

True ☐ False ☐

6. The range of the function $\sin^{-1} x + \tan^{-1}\frac{1}{x} + \tan^{-1} x$ is ________

7. If $(\sec^{-1} x)^2 + (\text{cosec}^{-1}\sqrt{2})^2 + 2\sec^{-1} x \cdot \frac{\pi}{4} = \frac{\pi^2}{4}$, then the value of $x \in [0, \pi]$ is ________

8. The value of

(i) $\cot^{-1}(-1) + \cot^{-1}(-2) + \cot^{-1}(-3)$ is ________

(ii) $\tan\left(\sin^{-1}\frac{3}{5} + \cot^{-1}\frac{3}{2}\right)$ is ________

9. $\sin^{-1}\left(\frac{8}{17}\right) + \sin^{-1}\left(\frac{3}{5}\right) = \sin^{-1}\left(\frac{77}{85}\right)$.

True ☐ False ☐

10. Evaluate $\sin\left\{\sec^{-1}\left(\frac{17}{8}\right) + \text{cosec}^{-1}\left(\frac{13}{5}\right)\right\}$ ________

11. (i) If a, b and c are three angles of a triangle and $\cot^{-1}\frac{a}{b} + \cot^{-1}\frac{a+b}{a-b} = \tan^{-1} c$, then the value of c is ________

(ii) The value of $\cot^{-1}\left[\frac{pq+1}{p-q}\right] + \cot^{-1}\left[\frac{qr+1}{q-r}\right] + \cot^{-1}\left[\frac{rp+1}{r-p}\right]$ is ________

12. State True or False.

(i) $\tan^{-1} 2, \tan^{-1} 3$ and $\frac{\pi}{4}$ are three interior angles of the triangle.

True ☐ False ☐

(ii) Sum of $\tan^{-1}\left(\frac{1}{3}\right), \tan^{-1}\left(\frac{1}{7}\right), \tan^{-1}\left(\frac{1}{13}\right) \ldots \infty$ is $\frac{\pi}{4}$.

True ☐ False ☐

(iii) The value of the function $\sin^{-1} x - \sin^{-1}\left(\frac{\sqrt{3}x - \sqrt{1-x^2}}{2}\right)$ is $\frac{\pi}{6}$.

True ☐ False ☐

13. Evaluate the following functions.

(i) $\tan\left[2\tan^{-1}\left(\frac{\sqrt{5}-1}{2}\right)\right]$ ____________________

(ii) $\tan\left[\frac{1}{2}\cos^{-1}\frac{\sqrt{5}}{3}\right]$ ____________________

14. State True or False.

(i) If $2\tan^{-1} x = \cos^{-1}\frac{1-x^2}{1+x^2}$, then $x \geq 1$.

True ☐ False ☐

(ii) If x, y and z are in GP and $\tan^{-1} x$, $\tan^{-1} y$ and $\tan^{-1} z$ are in AP, then the value of y is $x + z$.

True ☐ False ☐

(iii) The value of $2\cot^{-1} 5 + \tan^{-1}\left(\frac{1}{7}\right) + 2\cot^{-1} 8$ is $\frac{\pi}{2}$.

True ☐ False ☐

15. Solve the following equations.

(i) $\tan^{-1}\left(\frac{\sqrt{1+\cos x}}{\sqrt{1-\cos x}}\right) = \frac{\pi}{3}$ ____________________

(ii) $\sin^{-1} x - \cos^{-1} x = \sin^{-1}\left(\frac{1}{2}\right)$ ____________________

(iii) $3\tan^{-1} x + \cot^{-1} x = \pi$ ____________________

(iv) $(\sin^{-1} x)^2 + (\cos^{-1} x)^2 = \frac{5\pi^2}{8}$ ____________________

(v) $\tan\frac{1}{2}\left(\tan^{-1}\frac{2}{7} + \cot^{-1} y\right) = 1$ ____________________

(vi) $\tan^{-1}(1+x) + \tan^{-1}(1-x) = \frac{\pi}{2}$ ____________________

(vii) $\sec^{-1} x - \text{cosec}^{-1} x = \frac{\pi}{3}$ ____________________

(viii) $2\tan^{-1}(\sin x) = \tan^{-1}(2\sec x)$ ____________________

COMPETITION EDGE UP

1. Let the inverse trigonometric function take principal values. The number of real solution of the equation $2\sin^{-1}x + 3\cos^{-1}x = \frac{2\pi}{5}$, is .... **[JEE Main 2024]**

2. If the domain of the function $f(x) = \sin^{-1}\left(\frac{x-1}{2x+3}\right)$ is $R - (\alpha, \beta)$, then $12\alpha\beta$ is equal to **[JEE Main 2024]**

(a) 36 ☐
(b) 32 ☐
(c) 40 ☐
(d) 24 ☐

3. For $n \in N$, if $\cot^{-1} 3 + \cot^{-1} 4 + \cot^{-1} 5 + \cot^{-1} n = \frac{\pi}{4}$, then n is equal to .... **[JEE Main 2024]**

4. If the domain of the function $\sin^{-1}\left(\frac{3x-22}{2x-19}\right) + \log_e\left(\frac{3x^2-8x+5}{x^2-3x-10}\right)$ is $(\alpha, \beta]$, then $3\alpha + 10\beta$ is equal to **[JEE Main 2024]**

(a) 100 ☐
(b) 98 ☐
(c) 97 ☐
(d) 95 ☐

5. If $a = \sin^{-1}(\sin(5))$ and $b = \cos^{-1}(\cos(5))$, then $a^2 + b^2$ is equal to **[JEE Main 2024]**

(a) $4\pi^2 - 25$ ☐
(b) $4\pi^2 - 20\pi + 50$ ☐
(c) 25 ☐
(d) $8\pi^2 - 40\pi + 50$ ☐

6. For $\alpha, \beta, \gamma = \theta$, if $\sin^{-1}\alpha + \sin^{-1}\beta + \sin^{-1}\gamma = \pi$ and $(\alpha+\beta+\gamma)(\alpha-\gamma+\beta) = 3\alpha\beta$, then γ equals **[JEE Main 2024]**

(a) $\frac{\sqrt{3}-1}{2\sqrt{2}}$ ☐
(b) $\sqrt{3}$ ☐
(c) $\frac{\sqrt{3}}{2}$ ☐
(d) $\frac{1}{\sqrt{2}}$ ☐

7. If the domain of the function $f(x) = \log_e\left(\frac{2x+3}{4x^2+x-3}\right) + \cos^{-1}\left(\frac{2x-1}{x+2}\right)$ is $(\alpha, \beta]$, then the value of $5\beta - 4\alpha$ is equal to **[JEE Main 2024]**

(a 11 ☐
(b) 9 ☐
(c) 12 ☐
(d) 10 ☐

8. If the domain of the function $f(x) = \cos^{-1}\left(\frac{2-|x|}{4}\right) + \{\log_e(3-x)\}^{-1}$ is $[-\alpha, \beta] - [\gamma]$, then $\alpha + \beta + \gamma$ is equal to **[JEE Main 2024]**

(a) 8 ☐
(b) 12 ☐
(c) 9 ☐
(d) 11 ☐

9. Considering only the principal values of inverse trigonometric function, the number of positive real values of x satisfying $\tan^{-1}(x) + \tan^{-1}(2x) = \frac{\pi}{4}$ is **[JEE Main 2024]**

(a) 2 ☐
(b) 0 ☐
(c) More than 2 ☐
(d) 1 ☐

10. The range of $f(x) = 4\sin^{-1}\left(\frac{x^2}{x^2+1}\right)$ is **[JEE Main 2023]**

(a) $[0, \pi)$ ☐
(b) $[0, \pi]$ ☐
(c) $[0, 2\pi)$ ☐
(d) $[0, 2\pi]$ ☐

11. If the domain of the function $f(x) = \sec^{-1}\left(\frac{2x}{5x+3}\right)$ is $[\alpha, \beta) \cup (\gamma, \delta]$, then $|3\alpha + 10(\beta+\gamma) + 21\delta|$ is equal to .... **[JEE Main 2023]**

12. Let $S = \left\{ x \in R : 0 < x < 1 \text{ and } 2\tan^{-1}\left(\frac{1-x}{1+x}\right) = \cos^{-1}\left(\frac{1-x^2}{1+x^2}\right) \right\}$.

If $n(S)$ denotes the number of elements in S, then **[JEE Main 2023]**

(a) $n(S) = 1$ and the element in S is less than $\frac{1}{2}$. ☐

(b) $n(S) = 2$ and only one element in S is less than $\frac{1}{2}$. ☐

(c) $n(S) = 0$. ☐

(d) $n(S) = 1$ and the elements in S is more than $\frac{1}{2}$. ☐

13. If $\sin^{-1}\frac{\alpha}{17} + \cos^{-1}\frac{4}{5} - \tan^{-1}\frac{77}{36} = 0$, $0 < \alpha < 13$, then $\sin^{-1}(\sin\alpha) + \cos^{-1}(\cos\alpha)$ is equal to **[JEE Main 2023]**

(a) 0 ☐

(b) π ☐

(c) 16 ☐

(d) $16 - 5\pi$ ☐

14. Let $a_1 = 1, a_2, a_3, a_4, \ldots\ldots$ be consecutive natural numbers. Then,

$$\tan^{-1}\left(\frac{1}{1+a_1a_2}\right) + \tan^{-1}\left(\frac{1}{1+a_2a_3}\right) + \ldots + \tan^{-1}\left(\frac{1}{1+a_{2021}a_{2022}}\right)$$ is equal to

[JEE Main 2023]

(a) $\frac{\pi}{4} - \cot^{-1}(2022)$ ☐

(b) $\tan^{-1}(2022) - \frac{\pi}{4}$ ☐

(c) $\frac{\pi}{4} - \tan^{-1}(2022)$ ☐

(d) $\cot^{-1}(2022) - \frac{\pi}{4}$ ☐

15. $\tan^{-1}\left(\frac{1+\sqrt{3}}{3+\sqrt{3}}\right) + \sec^{-1}\left(\sqrt{\frac{8+4\sqrt{3}}{6+3\sqrt{3}}}\right)$ is equal to **[JEE Main 2023]**

(a) $\frac{\pi}{4}$ ☐

(b) $\frac{\pi}{6}$ ☐

(c) $\frac{\pi}{2}$ ☐

(d) $\frac{\pi}{3}$ ☐

Scan this QR code from your mobile phone to get the solutions of **Competition Edge Up** of this chapter.

Chapter 03

Matrices

Scan and take Chapter Test

TOPIC 1

Order, Types and Equality of Matrix

1. If the order of the matrix is $m \times n$, then how many elements will there be in the matrix?

(a) mn (b) m^2n^2 (c) mn^2 (d) $2mn$

2. Match the following number of orders with the number of the elements of the given matrix and choose the correct answer.

	Number of the elements of the matrix		Number of possible orders of the matrix
A.	12	1.	2
B.	7	2.	6
C.	8	3.	3
D.	9	4.	4

Choose the correct option.

(a) A → 2, B → 4, C → 1, D → 3

(b) A → 2, B → 1, C → 4, D → 3

(c) A → 4, B → 2, C → 1, D → 3

(d) A → 4, B → 1, C → 2, D → 3

3. If $A = \begin{bmatrix} 1 & 4 & 7 \\ 2 & 5 & 8 \\ 3 & 6 & 9 \end{bmatrix}$, then answer the following questions.

(i) The value of a_{32} is ______

(ii) The value of a_{31} is ______

(iii) The value of a_{22} is ______

(iv) The value of $a_{11} + a_{12} + a_{23} + a_{33}$ is ______

(v) The order of the matrix A is ______

*Concepts of all questions bearing * are important for JEE & CUET*

4. Determine the order of the matrix.

(i) $[-8]$ __________

(ii) $\begin{bmatrix} 7 \\ -5 \\ -1 \\ 3 \end{bmatrix}$ __________

(iii) $[2 \quad -4 \quad 0 \quad 9]$ __________

(iv) $\begin{bmatrix} 1 & -6 \\ -3 & 2 \\ 0 & 5 \end{bmatrix}$ __________

(v) $\begin{bmatrix} 1 & -5 & -8 \\ 6 & 4 & -2 \\ -3 & 0 & 7 \end{bmatrix}$ __________

(vi) $\begin{bmatrix} 13 & 2 & -6 & 4 \\ -1 & 18 & 5 & -12 \end{bmatrix}$ __________

***5.** (i) Construct a 2×3 matrix $B = [b_{ij}]_{2 \times 3}$, whose elements is $b_{ij} = \dfrac{i-j}{j+j}$ __________

(ii) Construct a 3×4 matrix $B = [b_{ij}]_{3 \times 4}$, whose elements are given by $b_{ij} = \dfrac{1}{2}(i+j)$ __________

6. Match the following for the matrix $A = [a_{ij}]_{m \times n}$

	Column I		Column II
A.	Row matrix	1.	$m \neq n$
B.	Square matrix	2.	$m = 1$
C.	Rectangular matrix	3.	$m = n = 1$
D.	Zero matrix	4.	$m = n$
E.	Singleton matrix	5.	$a_{ij} = 0$

Choose the correct option.

(a) A → 2, B → 4, C → 1, D → 5, E → 3
(b) A → 2, B → 1, C → 4, D → 3, E → 5
(c) A → 4, B → 2, C → 5, D → 3, E → 5
(d) A → 4, B → 1, C → 5, D → 3, E → 5

____

7. State True or False.

(i) A matrix that has all elements as 0 except diagonal elements is known as a diagonal matrix.

True ☐ False ☐

(ii) Scalar matrix is a kind of identity matrix.

True ☐ False ☐

(iii) The identity matrix can have any number of rows and columns.

True ☐ False ☐

(iv) A square matrix $B = [b_{ij}]_{n \times n}$ is said to be a scalar matrix, if $b_{ij} = 0$, where $i \neq j$.

True ☐ False ☐

(v) A matrix that has all elements as 0 is known as null matrix.

True ☐ False ☐

(vi) Every identity matrix is a scalar matrix.

True ☐ False ☐

8. Find the value of unknowns in the following equations.

(i) If $\begin{bmatrix} x+y & 2x+z \\ x-y & 2z+2p \end{bmatrix} = \begin{bmatrix} 4 & 7 \\ 0 & 16 \end{bmatrix}$ ________________

(ii) If $\begin{bmatrix} x+y+z & x+p \\ x+z & z+q \\ y+z & y-r \end{bmatrix} = \begin{bmatrix} 9 & 6 \\ 5 & 8 \\ 7 & 2 \end{bmatrix}$ ________________

(iii) If $\begin{bmatrix} x-y & 2x+z \\ 2x-y & 3z+p \end{bmatrix} = \begin{bmatrix} -1 & 5 \\ 0 & 13 \end{bmatrix}$ ________________

TOPIC 2

Operations of Matrices

9. Let $A = \begin{bmatrix} 3 & 5 \\ 4 & 8 \end{bmatrix}$, $B = \begin{bmatrix} 1 & 3 \\ -2 & 5 \end{bmatrix}$ and $C = \begin{bmatrix} -1 & 5 \\ 3 & 4 \end{bmatrix}$. Find the each of the following

(i) $A + B$ ________________

(ii) $A + B + C$ ________________

(iii) $A - B$ ________________

(iv) $A + B - C$ ________________

10. Choose the correct option.

(i) If $X = \begin{bmatrix} 3 & 1 & 3 \\ 2 & 3 & 4 \end{bmatrix}$ and $Y = \begin{bmatrix} -3 & 3 & 0 \\ 2 & 4 & 1 \end{bmatrix}$, then $X + Y$ is

(a) $\begin{bmatrix} 3 & 1 & 3 \\ 5 & 7 & 4 \end{bmatrix}$ (b) $\begin{bmatrix} 0 & 4 & 3 \\ 4 & 7 & 5 \end{bmatrix}$ (c) $\begin{bmatrix} 0 & 5 & 3 \\ 4 & 7 & 8 \end{bmatrix}$ (d) None of these

____

(ii) If $X + Y = \begin{bmatrix} 5 & 2 \\ 0 & 9 \end{bmatrix}$ and $X - Y = \begin{bmatrix} 3 & 6 \\ 0 & -1 \end{bmatrix}$, then the values of X and Y are

(a) $X = \begin{bmatrix} 4 & 0 \\ 0 & 4 \end{bmatrix}, Y = \begin{bmatrix} 4 & 4 \\ 0 & 4 \end{bmatrix}$ (b) $X = \begin{bmatrix} 4 & 4 \\ 0 & 4 \end{bmatrix}, Y = \begin{bmatrix} 1 & 0 \\ -2 & 5 \end{bmatrix}$

(c) $X = \begin{bmatrix} 4 & 4 \\ 0 & 4 \end{bmatrix}, Y = \begin{bmatrix} 1 & -2 \\ 0 & 5 \end{bmatrix}$ (d) None of these

____

11. Find the value of the following :

(i) If $2\begin{bmatrix}3 & 4\\5 & x\end{bmatrix}+\begin{bmatrix}1 & y\\0 & 1\end{bmatrix}=\begin{bmatrix}7 & 0\\10 & 5\end{bmatrix}$, then $x+y$ is ________

(ii) If $\begin{bmatrix}x & -5 & 3+x\\7 & y & 4\\y & 4+x & x+2\end{bmatrix}+\begin{bmatrix}y & 6 & y-2\\4+x & x & 3\\x+2 & y & y-2\end{bmatrix}=\begin{bmatrix}11 & 1 & 12\\22 & 11 & 7\\13 & 15 & 11\end{bmatrix}$, then $x-y$ is ________

(iii) If $\begin{bmatrix}2x+4y & 1\\3x-z & 2z\end{bmatrix}=\begin{bmatrix}26 & 1\\6 & 6\end{bmatrix}$, then $x+y+z$ is ________

12. Compute the indicated matrix by using the following matrices.

$A=\begin{bmatrix}1 & -2\\3 & 4\end{bmatrix}, B=\begin{bmatrix}2 & -3\\5 & -1\end{bmatrix}, C=\begin{bmatrix}0 & 6\\-4 & 2\end{bmatrix}, D=\begin{bmatrix}-2 & 3\\5 & -4\end{bmatrix}$ and $E=\begin{bmatrix}2 & 5\\7 & 3\end{bmatrix}$

(i) $3C+D$ ________

(ii) $4A-3B$ ________

(iii) $3A+2B-4C+2D+5E$ ________

***13.** Find a matrix A such that

(i) If $5A+B=\begin{bmatrix}4 & 3\\5 & 2\end{bmatrix}$ and $B=\begin{bmatrix}4 & -7\\0 & 7\end{bmatrix}$ ________

(ii) $2A-3B+5C=O$, where $B=\begin{bmatrix}-2 & 2 & 0\\3 & 1 & 4\end{bmatrix}$ and $C=\begin{bmatrix}2 & 0 & -2\\7 & 1 & 6\end{bmatrix}$ ________

***14.** Find the value of α and β in the following questions.

(i) If $A=\begin{bmatrix}\sin\alpha & -\sin\beta\\\sin\beta & \sin\alpha\end{bmatrix}$, then for what value of α and β, A is an identity matrix?

____

(ii) If $A=\begin{bmatrix}\alpha+\beta & 2\alpha\\2\beta & 3(\alpha-\beta)\end{bmatrix}$ and $B=\begin{bmatrix}5 & -4\beta\\-1 & 3\end{bmatrix}$, where $A+2B=15I$. ________

15. Determine whether the statement is True or False.

(i) If $k\begin{bmatrix}5 & 4\\3 & 2\end{bmatrix}-\begin{bmatrix}4 & a\\b & 4\end{bmatrix}=\begin{bmatrix}11 & 7\\6 & 2\end{bmatrix}$, then $k=a+b$.

True ☐ False ☐

(ii) $(k+l)A=kA+lA$, where k and l are scalars.

True ☐ False ☐

(iii) If $A=\text{diag}(1, 2, 3)$ and $B=\text{diag}(2, 3, 1)$, then $2A+3B=\text{diag}(8, 13, 9)$.

True ☐ False ☐

16. Compute AB and BA.

(i) $A=\begin{bmatrix}1 & -1\\ 2 & -2\end{bmatrix}$ and $B=\begin{bmatrix}3 & -4\\ -1 & 2\end{bmatrix}$ ______

(ii) $A=\begin{bmatrix}2 & -1 & -3\\ 0 & -4 & 7\end{bmatrix}$ and $B=\begin{bmatrix}2 & 1 & -1 & 4\\ 0 & -2 & 3 & 5\\ -6 & 4 & -2 & 0\end{bmatrix}$ ______

17. Find the value of $f(A)$.

(i) If $A=\begin{bmatrix}3 & 1\\ -1 & 2\end{bmatrix}$ and $f(x)=x^2-5x+7$, then $f(A)$ is ______

(ii) If $f(x)=x^2-4x+2$, where $A=\begin{bmatrix}1 & 0\\ -1 & 1\end{bmatrix}$, then $f(A)$ is ______

18. If $A=\begin{bmatrix}0 & 1 & 2\\ -1 & 2 & 0\\ 2 & -1 & -1\end{bmatrix}$, then the value of A^3 is ______

19. Find the value of λ.

(i) $\begin{bmatrix}1 & 4\\ 2 & 3\end{bmatrix}\begin{bmatrix}1 & 3\\ 2 & 4\end{bmatrix}=\begin{bmatrix}9 & \lambda\\ 8 & 18\end{bmatrix}$ ______

(ii) $A=\begin{bmatrix}2 & 1\\ 3 & -2\end{bmatrix}$ and $A^2=\lambda I$ ______

(iii) $A=\begin{bmatrix}1 & 2 & 2\\ 2 & 1 & 2\\ 2 & 2 & 1\end{bmatrix}$ and $A^2-4A=\lambda I$ ______

20. Find the value of A^n for the given matrix.

(i) $A=aI_3$ ______

(ii) $A=\begin{bmatrix}1 & x\\ 0 & 1\end{bmatrix}$ ______

***21.** Choose the correct option.

(i) $A=\begin{bmatrix}1 & -1\\ -1 & 1\end{bmatrix}$, then the matrix equation A^2-3A is equal to

(a) $-A$ (b) $3A$ (c) $-3A$ (d) A

______

(ii) If $A=\begin{bmatrix}1 & 2 & 3\\ 3 & -2 & 1\\ 4 & 2 & 1\end{bmatrix}$, then A^3-23A is equal to

(a) O (b) $40\,I$ (c) I (d) None of these

______

(iii) If $[1 \quad x \quad 1]\begin{bmatrix}1 & 3 & 2\\ 2 & 5 & 1\\ 15 & 3 & 2\end{bmatrix}\begin{bmatrix}1\\ 2\\ x\end{bmatrix} = O$, then the value of x is

(a) 14, 2 (b) 14, – 2

(c) – 14 , – 2 (d) None of these

(iv) If $f(x) = \begin{bmatrix}\cos x & \sin x\\ -\sin x & \cos x\end{bmatrix}$, then $f(\alpha)\, f(\beta)$ is

(a) $f(\alpha+\beta)$ (b) $f(\beta-\alpha)$ (c) $f(\alpha-\beta)$ (d) $f(\alpha\beta)$

(v) For two square matrix A and B, if $AB = A$ and $BA = B$, then the value of $A^2 + B^2 - (A + B)$ is

(a) 0 (b) 2

(c) 1 (d) None of these

***22.** Answer the following :

(i) If A is a matrix of order $m \times n$ and B is a matrix of order $n \times p$, then their product AB is of the order ______

(ii) If $[1 \quad 5 \quad 4]\begin{bmatrix}4 & 5 & 6\\ 1 & 2 & 3\\ \alpha & \beta & \gamma\end{bmatrix}\begin{bmatrix}a\\ b\\ c\end{bmatrix} = A$, then the order of matrix A is ______

TOPIC 3

Transpose, Symmetric Matrix, Skew-symmetric and Invertible Matrices

23. Find the transpose of the each of the following matrices.

(i) $\begin{bmatrix}6\\ 3\\ -4\end{bmatrix}$

(ii) $\begin{bmatrix}1 & 3 & 2\\ 3 & 6 & 5\end{bmatrix}$

(iii) $\begin{bmatrix}6 & -5 & 4\\ 2 & 7 & -6\\ 8 & 3 & -5\end{bmatrix}$

24. State True or False.

(i) If $A = \begin{bmatrix} -1 & 2 & 3 \\ 5 & 7 & 9 \\ 2 & 1 & 1 \end{bmatrix}$ and $B = \begin{bmatrix} -4 & 1 & -5 \\ 1 & 2 & 0 \\ 1 & 3 & 1 \end{bmatrix}$, then $(A+B)' = A' + B'$.

True ☐ False ☐

(ii) If $A' = \begin{bmatrix} -1 & 2 \\ 0 & 1 \end{bmatrix}$ and $B = \begin{bmatrix} -1 & 2 \\ 1 & 2 \end{bmatrix}$, then $(A - B)' = A' - B'$.

True ☐ False ☐

(iii) If $A = \begin{bmatrix} 3 & 4 & 3 \\ -1 & 2 & 4 \end{bmatrix}$, $B = \begin{bmatrix} 1 & 2 & 3 \\ 0 & -1 & 2 \end{bmatrix}$ and $C^T = \begin{bmatrix} 1 & 4 \\ 2 & 1 \\ -4 & 3 \end{bmatrix}$, then the value of $(A+B)^T - C^T$ is $\begin{bmatrix} 3 & -5 \\ 4 & 0 \\ 10 & 3 \end{bmatrix}$.

True ☐ False ☐

(iv) If $A = \begin{bmatrix} 1 \\ -4 \\ 2 \end{bmatrix}$ and $B = [1 \;\; 2 \;\; -1]$, then $(AB)' = B'A'$.

True ☐ False ☐

(v) If $A = \begin{bmatrix} 5 & 0 & 4 \\ 2 & 3 & 2 \\ 1 & 2 & 1 \end{bmatrix}$ and $B' = \begin{bmatrix} 1 & 3 & 3 \\ 1 & 4 & 3 \\ 1 & 3 & 4 \end{bmatrix}$, then $(AB)' = \begin{bmatrix} 17 & 17 & 10 \\ 17 & 20 & 12 \\ 21 & 19 & 11 \end{bmatrix}$

True ☐ False ☐

(vi) If $A = \begin{bmatrix} 1 & 2 & 2 \\ 2 & 1 & -2 \\ a & 2 & b \end{bmatrix}$ is a matrix satisfying $AA^T = 9I_3$, then the value of $a + b$ is $-\frac{1}{3}$.

True ☐ False ☐

25. Choose the correct option.

(i) If the matrix $\begin{bmatrix} 2 & 3 & 0 \\ a & 4 & 5 \\ b & c & 1 \end{bmatrix}$ is symmetric, then the value of $a + b + c$ is

(a) 5 (b) 6 (c) 4 (d) 8

(ii) The matrix $A = \begin{bmatrix} 0 & 1 & 2 \\ -1 & 0 & -5 \\ -2 & 5 & 0 \end{bmatrix}$ is a

(a) diagonal matrix (b) symmetric matrix

(c) skew-symmetric matrix (d) scalar matrix

____

*(iii) If A is skew-symmetric, then A^3 is a

(a) symmetric (b) skew-symmetric

(c) hermitian (d) None of these

____

26. If the matrix $\begin{bmatrix} 0 & 2 & 3 \\ a & b & c \\ d & 1 & 0 \end{bmatrix}$ is skew-symmetric, then find the value of a, b, c and d.

$a =$ ______________ $b =$ ______________

$c =$ ______________ $d =$ ______________

27. State True or False.

(i) The matrix $B^T AB$ is skew-symmetric, if A is a symmetric matrix.

True ☐ False ☐

(ii) If $A = \begin{bmatrix} 1 & 2 \\ 3 & 4 \end{bmatrix}$ is written as $A = P + Q$, where P is a symmetric matrix and Q is a skew-symmetric matrix, then the matrix P is $\begin{bmatrix} 1 & 5/2 \\ 5/2 & 4 \end{bmatrix}$.

True ☐ False ☐

***28.** Find the following matrices as the sum of a symmetric and a skew-symmetric matrix.

(i) $\begin{bmatrix} 4 & 5 \\ 1 & 2 \end{bmatrix}$ ______________________________

(ii) $\begin{bmatrix} 2 & 3 & 5 \\ 6 & -2 & 1 \\ 2 & -1 & 3 \end{bmatrix}$ ______________________________

(iii) $\begin{bmatrix} 1 & 2 & 3 \\ -6 & 8 & 3 \\ -4 & 6 & 5 \end{bmatrix}$ ______________________________

***29.** If $A^2 + 7I = O$, then the value of A^{-1} is equal to ______________________________

Assertion-Reason Questions

The following questions consist of two statements – Assertion (A) and Reason (R). Answer these questions by selecting the appropriate options given below.
(a) Both A and R are true and R is the correct explanation of A.
(b) Both A and R are true but R is not the correct explanation of A.
(c) A is true but R is false.
(d) A is false but R is true.

1. **Assertion** (A) $\begin{bmatrix} 0 & 1 \\ 1 & 0 \end{bmatrix}$ is an identity matrix.

Reason (R) A matrix $A = [a_{ij}]$ is an identity matrix if $a_{ij} = \begin{cases} 1, & \text{if } i = j \\ 0, & \text{if } i \neq j \end{cases}$

(a) ☐ (b) ☐ (c) ☐ (d) ☐

2. **Assertion** (A) Matrix $\begin{bmatrix} 1 \\ 7 \\ 2 \end{bmatrix}$ is an column matrix.

Reason (R) A matrix of order $m \times 1$ is called a column matrix.

(a) ☐ (b) ☐ (c) ☐ (d) ☐

3. **Assertion** (A) Transpose of the matrix $A = [2 \quad 5 \quad -1]$ is column matrix.

Reason (R) Transpose of a matrix of order $m \times n$ is a matrix of same order.

(a) ☐ (b) ☐ (c) ☐ (d) ☐

4. **Assertion** (A) If $\begin{bmatrix} xy & 4 \\ z+5 & x+y \end{bmatrix} = \begin{bmatrix} 4 & w \\ 0 & 4 \end{bmatrix}$, then $x = 2$, $y = 2$, $z = -5$ and $w = 4$.

Reason (R) Two matrices are equal. If their order are same and their corresponding elements are equal.

(a) ☐ (b) ☐ (c) ☐ (d) ☐

5. **Assertion** (A) Matrix $\begin{bmatrix} 3 & 2 & 2 \\ 2 & 3 & 2 \\ 2 & 2 & 3 \end{bmatrix}$ is a symmetric matrix.

Reason (R) A matrix is a symmetric if $A' = -A$.

(a) ☐ (b) ☐ (c) ☐ (d) ☐

6. **Assertion** (A) For two matrices $A = \begin{bmatrix} 2 & 0 \\ 0 & 3 \end{bmatrix}$ and $B = \begin{bmatrix} 5 & 0 \\ 0 & 0 \end{bmatrix}$ $(A + B)^2 = A^2 + 2AB + B^2$.

Reason (R) For given two matrices A and B, $AB = BA$.

(a) ☐ (b) ☐ (c) ☐ (d) ☐

7. **Assertion** (A) Let A be a square matrix give by $A = \begin{bmatrix} 1 & 2 & 4 \\ 6 & 8 & 2 \\ 2 & -2 & 7 \end{bmatrix}$, then skew-symmetric part of A is given by $\begin{bmatrix} 0 & -2 & 1 \\ 2 & 0 & 2 \\ -1 & -2 & 0 \end{bmatrix}$.

Reason (R) For every square matrix $A - A'$ is skew-symmetric.

(a) ☐ (b) ☐ (c) ☐ (d) ☐

8. **Assertion** (A) For the matrices $A = \begin{bmatrix} -3 & 2 \\ -5 & 4 \end{bmatrix}$ and $B = \begin{bmatrix} 4 & -2 \\ 5 & -3 \end{bmatrix}$ $A^{100} B = BA^{100}$.

Reason (R) $AB = BA^n$, implies integers.

(a) ☐ (b) ☐ (c) ☐ (d) ☐

9. **Assertion** (A) The sum of two orthogonal matrices is always orthogonal.

Reason (R) Two matrices A and B are orthogonal if $A^T A = I$ and $B^T B = I$.

(a) ☐ (b) ☐ (c) ☐ (d) ☐

10. **Assertion** (A) The transpose of a symmetric matrix is always symmetric.

Reason (R) Matrix A is symmetric if $A = A^T$.

(a) ☐ (b) ☐ (c) ☐ (d) ☐

Case Based Questions

Case 1 In a city there are two factories A and B. Each factory produces sports clothes for boys and girls. There are three types of clothes produces in the both factories, types I, II and III. For boys the of units number of types I, II and III respectively are 80, 70 and 65 in factory A and 85, 65 and 72 are in factory B. For girls the number of units of types I, II and III respectively are 80, 75, 90 in factory A and 50, 55, 80 are in factory B.

Based on the above information, answer the following questions.

(i) If P represent the matrix of number of units of each type produced by factory A for both boys and girls, then P is given by

(a) $\begin{array}{c} \\ \text{I} \\ \text{II} \\ \text{III} \end{array}\begin{array}{c} \text{Boys} \quad \text{Girls} \\ \begin{bmatrix} 85 & 50 \\ 65 & 55 \\ 72 & 80 \end{bmatrix} \end{array}$ ☐

(b) $\begin{array}{c} \\ \text{Boys} \\ \text{Girls} \end{array}\begin{array}{c} \text{I} \quad \text{II} \quad \text{III} \\ \begin{bmatrix} 50 & 55 & 80 \\ 85 & 65 & 72 \end{bmatrix} \end{array}$ ☐

(c) $\begin{array}{c} \\ \text{Boys} \\ \text{Girls} \end{array}\begin{array}{c} \text{I} \quad \text{II} \quad \text{III} \\ \begin{bmatrix} 80 & 75 & 90 \\ 80 & 70 & 65 \end{bmatrix} \end{array}$ ☐

(d) $\begin{array}{c} \\ \text{I} \\ \text{II} \\ \text{III} \end{array}\begin{array}{c} \text{Boys} \quad \text{Girls} \\ \begin{bmatrix} 80 & 80 \\ 70 & 75 \\ 65 & 90 \end{bmatrix} \end{array}$ ☐

(ii) If Q represents the matrix of number of units of each type produced by factory B for both boys and girls

(a) $\begin{array}{c} \\ \text{I} \\ \text{II} \\ \text{III} \end{array}\begin{array}{c} \text{Boys} \quad \text{Girls} \\ \begin{bmatrix} 85 & 50 \\ 65 & 55 \\ 72 & 80 \end{bmatrix} \end{array}$ ☐ (b) $\begin{array}{c} \\ \text{Boys} \\ \text{Girls} \end{array}\begin{array}{c} \text{I} \quad \text{II} \quad \text{III} \\ \begin{bmatrix} 50 & 55 & 80 \\ 85 & 65 & 72 \end{bmatrix} \end{array}$ ☐

(c) $\begin{array}{c} \\ \text{Boys} \\ \text{Girls} \end{array}\begin{array}{c} \text{I} \quad \text{II} \quad \text{III} \\ \begin{bmatrix} 80 & 75 & 90 \\ 80 & 70 & 65 \end{bmatrix} \end{array}$ ☐ (d) $\begin{array}{c} \\ \text{I} \\ \text{II} \\ \text{III} \end{array}\begin{array}{c} \text{Boys} \quad \text{Girls} \\ \begin{bmatrix} 80 & 80 \\ 70 & 75 \\ 65 & 90 \end{bmatrix} \end{array}$ ☐

(iii) The total production of sports clothes of each type for boys is given by the matrix.

(a) $\begin{array}{c} \text{I} \quad \text{II} \quad \text{III} \\ \begin{bmatrix} 165 & 130 & 137 \end{bmatrix} \end{array}$ ☐ (b) $\begin{array}{c} \text{I} \quad \text{II} \quad \text{III} \\ \begin{bmatrix} 130 & 165 & 137 \end{bmatrix} \end{array}$ ☐

(c) $\begin{array}{c} \text{I} \quad \text{II} \quad \text{III} \\ \begin{bmatrix} 165 & 135 & 137 \end{bmatrix} \end{array}$ ☐ (d) $\begin{array}{c} \text{I} \quad \text{II} \quad \text{III} \\ \begin{bmatrix} 137 & 135 & 165 \end{bmatrix} \end{array}$ ☐

(iv) The total production of sports clothes of each type for girls is given by the matrix.

(a) $\begin{array}{c} \text{I} \quad \text{II} \quad \text{III} \\ \begin{bmatrix} 130 & 130 & 170 \end{bmatrix} \end{array}$ ☐ (b) $\begin{array}{c} \text{I} \quad \text{II} \quad \text{III} \\ \begin{bmatrix} 170 & 130 & 130 \end{bmatrix} \end{array}$ ☐

(c) $\begin{array}{c} \text{I} \quad \text{II} \quad \text{III} \\ \begin{bmatrix} 130 & 170 & 130 \end{bmatrix} \end{array}$ ☐ (d) None of these ☐

Case 2 Consider 2 families A and B. Suppose, there are 4 men, 4 women and 4 children in family A and 2 men, 2 women, and 2 children in family B. The recommend daily amount of calories is 2400 for a man, 1900 for a woman, 1800 for a children and 45 grams of protein for a man, 55 grams for a woman and 33 grams for children.

Based on the above information, answer the following question.

(i) The requirement of calories and protein for each person in matrix form can be represented as

(a) $\begin{array}{c} \\ \text{Man} \\ \text{Woman} \\ \text{Children} \end{array}\begin{array}{c} \text{Calorie} \quad \text{Protein} \\ \begin{bmatrix} 2400 & 45 \\ 1900 & 55 \\ 1800 & 33 \end{bmatrix} \end{array}$ ☐ (b) $\begin{array}{c} \\ \text{Man} \\ \text{Woman} \\ \text{Children} \end{array}\begin{array}{c} \text{Calorie} \quad \text{Protein} \\ \begin{bmatrix} 1900 & 55 \\ 2400 & 45 \\ 1800 & 33 \end{bmatrix} \end{array}$ ☐

(c) $\begin{array}{c} \\ \text{Man} \\ \text{Woman} \\ \text{Children} \end{array}\begin{array}{c} \text{Calorie} \quad \text{Protein} \\ \begin{bmatrix} 1800 & 33 \\ 1900 & 55 \\ 2400 & 45 \end{bmatrix} \end{array}$ ☐ (d) $\begin{array}{c} \\ \text{Man} \\ \text{Woman} \\ \text{Children} \end{array}\begin{array}{c} \text{Calorie} \quad \text{Protein} \\ \begin{bmatrix} 2400 & 33 \\ 1900 & 55 \\ 1800 & 45 \end{bmatrix} \end{array}$ ☐

(ii) Requirement of calories of family A is

(a) 24000 ☐ (b) 24400 ☐ (c) 15000 ☐ (d) 15800 ☐

(iii) Requirement of protein for family B is

(a) 560 grams ☐ (b) 332 grams ☐

(c) 266 grams ☐ (d) 300 grams ☐

(iv) If A and B are two matrices such that $AB = B$ and $BA = A$, then $A^2 + B^2$ equals

(a) $2AB$ ☐ (b) $2BA$ ☐ (c) $A + B$ ☐ (d) AB ☐

COMPETITION EDGE UP

1. Let α and β be real numbers. Consider a 3×3 matrix A such that $A^2 = 3A + \alpha I$. If $A^4 = 21A + \beta I$, then **[JEE Main 2023]**

(a) $\alpha = 1$

(b) $\alpha = 4$

(c) $\beta = 8$

(d) $\beta = -8$

2. The number of square matrices of order 5 with entries from the set $\{0, 1\}$, such that the sum of all the elements in each row is 1 and the sum of all the elements in each column is also 1, is **[JEE Main 2023, 24]**

(a) 120

(b) 125

(c) 225

(d) 150

3. If A and B are two non-zero $n \times n$ matrices such that $A^2 + B = A^2 B$, then **[JEE Main 2023, 24]**

(a) $A^2 B = BA^2$

(b) $A^2 B = I$

(c) $A^2 = I$ or $B = I$

(d) $AB = I$

4. Let $A = \begin{bmatrix} 2 & a & 0 \\ 1 & 3 & 1 \\ 0 & 5 & b \end{bmatrix}$.

If $A^3 = 4A^2 - A - 21I$, where I is the identity matrix of order 3×3. Then, $2a + 3b$ is equal to **[JEE Main 2024]**

(a) -10

(b) -9

(c) -13

(d) -12

5. If $A = \frac{1}{2}\begin{bmatrix} 1 & \sqrt{3} \\ -\sqrt{3} & 1 \end{bmatrix}$, then **[2023, 1 Feb Shift-II]**

(a) $A^{30} - A^{25} = 2I$

(b) $A^{30} + A^{25} - A = I$

(c) $A^{30} + A^{25} + A = I$

(d) $A^{30} = A^{25}$

6. Let $A = \begin{bmatrix} 1 & \frac{1}{51} \\ 0 & 1 \end{bmatrix}$. If $B = \begin{bmatrix} 1 & 2 \\ -1 & -1 \end{bmatrix} A \begin{bmatrix} -1 & -2 \\ 1 & 1 \end{bmatrix}$, then the sum of all the elements of the matrix $\sum_{n=1}^{50} B^n$ is equal to **[JEE Main 2023]**

(a) 100

(b) 75

(c) 125

(d) 50

7. Let $A = \begin{bmatrix} 1 & 0 & 0 \\ 0 & 4 & -1 \\ 0 & 12 & -3 \end{bmatrix}$. Then, the sum of the diagonal elements of the matrix $(A + I)^{11}$ is equal to **[JEE Main 2023]**

(a) 2050

(b) 4094

(c) 6144

(d) 4097

8. Let $A = \begin{bmatrix} 2 & -1 \\ 1 & 1 \end{bmatrix}$. If the sum of the diagonal elements of A^{13} is 3^n, then n is equal to .... **[JEE Main 2024]**

9. Let $A = \begin{bmatrix} 0 & 1 & 2 \\ a & 0 & 3 \\ 1 & c & 0 \end{bmatrix}$, where $a, c \in R$. If $A^3 = A$ and the positive value of a belongs to the interval $(n-1, n]$, where $n \in N$, then n is equal to .... **[JEE Main 2023]**

10. Let $A = [a_{ij}]$, $a_{ij} \in Z \cap [0, 4]$, $1 \le i, j \le 2$. The number of matrices A such that the sum of all entries is a prime number $p \in (2, 13)$ is .... **[JEE Main 2023]**

11. Let A be a square matrix such that $AA^T = I$. Then, $\frac{1}{2} A[(A + A^T)^2 + (A - A^T)^2]$ is equal to **[JEE Main 2024]**

(a) $A^2 + A^T$

(b) $A^3 + A^T$

(c) $A^2 + I$

(d) $A^3 + I$

12. The number of symmetric matrices of order 3, with all the entries from the set $\{0, 1, 2, 3, 4, 5, 6, 7, 8, 9\}$, is **[JEE Main 2023]**

(a) 9^{10} ☐
(b) 10^6 ☐
(c) 10^9 ☐
(d) 6^{10} ☐

13. Let P be a square matrix such that $P^2 = I - P$. For $\alpha, \beta, \gamma, \delta \in N$. If $P^{\alpha} + P^{\beta} = \gamma I - 29P$ and $P^{\alpha} - P^{\beta} = \delta I - 13P$, then $\alpha + \beta + \gamma - \delta$ is equal to **[JEE Main 2023]**

(a) 22 ☐
(b) 18 ☐
(c) 24 ☐
(d) 40 ☐

14. Let $P = \begin{bmatrix} \frac{\sqrt{3}}{2} & \frac{1}{2} \\ -\frac{1}{2} & \frac{\sqrt{3}}{2} \end{bmatrix}$, $A = \begin{bmatrix} 1 & 1 \\ 0 & 1 \end{bmatrix}$ and $Q = PAP^T$. If $P^T Q^{2007} P = \begin{bmatrix} a & b \\ c & d \end{bmatrix}$, then $2a + b - 3c - 4d$ is equal to **[JEE Main 2023]**

(a) 2007 ☐
(b) 2004 ☐
(c) 2005 ☐
(d) 2006 ☐

15. Let A be a 2×2 matrix with real entries such that $A' = \alpha A + I$, where $\alpha \in R - \{-1, 1\}$. If $\det(A^2 - A) = 4$, then the sum of all possible values of α is equal to **[JEE Main 2023]**

(a) 5/2 ☐
(b) 2 ☐
(c) 3/2 ☐
(d) 0 ☐

16. If $A = \begin{bmatrix} 1 & 5 \\ \lambda & 10 \end{bmatrix}$, $A^{-1} = \alpha A + \beta I$ and $\alpha + \beta = -2$, then $4\alpha^2 + \beta^2 + \lambda^2$ is equal to **[JEE Main 2023]**

(a) 14 ☐
(b) 12 ☐
(c) 19 ☐
(d) 10 ☐

17. Let A, B and C be 3×3 matrices such that A is symmetric and B and C are skew-symmetric. Consider the statements

(S1) $A^{13} B^{26} - B^{26} A^{13}$ is symmetric.
(S2) $A^{26} C^{13} - C^{13} A^{26}$ is symmetric.

Then, **[JEE Main 2023]**

(a) Both S1 and S2 are false ☐
(b) only S1 is true ☐
(c) only S2 is true ☐
(d) Both S1 and S2 are true ☐

Scan this QR code from your mobile phone to get the solutions of **Competition Edge Up** of this chapter.

Chapter 04

Determinants

Scan and take Chapter Test

TOPIC 1

Expansion of Determinants

1. Matrix $A = [a_{ij}]$ is called square matrix, where i ______ j.

(a) = (equal to) (b) ≠ (not equal to)

(c) > (greater than) (d) < (less than)

2. Only square matrices have determinants.

True ☐ False ☐

***3.** Calculate the value of the following determinant.

(i) $\begin{vmatrix} 9 & -1 \\ -2 & 2/3 \end{vmatrix}$ ______

(ii) $\begin{vmatrix} a+b & -a \\ a-b & b \end{vmatrix}$ ______

(iii) $\begin{vmatrix} \sec\theta & \tan\theta \\ -\tan\theta & -\sec\theta \end{vmatrix}$ ______

(iv) $\begin{vmatrix} 21 & 22 & 23 \\ 24 & 25 & 26 \\ 27 & 28 & 29 \end{vmatrix}$ ______

(v) $\begin{vmatrix} a & b & c \\ b & c & a \\ c & a & b \end{vmatrix}$ ______

(vi) $\begin{vmatrix} \sin\theta & \cos\theta & 1 \\ 1 & \sin\theta & \cos\theta \\ \cos\theta & 1 & \sin\theta \end{vmatrix}$ ______

*Concepts of all questions bearing * are important for JEE & CUET*

4. State the given statements are True or False.

(i) If $A = \begin{bmatrix} 5 & -2 \\ 6 & 7 \end{bmatrix}$, then $|A| = 47$.

True ☐ False ☐

(ii) If $A = \begin{bmatrix} 1 & 0 & 1 \\ 0 & 2 & 1 \\ -1 & 0 & 3 \end{bmatrix}$, then $|A| = 5$.

True ☐ False ☐

***5.** Find the value of unknown variables in the following.

(i) If $\begin{vmatrix} 2x & 5 \\ 8 & 1 \end{vmatrix} = \begin{vmatrix} 6 & 6 \\ 3 & 1 \end{vmatrix}$, then x is ____________

(ii) If $\begin{vmatrix} 4 & -3 \\ 2 & 3 \end{vmatrix} = \begin{vmatrix} 6 & -1 \\ 8 & 9/y \end{vmatrix}$, then y is ____________

(iii) If $\begin{vmatrix} \sin\theta & \sec^2\theta \\ 1 & \operatorname{cosec}\theta \end{vmatrix} = \begin{vmatrix} \sin\theta & 1 \\ \sec^2\theta & \sec\theta \end{vmatrix}$, then θ is ____________

6. There are two values of a which makes determinant, $\begin{vmatrix} 1 & 2 & 2 \\ 2 & a & -1 \\ 3 & 4 & 2a \end{vmatrix} = 74$, then the sum of these numbers is ____________

7. If $\begin{vmatrix} x & -3 & 5 \\ 3 & x & -4 \\ 1 & 1 & -2 \end{vmatrix} = -1$, then the

(i) positive value of x is ____________

(ii) negative value of x is ____________

(iii) sum of positive and negative value of x is ____________

TOPIC 2

Area of a Triangle

NCERT Pg 82-83

8. Find the area of the ΔABC with vertices.

(i) $A(2, 3)$, $B(4, 5)$ and $C(8, 6)$ ____________

(ii) $A(2, 3)$, $B(-1, 0)$ and $C(2, -4)$ ____________

(iii) $A(-5, -1)$, $B(3, -5)$ and $C(5, -2)$ ____________

9. Find the area of the ΔABC shown in the graph.

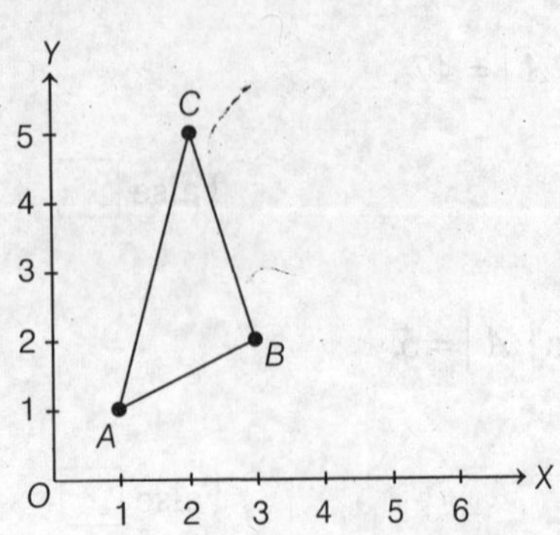

10. The points $(a, a^2 - bc)$, $(b, b^2 - ca)$ and $(c, c^2 - ab)$ are collinear.

True ☐ False ☐

11. Find the value of λ, if the given points are collinear.

(i) $(2, 4)$, (λ, λ) and $(1, 5)$ ____________________

(ii) $(2, 3)$, $(4, \lambda)$ and $(6, -3)$ ____________________

(iii) $(1, 0)$, $(3, \lambda^2)$ and $(5, 9)$ ____________________

12. If the area of ΔABC is 15 sq units, where the vertices of ΔABC are $(-1, -8)$, $(k, k-1)$ and $(3, 2)$, then the number of possible value of k is ____________________

13. Find the equation of the line joining the points $(3, -2)$ and $(7, 7)$, using determinant.

____

TOPIC 3

Minors and Cofactors

14. Calculate the minor and cofactor of following determinants.

(i) If $A = \begin{vmatrix} 3 & -1 \\ 0 & 2 \end{vmatrix}$, then the values of M_{22} and A_{21} are ____________________

(ii) If $\Delta = \begin{vmatrix} 2 & 1 & 5 \\ 0 & 3 & 4 \\ 7 & 8 & 2 \end{vmatrix}$, then the values of M_{31} and A_{22} are ____________________

(where minor of an element a_{ij} is denoted by M_{ij} and cofactor of an element a_{ij} is denoted by A_{ij})

15. The minor of the element of second row and third column of the square matrix $\begin{bmatrix} 1 & 2 & 3 \\ 4 & 0 & 5 \\ 2 & 1 & -1 \end{bmatrix}$ is ________

16. If $\Delta = \begin{vmatrix} 1 & 2 & 3 \\ 2 & 1 & 0 \\ 9 & 1 & 2 \end{vmatrix}$, then

(i) the minor of element 0 is ________

(ii) the minor of element 9 is ________

(iii) the minor of element 3 is ________

17. The cofactor of the element 3 of the matrix $\begin{bmatrix} 1 & 2 & 4 \\ 2 & 3 & -1 \\ 1 & 0 & 8 \end{bmatrix}$ is

(a) 2 (b) 3 (c) 4 (d) None of these

18. For the determinant $\Delta = \begin{vmatrix} 5 & 2 & -8 \\ 1 & 4 & 3 \\ 5 & 6 & -8 \end{vmatrix}$, then the minor and cofactor of the element 4 are non-zero.

True ☐ False ☐

19. For which of the following element in the matrix $A = \begin{bmatrix} 1 & 8 & 2 \\ 0 & -5 & 6 \\ -1 & 2 & 3 \end{bmatrix}$, then the cofactor is 58?

(a) 1 (b) 8 (c) −1 (d) 3

20. Find the minors and cofactors of the elements a_{21}, a_{22} and a_{32} of the matrix $\begin{bmatrix} 1 & 2 & -1 \\ 1 & 2 & 3 \\ 2 & -1 & 2 \end{bmatrix}$.

21. Using cofactor of elements of second row, expand $\begin{vmatrix} 1 & -1 & 2 \\ 5 & 3 & 8 \\ 1 & 2 & 3 \end{vmatrix}$

TOPIC 4

Adjoint and inverse of Matrix

22. The matrix $\begin{bmatrix} 1 & 2 & 4 \\ 3 & -1 & 0 \\ -7 & 2 & 1 \end{bmatrix}$ is singular matrix.

True ☐ False ☐

23. For what value of x, the matrix $\begin{bmatrix} 2 & 4 \\ 8-2x & x+1 \end{bmatrix}$ is singular?

______

24. Find the adjoint of the following matrices.

(i) $\begin{bmatrix} 1 & 3 \\ 4 & 5 \end{bmatrix}$ ______

(ii) $\begin{bmatrix} a & b^2 \\ -c & 3a \end{bmatrix}$ ______

(iii) $\begin{bmatrix} 1 & 2 & 3 \\ 1 & -1 & 0 \\ 4 & -2 & 3 \end{bmatrix}$ ______

(iv) $\begin{bmatrix} 1 & -1 & 0 \\ 2 & 1 & 4 \\ -3 & 2 & 5 \end{bmatrix}$ ______

25. If $A = \begin{bmatrix} \tan\theta & -\sec\theta \\ \sec\theta & -\tan\theta \end{bmatrix}$, then the value of $|\text{adj } A| = -1$.

True ☐ False ☐

***26.** If Δ is the determinant of a square matrix A of order n, then the $|\text{adj } A|$ is

(a) Δ (b) Δ^{n-1} (c) Δ^{n+1} (d) Δ^n

______

27. If A is a square matrix of order 3 such that adj $A = \begin{bmatrix} 64 & 0 & 0 \\ 0 & 64 & 0 \\ 0 & 0 & 64 \end{bmatrix}$, then the value of $|A|$ is

(a) 8 (b) 64 (c) 512 (d) None of these

______

28. The determinant of a skew-symmetric matrix of odd order is always zero.

True ☐ False ☐

***29.** If A is a square matrix of order 3 and $|A| = 5$, then the value of $|A(\text{adj } A)|$ is ______

30. If A and B are square matrices of the order 3 such that $|A| = 5$ and $AB = 10\,I$, then the value of $|B|$ is ______

***31.** For any 2×2 matrix, if $A(\text{adj } A) = \begin{vmatrix} 7 & 0 \\ 0 & 7 \end{vmatrix}$, then value of $|A|$ is ______

32. If $A = \begin{bmatrix} 3 & 1 \\ 4 & 2 \end{bmatrix}$, then the value of $A(\text{adj} A)$ is

(a) $\begin{bmatrix} 1 & 0 \\ 0 & 5 \end{bmatrix}$ (b) I (c) $\begin{bmatrix} 2 & 0 \\ 0 & 2 \end{bmatrix}$ (d) None of these

______

33. If A is a singular matrix of order n, then $A(\text{adj} A)$ is a ______ matrix.

34. Let A be a square matrix of order n, then $A(\text{adj} A) = (\text{adj} A)A = |A|\, I_n$. Justify your answer.

True ☐ False ☐

35. If K is a scalar and I is a unit matrix of order 3, then $\text{adj}\,(KI) = K^2 I_3$.

True ☐ False ☐

***36.** If $A = \begin{bmatrix} 1 & -1 & 1 \\ 0 & 2 & -3 \\ 2 & 1 & 0 \end{bmatrix}$, then the value of $\dfrac{|\text{adj}(\text{adj} A)|}{|5A|}$ is

(a) 0 (b) $|A|$ (c) 1 (d) None of these

37. If A is a singular matrix, then adj A is also a singular matrix.

True ☐ False ☐

38. If matrix $A\begin{bmatrix} 3 & 2 \\ 1 & 1 \end{bmatrix} = \begin{bmatrix} 4 & 1 \\ -1 & 2 \end{bmatrix}$, then A is ______

39. Write A^{-1} for $A = \begin{bmatrix} 4 & 1 \\ 5 & 2 \end{bmatrix}$.

______

40. Which of the following statement is correct or incorrect for the invertible function?

(i) $(A^T)^{-1} = (A^{-1})^T$

True ☐ False ☐

(ii) $(AB)^{-1} = B^{-1}A^{-1}$

True ☐ False ☐

(iii) $(\text{adj } A)^T = -(\text{adj } A)$

True ☐ False ☐

(iv) The inverse of an invertible symmetric matrix is a symmetric matrix.

True ☐ False ☐

***41.** If $A = \begin{bmatrix} 4 & 1 \\ -1 & 3 \end{bmatrix}$, then the value of $A^2 - 5A + 7I$ ____________ and A^{-1} ____________.

***42.** If $A = \begin{bmatrix} 2 & 7 \\ -6 & 4 \end{bmatrix}$, where $A^2 + aA + bI = O$, then the value of a and b are ____________

***43.** For the matrix $A = \begin{bmatrix} 1 & 1 & 1 \\ 1 & 3 & -4 \\ 3 & -1 & 5 \end{bmatrix}$, if $A^3 - 6A^2 - 5A + 11I = O$, then the value of A^{-1} is

____

TOPIC 5

Applications of Determinants and Matrices

44. Solve the following system of the equations using inverse of matrix.

(i) $x + 2y - 3z = -4$, $2x + 3y + 2z = 2$ and $3x - 3y - 4z = 11$

Then, $x =$ ____________, $y =$ ____________ and $z =$ ____________

(ii) $x - y + 2z = 7$, $3x + 4y - 5z = -5$ and $2x - y + 3z = 12$.

Then, $x =$ ____________, $y =$ ____________ and $z =$ ____________

45. The given system of equation is consistent

(i) $x + 2y = 2$ and $2x + 3y = 3$

True ☐ False ☐

(ii) $3x - y = 5$ and $6x - 2y = 3$

True ☐ False ☐

(iii) $3x - y - 2z = 2$, $2y - z = -1$ and $3x - 5y = 3$

True ☐ False ☐

46. The given system of the equation has unique solution.

(i) $y - z = 1$, $-x + 2z = -2$ and $x - 2y = 3$

True ☐ False ☐

(ii) $x + 3y + 3z = 2$, $x + 4y + 3z = 1$ and $x + 3y + 4z = 2$

True ☐ False ☐

47. If the system of the linear equations $x + 2ay + az = 0$, $x + 3by + bz = 0$ and $x + 4cy + cz = 0$ has no solution, then a, b and c are in AP.

True ☐ False ☐

Assertion-Reason Questions

The following questions consist of two statements – Assertion (A) and Reason (R). Answer these questions by selecting the appropriate options given below.
(a) Both A and R are true and R is the correct explanation of A.
(b) Both A and R are true but R is not the correct explanation of A.
(c) A is true but R is false.
(d) A is false but R is true.

1. **Assertion** (A) Minor of element 6 in the matrix $\begin{bmatrix} 0 & 2 & 6 \\ 1 & 2 & -1 \\ 2 & 1 & 3 \end{bmatrix}$ is –3.

Reason (R) Minor of an element a_{ij} of a matrix is the determinant obtained by deleting its ith row.

(a) ☐ (b) ☐ (c) ☐ (d) ☐

2. **Assertion** (A) For two matrices A and B of order 3, $|A| = 3$, $|B| = -4$, then $|2AB|$ is –96.

Reason (R) For a matrix A of an order n and a scalar k, $|kA| = k^n |A|$.

(a) ☐ (b) ☐ (c) ☐ (d) ☐

3. **Assertion** (A) For a matrix $A = \begin{bmatrix} 4 & 1 \\ 3 & 2 \end{bmatrix}$, $A\,(\text{adj}\ A) = \begin{bmatrix} 5 & 0 \\ 0 & 5 \end{bmatrix}$.

Reason (R) For a square matrix A, $A\,(\text{adj}\ A) = (\text{adj}\,A)\,A = |A|$. In

(a) ☐ (b) ☐ (c) ☐ (d) ☐

4. **Assertion** (A) For a square matrix of order $2A^{-1} = \frac{1}{5}$ adj A, so $|2A| = 20$.

Reason (R) For a square matrix of order n, $A^{-1} = \frac{1}{|A|}$ adj A and $|\text{adj}\ A| = |A|^{n-1}$.

(a) ☐ (b) ☐ (c) ☐ (d) ☐

5. **Assertion** (A) Value of x for which the matrix $\begin{bmatrix} 2 & 1 & 0 \\ 0 & 1 & 2 \\ 1 & -2 & x \end{bmatrix}$ is singular is –5.

Reason (R) A matrix A is singular, if $|A| \neq 0$.

(a) ☐ (b) ☐ (c) ☐ (d) ☐

6. **Assertion** (A) For a square matrix, $(2A)^{-1} = \frac{1}{2}A^{-1}$.

Reason (R) For any matrix A and scalar k, kA is a matrix obtained by multiplying each element of A by k.

(a) ☐ (b) ☐ (c) ☐ (d) ☐

7. **Assertion** (A) For a matrix $A = [a_{ij}]_3$, if det (adj A) = 49, then det $(A) = \pm 7$.

Reason (R) For a square matrix A of order n, $|\text{adj } A| = |A|^{n-1}$.

(a) ☐ (b) ☐ (c) ☐ (d) ☐

8. **Assertion** (A) adj (adj A) = $(\det A)^{n-2} A$.

Reason (R) $|\text{adj } A| = |A|^{n-1}$.

(a) ☐ (b) ☐ (c) ☐ (d) ☐

9. **Assertion** (A) If $|A|^2 = 25$, then $|A| = \pm \frac{1}{5}$.

Reason (R) $|AB| = |A||B|$.

(a) ☐ (b) ☐ (c) ☐ (d) ☐

10. **Assertion** (A) Value of k for which area of the triangle with vertices (1, 1), (0, 2), (k, 0) is 3 sq. units are 4 and 8.

Reason (R) Area of the triangle with vertices $(x_1, y_1), (x_2, y_2), (x_3, y_3)$ is $\frac{1}{2}\begin{vmatrix} x_1 & y_1 & 1 \\ x_2 & y_2 & 1 \\ x_3 & y_3 & 1 \end{vmatrix}$.

(a) ☐ (b) ☐ (c) ☐ (d) ☐

Case Based Questions

Case 1 Each triangular face of the Pyramid is made up of 30 smaller equilateral triangles as shown in the figure.

Using the above information and concept of determinants, answer the following questions.

(i) If the vertices of one of the smaller equilateral triangles are (0, 0), $(2, \sqrt{2})$ and $(2, -\sqrt{2})$, then the area of such triangle is

(a) $\sqrt{2}$ sq units ☐ (b) $3\sqrt{2}$ sq units ☐

(c) $2\sqrt{2}$ sq units ☐ (d) None of these ☐

(ii) The area of a face of the Pyramid is

(a) $25\sqrt{2}$ sq units ☐ (b) $50\sqrt{2}$ sq units ☐

(c) $60\sqrt{2}$ sq units ☐ (d) $35\sqrt{2}$ sq units ☐

(iii) The square of one side of smaller equilateral triangle is

(a) $3\sqrt{2}$ ☐ (b) $8\sqrt{2}$ ☐

(c) $2\sqrt{5}$ ☐ (d) 16 ☐

(iv) If (2, 4) and (2, 6) are two vertices of a smaller equilateral triangle, then the third vertex will lie on the line represented by

(a) $x + y = 5$ ☐ (b) $x = 1 + \sqrt{3}$ ☐

(c) $x = 2 + 2\sqrt{2}$ ☐ (d) $2x + y = 5$ ☐

(v) Let $A(a, 0)$, $B(0, b)$ and $C(1, 1)$ be three points. If $\frac{1}{a} + \frac{1}{b} = 1$, then the three points are

(a) vertices of an equilateral triangle. ☐

(b) vertices of a right angled triangle. ☐

(c) collinear. ☐

(d) vertices of an isosceles triangle. ☐

Case 2 Two schools A and B want to award their selected students on the values of Honesty, Hardwork and Punctuality. The school A wants to award ₹ x each, ₹ y each and ₹ z each for the three respective values to its 3, 2 and 1 students, respctively with a total award money of ₹ 2200, School B wants to spend ₹ 3100 to award its 4, 1 and 3 students on the respective values (by giving the same award money to the three values as school A). The total amount of award for one prize on each values is ₹1200.

Using the concept of matrices and determinants, answer the following questions.

(i) What is the award money for Honesty?

(a) ₹ 350 ☐ (b) ₹ 300 ☐

(c) ₹ 500 ☐ (d) ₹ 400 ☐

(ii) what is the award money for Punctuality?

(a) ₹ 300 ☐ (b) ₹ 280 ☐

(c) ₹ 450 ☐ (d) ₹ 500 ☐

(iii) What is the award money for Hard work?

(a) ₹ 500 ☐ (b) ₹ 400 ☐

(c) ₹ 360 ☐ (d) ₹ 550 ☐

(iv) If a matrix P is both symmetric and skew-symmetric, then $|P|$ is equal to

(a) 1 ☐ (b) −1 ☐

(c) 0 ☐ (d) None of these ☐

(v) If P and Q are two matrices such that $PQ = Q$ and $QP = P$, then $|Q^2|$ is equal to

(a) $|Q|$ ☐ (b) $|P|$ ☐

(c) 1 ☐ (d) 0 ☐

COMPETITION EDGE UP

1. Let $B = \begin{bmatrix} 1 & 3 \\ 1 & 5 \end{bmatrix}$ and A be a 2×2 matrix such that $AB^{-1} = A^{-1}$. If $BCB^{-1} = A$ and $C^4 + \alpha C^2 + \beta I = 0$, then $2\beta - \alpha$ is equal to **[JEE Main 2024]**

(a) 8 ☐
(b) 10 ☐
(c) 16 ☐
(d) 2 ☐

2. Let A be a non-singular matrix of order 3. If $\det(3\,adj\,(2\,adj\,((\det A)\,A))) = 3^{-13} \cdot 2^{-10}$ and $\det(3\,adj(2A)) = 2^m \cdot 3^n$, then $|3m + 2n|$ is equal to .... **[JEE Main 2024]**

3. If $\alpha \neq a$, $\beta \neq b$, $\gamma \neq c$ and $\begin{vmatrix} \alpha & b & c \\ a & \beta & c \\ a & b & \gamma \end{vmatrix} = 0$, then $\frac{a}{\alpha - a} + \frac{b}{\beta - b} + \frac{\gamma}{\gamma - c}$ is equal to **[JEE Main 2024]**

(a) 0 ☐
(b) 3 ☐
(c) 2 ☐
(d) 1 ☐

4. Let $A = \begin{bmatrix} 2 & a & 0 \\ 1 & 3 & 1 \\ 0 & 5 & b \end{bmatrix}$.

If $A^3 = 4A^2 - A - 21I$, where I is an identity matrix of order 3×3. Then, $2a + 3b$ is equal to **[JEE Main 2024]**

(a) -10 ☐
(b) -9 ☐
(c) -13 ☐
(d) -12 ☐

5. If A is a square matrix of order 3 such that $\det(A) = 3$ and $\det(adj(-4\,adj(-3\,adj(3\,adj(2A)^{-1})))) = 2^m 3^n$, then $m + 2n$ is equal to **[JEE Main 2024]**

(a) 3 ☐
(b) 4 ☐
(c) 6 ☐
(d) 2 ☐

6. For $\alpha, \beta \in R$ and a natural number n.

Let $A_r = \begin{vmatrix} r & 1 & \frac{n^2}{2} + \alpha \\ 2r & 2 & n^2 - \beta \\ 3r\;2 & 3 & \frac{n(3n-1)}{2} \end{vmatrix}$.

Then, $2A_{10} - A_8$ is **[JEE Main 2024]**

(a) $4\alpha + 2\beta$ ☐
(b) $2\alpha + 4\beta$ ☐
(c) 0 ☐
(d) $2n$ ☐

7. Let $\alpha\beta \neq 0$ and $A = \begin{bmatrix} \beta & \alpha & 3 \\ \alpha & \alpha & \beta \\ -\beta & \alpha & 2\alpha \end{bmatrix}$.

If $B = \begin{bmatrix} 3\alpha & -9 & 3\alpha \\ -\alpha & 7 & -2\alpha \\ -2\alpha & 5 & -2\beta \end{bmatrix}$ is the matrix of cofactors of the elements of A, then $\det(AB)$ is equal to **[JEE Main 2024]**

(a) 64 ☐
(b) 343 ☐
(c) 125 ☐
(d) 216 ☐

8. Let A and B be two square matrices of order 3 such that $|A| = 3$ and $|B| = 2$. Then, $|A^T A(adj(2A))^{-1}(adj(4B))(adj(AB))^{-1}AA^T|$ is equal to **[JEE Main 2024]**

(a) 32 ☐
(b) 108 ☐
(c) 81 ☐
(d) 64 ☐

9. Let $A = \begin{bmatrix} 1 & 2 \\ 0 & 1 \end{bmatrix}$ and

$B = I + adj\,(A) + (adj\,A)^2 + \ldots + (adj\,A)^{10}$.

Then, the sum of all the elements of the matrix B is **[JEE Main 2024]**

(a) -88 ☐
(b) -124 ☐
(c) -110 ☐
(d) 22 ☐

10. Let A be a 2×2 symmetric matrix such that $A\begin{bmatrix}1\\1\end{bmatrix} = \begin{bmatrix}3\\7\end{bmatrix}$ and the determinant of A be 1. If $A^{-1} = \alpha A + \beta I$, where I is an identity matrix of order 2×2, then $\alpha + \beta$ equals....... . **[JEE Main 2024]**

11. If $A = \begin{bmatrix}\sqrt{2} & 1\\ -1 & \sqrt{2}\end{bmatrix}$, $B = \begin{bmatrix}1 & 0\\ 1 & 1\end{bmatrix}$, $C = ABA^T$ and $X = A^T C^2 A$, then det X is equal to **[JEE Main 2024]**

(a) 243 ☐
(b) 729 ☐
(c) 891 ☐
(d) 27 ☐

12. Let A be a 3×3 matrix and $\det(A) = 2$. If $n = \det\underbrace{(\text{adj}(\text{adj}(\ldots(\text{adj } A))))}_{2024\text{-time}}$, then the remainder when n is divided by 9 is equal to .... **[JEE Main 2024]**

13. Let $A = \begin{bmatrix}1 & 0 & 0\\ 0 & \alpha & \beta\\ 0 & \beta & \alpha\end{bmatrix}$ and $|2A|^3 = 2^{21}$ where, $\alpha, \beta \in Z$. Then, a value of α is **[JEE Main 2024]**

(a) 3 ☐
(b) 5 ☐
(c) 9 ☐
(d) 17 ☐

14. The values of α, for which

$$\begin{vmatrix} 1 & \frac{3}{2} & \alpha + \frac{3}{2}\\ 1 & \frac{1}{3} & \alpha + \frac{1}{3}\\ 2\alpha + 3 & 3\alpha + 1 & 0 \end{vmatrix} = 0,$$

lie in the interval **[JEE Main 2024]**

(a) $(-2, 1)$ ☐
(b) $(-3, 0)$ ☐
(c) $\left(-\frac{3}{2}, \frac{3}{2}\right)$ ☐
(d) $(0, 3)$ ☐

15. If the system of equations $2x + 7y + \lambda z = 3$, $3x + 2y + 5z = 4$ and $x + \mu y + 32z = -1$ has infinitely many solutions, then $(\lambda - \mu)$ is equal to .... **[JEE Main 2024]**

16. Let $\alpha\beta\gamma = 45$, $\alpha, \beta, \gamma \in R$. If $x(\alpha, 1, 2) + y(1, \beta, 2) + z(2, 3, \gamma) = (0, 0, 0)$ for some $x, y, z \in R$, $xyz \neq 0$, then $6\alpha + 4\beta + \gamma$ is equal to .... **[JEE Main 2024]**

17. Let $A = \begin{bmatrix}2 & 0 & 1\\ 1 & 1 & 0\\ 1 & 0 & 1\end{bmatrix}$, $B = [B_1, B_2, B_3]$, where B_1, B_2, B_3 be column matrics and $AB_1 = \begin{bmatrix}1\\0\\0\end{bmatrix}$, $AB_2 = \begin{bmatrix}2\\3\\0\end{bmatrix}$, $AB_3 = \begin{bmatrix}3\\2\\1\end{bmatrix}$.

If $\alpha = |B|$ and β is the sum of all the diagonal elements of B, then $\alpha^3 + \beta^3$ is equal to .... **[JEE Main 2024]**

18. Let S be the set of values of λ, for which the system of equations $6\lambda x - 3y + 3z = 4\lambda^2$, $2x + 6\lambda y + 4z = 1$ and $3x + 2y + 3\lambda z = \lambda$ has no solution. Then, $12\sum_{\lambda \in S} |\lambda|$ is equal to .... **[JEE Main 2024]**

Scan this QR code from your mobile phone to get the solutions of **Competition Edge Up** of this chapter.

Chapter 05

Continuity and Differentiability

Scan and take Chapter Test

1. The function f given by

(i) $f(x) = 2x + 5$ at $x = 1$.

Continuous ☐ Discontinuous ☐

(ii) $f(x) = 3x^2 - 1$ at $x = 5$.

Continuous ☐ Discontinuous ☐

(iii) $f(x) = \dfrac{x^2 - 4}{2x - 3}$ at $x = -2$.

Continuous ☐ Discontinuous ☐

2. The given function

(i) $f(x) = \begin{cases} \dfrac{|x|}{x}, & x \neq 0 \\ 1, & x = 0 \end{cases}$ is not continuous at $x =$ ________

(ii) $f(x) = \begin{cases} x^3 + 3x + 3, & x \neq 0 \\ 1, & x = 0 \end{cases}$ is not continuous at $x =$ ________

3. The function $f(x)$ given by $f(x) = \begin{cases} \dfrac{e^{1/x} - 1}{e^{1/x} + 1}, & x \neq 0 \\ 0, & x = 0 \end{cases}$, is

(a) continuous everywhere in R (b) continuous at $x = 0$

(c) discontinuous at $x = 0$ (d) discontinuous except at $x = 0$

4. The function $f(x) = 2x - |x|$ is not continuous at $x = 0$.

True ☐ False ☐

*Concepts of all questions bearing * are important for JEE & CUET*

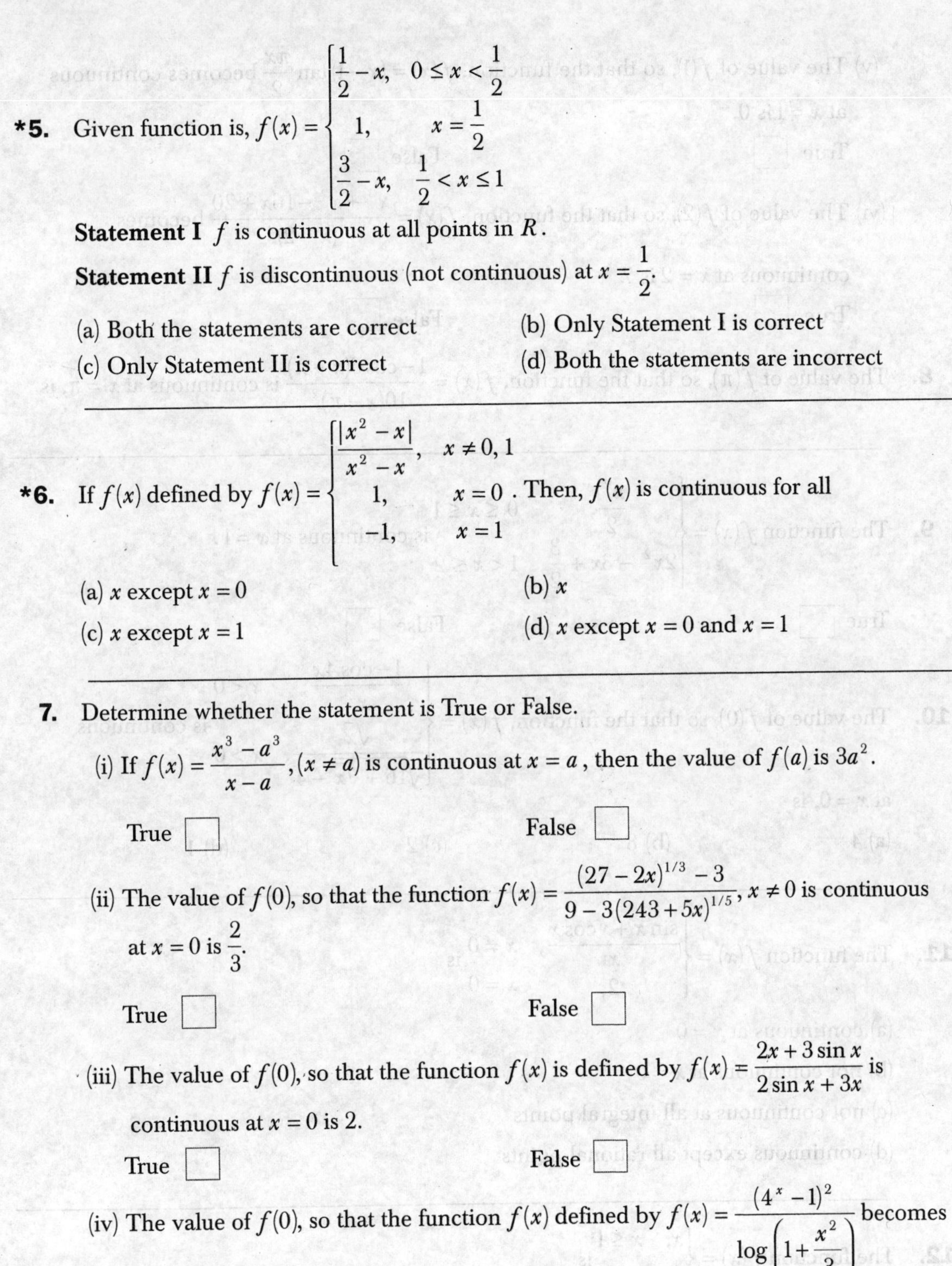

***5.** Given function is, $f(x)=\begin{cases}\frac{1}{2}-x, & 0\le x<\frac{1}{2}\\ 1, & x=\frac{1}{2}\\ \frac{3}{2}-x, & \frac{1}{2}<x\le 1\end{cases}$

Statement I f is continuous at all points in R.

Statement II f is discontinuous (not continuous) at $x=\frac{1}{2}$.

(a) Both the statements are correct
(b) Only Statement I is correct
(c) Only Statement II is correct
(d) Both the statements are incorrect

***6.** If $f(x)$ defined by $f(x)=\begin{cases}\frac{|x^2-x|}{x^2-x}, & x\ne 0,1\\ 1, & x=0\\ -1, & x=1\end{cases}$. Then, $f(x)$ is continuous for all

(a) x except $x=0$
(b) x
(c) x except $x=1$
(d) x except $x=0$ and $x=1$

---

7. Determine whether the statement is True or False.

(i) If $f(x)=\frac{x^3-a^3}{x-a}$, $(x\ne a)$ is continuous at $x=a$, then the value of $f(a)$ is $3a^2$.

True ☐ False ☐

(ii) The value of $f(0)$, so that the function $f(x)=\frac{(27-2x)^{1/3}-3}{9-3(243+5x)^{1/5}}$, $x\ne 0$ is continuous at $x=0$ is $\frac{2}{3}$.

True ☐ False ☐

(iii) The value of $f(0)$, so that the function $f(x)$ is defined by $f(x)=\frac{2x+3\sin x}{2\sin x+3x}$ is continuous at $x=0$ is 2.

True ☐ False ☐

(iv) The value of $f(0)$, so that the function $f(x)$ defined by $f(x)=\frac{(4^x-1)^2}{\log\left(1+\frac{x^2}{3}\right)}$ becomes continuous at $x=0$ is $(\log_e 4)^3$.

True ☐ False ☐

(v) The value of $f(1)$, so that the function, $f(x) = (x-1)\tan\frac{\pi x}{2}$ becomes continuous at $x = 1$ is 0.

True ☐ False ☐

(vi) The value of $f(2)$, so that the function, $f(x) = \frac{x^3 + x^2 - 16x + 20}{(x-2)^2}$ becomes continuous at $x = 2$ is 7.

True ☐ False ☐

8. The value of $f(\pi)$, so that the function, $f(x) = \frac{1-\cos 6(x-\pi)}{10(x-\pi)^2}$ is continuous at $x = \pi$, is

---

9. The function $f(x) = \begin{cases} \frac{x^2}{2}, & 0 \le x \le 1 \\ 2x^2 - 3x + \frac{3}{2}, & 1 < x \le 2 \end{cases}$ is continuous at $x = 1$.

True ☐ False ☐

10. The value of $f(0)$, so that the function, $f(x) = \begin{cases} \frac{1-\cos 4x}{x^2}, & x < 0 \\ \frac{\sqrt{x}}{\sqrt{16+\sqrt{x}} - 4}, & x > 0 \end{cases}$ is continuous at $x = 0$, is

(a) 4 (b) 8 (c) 2 (d) 1

***11.** The function $f(x) = \begin{cases} \frac{\sin x + x\cos x}{x}, & x \ne 0 \\ 2, & x = 0 \end{cases}$ is

(a) continuous at $x = 0$

(b) not continuous at $x = 0$

(c) not continuous at all integral points

(d) continuous except all rational points

***12.** The function $f(x) = \begin{cases} x, & x \le 1 \\ 2, & x > 1 \end{cases}$ is

(a) not continuous at $x = 0$

(b) continuous at $x = 1$

(c) continuous at all points in R except $x = 1$

(d) continuous at every real number

---

13. State True or False.

(i) The function $f(x)$ defined by $f(x)=\begin{cases}\dfrac{x^2-x-6}{x-3}, & x\neq 3\\ 5, & x=3\end{cases}$, is not continuous at $x=3$.

True ☐ False ☐

(ii) The function $f(x)=|x-5|$ is continuous at every real number R.

True ☐ False ☐

(iii) The function $f(x)=\begin{cases}\dfrac{2|x|+x^2}{x}, & x\neq 0\\ 0, & x=0\end{cases}$ is continuous at $x=0$.

True ☐ False ☐

(iv) The function $f(x)=\begin{cases}\dfrac{e^x-1}{\log(1+2x)}, & x\neq 0\\ 5, & x=0\end{cases}$ is continuous at $x=0$.

True ☐ False ☐

(v) The function $f(x)=\begin{cases}\dfrac{|x-a|}{x-a}, & x\neq a\\ 1, & x=a\end{cases}$ is continuous at $x=a$.

True ☐ False ☐

14. The point of discontinuity of the function, defined by

(i) $f(x)=\begin{cases}x+3, & x<1\\ 0, & x=1\\ x-3, & x>1\end{cases}$ is __________

(ii) $f(x)=\begin{cases}\dfrac{x^4+2x^3+3x^2}{(\tan^{-1}x)^2}, & x\neq 0\\ 5, & x=0\end{cases}$ is __________

(iii) $f(x)=\begin{cases}|x|+3, & x\leq -3\\ -2x, & -3<x<3\\ 6x+2, & x\geq 3\end{cases}$ is __________

(iv) $f(x)=\begin{cases}x-3, & x\geq 3\\ 6-5x, & 1<x<3\\ \dfrac{2x^2+3}{5}, & x\leq 1\end{cases}$ is __________

(v) $f(t)=\dfrac{1}{t^2+t-2}$, where $t=\dfrac{1}{x-2}$ is __________

***15.** The function $f(x) = \begin{cases} \dfrac{\log(1+3x)}{e^{2x}-1}, & x > 0 \\ \dfrac{3}{2}, & x = 0 \\ \dfrac{\sin 3x}{\tan 2x}, & x < 0 \end{cases}$ is

(a) discontinuous at $x = 0$
(b) continuous at $x = 0$
(c) discontinuous all points except $x = 1$
(d) discontinuous all integral points

---

16. The given function is $f(x) = \begin{cases} 3, & 1 \le x \le 2 \\ 4, & 2 < x < 3 \\ 5, & 3 \le x \le 5 \end{cases}$. Then,

(a) $f(x)$ is discontinuous at $x = 2, 3$
(b) $f(x)$ is continuous at $x = 2$ and 3
(c) $f(x)$ is continuous at $x = 1, 2$ and 3
(d) $f(x)$ is discontinuous at all points except 2 and 3

***17.** The function $f(x) = \begin{cases} \dfrac{x - |x|}{x}, & x \ne 0 \\ 1, & x = 0 \end{cases}$ is

(a) discontinuous at $x = 0$
(b) discontinuous at $x = 1$
(c) discontinuous all points except $x = 0$
(d) discontinuous at all integral points

---

18. The function defined by $f(x) = x - [x]$, here $[x]$ denotes the greatest integer less than or equal to x is discontinuous at all integral points.

True ☐ False ☐

19. The set of points at which the function $f(x) = \dfrac{1}{\log |x|}$ is not continuous, is

---

20. **Statement I** $x = 1$ is the only point of discontinuity of f, where f is defined by

$$f(x) = \begin{cases} x^{10} - 1, & x \le 1 \\ x^5, & x > 1 \end{cases}$$

Statement II The function $g(x) = \begin{cases} x + 5, & x \le 1 \\ x - 5, & x > 1 \end{cases}$ has no point of discontinuity.

(a) Both the statements are correct
(b) Both the statements are incorrect
(c) Only Statement I is correct
(d) Only Statement II is correct

***21.** The function $f(x) = \dfrac{4+x^2}{4x-x^3}$ is

(a) discontinuous at only one point

(b) discontinuous at exactly two points

(c) discontinuous at exactly three points

(d) None of the above

---

22. The point of discontinuity of f defined by $f(x) = |x| - |x+1|$ is 0 and 1.

True ☐ False ☐

23. The point of discontinuity of the function f given by $f(x) = \begin{cases} x^2 \sin \dfrac{1}{x^2}, & x \neq 0 \\ 0, & x = 0 \end{cases}$ is

(a) $x = 0$

(b) all points of $x \in R - \{0\}$

(c) no point of discontinuity

(d) all points $x \in R$

---

24. The function $f(x) = \begin{cases} \dfrac{\sin 2x}{x}, & x < 0 \\ x+2, & x \geq 0 \end{cases}$ is continuous ________

25. The point of discontinuity of the function $f(x)$ defined by $f(x) = \begin{cases} \sin x - \cos x, & x \neq 0 \\ -1, & x = 0 \end{cases}$, is $x = 0$.

True ☐ False ☐

26. **Statement I** The function f defined by $f(x) = |1 - x + |x||$ is everywhere continuous.

Statement II The function f defined by $f(x) = \sqrt{|x| - x}$ is continuous everywhere.

(a) Both the statements are true

(b) Both the statements are false

(c) Statement I is true but statement II is false

(d) Statement II is true but statement I is false

---

27. State True or False.

(i) $f(x) = \cos(x^2)$ is continuous function only in $[0, \infty)$.

True ☐ False ☐

(ii) $f(x) = |\cos x|$ is continuous everywhere.

True ☐ False ☐

28. **Statement I** The function $f(x) = \sin|x|$ is continuous everywhere.

Statement II The function $g(x) = \dfrac{1}{x+2}$, then the point of discontinuity of the function $g\{g(x)\}$ are -2 and $\dfrac{5}{2}$.

(a) Both the statements are true
(b) Both the statements are false
(c) Only Statement I is true
(d) Only Statement II is true

***29.** If $f(x) = 2x$ and $g(x) = \dfrac{x^2}{2} + 1$, then which of the following can be a discontinuous function?

(a) $f(x) + g(x)$ (b) $f(x) - g(x)$ (c) $fg(x)$ (d) $\dfrac{g(x)}{f(x)}$

***30.** Find the value of k so that the function f is continuous at the indicated point.

(i) $f(x) = \begin{cases} \dfrac{x^2 - 2x - 3}{x - 3}, & x \neq 3 \\ k, & x = 3 \end{cases}$ is continuous at $x = 3$ ________

(ii) $f(x) = \begin{cases} \dfrac{1 - \cos 2x}{4x^2}, & x \neq 0 \\ k, & x = 0 \end{cases}$ is continuous at $x = 0$ ________

(iii) $f(x) = \begin{cases} k(x^2 - 2x), & x < 0 \\ \cos x, & x \geq 0 \end{cases}$ is continuous at $x = 0$ ________

(iv) $f(x) = \begin{cases} \dfrac{\log(1 + 2x) - \log(1 - 3x)}{x}, & x \neq 0 \\ k, & x = 0 \end{cases}$ is continuous at $x = 0$ ________

(v) $f(x) = \begin{cases} \dfrac{\sqrt{2}\cos x - 1}{\cot x - 1}, & x \neq \dfrac{\pi}{4} \\ k, & x = \dfrac{\pi}{4} \end{cases}$ is continuous at $x = \dfrac{\pi}{4}$ ________

(vi) $f(x) = \begin{cases} \dfrac{1 - \cos 2x}{2x^2}, & x < 0 \\ k, & x = 0 \\ \dfrac{x}{|x|}, & x > 0 \end{cases}$ is continuous at $x = 0$ ________

***31.** The relation between a and b so that the function f defined by $f(x) = \begin{cases} ax + 1, & x \leq 3 \\ bx + 3, & x > 3 \end{cases}$ is continuous at $x = 3$, is ________

32. The value of a is 5 so that the function $f(x) = \begin{cases} 2x+1, & x < 2 \\ a, & x = 2 \\ 3x-1, & x > 2 \end{cases}$ is continuous at $x = 2$.

True ☐ False ☐

***33.** If $f(x) = \begin{cases} -2x^2 + a, & x < 0 \\ 2x^2 + a, & x \geq 0 \end{cases}$, then what should be the value of a so that $f(x)$ is continuous at $x = 0$?

(a) No value of a (b) $a = 1$ (c) $a = 0$ (d) Any value of a

---

34. The function $f(x)$ given by $f(x) = \begin{cases} 3ax + b, & x > 1 \\ 11, & x = 1 \\ 5ax - 2b, & x < 1 \end{cases}$, is continuous at $x = 1$.

	Column I		Column II
A.	Value of $a + b$ is	1.	True
B.	The relation $a + b < a$ is	2.	11
C.	Value of $f(1)$ is	3.	False
D.	The relation $a - b < b$ is	4.	5

So, which of the following is correct from the above table?

(a) A → 2, B → 3, C → 4, D → 1 (b) A → 4, B → 3, C → 2, D → 1

(c) A → 4, B → 1, C → 2, D → 3 (d) A → 2, B → 1, C → 4, D → 3

TOPIC 2

Differentiability

35. The value of $f'(1)$, so that the function $f(x) = x^2$ is differentiable at $x = 1$, is ______

36. The function f is given by $f(x) = x^2 - 6x + 9$.

	Column I		Column II
A.	The value of $f'(x)$ is	1.	9
B.	$f'(5) - 3f'(2)$ is	2.	$2x$
C.	$f'(8) - 1$ is	3.	10
D.	$f'(2x) - f'(x)$ is	4.	$2x - 6$

From the above table, which of the following is/are correct?

(a) A → 2, B → 3, C → 1, D → 4 (b) A → 4, B → 3, C → 1, D → 2

(c) A → 2, B → 1, C → 3, D → 4 (d) None of these

37. If $f(x)$ is differentiable at $x = a$, then the value of $\lim\limits_{x \to a} \dfrac{x^2 f(a) - a^2 f(x)}{x - a}$ is $2af(a) - a^2 f'(a)$.

True ☐ False ☐

***38.** The function $f(x) = |x-1| + |x+1|$, $\forall x \in R$ is

(a) non-differentiable only $x = 1$
(b) non-differentiable only $x = -1$
(c) non-differentiable at $x = 1$ and -1
(d) differentiable for all $x \in R$

39. The set of points where the function $f(x) = x|x|$ is differentiable, is

(a) $(-\infty, \infty)$
(b) $(-\infty, 0) \cup (0, \infty)$
(c) $[0, \infty)$
(d) $(-\infty, 0)$

40. The value of $f'(0)$ so that $f(x) = |x|^3$ is differentiable at $x = 0$, is ________

41. Let $f(x) = a + b|x| + c|x|^4$, where a, b and c are real constant. Then, $f(x)$ is differentiable if $b = 0$.

True ☐ False ☐

42. Let $f(x) = |\sin x|$, then

(a) $f(x)$ is everywhere differentiable
(b) $f(x)$ is everywhere continuous but non-differentiable at $x = n\pi$, $n \in Z$
(c) $f(x)$ is everywhere continuous but non-differentiable at $x = (2n+1)\dfrac{\pi}{2}$, $n \in Z$
(d) None of the above

43. The function $f(x) = e^{|x|}$ is non-differentiable at $x = 0$.

True ☐ False ☐

***44.** If $f(x) = \begin{cases} \dfrac{1}{1+e^{1/x}}, & x \neq 0 \\ 0, & x = 0 \end{cases}$, then $f(x)$ is

(a) continuous as well as differentiable at $x = 0$
(b) continuous but non-differentiable at $x = 0$
(c) differentiable but not continuous at $x = 0$
(d) not continuous as well as non-differentiable at $x = 0$

45. At $x = 1$, the function f defined by $f(x) = \begin{cases} 3^x, & -1 \le x < 1 \\ 4 - x, & 1 \le x < 4 \end{cases}$ is continuous and differentiable.

True ☐ False ☐

TOPIC 3

Derivatives of Composite Functions

46. Differentiate the function with respect to x in following questions.

(i) $(x+3)^2(x+4)^3\cdot(x+5)^4$ at $x=-3$ ______

(ii) $\tan(x^2+3)$ ______

(iii) $\sin(\cos x)$ ______

(iv) $\sin x^3\cdot\sin^2(x^4)$ ______

47. If $y=(x^2+x+1)^4$, then the value of $\frac{dy}{dx}$ at $x=-\frac{1}{2}$ is $\frac{3}{2}$.

True ☐ False ☐

***48.** If $y=\log(\sec x+\tan x)$, then the value of $\frac{dy}{dx}$ at $x=\frac{\pi}{3}$ is

(a) $\frac{1}{2}$ (b) $\frac{\sqrt{3}}{2}$ (c) $\frac{2}{\sqrt{3}}$ (d) 2

49. If $y=f(x^2)$ and $f'(x)=e^{\sqrt{x}}$, then $\frac{dy}{dx}$ is

(a) $2e^x$ (b) $2xe^{x^2}$ (c) $2xe^x$ (d) xe^x

50. If $y=\sqrt{\log\left\{\sin\left(\frac{x^2}{4}-1\right)\right\}}$, then $\frac{dy}{dx}$ is ______

***51.** If $y=e^{ax}\cdot\cos(bx+c)$, then $\frac{dy}{dx}$ is

(a) $e^{ax}\{a\cos(bx+c)-b\sin(bx+c)\}$ (b) $e^{ax}\{a\cos(bx+c)+b\sin(bx+c)\}$

(c) $e^{ax}\{a\cos(bx+c)\}$ (d) None of these

52. If $y=x^xe^{2(x+3)}$, then the value of $\frac{dy}{dx}$ at $x=1$ is ______

53. If $y=\cos x^3\cdot\sin^2(x^5)$, then the value of $\frac{dy}{dx}$ is ______

***54.** If $y=\frac{\sin(ax+b)}{\cos(cx+d)}$, then $\frac{dy}{dx}$ is

(a) $\frac{a\cos^2(ax+b)+c\sin^2(ax+b)}{\cos^2(cx+d)}$ (b) $\frac{\cos(cx+d)\cdot\cos(ax+b)+\sin(ax+b)\cdot\sin(cx+d)}{\cos^2(cx+d)}$

(c) $\frac{ax+b}{cx+d}\cdot\frac{\sin(ax+b)}{\cos(cx+d)}$ (d) $\frac{a\cos(ax+b)\cdot\cos(cx+d)+c\sin(ax+b)\cdot\sin(cx+d)}{\cos^2(cx+d)}$

TOPIC 4

Derivatives of Implicit Function and Inverse Trigonometric Function

55. Find $\frac{dy}{dx}$ of the following functions.

(i) $x\sqrt{1+y}+y\sqrt{1+x}=0$ and $x \neq y$ ______

(ii) $\sin y = x\sin(a+y)$ ______

(iii) $4x+3y=\log(4x-3y)$ ______

(iv) $y=\sin^{-1}\left(\frac{2x}{1+x^2}\right), 1<x<\infty$ ______

(v) $y=\tan^{-1}\left\{\sqrt{\frac{1-\cos x}{1+\cos x}}\right\}, -\pi<x<\pi$ ______

56. State True or False.

(i) If $x^2+2xy+y^3=100$, then $\frac{dy}{dx}$ is $-\frac{2(x+y)}{(2x+3y^2)}$.

True ☐ False ☐

(ii) If $\sin^2 y+\cos xy=k$, then the value of $\frac{dy}{dx}$ at $\left(1, \frac{\pi}{4}\right)$ is $8\left\{\frac{4}{\pi^2+16}-\frac{1}{\log 2}\right\}$.

True ☐ False ☐

(iii) If $e^{x-y}=\log\left(\frac{x}{y}\right)$, then the value of $\frac{dy}{dx}$ is $\frac{y}{x}\cdot\frac{(xe^{x-y}-1)}{(ye^{x-y}-1)}$.

True ☐ False ☐

(iv) If $e^x+e^y=e^{x+y}$, then the relation $\frac{dy}{dx}+e^{y-x}=0$ holds.

True ☐ False ☐

(v) If $xy^2=1$, then $\frac{dy}{dx}=-\frac{y^3}{2}$.

True ☐ False ☐

***57.** If $\log\sqrt{x^2+y^2}=\tan^{-1}\left(\frac{y}{x}\right)$, then $\frac{dy}{dx}$ is

(a) $\frac{x+y}{x-y}$

(b) $\frac{x-y}{x+y}$

(c) $\frac{dy}{dx}$ at (2, 1) is $\frac{3}{2}$

(d) None of these

______

58. State True or False.

(i) The derivative of f given by $f(x) = \tan^{-1} x$ (assuming it exists) is $\dfrac{1}{1+x^2}$.

True ☐ False ☐

(ii) If $y = \sin^{-1}\left(\dfrac{1-x^2}{1+x^2}\right), 0 < x < 1$, then $\dfrac{dy}{dx} = \dfrac{2}{1+x^2}$.

True ☐ False ☐

(iii) If $y = \sec^{-1}\left(\dfrac{1}{2x^2-1}\right), 0 < x < \dfrac{1}{\sqrt{2}}$, then $\dfrac{dy}{dx} = \dfrac{2}{\sqrt{1-x^2}}$.

True ☐ False ☐

(iv) If $y = \tan^{-1}\left(\dfrac{3x-x^3}{1-3x^2}\right), -\dfrac{1}{\sqrt{3}} < x < \dfrac{1}{\sqrt{3}}$, then $\dfrac{dy}{dx} = \dfrac{3}{1+x^2}$.

True ☐ False ☐

(v) If $y = \cos^{-1}(2x\sqrt{1-x^2}), -\dfrac{1}{\sqrt{2}} < x < \dfrac{1}{\sqrt{2}}$, then $\dfrac{dy}{dx} = -\dfrac{2}{\sqrt{1-x^2}}$.

True ☐ False ☐

***59.** If $y = \sin^{-1} x + \sin^{-1}\sqrt{1-x^2}$, $(0 < x < 1)$, then the value of $\dfrac{dy}{dx}$ is

(a) 1 (b) 0 (c) 2 (d) None of these

***60.** If $y = \tan^{-1}\left(\dfrac{a\cos x - b\sin x}{b\cos x + a\sin x}\right), -\dfrac{\pi}{2} < x < \dfrac{\pi}{2}$, then the value of $\dfrac{dy}{dx}$ at (0, 1) is ________

***61.** If $y = \sin^{-1}\left(\dfrac{2x}{1+x^2}\right) + \cos^{-1}\left(\dfrac{1-x^2}{1+x^2}\right), 0 < x < 1$, then the value of $\dfrac{dy}{dx}$ is

(a) $\dfrac{4}{1+x^2}$ (b) $\dfrac{2}{1+x^2}$ (c) $\dfrac{1}{1+x^2}$ (d) $\dfrac{1}{2(1+x^2)}$

TOPIC 5

Exponential and Logarithmic Functions (Derivatives)

62. Differentiate the following with respect to x.

(i) $e^x \cdot \sin x$ ________

(ii) $3e^x + 4\sin x \cdot e^x$ ________

(iii) $\cos e^x$ ________

(iv) $\sin(\log x), x > 0$ ________

(v) $\log(\cos e^x)$ ________

***63.** Differentiate $\sqrt{\dfrac{(x+3)(x^3+4)}{2x^2+3x+9}}$ with respect to x.

64. State True or False.

(i) If $y = \sin(\tan^{-1} e^x)$, then the value of $\dfrac{dy}{dx}$ is $\dfrac{e^x \cdot \cos(\tan^{-1} e^x)}{1+(e^x)^2}$.

True ☐ False ☐

(ii) If $y = x^{\sqrt{x}}$, then the value of $\dfrac{dy}{dx}$ at $x = 1$ is 1.

True ☐ False ☐

(iii) If $y = x^{\sin x}$, $x > 0$, then $\dfrac{dy}{dx} = \sin x \cdot x^{\sin x - 1} + x^{\sin x} \cos x \cdot \log x$.

True ☐ False ☐

(iv) If $y = e^x + a^x + x^x + x^a$, then the value of $\dfrac{dy}{dx}$ at $x = a$ is $e^a + 2a^a(1+\log a)$.

True ☐ False ☐

(v) If $x^{13}y^7 = (x+y)^{20}$, then the relation $x\dfrac{dy}{dx} - y = 0$ not satisfied.

True ☐ False ☐

(vi) If $y = (x)^{\log x} + (\log x)^x$, then at $x = 1$, the value of $\dfrac{dy}{dx}$ is greater than $\dfrac{3}{2}$.

[at $x = 1$, consider $(1 + \log x \cdot \log(\log x))$ = a constant value]

True ☐ False ☐

***65.** If $y = (\sin x)^x + \sin^{-1}(\sqrt{x})$, then the value of $\dfrac{dy}{dx}$ at $x = \dfrac{\pi}{2}$ is ____________

66. If $y = \log_5(\log_5 x)$, then the value of $\dfrac{dy}{dx}$ is ____________

67. If $y = \log \tan\left(\dfrac{\pi}{4} + \dfrac{x}{2}\right)$, then $\dfrac{dy}{dx}$ at $x = \dfrac{\pi}{4}$ is $\dfrac{1}{\sqrt{2}}$.

True ☐ False ☐

68. If $y = \log\left\{\dfrac{a + b\sin x}{a - b\sin x}\right\}$, then the value of $\dfrac{dy}{dx}$ at $x = \dfrac{\pi}{2}$ is $\dfrac{2ab}{a^2 - b^2}$.

True ☐ False ☐

***69.** If $x + y = e^{1/xy}$, then the value of $\dfrac{dy}{dx}$ is

(a) $\dfrac{-y(xy+x+y)}{x(xy+y)}$ (b) $-\dfrac{y^2(x^2y+x+y)}{x^2(xy^2+x+y)}$ (c) $-\dfrac{y(xy^2+x+y)}{x(x^2y+x+y)}$ (d) None of these

TOPIC 6

Derivatives of Functions in Parametric Forms

70. If x and y are connected parametrically by the equations given in following questions without eliminating the parameter, find $\frac{dy}{dx}$.

(i) $x = at^3$ and $y = 2at$ ______

(ii) $x = a(t - \sin t)$ and $y = a(1 - \cos t)$ ______

(iii) $x = \sqrt{a^{\sin^{-1} t}}$ and $y = \sqrt{a^{\cos^{-1} t}}$, $a > 0, |t| < 1$ ______

(iv) $y = \sin(2\cos^{-1} t)$ and $x = \cos(2\sin^{-1} t)$ ______

(v) $x = e^{\cos 2t}$ and $y = e^{\sin 2t}$ ______

***71.** If $x = 2\cos t - \cos 2t$ and $y = 2\sin t - \sin 2t$. Then, the value of $\frac{dy}{dx}$ at $t = \frac{\pi}{6}$ is

(a) $\sqrt{3}$ (b) 1

(c) $\frac{1}{\sqrt{3}}$ (d) 0

______

72. State True or False.

(i) If $x = \cos t$ and $y = \sin t$, then $\frac{dy}{dx} = \frac{1}{\sqrt{3}}$ at $t = \frac{2\pi}{3}$.

True ☐ False ☐

(ii) If $x = \sin^{-1}\left(\frac{2t}{1+t^2}\right)$ and $y = \tan^{-1}\left(\frac{2t}{1-t^2}\right)$, $-1 < t < 1$, then $\frac{dy}{dx} = 1$.

True ☐ False ☐

(iii) If $x = e^t\left(t + \frac{1}{t}\right)$ and $y = e^{-t}\left(t - \frac{1}{t}\right)$, then at $t = 1$, the value of $\frac{dy}{dx}$ is $\frac{1}{e^2}$.

True ☐ False ☐

(iv) If $x = a\cos^3 t$ and $y = a\sin^3 t$, then $\sqrt{1 + \left(\frac{dy}{dx}\right)^2}$ is $|\sec t|$.

True ☐ False ☐

TOPIC 7

Second Order Derivative

73. Find the second order derivative of

(i) $x^3 + \sin x$ ______

(ii) $\cos(\log x)$ ______

(iii) $\sin^{-1} x$ ______

(iv) $e^y(x+1) = 1$ ______

74. If $y = A\cos(\log x) + B\sin(\log x)$, then the relation $x^2 \dfrac{d^2y}{dx^2} + x\dfrac{dy}{dx} + y = 0$ holds.

True ☐ False ☐

***75.** Let $f(x)$ be a polynomial. Then, the second order derivative of $f(e^x)$ is

(a) $f''(e^x)e^{2x} + f'(e^x)\cdot e^x$ (b) $f''(e^x)$

(c) $f''(e^x)\cdot e^x + f'(e^x)$ (d) $f''(e^x)\cdot e^{2x} + f''(e^x)\cdot e^x$

______

76. If $x = f(t)\cos t - f'(t)\sin t$ and $y = f(t)\sin t + f'(t)\cos t$. Then, $\left(\dfrac{dx}{dt}\right)^2 + \left(\dfrac{dy}{dt}\right)^2 =$ ______

***77.** If $y = x\log\left(\dfrac{x}{a+bx}\right)$, then which of the following is true?

(a) $x^3\dfrac{d^2y}{dx^2} = \left(x\dfrac{dy}{dx} - y\right)$ (b) $x^3\dfrac{d^2y}{dx^2} = \left(x\dfrac{dy}{dx} - y\right)^2$

(c) $\dfrac{d^2y}{dx^2} = \left(\dfrac{dy}{dx} - \dfrac{y}{x}\right)^3$ (d) None of these

______

78. State True or False.

(i) If $y = e^{a\cos^{-1}x}$, then the relation $(1-x^2)\dfrac{d^2y}{dx^2} - x\dfrac{dy}{dx} - a^2y = 0$ holds.

True ☐ False ☐

(ii) If $x = \tan\left(\dfrac{1}{a}\log y\right)$, then the value of $(1+x^2)\dfrac{d^2y}{dx^2} + (2x-a)\dfrac{dy}{dx}$ is zero.

True ☐ False ☐

(iii) If $(x-a)^2 + (y-b)^2 = c^2$, then the value of the expression $\dfrac{\left\{1+\left(\dfrac{dy}{dx}\right)^2\right\}^{3/2}}{\dfrac{d^2y}{dx^2}}$ is $-2c$.

True ☐ False ☐

***79.** If $y^2 = ax^2 + bx + c$, then $y^3 \dfrac{d^2y}{dx^2}$ is

(a) constant
(b) a function of x only
(c) a function of y only
(d) a function of x and y

TOPIC 8

Differentiation of a Function with respect to Another Function

80. Differentiation of $\tan^{-1}\left(\dfrac{\sqrt{1+x^2}-1}{x}\right)$ with respect to $\tan^{-1} x \, (x \neq 0)$ is $\dfrac{1}{2}$.

True ☐ False ☐

***81.** Differentiation of $\tan^{-1}\left\{\dfrac{\sqrt{1+x^2}-\sqrt{1-x^2}}{\sqrt{1+x^2}+\sqrt{1-x^2}}\right\}$ with respect to $\cos^{-1} x^2$ is

(a) $\dfrac{1}{2}$
(b) $-\dfrac{1}{2}$
(c) 0
(d) None of these

---

82. Differentiation of $\tan^{-1}\left(\dfrac{2x}{1-x^2}\right)$ with respect to $\sin^{-1}\left(\dfrac{2x}{1+x^2}\right)$, where $-1 < x < 1$, is ______

***83.** If $x \in \left(\dfrac{1}{\sqrt{2}}, 1\right)$, then differentiation of $\tan^{-1}\left(\dfrac{\sqrt{1-x^2}}{x}\right)$ with respect to $\cos^{-1}(2x\sqrt{1-x^2})$ is

(a) $\dfrac{1}{2}$
(b) 0
(c) 1
(d) None of these

---

84. State True or False.

(i) The differentiate value of $\sin^2 x$ with respect to $e^{\cos x}$ is $-2e^{-\cos x} \cdot \cos x$.

True ☐ False ☐

(ii) The differentiate value of $\tan^{-1}\left(\dfrac{\sqrt{1+x^2}-1}{x}\right)$ with respect to $\sin^{-1}\left(\dfrac{2x}{1+x^2}\right)$, if $-1 < x < 1$, $x \neq 0$, is $\dfrac{1}{4}$.

True ☐ False ☐

Assertion-Reason Questions

The following questions consist of two statements – Assertion (A) and Reason (R). Answer these questions by selecting the appropriate option given below.
(a) Both A and R are true and R is the correct explanation of A.
(b) Both A and R are true but R is not the correct explanation of A.
(c) A is true but R is false.
(d) A is false but R is true.

1. **Assertion** (A) For $x < 0$, $\frac{d}{dx}(\ln|x|) = -\frac{1}{x}$

Reason (R) For $x < 0$, $|x| = -x$

(a) ☐ (b) ☐ (c) ☐ (d) ☐

2. **Assertion** (A) If $y = \log_{10} x + \log_e y$, then $\frac{dy}{dx} = \frac{\log_{10} e}{x}\left(\frac{y}{y-1}\right)$

Reason (R) $\frac{d}{dx}(\log_{10} x) = \frac{\log x}{\log e}$

(a) ☐ (b) ☐ (c) ☐ (d) ☐

3. **Assertion** (A) The value of k for which the function $f(x) = \begin{cases} 2x-1, & x < 2 \\ k, & x = 2 \\ x+1, & x > 2 \end{cases}$ is continuous at $x = 2$ is 4.

Reason (R) A function $f(x)$ is continuous at a point $x = a$ of its domain if $\lim_{x \to a} f(x) = f(a)$.

(a) ☐ (b) ☐ (c) ☐ (d) ☐

4. **Assertion** (A) The function $f(x) = |x| + |x-1|$ is continuous but not differentiable at $x = 0$ and $x = 1$.

Reason (R) Every differentiable function is continuous.

(a) ☐ (b) ☐ (c) ☐ (d) ☐

5. **Assertion** (A) If $y = \log(\sin e^x)$, then $\frac{dy}{dx} = e^x \cot(e^x)$.

Reason (R) For a function $y = f(g(x))$, $\frac{dy}{dx} = \frac{df}{dg} \cdot \frac{dg}{dx}$ and $\frac{d(\log x)}{dx} = \frac{1}{x}$

(a) ☐ (b) ☐ (c) ☐ (d) ☐

6. **Assertion** (A) If $x = a \sin\theta$ and $y = a\cos\theta$, then $\frac{d^2y}{dx^2} = -\sec^2\theta$.

Reason (R) For a parametric function $x = f(t)$ and $y = g(t)$, $\frac{d^2y}{dx^2} = \frac{d}{d\theta}\left(\frac{dy}{dx}\right)\frac{d\theta}{dx}$.

(a) ☐ (b) ☐ (c) ☐ (d) ☐

7. **Assertion** (A) If $\sin y = x \sin(a+y)$, then $\dfrac{dy}{dx} = \dfrac{\sin^2(a+y)}{\sin a}$

Reason (R) For two functions $f(x)$ and $g(x)$, $\dfrac{d}{dx}(f \cdot g) = f \cdot \dfrac{dg}{dx} + g\,\dfrac{df}{dx}$.

(a) ☐ (b) ☐ (c) ☐ (d) ☐

8. **Assertion** (A) $\dfrac{d}{dx} e^{\cos x} = e^{\cos x}(-\sin x)$

Reason (R) $\dfrac{d}{dx} e^x = e^x$

(a) ☐ (b) ☐ (c) ☐ (d) ☐

9. **Assertion** (A) $f(x)$ is continuous at $x = a$ iff $\lim_{x \to a} f(x)$ exists and equals to $f(a)$.

Reason (R) If $f(x)$ is continuous at a point, then $\dfrac{1}{f(x)}$ is also continuous at the point.

(a) ☐ (b) ☐ (c) ☐ (d) ☐

10. **Assertion** (A) $f(x) = [x]$ is not differentiable at $x = 2$.

Reason (R) $f(x) = [x]$ is not continuous at $x = 2$.

(a) ☐ (b) ☐ (c) ☐ (d) ☐

Case Based Questions

Case 1 If $y = f(u)$ is a differentiable function of u and $u = g(x)$ is differentiable function of x, then $y = f(g(x))$ is a differentiable function of x and $\dfrac{dy}{dx} = \dfrac{dy}{du} \times \dfrac{du}{dx}$. This rule is also known as Chain rule.

Based on the above information, answer the following questions.

Find the derivatives of functions w.r.t. x in the following questions.

(i) $\sqrt{\sin \sqrt{x}}$

(a) $\dfrac{1}{2\sqrt{\sin \sqrt{x}}}$ ☐ (b) $\dfrac{\cos \sqrt{x}}{\sqrt{x \sin \sqrt{x}}}$ ☐

(c) $\dfrac{\cos \sqrt{x}}{4\sqrt{x \sin \sqrt{x}}}$ ☐ (d) $-\dfrac{\cos \sqrt{x}}{4\sqrt{x \sin \sqrt{x}}}$ ☐

(ii) $\cos x^3$

(a) $\sin x^3$ ☐ (b) $-3x^2 \sin x^3$ ☐

(c) $-3x^2 \cos x^3$ ☐ (d) $3x^2 \sin x^3$ ☐

(iii) ln (sin x − cot x)

(a) $\dfrac{\cos x + \operatorname{cosec}^2 x}{\sin x - \cot x}$ ☐ (b) $\dfrac{\cos x + \tan^2 x}{\sin x - \cot x}$ ☐

(c) $\dfrac{1}{\sin x - \cot x}$ ☐ (d) $\cos x + \operatorname{cosec}^2 x$ ☐

Case 2 If a relation between x and y such that y cannot be expressed in terms of x, then y is called an implicit function of x. when a given relation expresses as an implicit function of x and we want to find $\frac{dy}{dx}$, then we differentiate every term of the given relation w.r.t. x remembering that a term in y is first differentiated w.r.t. y and then multiplied by $\frac{dy}{dx}$.

Based on the above information, find the value of $\frac{dy}{dx}$ in each of the following questions.

(i) $x^3 + x^2y + xy^2 + y^3 = 81$

(a) $\dfrac{(3x^2 + 2xy + y^2)}{x^2 + 2xy + 3y^2}$ (b) $\dfrac{-(3x^2 + 2xy + y^2)}{x^2 + 2xy + 3y^2}$

(c) $\dfrac{(3x^2 + 2xy - y^2)}{x^2 - 2xy + 3y^2}$ (d) $\dfrac{3x^2 + xy + y^2}{x^2 + xy + 3y^2}$

(ii) $x^y = e^{x-y}$

(a) $\dfrac{x-y}{(1+\log x)}$ (b) $\dfrac{x+y}{(1+\log x)}$ (c) $\dfrac{x-y}{x(1+\log x)}$ (d) $\dfrac{x+y}{x(1+\log x)}$

(iii) $\sin^2 x + \cos^2 y = 1$

(a) $\dfrac{\sin 2y}{\sin 2x}$ (b) $-\dfrac{\sin 2x}{\sin 2y}$ (c) $-\dfrac{\sin 2y}{\sin 2x}$ (d) $\dfrac{\sin 2x}{\sin 2y}$

COMPETITION CONNECT

Miscellaneous Exercise [NCERT (Old) Pg. 192]

1. If $y = \begin{vmatrix} f(x) & g(x) & h(x) \\ l & m & n \\ a & b & c \end{vmatrix}$, then $\dfrac{dy}{dx} = \begin{vmatrix} f'(x) & g'(x) & h'(x) \\ l & m & n \\ a & b & c \end{vmatrix}$.

True ☐ False ☐

2. If $f(x)$, $g(x)$ and $h(x)$ are three polynomial of degree 2 and $\phi(x) = \begin{vmatrix} f(x) & g(x) & h(x) \\ f'(x) & g'(x) & h'(x) \\ f''(x) & g''(x) & h''(x) \end{vmatrix}$, then $\phi(x)$ is

(a) polynomial of degree 2 (b) constant polynomial

(c) zero polynomial (d) None of these

COMPETITION EDGE UP

1. If the function

$$f(x) = \frac{\sin 3x + \alpha \sin x - \beta \cos 3x}{x^3},$$

$x \in R$, is continuous at $x = 0$, then $f(0)$ is equal to **[JEE Main 2024]**

(a) 2
(b) −2
(c) 4
(d) −4

2. Let : $R \to R$ be a function given by

$$f(x) = \begin{cases} \frac{1 - \cos 2x}{x^2}, & x < 0 \\ \alpha, & x = 0 \\ \frac{\beta\sqrt{1 - \cos x}}{x}, & x > 0 \end{cases}$$

where $\alpha, \beta \in R$. If f is continuous at $x = 0$, then $\alpha^2 + \beta^2$ is equal to **[JEE Main 2024]**

(a) 3
(b) 12
(c) 48
(d) 6

3. Let $f : [-1, 2] \to R$ be given by $f(x) = 2x^2 + x + [x^2] - [x]$, where $[t]$ denotes the greatest integer less than or equal to t. The number of points, where f is not continuous, is **[JEE Main 2024]**

(a) 3
(b) 6
(c) 4
(d) 5

4. If the function

$$f(x) = \begin{cases} \frac{72^x - 9^x - 8^x + 1}{\sqrt{2} - \sqrt{1 + \cos x}}, & x \neq 0 \\ a \log_e 2 \log_e 3, & x = 0 \end{cases}$$ is

continuous at $x = 0$, then the value of a^2 is equal to **[JEE Main 2024]**

(a) 1152
(b) 1250
(c) 968
(d) 746

5. For $a, b > 0$, let

$$f(x) = \begin{cases} \frac{\tan((a+1)x) + b \tan x}{x}, & x < 0 \\ 3, & x = 0 \\ \frac{\sqrt{ax + b^2x^2} - \sqrt{ax}}{b\sqrt{ax} \cdot \sqrt{x}}, & x > 0 \end{cases}$$

be a continuous function at $x = 0$.

Then, $\frac{b}{a}$ is equal to **[JEE Main 2024]**

(a) 4
(b) 5
(c) 8
(d) 6

6. Consider the function

$$f(x) = \begin{cases} \frac{a(7x - 12 - x^2)}{b|x^2 - 7x + 12|}, & x < 3 \\ 2^{\frac{\sin(x-3)}{x - [x]}}, & x > 3, \\ b, & x = 3 \end{cases}$$

where $[x]$ denotes the greatest integer less than or equal to x. If S denotes the set of all ordered pairs (a, b) such that $f(x)$ is continuous at $x = 3$, then the number of elements in S, is **[JEE Main 2024]**

(a) 4
(b) 2
(c) 1
(d) Infinitely many

7. Let $f : (-\infty, \infty) - \{0\} \to R$ be a differentiable function such that $f'(1) = \lim_{a \to \infty} a^2 f\left(\frac{1}{a}\right)$. Then,

$$\lim_{a \to \infty} \frac{a(a+1)}{2} \tan^{-1}\left(\frac{1}{a}\right) + a^2 - 2 \log_e a$$

is equal to **[JEE Main 2024]**

(a) $\frac{5}{2} + \frac{\pi}{8}$
(b) $\frac{3}{2} + \frac{\pi}{4}$
(c) $\frac{3}{4} + \frac{\pi}{8}$
(d) $\frac{3}{8} + \frac{\pi}{4}$

8. Let $f(x) = |2x^2 + 5|x| - 3|, x \in R$. If m and n denote the number of points where f is not continuous and not differentiable respectively, then $m + n$ is equal to **[JEE Main 2024]**

(a) 3 ☐
(b) 0 ☐
(c) 2 ☐
(d) 5 ☐

9. Consider the function $f : (0, \infty) \to R$, defined by $f(x) = e^{-|\log_e x|}$. If m and n are respectively, the number of points at which f is not continuous and f is not differentiable, then $m + n$ is **[JEE Main 2024]**

(a) 1 ☐
(b) 2 ☐
(c) 3 ☐
(d) 0 ☐

10. Consider the function $f : (0, 2) \to R$ defined by $f(x) = \frac{x}{2} + \frac{2}{x}$ and the function $g(x)$ defined by

$$g(x) = \begin{cases} \min\{f(t)\}, & 0 < t \le x \text{ and } 0 < x \le 1 \\ \frac{3}{2} + x, & 1 < x < 2 \end{cases}.$$

Then, **[JEE Main 2024]**

(a) g is neither continuous nor differentiable at $x = 1$ ☐
(b) g is not continuous for all $x \in (0, 2)$ ☐
(c) g is continuous but not differentiable at $x = 1$ ☐
(d) g is continuous and differentiable for all $x \in (0, 2)$ ☐

11. Let $f : R \to R$ be defined as

$$f(x) = \begin{cases} \frac{a - b\cos 2x}{x^2}, & x < 0 \\ x^2 + cx + 2, & 0 \le x \le 1 \\ 2x + 1, & x > 1 \end{cases}$$

If f is continuous everywhere in R and m is the number of points where f is not differential, then $m + a + b + c$ equals **[JEE Main 2024]**

(a) 4 ☐
(b) 2 ☐
(c) 3 ☐
(d) 1 ☐

12. Suppose for a differentiable function h, $h(0) = 0$, $h(1) = 1$ and $h'(0) = h'(1) = 2$. If $g(x) = h(e^x)e^{h(x)}$, then $g'(0)$ is equal to **[JEE Main 2024]**

(a) 3 ☐
(b) 5 ☐
(c) 4 ☐
(d) 8 ☐

13. Let $f : R - \{0\} \to R$ be a function satisfying $f\left(\frac{x}{y}\right) = \frac{f(x)}{f(y)}$ for all $x, y, f(y) = 0$. If $f'(1) = 2024$, then **[JEE Main 2024]**

(a) $xf'(x) + f(x) = 2024$ ☐
(b) $xf'(x) - 2023 f(x) = 0$ ☐
(c) $xf'(x) + 2024 f(x) = 0$ ☐
(d) $xf'(x) - 2024 f(x) = 0$ ☐

14. Let $f(x) = x^5 + 2x^3 + 3x + 1, x \in R$ and $g(x)$ be a function such that $g(f(x)) = x$, for all $x \in R$, then $\frac{g(7)}{g'(7)}$ is equal to **[JEE Main 2024]**

(a) 1 ☐
(b) 7 ☐
(c) 42 ☐
(d) 14 ☐

15. Let $f(x) = x^5 + 2e^{x/4}$ for all $x \in R$. Consider a function $g(x)$ such that $(gof)(x) = x$ for all $x \in R$. Then, the value of $8g'(2)$ is **[JEE Main 2024]**

(a) 4 ☐
(b) 2 ☐
(c) 8 ☐
(d) 16 ☐

16. If $f(x)=\begin{vmatrix} x^3 & 2x^2+1 & 1+3x \\ 3x^2+2 & 2x & x^3+6 \\ x^3-x & 4 & x^2-2 \end{vmatrix}$ for all $x \in R$, then $2f(0)+f'(0)$ is equal to [JEE Main 2024]

(a) 42 ☐
(b) 24 ☐
(c) 18 ☐
(d) 48 ☐

17. Suppose

$$f(x)=\frac{(2^x+2^{-x})\tan x\sqrt{\tan^{-1}(x^2-x+1)}}{(7x^2+3x+1)^3}.$$

Then, the value of $f'(0)$ is equal to [JEE Main 2024]

(a) 0 ☐
(b) $\frac{\pi}{2}$ ☐
(c) π ☐
(d) $\sqrt{\pi}$ ☐

18. Consider the function $f:\left[\frac{1}{2},1\right]\to R$ defined by $f(x)=4\sqrt{2}x^3-3\sqrt{2}x-1$. Consider the statements

I. The curve $y=f(x)$ intersects the X-axis exactly at one point.

II. The curve $y=f(x)$ intersects the X-axis at $x=\cos\frac{\pi}{12}$.

Then, [JEE Main 2024]

(a) Only I is correct ☐
(b) Both I and II are correct ☐
(c) Both I and II are incorrect ☐
(d) Only II is correct ☐

19. Let $g(x)$ be a linear function and

$$f(x)=\begin{cases} g(x), & x\le 0 \\ \left(\dfrac{1+x}{2+x}\right)^{\frac{1}{x}}, & x>0 \end{cases}$$, is continuous at $x=0$.

If $f'(1)=f(-1)$, then the value $g(3)$ is [JEE Main 2024]

(a) $\log_e\left(\frac{4}{9}\right)-1$ ☐
(b) $\log_e\left(\frac{4}{9e^{1/3}}\right)$ ☐
(c) $\frac{1}{3}\log_e\left(\frac{4}{9e^{1/3}}\right)$ ☐
(d) $\frac{1}{3}\log_e\left(\frac{4}{9}\right)+1$ ☐

20. If $\log_e y=3\sin^{-1}x$, then $(1-x^2)y''-xy'$ at $x=\frac{1}{2}$ is equal to [JEE Main 2024]

(a) $3e^{\pi/6}$ ☐
(b) $9e^{\pi/6}$ ☐
(c) $9e^{\pi/2}$ ☐
(d) $3e^{\pi/2}$ ☐

21. If $f(x)=\begin{cases} x^3\sin\left(\frac{1}{x}\right), & x\ne 0 \\ 0, & x=0 \end{cases}$, then [JEE Main 2024]

(a) $f''(0)=1$ ☐
(b) $f''(0)=0$ ☐
(c) $f''\left(\frac{2}{\pi}\right)=\frac{12-\pi^2}{2\pi}$ ☐
(d) $f''\left(\frac{2}{\pi}\right)=\frac{24-\pi^2}{2\pi}$ ☐

22. Let $g:R\to R$ be a non-constant twice differentiable function such that $g'\left(\frac{1}{2}\right)=g'\left(\frac{3}{2}\right)$. If a real valued function f is defined as $f(x)=\frac{1}{2}[g(x)+g(2-x)]$, then [JEE Main 2024]

(a) $f''(x)=0$ for exactly one x in $(0,1)$ ☐
(b) $f''(x)=0$ for atleast two x in $(0,2)$ ☐
(c) $f''(x)=0$ for no x in $(0,1)$ ☐
(d) $f'\left(\frac{3}{2}\right)+f'\left(\frac{1}{2}\right)=1$ ☐

Scan this QR code from your mobile phone to get the solutions of **Competition Edge Up** of this chapter.

Chapter 06

Application of Derivatives

Scan and take Chapter Test

TOPIC 1

Rate of Change of Quantities

1. Find the rate of change of the following.

(i) The rate of change of volume of a sphere with respect to surface area is ________

(ii) The rate of change of volume of cube with respect to surface area is (whose side is x cm) ________

2. State True or False for the statements.

(i) The rate of change of area of a circle with respect to radius r, when $r = 2.2$ cm, is $8\pi^2$ cm.

True ☐ False ☐

(ii) The rate of change of area of equilateral triangle with respect to side x, when $x = 4$ cm, is $2\sqrt{3}$ cm.

True ☐ False ☐

(iii) The rate of change of area of square with respect to side x, when $x = 5$ cm, is 10 cm.

True ☐ False ☐

3. A stone is dropped into a quiet lake and waves moves in circles at a speed of 5 cm/s. At the instant when the radius of the circular wave is 9 cm. Then, the enclosed area is increasing at the rate of

(a) $80\ \pi\ \text{cm}^2/\text{s}$ ☐ (b) $81\pi\ \text{cm}^2/\text{s}$ ☐

(c) $80\ \text{cm}^2/\text{s}$ ☐ (d) None of these ☐

*Concepts of all questions bearing * are important for JEE & CUET*

4. A balloon which always remains spherical, has a variable radius. The rate at which its volume is increasing with respect to its radius when radius 7 cm, is $196\,\pi$ cm^2.

True ☐ False ☐

5. An edge of a cube is increasing at the rate 3 cm/s. How fast is the volume of the cube increasing when the edge is 9 cm long?

---

6. The volume of a cube is increasing at the rate of 9 cm^3/s. How fast is the surface area increasing when the length of an edge is 9 cm?

(a) 3.6 cm^2/s ☐ (b) 3.8 cm^2/s ☐
(c) 1.8 cm^2/s ☐ (d) 4 cm^2/s ☐

---

7. For the curve $y = 5x - 2x^3$, if x increases at the rate of 2 units/s, then at $x = 3$, the slope of the curve is decreasing at the rate of 72 units/s.

True ☐ False ☐

8. If a and b are the sides of two squares such that $b = a + a^2$. Then, the change of the area of second square with respect to the area of the first square is

(a) $1 - 3a + 2a^2$ ☐ (b) $1 + 3a + 2a^2$ ☐
(c) $1 + 3a - 2a^2$ ☐ (d) None of these ☐

---

9. The length x of a rectangle is decreasing at the rate of 2 cm/s and the width y increasing at the rate of 2 cm/s, when $x = 12$ cm and $y = 5$ cm.

Statement I The rate of change of the perimeter remains constant.

Statement II The rate of change of area of the rectangle is 14 cm^2/s.

(a) Both statement are true ☐
(b) Both statements are false ☐
(c) Only Statement I is true ☐
(d) Only Statement II is true ☐

---

10. A water tank has the shape of an inverted right circular cone with its axis vertical and vertex lower most. Its semi-vertical angle is $\tan^{-1}\left(\frac{1}{3}\right)$. Water is poured into it at a constant rate of 7 cu m/s. The rate of change of water level is $\frac{441}{352}$ m/s, when depth of water in the tank is 4 m.

True ☐ False ☐

11. A ladder 10 m long is leaning against a wall. The bottom of the ladder is pulled along the ground away from the wall at the rate of 2 m/s. How fast its height on the wall decreasing when the foot of the ladder is 6 m away from the wall?

(a) $\frac{3}{2}$ m/s ☐ (b) $\frac{4}{3}$ m/s ☐

(c) $-\frac{4}{3}$ m/s ☐ (d) 8 m/s ☐

12. Sand is pouring from a pipe at the rate of 12 cm^3/s. The falling sand forms a cone on the ground in such a way that the height of the cone is always one-sixth of the radius of the base. The height of the sand cone is increasing at the rate $\frac{1}{48}$ cm/s when the height is 4 cm.

True ☐ False ☐

13. Two equal sides of an isosceles triangle with fixed base b are decreasing at the rate of 6 cm/s. Then, the area is decreasing by $\sqrt{3}b$ cm^2/s, when two equal sides are equal to the base.

True ☐ False ☐

14. **Statement I** The volume of a cube is increasing at a constant rate. Then, the increase in surface area varies inversely with the length of the edge of the cube.

Statement II The volume of a cube is increasing at a rate of 7 cm^3/s. Then, the surface area is increasing at the rate of 7 cm^2/s, when the length of an edge is 12 cm.

(a) Both statements are true ☐

(b) Both statements are false ☐

(c) Only Statement I is true ☐

(d) Only Statement II is true ☐

15. **Statement I** If the area of a circle increases at a uniform rate, then the perimeter varies inversely as the radius.

Statement II If a spherical ball of salt is dissolving in water in such a manner that the rate of decrease of volume at any instant is proportional to the surface. Then, the radius is decreasing at a constant rate.

Which of the following statement/statements is/are correct?

(a) Only I ☐ (b) I and II ☐

(c) Only II ☐ (d) None of these ☐

16. The total cost $C(x)$ associated with the production of x units of an item is given by $C(x) = 0.005x^3 - 0.02x^2 + 30x + 5000$. Then, the marginal cost when 3 units are produced, is ₹ 30.02.

True ☐ False ☐

17. The total revenue received from the sale of x units of product is given by $R(x) = 13x^2 + 26x + 15$. Then, the marginal revenue when $x = 7$, is

(a) 208 ☐ (b) 209 ☐

(c) 104 ☐ (d) 104.5 ☐

TOPIC 2

Increasing and Decreasing Functions

NCERT Pg 152-158

18. State True or False for the statements.

(i) The function $f(x) = x^2$ is strictly increasing function on $[0, \infty)$.

True ☐ False ☐

(ii) The function $f(x) = 7x - 3$ is increasing on R.

True ☐ False ☐

(iii) The function $f(x) = -3x + 4$ is strictly decreasing function on R.

True ☐ False ☐

(iv) The function $f(x) = x^2$ is neither strictly increasing nor strictly decreasing on R.

True ☐ False ☐

19. The given function $f(x) = \log_a x, x \in (0, \infty)$.

Statement I The above function is increasing on $(0, \infty)$, if $0 < a < 1$.

Statement II The above function is decreasing on $(0, \infty)$, if $a > 1$.

(a) Both statements are true ☐

(b) Both statements are false ☐

(c) Only Statement I is true ☐

(d) Only Statement II is true ☐

20. The given function $f(x) = a^x, a \in R$.

Statement I The above function is strictly increasing on R, if $a > 1$.

Statement II The above function is strictly decreasing on R, if $0 < a < 1$.

(a) Both statements are true ☐

(b) Only Statement I is true ☐

(c) Only Statement II is true ☐

(d) None of the above ☐

***21.** Fill in the blanks in each of the following questions.

(i) The function f given by $f(x) = x^3 - 3x^2 + 4x$, $x \in R$ is decreasing in the interval ______

(ii) The function $f(x) = 2x^3 - 9x^2 + 12x + 25$ is increasing in the interval ______

(iii) The interval in which $f(x) = \dfrac{4x^2 + 1}{x}$ is decreasing. is ______

(iv) The interval in which $f(x) = \dfrac{x}{2} + \dfrac{2}{x}$, $x \neq 0$ is increasing, is ______

***22.** The function f is given by $f(x) = (x+1)^3 (x-3)^3$.

Statement I f is increasing on the interval $(1, 3) \cup (3, \infty)$.

Statement II f is decreasing on the interval $(-\infty, -1) \cup (-1, 1)$.

(a) Both statements are true ☐

(b) Only Statement I is true ☐

(c) Only Statement II is true ☐

(d) None of the above ☐

***23.** The function $f(x) = \cos\left(2x + \dfrac{\pi}{4}\right)$ is an increasing function on $\left(\dfrac{3\pi}{8}, \dfrac{7\pi}{8}\right)$.

True ☐ False ☐

***24.** Find the intervals in which the following functions are increasing or decreasing.

(i) $f(x) = \sin 3x - \cos 3x$, $0 < x < \pi$ is increasing in ______

(ii) $f(x) = \tan^{-1}(\sin x + \cos x)$, $x \in (0, \pi/2)$ is increasing in ______ and decreasing in ______.

(iii) $f(x) = \log \cos x$, $x \in \left(-\dfrac{\pi}{2}, \dfrac{\pi}{2}\right)$ is increasing in ______ and decreasing in ______.

(iv) $f(x) = \dfrac{4\sin x - 2x - x\cos x}{2 + \cos x}$, $x \in (0, 2\pi)$ is increasing in ______ and decreasing in ______.

(v) $f(x) = x^x$, $x > 0$ is decreasing in ______

25. State True or False.

(i) The function $f(x) = \log(1 + x) - \dfrac{2x}{2 + x}$ is increasing on $(-1, 0) \cup (0, \infty)$.

True ☐ False ☐

(ii) The function $f(x) = \log \sin x$ is increasing on $\left(0, \dfrac{\pi}{2}\right)$.

True ☐ False ☐

(iii) The function $f(x) = \cos^2 x$ is decreasing on $\left(0, \frac{\pi}{2}\right)$.

True ☐ False ☐

(iv) The function $f(x) = \sqrt{3}\sin x - \cos x - 2ax + b$ is decreasing on R, where $a \geq 1$.

True ☐ False ☐

26. Choose the correct option.

(i) Which of the following function is decreasing on $\left(0, \frac{\pi}{2}\right)$?

(a) $\sin x$ ☐ (b) $\cos 2x$ ☐

(c) $\tan x$ ☐ (d) $\cos 3x$ ☐

(ii) The interval of increase of the function $f(x) = x - e^x + \tan\left(\frac{2\pi}{7}\right)$ is

(a) $(0, \infty)$ ☐ (b) $(-\infty, 0)$ ☐

(c) $(1, \infty)$ ☐ (d) $(-\infty, 1)$ ☐

27. Mark the correct alternative in the following.

The function $f(x) = \log_e(x^3 + \sqrt{x^6 + 1})$ is of the following types.

(a) Even function and increasing ☐

(b) Odd function and decreasing ☐

(c) Even function and decreasing ☐

(d) Odd function and increasing ☐

28. The values of k for which $f(x) = kx^3 - 9kx^2 + 9x + 3$ is increasing on R, is ______

29. Find the value of k for which $(k+2)x^3 - 3kx^2 + 9kx - 1$ decreases monotonically for all real x.

30. Find the value of k for which $f(x) = \sin x - kx + c$ is a decreasing function on R.

31. Find the value of k in order that $f(x) = \sqrt{3}\sin x - \cos x - 2kx + b$ decreases for all real values of x.

TOPIC 3

Maxima and Minima

NCERT Pg 159-174

32. Find the maximum and minimum values, if any of the following functions is given by

(i) $f(x) = -|x-1|+5$ ______

(ii) $f(x) = \sin 3x + 4$ ______

(iii) $f(x) = 4x^2 - 4x + 4$ on R ______

33. State True or False.

(i) The function $f(x) = |x+2|, \forall x \in R$ has maximum value at $x = -3$.

True ☐ False ☐

(ii) The function $f(x) = -(x-1)^2 + 10, \forall x \in R$ has maximum value 10.

True ☐ False ☐

(iii) The function $g(x) = |\sin 2x + 3|$ has maximum value greater than minimum value.

True ☐ False ☐

***34.** Find the local maximum and the local minimum values, as the case may be

(i) $f(x) = (x-1)(x+2)^2$ ______

(ii) $f(x) = \sin x - \cos x, 0 < x < 2\pi$ ______

(iii) $f(x) = x\sqrt{1-x}, x > 0$ ______

(iv) $f(x) = \sin^4 x + \cos^4 x, 0 < x < \frac{\pi}{2}$ ______

***35.** The function $f(x) = 2x^3 - 6x^2 + 6x + 5$ has point of inflexion at $x =$ ______

36. Find the points of local maxima or local minima and corresponding local maximum and local minimum value by using second derivative test.

(i) $f(x) = x^3 - 6x^2 + 9x + 15$ ______

(ii) $f(x) = \sin 2x - x$, where $-\frac{\pi}{2} < x < \frac{\pi}{2}$ ______

(iii) $f(x) = (x-1)(x-2)^2$ ______

(iv) $f(x) = x^3 - 2ax^2 + a^2x, a > 0, x \in R$ ______

37. If $f(x) = a\log|x| + bx^2 + x$ has extreme value at $x = -1$ and $x = 2$, then the value of $a + b$ is

______

***38.** State True or False.

(i) The maximum value of $\left(\frac{1}{x}\right)^x$ is $e^{1/e}$.

True ☐ False ☐

(ii) The function $\frac{\log x}{x}$ has a maximum value as $\frac{1}{e}$ at $x = e$.

True ☐ False ☐

(iii) The function $f(x) = \sin x + \sqrt{3}\cos x$ has maximum value at $x = \frac{\pi}{6}$.

True ☐ False ☐

39. Find the absolute maximum and the absolute minimum values of the following functions in the given intervals.

(i) $f(x) = 2x^3 - 24x + 107$ in $[1, 3]$ __________

(ii) $f(x) = \left(\frac{1}{2} - x\right)^2 + x^3$ in $\left[-2, \frac{5}{2}\right]$ __________

(iii) $f(x) = \cos^2 x + \sin x$ in $[0, \pi]$ __________

(iv) $f(x) = 3x^4 - 8x^3 + 12x^2 - 48x + 1$ in $[1, 4]$ __________

***40.** Two positive numbers whose sum is 15 and the sum of whose squares is minimum. Then, the numbers are $\frac{15}{2}$ and $\frac{15}{2}$.

True ☐ False ☐

41. Two positive numbers x and y such that $x + y = 60$ and xy^3 is maximum. Then, the relation between x and y is

(a) $x = y$ ☐ (b) $x > y$ ☐

(c) $x < y$ ☐ (d) None of these ☐

42. Amongst all pairs of positive numbers with product 256 whose sum is least, then these numbers are __________

43. The minimum value of $ax + by$, where $xy = c^2$ and $a > 0$, $b > 0$, $c > 0$ is

(a) $\sqrt{\frac{b}{a}}$ ☐ (b) $\sqrt{\frac{2b}{a}}\,c$ ☐

(c) $-\sqrt{\frac{b}{2a}}\,c$ ☐ (d) None of these ☐

***44.** If all rectangles inscribed in a given circle, then the square has the maximum area.

True ☐ False ☐

***45.** **Statement I** If sum of the lengths of the hypotenuse and a side of a right angled triangle is given, then the area of triangle is maximum when the angle between them is $\frac{\pi}{6}$.

Statement II An open tank with a square base and vertical sides is to be constructed from a metal sheet so as to hold a given quantity of water. Then, the cost of the material will be least when depth of the tank is half of its width.

(a) Both statements are true ☐
(b) Both statements are false ☐
(c) Only Statement I is true ☐
(d) Only Statement II is true ☐

---

46. The semi-vertical angle of a right circular cone of given surface area and maximum volume is $\sin^{-1}\left(\frac{1}{3}\right)$.

True ☐ False ☐

***47.** If length of three sides of a trapezium other than base are equal to 10 cm, then the area of trapezium when it is maximum, is

(a) $75\sqrt{3}$ cm^2 ☐
(b) $\frac{75\sqrt{3}}{2}$ cm^2 ☐
(c) $\frac{7\sqrt{3}}{2}$ cm^2 ☐
(d) $7\sqrt{3}$ cm^2 ☐

***48.** The volume of the longest cone that can be inscribed in a sphere of radius R is $\frac{8}{27}$ of the volume of the sphere.

True ☐ False ☐

49. The shortest distance of the point $(0, c)$ from the parabola $y = x^2$, where $\frac{1}{2} \leq c \leq 5$, is ______

50. A point on the hypotenuse of a right triangle is at distance a and b from the sides of the triangle. Then, the minimum length of the hypoteneous is

(a) $(a^2 + b^2)^{2/3}$ ☐
(b) $(a^{2/3} + b^{2/3})^3$ ☐
(c) $(a^{2/3} + b^{2/3})^{3/2}$ ☐
(d) $(a^3 + b^3)^{2/3}$ ☐

Assertion-Reason Questions

The following questions consist of two statements– Assertion (A) and Reason (R). Answer these questions by selecting the appropriate options given below.
(a) Both A and R are true and R is the correct explanation of A.
(b) Both A and R are true but R is not the correct explanation of A.
(c) A is true but R is false.
(d) A is false but R is true.

1. **Assertion** (A) The function $5 + \frac{6}{x}, x \neq 0$ is strictly decreasing.

Reason (R) For strictly decreasing function $f'(x) < 0$.

2. **Assertion** (A) The function $f(x) = x^2 - 8x + 15$ is strictly increasing in the interval $(4, \infty)$.

Reason (R) The function $f(x) = x^2 - 8x + 15$ is strictly decreasing in the interval $(-\infty, 4)$.

3. **Assertion** (A) The interval in which $f(x) = \log \sin x, 0 \leq x \leq \pi$ is increasing in $\left(0, \frac{\pi}{2}\right)$.

Reason (R) The function $\tan x$ is positive in first quadrant.

4. **Assertion** (A) The function $y = \frac{e^x + e^{-x}}{2}$ is an increasing function on $[0, \infty)$.

Reason (R) The function $y = \frac{e^x - e^{-x}}{2}$ is an increasing function on $(-\infty, \infty)$.

5. **Assertion** (A) The local maximum value of $f(x) = -x^3 + 6x^2 - 9x + 10$ is 10.

Reason (R) For local maximum, $f''(x) > 0$.

6. **Assertion** (A) The function $f(x) = \sin x$ decreases on the interval $\left(0, \frac{\pi}{2}\right)$.

Reason (R) The function $f(x) = \cos x$ decreases on the interval $\left(0, \frac{\pi}{2}\right)$.

7. **Assertion** (A) The point of local maxima of function $f(x) = x^3 - 3x + 3$ is $x = -1$.

Reason (R) For local minima, $f''(x) > 0$.

8. **Assertion** (A) Function $f(x) = 2x^3 - 9x^2 + 12x - 3$ is increasing outside the interval (1, 2).

Reason (R) $f'(x) < 0$ for $x \in (1, 2)$. ______________________

9. **Assertion** (A) Two numbers whose sum is 24 and product is as large as possible are 8 and 16.

Reason (R) A function $f(x)$ is minimum at $x = a$, if $f'(a) = 0$ and $f''(a) \geq 0$.

____

10. **Assertion** (A) The function $y = [x(x-2)]^2$ is increasing in $(0, 1) \cup (2, \infty)$.

Reason (R) $\frac{dy}{dx} = 0$, when $x = 0, 1, 2$.

____

Case Based Questions

Case 1 The relation between the height of the plant (y cm) with respect to exposure to sunlight is governed by the following equation. $y = 4x - \frac{1}{2}x^2$, where x is the number of days exposed to sunlight.

Based on the above information, answer the following questions.

(i) The rate of growth of the plant with respect to sunlight is ....

(a) $x - \frac{1}{2}x^2$ ☐ (b) $x - 4$ ☐

(c) $4 - x$ ☐ (d) $4x - \frac{1}{2}x^2$ ☐

(ii) What is the number of days it will take for the plant to grow to the maximum height?

(a) 4 ☐ (b) 7 ☐

(c) 6 ☐ (d) 10 ☐

(iii) What is the maximum height of the plant?

(a) 10 cm ☐ (b) 12 cm ☐

(c) 6 cm ☐ (d) 8 cm ☐

Case 2 Megha's father wants to construct a rectangular garden using a brick wall on one side of the garden and wire fencing for the other three sides. He has 200 ft of wire fencing.

Based on the above information, answer the following questions.

(i) If x denote the length of side of graden perpendicular to brick wall and y denote the length of side parallel to brick wall, then find the relation representing total amount of fencing wire.

(ii) Find the area of the garden, $A(x)$ as a function of x.

(iii) Find the value of x for which $A(x)$ will be maximum.

(iv) Find the maximum value of $A(x)$.

COMPETITION EDGE UP

1. The function $f(x)=\frac{x}{x^2-6x-16}$, $x \in R-\{-2, 8\}$ [JEE Main 2024]
(a) decreases in $(-\infty, -2)$ and increases in $(8, \infty)$ ☐
(b) increases in $(-\infty, -2) \cup (-2, 8) \cup (8, \infty)$ ☐
(c) decreases in $(-\infty, -2) \cup (-2, 8) \cup (8, \infty)$ ☐
(d) decreases in $(-2, 8)$ and increases in $(-\infty, -2) \cup (8, \infty)$ ☐

2. The number of critical points of the function $f(x)=(x-2)^{2/3}(2x+1)$ is [JEE Main 2024]
(a) 1 ☐ (b) 3 ☐
(c) 0 ☐ (d) 2 ☐

3. For the function $f(x)=\sin x+3x-\frac{2}{\pi}(x^2+x)$, where $x \in \left[0, \frac{\pi}{2}\right]$, consider the following two statements: [JEE Main 2024]
I. f is increasing in $\left(0, \frac{\pi}{2}\right)$.
II. f' is decreasing in $\left(0, \frac{\pi}{2}\right)$.
Between the above two statements,
(a) Neither I nor II is true ☐
(b) Both I and II are true ☐
(c) Only I is true ☐
(d) Only II is true ☐

4. Let $f: R \to (0, \infty)$ be strictly increasing function such that $\lim_{x \to \infty} \frac{f(7x)}{f(x)}=1$. Then, the value of $\lim_{x \to \infty}\left[\frac{f(5x)}{f(x)}-1\right]$ is equal to [JEE Main 2024]
(a) 7/5 ☐
(b) 1 ☐
(c) 0 ☐
(d) 4 ☐

5. Let $g(x)=3f\left(\frac{x}{3}\right)+f(3-x)$ and $f''(x)>0$ for all $x \in (0, 3)$. If g is decreasing in $(0, \alpha)$ and increasing in $(\alpha, 3)$, then 8α is [JEE Main 2024]
(a) 0 ☐
(b) 20 ☐
(c) 18 ☐
(d) 24 ☐

6. If $5f(x)+4f\left(\frac{1}{x}\right)=x^2-2, \forall x \neq 0$ and $y=9x^2 f(x)$, then y is strictly increasing in [JEE Main 2024]
(a) $\left(0, \frac{1}{\sqrt{5}}\right) \cup \left(\frac{1}{\sqrt{5}}, \infty\right)$ ☐
(b) $\left(-\frac{1}{\sqrt{5}}, 0\right) \cup \left(\frac{1}{\sqrt{5}}, \infty\right)$ ☐
(c) $\left(-\frac{1}{\sqrt{5}}, 0\right) \cup \left(0, \frac{1}{\sqrt{5}}\right)$ ☐
(d) $\left(-\infty, \frac{1}{\sqrt{5}}\right) \cup \left(0, \frac{1}{\sqrt{5}}\right)$ ☐

7. Let the set of all values of p, for which $f(x)=(p^2-6p+8)(\sin^2 2x-\cos^2 2x)+2(2-p)x+7$ does not have any critical point, be the interval (a, b). Then, $16ab$ is equal to .... [JEE Main 2024]

8. Let the sum of the maximum and the minimum values of the function $f(x)=\frac{2x^2-3x+8}{2x^2+3x+8}$ be $\frac{m}{n}$, where gcd $(m, n)=1$. Then, $m+n$ is equal to [JEE Main 2024]
(a) 201 ☐
(b) 217 ☐
(c) 195 ☐
(d) 182 ☐

9. Let $f(x)=(x+3)^2(x-2)^3$, $x \in [-4, 4]$. If M and m are the maximum and minimum values of f, respectively in $[-4, 4]$, then the value of $M-m$ is [JEE Main 2024]
(a) 392 ☐ (b) 108 ☐
(c) 608 ☐ (d) 600 ☐

10. The function $f(x) = 2x + 3(x)^{2/3}, x \in R$ has **[JEE Main 2024]**

(a) exactly one point of local minima and no point of local maxima ☐

(b) exactly two points of local maxima and exactly one point of local minima ☐

(c) exactly one point of local maxima and exactly one point of local minima ☐

(d) exactly one point of local maxima and no point of local minima ☐

11. Let $f(x) = 4\cos^3 x + 3\sqrt{3}\cos^2 x - 10$. The number of points of local maxima of f in interval $(0, 2\pi)$ is **[JEE Main 2024]**

(a) 3 ☐
(b) 1 ☐
(c) 2 ☐
(d) 4 ☐

12. If the function $f(x) = \left(\frac{1}{x}\right)^{2x}; x > 0$ attains the maximum value at $x = \frac{1}{e}$, then **[JEE Main 2024]**

(a) $e^{2\pi} < (2\pi)^e$ ☐
(b) $e^{\pi} > \pi^e$ ☐
(c) $e^{\pi} < \pi^e$ ☐
(d) $(2e)^{\pi} > \pi^{(2e)}$ ☐

13. Let a rectangle ABCD of sides 2 and 4 be inscribed in another rectangle PQRS such that the vertices of the rectangle ABCD lie on the sides of the rectangle PQRS. Let a and b be the sides of the rectangle PQRS when its area is maximum. Then, $(a + b)^2$ is equal to **[JEE Main 2024]**

(a) 72 ☐
(b) 64 ☐
(c) 60 ☐
(d) 80 ☐

14. Let $f(x) = 3\sqrt{x-2} + \sqrt{4-x}$ be a real valued function. If α and β are respectively the minimum and the maximum values of f, then $\alpha^2 + 2\beta^2$ is equal to **[JEE Main 2024]**

(a) 42 ☐
(b) 38 ☐
(c) 44 ☐
(d) 24 ☐

15. Let the set of all positive values of λ, for which the point of local minimum of the function $(1 + x(\lambda^2 - x^2))$ satisfies $\frac{x^2 + x + 2}{x^2 + 5x + 6} < 0$, be (α, β).

Then, $\alpha^2 + \beta^2$ is equal to .... **[JEE Main 2024]**

16. Let A be the region enclosed by the parabola $y^2 = 2x$ and the line $x = 24$. Then, the maximum area of the rectangle inscribed in the region A is .... **[JEE Main 2024]**

17. Let the maximum and minimum values of $(\sqrt{8x - x^2 - 12} - 4)^2 + (x - 7)^2, x \in R$ be M and m, respectively. Then, $M^2 - m^2$ is equal to .... **[JEE Main 2024]**

18. Let $S = \{\sin^2 2\theta : (\sin^4\theta + \cos^4\theta)x^2 + (\sin 2\theta)x + (\sin^6\theta + \cos^6\theta) = 0$ has real roots$\}$.

If α and β are the smallest and largest elements of the set S, respectively, then $3((\alpha - 2)^2 + (\beta - 1)^2)$ equals .... **[JEE Main 2024]**

Scan this QR code from your mobile phone to get the solutions of **Competition Edge Up** of this chapter.

Chapter 07

Integrals

Scan and take Chapter Test

TOPIC 1

Integration and Its Properties

1. State True or False.

(i) $\frac{d}{dx}\left(\frac{x^n+1}{n+1}\right)=x^n$ and $\int x^n\,dx=\frac{x^n}{n+1}+C, n\neq -1$

True ☐ False ☐

(ii) $\frac{d}{dx}(\tan x)=\sec^2 x$ and $\int \sec^2 x\,dx=-\tan x+C$

True ☐ False ☐

(iii) $\frac{d}{dx}(\sin^{-1} x)=\frac{1}{\sqrt{1-x^2}}$ and $\int\frac{1}{\sqrt{1-x^2}}dx=\sin^{-1} x+C$

True ☐ False ☐

(iv) $\frac{d}{dx}(\cot^{-1} x)=\frac{-1}{1+x^2}$ and $\int\frac{dx}{1+x^2}=\cot^{-1} x+C$

True ☐ False ☐

2. The anti-derivative 'F' of f defined by $f(x)=4x^3+6$, where $F(0)=3$, is ______

3. Find the value of

(i) $\int x^3\left(1+\frac{1}{x^2}\right)dx$ ______

(ii) $\int (ax^3+bx^2+C)\,dx$ ______

(iii) $\int\left(x^{3/2}+2e^x-\frac{1}{x}\right)dx$ ______

(iv) $\int(\sin x-\cos x+x)\,dx$ ______

*Concepts of all questions bearing * are important for JEE & CUET*

(v) $\int \sec^2 (7 + x)\, dx$ ______

(vi) $\int \operatorname{cosec} x (\operatorname{cosec} x + \cot x)\, dx$ ______

(vii) $\int (\cos x + \sin x)\, dx$ ______

(viii) $\int (\sin x - 4e^x)\, dx$ ______

(ix) $\int (e^x + \cos x) dx$ ______

(x) $\int \left\{(x+3)^5 + \dfrac{1}{(x-5)^3} + \dfrac{1}{\sqrt{x-4}} + \sqrt{x+2}\right\} dx$ ______

4. State True or False.

(i) $\int \left(\sqrt{x} - \dfrac{1}{\sqrt{x}}\right)^2 dx = \dfrac{x^2}{2} + \log|x| - 2x + C.$

True ☐ False ☐

(ii) $\int \sqrt{x}(3x^2 + 2x + 3)\, dx = \dfrac{6}{7}x^{7/2} + \dfrac{4}{5}x^{5/2} + 2x^{3/2} + C.$

True ☐ False ☐

(iii) $\int \dfrac{x^3 - x^2 + x - 1}{x - 1}\, dx = \dfrac{x^3}{3} + x + C.$

True ☐ False ☐

(iv) $\int (x^2 + e^{\log x} + e^x)\, dx = \dfrac{x^3}{3} + \dfrac{x^2}{2} + \dfrac{e^x}{\log(e)} + C.$

True ☐ False ☐

(v) $\int \dfrac{x^5 + x^{-2} + 2}{x^2}\, dx = \dfrac{x^4}{4} + \dfrac{x^3}{3} - \dfrac{2}{x} + C.$

True ☐ False ☐

(vi) $\int \dfrac{5\cos^3 x + 6\sin^3 x}{2\sin^2 x \cos^2 x}\, dx = \dfrac{5}{2}\operatorname{cosec} x + 3\sec x + C.$

True ☐ False ☐

5. The value of $\int \sqrt{1 - \sin 2x}\, dx, \dfrac{\pi}{4} < x < \dfrac{\pi}{2}$ is ______

6. If $I = \int \tan^{-1}\left(\sqrt{\dfrac{1 - \sin x}{1 + \sin x}}\right) dx, -\dfrac{\pi}{2} < x < \dfrac{\pi}{2}$, then the value of I is ______

7. Match the following columns.

	Column I		Column II
A.	$\int \tan^{-1}(\sec x + \tan x)\, dx, -\frac{\pi}{2} < x < \frac{\pi}{2}$	1.	$2 \tan x - 3 \sec x + C$
B.	$\int \left(\frac{x}{m} + \frac{m}{x} + x^m + m^x\right) dx$	2.	$\frac{\pi}{4} x + \frac{x^2}{4} + C$
C.	$\int \frac{2 - 3 \sin x}{\cos^2 x} dx$	3.	$x^3 + \frac{1}{x^2} - 2$
D.	If $f'(x) = 3x^2 - \frac{2}{x^3}$ and $f(1) = 0$, then $f(x)$ is	4.	$\frac{x^2}{2m} + m \log\|x\| + \frac{x^{m+1}}{m+1} + \frac{m^x}{\log m} + C$

Which of the following option is correct?

(a) A → 2, B → 4, C → 1, D → 3 ☐
(b) A → 2, B → 1, C → 4, D → 3 ☐
(c) A → 3, B → 1, C → 4, D → 2 ☐
(d) None of these ☐

TOPIC 2

Method of Integral-Substitution

8. Make the substitution for the following integrals.

(i) $\int 5x^4 \sqrt{1 + x^5}\, dx$ ______

(ii) $\int \frac{6x^2}{3 + 2x^3} dx$ ______

(iii) $\int x e^{x^2} dx$ ______

(iv) $\int \sin mx\, dx$ ______

(v) $\int 3x^2 \cos(x^3 + 1)\, dx$ ______

(vi) $\int x(x^2 + 3)^5\, dx$ ______

9. To find $\int \frac{1}{4x} dx$, Roy's answer was $\int \frac{1}{4x} dx = \frac{1}{4} \ln|4x| + C$ and Robert's answer was $\int \frac{1}{4x} dx = \frac{1}{4} \int \frac{1}{x} dx = \frac{1}{4} \ln|x| + C.$

Which of them has found the correct answer? Prove your statement.

______

10. Evaluate the following integrals.

(i) $\int \frac{3x^2}{2 + x^3} dx$ ______

(ii) $\int \frac{(1 + \log x)}{x} dx$ ____________________

(iii) $\int \cos x \cos(\sin x)\, dx$ ____________________

11. $\int \{f(ax + b)\}^n \cdot f'(ax + b)\, dx, n \neq -1$ is equal to ____________________

12. $\int 2^{2^{2^x}} \cdot 2^{2^x} \cdot 2^x\, dx$ is equal to

(a) $\frac{1}{(\log_e 2)} \cdot 2^{2^{2^x}} + C$ ☐

(b) $\frac{1}{(\log_e 2)^2} \cdot 2^{2^{2x}} + C$ ☐

(c) $\frac{2^{2^{2^x}}}{(\log_e 2)^3} + C$ ☐

(d) $\frac{1}{(\log_e 2)^3} \cdot 2^{2^x} + C$ ☐

---

13. Which of the following is correct or incorrect?

(i) $\int \cot x\, dx = -\log|\sin x| + C$ ____________________

(ii) $\int \sec x\, dx = -\log|\sec x + \tan x| + C$ ____________________

(iii) $\int \text{cosec}\, x\, dx = \log|\text{cosec}\, x - \cot x| + C$ ____________________

(iv) $\int \tan x\, dx = -\log|\sec x| + C$ ____________________

14. State True or False.

(i) $\int \frac{dx}{\sqrt{3x+4} - \sqrt{3x+1}} = \frac{2}{27}[(3x+4)^{3/2} + (3x+1)^{3/2}] + C.$

True ☐ False ☐

(ii) $\int \tan^2(2x - 3)\, dx = \frac{1}{2}\tan(2x - 3) - x + C.$

True ☐ False ☐

(iii) $\int \frac{dx}{x + x\log x} = \log|1 + \log x| + C.$

True ☐ False ☐

(iv) $\int (4x + 2)\sqrt{x^2 + x + 1}\, dx = \frac{4}{3}(x^2 + x + 1)^{1/2} + C.$

True ☐ False ☐

(v) $\int \frac{dx}{x(\log x)^m}, x > 0 = \frac{(\log x)^{1-m}}{1 - m} + C.$

True ☐ False ☐

15. Match the following columns.

	Column I		Column II
A.	$\int \frac{e^{\tan^{-1} x}}{1+x^2} dx$	1.	$2\sqrt{\tan x} + C$
B.	$\int \frac{1}{\cos^2 x (1 - \tan x)^2} dx$	2.	$e^{\tan^{-1} x} + C$
C.	$\int \frac{(1 + \log x)^2}{x} dx$	3.	$\frac{1}{(1 - \tan x)} + C$
D.	$\int \frac{\sqrt{\tan x}}{\sin x \cos x} dx$	4.	$\frac{1}{3}(1 + \log x)^3 + C$

From the above table, which of the following is/are correct?

(a) A → 3, B → 2, C → 4, D → 1 ☐

(b) A → 2, B → 3, C → 4, D → 1 ☐

(c) A → 2, B → 4, C → 3, D → 1 ☐

(d) None of these ☐

16. $\int \frac{x^3 \sin (\tan^{-1} x^4)}{1+x^8} dx$ equals $-\frac{1}{4} \cos \{\tan^{-1} (x^4)\} + C$.

True ☐ False ☐

17. $\int \frac{(10x^9 + 10^x \log_e 10)}{x^{10} + 10^x} dx$ is equal to ____________

18. Find the integrals of the following.

(i) $\int \frac{e^{2x} - e^{-2x}}{e^{2x} + e^{-2x}} dx$ ____________

(ii) $\int \frac{e^{2x} - 1}{e^{2x} + 1} dx$ ____________

(iii) $\int \frac{x^2}{(3x^3 + 2)^3} dx$ ____________

(iv) $\int \frac{8x + 13}{\sqrt{4x + 7}} dx$ ____________

(v) $\int (7x - 2)\sqrt{3x + 2}\, dx$ ____________

(vi) $\int \frac{\sin x}{(1+\cos x)^2} dx$ ____________

19. The value of the integral $\int \sin^3 x \cos^2 x\, dx$ is ____________

20. $\int \frac{\sin x - x\cos x}{x(x+\sin x)}\,dx$ is equal to

(a) $\log\left|\frac{x}{x+\cos x}\right| + C$ ☐
(b) $\log\left|\frac{x}{x+\sin x}\right| + x + C$ ☐

(c) $x - \log\left|\frac{x}{x+\sin x}\right| + C$ ☐
(d) $\log\left|\frac{x}{x+\sin x}\right| + C$ ☐

---

21. The value of the integral $\int \frac{dx}{1+\tan x}$ is

(a) $\frac{x}{2} + \frac{1}{2}\log|\sin x + \cos x| + C$ ☐
(b) $\frac{x}{2} - \frac{1}{2}\log|\sin x + \cos x| + C$ ☐

(c) $\frac{1}{2}\log|\sin x + \cos x| + C$ ☐
(d) $\frac{1}{2}\log|\sin x - \cos x| + C$ ☐

---

22. $\int \frac{8^{1+x} + 4^{1-x}}{2^x}\,dx$ equals $\frac{2^{x+2}}{\log 2} - \frac{2^{2-3x}}{3\log 2} + C.$

True ☐ False ☐

23. Evaluate the integral of the following functions.

(i) $\int \frac{e^x\,dx}{(1+e^x)^2}$ ____________________

(ii) $\int x^{2x}(1+\log x)\,dx$ ____________________

TOPIC 3

Integration using Trigonometric Indentities

24. Evaluate the following integrals.

(i) $\int \frac{\sin x}{1+\cos x}\,dx$ ____________________

(ii) $\int \sin 2x \cdot \cos 3x\,dx$ ____________________

(iii) $\int \sin^2 x \cos^2 x\,dx$ ____________________

(iv) $\int \sin^2(2x+5)\,dx$ ____________________

(v) $\int (\sin^4 x + \cos^4 x)\,dx$ ____________________

25. Use the identity $\cos^2\theta = \frac{1}{2} + \frac{1}{2}\cos(2\theta)$ to show that $\cos^4 x = \frac{1}{8}\cos(4x) + \frac{1}{2}\cos(2x) + \frac{3}{8}$ and hence find $\int \cos^4 x\, dx$.

---

26. $\int \frac{\cos 2x}{(\cos x + \sin x)^2} dx$ is equal to $\frac{1}{2}\log|1 + \sin 2x| + C$.

True ☐ False ☐

27. The value of the integral $\int \frac{\sin x}{\sin(x+a)} dx$ is

(a) $x\cos a + \sin a \log|\sin(x+a)| + C$ (b) $x\cos a - \sin a \log|\sin(x+a)| + C$

(c) $x\sin a - \cos a \log|\sin(x+a)| + C$ (d) $x\sin a + \cos a \log|\sin(x+a)| + C$

---

28. If $I = \int \sin x \cdot \sin 2x \cdot \sin 3x\, dx$, then the value of I is

(a) $\frac{1}{4}\left\{\frac{\cos 4x}{4} + \frac{\cos 2x}{2} + \frac{\cos 6x}{6}\right\} + C$ (b) $-\frac{1}{4}\left\{\frac{\cos 4x}{4} + \frac{\cos 2x}{2} - \frac{\cos 6x}{6}\right\} + C$

(c) $\frac{1}{4}\left\{\frac{\cos 4x}{4} - \frac{\cos 2x}{2} - \frac{\cos 6x}{6}\right\} + C$ (d) $\frac{1}{4}\left\{-\frac{\cos 4x}{4} - \frac{\cos 2x}{2} + \frac{\cos 6x}{6}\right\} + C$

---

29. $\int \frac{\cos 5x + \cos 4x}{1 - 2\cos 3x} dx$ is equal to $-\left(\sin 2x + \frac{\sin x}{2}\right) + C$.

True ☐ False ☐

30. $\int \sqrt{\frac{1 - \cos 2x}{1 + \cos 2x}}\, dx$ is equal to ______

***31.** $\int \frac{\sin 2x}{a^2 \sin^2 x + b^2 \cos^2 x} dx$ is equal to

(a) $\frac{1}{(a^2 - b^2)}\log|a^2 \sin^2 x + b^2 \cos^2 x| + C$ (b) $\frac{1}{a^2 - b^2}\log|a^2 \cos^2 x + b^2 \sin^2 x| + C$

(c) $\frac{1}{a^2 + b^2}\log|a^2 \sin^2 x - b^2 \cos^2 x| + C$ (d) None of these

---

32. $\int \frac{\sin 2x}{\sin\left(x - \frac{\pi}{6}\right)\sin\left(x + \frac{\pi}{6}\right)} dx$ is equal to $\log\left|\sin\left(x - \frac{\pi}{6}\right)\right| + \log\left|\sin\left(x + \frac{\pi}{6}\right)\right| + C$.

True ☐ False ☐

33. $\int \frac{\sin(x-\alpha)}{\sin(x+\alpha)}\,dx$ is equal to ______

34. $\int \frac{\cos^3 x}{\sin^2 x + \sin x}\,dx$ is equal to $\log|\sin x| + \sin x + C$.

True ☐ False ☐

35. $\int \sec^4 x\,dx$ is equal to ______

TOPIC 4

Integrals of Some Particular Functions

NCERT Pg 243-252

36. State True or False.

(i) $\int \frac{dx}{x^2 - a^2} = \frac{1}{2a}\log\left|\frac{x+a}{x-a}\right| + C$

True ☐ False ☐

(ii) $\int \frac{dx}{x^2 + a^2} = \frac{1}{2a}\tan^{-1}\frac{x}{a} + C$

True ☐ False ☐

(iii) $\int \frac{dx}{\sqrt{x^2 + a^2}} = \frac{1}{a}\log|x + \sqrt{x^2 + a^2}| + C$

True ☐ False ☐

(iv) $\int \frac{dx}{\sqrt{a^2 - x^2}} = \sin^{-1}\frac{x}{a} + C$

True ☐ False ☐

37. Evaluate the following integrals.

(i) $\int \frac{dx}{9x^2 - 4}$ ______

(ii) $\int \frac{dx}{\sqrt{2x - x^2}}$ ______

*(iii) $\int \frac{dx}{\sqrt{16x^2 + 25}}$ ______

(iv) $\int \frac{dx}{\sqrt{9 - 25x^2}}$ ______

***38.** State True or False.

(i) $\int \frac{3x^2}{x^6+1}\,dx = \frac{1}{2}\tan^{-1}(x^3) + C.$

True ☐ False ☐

(ii) $\int \frac{dx}{a^2x^2 - b^2} = \frac{1}{2ab}\log\left|\frac{ax-b}{ax+b}\right| + C.$

True ☐ False ☐

(iii) $\int \frac{dx}{\sqrt{(2-x)^2+1}} = \log|(2-x)+\sqrt{(2-x)^2+1}| + C.$

True ☐ False ☐

39. $\int \frac{dx}{2x^2+x-1}$ is equal to ________________

40. $\int \frac{dx}{x^2+4x+8}$ is equal to

(a) $\frac{1}{2\sqrt{2}}\tan^{-1}\left(\frac{2x-1}{\sqrt{2}}\right) + C$ ☐

(b) $\frac{1}{2}\tan^{-1}\left(\frac{2x-1}{\sqrt{2}}\right) + C$ ☐

(c) $\frac{1}{\sqrt{2}}\tan^{-1}\left(\frac{2x-1}{\sqrt{2}}\right) + C$ ☐

(d) None of these ☐

____

41. $\int \frac{dx}{\sqrt{5x^2-2x}}$ is equal to $\frac{1}{\sqrt{5}}\log\left|\left(x-\frac{1}{5}\right)+\sqrt{x^2-\frac{2x}{5}}\right| + C.$

True ☐ False ☐

42. $\int \frac{dx}{x\,\{6(\log x)^2 + 7\log x + 2\}}$ is equal to

(a) $\log\left|\frac{2\log x+1}{3\log x+1}\right| + C$ ☐

(b) $\log\left|\frac{2\log x+1}{3\log x+2}\right| + C$ ☐

(c) $\log\left|\frac{2\log x+1}{2\log x+3}\right| + C$ ☐

(d) None of these ☐

____

43. $\int \frac{\sin x + \cos x}{9 + 16\sin 2x}\,dx$ is equal to ________________

44. State True or False.

(i) $\int \frac{dx}{\sqrt{9+8x-x^2}} = \sin^{-1}\left(\frac{x-4}{5}\right) + C.$

True ☐ False ☐

(ii) $\int \frac{dx}{\sqrt{2x^2+3x-2}} = \frac{1}{\sqrt{2}} \log \left| \left(x + \frac{3}{4} \right) + \sqrt{x^2 + \frac{3}{2}x - 1} \right| + C.$

True ☐ False ☐

(iii) $\int \frac{\sec^2 x}{\sqrt{\tan^2 x + 4}} dx = \log |\tan x + \sqrt{\tan^2 x + 4}| + C.$

True ☐ False ☐

45. $\int \frac{e^x dx}{\sqrt{5 - 4e^x - e^{2x}}}$ is equal to ______________

46. $\int \frac{\sin 2x \cos 2x}{\sqrt{9 - \cos^4 2x}} dx$ is equal to

(a) $\frac{1}{4} \sin^{-1} \left(\frac{\cos^2 2x}{3} \right) + C$ (b) $\frac{1}{4} \sin^{-1} \left(\frac{\cos 2x}{3} \right) + C$

(c) $-\frac{1}{4} \sin^{-1} \left(\frac{\cos^2 2x}{3} \right) + C$ (d) $\frac{1}{4} \tan^{-1} \left(\frac{\cos^2 2x}{3} \right) + C$

---

47. $\int \frac{dx}{\sqrt{1 - e^{2x}}}$ is equal to $\log |e^{-x} - \sqrt{e^{-2x} - 1}| + C.$

True ☐ False ☐

48. $\int \frac{(4x+1)}{x^2 + 3x + 2} dx$ is equal to ______________

49. $\int \frac{2x+3}{\sqrt{x^2 + 4x + 1}} dx$ is equal to

(a) $2\sqrt{x^2 + 4x + 1} + \log |x + 2 + \sqrt{x^2 + 4x + 1}| + C$

(b) $2\sqrt{x^2 + 4x + 1} - \log |x + 2 + \sqrt{x^2 + 4x + 1}| + C$

(c) $2\sqrt{x^2 + 4x + 1} - \log |x + 2 - \sqrt{x^2 + 4x + 1}| + C$

(d) $\log |(x + 2) + \sqrt{x^2 + 4x + 1}| + C$

---

50. $\int \frac{x^2 + 5x + 3}{x^2 + 3x + 2} dx$ is equal to ______________

51. State True or False.

(i) $\int \frac{(3\sin x - 2)\cos x}{5 - \cos^2 x - 4\sin x} dx = 3\log|2 - \sin x| - 4\left(\frac{1}{2 - \sin x}\right) + C.$

True ☐ False ☐

(ii) $\int \frac{(3x + 5)}{x^2 + 3x - 18} dx = \frac{3}{2}\log|x^2 + 3x - 18| + \frac{1}{18}\left(\frac{x - 3}{x + 3}\right) + C.$

True ☐ False ☐

(iii) $\int \frac{x^3 + 1}{x^3 - x} dx = x + \log\left|\frac{x - 1}{x}\right| + C.$

True ☐ False ☐

TOPIC 5

Integration by Partial Fraction

52. Match the following columns.

	Column I (Form of fraction)		Column II (Form of partial fraction)
A.	$\frac{px + q}{(x - a)(x - b)}, a \neq b$	1.	$\frac{A}{(x - a)} + \frac{B}{(x - a)^2}$
B	$\frac{px^2 + qx + r}{(x - a)(x - b)(x - c)}$	2.	$\frac{A}{(x - a)} + \frac{B}{(x - b)}$
C.	$\frac{px^2 + qx + r}{(x - a)(x^2 + bx + c)}$	3.	$\frac{A}{(x - a)} + \frac{B}{(x - b)} + \frac{C}{(x - c)}$
D	$\frac{(px + q)}{(x - a)^2}$	4.	$\frac{A}{(x - a)} + \frac{Bx + C}{(x^2 + bx + c)}$

From the above table, which of the following is/are correct?

(a) A → 2, B → 3, C → 4, D → 1 ☐
(b) A → 2, B → 3, C → 1, D → 4 ☐
(c) A → 3, B → 2, C → 1, D → 4 ☐
(d) None of these ☐

53. Evaluate the following integrals.

(i) $\int \frac{\cos\theta}{(2 + \sin\theta)(3 + 4\sin\theta)} d\theta$ ______

(ii) $\int \frac{(3x - 1)}{(x + 2)^2} dx$ ______

(iii) $\int \frac{x\, dx}{(x - 1)^2 (x + 2)}$ ______

(iv) $\int \frac{(x^2 + 1)\, dx}{(x - 1)^2 (x + 3)}$ ______

(v) $\int \frac{8dx}{(x + 2)(x^2 + 4)}$ ______

54. $\int \frac{(2x-3)}{(x^2-1)(2x+3)} dx$ is equal to

(a) $\frac{5}{2} \log|x+1| - \frac{1}{10} \log|x-1| - \frac{12}{5} \log|2x+3| + C$ ☐

(b) $\frac{5}{2} \log|x+1| + \frac{1}{10} \log|x-1| - \frac{12}{5} \log|2x+3| + C$ ☐

(c) $\frac{5}{2} \log|x+1| + \frac{1}{10} \log|x-1| + \frac{12}{5} \log|2x+3| + C$ ☐

(d) None of the above ☐

---

55. $\int \frac{2\,dx}{(1-x)(1+x^2)}$ is equal to $-\log|x-1| + \frac{1}{2}\log|1+x^2| + \tan^{-1} x + C$.

True ☐ False ☐

56. $\int \frac{x^2}{(x^2+1)(x^2+4)} dx$ is equal to

(a) $-\frac{1}{3}\tan^{-1} x + \frac{1}{3}\tan^{-1}\left(\frac{x}{2}\right) + C$ ☐ (b) $-\frac{1}{3}\tan^{-1} x + \frac{2}{3}\tan^{-1}\left(\frac{x}{2}\right) + C$ ☐

(c) $-\frac{1}{3}\tan^{-1} x - \frac{2}{3}\tan^{-1}\left(\frac{x}{2}\right) + C$ ☐ (d) None of these ☐

---

57. $\int \frac{(3\sin\phi - 2)\cos\phi}{5 - \cos^2\phi - 4\sin\phi} d\phi$ is equal to ____________

58. $\int \frac{(x^2+1)(x^2+2)}{(x^2+3)(x^2+4)} dx = x + \frac{2}{\sqrt{3}}\tan^{-1}\frac{x}{\sqrt{3}} - 3\tan^{-1}\frac{x}{2} + C.$

True ☐ False ☐

TOPIC 6

Integration by Parts

59. Evaluate the following integrals.

(i) $\int x^n \log x \, dx$ ____________

(ii) $\int x \log x \, dx$ ____________

(iii) $\int (x+1) \log x \, dx$ ____________

(iv) $\int x^3 \cos x^2 \, dx$ ____________

(v) $\int e^x \sin x \, dx$ ____________

(vi) $\int x^2 e^x dx$ ______

(vii) $\int \tan^{-1} x \, dx$ ______

60. $\int x \tan^{-1} x \, dx$ is equal to

(a) $\frac{x^2}{2} \tan^{-1} x + \frac{1}{2}(x - \tan^{-1} x) + C$ ☐

(b) $\frac{x^2}{2} \tan^{-1} x - \frac{1}{2}(x - \tan^{-1} x) + C$ ☐

(c) $\frac{x^2}{2} \tan^{-1} x - \frac{1}{2}(x + \tan^{-1} x) + C$ ☐

(d) None of the above ☐

---

61. State True or False.

(i) $\int x^3 \cdot e^x \, dx = (x^3 - 3x^2 + 6x - 6) \cdot e^x + C.$

True ☐ False ☐

(ii) $\int \frac{x \cos^{-1} x}{\sqrt{1-x^2}} dx = -\{\sqrt{1-x^2} \cdot \cos^{-1} x + x\} + C.$

True ☐ False ☐

62. $\int e^x \left(\frac{1}{x} - \frac{1}{x^2}\right) dx$ is equal to

(a) $\frac{e^x}{x} + C$ ☐ (b) $-\frac{e^x}{x} + C$ ☐

(c) $\frac{e^x}{x^2} + C$ ☐ (d) $-\frac{e^x}{x^2} + C$ ☐

---

63. Find $\frac{d}{dx}(e^x \sin x)$ and hence find $\int e^x (\sin x + \cos x) \, dx$.

---

64. $\int \frac{(x^2+1)}{(x+1)^2} e^x \, dx$ is equal to ______

65. $\int e^x \left(\frac{2 + \sin 2x}{1 + \cos 2x}\right) dx$ is equal to $e^x \tan x + C$.

True ☐ False ☐

66. Match the following columns.

	Column I		Column II
A.	$\int e^x \cdot \frac{x}{(x+1)^2}\,dx$	1.	$2\left\{x\tan^{-1}x - \frac{1}{2}\log\lvert 1+x^2\rvert\right\} + C$
B.	$\int\left\{\frac{1}{\log x} - \frac{1}{(\log x)^2}\right\}dx$	2.	$\frac{e^{2x}}{2}\tan x + C$
C.	$\int e^{2x}\left(\frac{1+\sin 2x}{1+\cos 2x}\right)dx$	3.	$\frac{x}{\log x} + C$
D.	$\int \sin^{-1}\left(\frac{2x}{1+x^2}\right)dx$	4.	$\frac{e^x}{x+1} + C$

From the above table, which of the following is/are correct?

(a) A → 4, B → 3, C → 2, D → 1 ☐
(b) A → 2, B → 3, C → 4, D → 1 ☐
(c) A → 2, B → 4, C → 3, D → 1 ☐
(d) None of these ☐

TOPIC 7

Integral of Some More Types

67. State True or False.

(i) $\int\sqrt{x^2+2x+5}\,dx = \frac{(x+1)}{2}\sqrt{x^2+2x+5} + 2\log\lvert(x+1)+\sqrt{(x^2+2x+5}\rvert + C.$

True ☐ False ☐

(ii) $\int\sqrt{3-2x-x^2}\,dx = \frac{1}{2}(x+1)\sqrt{3-2x-x^2} + 2\sin^{-1}\left(\frac{x+1}{2}\right) + C.$

True ☐ False ☐

(iii) $\int\frac{\sqrt{16+(\log x)^2}}{x}\,dx$ is equal to $\frac{\log x}{2}\sqrt{16+(\log x)^2} + 8\log\lvert\log x + \sqrt{16+(\log x)^2}\rvert + C.$

True ☐ False ☐

(iv) $\int\sqrt{x^2-8x+7}\,dx = \frac{(x-4)\sqrt{x^2-8x+7}}{2} - \frac{9}{2}\log\lvert(x-4)+\sqrt{(x^2-8x+7\}}\rvert + C.$

True ☐ False ☐

(v) $\int\cos x\sqrt{4-\sin^2 x}\,dx = \frac{\sin x\sqrt{4-\sin^2 x}}{2} + 2\sin^{-1}\left(\frac{\sin x}{2}\right) + C.$

True ☐ False ☐

68. $\int \sqrt{4x^2 + 9}\, dx$ is equal to ______

69. $\int \sqrt{x^2 - 2x}\, dx$ is equal to ______

70. $\int \sqrt{(x-3)(5-x)}\, dx$ is equal to ______

TOPIC 8

Definite Integral

71. Evaluate the following integrals.

(i) $\int_4^5 e^x\, dx$ ______

(ii) $\int_1^2 (4x^3 - 5x^2 + 6x + 9)\, dx$ ______

(iii) $\int_1^2 \frac{x\, dx}{(x+1)(x+2)}$ ______

(iv) $\int_0^{\pi/2} \cos 2x\, dx$ ______

(v) $\int_0^{\pi/4} \sin^3 2x \cos 2x\, dx$ ______

72. State True or False.

(i) $\int_0^1 \frac{dx}{\sqrt{1-x^2}} = \pi$

True ☐ False ☐

(ii) The value of $\int_0^{\pi/2} \cos^2 x\, dx = \frac{\pi}{4}$.

True ☐ False ☐

(iii) The value of $\int_0^1 \frac{2x+3}{5x^2+1}\, dx = \frac{1}{5} \log 6 + \frac{3}{\sqrt{5}} \tan^{-1} \sqrt{5}$.

True ☐ False ☐

73. The value of $\int_0^{\pi/4} (\sec^2 x + x^3 + 2)\, dx$ is equal to

(a) $1 + \frac{\pi}{2} + \frac{\pi^4}{1024}$ ☐

(b) $2 + \frac{\pi}{2} + \frac{\pi^4}{1024}$ ☐

(c) $1 + \frac{\pi}{2} + \frac{\pi^4}{512}$ ☐

(d) None of these ☐

74. $\int_0^1 \left(xe^x + \sin \frac{\pi x}{4} \right) dx$ is equal to ________________

***75.** $\int_0^{2/3} \frac{dx}{4 + 9x^2}$ is equal to

(a) $\frac{\pi}{6}$ (b) $\frac{\pi}{12}$ (c) $\frac{\pi}{24}$ (d) $\frac{\pi}{4}$

____

76. Evaluate the following integrals.

(i) $\int_0^1 \frac{\tan^{-1} x}{1 + x^2} dx$ ________________

(ii) $\int_0^{\frac{\pi}{2}} \sqrt{\sin \phi} \cos^5 \phi \, d\phi$ ________________

(iii) $\int_0^1 \sin^{-1} \left(\frac{2x}{1 + x^2} \right) dx$ ________________

(iv) $\int_0^{\frac{\pi}{2}} \frac{\sin x}{1 + \cos^2 x} dx$ ________________

77. If $\int_1^a (3x^2 + 2x + 1) \, dx = 11$, then the value of a is

(a) 2 (b) 3 (c) 1 (d) $\frac{5}{2}$

____

78. $\int_0^{\pi/2} \cos^3 x \, dx =$ ________________

79. State True or False.

(i) $\int_0^{\pi/4} \sin 3x \cdot \sin 2x \, dx = \frac{3\sqrt{2}}{10}$.

True ☐ False ☐

(ii) $\int_0^4 \frac{dx}{\sqrt{x^2 + 2x + 3}} = \log \left(\frac{5 + 3\sqrt{3}}{1 + \sqrt{3}} \right)$.

True ☐ False ☐

(iii) $\int_{-1}^1 \frac{dx}{x^2 + 2x + 5} = \frac{\pi}{8}$.

True ☐ False ☐

80. $\int_1^2 \frac{5x^2}{x^2 + 4x + 3} dx$ is equal to ________________

81. If $f(x) = a + bx + cx^2$, then the value of $\int_0^1 f(x)\,dx$ is equal to

(a) $\frac{1}{6}\left\{f(0) + 4f\left(\frac{1}{2}\right) + f(1)\right\}$ ☐ (b) $\frac{1}{6}\left\{f(0) + 4f\left(\frac{1}{2}\right) + 6f(1)\right\}$ ☐

(c) $\frac{1}{12}\left\{f(0) + 4f\left(\frac{1}{2}\right) + f(1)\right\}$ ☐ (d) None of these 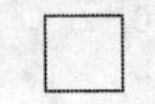

---

82. $\int_{\pi/6}^{\pi/3} \frac{\cos x + \sin x}{\sqrt{\sin 2x}}\,dx$ is equal to $2\sin^{-1}\frac{\sqrt{3}-1}{2}$.

True ☐ False ☐

83. $\int_0^1 (\tan^{-1} x)^2 \cdot x\,dx =$ ____________________

TOPIC 9

Some Properties of Definite Integral

84. Using given information, evaluate the following integrals.

$$\int_{-3}^{2} f(x)\,dx = 5,\ \int_{-3}^{2} g(x)\,dx = -2,\ \int_{-3}^{1} f(x)\,dx = 0 \text{ and } \int_{-3}^{1} g(x)\,dx = 4$$

(i) $\int_{-3}^{2} [-2f(x) + 5g(x)]\,dx$ ____________________

(ii) $\int_{2}^{-3} f(x)\,dx$ ____________________

(iii) $\int_{-3}^{1} [2f(x) + 3g(x)]\,dx$ ____________________

(iv) $\int_{1}^{-3} g(x)\,dx$ ____________________

85. If $\int_1^3 f(x)\,dx = 4$ and $\int_1^6 f(x)\,dx = -8$, then find $\int_3^6 f(x)\,dx$.

---

86. Given, $f(x) = \begin{cases} 2x + 8, & 1 \le x \le 2 \\ 6x, & 2 \le x \le 4 \end{cases}$, then $\int_1^4 f(x)\,dx =$ ____________________

87. $\int_{-1}^{2} |x^3 - x|\,dx = \frac{11}{4}$.

True ☐ False ☐

88. $\int_0^{\pi/2} |\cos 2x|\,dx =$ ____________________

89. The value of $\int_2^8 |x-5|\, dx$ is

(a) $\frac{15}{2}$ ☐ (b) 9 ☐

(c) 7 ☐ (d) $\frac{9}{2}$ ☐

---

90. $\int_1^4 \{|x-1|+|x-2|+|x-4|\}\, dx =$ ________

91. $\int_a^b \frac{f(x)}{f(x)+f(a+b-x)}\, dx = \frac{b-a}{2}$.

True ☐ False ☐

92. $\int_{\pi/6}^{\pi/3} \frac{dx}{1+\sqrt{\cot x}}$ is equal to

(a) $\frac{\pi}{6}$ ☐ (b) $\frac{\pi}{12}$ ☐

(c) $\frac{\pi}{36}$ ☐ (d) $\frac{\pi}{24}$ ☐

---

93. $\int_0^{2\pi} \frac{e^{\sin x}}{e^{\sin x}+e^{-\sin x}}\, dx =$ ________

94. $\int_{-a}^{a} \frac{1}{1+a^x}\, dx =$ ________

95. $\int_0^7 \frac{\sqrt[3]{x}}{\sqrt[3]{x}+\sqrt[3]{7-x}}\, dx$ is equal to

(a) $\frac{7}{2}$ ☐ (b) 7 ☐

(c) 14 ☐ (d) $\frac{15}{2}$ ☐

---

96. $\int_0^{\pi/2} \frac{\sin x}{\sin x+\cos x}\, dx =$ ________

97. $\int_0^{\pi/4} \log(1+\tan x)\, dx = \frac{\pi}{8}\log 2$.

True ☐ False ☐

98. $\int_0^{\pi/2} \sin 2x \cdot \log \tan x\, dx =$ ________

99. $\int_0^{\pi/2} \frac{\sin^2 x \, dx}{\sin x + \cos x}$ is equal to

(a) $-\frac{1}{\sqrt{2}} \log(\sqrt{2}-1)$ ☐ (b) $\frac{1}{\sqrt{2}} \log(\sqrt{2}-1)$ ☐

(c) 0 ☐ (d) $\log(\sqrt{2}-1)$ ☐

---

100. $\int_0^{2\pi} \frac{dx}{1+e^{\sin x}} =$ ________________

***101.** $\int_0^{\pi} \frac{x \, dx}{a^2 \cos^2 x + b^2 \sin^2 x}$ is

(a) $\frac{\pi^2}{2ab}$ ☐ (b) $\frac{\pi^2}{ab}$ ☐

(c) $\frac{\pi^2}{2a}$ ☐ (d) $\frac{\pi^2}{2b}$ ☐

***102.** $\int_0^{2\pi} \cos^5 x \, dx = 0.$

True ☐ False ☐

103. $\int_0^{2\pi} \frac{x \sin^{2n} x}{\sin^{2n} x + \cos^{2n} x} dx =$ ________________

104. $\int_{-\pi/2}^{\pi/2} \sin^7 x \, dx = \pi.$

True ☐ False ☐

105. The value of $\int_{-1}^{1} \sin^5 x \cos^4 x \, dx$ is ________________

106. $\int_{-1}^{1} \frac{x^3 + |x| + 1}{x^2 + 2|x| + 1} dx$ is equal to

(a) log 2 ☐ (b) 2 log 2 ☐

(c) log 2 – 1 ☐ (d) None of these 

---

107. $\int_{-\pi/2}^{\pi/2} |\sin x| \, dx =$ ________________

108. $\int_{-\pi/2}^{\pi/2} \sin^2 x \, dx = \frac{\pi}{2}.$

True ☐ False ☐

Assertion-Reason Questions

Direction In each of the following questions, a statement of Assertion is given followed by a corresponding statement of Reason just below it. Of the statements, mark the correct answer as
(a) Both assertion and reason are true and reason is the correct explanation of assertion.
(b) Both assertion and reason are true but reason is not the correct explanation of assertion.
(c) Assertion is true but reason is false.
(d) Assertion is false but reason is true.

1. **Assertion** (A) $\int \frac{dx}{x^2 + 2x + 3} = \frac{1}{\sqrt{2}} \tan^{-1}\left(\frac{x+1}{\sqrt{2}}\right) + C$

Reason (R) $\int \frac{dx}{x^2 + a^2} = \frac{1}{a} \tan^{-1}\left(\frac{x}{a}\right) + C$

(a) ☐ (b) ☐ (c) ☐ (d) ☐

2. **Assertion** (A) $\int e^x [\sin x - \cos x]\, dx = e^x \sin x + C$

Reason (R) $\int e^x [f(x) + f'(x)]\, dx = e^x f(x) + C$

(a) ☐ (b) ☐ (c) ☐ (d) ☐

3. **Assertion** (A) $\int x^x (1 + \log x)\, dx = x^x + C$

Reason (R) $\frac{d}{dx}(x^x) = x^x (1 + \log x)$

(a) ☐ (b) ☐ (c) ☐ (d) ☐

4. **Assertion** (A) $\int x^2 dx = \frac{x^3}{3} + C$

Reason (R) $\int e^{x^2} dx = e^{x^3/3} + C$

(a) ☐ (b) ☐ (c) ☐ (d) ☐

5. **Assertion** (A) $\int_0^{\pi/2} \frac{\cos x}{\sin x + \cos x} dx = \frac{\pi}{4}$

Reason (R) $\int_0^{\pi/2} \frac{\sin x}{\sin x + \cos x} dx = \frac{\pi}{4}$

(a) ☐ (b) ☐ (c) ☐ (d) ☐

6. **Assertion** (A) $\int_{-3}^{3} (x^3 + 5) dx = 30.$

Reason (R) $f(x) = x^3 + 5$ in an odd function.

(a) ☐ (b) ☐ (c) ☐ (d) ☐

7. Assertion (A) $\frac{d}{dx}\left[\int_0^{x^2} \frac{dt}{t^2+4}\right] = \frac{2x}{x^4+4}$

Reason (R) $\int \frac{dx}{x^2+a^2} = \frac{1}{a}\tan^{-1}\left(\frac{x}{a}\right) + C$

(a) ☐ (b) ☐ (c) ☐ (d) ☐

8. Assertion (A) $\int_{-1}^{1} (x^3 + \sin x + 2)\, dx = 0$

Reason (R) $\int_{-a}^{a} f(x)\, dx = \begin{cases} 2\int_0^a f(x)\, dx, & \text{if } f(x) \text{ is an even function i.e. } (-x) = f(x) \\ 0, & \text{if } f(x) \text{ is an odd function i.e. } f(-x) = -f(x) \end{cases}$

(a) ☐ (b) ☐ (c) ☐ (d) ☐

9. Assertion (A) $\int_{-2}^{2} \log\left(\frac{1+x}{1-x}\right) dx = 0$

Reason (R) If f is an odd function, then $\int_{-a}^{a} f(x)dx = 0$.

(a) ☐ (b) ☐ (c) ☐ (d) ☐

10. Assertion (A) The value of the integral $\int e^x [\tan x + \sec^2 x]dx$ is $e^x \tan x + C$.

Reason (R) The value of the integral $e^x \{f(x) + f'(x)\}dx$ is $e^x f(x) + C$.

(a) ☐ (b) ☐ (c) ☐ (d) ☐

Case Based Questions

Case 1

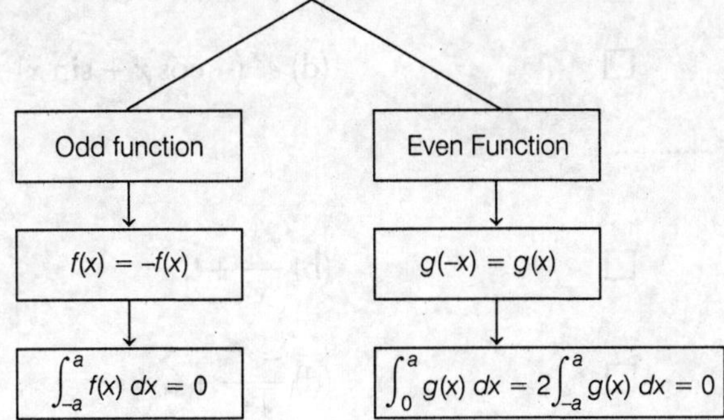

Based on the above information, answer any four of the following questions.

(i) $\int_{-1}^{1} x^{99}\, dx =$ ....

(a) 0 ☐ (b) 1 ☐

(c) – 1 ☐ (d) 2 ☐

(ii) $\int_{-\pi}^{\pi} x \cos x \, dx =$ ....

(a) 1 ☐ (b) 0 ☐

(c) -1 ☐ (d) $\frac{\pi}{2}$ ☐

(iii) $\int_{-\frac{\pi}{2}}^{\frac{\pi}{2}} \sin^3 x \, dx =$ ....

(a) 1 ☐ (b) 0 ☐

(c) -1 ☐ (d) π ☐

(iv) $\int_{-\pi}^{\pi} x \sin x \, dx =$ ....

(a) π ☐ (b) 0 ☐

(c) 2π ☐ (d) $\frac{\pi}{2}$ ☐

(v) $\int_{-\pi}^{\pi} \tan x \sec^2 x \, dx =$ ....

(a) 1 ☐ (b) -1 ☐

(c) 0 ☐ (d) 2 ☐

Case 2 $\int e^x [f(x) + f'(x)] \, dx = \int e^x f(x) \, dx + \int e^x f'(x) dx$

Using the integration by parts

$$= f(x) \int e^x \, dx - \int f'(x) e^x dx + \int f'(x) e^x dx$$

$$= f(x) e^x - \int f'(x) e^x dx + \int f'(x) e^x dx = e^x f(x) + C$$

Based on the above information, answer the following questions.

(i) $\int e^x (\sin x + \cos x) \, dx =$ ....

(a) $e^x \cos x + C$ ☐ (b) $e^x \sin x + C$ ☐

(c) $e^x + C$ ☐ (d) $e^x(-\cos x + \sin x) + C$ ☐

(ii) $\int e^x \left(\frac{x-1}{x^2} \right) dx =$ ....

(a) $e^x + C$ ☐ (b) $\frac{e^x}{x} + C$ ☐

(c) $\frac{e^x}{x^2} + C$ ☐ (d) $\frac{-e^x}{x^2} + C$ ☐

(iii) $\int e^x (1 + x) dx =$ ....

(a) $xe^x + C$ ☐ (b) $e^x + C$ ☐

(c) $e^{-x} + C$ ☐ (d) None of these ☐

(iv) $\int_0^{\pi} e^x (\tan x + \sec^2 x) dx = \ldots\ldots$

(a) 0 ☐ (b) 1 ☐

(c) -1 ☐ (d) $-e^{\pi}$ ☐

(v) $\int \frac{xe^x}{(1+x)^2} dx = \ldots\ldots\ldots$

(a) $xe^x + C$ ☐ (b) $\frac{e^x}{(x+1)^2} + C$ ☐

(c) $\frac{xe^x}{x+1} + C$ ☐ (d) $\frac{e^x}{x+1} + C$ ☐

COMPETITION EDGE UP

1. Let $\int \frac{2 - \tan x}{3 + \tan x} dx = \frac{1}{2} (\alpha x + \log_e |\beta \sin x + \gamma \cos x|) + C$, where C is the constant of integration. Then, $\alpha + \frac{\gamma}{\beta}$ is equal to **[JEE Main 2024]**

(a) 1 ☐

(b) 3 ☐

(c) 7 ☐

(d) 4 ☐

2. Let $I(x) = \int \frac{6}{\sin^2 x (1 - \cot x)^2} dx$.

If $I(0) = 3$, then $I(\pi/12)$ is equal to **[JEE Main 2024]**

(a) $2\sqrt{3}$ ☐

(b) $6\sqrt{3}$ ☐

(c) $\sqrt{3}$ ☐

(d) $3\sqrt{3}$ ☐

3. If $\int \frac{1}{a^2 \sin^2 x + b^2 \cos^2 x} dx = \frac{1}{12} \tan^{-1} (3 \tan x) +$ constant, then the maximum value of $a \sin x + b \cos x$, is **[JEE Main 2024]**

(a) $\sqrt{42}$ ☐

(b) $\sqrt{41}$ ☐

(c) $\sqrt{40}$ ☐

(d) $\sqrt{39}$ ☐

4. If $\int \frac{\sin^{3/2} x + \cos^{3/2} x}{\sqrt{\sin^3 x \cos^3 x \sin(x - \theta)}} dx = A\sqrt{\cos\theta \tan x - \sin\theta} + B\sqrt{\cos\theta - \sin\theta \cot x} + C$, where C is the integration constant, then AB is equal to **[JEE Main 2024]**

(a) $4 \text{ cosec } (2\theta)$ ☐

(b) $4 \sec\theta$ ☐

(c) $8 \text{ cosec } (2\theta)$ ☐

(d) $2 \sec\theta$ ☐

5. For $x \in \left(-\frac{\pi}{2}, \frac{\pi}{2}\right)$, if

$y(x) = \int \frac{\text{cosec } x + \sin x}{\text{cosec } x \sec x + \tan x \sin^2 x} dx$

and $\lim_{x \to \left(\frac{\pi}{2}\right)^-} y(x) = 0$, then $y\left(\frac{\pi}{4}\right)$ is equal to **[JEE Main 2024]**

(a) $\frac{1}{2} \tan^{-1}\left(\frac{1}{\sqrt{2}}\right)$ ☐

(b) $\frac{1}{\sqrt{2}} \tan^{-1}\left(-\frac{1}{2}\right)$ ☐

(c) $\tan^{-1}\left(\frac{1}{\sqrt{2}}\right)$ ☐

(d) $-\frac{1}{\sqrt{2}} \tan^{-1}\left(\frac{1}{\sqrt{2}}\right)$ ☐

6. The integral $\int \frac{(x^8 - x^2)dx}{(x^{12} + 3x^6 + 1)\tan^{-1}\left(x^3 + \frac{1}{x^3}\right)}$ is equal to **[JEE Main 2024]**

(a) $\log_e\left(\left|\tan^{-1}\left(x^3 + \frac{1}{x^3}\right)\right|\right) + C$ ☐

(b) $\log_e\left(\left|\tan^{-1}\left(x^3 + \frac{1}{x^3}\right)\right|\right)^{1/2} + C$ ☐

(c) $\log_e\left(\left|\tan^{-1}\left(x^3 + \frac{1}{x^3}\right)\right|\right)^{3} + C$ ☐

(d) $\log_e\left(\left|\tan^{-1}\left(x^3 + \frac{1}{x^3}\right)\right|\right)^{1/3} + C$ ☐

7. If $\int \frac{1}{\sqrt[5]{(x-1)^4(x+3)^6}}dx$ $= A\left(\frac{\alpha x - 1}{\beta x + 3}\right)^B + C$, where C is the constant of integration, then the value of $\alpha + \beta + 20AB$ is .... **[JEE Main 2024]**

8. If $\int \text{cosec}^5 x\, dx = \alpha \cot x \,\text{cosec}\, x \left(\text{cosec}^2 x + \frac{3}{2}\right) + \beta \log_6\left|\tan\frac{x}{2}\right| + C$, where $\alpha, \beta \in R$ and C is the constant of integration, then the value of $8(\alpha + \beta)$ equals .... **[JEE Main 2024]**

9. The integral $\int_{1/4}^{3/4} \cos\left(2\cot^{-1}\sqrt{\frac{1-x}{1+x}}\right) dx$ is equal to **[JEE Main 2024]**

(a) 1/4 ☐

(b) −1/4 ☐

(c) 1/2 ☐

(d) −1/2 ☐

10. The value of the integral $\int_{-1}^{2} \log_e(x + \sqrt{x^2+1})\, dx$ is **[JEE Main 2024]**

(a) $\sqrt{2} - \sqrt{5} + \log_e\left(\frac{9 + 4\sqrt{5}}{1 + \sqrt{2}}\right)$ ☐

(b) $\sqrt{5} - \sqrt{2} + \log_e\left(\frac{9 + 4\sqrt{5}}{1 + \sqrt{2}}\right)$ ☐

(c) $\sqrt{5} - \sqrt{2} + \log_e\left(\frac{7 + 4\sqrt{5}}{1 + \sqrt{2}}\right)$ ☐

(d) $\sqrt{2} - \sqrt{5} + \log_e\left(\frac{7 + 4\sqrt{5}}{1 + \sqrt{2}}\right)$ ☐

11. $\lim_{x \to \frac{\pi}{2}} \left(\frac{\int_{x^3}^{(\pi/2)^3} (\sin(2t^{1/3}) + \cos(t^{1/3}))\, dt}{\left(x - \frac{\pi}{2}\right)^2}\right)$ is equal to **[JEE Main 2024]**

(a) $\frac{3\pi^2}{2}$ ☐

(b) $\frac{9\pi^2}{8}$ ☐

(c) $\frac{11\pi^2}{10}$ ☐

(d) $\frac{5\pi^2}{9}$ ☐

12. Let $\int_{\alpha}^{\log_e 4} \frac{dx}{\sqrt{e^x - 1}} = \frac{\pi}{6}$. Then, e^{α} and $e^{-\alpha}$ are the roots of the equation **[JEE Main 2024]**

(a) $x^2 - 2x - 8 = 0$ ☐

(b) $2x^2 - 5x - 2 = 0$ ☐

(c) $2x^2 - 5x + 2 = 0$ ☐

(d) $x^2 + 2x - 8 = 0$ ☐

13. The value of $k \in N$ for which the integral $I_n = \int_0^1 (1 - x^k)^n\, dx$, $n \in N$, satisfies $147I_{20} = 148I_{21}$ is **[JEE Main 2024]**

(a) 14 ☐

(b) 7 ☐

(c) 10 ☐

(d) 8 ☐

14. $\int_0^{\frac{\pi}{4}} \frac{\cos^2 x \sin^2 x}{(\cos^3 x + \sin^3 x)^2} dx$ is equal to **[JEE Main 2024]**

(a) $\frac{1}{6}$ ☐

(b) $\frac{1}{12}$ ☐

(c) $\frac{1}{9}$ ☐

(d) $\frac{1}{3}$ ☐

15. Let $\beta(m, n) = \int_0^1 x^{m-1}(1-x)^{n-1} dx$, $m, n > 0$.
If $\int_0^1 (1 - x^{10})^{20} dx = a \times \beta(b, c)$, then $100(a + b + c)$ equals **[JEE Main 2024]**

(a) 2120
(b) 2012
(c) 1120
(d) 1021

16. The value of $\int_{-\pi}^{\pi} \frac{2y(1 + \sin y)}{1 + \cos^2 y} dy$ is **[JEE Main 2024]**

(a) π^2
(b) $2\pi^2$
(c) $\frac{\pi}{2}$
(d) $\frac{\pi^2}{2}$

17. The integral $\int_0^{\pi/4} \frac{136 \sin x}{3 \sin x + 5 \cos x} dx$ is equal to **[JEE Main 2024]**

(a) $3\pi - 50 \log_e 2 + 20 \log_e 5$
(b) $3\pi - 25 \log_e 2 + 10 \log_e 5$
(c) $3\pi - 10 \log_e(2\sqrt{2}) + 10 \log_e 5$
(d) $3\pi - 30 \log_e 2 + 20 \log_e 5$

18. If the value of the integral $\int_{-1}^{1} \frac{\cos \alpha x}{1 + 3^x} dx$ is $\frac{2}{\pi}$. Then, a value of α is **[JEE Main 2024]**

(a) $\pi / 3$
(b) $\pi / 4$
(c) $\pi / 6$
(d) $\pi / 2$

19. Let $f(x) = \int_0^x (t + \sin(1 - e^t)) dt, x \in R$. Then, $\lim_{x \to 0} \frac{f(x)}{x^3}$ is equal to **[JEE Main 2024]**

(a) $\frac{1}{6}$
(b) $-\frac{2}{3}$
(c) $\frac{2}{3}$
(d) $-\frac{1}{6}$

20. Let $f(x) = \begin{cases} -2, & -2 \le x \le 0 \\ x - 2, & 0 < x \le 2 \end{cases}$ and $h(x) = f(|x|) + |f(x)|$. Then, $\int_{-2}^{2} h(x) dx$ is equal to **[JEE Main 2024]**

(a) 1
(b) 6
(c) 4
(d) 2

Scan this QR code from your mobile phone to get the solutions of **Competition Edge Up** of this chapter.

Chapter 08

Application of Integrals

Scan and take Chapter Test

TOPIC 1

Area Under Simple Curve

NCERT Pg 292-296

***1.** Find the area of the region bounded by the curve $y^2 = x$ and the lines $x = 1$ and $x = 3$ and the X-axis in the first quadrant.

***2.** Find the area of the region bounded by the curve $4x^2 = y$ and the lines $y = 2$, $y = 4$ and the Y-axis in the first quadrant.

***3.** The area lying in the first quadrant and bounded by the circle $x^2 + y^2 = 4$ and the lines $x = 0$ and $x = 2$ (in sq units) is

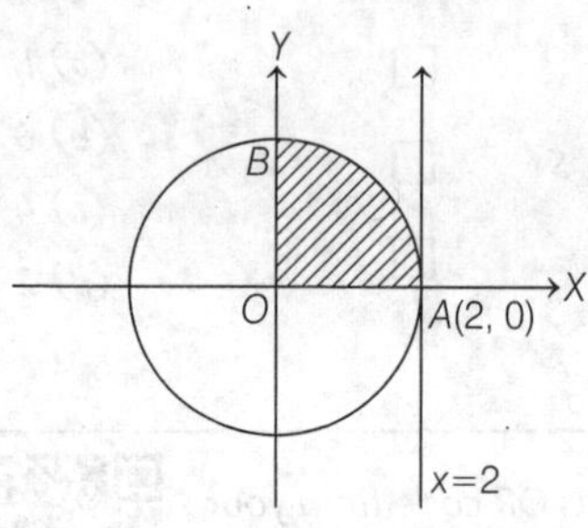

(a) π (b) $\frac{\pi}{2}$

(c) $\frac{\pi}{3}$ (d) $\frac{\pi}{4}$

***4.** The area of the region in the first quadrant enclosed by X-axis, line $x = \sqrt{3}y$ and the circle $x^2 + y^2 = 4$ is ______

*Concepts of all questions bearing * are important for JEE & CUET*

***5.** Find the area of the shaded region

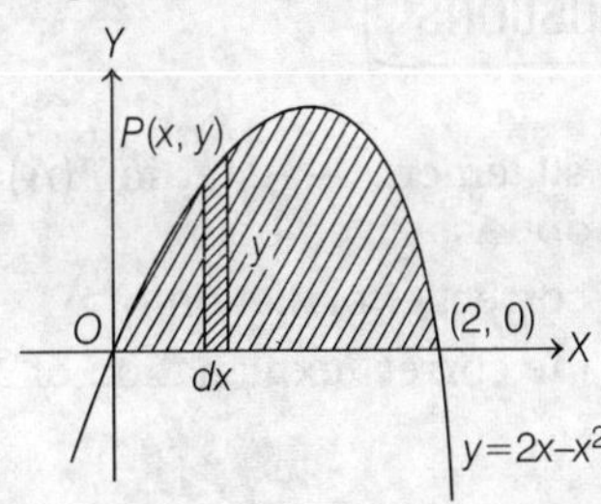

(a) $\frac{4}{3}$ sq units (b) 3 sq units

(c) $\frac{1}{3}$ sq unit (d) $\frac{16}{3}$ sq units

***6.** The area of the region bounded by the line $x = 4$ and the parabola $y^2 = 16x$ is

---

7. The area bounded by the curve $y = \cos x$ between $x = 0$ and $x = 2\pi$ (in sq units) is

(a) 4 (b) [illegible]

(c) 8 (d) 0

***8.** The area of the region bounded by the line $2y = -x + 8$, X-axis and the lines $x = 2$ and $x = 4$ is ______

9. If the area above X-axis bounded by the curve $y = 2^{kx}$, the line $x = 0$ and $x = 2$ is $\frac{3}{\log_e 2}$, then the value of k is 1.

True ☐ False ☐

***10.** The area between $x = y^2$ and $x = 4$ is divided into two equal parts by the line $x = a$, then the value of a is ______

***11.** The area of the region lying in the first quadrant and bounded by $y = 4x^2$, $x = 0$, $y = 1$ and $y = 4$ is $\frac{7}{3}$ sq units.

True ☐ False ☐

Assertion-Reason Questions

The following questions consist of two statements – Assertion (A) and Reason (R). Answer these questions by selecting the appropriate options given below.
(a) Both A and R are true and R is the correct explanation of A.
(b) Both A and R are true but R is not the correct explanation of A.
(c) A is true but R is false.
(d) A is false but R is true.

1. **Assertion** (A) The area bounded by $y^2 = 4x$ and $y = x$ is $\frac{8}{3}$ sq units.

Reason (R) The area bounded by $y^2 = 4ax$ and $y = mx$ is $\frac{8a^2}{3m^3}$ sq units.

(a) ☐ (b) ☐ (c) ☐ (d) ☐

2. **Assertion** (A) The area enclosed by the circle $x^2 + y^2 = 9^2$ is $\pi 9^2$.

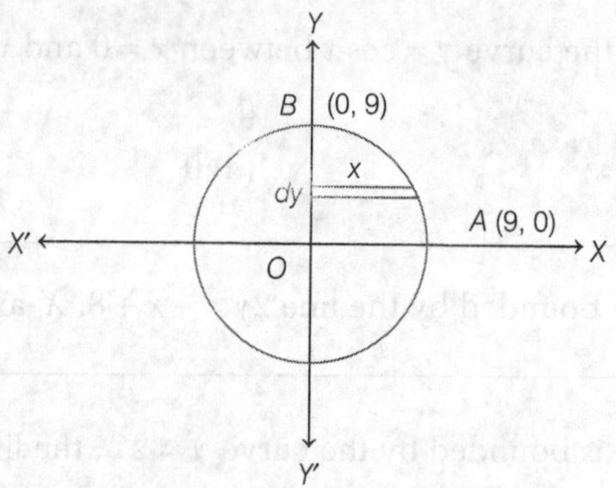

Reason (R) The area enclosed by the circle $x^2 + y^2 = a^2$ is πa^2.

(a) ☐ (b) ☐ (c) ☐ (d) ☐

3. **Assertion** (A) The area of the region bounded by the curve $y = x^2$ and the line $y = 4$ is $\frac{3}{32}$.

Reason (R)

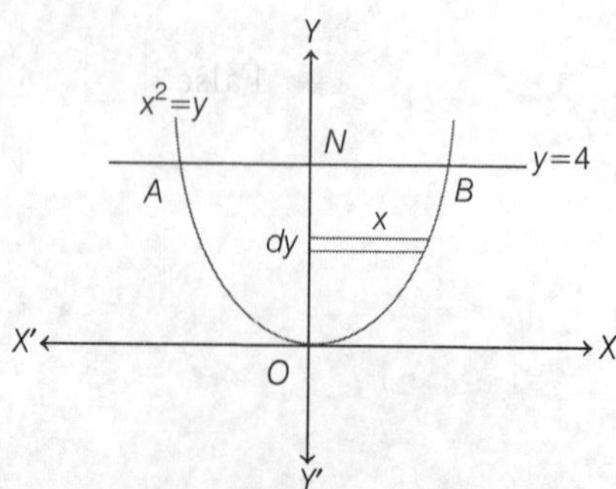

(a) ☐ (b) ☐ (c) ☐ (d) ☐

4. **Assertion** (A) The area under the curve $y = f(x)$ from $x = a$ to $x = b$ is given by the integral $\int_a^b f(x)\, dx$.

Reason (R) The definite integral $\int_a^b f(x)\, dx$ represents the sum of the areas of infinitesimally small rectangles under the curve $y = f(x)$ from $x = a$ to $x = b$.

(a) ☐ (b) ☐ (c) ☐ (d) ☐

***5.** **Assertion** (A) The integral $\int_0^{\pi} \sin x\, dx = 2$.

Reason (R) The function $f(x) = \sin x$ has a maximum value of 1 and a minimum value of -1 within the interval $[0, \pi]$.

(a) ☐ (b) ☐ (c) ☐ (d) ☐

6. **Assertion** (A) Area of the region bounded by the parabola $x^2 = y$, $y = 2x$ is $\frac{4}{3}$ sq units.

Reason (R) Area of the region bounded by the circle $x^2 + y^2 = 4$, $y = x$ and $y = 0$ is $\left(\frac{\pi}{2} + 1\right)$ sq units.

(a) ☐ (b) ☐ (c) ☐ (d) ☐

7. **Assertion** (A) The area bounded by the curve $y = f(x)$, the X-axis and $x = a$ and $x = b$ is given by $\int_a^b f(x)\, dx$.

Reason (R) If the curve $y = f(x)$ lies below X-axis, then the area bounded by the curve $y = f(x)$, the X-axis and $\int_a^b f(x)\, dx$ is given by.

(a) ☐ (b) ☐ (c) ☐ (d) ☐

8. **Assertion** (A) The area bounded by the parabola $y^2 = 4ax$ and its latus rectum is $\frac{8}{3}a^2$ sq unit.

Reason (R) The area bounded by the parabola $x^2 = 4ay$ and its latus rectum is $\frac{8}{3}a^2$ sq unit.

(a) ☐ (b) ☐ (c) ☐ (d) ☐

9. **Assertion** (A) Area of the region bounded by the parabola $y^2 = 4x$, $x = 1$, $x = 4$ and $y = 0$ is $\frac{28}{3}$ sq units.

Reason (R) Area under a curve $y = f(x)$ and above X-axis lying between $x = a$ and $x = b$ is given by $\int_a^b f(x)\, dx$.

(a) ☐ (b) ☐ (c) ☐ (d) ☐

10. **Assertion** (A) Area of the region bounded by the curves $y = \sin x$, $y = \cos x$, $0 \le x \le \frac{\pi}{2}$ is $2(\sqrt{2} - 1)$ sq units.

Reason (R) Area under a curve $y = \sin x$, $y = 0$, $0 \le x \le \frac{\pi}{2}$ is $\frac{1}{2}$ sq unit.

(a) ☐ (b) ☐ (c) ☐ (d) ☐

Case Based Questions

Case 1 Consider the following equation of curves $x^2 = y$ and $y = x$ on the basis of above information, answer the following questions.

(i) The point(s) of intersection of both the curves is (are)

(a) (0, 0), (2, 2) ☐ (b) (0, 0), (1, 1) ☐
(c) (0, 0), (–1, –1) ☐ (d) (0, 0), (–2, –2) ☐

(ii) Area bounded by the curves is represented by which of the following graph?

(a)
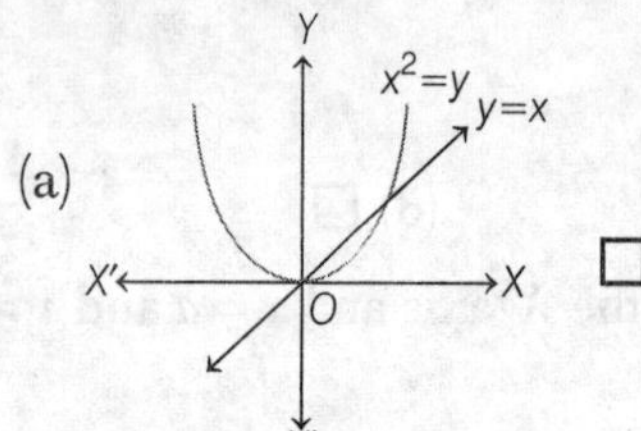

☐

(b)
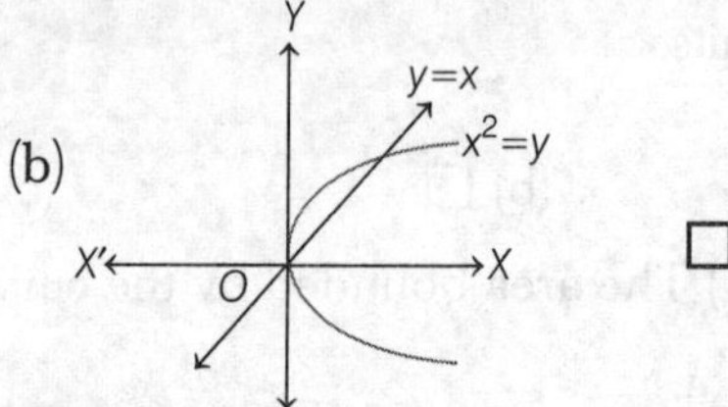

☐

(c)
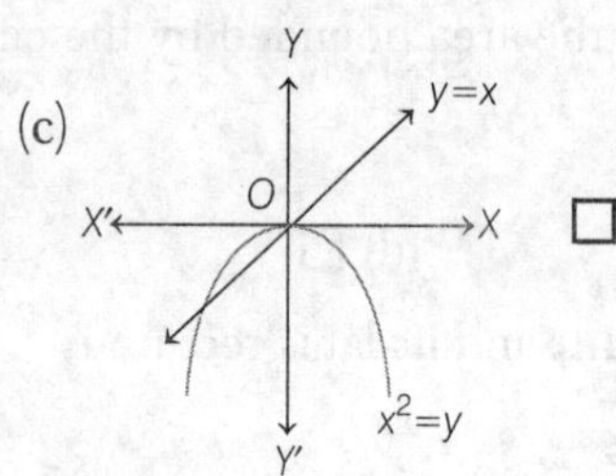

☐

(d)
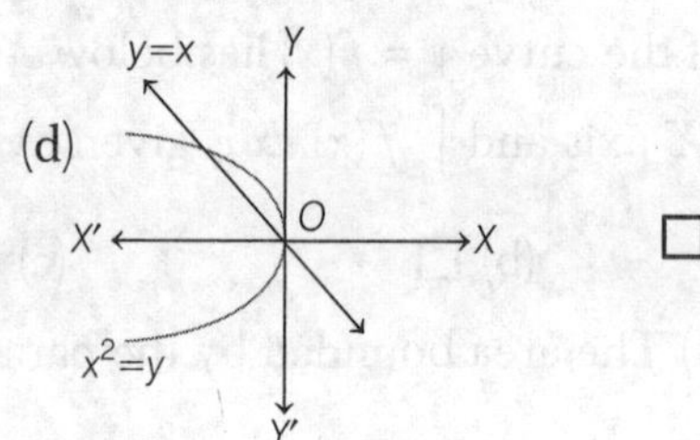

☐

(iii) The value of the integral $\int_0^1 x\,dx$ is

(a) $\frac{1}{4}$ ☐ (b) $\frac{1}{3}$ ☐
(c) $\frac{1}{2}$ ☐ (d) 1 ☐

(iv) The value of the integral $\int_0^1 x^2\,dx$ is

(a) $\frac{1}{4}$ ☐ (b) $\frac{1}{3}$ ☐
(c) $\frac{1}{2}$ ☐ (d) 1 ☐

Case 2 Consider the following equation of curves $y = \cos x$, $y = x + 1$ and $y = 0$. On the basis of above information, answer the following questions.

(i) The curves $y = \cos x$ and $y = x + 1$ meet at

(a) (1, 0) ☐ (b) (0, 1) ☐

(c) (1, 1) ☐ (d) (0, 0) ☐

(ii) $y = \cos x$ meet the X-axis at

(a) $\left(-\frac{\pi}{2}, 0\right)$ ☐ (b) $\left(\frac{\pi}{2}, 0\right)$ ☐

(c) both (a) and (b) ☐ (d) none of these ☐

(iii) Value of the integral $\int_{-1}^{0} (x + 1)\, dx$ is

(a) $\frac{1}{2}$ ☐ (b) $\frac{2}{3}$ ☐

(c) $\frac{3}{4}$ ☐ (d) $\frac{1}{3}$ ☐

(iv) Value of the integral $\int_{0}^{\frac{\pi}{2}} \cos x\, dx$ is

(a) 0 ☐ (b) −1 ☐

(c) 2 ☐ (d) 1 ☐

COMPETITION CONNECT

Area Between Two Curves [NCERT (Old) Pg. 366-372]

1. The area of the region bounded by the two parabolas $y = x^2$ and $y^2 = x$ is $\frac{1}{3}$ sq unit.

True ☐ False ☐

2. The area of the region included between the parabolas $y^2 = 4\,ax$ and $x^2 = 4ay$, where $a > 0$, is

(a) $16a^2$ sq units

(b) $\frac{16a^2}{3}$ sq units

(c) $\frac{32a^2}{3}$ sq units

(d) None of the above

***3.** Find the area of the shaded region.

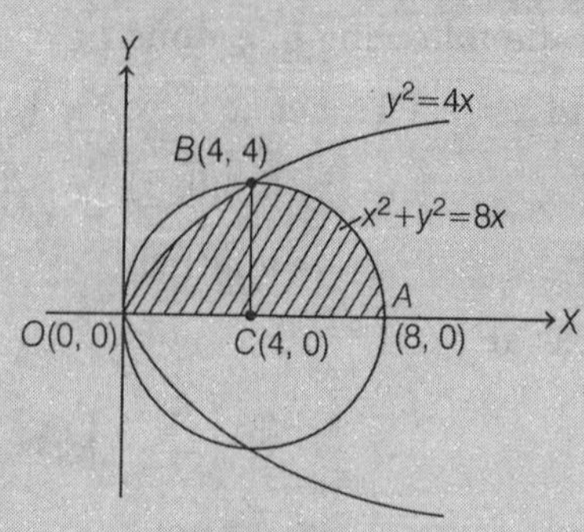

4. State True or False.

(i) The area of the triangular region whose sides have the equation $y = 2x + 1$, $y = 3x + 1$ and $x = 4$ is 8 sq units.

True ☐ False ☐

(ii) The smaller area enclosed by the circle $x^2 + y^2 = 4$ and the line $x + y = 2$ is $(\pi + 2)$ sq units.

True ☐ False ☐

(iii) The area of the region bounded by the triangle whose vertices are (1, 0), (2, 2) and (3, 1) is $\frac{3}{2}$ sq units.

True ☐ False ☐

5. The area of the triangle formed by positive X-axis, tangent and normal to the circle $x^2 + y^2 = 4$ at $(1, \sqrt{3})$ is

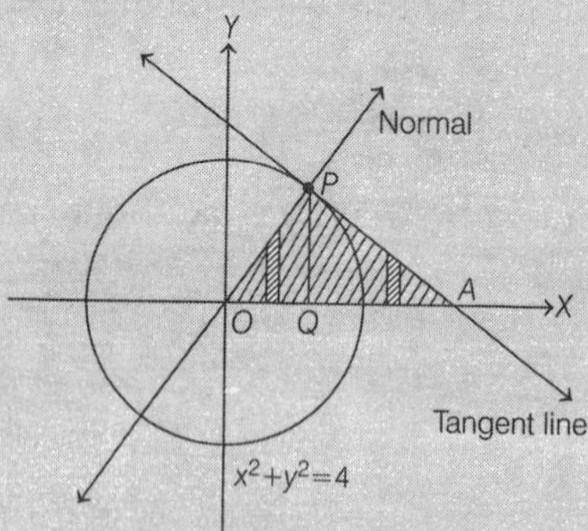

(a) $2\sqrt{3}$ sq units
(b) $\sqrt{3}$ sq units
(c) 2 sq units
(d) $3\sqrt{3}$ sq units

6. The area of the region bounded by the line $y = 3x + 2$, the X-axis and the $x = -1$ and $x = 1$, is

(a) $\frac{13}{3}$ sq units (b) $\frac{26}{3}$ sq units

(c) $\frac{2}{3}$ sq units (d) None of these

---

7. Using the method of integration, the area bounded by the curve $|x| + |y| = 1$ is

(a) 2 sq units (b) 3 sq units

(c) 4 sq units (d) None of these

---

8. The area of the region $\{(x, y); x^2 \le y \le x\}$ is

(a) $\frac{1}{3}$ sq unit (b) $\frac{1}{6}$ sq unit

(c) $\frac{1}{8}$ sq unit (d) 1 sq unit

---

9. Using integration, the area of the region bounded by the curves $y = 1 + |x + 1|$, $x = -3$, $x = 3$ and $y = 0$ is ______

10. The area of the region $\{(x, y); x^2 + y^2 \le 1 \le x + y\}$ is

(a) $\left(\frac{\pi}{4} + \frac{1}{2}\right)$ sq units (b) $\left(\frac{\pi}{4} - \frac{1}{2}\right)$ sq units

(c) $\left(\frac{\pi}{2} - 1\right)$ sq units (d) $\left(\frac{\pi}{4} + 1\right)$ sq units

---

11. The area of the region $\{(x, y); y^2 \le 4x, 4x^2 + 4y^2 \le 9\}$ (in sq units) is

(a) $\frac{9\pi}{8} - \frac{9}{4}\sin^{-1}\left(\frac{1}{3}\right) + \frac{1}{3\sqrt{2}}$ (b) $\frac{3\pi}{8} + \frac{9}{4}\sin^{-1}\left(\frac{1}{3}\right) + \frac{1}{3\sqrt{2}}$

(c) $\frac{9\pi}{8} - \frac{9}{4}\sin^{-1}\left(\frac{1}{3}\right) + \frac{1}{\sqrt{2}}$ (d) $\frac{8\pi}{3} + \frac{4}{9}\sin^{-1}\left(\frac{1}{3}\right) + \frac{1}{\sqrt{2}}$

---

12. The area enclosed between the parabola $y^2 = 4ax$ and the line $y = mx$ is

(a) $\frac{8a^2}{2m^2}$ sq units (b) $\frac{8a^2}{3m^3}$ sq units

(c) $\frac{3a^2}{8m^3}$ sq units (d) None of these

---

13. The curves $y^2 = 4x$ and $x^2 = 4y$ divide the area of the square bounded by $x = 0$, $x = 4$, $y = 4$ and $y = 0$ into three equal parts.

True ☐ False ☐

14. The area bounded by the curve $x^2 = 4y$ and straight line $x = 4y - 2$ is ________.

15. The area of the smaller region bounded by the ellipse $\frac{x^2}{a^2} + \frac{y^2}{b^2} = 1$ and the straight line $\frac{x}{a} + \frac{y}{b} = 1$ is $\frac{1}{2ab}\left(\frac{\pi}{2} - 1\right)$ sq units.

True ☐ False ☐

16. From this figure, $AOBA$ is the part of the ellipse $9x^2 + y^2 = 36$ in the first quadrant such that $OA = 2$ and $OB = 6$. Then, area between the arc AB and the chord AB is

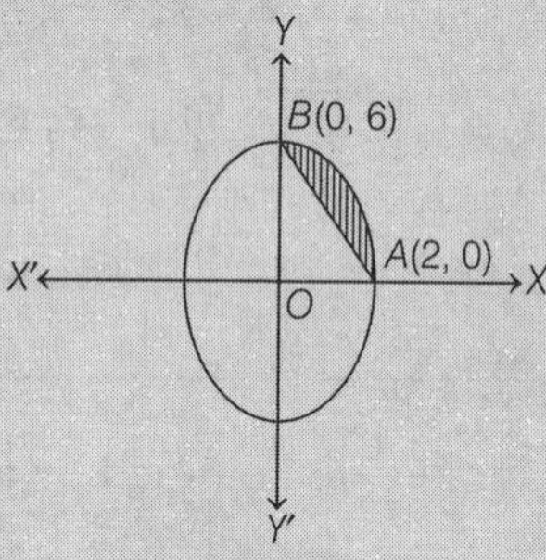

(a) $(3\pi + 6)$ sq units
(b) $(3\pi - 6)$ sq units
(c) $\left(\frac{3\pi + 6}{2}\right)$ sq units
(d) $\left(\frac{3}{2}\pi - 6\right)$ sq units

---

17. The area enclosed between the curves $y = ax^2$ and $x = ay^2$ $(a > 0)$ is 1 sq unit, then the value of a is

(a) $\frac{1}{3}$
(b) $\frac{1}{\sqrt{3}}$
(c) $\frac{2}{\sqrt{3}}$
(d) $\left(1 - \frac{1}{\sqrt{3}}\right)$

---

18. Sketch of the curves $y = \sin x$ and $y = \cos x$ as x varies from 0 to $\frac{\pi}{2}$, then the area of the region enclosed by them and X-axis is $2 - \sqrt{2}$ sq units.

True ☐ False ☐

19. The area of the figure bounded by the straight lines $x = 0$, $x = 2$ and the curves $y = 2^x$, $y = 2x - x^2$ is ________

COMPETITION EDGE UP

1. The area (in sq units) of the region described by $\{(x, y): y^2 \le 2x$ and $y \ge 4x - 1\}$ is **[JEE Main 2024]**

(a) $\frac{11}{12}$ ☐

(b) $\frac{9}{32}$ ☐

(c) $\frac{8}{9}$ ☐

(d) $\frac{11}{32}$ ☐

2. The area bounded by the curves $y = |x - 1| + |x - 2|$ and $y = 3$ is equal to **[JEE Main 2024]**

(a) 4 ☐

(b) 5 ☐

(c) 6 ☐

(d) 3 ☐

3. The area (in sq units) of the region enclosed by the ellipse $x^2 + 3y^2 = 18$ in the first quadrant below the line $y = x$ is **[JEE Main 2024]**

(a) $\sqrt{3}\pi$ ☐

(b) $\sqrt{3}\pi - \frac{3}{4}$ ☐

(c) $\sqrt{3}\pi + \frac{3}{4}$ ☐

(d) $\sqrt{3}\pi + 1$ ☐

4. The area of the region enclosed by the curve $y = x^3$ and its tangent at the point $(-1, -1)$ is **[JEE Main 2024]**

(a) $\frac{23}{4}$ ☐

(b) $\frac{19}{4}$ ☐

(c) $\frac{31}{4}$ ☐

(d) $\frac{27}{4}$ ☐

5. Let the area of the region enclosed by the curve $y = \min\{\sin x, \cos x\}$ and the X-axis between $x = -\pi$ to $x = \pi$ be A. Then, A^2 is equal to .... **[JEE Main 2024]**

6. Let α be the area of the larger region bounded by the curve $y^2 = 8x$ and the lines $y = x$ and $x = 2$, which lies in the first quadrant. Then, the value of 3α is equal to .... **[JEE Main 2024]**

7. The area of the region in the first quadrant inside the circle $x^2 + y^2 = 8$ and outside the parabola $y^2 = 2x$ is equal to **[JEE Main 2024]**

(a) $\pi - \frac{2}{3}$ ☐

(b) $\frac{\pi}{2} - \frac{2}{3}$ ☐

(c) $\frac{\pi}{2} - \frac{1}{3}$ ☐

(d) $\pi - \frac{1}{3}$ ☐

8. If the area of the region

$$\left\{(x, y) : \frac{a}{x^2} \le y \le \frac{1}{x}, 1 \le x \le 2, 0 < a < 1\right\}$$

is $(\log_e 2) - \frac{1}{7}$, then the value of $7a - 3$ is equal to **[JEE Main 2024]**

(a) 1 ☐

(b) 0 ☐

(c) 2 ☐

(d) -1 ☐

9. The area enclosed by the curves $xy + 4y = 16$ and $x + y = 6$ is equal to **[JEE Main 2024]**

(a) $30 - 32 \log_e 2$ ☐

(b) $32 - 30 \log_e 2$ ☐

(c) $30 - 28 \log_e 2$ ☐

(d) $28 - 30 \log_e 2$ ☐

10. The area (in sq units) of the region bounded by the parabola $y^2 = 4(x - 2)$ and the line $y = 2x - 8$, is **[JEE Main 2024]**

(a) 6 ☐

(b) 9 ☐

(c) 7 ☐

(d) 8 ☐

11. Area of the region $\{(x, y) : x^2 + (y-2)^2 \le 4, x^2 \ge 2y\}$ is **[JEE Main 2024]**

(a) $\pi - \frac{8}{3}$ ☐

(b) $2\pi + \frac{16}{3}$ ☐

(c) $2\pi - \frac{16}{3}$ ☐

(d) $\pi + \frac{8}{3}$ ☐

12. The area of the region $\{(x, y) : x^2 \le y \le 8 - x^2, y \le 7\}$ is **[JEE Main 2024]**

(a) 21 ☐

(b) 20 ☐

(c) 18 ☐

(d) 24 ☐

13. The area of the region given by $\{(x, y) : xy \le 8, 1 \le y \le x^2\}$ is **[JEE Main 2024]**

(a) $16 \log_e 2 + \frac{7}{3}$ ☐

(b) $16 \log_e 2 - \frac{14}{3}$ ☐

(c) $8 \log_e 2 + \frac{7}{6}$ ☐

(d) $8 \log_e 2 - \frac{13}{3}$ ☐

14. The area of the region $A = \left\{\begin{matrix}(x, y) : |\cos x - \sin x| \\ \le y \le \sin x, 0 \le x \le \frac{\pi}{2}\end{matrix}\right\}$ is **[JEE Main 2024]**

(a) $\sqrt{5} + 2\sqrt{2} - 4.5$ ☐

(b) $\frac{3}{\sqrt{5}} - \frac{3}{\sqrt{2}} + 1$ ☐

(c) $1 - \frac{3}{\sqrt{2}} + \frac{4}{\sqrt{5}}$ ☐

(d) $\sqrt{5} - 2\sqrt{2} + 1$ ☐

15. The parabola $y^2 = 4x$ divides the area of the circle $x^2 + y^2 = 5$ in two parts. The area of the smaller part of equal to **[JEE Main 2024]**

(a) $\frac{1}{3} + 5\sin^{-1}\left(\frac{2}{\sqrt{5}}\right)$ ☐

(b) $\frac{2}{3} + 5\sin^{-1}\left(\frac{2}{\sqrt{5}}\right)$ ☐

(c) $\frac{2}{3} + \sqrt{5}\sin^{-1}\left(\frac{2}{\sqrt{5}}\right)$ ☐

(d) $\frac{1}{3} + \sqrt{5}\sin^{-1}\left(\frac{2}{\sqrt{5}}\right)$ ☐

Scan this QR code from your mobile phone to get the solutions of **Competition Edge Up** of this chapter.

Chapter 09

Differential Equations

Scan and take Chapter Test

TOPIC 1

Order and Degree of Differential Equation

1. Find the order of the differential equations.

(i) $xy\dfrac{d^2y}{dx^2}+\sin\left(\dfrac{x}{y}\right)=0$ ______

(ii) $xy\dfrac{d^3y}{dx^3}+x\left(\dfrac{dy}{dx}\right)^2-y\dfrac{dy}{dx}+y=0$ ______

(iii) $\left(\dfrac{d^2y}{dx^2}\right)^3+\left(\dfrac{dy}{dx}\right)^2+\sin\left(\dfrac{dy}{dx}\right)+1=0$ ______

(iv) $e^{\frac{dy}{dx}}+\dfrac{d^2y}{dx^2}=0$ ______

(v) $\dfrac{d^2y}{dx^2}+\sin\left(\dfrac{dy}{dx}\right)=0$ ______

2. Find the degree of the differential equations.

(i) $\left(\dfrac{d^2y}{dx^2}\right)^2+5\dfrac{dy}{dx}+\sin x=0$ ______

(ii) $\dfrac{d^2y}{dx^2}+\log(y)=\cos 3x$ ______

(iii) $\left(\dfrac{d^2y}{dx^2}\right)^2+\left(\dfrac{dy}{dx}\right)^2=x\sin\left(\dfrac{dy}{dx}\right)$ ______

*Concepts of all questions bearing * are important for JEE & CUET*

3. Fill in the blanks.

(i) If p and q are the order and degree of the differential equation

$$\left(\frac{d^2y}{dx^2}\right)^5 + 4\frac{\left(\frac{d^2y}{dx^2}\right)^3}{\left(\frac{d^3y}{dx^3}\right)} + \left(\frac{d^3y}{dx^3}\right) = x, \text{ then value of } p+q \text{ is } \_\_\_\_\_\_\_\_\_\_$$

(ii) The sum of the order and degree of the differential equation $\frac{d^2y}{dx^2} + \sqrt[3]{\frac{dy}{dx}} + (1+x) = 0$ is __________

4. Do the given differential equations have same order and degree?

(i) $\left[1+\left(\frac{dy}{dx}\right)^3\right]^{2/3} = 4\left(\frac{d^3y}{dx^3}\right)$

Yes ☐ No ☐

(ii) $\frac{d^2y}{dx^2} + 8\left(\frac{dy}{dx}\right)^3 + 5y = e^x + 2x + 7$

Yes ☐ No ☐

(iii) $5\left(\frac{d^3y}{dx^3}\right)^4 + 8\left(1+\frac{dy}{dx}\right)^3 + 5y = x^7$

Yes ☐ No ☐

(iv) $y = x^2\frac{dy}{dx} + \sqrt{1+\left(\frac{dy}{dx}\right)^2}$

Yes ☐ No ☐

5. If m and n are degree and order of the equation $\left[1+\left(\frac{dy}{dx}\right)^2\right]^{2/3} = \left(\frac{d^2y}{dx^2}\right)$, then m and n satisfies,

(a) $m < n, \frac{m-n}{m+n} = \frac{5}{2}$ ☐

(b) $m < n, \frac{m+n}{m-n} > \frac{5}{2}$ ☐

(c) $m > n, \frac{m+n}{m-n} > \frac{5}{2}$ ☐

(d) $m < n, \frac{m+n}{m-n} < \frac{5}{2}$ ☐

TOPIC 2

Solutions of Differential Equations and Variable Separable Method

6. If the differential equation has order n, then the number of arbitrary constant in the general solution is ________

7. State True or False.

(i) If $y = e^{ax} \sin bx$, then the value of $\frac{d^2y}{dx^2} - 2a\frac{dy}{dx} + a^2 y$ is $-b^2 y$.

True ☐ False ☐

(ii) $\frac{d^2y}{dx^2} - x^2 \frac{dy}{dx} + xy = x$ is differential equation and $y = x$ is one of its particular solution.

True ☐ False ☐

(iii) The order of the differential equation whose general solution is given by $y = (c_1 + c_2)\cos(x + c_3) - c_4 e^{x+c_5}$, where c_1, c_2, c_3, c_4 and c_5 are arbitrary constants, is 5.

True ☐ False ☐

***8.** Find the general solution of given differential equation by variable separable method.

(i) $\cos y \log(\sec x + \tan x)\, dx = \cos x \log(\sec y + \tan y) dy$ ________

(ii) $\frac{dy}{dx} = \sqrt{y - x}$ ________

(iii) $\frac{dy}{dx} = \frac{y^2 - y - 2}{x^2 + 2x - 3}$ ________

(iv) $\frac{dy}{dx} = \cos(x + y)$ ________

(v) $\frac{x \log x^2 + x}{\sin y + y \cos y} = \frac{dy}{dx}$ ________

9. Answer the following.

*(i) Given differential equation is $\frac{dy}{dx} = y \sin 2x$. If $y(0) = 1$, then the particular solution is ________

(ii) If $\frac{dy}{dx} = e^{-2y}$ and $y = 0$, when $x = 5$, then the value of x, when $y = 3$, is ________

*(iii) Given differential equation is $\frac{dy}{dx} = \left(\frac{y}{x}\right)^{1/3}$. If $y(1) = -1$, then particular solution is __

10. A continuously differentiable function in $(0, \pi)$ satisfies $\frac{dy}{dx} = 1 + y^2$, $y(0) = 0 = y(\pi)$, exist.

True ☐ False ☐

11. Let a solution $y = y(x)$ of the differential equation

$$x\sqrt{x^2 - 1}\, dy - y\sqrt{y^2 - 1}\, dx = 0 \text{ and } y(2) = \frac{2}{\sqrt{3}}.$$

(a) $y(x) = \sec\left(\sec^{-1} x - \frac{\pi}{6}\right)$ ☐ (b) $y(x) = \frac{2\sqrt{3}}{x} - \sqrt{1 - \frac{1}{x^2}}$ ☐

(c) $y(x) = \cos\left(\cos^{-1} x - \frac{\pi}{6}\right)$ ☐ (d) $y(x) = \sec^{-1}\left(\sec \frac{\pi}{6}\right)$ ☐

***12.** Answer the following.

(i) For the differential equation $\frac{dy}{dx} = 1 + x + y + xy$ and $y(-1) = 0$, the function y is ______

(ii) For the differential equation $y dx + (1 + x^2) \tan^{-1} x\, dy = 0$ and $y(1) = 1$ at $x = -1$, the value of y is ______

*(iii) The particular solution of $\frac{dy}{dx} = 1 + x + y^2 + xy^2$ and $y(0) = 0$ at $x = \pi$ is ______

*(iv) For the differential equation $\left(\frac{2 + \sin x}{1 + y}\right)\frac{dy}{dx} = -\cos(x)$ at $y(0) = 1$, $y\left(\frac{\pi}{2}\right)$ is equal to ______

13. Choose the correct option.

(i) The solution of differential equation $xdy - ydx = 0$ represents

(a) a circle whose centre is at (0, 0) ☐

(b) rectangular hyperbola ☐

(c) straight line passing through the origin ☐

(d) None of the above ☐

(ii) The equation of a curve passing through the point $(-2, 3)$, given that the slope of the tangent to the curve at any point (x, y), is $\frac{2x}{y^2}$, when $x = 4$, then the value of y is

(a) $\sqrt[3]{63}$ ☐ (b) $\sqrt[2]{63}$ ☐ (c) $\sqrt[3]{67}$ ☐ (d) $\sqrt[2]{67}$ ☐

*(iii) Let P be the purchase value of an equipment and $V(t)$ be the value after it has been used for t yr. The value of $V(t)$ depreciates at a rate given by differential equation $\frac{dV(t)}{dt} = -K(T - t)$, where $K > 0$ is a constant and T is the total life in years of the equipment. Then, the scrap value $V(T)$ of the equipment is

(a) $P - \frac{KT^2}{2}$ ☐ (b) $T^2 - \frac{P}{K}$ ☐ (c) e^{-PT} ☐ (d) $P - \frac{KT}{2}$ ☐

(iv) In a private limited company, principal increases continuously at the rate of 10% per year. In how many years ₹ 100 double itself?

(a) $10\log_e 2$ ☐ (b) $5\log_e 2$ ☐ (c) $\log_e\left(\frac{1}{2}\right)$ ☐ (d) $5\log_e\left(\frac{1}{2}\right)$ ☐

TOPIC 3

Homogeneous Method

14. Which of the following differential equations are homogeneous and non-homogeneous?

(i) $(t - P)\frac{dP}{dt} = t + 2P$ ________

(ii) $x\frac{dy}{dx} = 5y(\log x - \log y)$ ________

(iii) $x\cos\left(\frac{y}{x}\right)\frac{dy}{dx} = y\cos\left(\frac{y}{x}\right) + x$ ________

***15.** Find the general solution of the following homogeneous differential equations.

(i) $x\sin\frac{y}{x}\,dy = \left(y\sin\frac{y}{x} - 1\right)dx$ ________

(ii) $(1 + e^{x/y})\,dx + e^{x/y}\left(1 - \frac{x}{y}\right)dy = 0$ ________

(iii) $\frac{dy}{dx} = \frac{x + y}{x - y}$ ________

(iv) $xdy - ydx = (\sqrt{x^2 + y^2})\,dx$ ________

(v) $(x + y - 1)dx + (2x + 2y - 3)\,dy = 0$ ________

(vi) $x(x - y)dy + y^2 dx = 0$ ________

(vii) $x^2\frac{dy}{dx} = x^2 + xy + y^2$ is ________

(viii) $x\frac{dy}{dx} = y - x\cos^2\left(\frac{y}{x}\right)$ at $y(1) = \frac{\pi}{4}$ ________

16. Given differential equation is $x^2 dy + (xy + y^2)\, dx = 0$.

(i) General solution is $x^2 y = c(2x + y)$.

True ☐ False ☐

(ii) Particular solution at (1, 1) is $2x + y = 3x^2 y$.

True ☐ False ☐

17. Fill in the blanks.

(i) The slope of the tangent at (x, y) to a curve passing through the point (2, 1) is $\frac{x^2 + y^2}{2xy}$, then the equation of the curve is ____________

(ii) The slope of the tangent at (x, y) to a curve passing through $\left(1, \frac{\pi}{4}\right)$ is given by $\frac{y}{x} - \cos^2 \frac{y}{x}$, then the equation of the curve is ____________

TOPIC 4

Linear Differential Equations

18. Which of the following equations are linear or non-linear.

(i) $y\frac{dy}{dx} + 4x^2 = 0$ ____________

(ii) $x^2 \frac{d^2 y}{dx^2} + x\frac{dy}{dx} + y = \sin x$ ____________

(iii) $\frac{dy}{dx} + \frac{y}{x} = \log x$ ____________

(iv) $\frac{d^2 y}{dx^2} + y = \cos x$ ____________

(v) $\left(\frac{d^2 y}{dx^2}\right)^2 + x^2\left(\frac{dy}{dx}\right) = 0$ ____________

(vi) $x^2 \frac{d^2 y}{dx^2} + x\frac{dy}{dx} + y = 0$ ____________

(vii) $y = \frac{dy}{dx} + \sqrt[3]{1 + \left(\frac{dy}{dx}\right)^2}$ ____________

19. Find the integrating factor of the given differential equations.

(i) $(1 + x^2)\frac{dy}{dx} + y = e^{\tan^{-1} x}$ ____________

(ii) $x\, dy + (2x^2 y - y - ax^3)\, dx = 0$ ____________

(iii) $\frac{dy}{dx} + y \tan x + \sec x = 0$ ____________

(iv) $x\frac{dy}{dx} + \log x \cdot y = xe^x x^{-\frac{1}{2}\log x}$ $(x > 0)$ at $x = 2$ ____________

***20.** Find the solution of the following linear differential equations.

(i) $dy + 2xy\,dx = 2e^{-x^2}\,dx$ ____________

(ii) $\frac{dy}{dx} = \frac{1}{1 + x + y}$ ____________

(iii) $\frac{dy}{dx} + 2y\cot x = 3x^2 \operatorname{cosec}^2 x$ ____________

(iv) $\frac{dy}{dx} + \frac{y}{x} = x^3$ ____________

(v) $\frac{dy}{dx} + 3y = e^{-2x}$ ____________

(vi) $\frac{dy}{dx} + 2y = xe^{4x}$ ____________

21. Choose the correct option.

(i) The differential equation $\frac{dy}{dx} + P\,y = Q\,y^n$, $(n > 1)$ can be reduced to linear form by substituting

(a) $z = y^{n-1}$ ☐
(b) $z = y^{n+1}$ ☐
(c) $z = y^{1-n}$ ☐
(d) All of these ☐

*(ii) If $y(x)$ satisfies the differential equation $\frac{dy}{dx} - y\tan x = 2x\sec x$ and $y(0) = 0$, then

(a) $y\left(\frac{\pi}{3}\right) = \frac{\pi^2}{9}$ ☐
(b) $y'\left(\frac{\pi}{3}\right) = \frac{4\pi}{3} + \frac{2\pi^2}{2\sqrt{3}}$ ☐
(c) $y\left(\frac{\pi}{4}\right) = \frac{\pi^2}{8\sqrt{2}}$ ☐
(d) $y'\left(\frac{\pi}{4}\right) = \frac{\pi^2}{18}$ ☐

*(iii) The solution of $x^3\frac{dy}{dx} + 4x^2\tan y = e^x \sec y$ satisfied $y(1) = 0$ is

(a) $\tan y = (x-1)e^x x^{-3}$ ☐
(b) $\tan y = (x-2)e^x \log x$ ☐
(c) $\sin y = e^x (x-1)\,x^{-4}$ ☐
(d) $\sin y = e^x (x-1)\,x^{-3}$ ☐

***22.** The solution of $\frac{dy}{dx} = \frac{y \cdot \phi'(x) - y^2}{\phi(x)}$ with $\phi(0) = 1$ and $y(0) = 2$ is ____________

23. Let $f : [1, \infty) \to [2, \infty)$ be a differentiable function such that $f(1) = 2$.

If $6\int_1^x f(t)\,dt = -x^3 + 3xf(x) - 5\ \forall\ x \geq 1$, then the value of $f(2)$ is

(a) 1 (b) 3 (c) 6 (d) 2

24. Let $y'(x) + P'(x)\, y(x) = P(x)\, P'(x)$, $y(0) = 0$, $x \in R$, where $f'(x)$ denotes $\frac{df(x)}{dx}$ and $P(x)$ is a given non-constant differentiable function on R and $P(0) = 0$, $P(3) = 0$. Then, the value of $y(3)$ is ____________

25. Let f be a real-valued differentiable function on set of all real numbers (R) such that $f(1) = 1$. If the y-intercept of the tangent at any point $P(x, y)$ on the curve $y = f(x)$ is equal to the cube of the abscissa of P, then the value of $f(2)$ is

(a) 2 ☐ (b) 8 ☐

(c) 4 ☐ (d) None of these ☐

26. The equation of the curve passing through the point (0, 2), given that the sum of the coordinates of any point in the curve exceeds the magnitude of the slope of the tangent to the curve at point by 5, is $y(x) = (4 - x) + Ce^x$, where C is an arbitrary constant.

True ☐ False ☐

Assertion-Reason Questions

The following questions consist of two statements – Assertion (A) and Reason (R). Answer these questions by selecting the appropriate options given below.

(a) Both A and R are true and R is the correct explanation of A.
(b) Both A and R are true but R is not the correct explanation of A.
(c) A is true but R is false.
(d) A is false but R is true.

1. **Assertion** (A) The order of the differential equation given by $\frac{dy}{dx} + 3y = \cos x$ is 1.

Reason (R) The order of a differential equation is defined as the order of the highest derivative occurring in the differential equation.

(a) ☐ (b) ☐ (c) ☐ (d) ☐

2. **Assertion** (A) The degree of the differential equation given by $\left(\frac{dy}{dx}\right)^2 = \frac{x^6 - y^6}{(x^2 + y^2)\, xy}$ is 2.

Reason (R) The degree of a differential equation is the degree of the highest order derivative when differential coefficients are free from radicals and fraction.

(a) ☐ (b) ☐ (c) ☐ (d) ☐

3. **Assertion** (A) The order and degree of the differential equation $\sqrt{\frac{d^2y}{dx^2}} = \sqrt{\frac{dy}{dx}} + 5$ are 2 and 1, respectively.

Reason (R) The differential equation $\left(\frac{dx}{dy}\right)^3 + 2y^{\frac{1}{2}} = x$ is of order 1 and degree 3.

(a) ☐ (b) ☐ (c) ☐ (d) ☐

4. Assertion (A) The differential equation $\frac{dy}{dx} + x^2 y = 5$ is a first order linear differential equation.

Reason (R) If P and Q are functions of x only or constant, then differential equation of the form $\frac{dy}{dx} + Py = Q$ is a first order linear differential equation.

(a) ☐ (b) ☐ (c) ☐ (d) ☐

5. Assertion (A) The degree of the differential equation $\frac{d^2y}{dx^2} + 3\left(\frac{dy}{dx}\right)^2 = x^2 \log\left(\frac{d^2y}{dx^2}\right)$ is not defined.

Reason (R) If the differential equation is a polynomial in terms of its derivatives, then its degree is defined.

(a) ☐ (b) ☐ (c) ☐ (d) ☐

6. Assertion (A) The function $x + y = \tan^{-1} y$ is a solution of the differential equation $y^2 \frac{dy}{dx} + y^2 + 1 = 0$.

Reason (R) A function which satuisfiers the given differential equation is called its solution.

(a) ☐ (b) ☐ (c) ☐ (d) ☐

7. Assertion (A) Equation $\frac{dy}{dx} = \frac{\sin y}{\sin x}$ is a homogeneous differential equation of order 0.

Reason (R) To solve a differential equation of the form $\frac{dy}{dx} = f\left(\frac{y}{x}\right)$, we put $y = vx$.

(a) ☐ (b) ☐ (c) ☐ (d) ☐

8. Assertion (A) Integrating factor for the differential equation $(x + y)\frac{dy}{dx} = 1$ is e^{-y}.

Reason (R) Integrating factor for the differential equation $\frac{dy}{dx} + Py = Q$, where P and Q are functions of x is $e^{\int Q\,dx}$.

(a) ☐ (b) ☐ (c) ☐ (d) ☐

9. Assertion (A) The general solution of the differential equation $(x + 2)\frac{dy}{dx} = x^2 + 5x - 3$, $x \neq 2$ is $y = \frac{x^2}{2} + 3x - 9\log|x + 2| + C$.

Reason (R) The number of arbitrary constant in the general solution is equal to the order of the differential equation.

(a) ☐ (b) ☐ (c) ☐ (d) ☐

10. Assertion (A) The order of the differential equation whose solution is $y = C_1 e^{x + C_2} + C_3 e^{x + C_4}$ is 4.

Reason (R) Order of the differential equation is the order of the highest order derivatives occurring in the differential equation.

(a) ☐ (b) ☐ (c) ☐ (d) ☐

Case Based Questions

Case 1 A thermometer reading 80°F is taken outside. Five minutes later the thermometer reads 60°F. After another 5 min the thermometer reads 50°F. At any time t the thermometer reading be T°F and the outside temperature be S°F.

Based on the above information, answer the following questions

(i) If λ is the positive constant of proportionality, then $\frac{dT}{dt}$ is

(a) $\lambda(T+S)$ ☐ (b) $-\lambda(T-S)$ ☐

(c) $\lambda(T-S)$ ☐ (d) λTS ☐

(ii) Find the general solution of differential equation formed.

(a) $\log T = St + C$ ☐

(b) $\log(T+S) = \lambda t + C$ ☐

(c) $\log(T-S) = -\lambda t + C$ ☐

(d) $\log S = tT + C$ ☐

(iii) Find the value of constant of integration C in the solution of differential equation formed.

(a) $\log(60 - S)$ ☐

(b) $\log(60 + S)$ ☐

(c) $\log(80 + S)$ ☐

(d) $\log(80 - S)$ ☐

Case 2 If an equation is of the form $\frac{dy}{dx} + Py = Q$, where P and Q are function of x, then such equation is known as linear differential equation.

Its solution is given by

$$y(\text{IF}) = \int Q \cdot (\text{IF})\, dx + C, \text{ where IF} = e^{\int P\, dx}.$$

Now, suppose the given equation

$$(1+\sin x)\frac{dy}{dx} + y\cos x + x = 0$$

Based on the above information, answer the following questions.

(i) The value of P and Q respectively are ....

(ii) Find the value of IF

(iii) Find the solution of the given differential equation.

(iv) If $y(0) = 1$, then y equals ....

COMPETITION EDGE UP

1. The differential equation of the family of circles passing through the origin and having centre at the line $y = x$ is **[JEE Main 2024]**

(a) $(x^2 - y^2 + 2xy)dx = (x^2 - y^2 + 2xy)dy$ ☐

(b) $(x^2 + y^2 - 2xy)dx = (x^2 + y^2 + 2xy)dy$ ☐

(c) $(x^2 + y^2 + 2xy)dx = (x^2 + y^2 - 2xy)dy$ ☐

(d) $(x^2 - y^2 + 2xy)dx = (x^2 - y^2 - 2xy)dy$ ☐

2. Let $f(x)$ be a positive function such that the area bounded by $y = f(x)$, $y = 0$ from $x = 0$ to $x = a > 0$ is $e^{-a} + 4a^2 + a - 1$. Then, the differential equation, whose general solution is $y = c_1 f(x) + c_2$, where c_1 and c_2 are arbitrary constants, is **[JEE Main 2024]**

(a) $(8e^x - 1)\dfrac{d^2y}{dx^2} + \dfrac{dy}{dx} = 0$ ☐

(b) $(8e^x + 1)\dfrac{d^2y}{dx^2} - \dfrac{dy}{dx} = 0$ ☐

(c) $(8e^x + 1)\dfrac{d^2y}{dx^2} + \dfrac{dy}{dx} = 0$ ☐

(d) $(8e^x - 1)\dfrac{d^2y}{dx^2} - \dfrac{dy}{dx} = 0$ ☐

3. The solution curve, of the differential equation $2y\dfrac{dy}{dx} + 3 = 5\dfrac{dy}{dx}$, passing through the point $(0, 1)$ is a conic, whose vertex lies on the line. **[JEE Main 2024]**

(a) $2x + 3y = 9$ ☐

(b) $2x + 3y = -9$ ☐

(c) $2x + 3y = 6$ ☐

(d) $2x + 3y = -6$ ☐

4. Let $y = y(x)$ be the solution of the differential equation $(1 + y^2)e^{\tan x}dx + \cos^2 x(1 + e^{2\tan x})dy = 0$, $y(0) = 1$. Then, $y\left(\dfrac{\pi}{4}\right)$ is equal to **[JEE Main 2024]**

(a) $\dfrac{2}{e}$ ☐ (b) $\dfrac{2}{e^2}$ ☐

(c) $\dfrac{1}{e^2}$ ☐ (d) $\dfrac{1}{e}$ ☐

5. The temperature $T(t)$ of a body at time $t = 0$ is 160°F and it decreases continuously as per the differential equation $\dfrac{dT}{dt} = -K(T - 80)$, where K is a positive constant. If $T(15) = 120°F$, then $T(45)$ is equal to **[JEE Main 2024]**

(a) 85°F ☐ (b) 95°F ☐

(c) 80°F ☐ (d) 90°F ☐

6. The solution curve of the differential equation $y\dfrac{dx}{dy} = x(\log_e x - \log_e y + 1)$, $x > 0, y > 0$ passing through the point $(e, 1)$ is **[JEE Main 2024]**

(a) $\left|\log_e \dfrac{y}{x}\right| = x$ ☐

(b) $\left|\log_e \dfrac{x}{y}\right| = y$ ☐

(c) $\left|\log_e \dfrac{y}{x}\right| = y^2$ ☐

(d) $2\left|\log_e \dfrac{x}{y}\right| = y + 1$ ☐

7. If $\sin\left(\dfrac{y}{x}\right) = \log_e |x| + \dfrac{\alpha}{2}$ is the solution of the differential equation $x\cos\left(\dfrac{y}{x}\right)\dfrac{dy}{dx} = y\cos\left(\dfrac{y}{x}\right) + x$ and $y(1) = \dfrac{\pi}{3}$, then α^2 is equal to **[JEE Main 2024]**

(a) 3 ☐

(b) 12 ☐

(c) 9 ☐

(d) 4 ☐

8. The solution of the differential equation $(x^2 + y^2)dx - 5xy\,dy = 0$, $y(1) = 0$, is **[JEE Main 2024]**

(a) $|x^2 - 2y^2|^6 = x$ ☐

(b) $|x^2 - 4y^2|^6 = x$ ☐

(c) $|x^2 - 4y^2|^5 = x^2$ ☐

(d) $|x^2 - 2y^2|^5 = x^2$ ☐

9. If the solution $y = y(x)$ of the differential equation $(x^4 + 2x^3 + 3x^2 + 2x + 2)dy - (2x^2 + 2x + 3)dx = 0$ satisfies $y(-1) = -\frac{\pi}{4}$, then $y(0)$ is equal to **[JEE Main 2024]**

(a) $-\frac{\pi}{12}$ ☐ (b) $\frac{\pi}{4}$ ☐

(c) $\frac{\pi}{2}$ ☐ (d) 0 ☐

10. Let α be a non-zero real number. Suppose $f : R \to R$ is a differentiable function such that $f(0) = 2$ and $\lim_{x \to -\infty} f(x) = 1$. If $f'(x) = \alpha f(x) + 3$, for all $x \in R$, then $f(-\log_e 2)$ is equal to ...... **[JEE Main 2024]**

(a) 5 ☐ (b) 9 ☐

(c) 7 ☐ (d) 3 ☐

11. Let $y = y(x)$ be the solution of the differential equation $\sec x\, dy + [2(1 - x) \tan x + x(2 - x)]\, dx = 0$ such that $y(0) = 2$. Then, $y(2)$ is equal to **[JEE Main 2024]**

(a) 2 ☐

(b) $2\{1 - \sin(2)\}$ ☐

(c) 1 ☐

(d) $2\{\sin(2) + 1\}$ ☐

12. A function $y = f(x)$ satisfies $f(x) \sin 2x + \sin x - (1 + \cos^2 x) f'(x) = 0$ with condition $f(0) = 0$. Then, $f\left(\frac{\pi}{2}\right)$ is equal to **[JEE Main 2024]**

(a) 0 ☐

(b) -1 ☐

(c) 2 ☐

(d) 1 ☐

13. Let $y = y(x)$ be the solution curve of the differential equation $\sec y \frac{dy}{dx} + 2x \sin y = x^3 \cos y$, $y(1) = 0$. Then, $y(\sqrt{3})$ is equal to **[JEE Main 2024]**

(a) $\frac{\pi}{3}$ ☐

(b) $\frac{\pi}{12}$ ☐

(c) $\frac{\pi}{6}$ ☐

(d) $\frac{\pi}{4}$ ☐

14. Let $y = y(x)$ be the solution of the differential equation $(1 + x^2)\frac{dy}{dx} + y = e^{\tan^{-1} x}$, $y(1) = 0$. Then, $y(0)$ is **[JEE Main 2024]**

(a) $\frac{1}{2}\left(1 - e^{\frac{\pi}{2}}\right)$ ☐

(b) $\frac{1}{2}\left(e^{\frac{\pi}{2}} - 1\right)$ ☐

(c) $\frac{1}{4}\left(1 - e^{\frac{\pi}{2}}\right)$ ☐

(d) $\frac{1}{4}\left(e^{\frac{\pi}{2}} - 1\right)$ ☐

15. If $y = y(x)$ is the solution of the differential equation $\frac{dy}{dx} + 2y = \sin(2x)$, $y(0) = \frac{3}{4}$, then $y\left(\frac{\pi}{8}\right)$ is equal to **[JEE Main 2024]**

(a) $e^{\pi/4}$ ☐ (b) $e^{-\pi/8}$ ☐

(c) $e^{\pi/8}$ ☐ (d) $e^{-\pi/4}$ ☐

Scan this QR code from your mobile phone to get the solutions of **Competition Edge Up** of this chapter.

Chapter 10

Vector Algebra

Scan and take Chapter Test

TOPIC 1

Basic Concept and Types of Vector

1. Classify the following measures as scalars and vectors.

(i) 5 L ______

(ii) 3 min ______

(iii) 2 N ______

(iv) 8 km/hr ______

(v) 10 m/s towards East ______

2. The position vector of a point $P(x, y, z)$ with respect to origin O is ______ and $\sqrt{x^2 + y^2 + z^2} =$ ______

(a) $\overrightarrow{PO}, |\overrightarrow{PO}|$ (b) $\overrightarrow{OP}, 2|\overrightarrow{PO}|$ (c) $\overrightarrow{OP}, |\overrightarrow{OP}|$ (d) $\overrightarrow{PO}, |\overrightarrow{OP}|$

______

3. Find magnitude of the following vectors $(\vec{a})$.

(i) $\frac{1}{\sqrt{3}}\hat{i} + \frac{1}{\sqrt{3}}\hat{j} - \frac{1}{\sqrt{3}}\hat{k}$ ______

(ii) $\sqrt{5}\,\hat{i} - \frac{1}{\sqrt{5}}\hat{j} - 2\hat{k}$ ______

(iii) $2\sqrt{2}\hat{i} + 3\hat{j} + 1\hat{k}$ ______

4. The direction ratios and direction cosines of the vector $\vec{a} = \hat{i} + \hat{j} - 2\hat{k}$ is

(a) $(-1, -1, 2), \left(\frac{1}{\sqrt{6}}, \frac{-1}{\sqrt{6}}, \frac{-2}{\sqrt{6}}\right)$ (b) $(1, 1, -2), \left(\frac{1}{\sqrt{6}}, \frac{1}{\sqrt{6}}, \frac{-2}{\sqrt{6}}\right)$

(c) $(-1, -1, 2), \left(\frac{-1}{\sqrt{6}}, \frac{-1}{\sqrt{6}}, \frac{2}{\sqrt{6}}\right)$ (d) $(1, 1, -2), \left(\frac{-1}{\sqrt{6}}, \frac{-1}{\sqrt{6}}, \frac{-2}{\sqrt{6}}\right)$

______

*Concepts of all questions bearing * are important for JEE & CUET*

5. If α, β and γ are the angles made by vector $\vec{r} = x\hat{i} + y\hat{j} + z\hat{k}$ with positive directions of X, Y and Z-axes respectively, then match the following.

	Column I		Column II
A.	$\cos\alpha$	1.	$\frac{y}{r}$
B.	$\cos\beta$	2.	$\frac{z}{r}$
C.	$\cos\gamma$	3.	$\frac{x}{r}$
D.	$\cos^2\alpha + \cos^2\beta + \cos^2\gamma$	4.	1

Choose the correct option.

(a) A → 3, B → 1, C → 2, D → 4
(b) A → 3, B → 2, C → 1, D → 4
(c) A → 2, B → 1, C → 3, D → 4
(d) A → 1, B → 2, C → 3, D → 4

6. Match the following columns.

	Column I		Column II
A.	Equal vectors	1.	Initial and terminal points coincide
B.	Unit vector	2.	Magnitude is 1
C.	Zero vector	3.	Parallel to the same line
D.	Collinear vector	4.	Same magnitude and direction

Choose the correct option.

(a) A → 1, B → 2, C → 3, D → 4
(b) A → 4, B → 2, C → 1, D → 3
(c) A → 4, B → 1, C → 2, D → 3
(d) A → 1, B → 3, C → 4, D → 2

7. State the following statements are True or False.

(i) $\overrightarrow{OA}$ and $\overrightarrow{OB}$ are coinitial vectors.

True ☐ False ☐

(ii) $\vec{a}$ and $-\vec{a}$ are collinear.

True ☐ False ☐

(iii) Two collinear vectors are always equal in magnitude.

True ☐ False ☐

(iv) Two vectors having same magnitude are collinear.

True ☐ False ☐

(v) Two collinear vectors having the same magnitude are equal.

True ☐ False ☐

8. Match the following based on the diagram.

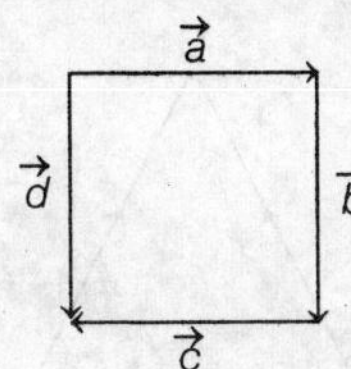

	Column I		Column II
A.	Coinitial	1.	$\vec{a}$ and $\vec{c}$
B.	Equal	2.	$\vec{a}$ and $\vec{d}$
C.	Collinear but not equal	3.	$\vec{b}$ and $\vec{d}$

Choose the correct option.

(a) A → 2, B → 3, C → 1
(b) A → 2, B → 1, C → 3
(c) A → 1, B → 2, C → 3
(d) A → 1, B → 3, C → 2

9. The negative of the vector $\overrightarrow{AB}$ is

(a) $\overrightarrow{BA}$
(b) $-\overrightarrow{AB}$
(c) $-\overrightarrow{BA}$
(d) None of these

TOPIC 2

Addition of Vectors

***10.** From the diagram,

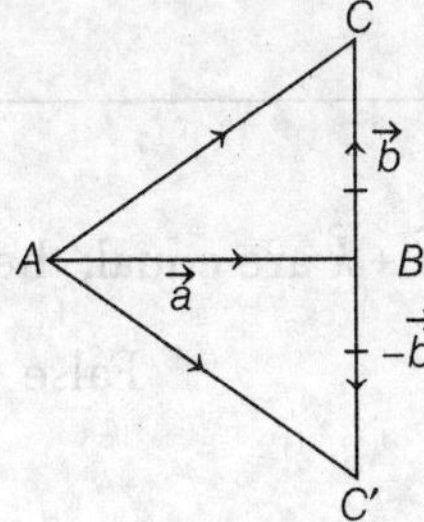

$\overrightarrow{AC}$ = ______________ and $\overrightarrow{AC'}$ = ______________

(a) $\vec{b} - \vec{a}$ and $\vec{a} - \vec{b}$
(b) $\vec{a} + \vec{b}$ and $\vec{a} - \vec{b}$
(c) $\vec{a} + \vec{b}$ and $-\vec{a} + \vec{b}$
(d) $-\vec{a} + \vec{b}$ and $-\vec{a} - \vec{b}$

11. State the following statements are True or False.

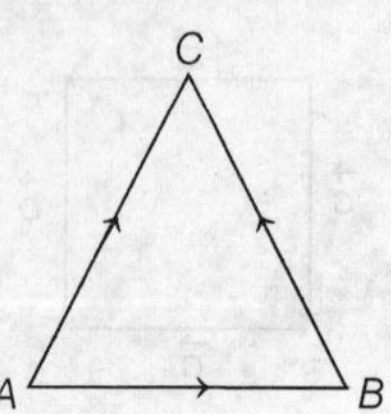

(i) $\overrightarrow{AB} + \overrightarrow{BC} - \overrightarrow{AC} = 0$

True ☐ False ☐

(ii) $\overrightarrow{AB} + \overrightarrow{BC} + \overrightarrow{CA} = 0$

True ☐ False ☐

(iii) $\overrightarrow{AB} + \overrightarrow{BC} - \overrightarrow{CA} = 0$

True ☐ False ☐

(iv) $\overrightarrow{AB} - \overrightarrow{CB} + \overrightarrow{CA} = 0$

True ☐ False ☐

TOPIC 3

Multiplication of a Vector by a Scalar

12. If $\vec{a} = 2\hat{i} - 4\hat{j} + \hat{k}$, then

(i) $\frac{1}{2}\vec{a} =$ ______

(ii) $3\vec{a} =$ ______

(iii) $-\frac{1}{4}\vec{a} =$ ______

13. If $\vec{a} = x\hat{i} + 2\hat{j} + z\hat{k}$ and $\vec{b} = 2\hat{i} + y\hat{j} + \hat{k}$ are equal, then the values of x, y and z are 2, 2 and 1.

True ☐ False ☐

14. Let $\vec{a} = \hat{i} + 2\hat{j}$ and $\vec{b} = 2\hat{i} + \hat{j}$.

Is $\vec{a}$ and $\vec{b}$ are equal?

______

15. $x(\hat{i} + \hat{j} + \hat{k})$ is a unit vector. The value of x is

(a) $\frac{1}{\sqrt{2}}$ (b) $\pm\frac{1}{\sqrt{3}}$ (c) $\frac{1}{\sqrt{5}}$ (d) $\sqrt{3}$

______

16. The vector in the direction of vector $5i - j + 2k$ that has magnitude 8 units, is $\frac{8(5\hat{i} - \hat{j} + 2\hat{k})}{\sqrt{30}}$.

True ☐ False ☐

17. The unit vector in the direction of sum of the vectors $\vec{a} = 2\hat{i} + 2\hat{j} - 5\hat{k}$ and $\vec{b} = 2\hat{i} + \hat{j} + 3\hat{k}$ is ____________

TOPIC 4

Component of a Vector, Vector Joining Two Points and Section Formula

18. If $\vec{r} = x\hat{i} + y\hat{j} + z\hat{k}$, then

(i) scalar components of $\vec{r}$ = ________, ________ and ________

(ii) vector components of $\vec{r}$ = ________, ________ and ________

19. The scalar components and vector components of the vector with initial point (2, 1)and terminal point (– 5, 7), respectively are ________ and ________.

(a) $-7\hat{i}, 6\hat{j}$ and $-7, 6$ (b) $-7, 6$ and $-7\hat{i}, 6\hat{j}$

(c) $6, -7$ and $6\hat{i}, -7\hat{j}$ (d) $7, -6$ and $7\hat{i} - 6\hat{j}$

20. The unit vector in the direction of $\overrightarrow{PQ}$, where P and Q are the points (1, 2, 3) and (4, 5, 6), respectively, is ____________

21. The vector joining the points P (2, 3, 0) and Q (–1, – 2, – 4) directed from P to Q, is ____________

22. The direction cosines of the vector joining the points $A(1, 2, -3)$ and $B(-1, -2, 1)$ directed from A to B, is

(a) $\left(\frac{1}{3}, \frac{2}{3}, \frac{2}{3}\right)$ (b) $\left(-\frac{1}{3}, \frac{2}{3}, -\frac{2}{3}\right)$ (c) $\left(-\frac{1}{3}, -\frac{2}{3}, \frac{2}{3}\right)$ (d) $\left(-\frac{1}{3}, -\frac{2}{3}, -\frac{2}{3}\right)$

23. If $\vec{a} = a_1\hat{i} + b_1\hat{j} + c_1\hat{k}$ and $\vec{b} = a_2\hat{i} + b_2\hat{j} + c_2\hat{k}$ are collinear, then

(a) $\frac{a_1}{a_2} + \frac{b_1}{b_2} = \frac{c_1}{c_2}$ (b) $\frac{a_1}{a_2} \neq \frac{b_1}{b_2} \neq \frac{c_1}{c_2}$ (c) $\frac{a_1}{a_2} = \frac{b_1}{b_2} = \frac{c_1}{c_2}$ (d) $\frac{a_1}{a_2} = \frac{b_1}{b_2} \neq \frac{c_1}{c_2}$

24. In what ratio the point $B(5, 0, -2)$ divides $A(1, -2, -8)$ and $C(11, 3, 7)$, ________

25. The position vector of the mid-point of the vector joining the points $P(2, 3, 4)$ and $Q(4, 1, -2)$, is ________

26. Two points P and Q with position vectors $\overrightarrow{OP} = 3\vec{a} - 2\vec{b}$ and $\overrightarrow{OQ} = \vec{a} + \vec{b}$. The position vector of a point R, which divides the line joining P and Q in the ratio 2 : 1 internally, is

(a) $4\vec{b} - \vec{a}$ (b) $4\vec{a} - \vec{b}$ (c) $\frac{5\vec{a}}{3}$ (d) $-\frac{5\vec{a}}{3}$

27. The position vector of a point C which divides the line segment joining A and B, whose position vectors are $2\vec{a} + \vec{b}$ and $\vec{a} - 3\vec{b}$, externally in the ratio 1 : 2, is

(a) $3\vec{a} - 5\vec{b}$ (b) $3\vec{a} + 5\vec{b}$

(c) $3\vec{a} - 2\vec{b}$ (d) $-3\vec{a} - 5\vec{b}$

TOPIC 5

Scalar Product

NCERT Pg 355-357

28. If θ is the angle between two vectors $\vec{a}$ and $\vec{b}$, then $\vec{a} \cdot \vec{b} \geq 0$ only, when

(a) $0 < \theta < \frac{\pi}{2}$ (b) $0 \leq \theta \leq \frac{\pi}{2}$ (c) $0 < \theta < \pi$ (d) $0 \leq \theta \leq \pi$

29. If $\vec{a} \cdot \vec{b} = 0$, then $\vec{a}$ is ________ to $\vec{b}$.

(a) perpendicular (b) parallel

(c) collinear (d) skew lines

30. Fill in the following statements.

(i) If $\vec{a} = 2\hat{i} + 2\hat{j} + 3\hat{k}$, $\vec{b} = -\hat{i} + 2\hat{j} + \hat{k}$ and $\vec{c} = 3\hat{i} + \hat{j}$ are such that $\vec{a} + \lambda\vec{b}$ is perpendicular to $\vec{c}$, then the value of λ is ________

(ii) If $\vec{a} = \hat{i} + 4\hat{j} + 2\hat{k}$, $\vec{b} = 3\hat{i} - 2\hat{j} + 7\hat{k}$, $\vec{c} = 2\hat{i} - \hat{j} + 4\hat{k}$ and $\vec{d}$ is perpendicular to both $\vec{a}$ and $\vec{b}$, and $\vec{c} \cdot \vec{d} = 15$, then $\vec{d}$ is ________

31. Let $\vec{a}$ and $\vec{b}$ be two vectors. Then, match the following columns.

	Column I		Column II
A.	$\vec{a}\cdot\vec{b} = \lvert\vec{a}\rvert\lvert\vec{b}\rvert$	1.	$\theta = 0$
B.	$\vec{a}\cdot\vec{b} = -\lvert\vec{a}\rvert\lvert\vec{b}\rvert$	2.	$\theta = \frac{\pi}{2}$
C.	$\vec{a}\cdot\vec{b} = 0$	3.	$\theta = \pi$

Choose the correct option.

(a) A → 1, B → 2, C → 3 (b) A → 1, B → 3, C → 2

(c) A → 3, B → 2, C → 1 (d) A → 2, B → 3, C → 1

32. State the following statements are True or False.

(i) $\hat{i}\cdot\hat{i} = 1$

True ☐ False ☐

(ii) $\hat{j}\cdot\hat{k} = i$

True ☐ False ☐

(iii) $\hat{k}\cdot\hat{i} = 0$

True ☐ False ☐

(iv) $\hat{j}.\hat{j} = 1$

True ☐ False ☐

***33.** If $|\vec{a}| = 1, |\vec{b}| = 2$ and $\vec{a}\cdot\vec{b} = 1$, then the angle between $\vec{a}$ and $\vec{b}$ is ____________

***34.** The angle θ between the vectors $\vec{a} = \hat{i} + \hat{j} - \hat{k}$ and $\vec{b} = \hat{i} - \hat{j} + \hat{k}$ is ____________

35. If $|\vec{a}| = 2, |\vec{b}| = 3$ and $\vec{a}\cdot\vec{b} = 4$, then $|\vec{a} - \vec{b}|^2$ is equal to

(a) 5 (b) $\sqrt{5}$ (c) $-\sqrt{5}$ (d) -5

36. If the vertices of a ΔABC are (1, 2, 3), (− 1, 0, 0) and (0, 1, 2) respectively, then $\angle ABC = \left(\cos^{-1}\frac{3}{\sqrt{5}}\right)$.

True ☐ False ☐

37. Find the value of $|\vec{a}|$, when the following conditions are given.

(i) $(\vec{a} + \vec{b})\cdot(\vec{a} - \vec{b}) = 8$ and $|\vec{a}| = 8\,|\vec{b}|$ ____________

(ii) $(\vec{a} + \vec{b})\cdot(\vec{a} - \vec{b}) = 2$ and $|\vec{a}| = \frac{7}{2}|\vec{b}|$ ____________

(iii) $(\vec{a} + \vec{b})\cdot(\vec{a} - \vec{b}) = 1$ and $|\vec{b}| = \frac{1}{\sqrt{5}}|\vec{a}|$ ____________

38. For any two vectors $\vec{a}$ and $\vec{b}$, prove $|\vec{a} \cdot \vec{b}| \leq |\vec{a}||\vec{b}|$.

***39.** The points A, B and C with position vectors $\vec{a} = 2\hat{i} - \hat{j} + \hat{k}$, $\vec{b} = \hat{i} - 3\hat{j} - 5\hat{k}$ and $\vec{c} = 3\hat{i} - 4\hat{j} - 4\hat{k}$, respectively are the vertices of ________________ triangle.

40. Let $\vec{a}$, $\vec{b}$ and $\vec{c}$ be three vectors such that $|\vec{a}| = 3$, $|\vec{b}| = 4$, $|\vec{c}| = 5$ and each of them being perpendicular to the sum of the other two, then $|\vec{a} + \vec{b} + \vec{c}|$ is equal to

(a) $\sqrt{5}$ (b) 5 (c) $5\sqrt{2}$ (d) $\sqrt{10}$

---

41. If $\vec{\alpha} = 3\hat{i} - \hat{j}$ and $\vec{\beta} = 2\hat{i} + \hat{j} - 3\hat{k}$, expressed $\vec{\beta}$ in the form of $\vec{\beta} = \vec{\beta}_1 + \vec{\beta}_2$, where $\vec{\beta}_1$ is parallel to $\vec{\alpha}$ and $\vec{\beta}_2$ is perpendicular to $\vec{\alpha}$, then $\vec{\beta}_1 =$ ____________, $\vec{\beta}_2 =$ ____________

(a) $\vec{\beta}_1 = \frac{3}{2}\hat{i} - \frac{1}{2}\hat{j}$, $\vec{\beta}_2 = \frac{1}{2}\hat{i} + \frac{3}{2}\hat{j} - 3\hat{k}$

(b) $\vec{\beta}_1 = \frac{1}{2}\hat{i} + \frac{3}{2}\hat{j} - 3\hat{k}$, $\vec{\beta}_2 = \frac{3}{2}\hat{i} - \frac{1}{2}\hat{j}$

(c) $\vec{\beta}_1 = \frac{3}{2}\hat{i} + \frac{1}{2}\hat{j}$, $\vec{\beta}_2 = \frac{1}{2}\hat{i} + \frac{3}{2}\hat{j} + 3\hat{k}$

(d) $\vec{\beta}_1 = \frac{1}{2}\hat{i} - \frac{3}{2}\hat{j} + 3\hat{k}$, $\vec{\beta}_2 = \frac{3}{2}\hat{i} + \frac{1}{2}\hat{j}$

42. The points $A(-2\hat{i} + 3\hat{j} + 5\hat{k})$, $B(\hat{i} + 2\hat{j} + 3\hat{k})$ and $C(7\hat{i} - \hat{k})$ are non-collinear.

True ☐ False ☐

TOPIC 6

Projection

NCERT Pg. 357-361

43. Projection of a vector $\vec{a}$ on other vector $\vec{b}$ is given by

(a) $\vec{a} \cdot \vec{b}$ (b) $\vec{a} \cdot \frac{\vec{b}}{|\vec{b}|}$

(c) $\vec{a} \times \vec{b}$ (d) $\frac{\vec{b} \cdot \vec{a}}{|\vec{a}|}$

---

44. Fill in the blanks.

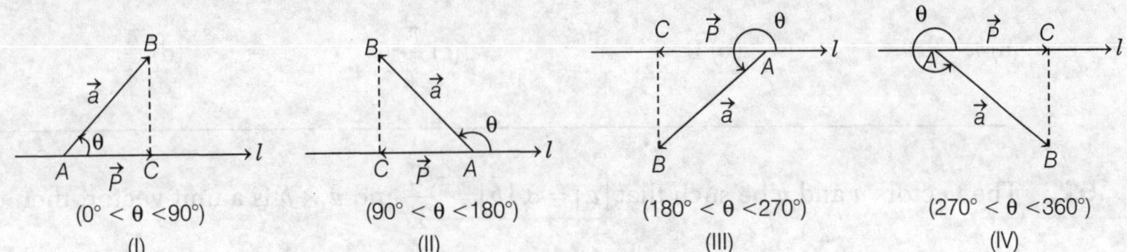

(i) The projection vector of $\overrightarrow{AB}$ will be zero vector if $\theta =$ ________ or ________ .

(ii) The projection vector of $\overrightarrow{AB}$ will be $\overrightarrow{AB}$ and $\overrightarrow{BA}$ if $\theta =$ ________ and ________ , respectively.

45. If α, β and γ are the direction angles of the vector $\vec{a} = a_1\hat{i} + a_2\hat{j} + a_3\hat{k}$, then projections of $\vec{a}$ along OX, OY and OZ are

(a) $|\vec{a}|\cos\alpha, |\vec{a}|\cos\beta, |\vec{a}|\cos\gamma$
(b) $|\vec{a_1}|\cos\alpha, |\vec{a_2}|\cos\beta, |\vec{a_3}|\cos\gamma$
(c) $|\vec{a}|\sin\alpha, |\vec{a}|\sin\beta, |\vec{a}|\sin\gamma$
(d) $|\vec{a_1}|\sin\alpha, |\vec{a_2}|\sin\beta, |\vec{a_3}|\sin\gamma$

---

46. If a unit vector $\vec{a}$ makes angles $\frac{\pi}{3}$ with $\hat{i}$, $\frac{\pi}{4}$ with $\hat{j}$ and $\frac{\pi}{3}$ with $\hat{k}$, then the components of $\vec{a}$ is

(a) $\left(\frac{1}{\sqrt{2}}, \frac{1}{\sqrt{2}}, \frac{1}{\sqrt{2}}\right)$ (b) $\left(\frac{1}{\sqrt{2}}, \frac{1}{\sqrt{2}}, \frac{1}{2}\right)$ (c) $\left(\frac{1}{2}, \frac{1}{\sqrt{2}}, \frac{1}{2}\right)$ (d) $\left(\frac{1}{2}, \frac{1}{2}, \frac{1}{\sqrt{2}}\right)$

---

47. Find the projection
(i) of the vector $\hat{i} + 3\hat{j} + 7\hat{k}$ on the vector $7\hat{i} - \hat{j} + 8\hat{k}$ is ________
(ii) of the vector $\hat{i} - \hat{j}$ on the vector $\hat{i} + \hat{j}$ is ________

TOPIC 7

Vector Product

48. Unit vector perpendicular to both $\vec{a}$ and $\vec{b}$ is ________

49. If $\vec{a} \times \vec{b} = 0$, then $\vec{a}$ and $\vec{b}$ are

(a) perpendicular (b) equal (c) collinear (d) parallel

---

50. If $|\vec{a} \times \vec{b}| = |\vec{a}||\vec{b}|$, then θ is equal to

(a) π (b) 0 (c) $\frac{\pi}{2}$ (d) $\frac{\pi}{4}$

51. The vectors $\vec{a}$ and $\vec{b}$ be such that $|\vec{a}| = 3$, $|\vec{b}| = \frac{\sqrt{2}}{3}$ and $\vec{a} \times \vec{b}$ is a unit vector, then the angle between $\vec{a}$ and $\vec{b}$ is

(a) $\frac{\pi}{6}$ (b) $\frac{\pi}{4}$ (c) $\frac{\pi}{3}$ (d) $\frac{\pi}{2}$

52. Which of the following is/are true?

(i) $\hat{i} \times \hat{j} = \hat{k}, \hat{j} \times \hat{k} = \hat{i}$ and $\hat{k} \times \hat{i} = \hat{j}$

(ii) $\hat{i} \times \hat{i} = 0, \hat{j} \times \hat{j} = 0$ and $\hat{k} \times \hat{k} = 0$

(iii) $\hat{j} \times \hat{i} = -\hat{k}, \hat{k} \times \hat{j} = -\hat{i}$ and $\hat{i} \times \hat{k} = -\hat{j}$

(a) Only (i) (b) Only (iii) (c) (i), (ii) and (iii) (d) (i) and (iii)

53. Find the value of $|\vec{a} \times \vec{b}|$, when the following vectors are given.

(i) $\vec{a} = \hat{i} - 7\hat{j} + 7\hat{k}$ and $\vec{b} = 3\hat{i} - 2\hat{j} + 2\hat{k}$ ________

(ii) $\vec{a} = 2\hat{i} - 2\hat{j}$ and $\vec{b} = \hat{i} - \hat{j} + \hat{k}$ ________

(iii) $\vec{a} = \hat{i}$ and $\vec{b} = \hat{k}$ ________

(iv) $\vec{a} = 2\sqrt{2}\hat{i} + \sqrt{2}\hat{j}$ and $\vec{b} = \hat{i} - 2\sqrt{2}\hat{j} + \hat{k}$ ________

54. If $\vec{a} = 3\hat{i} + 2\hat{j} + 2\hat{k}$ and $\vec{b} = \hat{i} + 2\hat{j} - 2\hat{k}$, then the unit vector perpendicular to each of the vectors $\vec{a} + \vec{b}$ and $\vec{a} - \vec{b}$ is

(a) $\pm\frac{1}{3}(\hat{i} - \hat{j} - \hat{k})$ (b) $\pm\frac{2}{3}\hat{i} \pm \frac{2}{3}\hat{j} \pm \frac{1}{3}\hat{k}$ (c) $\pm\frac{1}{3}(2\hat{i} - 2\hat{j} - \hat{k})$ (d) $\pm\frac{1}{3}(\hat{i} + \hat{j} - \hat{k})$

55. If A, B and C are the vertices of a triangle, then area is equal to

(a) $\frac{1}{2}|\overrightarrow{AB} \times \overrightarrow{AC}|$ (b) $\frac{1}{2}(\overrightarrow{AB} \cdot \overrightarrow{AC})$ (c) $\overrightarrow{AB} \times \overrightarrow{AC}$ (d) None of these

56. Find the area of the triangle, when its vertices are given below.

(i) $A(1, 1, 1)$, $B(1, 2, 3)$ and $C(2, 3, 1)$ ________

(ii) $A(1, -1, 1)$, $B(1, 0, 1)$ and $C(1, -1, 0)$ ________

(iii) $A(2, 1, 0)$, $B(-1, 0, 2)$ and $C(1, 1, 1)$ ________

57. If $\vec{a}$ and $\vec{b}$ are adjacent sides of a parallelogram, then area is equal to

(a) $|\vec{a} \times \vec{b}|$ (b) $\vec{a} \times \vec{b}$ (c) $\frac{1}{2}|\vec{a} \times \vec{b}|$ (d) $\frac{1}{2}|\vec{a} \times \vec{b}|$

---

58. The area of the parallelogram whose adjacent sides are determined by the vectors $\vec{a} = \hat{i} - \hat{j} + 3\hat{k}$ and $\vec{b} = 2\hat{i} - 7\hat{j} + \hat{k}$ is ______

59. If $(2\hat{i} + 6\hat{j} + 27\hat{k}) \times (\hat{i} + \lambda\hat{j} + \mu\hat{k}) = \vec{0}$, then λ and μ are equal to

(a) $\frac{27}{2}$ and 3 (b) 3 and $\frac{27}{2}$ (c) 4 and $\frac{17}{2}$ (d) 4 and $\frac{27}{2}$

Assertion-Reason Questions

The following questions consist of two statements – Assertion (A) and Reason (R). Answer these questions by selecting the appropriate options given below.
(a) Both A and R are true and R is the correct explanation of A.
(b) Both A and R are true but R is not the correct explanation of A.
(c) A is true but R is false.
(d) A is false but R is true.

1. Assertion (A) Two vectors $\vec{a} = 3\hat{i} - \hat{j} + 2\hat{k}$ and $\vec{b} = \hat{i} + 7\hat{j} + 2\hat{k}$ are perpendicular.

Reason (R) Two non-zero vectors are $\vec{a}$ and $\vec{b}$ are parallel if and only if $\vec{a} \times \vec{b} = 0$.

(a) ☐ (b) ☐ (c) ☐ (d) ☐

2. Assertion (A) Projection of the vector $\vec{a} = 2\hat{i} + 2\hat{j} + \hat{k}$ along $\vec{b} = \hat{i} + 3\hat{j} - \hat{k}$ is $\frac{7\sqrt{11}}{11}$.

Reason (R) Projection of $\vec{p}$ along $\vec{q} = \frac{\vec{p} \cdot \vec{q}}{|\vec{p}|}$.

(a) ☐ (b) ☐ (c) ☐ (d) ☐

3. Assertion (A) If two vectors $\vec{a} = x\hat{i} + \hat{j} + 3\hat{k}$ and $\vec{b} = 2\hat{i} + 3\hat{j} - y\hat{k}$ are parallel, then $x = \frac{2}{3}$ and $y = -\frac{9}{2}$.

Reason (R) Two vectors $\vec{a} = a_1\hat{i} + a_2\hat{j} + a_3\hat{k}$ and $\vec{b} = b_1\hat{i} + b_2\hat{j} + b_3\hat{k}$ are parallel if and only if, then $\frac{a_1}{b_1} = \frac{a_2}{b_2} = \frac{a_3}{b_3}$.

(a) ☐ (b) ☐ (c) ☐ (d) ☐

4. **Assertion** (A) Area of a triangle with two of adjacent sides as $\vec{a} = \hat{i} + \hat{j} + 2\hat{k}$ and $\vec{b} = 2\hat{i} - \hat{j} - \hat{k}$ is $\sqrt{35}$ units.

Reason (R) Area of a parallelogram with sides $\vec{a}$ and $\vec{b}$ is $|\vec{a} \times \vec{b}|$.

(a) ☐ (b) ☐ (c) ☐ (d) ☐

5. **Assertion** (A) Angle between the diagonals of a parallelogram with adjacent sides as $\vec{a} = 3\hat{i} + \hat{j} - \hat{k}$ and $\vec{b} = 2\hat{i} + \hat{j} + \hat{k}$ is $\frac{\pi}{3}$.

Reason (R) Two non-zero vectors $\vec{a}$ and $\vec{b}$ are perpendicular if $\vec{a} \cdot \vec{b} = 0$.

(a) ☐ (b) ☐ (c) ☐ (d) ☐

6. **Assertion** (A) Position vector of the point P which divides the vector joining the points $A\,(2\vec{a} + \vec{b})$ and $B\,(3\vec{a} + 2\vec{b})$, externally in the ratio $3:2$ is $5\vec{a} + 4\vec{b}$.

Reason (R) For three points $A\,(2\vec{a} + \vec{b})$, $B\,(3\vec{a} + 2\vec{b})$ and $P\,(5\vec{a} + 4\vec{b})$. B is the mid-point of vector AP.

(a) ☐ (b) ☐ (c) ☐ (d) ☐

7. **Assertion** (A) If $\vec{a}, \vec{b}$ and $\vec{c}$ are unit vectors such that $\vec{a} + \vec{b} + \vec{c} = 0$, then $\vec{a} \cdot \vec{b} + \vec{b} \cdot \vec{c} + \vec{c} \cdot \vec{a} = -\frac{3}{2}$.

Reason (R) $(\vec{x} + \vec{y})^2 = \vec{x}^2 + \vec{y}^2 + 2\vec{x} \cdot \vec{y}$.

(a) ☐ (b) ☐ (c) ☐ (d) ☐

8. **Assertion** (A) If the magnitude of displacement is zero, then it is not a vector quantity.

Reason (R) A vector have both magnitude and direction.

(a) ☐ (b) ☐ (c) ☐ (d) ☐

9. **Assertion** (A) Two vectors are said to be like vectors, if they have the same direction but different magnitude.

Reason (R) Vector quantities do not have a specific direction.

(a) ☐ (b) ☐ (c) ☐ (d) ☐

10. **Assertion** (A) If $a_1 = x\hat{i} - \hat{j} + \hat{k}$ and $a_2 = \hat{i} + y\hat{j} + z\hat{k}$ are collinear, then a possible unit vector parallel to the vector $x\hat{i} + y\hat{j} + z\hat{k}$ is $\frac{1}{\sqrt{3}}(\hat{i} - \hat{j} + \hat{k})$.

Reason (R) If A_1 and A_2 are collinear, then $\frac{a_1}{b_1} = \frac{a_2}{b_2} = \frac{a_3}{b_3}$.

(a) ☐ (b) ☐ (c) ☐ (d) ☐

Case Based Questions

Case 1 Teams A, B and C went for playing a tug of war game. Teams A, B and C have attached a rope to metal ring and is trying to pull the ring into their own area (force applied on point by team is shown below)

Team A pulls with force $F_1 = 4\hat{i} + 0\hat{j}$ KN

Team $B \rightarrow F_2 = -2\hat{i} + 4\hat{j}$ KN

Team $C \rightarrow F_3 = -3\hat{i} - 3\hat{j}$ KN

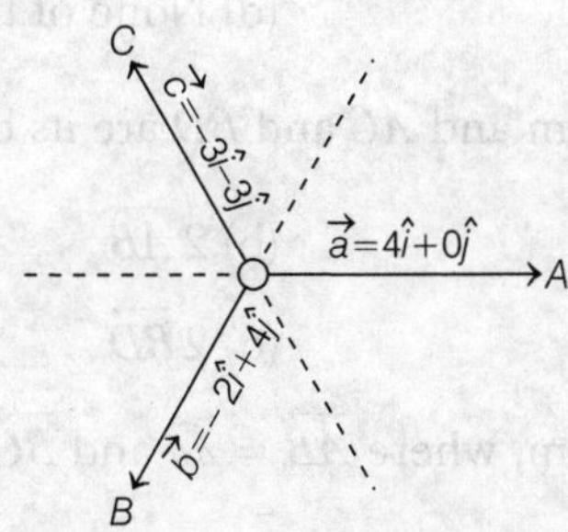

Based on the above information, answer the following questions.

(i) Which team will win the game

(a) Team B ☐ (b) Team A ☐

(c) Team C ☐ (d) No one ☐

(ii) What is the magnitude of the teams combined force?

(a) 7 KN ☐ (b) 1.4 KN ☐

(c) 1.5 KN ☐ (d) 2 KN ☐

(iii) In what direction is the ring getting pulled?

(a) 2.0 radian ☐ (b) 2.5 radian ☐

(c) 2.4 radian ☐ (d) 3 radian ☐

(iv) What is the magnitude of the force of Team B?

(a) $2\sqrt{5}$ KN ☐ (b) 6 KN ☐

(c) 2 KN ☐ (d) 4 KN ☐

Case 2 If two vectors are represented by the two sides of triangle taken in order, then their sum is represented by the third side of the triangle taken in opposite order and this is known as triangle law of vector addition.

Based on the above information, answer the following questions.

(i) If $\vec{p}, \vec{q}, \vec{r}$ are the vectors represented by the sides of a triangle taken in order, then $\vec{q} + \vec{r} =$

(a) $\vec{p}$ ☐ (b) $2\vec{p}$ ☐

(c) $-\vec{p}$ ☐ (d) None of these ☐

(ii) If *ABCD* is a parallelogram and *AC* and *BD* are its diagonals, then $\overrightarrow{AC} + \overrightarrow{BD}$ is equal to

(a) $2\overrightarrow{DA}$ ☐ (b) $2\overrightarrow{AB}$ ☐

(c) $2\overrightarrow{BC}$ ☐ (d) $2\overrightarrow{BD}$ ☐

(iii) If *ABCD* is a parallelogram, where $\overrightarrow{AB} = 2\vec{a}$ and $\overrightarrow{BC} = 2\vec{b}$, then $\overrightarrow{AC} - \overrightarrow{BD}$ is equal to

(a) $3\vec{a}$ ☐ (b) $4\vec{a}$ ☐

(c) $2\vec{b}$ ☐ (d) $4\vec{b}$ ☐

(iv) If *ABCD* is a quadrilateral whose diagonals are $\overrightarrow{AC}$ and $\overrightarrow{BD}$, then $\overrightarrow{BA} + \overrightarrow{CD}$ is equal to

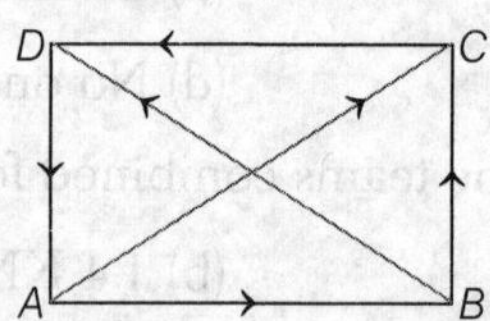

(a) $\overrightarrow{AC} + \overrightarrow{DB}$ ☐ (b) $\overrightarrow{AC} + \overrightarrow{BD}$ ☐

(c) $\overrightarrow{BC} + \overrightarrow{AD}$ ☐ (d) $\overrightarrow{BD} + \overrightarrow{CA}$ ☐

COMPETITION EDGE UP

1. Let $\vec{a} = \hat{i} + 2\hat{j} + 3\hat{k}, \vec{b} = 2\hat{i} + 3\hat{j} - 5\hat{k}$ and $\vec{c} = 3\hat{i} - \hat{j} + \lambda\hat{k}$ be three vectors.

Let r be a unit vector along b + c. If $r \cdot a = 3$, then 3λ is equal to **[JEE Main 2024]**

(a) 27 ☐
(b) 30 ☐
(c) 25 ☐
(d) 21 ☐

2. For $\lambda > 0$, let θ be the angle between the vectors $\vec{a} = \hat{i} + \lambda\hat{j} - 3\hat{k}$ and $\vec{a} = 3\hat{i} - \hat{j} + 2\hat{k}$.

If the vectors $\vec{a} + \vec{b}$ and $\vec{a} - \vec{b}$ are mutually perpendicular, then the value of $(14\cos\theta)^2$ is equal to **[JEE Main 2024]**

(a) 20 ☐
(b) 50 ☐
(c) 40 ☐
(d) 25 ☐

3. Let $\vec{a} = \hat{i} + \alpha\hat{j} + \beta\hat{k}, \alpha, \beta \in R$. Let a vector b be such that the angle between a and b is $\frac{\pi}{4}$ and $|b|^2 = 6$. If $a \cdot b = 3\sqrt{2}$, then the value of $(\alpha^2 + \beta^2)\,|a \times b|^2$ is equal to **[JEE Main 2024]**

(a) 90 ☐
(b) 85 ☐
(c) 95 ☐
(d) 75 ☐

4. Let P(3, 2, 3), Q(4, 6, 2) and R(7, 3, 2) be the vertices of ΔPQR. Then, the $\angle QPR$ is **[JEE Main 2024]**

(a) $\frac{\pi}{6}$ ☐
(b) $\cos^{-1}\left(\frac{1}{18}\right)$ ☐
(c) $\cos^{-1}\left(\frac{7}{18}\right)$ ☐
(d) $\frac{\pi}{3}$ ☐

5. An arc PQ of a circle subtends a right angle at its centre O. The mid-point of the arc PQ is R. If OP = u, OR = v and $OQ = \alpha u + \beta v$, then α, β^2 are the roots of the equation **[JEE Main 2024]**

(a) $3x^2 - 2x - 1 = 0$ ☐
(b) $3x^2 + 2x - 1 = 0$ ☐
(c) $x^2 - x - 2 = 0$ ☐
(d) $x^2 + x - 2 = 0$ ☐

6. Let the position vectors of the vertices A, B and C of a triangle be $2\hat{i} + 2\hat{j} + \hat{k}$, $\hat{i} + 2\hat{j} + 2\hat{k}$ and $2\hat{i} + \hat{j} + 2\hat{k}$, respectively. Let l_1, l_2 and l_3 be the lengths of perpendiculars drawn from the orthocenter of the triangle on the sides AB, BC and CA respectively, then $l_1^2 + l_2^2 + l_3^2$ equals **[JEE Main 2024]**

(a) $\frac{1}{5}$ ☐
(b) $\frac{1}{4}$ ☐
(c) $\frac{1}{3}$ ☐
(d) $\frac{1}{2}$ ☐

7. The position vectors of the vertices A, B and C of a triangle are $2\hat{i} - 3\hat{j} + 3\hat{k}$, $2\hat{i} + 2\hat{j} + 3\hat{k}$ and $-\hat{i} + \hat{j} + 3\hat{k}$, respectively. Let l denotes the length of the angle bisector AD of $\angle BAC$, where D is on the line segment BC, then $2l^2$ equals **[JEE Main 2024]**

(a) 49 ☐
(b) 42 ☐
(c) 45 ☐
(d) 50 ☐

8. If the points with position vectors $\alpha\hat{i} + 10\hat{j} + 13\hat{k}, 6\hat{i} + 11\hat{j} + 11\hat{k}$, $\frac{9}{2}\hat{i} + \beta\hat{j} - 8\hat{k}$ are collinear, then $(19\alpha - 6\beta)^2$ is equal to **[JEE Main 2024]**

(a) 36 ☐
(b) 25 ☐
(c) 49 ☐
(d) 16 ☐

9. If the points P and Q are respectively the circumcenter and the orthocentre of a ΔABC, then $PA + PB + PC$ is equal to **[JEE Main 2024]**

(a) $\overrightarrow{PQ}$ ☐

(b) $2\overrightarrow{QP}$ ☐

(c) $\overrightarrow{QP}$ ☐

(d) $2\overrightarrow{PQ}$ ☐

10. Let ABCD be a quadrilateral. If E and F are the mid-points of the diagonals AC and BD respectively and $(\overrightarrow{AB} - \overrightarrow{BC}) + (\overrightarrow{AD} - \overrightarrow{DC}) = k\,\overrightarrow{FE}$, then k is equal to **[JEE Main 2024]**

(a) 4 ☐

(b) − 4 ☐

(c) − 2 ☐

(d) 2 ☐

11. For any vector $\vec{a} = a_1\hat{i} + a_2\hat{j} + a_3\hat{k}$, with $10|a_i| < 1, i = 1, 2, 3$, consider the following statements

(A) $\max\{|a_1|, |a_2|, |a_3|\} \le |a|$

(B) $|a| \le 3\max\{|a_1|, |a_2|, |a_3|\}$

[JEE Main 2024]

(a) Neither (A) nor (B) is true. ☐

(b) Both (A) and (B) are true. ☐

(c) Only (B) is true. ☐

(d) Only (A) is true. ☐

12. Let $\vec{a}, \vec{b}$ and $\vec{c}$ be three non-zero vectors such that $\vec{b}$ and $\vec{c}$ are non-collinear. If $\vec{a} + 5\vec{b}$ is collinear with $\vec{c}$, $\vec{b} + 6\vec{c}$ is collinear with $\vec{a}$ and $\vec{a} + \alpha\vec{b} + \beta\vec{c} = 0$, then $\alpha + \beta$ is equal to **[JEE Main 2024]**

(a) −25 ☐

(b) 35 ☐

(c) 30 ☐

(d) −30 ☐

13. The set of all α, for which the vectors $\vec{a} = \alpha t\hat{i} + 6\hat{j} - 3\hat{k}$ and $\vec{b} = t\hat{i} - 2\hat{j} - 2\alpha t\hat{k}$ are inclined at an obtuse angle for all $t \in R$ is **[JEE Main 2024]**

(a) $(-2, 0]$ ☐

(b) $\left(-\frac{4}{3}, 0\right]$ ☐

(c) $[0, 1)$ ☐

(d) $\left(-\frac{4}{3}, 1\right)$ ☐

14. Let a unit vector which makes an angles of 60° with $2\hat{i} + 2\hat{j} - \hat{k}$ and an angle of 45° with $\hat{i} - \hat{k}$ be c.

Then, $\vec{c} + \left(-\frac{1}{2}\hat{i} + \frac{1}{3\sqrt{2}}\hat{j} - \frac{\sqrt{2}}{3}\hat{k}\right)$ is **[JEE Main 2024]**

(a) $\left(\frac{1}{\sqrt{3}} + \frac{1}{2}\right)\hat{i} + \left(\frac{1}{\sqrt{3}} - \frac{1}{3\sqrt{2}}\right)\hat{j} + \left(\frac{1}{\sqrt{3}} + \frac{\sqrt{2}}{3}\right)\hat{k}$ ☐

(b) $-\frac{\sqrt{2}}{3}\hat{i} + \frac{\sqrt{2}}{3}\hat{j} + \left(\frac{1}{2} + \frac{2\sqrt{2}}{3}\right)\hat{k}$ ☐

(c) $\frac{\sqrt{2}}{3}\hat{i} - \frac{1}{2}\hat{k}$ ☐

(d) $\frac{\sqrt{2}}{3}\hat{i} + \frac{1}{3\sqrt{2}}\hat{j} - \frac{1}{2}\hat{k}$ ☐

15. Consider a ΔABC where A(1, 3, 2), B (−2, 8, 0) and C (3, 6, 7). If the angle bisector of $\angle BAC$ meets the line BC at D, then the length of the projection of the vector AD on the vector AC is **[JEE Main 2024]**

(a) $\frac{39}{2\sqrt{38}}$ ☐

(b) $\frac{\sqrt{38}}{2}$ ☐

(c) $\sqrt{19}$ ☐

(d) $\frac{37}{2\sqrt{38}}$ ☐

Scan this QR code from your mobile phone to get the solutions of **Competition Edge Up** of this chapter.

Chapter 11

Three Dimensional Geometry

Scan and take Chapter Test

TOPIC 1

Direction Cosine and Direction Ratio

1. The relation between the direction cosines of a line is ______

2. If a line makes angles α, β, γ with positive direction of coordinate axes, then

$\sin^2 \alpha + \sin^2 \beta + \sin^2 \gamma$ ______

3. Find direction cosines.

(i) If a line makes an angle 90°, 60°, 30° with the X, Y and Z-axes, respectively.

______

(ii) If a line has the direction ratios – 18, 12, – 4.

______

4. The direction ratio of a line joining points $P(x_1, y_1, z_1)$ and $Q(x_2, y_2, z_2)$ may be taken as

______

5. The direction cosines of the line segment joining point $P(x_1, y_1, z_1)$ and $Q(x_2, y_2, z_2)$ is

______

6. The direction cosines of a line passing through the given points are

(i) $(-2, 4, -5)$ and $(1, 2, 3)$ ______

(ii) $(2, -4, 6)$ and $(2, 3, 4)$ ______

7. The direction cosines of X-axis, Y-axis and Z-axis are ______

8. $A(2, 3, -4)$, $B(1, -2, 3)$ and $C(3, 8, -11)$ are collinear.

True ☐ False ☐

*Concepts of all questions bearing * are important for JEE & CUET*

TOPIC 2

Line in Three Dimensional Geometry

NCERT Pg 381-389

9. The vector equation of the line through the point (5, 2, – 4) and which is parallel to the vector $3\hat{i} + 2\hat{j} - 8\hat{k}$ is

(a) $\vec{r} = 5\hat{i} + 2\hat{j} + 4\hat{k} + \lambda(3\hat{i} + 2\hat{j} + 8\hat{k})$
(b) $\vec{r} = 5\hat{i} + 2\hat{j} - 4\hat{k} - \lambda(3\hat{i} + 2\hat{j} + 8\hat{k})$
(c) $\vec{r} = 5\hat{i} + 2\hat{j} - 4\hat{k} + \lambda(3\hat{i} + 2\hat{j} - 8\hat{k})$
(d) $\vec{r} = 5\hat{i} - 2\hat{j} - 4\hat{k} + \lambda(3\hat{i} + 2\hat{j} + 8\hat{k})$

10. The cartesian equation of the line through the point (1, 2, –3) and which is parallel to the vector $3\hat{i} + 2\hat{j} - 2\hat{k}$ is ________

11. Match the following.

	Column I		Column II
A.	The line through the points (1, –1, 2), (3, 4, – 2) and the line through the points (0, 3, 2), (3, 5, 6)	1.	Perpendicular lines
B.	The line through the points (4, 7, 8), (2, 3, 4) and the line through the points (– 1, – 2, 1) (1, 2, 5) are	2.	Parallel lines
C.	The three lines with direction cosines $\frac{12}{13}, \frac{-3}{13}, \frac{-4}{13}; \frac{4}{13}, \frac{12}{13}, \frac{3}{13}$ and $\frac{3}{13}, \frac{-4}{13}, \frac{12}{13}$ are	3.	Mutually perpendicular lines

Choose the correct option.

(a) A → 2, B → 1, C → 3
(b) A → 1, B → 2, C → 3
(c) A → 3, B → 2, C → 1
(d) None of these

12. Write the vector equation of the given lines

(i) $\frac{x+3}{2} = \frac{y-5}{4} = \frac{z+6}{2}$ ________

(ii) $\frac{5-x}{3} = \frac{y+4}{7} = \frac{z-6}{2}$ ________

13. The cartesian equation of the line passes through the point (– 2, 4, – 5) and parallel to the given line $\frac{x+3}{3} = \frac{y-4}{5} = \frac{z+8}{6}$ is

(a) $\frac{x+3}{3} = \frac{y-4}{5} = \frac{z+8}{6}$
(b) $\frac{x-2}{3} = \frac{y-4}{5} = \frac{z+5}{6}$
(c) $\frac{x+2}{3} = \frac{y-4}{5} = \frac{z+5}{6}$
(d) None of these

14. Find the angle between the given pair of lines

(i) $\vec{r} = 3\hat{i} + 2\hat{j} - 4\hat{k} + \lambda(\hat{i} + 2\hat{j} + 2\hat{k})$ and $\vec{r} = 5\hat{i} - 2\hat{j} + \mu(3\hat{i} + 2\hat{j} + 6\hat{k})$ ________

(ii) $\dfrac{x+3}{3} = \dfrac{y-1}{5} = \dfrac{z+3}{4}$ and $\dfrac{x+1}{1} = \dfrac{y-4}{1} = \dfrac{z-5}{2}$ ________

***15.** If the angle between the pair of lines $\dfrac{1-x}{3} = \dfrac{7y-14}{2p} = \dfrac{z-3}{2}$ and $\dfrac{7-7x}{3p} = \dfrac{y-5}{1} = \dfrac{6-z}{5}$ is right angle, then the value of p is ________

***16.** The shortest distance between the lines whose vector equations are

(i) $\vec{r} = \hat{i} + \hat{j} + \lambda(2\hat{i} - \hat{j} + \hat{k})$ and $\vec{r} = 2\hat{i} + \hat{j} - \hat{k} + \mu(3\hat{i} - 5\hat{j} + 2\hat{k})$ is ________

(ii) $\vec{r} = 2\hat{i} - 5\hat{j} + \hat{k} + \lambda(3\hat{i} + 2\hat{j} + 6\hat{k})$ and $\vec{r} = 7\hat{i} - 6\hat{k} + \mu(\hat{i} + 2\hat{j} + 2\hat{k})$ is ________

***17.** The distance between the lines $\vec{r} = \hat{i} + 2\hat{j} - 4\hat{k} + \lambda(2\hat{i} + 3\hat{j} + 6\hat{k})$ and $\vec{r} = 3\hat{i} + 3\hat{j} - 5\hat{k} - \mu(2\hat{i} + 3\hat{j} + 6\hat{k})$ is ________

***18.** The shortest distance between the lines whose cartesian equation are

(i) $\dfrac{x+1}{7} = \dfrac{y+1}{-6} = \dfrac{z+1}{1}$ and $\dfrac{x-3}{1} = \dfrac{y-5}{-2} = \dfrac{z-7}{1}$ is ________

(ii) $\dfrac{x-1}{6} = \dfrac{y-1}{7} = \dfrac{z-1}{1}$ and $\dfrac{x+3}{1} = \dfrac{y+5}{2} = \dfrac{z-7}{1}$ is ________

Assertion-Reason Questions

The following questions consist of two statements-Assertion (A) and Reason (R). Answer these questions by selecting the appropriate option given below.
(a) Both A and R are true and R is correct explanation of A.
(b) Both A and R are true, but R is not the correct explanation of A
(c) A is true but R is false.
(d) A is false but R is true.

1. Assertion (A) Direction cosines of a line are the cosines of the angels made by the line with the negative directions of the coordinate axes.

Reason (R) The acute angle between the lines $x - 2 = 0$ and $\sqrt{3x} - y - 2$ is 30.

(a) ☐ (b) ☐ (c) ☐ (d) ☐

2. Assertion (A) The points $A(2, 3, -4)$, $B(1, -2, 3)$ and $C(3, 8, -11)$ are collinear.

Reason (R) If a line makes 90°, 135°, 45° with the X, Y and Z-axes, respectively, then its direction cosines are $0, \dfrac{-1}{2}$ and $\dfrac{1}{\sqrt{2}}$.

(a) ☐ (b) ☐ (c) ☐ (d) ☐

3. **Assertion** (A) If a line has direction ratios −2, 1,− 2, then its direction cosines are $\frac{-2}{3}, \frac{1}{3}, \frac{-2}{3}$.

Reason (R) If a, b and c are the direction ratios of a line, then its direction cosines are

$$\frac{a}{\sqrt{a^2+b^2+c^2}}, \frac{b}{\sqrt{a^2+b^2+c^2}}, \frac{c}{\sqrt{a^2+b^2+c^2}}$$

(a) ☐ (b) ☐ (c) ☐ (d) ☐

4. **Assertion** (A) The cartesian equation of line passing through the points $A(-1, 1, 2)$ and $B(2, 4, 5)$, is $\frac{x+1}{3} = \frac{y-1}{4} = \frac{z-2}{5}$

Reason (R) The cartesian equation of a line passing through the two points A (x_1, y_1, z_1) and B (x_2, y_2, z_2) is given by $\frac{x-x_1}{x_2-x_1} = \frac{y-y_1}{y_2-y_1} = \frac{z-z_1}{z_2-z_1}$

(a) ☐ (b) ☐ (c) ☐ (d) ☐

5. **Assertion** (A) The shortest distance between the lines $\vec{r} = -\hat{i} + 4\hat{j} + 3\hat{k} + \lambda(4\hat{i} + \hat{j} + \hat{k})$ and $\vec{r} = -4\hat{i} + \hat{j} + \mu(5\hat{i} + 2\hat{j} + \hat{k})$ is zero.

Reason (R) The shortest distance between two lines $\vec{r} = \vec{a_1} + \lambda \vec{b_1}$ and $\vec{r} = \vec{a_2} + \mu \vec{b_2}$ is zero if $(\vec{a}_2 - \vec{a}_1) \cdot (\vec{b}_1 \times \vec{b}_2) = 0$.

(a) ☐ (b) ☐ (c) ☐ (d) ☐

6. **Assertion** (A) P is a point on the line segment joining the points (3, 2, −1) and (6, −4, − 2). If x coordinate of P is 5, then its y coordinate is −2.

Reason (R) The two lines $x = ay + b, z = cy + d$ and $x = a'y + b', z = c'y + d'$ will be perpendicular, if $aa' + bb' + cc' = 0$.

(a) ☐ (b) ☐ (c) ☐ (d) ☐

7. **Assertion** (A) The vector equation of line passing through the points (−1, 0, 2) and (3, 4, 6) is $-\hat{i} + 2\hat{k} + \lambda(4\hat{i} + 4\hat{j} + 4\hat{k})$.

Reason (R) The vector equation of line passing through $\vec{a}$ and $\vec{b}$ is $\vec{r} = \vec{a} + \lambda(\vec{b} - \vec{a})$.

(a) ☐ (b) ☐ (c) ☐ (d) ☐

8. **Assertion** (A) Vector form of the equation of a line $\frac{x-2}{3} = \frac{y-1}{2} = \frac{3-z}{-1}$ is $\vec{r} = (2\hat{i} + \hat{j} + 3\hat{k}) + \lambda(3\hat{i} + 2\hat{j} + \hat{k})$.

Reason (R) Cartesian equation of a line passing through the point (2, 1, 3) and parallel to the line $\frac{x-3}{1} = \frac{y-2}{2} = \frac{z-4}{-2}$ is $2x - 4 = y - 1 = 3 - z$.

(a) ☐ (b) ☐ (c) ☐ (d) ☐

9. **Assertion** (A) Equation of a line passing through the point (1, 1, 0) and parallel to the vector $\hat{i} + \hat{j} + \hat{k}$ is $\vec{r} = (\hat{i} + \hat{j}) + \lambda(\hat{i} + \hat{j} + \hat{k})$.

Reason (R) Position vector of a point (a, b, c) is $a\hat{i} + b\hat{j} + c\hat{k}$ and vector equation of a line passing through the point with position vector $\vec{a}$ and parallel to the vector $\vec{b}$ is $\vec{r} = \vec{a} + \lambda\vec{b}$.

(a) ☐ (b) ☐ (c) ☐ (d) ☐

10. **Assertion** (A) Two lines $\vec{r} = (\hat{i} + \hat{j} + 2\hat{k}) + \lambda(2\hat{i} - \hat{j} + 3\hat{k})$ and $\vec{r} = (\hat{i} + \hat{j}) + \mu(6\hat{i} - 3\hat{j} + 9\hat{k})$ are parallel.

Reason (R) Two lines are parallel if the vector product of their direction vectors is zero.

(a) ☐ (b) ☐ (c) ☐ (d) ☐

Case Based Questions

Case 1 Two motor cycles A and B are running at the speed more than allowed speed on the road along the lines $\vec{r} = \lambda(\hat{i} + 2\hat{j} - \hat{k})$ and $\vec{r} = 3\hat{i} + 3\hat{j} + \mu(2\hat{i} + \hat{j} + \hat{k})$.

Based on the above information, answer the following questions.

(i) The cartesian equation of the line along which motor cycle *A* is running, is

(a) $\frac{x+1}{1} = \frac{y+1}{2} = \frac{z-1}{-1}$ ☐ (b) $\frac{x}{1} = \frac{y}{2} = \frac{z}{-1}$ ☐

(c) $\frac{x}{1} = \frac{y}{2} = \frac{z}{1}$ ☐ (d) None of these ☐

(ii) The direction cosines of the line along which motor cycle *A* is running, are

(a) <1, –2, 1> ☐ (b) $< \frac{1}{\sqrt{6}}, \frac{-2}{\sqrt{6}}, \frac{1}{\sqrt{6}}$. ☐

(c) $< \frac{1}{\sqrt{6}}, \frac{2}{\sqrt{6}}, \frac{-1}{\sqrt{6}}$ ☐ (d) < 1, 2, – 1> ☐

(iii) The direction ratios of line along which motor cycle *B* is running, are

(a) < 1, 0, 2 > ☐ (b) < 1, 1, 2 > ☐

(c) < 2, 1, 1 > ☐ (d) < 2, 1, 0 > ☐

(iv) The shortest distance between the given lines is

(a) 0 unit ☐ (b) 4 units ☐

(c) $2\sqrt{3}$ units ☐ (d) $5\sqrt{2}$ units ☐

Case 2 In a diamond exhibition, a diamond is covered in cubical glass box having coordinates *O* (0, 0, 0), *A* (1, 0, 0), *B* (1, 2, 0), *C* (0, 2, 0), *O* (0, 0, 3), *A′* (1, 0, 3), *B′* (1, 2, 3) and C′ (0, 2, 3)

Based on the above information, answer the following questions.

(i) Find the direction ratio of *OA*. ________________

(ii) Find the equation of diagonal *OB′* ________________

(iii) Find the direction cosines of *AB*. ________________

COMPETITION EDGE UP

1. The shortest distance between the lines

$$\frac{x-3}{4}=\frac{y+7}{-11}=\frac{z-1}{5} \text{ and } \frac{x-5}{3}=\frac{y-9}{-6}=\frac{z+2}{1} \text{ is}$$

[JEE Main 2024]

(a) $\frac{178}{\sqrt{563}}$ ☐
(b) $\frac{185}{\sqrt{563}}$ ☐
(c) $\frac{179}{\sqrt{563}}$ ☐
(d) $\frac{187}{\sqrt{563}}$ ☐

2. If the shortest distance between the lines

$L_1 : \vec{r} = (2+\lambda)\hat{i} + (1-3\lambda)\hat{j} + (3+4\lambda)\hat{k}, \lambda \in R$

$L_2 : \vec{r} = 2(1+\mu)\hat{i} + 3(1+\mu)\hat{j} + (5+\mu)\hat{k}, \mu \in R$

is $\frac{m}{\sqrt{n}}$, where gcd $(m, n) = 1$, then the value of $m + n$ equals **[JEE Main 2024]**

(a) 387 ☐
(b) 377 ☐
(c) 384 ☐
(d) 390 ☐

3. The shortest distance between the lines

$$\frac{x-3}{2}=\frac{y+15}{-7}=\frac{z-9}{5} \text{ and } \frac{x+1}{2}=\frac{y-1}{1}=\frac{z-9}{-3} \text{ is}$$

[JEE Main 2024]

(a) $5\sqrt{3}$ ☐
(b) $4\sqrt{3}$ ☐
(c) $8\sqrt{3}$ ☐
(d) $6\sqrt{3}$ ☐

4. Let (α, β, γ) be the image of the point $(8, 5, 7)$ in the line

$$\frac{x-1}{2}=\frac{y+1}{3}=\frac{z-2}{5}.$$

Then, $\alpha+\beta+\gamma$ is equal **[JEE Main 2024]**

(a) 16 ☐
(b) 14 ☐
(c) 18 ☐
(d) 20 ☐

5. If the line $\frac{2-x}{3}=\frac{3y-2}{4\lambda+1}=4-z$ makes a right angle with the line $\frac{x+3}{3\mu}=\frac{1-2y}{6}=\frac{5-z}{7}$, then $4\lambda+9\mu$ is equal to **[JEE Main 2024]**

(a) 13 ☐
(b) 6 ☐
(c) 4 ☐
(d) 5 ☐

6. Let the point on the line passing through the points $P(1, -2, 3)$ and $Q(5, -4, 7)$, farther from the origin and at a distance of 9 units from the point P be (α, β, γ). Then, $\alpha^2+\beta^2+\gamma^2$ is equal to **[JEE Main 2024]**

(a) 155 ☐
(b) 165 ☐
(c) 150 ☐
(d) 160 ☐

7. If the shortest distance between the lines $\frac{x-\lambda}{-2}=\frac{y-2}{1}=\frac{z-1}{1}$ and $\frac{x-\sqrt{3}}{1}=\frac{y-1}{-2}=\frac{z-2}{1}$ is 1, then the sum of all possible values of λ is **[JEE Main 2024]**

(a) 13 ☐
(b) 6 ☐
(c) 4 ☐
(d) 5 ☐

8. Let (α, β, γ) be the mirror image of the point $(2, 3, 5)$ in the line $\frac{x-1}{2}=\frac{y-2}{3}=\frac{z-3}{4}$. Then, $2\alpha+3\beta+4\gamma$ is equal to **[JEE Main 2024]**

(a) 34 ☐
(b) 31 ☐
(c) 33 ☐
(d) 32 ☐

9. Consider the line L passing through the points (1, 2, 3) and (2, 3, 5). The distance of the point $\left(\frac{11}{3}, \frac{11}{3}, \frac{19}{3}\right)$ from the line L along the line $\frac{3x-11}{2} = \frac{3y-11}{1} = \frac{3z-19}{2}$ is equal to **[JEE Main 2024]**

(a) 3 ☐
(b) 5 ☐
(c) 6 ☐
(d) 4 ☐

10. If the shortest distance between the lines $\frac{x-\lambda}{2} = \frac{y-4}{3} = \frac{z-3}{4}$ and $\frac{x-2}{4} = \frac{y-4}{6} = \frac{z-7}{8}$ is $\frac{13}{\sqrt{29}}$, then a value of λ is **[JEE Main 2024]**

(a) $\frac{13}{25}$ ☐
(b) $-\frac{13}{25}$ ☐
(c) 1 ☐
(d) −1 ☐

11. Let d be the distance of the point of intersection of the lines $\frac{x+6}{3} = \frac{y}{2} = \frac{z+1}{1}$ and $\frac{x-7}{4} = \frac{y-9}{3} = \frac{z-4}{2}$ from the point (7, 8, 9). Then, $d^2 + 6$ is equal to **[JEE Main 2024]**

(a) 72 ☐
(b) 78 ☐
(c) 69 ☐
(d) 75 ☐

12. The shortest distance between lines L_1 and L_2, where $L_1 : \frac{x-1}{2} = \frac{y+1}{-3} = \frac{z+4}{2}$ and L_2 is the line passing through the points A(− 4, 4, 3), B(− 1, 6, 3) and perpendicular to the line $\frac{x-3}{-2} = \frac{y}{3} = \frac{z-1}{1}$ is **[JEE Main 2024]**

(a) $\frac{121}{\sqrt{221}}$ ☐
(b) $\frac{24}{\sqrt{117}}$ ☐
(c) $\frac{42}{\sqrt{117}}$ ☐
(d) $\frac{141}{\sqrt{221}}$ ☐

13. If the shortest distance between the lines $\frac{x-4}{1} = \frac{y+1}{2} = \frac{z}{-3}$ and $\frac{x-\lambda}{2} = \frac{y+1}{4} = \frac{z-2}{-5}$ is $\frac{6}{\sqrt{5}}$, then the sum of all possible values of λ is **[JEE Main 2024]**

(a) 7 ☐
(b) 8 ☐
(c) 5 ☐
(d) 10 ☐

14. The distance of the point (7, − 2, 11) from the line $\frac{x-6}{1} = \frac{y-4}{0} = \frac{z-8}{3}$ along the line $\frac{x-5}{2} = \frac{y-1}{-3} = \frac{z-5}{6}$, is **[JEE Main 2024]**

(a) 14 ☐
(b) 12 ☐
(c) 18 ☐
(d) 21 ☐

15. Let the line L intersect the lines $x-2 = -y = z-1$, $2(x+1) = 2(y-1) = z+1$ and be parallel to the lines $\frac{x-2}{3} = \frac{y-1}{1} = \frac{z-2}{2}$. Then, which of the following points lies on L? **[JEE Main 2024]**

(a) $\left(-\frac{1}{3}, -1, -1\right)$ ☐
(b) $\left(-\frac{1}{3}, -1, 1\right)$ ☐
(c) $\left(-\frac{1}{3}, 1, 1\right)$ ☐
(d) $\left(-\frac{1}{3}, 1, -1\right)$ ☐

16. Let $P(\alpha, \beta, \gamma)$ be the image of the point $Q(3, -3, 1)$ in the line $\frac{x-0}{1} = \frac{y-3}{1} = \frac{z-1}{-1}$ and R be the point $(2, 5, -1)$. If the area of the ΔPQR is λ and $\lambda^2 = 14K$, then K equal to **[JEE Main 2024]**

(a) 18 ☐
(b) 72 ☐
(c) 36 ☐
(d) 81 ☐

17. Let P be the point of intersection of the lines $\frac{x-2}{1} = \frac{y-4}{5} = \frac{z-2}{1}$ and $\frac{x-3}{2} = \frac{y-2}{3} = \frac{z-3}{2}$. Then, the shortest distance of P from the line $4x = 2y = z$ is **[JEE Main 2024]**

(a) $\frac{3\sqrt{14}}{7}$ ☐
(b) $\frac{\sqrt{14}}{7}$ ☐
(c) $\frac{5\sqrt{14}}{7}$ ☐
(d) $\frac{6\sqrt{14}}{7}$ ☐

18. If the mirror image of the point $P(3, 4, 9)$ in the line $\frac{x-1}{3} = \frac{y+1}{2} = \frac{z-2}{1}$ is (α, β, γ), then $14(\alpha + \beta + \gamma)$ is **[JEE Main 2024]**

(a) 132 ☐
(b) 138 ☐
(c) 108 ☐
(d) 102 ☐

19. The distance of the point $Q(0, 2, -2)$ form the line passing through the point $P(5, -4, 3)$ and perpendicular to the lines $\vec{r} = (-3\hat{i} + 2\hat{k}) + \lambda(2\hat{i} + 3\hat{j} + 5\hat{k})$, $\lambda \in R$ and $\vec{r} = (\hat{i} - 2\hat{j} + \hat{k}) + \mu(-\hat{i} + 3\hat{j} + 2\hat{k}), \mu \in R$ is **[JEE Main 2024]**

(a) $\sqrt{20}$ ☐
(b) $\sqrt{86}$ ☐
(c) $\sqrt{54}$ ☐
(d) $\sqrt{74}$ ☐

20. Let a line l pass through the origin and be perpendicular to the lines $\vec{r} = (\hat{i} - 11\hat{j} - 7\hat{k}) + \lambda(\hat{i} + 2\hat{j} + 3\hat{k})$, $\lambda \in R$ and l_2: $\vec{r} = (-\hat{i} + \hat{k}) + \mu(2\hat{i} + 2\hat{j} + \hat{k}), \mu \in R$.

If P is the point of intersection of l and l_1, and $Q(\alpha, \beta, \gamma)$ is the foot of perpendicular from P on l_2, then $9(\alpha + \beta + \gamma)$ is equal to .... **[JEE Main 2023]**

21. If the lines $\frac{x-1}{2} = \frac{2-y}{-3} = \frac{z-3}{\alpha}$ and $\frac{x-4}{5} = \frac{y-1}{2} = \frac{z}{\beta}$ intersect, then the magnitude of the minimum value of $8\alpha\beta$ is .... **[JEE Main 2023]**

22. One vertex of a rectangular parallelopiped is at the origin O and the lengths of its edges along X, Y and Z axes are 3, 4 and 5 units respectively. Let P be the vertex (3, 4, 5). Then, the shortest distance between the diagonal OP and an edge parallel to Z-axis, not passing through O or P is **[JEE Main 2023]**

23. Let a line L pass through the point $P(2, 3, 1)$ and be parallel to the line $x + 3y - 2z - 2 = 0 = x - y + 2z$. If the distance of L from the point $(5,3,8)$ is α, then $3\alpha^2$ is equal to .... **[JEE Main 2023]**

Scan this QR code from your mobile phone to get the solutions of **Competition Edge Up** of this chapter.

Chapter 12

Linear Programming Problems

TOPIC 1

LPP and Its Mathematical Formulation

1. Which one is representation of the following statement?
If x is the number of tables and y be the number of chairs, which are non-negative.

(a) $x \geq 0, y \geq 0$
(b) $x \leq 0, y \leq 0$
(c) $x + y = 0$
(d) None of these

2. Observe the following problem and state the dealer (z) will get profit or loss?
Maximise $Z = 250x + 5y$
Subject to constraints are $5x + y \leq 60$, $x \geq 0$ and $y \geq 0$.

3. Linear function $Z = ax + by$, where a and b are constants, then the function is called ________________, when its value is maximised and minimised.

4. In graphical representation of linear programming problems, the region covered by the linear inequality is called ________________

5. The optimum value must occur in the feasible region.

True ☐ False ☐

6. Every point of the feasible region is called

(a) feasible solution
(b) optimal
(c) feasible choice
(d) None of these

*Concepts of all questions bearing * are important for CUET*

7. **Statement I** Every point in the feasible region is a feasible solution of the given linear programming.

Statement II Every point in the feasible region, which does not give maximum or minimum value of the objective function is called an optimal solution.

(a) Only Statement I is correct

(b) Only Statement II is correct

(c) Both statements are correct

(d) Neither Statement I nor Statement II are correct.

---

8. Fill in the blanks

(i) Any point ________ (inside/outside) of the feasible region is called infeasible solution.

(ii) Optimal values of the objective function is called an ________ (optimal solution/linear solution).

(iii) ________ (finite/infinite) points occur in the given problem, when every point of the feasible region is satisfying all the constraints.

(iv) A point ________ (at corner/outside/inside) of a feasible region is a point in the region, which is the intersection of two boundary lines.

(v) A maximum or minimum may not exist for a linear programming problem, if the feasible region is ________ (bounded/unbounded).

9. Match the following .

	Column I		Column II
A.	Feasible region	1.	enclosed within a circle
B.	Bounded feasible region	2.	extends indefinitely in any direction
C.	Unbounded feasible region	3.	common region determined by constraints and non-negative restrictions

Which of the following option is correct?

(a) A $\rightarrow$ 2, B $\rightarrow$ 3, C $\rightarrow$ 1

(b) A $\rightarrow$ 3, B $\rightarrow$ 1, C $\rightarrow$ 2

(c) A $\rightarrow$ 3, B $\rightarrow$ 2, C $\rightarrow$ 1

(d) A $\rightarrow$ 2, B $\rightarrow$ 1, C $\rightarrow$ 3

---

10. Shape of the feasible region formed by the following constraints $x + y \geq 5$, $2x + y \leq 10$, $x \geq 0$ and $y \geq 0$, is

(a) no feasible region

(b) triangular region

(c) unbounded region

(d) trapezium

***11.** Let $Z = 140x + 75y$ is a linear objective function. Then, variables x and y are known as

(a) independent variables (b) continuous variables
(c) decision variables (d) dependent variables

---

12. State whether the statement is True or False.

(i) Maximum $Z = 4x + y$, subject to the constraints are $x + y \leq 50$, $3x + y \leq 90$ and $x, y \geq 0$ occur's at (30, 0).

True ☐ False ☐

(ii) For the linear function $Z = 5x + 7y$, subject to constraints are $x + 2y \leq 8$, $3x + 2y \leq 12$, $x \geq 0$ and $y \geq 0$.

(a) The maximum value of the function is 31 at (2, 3).

True ☐ False ☐

(b) The minimum value of the function is 0 at (0, 0).

True ☐ False ☐

(iii) Maximise $Z = 4x + y$, subject to constraints are $x + y \leq 50$, $x + y \geq 100$ and $x, y \geq 0$, then maximum of Z is 50.

True ☐ False ☐

***13.** Fill in the blanks on the basis of maximum value of objective function (Z).

(i) Objective function $Z = 5x + 10y$, subject to the constraints are $x + 4y \leq 120$, $x + y \geq 30$, $x - 4y \geq 0$, $x \geq 0$ and $y \geq 0$. Maximum value of Z is ______________.

(ii) Objective function $Z = 11x + 8y$, subject to constraints are $x \leq 3$, $y \leq 7$, $x + y \leq 7$, $x \geq 0$ and $y \geq 0$. The maximum value of Z is ______________.

(iii) The objective function $Z = x + 2y$, subject to constraints are $(x - y) \leq 10$, $2x + 3y \leq 20$, $x \geq 0$, $y \geq 0$. The maximum value of Z is __________ at __________.

***14.** The corner points of the feasible region determined by the system of linear constraints are (0, 0), (0, 40), (20, 40), (60, 20) and (60, 0). The objective function is $Z = 7x + 4y$. Compare the quantity in column I and column II.

Column I	Column II
Maximum value of Z	325

(a) The quantity in column I is greater
(b) The quantity in column II is greater
(c) The two quantities are equal
(d) The relationship cannot be determined on the basis of the information supplied

---

15. The feasible region for a LPP is shown shaded in the figure. Let $Z = 3x - 4y$ be the objective function. Minimum value of Z occurs at the point (0, 8).

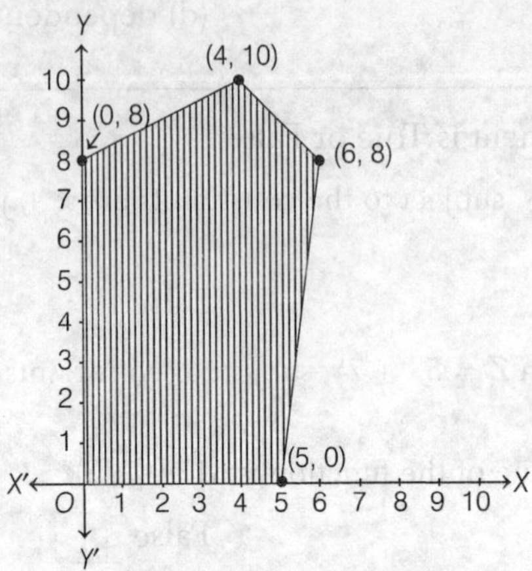

True ☐ False ☐

16. The corner points of the bounded feasible region for an LPP are (0, 4), (6, 0), (12, 0), (12, 16) and (0, 10). Let $Z = 8x + 12y$ be the objective function.

Column I	Column II
A. Minimum value of z occurs at	1. 288
B. Maximum value of z occurs at	2. (0, 4) and (6, 0)
C. Maximum of z is	3. 48
D. Minimum of z is	4. (12, 16)

Which of the following option is correct?

(a) A → 2, B → 4, C → 1, D → 3

(b) A → 2, B → 4, C → 3, D → 1

(c) A → 4, B → 2, C → 1, D → 3

(d) A → 4, B → 2, C → 3, D → 1

17. The corner points of the feasible region determined by the linear inequalities are (0, 0), (4, 5), (4, 0) and (5, 0). If the maximum value of $Z = ax + by$, where $a, b > 0$ occur at (4, 5) and (5, 0), then the relation between a and b is ____________

Assertion-Reason Questions

The following questions consist of two statements – Assertion (A) and Reason (R). Answer these questions by selecting the appropriate options given below.
(a) Both A and R are true and R is the correct explanation of A.
(b) Both A and R are true, but R is not the correct explanation of A.
(c) A is true, but R is false.
(d) A is false, but R is true.

1. **Assertion** (A) Some of the feasible solutions for the system of inequalities : $x + 2y \leq 6$, $4x + 3y \leq 12$, $x \geq 0$, $y \geq 0$ are (0, 3), (3, 0), (1, 2), (2, 1).

Reason (R) Any point inside the feasible region for an LPP is called a feasible solution.

(a) ☐ (b) ☐ (c) ☐ (d) ☐

2. **Assertion** (A) Consider the graph for the system of inequalities : $5x + 2y \geq 100$, $x + y \leq 40$, $x \geq 0$, $y \geq 0$. Feasible region for it is unbounded.

Reason (R) Graph for the system of inequalities.

(a) ☐ (b) ☐ (c) ☐ (d) ☐

3. **Assertion** (A) Solution of the linear programming problem, maximize $Z = 2x + y$, subject to constraints. $x + 2y \leq 10$, $3x + 2y \leq 12$, $x \geq 0$, $y \geq 0$ is 6.5

Reason (R) To obtain maximum value of the objective function Z in a linear programming problem, we need to compare value of Z at all the corner points of the shaded region.

(a) ☐ (b) ☐ (c) ☐ (d) ☐

4. **Assertion** (A) Feasible region for $x \geq 1$ and $y \leq 2$ lines in 1st and 2nd quadrant.

Reason (R) Graph for the inequalities $x \geq 1$ and $y \leq 2$ is

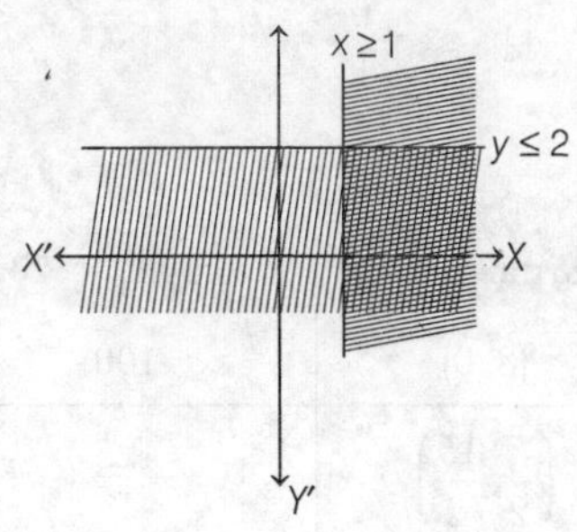

(a) ☐ (b) ☐ (c) ☐ (d) ☐

5. **Assertion** (A) Solution of the linear programming problem, maximize $Z = 2x + 3y$, subject to constraints $x + y \leq 20$, $x + y \geq 40$, $x \geq 0$, $y \geq 0$ is 20.

Reason (R) If the feasible region of a LPP is bounded, then both maximum and minimum values of Z exists.

(a) ☐ (b) ☐ (c) ☐ (d) ☐

6. **Assertion** (A) There is no feasible region for the constraints defined in the LPP. Maximize $Z = 2x + 3y$, subject to constraints $x + y \leq 7$, $x + y \geq 14$, $x \geq 0$, $y \geq 0$.

Reason (R) If the feasible region of a LPP is unbounded, then it may or may not have optional solution.

(a) ☐ (b) ☐ (c) ☐ (d) ☐

7. **Assertion** (A) Some of the feasible solutions for the linear inequalities, $5x + y \leq 100$, $x + y \leq 60$, $x \geq 0$, $y \geq 0$ are (10, 50), (0, 60) and (20, 0).

Reason (R) Points within and on the boundary of the feasible region represent feasible solutions of the constraints.

(a) ☐ (b) ☐ (c) ☐ (d) ☐

8. **Assertion** (A) The intermediate solutions of constraints must be checked by substituting them back into objective function, linear inequalities $5x + 3y \leq 15$, $2x + 3y \leq 6$, $x \geq 0$, $y \geq 0$.

Reason (R) Here (0, 2), (0, 0) and (3, 0) all are vertices of feasible region.

(a) ☐ (b) ☐ (c) ☐ (d) ☐

9. **Assertion** (A) For the constraints of linear optimizing $z = x_1 + x_2$ are given by $x_1 + x_2 \leq 1$, $3x_1 + x_2 \geq 1$ there is no feasible region. (Hints $x_1 = x$, $x_2 = y$.)

Reason (R) $Z = 7x + y$, subject to constraints $5x + y \leq 5$, $x + y \geq 3$, $x \geq 0$, $y \geq 0$. Out of the corner points of feasible region (3, 0), $\left(\frac{1}{2}, \frac{5}{2}\right)$, (7, 0) and (0, 5) the maximum value of z occurs at (7, 0).

(a) ☐ (b) ☐ (c) ☐ (d) ☐

10. **Assertion** (A) $z = 20x_1 + 20x_2$, subject to constraint $x_1 \geq 0$, $x_2 \geq 0$, $x_1 + 2x_2 \geq 8$, $3x_1 + 2x_2 \geq 15$, $5x_1 + 2x_2 \geq 20$.

Out of the corner points of feasible region (8, 0), $\left(\frac{5}{2}, \frac{15}{2}\right)$, $\left(\frac{7}{2}, \frac{9}{4}\right)$ and (0, 10) the minimum value of z occurs at $\left(\frac{7}{2}, \frac{9}{4}\right)$.

Reason (R)

Corner points	$Z = 20x_1 + 20x_2$
(8, 0)	100
$\left(\frac{5}{2}, \frac{15}{2}\right)$	125
$\left(\frac{7}{2}, \frac{9}{4}\right)$	115 minimum
(0, 10)	200

(a) ☐ (b) ☐ (c) ☐ (d) ☐

Case Based Questions

Case 1 Linear programming is a method for finding the optimal values (maximum or minimum) of quantities subject to the constraints when relationship is expressed as linear equations or inequations.

Based on the above information, answer the following questions.

(i) The optimal value of the objective function is attained at the points

(a) on X-axis ☐

(b) on Y-axis ☐

(c) which are corner points of the feasible region ☐

(d) None of the above ☐

(ii) The graph of the inequality $3x + 4y < 12$ is

(a) Half plane that contains the origin ☐

(b) Half plane that neither contains the origin nor the points of the line $3x + 4y = 12$ ☐

(c) whole XOY-plane excluding the points on line $3x + 4y = 12$ ☐

(d) None of the above ☐

(iii) The feasible region for an LPP is shown in the figure. Let $Z = 2x + 5y$ be the objective function. Maximum of Z occurs at

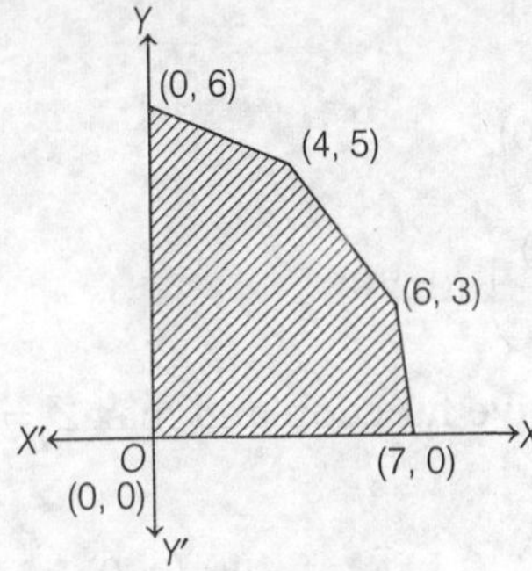

(a) (7, 0) ☐ (b) (6, 3) ☐

(c) (0, 6) ☐ (d) (4, 5) ☐

(iv) The corner points of the feasible region determined by the system of linear constraints are (0, 10), (5, 5), (15, 15), (0, 20). Let $Z = px + qy$, where $p, q > 0$. Condition on p and q so that the maximum of z occurs at both points (15, 15) and (0, 20) is

(a) $p = q$ ☐ (b) $p = 2q$ ☐

(c) $q = 2p$ ☐ (d) $q = 3p$ ☐

Case 2 Deepa rides her car at 25 km/hr. She has to spend ₹2 per km. She has ₹100 to spend on diesel. Let the travel x kms with speed 25 km/hr and y kms with speed 40 km/hr. The feasible region for the LPP is shown below.

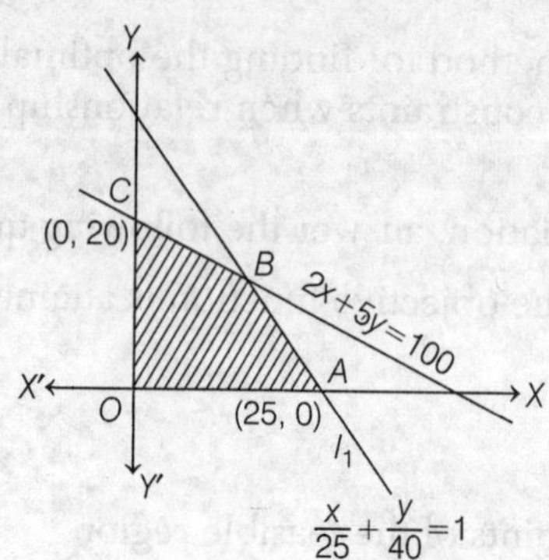

Based on the above information, answer the following questions.

(i) What is the point of intersection of line l_1 and l_2

(a) $\left(\frac{40}{3}, \frac{50}{3}\right)$ ☐ (b) $\left(\frac{50}{3}, \frac{40}{3}\right)$ ☐

(c) $\left(\frac{-50}{3}, \frac{40}{3}\right)$ ☐ (d) $\left(-\frac{50}{3}, -\frac{40}{3}\right)$ ☐

(ii) The corner points of the feasible region shown in the above graph are

(a) (0, 25), (20, 0), $\left(\frac{40}{3}, \frac{50}{3}\right)$ ☐

(b) (0, 0), (25, 0), (0, 20) ☐

(c) (0, 0), $\left(\frac{40}{3}, \frac{50}{3}\right)$, (0, 20) ☐

(d) (0, 0), (25, 0), $\left(\frac{50}{3}, \frac{40}{3}\right)$, (0, 20) ☐

(iii) If $Z = x + y$ be the objective function and max $Z = 30$. The maximum value occurs at point

(a) $\left(\frac{50}{3}, \frac{40}{3}\right)$ ☐ (b) (0, 0) ☐

(c) (25, 0) ☐ (d) (0, 20) ☐

(iv) If $Z = 6x - 9y$ be the objective function, then the maximum value of Z is

(a) –20 ☐ (b) 150 ☐

(c) 180 ☐ (d) 20 ☐

Chapter 13

Probability

Scan and take Chapter Test

TOPIC 1

Conditional Probability

1. Find the following probabilities.

(i) If $P(A) = \frac{7}{19}$, $P(B) = \frac{11}{19}$ and $P(A \cap B) = \frac{3}{19}$, then find $P(A / B)$.

(ii) If $P(A) = 0.6$, $P(B) = 0.4$ and $P(A \cap B) = 0.3$, then find $P(A / B)$.

(iii) If $2P(A) = 3P(B) = 5P(A \cap B) = 1$, then find $P(A / B)$.

(iv) If $3P(A) = 2P(B) = \frac{4}{5}$ and $P(A / B) = \frac{1}{3}$, then find $P(A \cup B)$.

2. If $P(A) = \frac{1}{6}$, $P(B) = \frac{1}{2}$ and $P(A \cup B) = \frac{7}{12}$, find

(i) $P(A \cap B)$

(ii) $P(A / B)$

(iii) $P(B / A)$

3. A coin is tossed three times. Determine $P(E / F)$, where

(i) E : Head on second toss; F: Tails on first two tosses

(ii) E : Atleast two tails; F : Head on third toss

(iii) E : Atmost two heads; F : Atleast one tail

4. A die is thrown two times. Determine $P(E / F)$ where

(i) E : 3 appears on the second toss; F : 2 appears on the first toss

(ii) E : Sum of the numbers is less than 5; F : 1 appears on the second toss

(iii) E : Product of the numbers is 6; F : Atleast one 6 appears

*Concepts of all questions bearing * are important for JEE & CUET*

5. If A and B are two events such that $P(A) \neq 0$ and $P(B) \neq 1$, then $P(\bar{A}/\bar{B}) = \dfrac{1 - P(A \cap B)}{P(\bar{B})}$.

True ☐ False ☐

6. If $P(A \cup B / F) = P(A/F) + P(B/F)$, then A and B are ______ events.

7. A fair die is rolled. Consider events $E = \{1, 2, 3\}$, $F = \{3, 5\}$ and $G = \{1, 2, 3, 4, 5\}$. Find

(i) $P(E/F)$ ______

(ii) $P(F/E)$ ______

(iii) $P(E/G)$ ______

(iv) $P(G/E)$ ______

(v) $P\{(E \cup F)/G\}$ ______

8. A family has two children. If one of them is a girl, then find the probability the other is also a girl.

______

9. Three coins are tossed. If one of them shows tails, then the probability that all three coins show tail is ______

***10.** One-dice is thrown three times and the sum of the thrown numbers is 14. The probability for which the number 3 appears in first throw is

(a) $\dfrac{1}{18}$ (b) $\dfrac{1}{36}$ (c) $\dfrac{1}{9}$ (d) $\dfrac{1}{3}$

______

11. In a school there are 1200 students, out of which 450 are girls. It is known that out of 450, 20% of the girls study in class XII. What is the probability that a student chosen randomly studies in class XII given that the chosen student is a girl?

______

12. Which of the following statement is correct?

Statement I $P(A'/B) = 1 - P(A/B)$.

Statement II $P(F/F) = 1$.

(a) Only Statement I is correct (b) Only Statement II is correct

(c) Both statements are correct (d) Both statements are incorrect

______

***13.** In a hostel, 40% of the students go to swimming, 60% go to gym and 20% go to both swimming and gym. A student is selected at random.

(i) Find the probability that he goes neither to swimming nor gym.

______

(ii) If he goes to swimming, find the probability that he goes to gym.

______

(iii) If he goes to gym, find the probability that he goes to swimming.

______

TOPIC 2

Multiplication Theorem on Probability and Independent Events

14. Let A and B be the events with $P(A) = \frac{2}{7}, P(B) = \frac{5}{14}$ and $P(A \cup B) = \frac{1}{2}$, then A and B are independent event.

True ☐ False ☐

15. A box contains 8 black and 5 white marbles. The probability of drawing a black marble without replacement, if the first marble is white, is ________

***16.** The probability that Ram goes to the market is 0.15 and if he goes to the market, the probability that he drinks the cold drink is 0.9. The probability that he goes to the market and drink cold drink is

(a) 0.6 (b) 0.135 (c) 0.25 (d) 0.14

17. From a deck of 52 cards, choose a card and keep it and then choose a second card from the deck. Let A be the event that the first card is a spade. Let B be the event that second card is a black card. Find $P(B \cap A)$.

***18.** 20% of the emails that a man receives are spam emails. His spam filter catches spam 90% of the time. His spam filter misidentifies non-spam as spam 2% of the time. The probability of an email chosen at random of being a spam mail is

(a) 18% (b) 20% (c) 25% (d) 22%

19. If the probability of solving a problem A and B individually are $\frac{1}{2}$ and $\frac{2}{3}$, then probability that the problem is solved, is ________

20. In a cricket match, if the probability that Rahul will hit a boundary is $\frac{2}{3}$, then the probability that he will hit atleast one boundary in three balls is 26/27.

True ☐ False ☐

21. P speaks the truth in 70% of the cases and Q speaks the truth in 60% cases. Find the probability that they will contradict each other in a case.

22. If A and B are independent event, then which of the following statement is incorrect?

Statement I $P(A \cap B) = 1 - P(A')P(B')$.

Statement II $P(A \cup B) = P(A) + P(B)$.

Statement III $P(A \cap B) = P(A) \cdot P(B)$.

(a) Only Statement I (b) Only Statement II
(c) Both Statements I and II (d) None of these

23. If A and B are independent events, then A' and B are dependent event, while A' and B' are independent event.

True ☐ False ☐

***24.** A coin is tossed twice. If E and F denote the occurrence of head on first toss and second toss respectively, then $P(E \cap F)$ is equal to

(a) $\frac{1}{4}$ (b) $\frac{1}{2}$ (c) $\frac{3}{4}$ (d) $\frac{1}{3}$

25. A player throws a ball at a basket kept at a distance. The probability that the ball falls into the basket in a single attempt is 0.2. The player attempts to throw the ball twice. Considering each attempt to be independent, the probability that this player puts the ball into the basket only in the second attempt is 0.16

True ☐ False ☐

26. Let A and B be independent events with $P(A) = \frac{1}{2}$ and $P(B) = \frac{3}{5}$. Find

(i) $P(A \cap B)$ ________

(ii) $P(A \cup B)$ ________

(iii) $P(A / B)$ ________

(iv) $P(B / A)$ ________

***27.** Given two independent events A and B such that $P(A) = \frac{1}{2}$ and $P(B) = \frac{1}{3}$. Find

(i) P (A and B) ________

(ii) P (A and not B) ________

(iii) P (A or B) ________

(iv) P (neither A nor B) ________

***28.** Two balls are drawn at random with replacement from a box containing 9 white balls and 7 red balls. Find the probability that

(i) both balls are red ________

(ii) first ball is white and second ball is red ________

(iii) one of them is white and other is red ________

29. One card is drawn at random from a well-shuffled deck of 52 cards. In which of the following cases are the events E and F independent?

(i) E : The card drawn is a club; F : The card drawn is a king

____

(ii) E : The card drawn is red; F : The card drawn is a queen

____

(iii) E : The card drawn is an ace or king; F : The card drawn is king or jack

____

TOPIC 3

Theorem of Total Probability and Baye's Theorem

30. In a class, 40% of the boys opted for Maths and 50% of the girls opted for Maths. If half of the class's population is girls, then find the probability of selecting a Maths student______

***31.** A problem is given to three students P, Q and R. If the probability of solving the problem by them is $\frac{1}{2}, \frac{1}{3}$ and $\frac{2}{3}$, respectively the probability that the problem is solved, is

(a) $\frac{1}{2}$ (b) $\frac{4}{9}$ (c) $\frac{5}{9}$ (d) $\frac{7}{9}$

***32.** A factory has two Machines I and II. Machine I produces 50% of the items and Machine II produces 30% of the items of the total output. Further 2% of the items produced by Machine I are defective, whereas 3% produced by Machine II are defective. If an item is chosen at random, what is the probability that it is defective?

33. A Bag I contains 4 white and 6 black balls and another Bag II contains 4 white and 5 blacks balls. One ball is drawn at random from one of the bags and it is found to be white. Find the probability that it was drawn from bag I.

34. A man is known to speak the truth 3 out of 4 times. He throws a coins and reports that he got head. The probability that he actually got head is ______

***35.** An insurance company insured 1000 light vehicle drivers, 2000 medium vehicle drivers and 3000 heavy vehicle drivers. The probability of them meeting an accident are 0.01, 0.02 and 0.25. If one of the insured drivers meets with an accidents, then the probability that he/she was a heavy vehicle driver, is

(a) $\frac{13}{16}$ (b) $\frac{15}{16}$

(c) $\frac{12}{13}$ (d) $\frac{11}{13}$

***36.** In an entrance test there are multiple choice questions, with four possible answer to each question of which one is correct. The probability that a student knows the answer to a question is 80%. If a student gets the correct answer to a question, then the probability that he was guessing is ______

37. A and B are independent witnesses in a case, the chance that A speaks truth is a and B speaks truth is b. If A and B agree on certain statements, the probability that the statement is true, is ______

***38.** There are 3 coins in a box. One is a two-headed coin, another is a fair coin and third is a biased coins that comes up heads 70% of time. When one of the three coins is selected at random and flipped, its shows tail. The probability that it was a biased coin is

(a) $\frac{5}{8}$ (b) $\frac{7}{8}$ (c) $\frac{3}{8}$ (d) None of these

39. A man speaks truth 2 out of 3 times. He picks one of the cards in which the numbers from 1 to 10 are written and reports that it is a prime number. The probability that it is actually a prime number is $\frac{4}{7}$.

True ☐ False ☐

***40.** A company manufactures three types of bulbs X, Y and Z with respective probabilities 0.25, 0.45, 0.30. Out of their output, 5%, 3% and 2% respectively are defective bulbs. A bulb is drawn at random and found to be defective. What is the probability that it is Z type of bulb.

Assertion-Reason Questions

In each of the following questions, a statement of Assertion is given followed by a corresponding statement of Reason just below it. Of the statements, mark the correct answer as
(a) Both assertion and reason are true and reason is the correct explanation of assertion.
(b) Both assertion and reason are true but reason is not the correct explanation of assertion.
(c) Assertion is true but reason is false
(d) Assertion is false but reason is true

1. **Assertion** (A) Let A and B be two events such that $P(A) = \frac{1}{5}$, while $P(A \text{ or } B) = \frac{1}{2}$. Let $P(B) = P$, then for $P = \frac{3}{8}$, A and B independent.

Reason (R) For independent events,

$$P(A \cap B) = P(A)P(B)$$
$$P(A \cup B) = P(A) + P(B) - P(A \cap B) = P(A) + P(B) - P(A)P(B)$$
$$= \frac{1}{5} + P - \left(\frac{1}{5}\right)P$$
$$\Rightarrow \quad \frac{1}{2} = \frac{1}{5} + \frac{4}{5}P \Rightarrow P = \frac{3}{8}.$$

(a) ☐ (b) ☐ (c) ☐ (d) ☐

2. **Assertion** (A) If A and B are two mutually exclusive events with $P(\overline{A}) = \frac{5}{6}$ and $P(B) = \frac{1}{3}$. Then $P\left(\frac{A}{\overline{B}}\right)$ is equal to $\frac{1}{4}$.

Reason (R) If A and B are two events such that $P(A) = 0.2$, $P(B) = 0.6$ and $P(A \mid B) = 0.2$, then the value of $P(A \mid \overline{B})$ is 0.2.

(a) ☐ (b) ☐ (c) ☐ (d) ☐

3. **Assertion** (A) Let A and B be two events such that the occurrence of A implies occurrence of B, but not vice-verse, then the correct relation between $P(A)$ and $P(B)$ is $P(B) \geq P(A)$.

Reason (R) Here, according to the given statement

$$A \subseteq B$$

$$P(B) = P(A \cup (A \cap B)) \qquad [\because A \cap B = A]$$

$$= P(A) + P(A \cap B)$$

Therefore, $P(B) \geq P(A)$

(a) ☐ (b) ☐ (c) ☐ (d) ☐

4. **Assertion** (A) If $A \subset B$ and $B \subset A$, then $P(A) = P(B)$.

Reason (R) If $A \subset B$, then $P(A) \leq P(B)$.

(a) ☐ (b) ☐ (c) ☐ (d) ☐

5. **Assertion** (A) The probability of an impossible events is 1.

Reason (R) If A is a perfect subset of B and $P(A) < P(B)$, then $P(B - A)$ is equal to $P(B) - P(A)$.

(a) ☐ (b) ☐ (c) ☐ (d) ☐

6. **Assertion** (A) If $A = A_1 \cup A_2 ... \cup A_n$ where $A_1 ... A_n$ are mutually exclusive events, then $\Sigma_{i=1}^{n} P(A_i) = P(A)$

Reason (R) Given, $A = A_1 \cup A_2 ... \cup A_n$

Since $A_1 ... A_n$ are mutually exclusive $P(A) = P(A_{1)} + P(A_{2)} + ... + P(A_n)$

Therefore, $P(A) = \Sigma_{i=1}^{n} P(A_i)$

(a) ☐ (b) ☐ (c) ☐ (d) ☐

7. **Assertion** (A) There are two bags (i) and (ii), bag (i) contains 3 red and 4 black balls and bag (ii) contains 5 red and 6 black balls. If one ball is drawn at random from one of the bags and found to be red, then the probability that it was drawn from bag (ii) is $\frac{35}{68}$.

Reason (R) If E_1 and E_2 event constitute a partition of sample space S and A is any event of non-zero probability, then $P\left(\frac{E_i}{A}\right) = \frac{P(E_i)P\left(\frac{A}{E_i}\right)}{P(A)}$, $(i = 1, 2)$.

(a) ☐ (b) ☐ (c) ☐ (d) ☐

8. **Assertion** (A) Two coins are tossed simultaneously. The probability of getting two heads, if it is known that at least one head comes up, is $\frac{1}{3}$.

Reason (R) Let E and F be two events with a random experiment, then $P\left(\frac{E}{F}\right) = \frac{P(E \cap F)}{P(E)}$.

(a) ☐ (b) ☐ (c) ☐ (d) ☐

Case Based Questions

Case 1 Three friends, A, B and C are playing a dice game. The numbers rolled up by them in their first three chances were noted and given by $A = (1, 2)$, $B = (2, 4, 5)$ and $C = (1, 2, 5)$ as A reaches the cell 'SKIP YOUR NEXT TURN' in second throw.

Based on the above information, answer the following questions.

(i) $P(A \mid B) =$

(a) $\frac{1}{6}$ ☐ (b) $\frac{1}{3}$ ☐

(c) $\frac{1}{2}$ ☐ (d) $\frac{2}{3}$ ☐

(ii) $P(B \mid C) =$

(a) $\frac{2}{3}$ ☐ (b) $\frac{1}{12}$ ☐

(c) $\frac{1}{9}$ ☐ (d) 0 ☐

(iii) $P(A \cap B \mid C) =$

(a) $\frac{1}{6}$ ☐ (b) $\frac{1}{2}$ ☐

(c) $\frac{1}{12}$ ☐ (d) $\frac{1}{3}$ ☐

(iv) $P(A \mid C) =$

(a) $\frac{1}{4}$ ☐ (b) 1 ☐

(c) $\frac{2}{3}$ ☐ (d) None of these ☐

(v) $P(A \cup B \mid C) =$

(a) 0 ☐ (b) $\frac{1}{2}$ ☐

(c) $\frac{2}{3}$ ☐ (d) 1 ☐

Case 2 Two cards is lost from a pack of 52 cards. From the remaining cards two cards are drawn at random.

Based on the above information, answer the following questions.

(i) The probability of drawing two diamonds given that two card of diamond is missing, is

(a) $\frac{21}{425}$ ☐ (b) $\frac{11}{245}$ ☐

(c) $\frac{23}{425}$ ☐ (d) $\frac{1}{425}$ ☐

(ii) The probability of drawing two diamonds given that two card of heart is missing, is

(a) $\frac{78}{245}$ ☐ (b) $\frac{22}{425}$ ☐

(c) $\frac{19}{425}$ ☐ (d) $\frac{23}{425}$ ☐

(iii) Let A be the event of drawing two diamonds from remaining 50 cards and E_1, E_2, E_3 and E_4 be the events that lost card is of diamond, club, spade and heart respectively, then the approximate value of $\sum_{i=1}^{4} P(A \mid E_i)$ is

(a) 0.17 ☐ (b) 0.24 ☐

(c) 0.25 ☐ (d) 0.18 ☐

(iv) All of a sudden, missing card is found and, then two cards are drawn simultaneously without replacement. Probability that both drawn cards are king is

(a) $\frac{1}{52}$ ☐ (b) $\frac{1}{221}$ ☐

(c) $\frac{1}{121}$ ☐ (d) $\frac{2}{221}$ ☐

(v) If two cards are drawn from a well shuffled pack of 52 cards, one by one with replacement, then probability of getting not a king in 1st and 2nd draw is

(a) $\frac{144}{169}$ ☐ (b) $\frac{12}{169}$ ☐

(c) $\frac{64}{169}$ ☐ (d) None of these ☐

COMPETITION CONNECT

Random Variable and Its Probability Distribution [NCERT (Old) Pg. 557-571]

1. Do the following represents the probability distribution of a random variable?

(i)

X	0	1	2	3	4
$P(X)$	0.2	0.5	0.4	– 0.1	0

Yes ☐ No ☐

(ii)

X	0	1	2
$P(X)$	0.3	0.4	0.3

Yes ☐ No ☐

(iii)

X	0	1	2	3
$P(X)$	0.3	0.2	0.2	0.3

Yes ☐ No ☐

(iv)

X	0	1	2	3	4
$P(X)$	0.2	0.3	0.4	0.1	0

Yes ☐ No ☐

(v)

X	0	1	2
$P(X)$	0.3	0.5	0.4

Yes ☐ No ☐

2. A month has atleast 28 days. If X denotes number of days in a month, then X is a discrete random variable.

True ☐ False ☐

3. A bag contains 1 black and 2 green marbles. One marbles is drawn at random and then put back in the bag without noting its colour. The process is repeated again. If X denotes the number of black marbles recorded in two draws, then describe X.

____

4. If X is a random variable taking values 0, 1, 2, 3, where $P(X = 0) = 0$, $P(X = 1) = \frac{1}{4}$ and $P(X = 2) = \frac{1}{4}$, then the value of $P(X = 3)$ is ______________________________

5. Let X be the random variable, $P(X = x)$ is given by

X	0	1	2	3
$P(X = x)$	0	K	$2K$	$3K$

The value of K is

(a) $\frac{1}{5}$ (b) $\frac{2}{5}$ (c) $\frac{1}{6}$ (d) $\frac{1}{2}$

____

6. Two cards are drawn successively with replacement from a well-shuffled deck of 52 cards. Find the probability distribution of the number of

(i) kings ______________________________

(ii) jack ______________________________

(iii) spade ______________________________

7. Two cards are drawn at random from a well shuffled deck of 52 cards with replacement. The probability distribution of number of diamond card is given in the table below.

X	0	1	2
$P(X)$	K_1	K_2	K_3

Which of the following option is correct?

(a) $K_1 = \frac{9}{16}, K_2 = \frac{1}{16}$ (b) $K_1 = \frac{3}{8}, K_2 = \frac{9}{16}$

(c) $K_2 = \frac{3}{8}, K_3 = \frac{1}{16}$ (d) $K_1 = \frac{3}{8}, K_3 = \frac{1}{16}$

8. The probability distribution of the number of success in two tosses of a die, where a success is defined as prime number on atleast one die, is

X	0	1	2
$P(X)$	1/4	1/2	1/4

True ☐ False ☐

9. A random variable X has the following probability distribution.

X	0	1	2	3	4	5
$P(X)$	K	$2K$	$3K$	$4K^2 + K$	$6K^2$	$2K$

Determine

(i) K __________

(ii) $P(X < 3)$ __________

(iii) $P(X > 3)$ __________

(iv) $P(0 < X < 4)$ __________

10. The mean number of six in three tosses of a die is $\frac{1}{2}$.

True ☐ False ☐

11. Find the variance of the following.

(i) The number of tails in three tosses of a coin.

____

(ii) The variance of X, when two dice are thrown simultaneously and X denotes the composite number.

____

12. A random variable X has the distribution law as given below

X	1	2	3
$P(X)$	0.3	0.4	0.3

The variance of the distribution is 0.6.

True ☐ False ☐

13. X is a non-negative integer valued random variable with $P(X=x)=\begin{cases}\dfrac{x+1}{2^{(x+2)}}, & x=0,1,2\\ \dfrac{x^2+1}{2^{(x+2)}}, & x=3\end{cases}$.

The mean and variance of X are respectively

(a) 2 and 3 (b) 3 and 2 (c) 2 and 4 (d) None of these

COMPETITION EDGE UP

1. Let the sum of two positive integers be 24. If the probability that their product is not less than 3/4 times their greatest possible product is m/n, where gcd $(m, n) = 1$, then $n - m$ equals [JEE Main 2024]

(a) 8 ☐

(b) 10 ☐

(c) 11 ☐

(d) 9 ☐

2. A company has two plants A and B to manufacture motorcycles. 60% motorcycles are manufactured at plant A and the remaining are manufactured at plant B. 80% of the motorcycles manufactured at plant A are rated of the standard quality, while 90% of the motorcycles manufactured at plant B are rated of the standard quality. A motorcycle picked up randomly from the total production is found to be of the standard quality. If p is the probability that it was manufactured at plant B, then $126p$ is [JEE Main 2024]

(a) 66 ☐

(b) 56 ☐

(c) 64 ☐

(d) 54 ☐

3. Three urns A, B and C contain 7 red, 5 black; 5 red, 7 black and 6 red, 6 black balls, respectively. One of the urn is selected at random and a ball is drawn from it. If the ball drawn is black, then the probability that it is drawn from urn A is [JEE Main 2024]

(a) 4/17 ☐

(b) 5/16 ☐

(c) 5/18 ☐

(d) 7/18 ☐

4. A bag contains 8 balls, whose colours are either white or black. 4 balls are drawn at random without replacement and it was found that 2 balls are white and other 2 balls are black. The probability that the bag contains equal number of white and black balls is [JEE Main 2024]

(a) 2/7 ☐

(b) 1/5 ☐

(c) 2/5 ☐

(d) 1/7 ☐

5. Bag A contains 3 white, 7 red balls and Bag B contains 3 white, 2 red balls. One bag is selected at random and a ball is drawn from it. The probability of drawing the ball from the bag A, if the ball drawn is white, is [JEE Main 2024]

(a) 1/4 ☐

(b) 1/3 ☐

(c) 3/10 ☐

(d) 1/9 ☐

6. Two integers x and y are chosen with replacement from the set [0, 1, 2, 3, ..., 10]. Then, the probability that $|x - y| \geq 5$, is **[JEE Main 2024]**
(a) 62/121
(b) 30/121
(c) 60/121
(d) 31/121

7. A fair die is thrown until 2 appears. Then, the probability that 2 appears in even number of throws, is **[JEE Main 2024]**
(a) 5/11
(b) 1/6
(c) 5/6
(d) 6/11

8. Three balls are drawn at random from a bag containing 5 blue and 4 yellow balls. Let the random variables X and Y, respectively denote the number of blue and yellow balls. If $\overline{X}$ and $\overline{Y}$ are the means of X and Y, respectively. Then, $7\overline{X} + 4\overline{Y}$ is equal to .... **[JEE Main 2024]**

9. Let the mean and the standard deviation of the probability distribution

X	α	1	0	-3
P(X)	$\frac{1}{3}$	K	$\frac{1}{6}$	$\frac{1}{4}$

be μ and α, respectively. If $\sigma - \mu = 2$, then $\sigma + \mu$ is equal to .... **[JEE Main 2024]**

10. From a lot of 10 items which include 3 defective items, a sample of 5 items is drawn at random. Let the random variable X denote the number of defective items in the sample. If the variance of X is σ^2, then $96\sigma^2$ is equal to **[JEE Main 2024]**

11. In a tournament, a team plays 10 matches with probabilities of winning and losing each match as $\frac{1}{3}$ and $\frac{2}{3}$, respectively. Let x be the number of matches that the team wins and y be the number of matches that team loses. If the probability $P(|x - y| \leq 2)$ is p, then 3^9 p equals...... . **[JEE Main 2024]**

12. A fair die is tossed repeatedly until a six is obtained. Let X denote the number of tosses required and let $a = P(X = 3)$, $b = P(X \geq 3)$ and $c = P(X \geq 6 \mid X > 3)$. Then, $\frac{b + c}{a}$ is equal to .... **[JEE Main 2024]**

13. Three dice are rolled. If the probability of getting different numbers on the three dice is $\frac{p}{q}$, where p and q are co-prime, then $q - p$ is equal to **[JEE Main 2024]**
(a) 4
(b) 3
(c) 1
(d) 2

14. Let Ω be the sample space and $A \subseteq \Omega$ be an event.
Given below are two statements
(S1) : If $P(A) = 0$, then $A = \phi$
(S2) : If $P(A) = 1$, then $A = \Omega$.
Then, **[JEE Main 2024]**
(a) only (S2) is true
(b) Both (S1) and (S2) are true
(c) only (S1) is true
(d) Both (S1) and (S2) are false

15. Let N be the sum of the numbers appeared when two fair dice are rolled and let the probability that $N - 2$, $\sqrt{3N}$, $N + 2$ are in geometric progression be $k/48$. Then, the value of k is **[JEE Main 2024]**
(a) 2
(b) 8
(c) 16
(d) 4

16. A fair $n(n > 1)$ faces die is rolled repeatedly until a number less than n appears. If the mean of the number of tosses required is $n/9$, then n is equal to .... **[JEE Main 2023]**

17. A bag contains six balls of different colours. Two balls are drawn in succession with replacement. The probability that both the balls are of the same colour is p. Next four balls are drawn in succession with replacement and the probability that exactly three balls are of the same colour is q. If $p : q = m : n$, where m and n are coprime, then $m + n$ is equal to .... **[JEE Main 2023]**

Scan this QR code from your mobile phone to get the solutions of **Competition Edge Up** of this chapter.

NCERT
REVISION WORK BOOK

Solutions

Solutions

Chapter-1

Relations and Functions

1. No student of the school can be father of any student of the school as the father and child will not study in the same school. Hence, $R = \phi \Rightarrow R$ is the empty relation.

2. (c) A relation R in a set A is called empty relation, if no element of A is related to any element of A

i.e. $R = \phi \subset A \times A$.

e.g. If set $A = \{1, 2, 3, 4\}$, then one of the void relations can be $R = \{x, y\}$, where $|x - y| = 8$.

For empty relation,

$$R = \phi \subset A \times A$$

A relation R in set A is called universal relation, if each element of A is related to every element of A

i.e. $R = A \times A$

Consider, set $A = \{a, b, c, d\}$

Now, one of the universal relation will be $R = \{x, y\}$, where $|x - y| \geq 0$.

For universal relation, $R = A \times A$.

3. $A = \{x \in Z : 1 \leq x \leq 9\}$

$= \{1, 2, 3, 4, 5, 6, 7, 8, 9\}$

$R = \{(a, b)$: the product of a and b end with zero$\}$

$= \{(2, 5), (4, 5), (6, 5), (8, 5), (5, 2), (5, 4), (5, 6), (5, 8)\}$

The number of set of elements is 8.

4. (i) Since, x and x are the same person, he cannot be younger than himself.

$\Rightarrow (x, x) \notin R$

If x is exactly five years younger than y, then y is five years older than x.

So, if $(x, y) \in R$

$\Rightarrow \quad (y, x) \notin R$

If x is exactly five years younger than y and y is exactly five years younger than z, then x is not five years younger than z.

So, if $(x, y) \in R$ and $(y, z) \in R$

$\Rightarrow (x, z) \notin R$

Hence, the relation is neither reflexive nor symmetric nor transitive.

(ii) $N = \{1, 2, 3, \ldots\ldots\}$ and $R = \{(1, 7), (2, 9), (3, 11)\}$ because $x < 4$.

R is not reflexive as $(1, 1) \notin R$

R is not symmetric as 3 $(2, 9) \in R$ but $(9, 2) \notin R$

R is transitive as transitivity is not contradicted.

(iii) Let set $A = \{1, 2, 3, 4\}$. The relation $R = \{(1, 1), (2, 2), (3, 3), (4, 4), (1, 2), (2, 1), (2, 3), (3, 2)\}$

R is reflexive as $(1, 1), (2, 2), (3, 3), (4, 4) \in R$

R is symmetric as $(1, 2) \in R$ $\Rightarrow (2, 1) \in R$ and $(2, 3) \in R$ $\Rightarrow (3, 2) \in R$

R is not transitive as $(1, 2), (2, 3) \in R$ $\Rightarrow (1, 3) \notin R$.

(iv) R is not reflexive as x cannot be the mother of x.

R is not symmetric as if x is the mother of y, then y cannot be the mother of x.

R is not transitive as if x is the mother of y and y is the mother of z, then x cannot be the mother of z.

(v) $9x - 3y = 0 \Rightarrow y = 3x$

$R = \{(1, 3), (2, 6), (3, 9), \ldots\ldots, (14, 42)\}$

The relation is neither reflexive nor symmetric nor transitive.

(vi) $R = \{(x, y) : y = x + 1, x \leq 4\}$

$R = \{(1, 2), (2, 3), (3, 4), (4, 5)\}$

The relation is neither reflexive nor symmetric nor transitive.

(vii) $A = \{1, 2, 3, 4, 5, 6\}$

$R = \{(1, 1), (1, 2), (1, 3), (1, 4), (1, 5), (1, 6), (2, 2), (2, 4), (2, 6), (3, 3), (3, 6), (4, 4), (5, 5), (6, 6)\}$

Clearly, $(1, 1), (2, 2), (3, 3), (4, 4), (5, 5), (6, 6) \in R$

Therefore, R is reflexive.

As, $(1, 2) \in R$ but $(2, 1) \notin R$

Therefore, R is not symmetric.

For each (a, b) and $(b, c) \in R$.

Clearly, $(a, c) \in R$

Therefore, R is transitive.

5. (i) Let R_1 be the relation which is reflexive, transitive but not symmetric.

As, the relation is reflexive, $(1, 1), (2, 2), (3, 3), (4, 4) \in R_1$

As, the relation is transitive, $(1, 2), (2, 3), (1, 3) \in R_1$

Therefore, $R_1 = \{(1, 1), (2, 2), (3, 3), (4, 4), (1, 2), (2, 3), (1, 3)\}$

(ii) Let R_2 be the relation, which is symmetric but neither reflexive nor transitive.

As, the relation is symmetric, $(1, 2), (2, 1) \in R_2$

Therefore, $R_2 = \{(1, 2), (2, 1)\}$

(iii) Let R_3 be the relation, which is reflexive, symmetric and transitive.

As, the relation is reflexive, $(1, 1), (2, 2), (3, 3), (4, 4) \in R_3$

As, the relation is transitive, $(1, 2), (2, 3), (1, 3) \in R_3$

As, the relation is symmetric, $(1, 2), (2, 1), (2, 3), (3, 2), (3, 1), (1, 3) \in R_3$

Therefore, $R_3 = \{(1, 1), (2, 2), (3, 3), (4, 4), (1, 2), (2, 1), (3, 2), (3, 1), (2, 3), (1, 3)\}$.

6. (i) Let $A = \{5, 6, 7\}$

Now, consider the relation R on A as $R = \{(5, 6), (6, 5)\}$.

$\because (5, 5) \notin R$

$\therefore R$ is not reflexive.

$\because (5, 6) \in R$ and also $(6, 5) \in R$

$\therefore R$ is symmetric.

Here, $(5, 6), (6, 5) \in R$ but $(5, 5) \notin R$.

$\therefore R$ is not transitive.

(ii) Consider a relation R in R defined as

$$R = \{(a, b) : a < b\}$$

Here, for any $a \in R, (a, a) \notin R$

$\therefore R$ is not reflexive.

Now, $(1, 2) \in R$ but $(2, 1) \notin R$

$\therefore R$ is not symmetric.

Now, let $(a, b), (b, c) \in R$

$\Rightarrow a < b$ and $b < c$

$\Rightarrow a < c$

$\Rightarrow (a, c) \in R$

$\therefore R$ is transitive.

(iii) Let $A = \{4, 6, 8\}$

Now, consider the relation R on A as

$R = \{(4, 4), (6, 6), (8, 8), (4, 6), (6, 4), (6, 8), (8, 6)\}$

$\because$ $(4, 4), (6, 6), (8, 8) \in R$

$\therefore$ R is reflexive.

$\because$ $(a, b) \in R$

$\Rightarrow (b, a) \in R \forall a, b \in R$

$\therefore$ R is symmetric.

Here, $(4, 6), (6, 8) \in R$ but $(4, 8) \notin R$

$\therefore$ R is not transitive.

(iv) Let $A = \{-5, -6\}$

Now, consider the relation R on A as

$R = \{(-5, -6), (-6, -5), (-5, -5)\}$

$\because (-6, -6) \notin R$

$\therefore$ R is not reflexive.

$\because (-5, -6) \in R$ and $(-6, -5) \in R$

$\therefore$ R is symmetric.

Here, $(-5, -6), (-6, -5) \in R$ and also $(-5, -5) \in R$

$\therefore$ R is transitive.

7. (b) R is not reflexive as x is not more than $x \ \forall \ x \in R$.

R is not symmetric as $a > b$ $\Rightarrow b$ is not more than $a \ \forall \ a, b \in R$

R is transitive as $a > b$ and $b > c$ $\Rightarrow a$ is more than $c \ \forall \ a, b, c \in R$

Hence, R is a transitive relation.

8. (d) Given,

$R = \{(x, y) : 2x + 3y \text{ is an integer}\}$

As, $2x + 3x = 5x$ is an integer, $(x, x) \in R \ \forall \ x \in Z$

Therefore, R is reflexive.

Let $x, y \in Z$, where $(x, y) \in R$

If $2x + 3y$ is an integer, then $2y + 3x$ is also an integer.

i.e. $(y, x) \in R$.

Therefore, R is symmetric

Let $(x, y) \in R$ and $(y, z) \in R$, where $x, y, z \in Z$.

If $2x + 3y$ and $2y + 3z$ are integers, then

$2x + 3z$ is also an integer.

i.e. $(x, z) \in R$.

Therefore, R is transitive.

As, R is reflexive, symmetric and transitive, R is equivalence.

9. (False)

R is not reflexive as a is not less than $a^2 \ \forall \ a \in R$. $\left[\text{taking } a = \frac{1}{2}\right]$

R is not symmetric as $a < b^2 \Rightarrow b$ is not less than $a^2 \ \forall \ a, b \in R$.

[taking $a = 1$ and $b = 2$]

R is not transitive as $a < b^2$ and $b < c^2 \Rightarrow a$ is not less than $c^2 \ \forall \ a, b, c \in R$.

[taking $a = 3$, $b = 2$ and $c = \sqrt{3}$]

Hence, R is not an equivalence relation.

10. (True)

$(Q, Q) \in R$

$\Rightarrow$ The diagonals of Q and Q are equal in length.

Therefore, R is reflexive.

$(Q_1, Q_2) \in R \Rightarrow$ The diagonals of Q_1 and Q_2 are equal in length.

$\Rightarrow$ The diagonals of Q_2 and Q_1 are equal in length.

$\Rightarrow$ $(Q_2, Q_1) \in R$

Therefore, R is symmetric.

$(Q_1, Q_2) \in R \Rightarrow$ The diagonals of Q_1 and Q_2 are equal in length and $(Q_2, Q_3) \in R$

$\Rightarrow$ The diagonals of Q_2 and Q_3 are equal in length.

$\Rightarrow$ The diagonals of Q_1 and Q_3 are equal in length

$\Rightarrow (Q_1, Q_3) \in R$

Therefore, R is transitive.

Hence, the relation R is equivalence.

11. (d) $(m, m) \in R \Rightarrow$ The lines m and m lie on the same plane.

Therefore, R is reflexive.

$(m, n) \in R \Rightarrow$ The lines m and n lie on the same plane.

$\Rightarrow$ The lines n and m lie on the same plane $\Rightarrow (n, m) \in R$.

Therefore, R is symmetric.

$(m, n) \in R \Rightarrow$ The lines m and n lie on the same plane and

$(n, p) \in R \Rightarrow$ The lines n and p lie on the same plane

$\Rightarrow$ The lines m and p lie on the same plane $\Rightarrow (m, p) \in R$

Therefore, R is transitive.

Hence, the relation R is an equivalence.

12. R is reflexive, since $(1, 1)$, $(2, 2)$ and $(3, 3)$ lie in R.

R will be symmetric if $(2, 1)$ and $(3, 2)$ included in the relation R.

R will be transitive if $(1, 3)$ included in the relation R.

Hence, $\{(1, 1), (2, 2), (3, 3), (1, 2), (2, 3), (2, 1), (3, 2), (1, 3)\}$ is an equivalence relation.

13. (False)

R is reflexive as $x + x = 2x$, which is an even number for all $x \in Z$.

Let $x, y \in Z$, where $(x, y) \in R$.

If $x + y$ is an even integer, then $y + x$ is also an even integer.

Therefore, R is symmetric.

Let $x, y, z \in Z$, where $(x, y) \in R$ and $(y, z) \in R$

If $x + y$ and $y + z$ are even integers, then $x + z$ is also an even integer.

Therefore, R is transitive.

As, R is reflexive, symmetric and transitive, R is equivalence.

14. (d) S is reflexive as

$(a, a) \in S \Leftrightarrow a \times a = a^2 \geq 0$

S is symmetric as

$(a, b) \in S \Leftrightarrow a \times b \geq 0$

$\Leftrightarrow b \times a \geq 0 \Leftrightarrow (b, a) \in S$

S is transitive as

$(a, b) \in S$ and $(b, c) \in S$

$\Leftrightarrow a \times b \geq 0$

and $b \times c \geq 0 \Rightarrow a \times c \geq 0$

$\Leftrightarrow (a, c) \in S$.

15. (True) Let any $x, y, z \in Z$

R is reflexive as

$x - x = 0 = 5 \times 0 \ \forall \ x \in Z$

Let $(x, y) \in R$, where $x, y \in Z$

If $x - y$ is multiple of 5, then $y - x$ is also a multiple of 5.

Therefore, R is symmetric.

Let $(x, y) \in R$ and $(y, z) \in R$, where $x, y, z \in Z$

If $x - y = 5m$ and $y - z = 5n$, then

$x - z = x - y + y - z$

$= 5m + 5n = 5(m + n)$

If $x - y$ and $y - z$ are multiples of 5, then $x - z$ is also a multiple of 5.

Therefore, R is transitive.

As, R is reflexive, symmetric and transitive, R is equivalence.

16. (False)

R is reflexive as $x - x + \sqrt{2} = \sqrt{2}$, which is irrational $\forall\ x \in Z$.

Let $(x, y) \in R$, where $x, y \in Z$.

If $x - y + \sqrt{2}$ is an irrational number, then $y - x + \sqrt{2}$ is also an irrational number.

Therefore, R is symmetric.

Let $(x, y) \in R$ and $(y, z) \in R$, where $x, y, z \in Z$.

If $x - y + \sqrt{2}$ and $y - z + \sqrt{2}$ are irrational numbers, then

$$x - z + \sqrt{2} = (x - y + \sqrt{2}) + (y - z + \sqrt{2}) - \sqrt{2}$$

is irrational.

Therefore, R is transitive.

As, R is reflexive, symmetric and transitive, R is equivalence.

17. (d) The relation $aR_1b \Leftrightarrow a$ is the son of b, is not reflexive as a cannot be the son of a.

The relation $aR_2b \Leftrightarrow a$ is perpendicular to b, is also not reflexive as a cannot be perpendicular to a.

The relation $aR_3b \Leftrightarrow a \geq b$ is not symmetric as if $a \geq b$, then $b \leq a$.

The relation $aR_4b \Leftrightarrow |a| = |b|$ is reflexive as $|x| = |x|, \forall\ x \in Z$

The relation $aR_4b \Leftrightarrow |a| = |b|$ is symmetric as

$|x| = |y| \Rightarrow |y| = |x|, \forall\ x, y \in Z$

The relation $aR_4b \Leftrightarrow |a| = |b|$ is transitive as

$|x| = |y|$ and $|y| = |z|$

$\Rightarrow |x| = |z|, \forall\ x, y, z \in Z$.

Hence, the relation $aR_4b \Leftrightarrow |a| = |b|$ is an equivalence relation.

18. The smallest equivalence relation is the identity relation

$R_1 = \{(a, a), (b, b), (c, c)\}$

Then, two ordered pairs of two distinct elements can be added to give three more equivalence relations.

$R_2 = \{(a, a), (b, b), (c, c), (a, b), (b, a)\}$

Similarly,

$R_3 = \{(a, a), (b, b), (c, c), (b, c), (c, b)\}$

$R_4 = \{(a, a), (b, b), (c, c), (a, c), (c, a)\}$

$R_5 = \{(a, a), (b, b), (c, c), (a, b), (b, a), (a, c), (c, a), (b, c), (c, b)\}$

Hence, the total number of equivalence relation is 5.

19. (c) $R_1 = \{(1, 2), (1, 8), (3, 6), (5, 4), (7, 2), (7, 8)\}$

$R_2 = \{(2, 2), (4, 4), (6, 2), (6, 4), (8, 2)\}$

Hence, $R_1oR_2 = \{(1, 2), (3, 2), (3, 4), (5, 4), (7, 2)\}$

20. $(1, 2)\ R(c, d)$

$\Rightarrow \quad c = 2d$

This is possible, if the value of d is 1 or 2.

When $d = 1$, then $c = 2$

and when $d = 2$, then $c = 4$

Hence, the equivalence classes are (2, 1) and (4, 2).

21. (d) The figure in the option (d) is not the function, as the element c has no image.

22. (True)

Let (a, b) and $(c, d) \in A \times B$

and $f(a, b) = f(c, d)$

$(b, a) = (d, c)$

$\Rightarrow \quad b = d$ and $a = c$

$\Rightarrow \quad (a, b) = (c, d)$

Hence, f is one-one.

23. If the given function is one-one and onto, then every element has only one image, then the value of M should be 4.

24. (i) As, x^6 is an even number, so the function is not onto.

Also, $f(-2) = f(2) = 64$, the function is not one-one.

Hence, the given function is neither one-one nor onto.

(ii) f is one-one as

$f(x_1) = f(x_2)$

$\Rightarrow \quad 3 - 4x_1 = 3 - 4x_2$

$\Rightarrow \quad x_1 = x_2$

f is onto as given any $y \in R$, we can choose x as $\frac{1}{4}(3 - y)$ such that

$$f\left(\frac{1}{4}(3-y)\right) = 3 - 4\left(\frac{1}{4}(3-y)\right) = y$$

Hence, the function $f(x) = 3 - 4x$ is bijective.

(iii) $f(x) = (x - 1)(x - 2)(x - 3)$

$f(x) = x^3 - 6x^2 + 11x - 6$

In this cubic function,

$f(1) = f(2) = f(3) = 0$

Hence, the function is many-one and onto function.

(iv) Given, $f(n) = n - (-1)^n$

$$f(n) = \begin{cases} n - 1, & \text{if } n \text{ is even} \\ n + 1, & \text{if } n \text{ is odd} \end{cases}$$

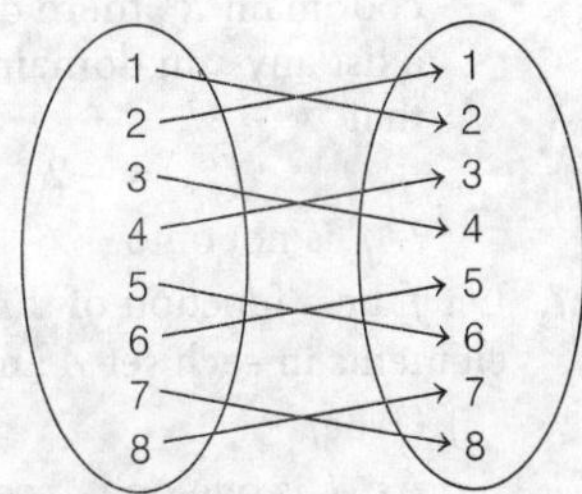

Hence, the function is bijective.

25. (False)

Given, function $f : R \rightarrow R$

such that $f(x) = \frac{1}{x^2}$

Let $f(x_1) = f(x_2)$

$$\frac{1}{x_1^2} = \frac{1}{x_2^2} \Rightarrow x_1 = \pm\, x_2$$

Hence, the function is not one-one and the statement is false.

26. (i) (True)

For $1 \leq x < 2$, $f(x) = 1$

Therefore, the function is not one-one.

Also, the function does not attain non-integral values, so the function is not onto.

(ii) (True)

$$f(x) = |x| = \begin{cases} x, & \text{if } x \geq 0 \\ -x, & \text{if } x < 0 \end{cases}$$

It is seen that

$f(-1) = |-1| = 1$, $f(1) = |1| = 1$

$\therefore f(-1) = f(1)$ but $-1 \neq 1$

$\therefore f$ is not one-one.

Now, consider $-1 \in R$

But it is known that $f(x) = |x|$ is always non-negative.

Thus, there does not exist any element x in domain R such that

$f(x) = |x| = -1$

$\therefore f$ is not onto.

(iii) (True)

$$f(x)=\begin{cases}1, & \text{if } x>0\\ 0, & \text{if } x=0\\ -1, & \text{if } x<0\end{cases}$$

Here, $f(1)=f(2)=1$ but $1 \neq 2$

$\therefore f$ is not one-one.

Now, as $f(x)$ takes only 3 values (1, 0 or -1).

For the element -2 in codomain R, there does not exist any x in domain R such that

$$f(x)=-2$$

$\therefore f$ is not onto.

27. Let f be a function of three elements in each set A and B.

(i) (True)

As, f is one-one, three elements must be taken to three different elements of the codomain under f.

Hence, f has to be onto.

(ii) (True)

As, f is onto, all three images must have three different pre-images.

Hence, f must be one-one.

28. (b) Let $f(x_1)=f(x_2)$

$$\Rightarrow \frac{2x_1-4}{3x_1-9}=\frac{2x_2-4}{3x_2-9}$$

$$\Rightarrow 6x_1x_2-12x_2-18x_1+36 = 6x_1x_2-12x_1-18x_2+36$$

$$\Rightarrow x_1=x_2$$

Therefore, the function is one-one.

Let $y=\dfrac{2x-4}{3x-9}$

$$\Rightarrow 3xy-9y=2x-4 \Rightarrow x=\frac{9y-4}{3y-2}$$

Now, $f(x)=\dfrac{2x-4}{3x-9}$

$$f\left(\frac{9y-4}{3y-2}\right)=\frac{2\left(\frac{9y-4}{3y-2}\right)-4}{3\left(\frac{9y-4}{3y-2}\right)-9}=y$$

Therefore, the function is onto.

As, the function is one-one and onto, so the function is bijective.

29. Number of one-one functions from A to $B={}^4P_3=24$.

30. The total number of functions are $2^4=16$. There were two such functions, which do not have 1 and 2 as a range.

So, the number of onto functions is $16-2=14$.

31. The function

$f:\{3, 6, 7\}\to\{3, 2, 5\}$

and $g:\{3, 2, 5\}\to\{3, 6\}$

be given by $f=\{(3, 2), (6, 5), (7, 3)\}$

and $g=\{(3, 6), (2, 6), (5, 3)\}$

(i) $gof(3)=g\{f(3)\}=g(2)=6$

$[\because f(3)=2 \text{ and } g(2)=6]$

(ii) $gof(6)=g\{f(6)\}=g(5)=3$

$[\because f(6)=5 \text{ and } g(5)=3]$

(iii) $gof(7)=g\{f(7)\}=g(3)=6$

$[\because f(7)=3 \text{ and } g(3)=6]$

32. (i) $gof(1)=g[f(1)]=g[7]=10$

(ii) $gof(2)=g[f(2)]=g[8]=12$

(iii) $gof(3)=g[f(3)]=g[9]=13$

(iv) $gof(4)=g[f(4)]=g[3]=14$

33. (i) $(gof)(x)=g\{f(x)\}=g\left(\dfrac{2x-1}{2}\right)$

$$=4\times\frac{(2x-1)}{2}+2=4x$$

and $fog(x)=f\{g(x)\}$

$$=f\{4x+2\}$$

$$=\frac{2(4x+2)-1}{2}$$

$$=\frac{8x+4-1}{2}=\frac{8x+3}{2}$$

(ii) Given, $f(x)=x^2+x$

and $g(x)=\log x$

$gof=g[f(x)]=g[x^2+x]$

$=\log(x^2+x)$

$fog=f[g(x)]=f[\log x]$

$=(\log x)^2+\log x$

34. $(gof)(x)=x^2+17x+69$

$f^2(x)+7f(x)+9=x^2+17x+69$

$f^2(x)+7f(x)=x^2+10x+7x+60$

$f^2(x)+7f(x)=x^2+10x+25+7x+35$

$f^2(x)+7f(x)=(x+5)^2+7(x+5)$

Therefore, $f(x)=x+5$

35. (False)

As, g is one-one,

$g\{f(x_1)\}=g\{f(x_2)\}$

$\Rightarrow \quad f(x_1)=f(x_2)$

As, f is one-one, $f(x_1)=f(x_2)$

$\Rightarrow \quad x_1=x_2$

As, $g\{f(x_1)\}=g\{f(x_2)\}$

$\Rightarrow \quad x_1=x_2$, gof is one-one.

Given, an arbitrary element $z\in C$, there exists a pre-image y of z under g such that $g(y)=z$, since g is onto.

Further, for $y\in B$, there exists an element x in A with $f(x)=y$, since f is onto.

Therefore,

$$gof(x)=g\{f(x)\}=g(y)=z,$$

showing that gof is onto.

But the *vice-versa* is not true.

Consider, $f:\{1, 2, 3, 4\}\to\{1, 2, 3, 4\}$

and $g:\{1, 2, 3, 4\}\to\{1, 2, 3\}$ defined as $f(1)=1$, $f(2)=2$, $f(3)=f(4)=3$, $g(1)=1$, $g(2)=2$ and $g(3)=g(4)=3$.

It can be seen that gof is onto but f is not onto.

36. (True)

$$gof(x)=g[f(x)]=g\left[\frac{5x-9}{4x-3}\right]$$

$$=\frac{3\left[\frac{5x-9}{4x-3}\right]-9}{4\left[\frac{5x-9}{4x-3}\right]-5}$$

$$=x\in R$$

Similarly, $fog(x)=x\in R$

Hence, gof and fog are the identity function.

37. (i) $fog(x)=f\{g(x)\}$

$$=f\left(\frac{x+1}{2x+5}\right)=\frac{1}{\frac{x+1}{2x+5}+5}$$

$$=\frac{2x+5}{x+1+5(2x+5)}=\frac{2x+5}{11x+26}$$

(ii) $fog(x)=\dfrac{2x+5}{11x+26}$

At $x=-\dfrac{26}{11}$,

$fog(x)$ does not exist.

Hence, domain of $fog(x)$

$$=\left(R-\left\{-\frac{26}{11}\right\}\right)$$

38. (True)

$$f\{f(x)\}=f\left(\frac{ax-b}{bx-a}\right)$$

$$=\frac{a\left(\frac{ax-b}{bx-a}\right)-b}{b\left(\frac{ax-b}{bx-a}\right)-a}$$

$$=\frac{a^2x-ab-b^2x+ab}{abx-b^2-abx+a^2}$$

$$=\frac{x(a^2-b^2)}{a^2-b^2}=x$$

39. Given, $f(x)=\sqrt[3]{3-x^3}$

$\Rightarrow f\{f(x)\}=\sqrt[3]{3-(\sqrt[3]{3-x^3})^3}$

$=\sqrt[3]{3-3+x^3}=x$

40. (False)

$ho(gof)(x)=h[g\{f(x)\}]$

$=h[g(2x+3)]$

$=h[4(2x+3)+3]$

$=h[8x+15]$

$=\cos(8x+15)$

$hog(x)=h\{g(x)\}$

$=\cos(4x+3)$

$(hog)of(x)=\cos[4f(x)+3]$

$=\cos[4(2x+3)+3]$

$=\cos(8x+15)$

Hence, $ho(gof)=(hog)of$

41. Given, $f(x)=3x+5$

and $fog(x)=gof(x)=I_R$

$3[g(x)]+5=g(3x+5)=x$

$3[g(x)]+5=x$

$g(x)=\dfrac{x-5}{3}$

42. (False)

$(f^{-1}og^{-1})o(gof)$

$=\{(f^{-1}og^{-1})og\}of$

$=\{f^{-1}o(g^{-1}og)\}of$

$=(f^{-1}oI)\ of=(f^{-1}of)=I_x$

Hence, $(gof)^{-1}=f^{-1}og^{-1}$.

43. (i) $f=\{(1,10),(2,10),(3,9)\}$

Since, the elements 1 and 2 have image 10, they do not have unique image.

$\therefore f$ is not one-one and the function is non-invertible.

(ii) $g=\{(1,6),(2,5),(8,4)\}$

Since, the element 1 does not have pre-image, function f is not onto and the function is non-invertible.

(iii) $h=\{(1,7),(4,8),(5,10),(8,13)\}$

Since, the function is one-one and onto, the function is invertible.

44. (a) $f^{-1}(a)=1, f^{-1}(b)=2$ and $f^{-1}(c)=3$

$\dfrac{f^{-1}(c)-f^{-1}(a)}{f^{-1}(b)}=\dfrac{3-1}{2}=1$

45. Let $f^{-1}(-3)=x \Rightarrow -3=f(x)$

$x^2+7x+9=-3$, then

$x^2+7x+12=0 \Rightarrow x=-4,-3$

As, there are two different values of x, $f^{-1}(x)$ does not exist.

Hence, no solution.

46. As, the function is one-one and onto, the function is invertible.

Let $y=5x+7 \Rightarrow x=\dfrac{y-7}{5}$

Hence, $f^{-1}(x)=\dfrac{x-7}{5}$

47. (d) Let $y=\dfrac{2x}{x+5}$

$xy+5y=2x \Rightarrow x=\dfrac{5y}{2-y}$

Hence, $f^{-1}(x)=\dfrac{5x}{2-x}$

48. Let $y=\dfrac{1}{2}(kx-1)$

$\Rightarrow 2y=kx-1 \Rightarrow x=\dfrac{2y+1}{k}$

Therefore, $f^{-1}(x)=\dfrac{2x+1}{k}$

According to question,

$\dfrac{kx-1}{2}=\dfrac{2x+1}{k}$

$k^2x-k=4x+2$

Comparing the coefficient of x

$k^2=4$ and $k=-2$

Hence, $k=-2$

49. (a) Let $y=x^5+6$

$x^5=y-6 \Rightarrow x=(y-6)^{1/5}$

Hence, $f^{-1}(x)=(x-6)^{1/5}$

Assertion-Reason

1. (d) We have, $f(x)=\sin x$

We know that $f(0)=\sin(0)=0$ and $f(\pi)=\sin(\pi)=0$

Thus, 0 and π have same image

$\therefore f$ is not one-one.

Also, range of $f=[-1,1]\subset R$

$\therefore f$ is not onto.

Hence, f is not bijection.

$\therefore$ Assertion is false but reason is true.

2. (c) We have, $f:R\rightarrow R$ such that

$f(x)=\dfrac{2x+1}{3}$

Let $y=\dfrac{2x+1}{3}$

$\Rightarrow 2x=3y-1 \Rightarrow x=\dfrac{3y-1}{2}$

$\therefore f^{-1}(x)=\dfrac{3x-1}{2}$

Hence, Assertion (A) is true.

For one-one.

$f(x_1)=f(x_2)$

$\Rightarrow \dfrac{2x_1+1}{3}=\dfrac{2x_2+1}{3} \Rightarrow x_1=x_2$

$\therefore f$ is one-one.

For onto

For every $y\in R$,

$\exists\ x=\dfrac{3y-1}{2}\in R$

such that $f(x)=y$

$\therefore f$ is onto.

Hence, Reason (R) is false.

3. (a) We have, $f(-x)=f(x)$ and $g(-x)=-g(x)$

Let $h(x)=\dfrac{f(x)}{g(x)}$

So, $h(-x)=\dfrac{f(-x)}{g(-x)}$

$=\dfrac{f(x)}{-g(x)}=-\dfrac{f(x)}{g(x)}$

$\therefore h(x)$ is an odd function.

Both Assertion and Reason are true and reason is the correct explanation of assertion.

4. (d) We have, $f:R\rightarrow R$ such that

$f(x)=\dfrac{1}{x}$

For one-one

$f(x_1)=f(x_2)$

$\Rightarrow \dfrac{1}{x_1}=\dfrac{1}{x_2}$

$\Rightarrow x_1=x_2$

$\therefore f$ is one-one.

For onto

Let $y=\dfrac{1}{x}$ such that $y\in R$

$\Rightarrow x=\dfrac{1}{y}$

Here, $y\neq 0$

$\therefore$ Range $=R-\{0\}\neq R$

$=$ codomain

Hence, f is not onto.

So, $x=0$ does not belong to domain of f.

Assertion is false but reason is true.

5. (a) We have, $f:R\rightarrow R$ such that $f(x)=x^3$

For one-one,

$f(x_1)=f(x_2)$

$\Rightarrow x_1^3=x_2^3$

$\Rightarrow x_1=x_2$

$\therefore f$ is an injective function.

Both Assertion and Reason are true and reason is the correct explanation of assertion.

6. (c) We have, $f: R \to R$ and $g: R \to R$ such that $f(x) = \sin x$ and $g(x) = x^2$

So, $fog(x) = f(g(x))$ $[\because fog(x) = f(g(x))]$

$= f(x^2) = \sin x^2$

$gof(x) = g(f(x))$ $[\because gof(x) = g(f(x))]$

Thus, $fog(x) \neq gof(x)$

$\therefore$ Assertion (A) is true.

$fog(x) \neq f(x)g(x) \neq gof(x)$

$\therefore$ Reason (R) is false.

7. (b) We have, relation R defined in $A = \{1, 2, 3\}$ by aRb such that $|a^2 - b^2| \leq 5$

$\Rightarrow R = \{(a, b) : |a^2 - b^2| \leq 5, a, b \in A\}$

So, $R^{-1} = \{(b, a) : |b^2 - a^2| \leq 5, a, b \in A\}$

$\Rightarrow R^{-1} = R$

We can see that the domain of R^{-1} = Range of R.

8. (a) We have, $R = \{(L_1, L_2) : L_1$ is perpendicular to $L_2\}$

For reflexive

Line L cannot be perpendicular to itself.

So, line L is not perpendicular to line L.

$\Rightarrow (L, L) \notin R$

$\therefore R$ is not reflexive.

For symmetric

If L_1 is perpendicular to L_2, then L_2 is perpendicular.

So, if $(L_1, L_2) \in R \Rightarrow (L_2, L_1) \in R$

$\therefore R$ is symmetric.

For transitive

If L_1 is perpendicular to L_2 and L_2 is perpendicular to L_3, then L_1 is parallel to L_2.

So, if $(L_1, L_2) \in R$ and $(L_2, L_3) \in R$ then $(L_1, L_3) \notin R$

$\therefore R$ is not transitive.

Hence, R is not an equivalence relation.

9. (a) We have,

$f(-x) = f(x)$ and $g(-x) = -g(x)$

So, $fog(x) = f(g(x))$

Let $g(x) = y$

$\Rightarrow fog(x) = f(y)$

Also, $fog(x) = f(g(-x))$

$= f(-g(x))$

$= f(-y)$

$= f(y)$

$\Rightarrow fog(x) = fog(-x)$

$\therefore fog$ is an even function.

Both Assertion and Reason are true and reason is the correct explanation of assertion.

10. (a) We have, $R = \{(1, 1), (1, 2), (2, 2), (2, 3), (3, 3)\}$ defined on the set $A = \{1, 2, 3\}$.

Here, $(1, 1), (2, 2), (3, 3) \in R \; \forall \; 1, 2, 3 \in A$

$\therefore R$ is reflexive.

Both Assertion and Reason are true and reason is the correct explanation of assertion.

Case Based

1. (i) (a) We have, $R : B \to B$ such that $R = \{(x, y) : y$ is divisible by $x\}$

For reflexive

x is divisible by x

$\therefore$ For every $x \in B$, x is divisible by x

$\Rightarrow (x, x) \in R \; \forall \; x \in B$

Hence, R is reflexive.

For symmetric

Here, $(2, 4) \in R$ $[\because 4$ is divisible by $2]$

but $(4, 2) \notin R$ $[\because 2$ is not divisible by $4]$

$\therefore R$ is not symmetric.

For transitive

Let $(x, y), (y, z) \in R$.

Then, y is divisible by x and z is divisible by y.

$\Rightarrow z$ is divisible by x

$\Rightarrow (x, z) \in R$

$\therefore R$ is transitive.

(ii) (c) Here, $n(A) = 2$ and $n(B) = 6$

So, number of function from A to $B = 6^2$.

(iii) (d) We have,

$R = \{(1, 2), (2, 2), (1, 3), (3, 4), (3, 1), (4, 3), (5, 5)\}$

For reflexive

Here, $(1, 1), (3, 3), (4, 4), (5, 5) \notin R$

$\Rightarrow (x, x) \notin R \; \forall \; x \in B$

$\therefore R$ is not reflexive.

For symmetric

Here, $(1, 2) \in R$ but $(2, 1) \notin R$

$\therefore R$ is not symmetric.

For transitive

Here, $(1, 3) \in R$ and $(3, 1) \in R$ but $(1, 1) \notin R$

$\therefore R$ is not transitive.

Here, R is not reflexive, not symmetric and not transitive.

2. (i) (a) We have, $f : R \to R$ such that $f(x) = 2x^2$

For one-one

For $x = 1 = 2(1)^2 = 2$

For $x = -1$

$f(x) = f(-1)$

$= 2(-1)^2 = 2$

So, $f(x_1) = f(x_2)$

$\Rightarrow$ but $x_1 \neq x_2$

$\therefore f$ is not one-one.

For onto

Let $y = -3 \in R$

$\Rightarrow f(x) = y$

$\Rightarrow 2x^2 = -3$

$\Rightarrow x^2 = -\dfrac{3}{2}$

$\Rightarrow x = \pm\sqrt{\dfrac{-3}{2}} \notin R$

$\therefore f$ is not onto.

Hence, $f(x)$ is neither one-one nor onto.

(ii) (c) We have, $f : N \to N$ such that $f(x) = 2x^2$

For one-one

Let, $x_1, x_2 \in N$

So, $f(x_1) = f(x_2)$

$\Rightarrow 2x_1^2 = 2x_2^2$

$\Rightarrow x_1 = x_2$

$\therefore f$ is one-one.

For onto

Let $y = 3 \in N$

$\Rightarrow f(x) = y$

$\Rightarrow 2x^2 = 3 \Rightarrow x^2 = \dfrac{3}{2}$

$\Rightarrow x = \pm\sqrt{\dfrac{3}{2}} \notin N$

$\therefore f$ is not onto.

(iii) (b) We have,

$f : N \to R$ such that $f(x) = 2x^2$

So, $f(1) = 2(1)^2 = 2$

$f(2) = 2(2)^2 = 8$

$f(3) = 2(3)^2 = 18$

$f(4) = 2(4)^2 = 32$

So on

$\therefore$ Range of f is $\{2, 8, 18, 32, \ldots\ldots\}$

Chapter-2

Inverse Trigonometric Function

1. (c) **2.** (b)

3. (d) $(f^{-1}of)(x) = f^{-1}\{f(x)\}$

$= f^{-1}(y) = x$

4. (i) (False)

$\because$ If sine function is restricted with the domain $\left[-\frac{\pi}{2}, \frac{\pi}{2}\right]$, then its range is $[-1, 1]$.

(ii) (True)

(iii) (True)

We know that the graph of inverse function can be obtain from the corresponding graph of original function as a mirror image (reflection) along the line $y = x$.

(iv) (False)

The range of the function $\sec^{-1} x$ is $[0, \pi] - \left\{\frac{\pi}{2}\right\}$.

(v) (True)

The tangent function for the intervals $(-3\pi/2, -\pi/2)$, $(-\pi/2, \pi/2)$, $(\pi/2, 3\pi/2)$, etc is bijective and thus possess inverse.

5. The graph of the function $y = \sin^{-1} x$ can be obtained from the graph of $y = \sin x$ by interchanging X and Y-axes. So, if (a, b) is a point on the graph of sine function, then (b, a) becomes the corresponding point on the graph of inverse of sine function.

6. Secant function restricted to any of the intervals $[-\pi, 0] - \left\{-\frac{\pi}{2}\right\}$, $[0, \pi] - \left\{\frac{\pi}{2}\right\}$, $[\pi, 2\pi] - \left\{\frac{3\pi}{2}\right\}$, $[2\pi, 3\pi] - \left\{\frac{5\pi}{2}\right\}$ etc., is bijective and its range is $R - (-1, 1)$.

Hence, the branch of $\sec^{-1} x$ other than the principal value branch corresponds to $[\pi, 2\pi] - \left\{\frac{3\pi}{2}\right\}$ and $[2\pi, 3\pi] - \left\{\frac{5\pi}{2}\right\}$.

7. (i) Let $\sin^{-1}(5x+1) = \theta$

$$5x + 1 = \sin\theta$$

Since, $-1 \le \sin\theta \le 1$

$\Rightarrow \quad -1 \le 5x + 1 \le 1$

$\Rightarrow \quad -\frac{2}{5} \le x \le 0$

$\therefore \quad x \in \left[-\frac{2}{5}, 0\right]$

Hence, the domain of $\sin^{-1}(5x+1)$ is $\left[\frac{-2}{5}, 0\right]$

(ii) The domain of $\sqrt{x-1}$ is $[1, \infty)$.

$$x - 1 \ge 0 \Rightarrow x \ge 1$$

The domain of $\cos^{-1} x$ is $[-1, 1]$.

So, $\quad 0 \le \sqrt{x-1} \le 1$

$$0 \le x - 1 \le 1$$

$$1 \le x \le 2$$

Hence, the domain of the function $\cos^{-1}(\sqrt{x-1})$ is $[1, 2]$.

(iii) For $\sec^{-1}(3-2x)$ to be defined

$$|3 - 2x| \ge 1$$

$$3 - 2x \ge 1 \text{ or } 3 - 2x \le -1$$

$$-2x \ge -2 \text{ or } -2x \le -4$$

$$x \le 1 \text{ or } x \ge 2$$

So, the domain of $\sec^{-1}(3-2x)$ is $(-\infty, 1] \cup [2, \infty)$.

8. (i) True (ii) True (iii) False as range of the function $\cot^{-1} x$ is $[0, \pi]$.

9. (b)

10. (i) As, $\sin^{-1} x \in \left[-\frac{\pi}{2}, \frac{\pi}{2}\right]$

$$\sin^{-1}\left(\frac{\sqrt{3}}{2}\right) = \frac{\pi}{3} \in \left[-\frac{\pi}{2}, \frac{\pi}{2}\right]$$

(ii) Let $x = \text{cosec}^{-1}\left(-\frac{2}{\sqrt{3}}\right)$

Then, $y = \text{cosec}^{-1} x$ is defined for all $x \in (-\infty, -1] \cup [1, \infty)$ and $y \in \left[-\frac{\pi}{2}, 0\right) \cup \left(0, \frac{\pi}{2}\right]$.

$$\text{cosec}\, x = -\frac{2}{\sqrt{3}}$$

$$\text{cosec}\, x = \text{cosec}\left(-\frac{\pi}{3}\right)$$

$$x = -\frac{\pi}{3}$$

(iii) Let $x = \sec^{-1}(-\sqrt{2})$

Then, $y = \sec^{-1} x$ is defined for all $x \in (-\infty, -1] \cup [1, \infty)$ and $y \in \left[0, \frac{\pi}{2}\right) \cup \left(\frac{\pi}{2}, \pi\right]$

$$\sec x = -\sqrt{2}$$

$$\sec x = \sec\left(\pi - \frac{\pi}{4}\right) \Rightarrow x = \frac{3\pi}{4}$$

11. (i) (False)

If $\sin^{-1} x = y$, then $y \in \left[-\frac{\pi}{2}, \frac{\pi}{2}\right]$

The range of $\sin^{-1} x$ is $\left[-\frac{\pi}{2}, \frac{\pi}{2}\right]$

$$\sin^{-1}\left(\frac{1}{2}\right) = \frac{5\pi}{6}$$

$$\frac{5\pi}{6} \notin \left[-\frac{\pi}{2}, \frac{\pi}{2}\right]$$

(ii) (False)

If $\tan^{-1} x = y$, then $y \in \left(-\frac{\pi}{2}, \frac{\pi}{2}\right)$

The range of $\tan^{-1} x$ is $\left(-\frac{\pi}{2}, \frac{\pi}{2}\right)$

$$\tan^{-1}(\sqrt{3}) = \frac{4\pi}{3}$$

$$\frac{4\pi}{3} \notin \left(-\frac{\pi}{2}, \frac{\pi}{2}\right)$$

12. (i) $\cos^{-1}\left(-\frac{1}{2}\right) + 2\sin^{-1}\left(\frac{1}{2}\right)$

$$= \frac{2\pi}{3} + \frac{2 \cdot \pi}{6} = \pi$$

(ii) $\sin^{-1}\left(\frac{1}{2}\right) = \frac{\pi}{6} \in \left[-\frac{\pi}{2}, \frac{\pi}{2}\right]$

$$\sec^{-1}(-2) = \frac{2\pi}{3} \in [0, \pi] - \left\{\frac{\pi}{2}\right\}$$

$$\sin^{-1}\left(\frac{1}{2}\right) - \sec^{-1}(-2)$$

$$= \frac{\pi}{6} - \frac{2\pi}{3} = -\frac{\pi}{2}$$

(iii) $\cos^{-1}\left(\frac{-1}{\sqrt{2}}\right) + \tan^{-1}(-\sqrt{3}) - \text{cosec}^{-1}(2)$

$$= \frac{3\pi}{4} + \left(-\frac{\pi}{3}\right) - \frac{\pi}{6}$$

$$= \frac{3\pi}{4} - \frac{\pi}{3} - \frac{\pi}{6}$$

$$= \frac{9\pi - 4\pi - 2\pi}{12} = \frac{3\pi}{12} = \frac{\pi}{4}$$

(iv) $\sin^{-1}\left(\frac{-\sqrt{3}}{2}\right) + \cos^{-1}\left(\frac{-\sqrt{2}}{2}\right) - \tan^{-1}\left(\frac{\sqrt{3}}{3}\right) + \cot^{-1}\left(\frac{-\sqrt{3}}{3}\right)$

$$= \frac{-\pi}{3} + \frac{3\pi}{4} - \frac{\pi}{6} + \frac{2\pi}{3}$$

$$= \frac{-4\pi + 9\pi - 2\pi + 8\pi}{12} = \frac{11\pi}{12}$$

13. (i) True (ii) True (iii) True

(iv) False as $\operatorname{cosec}^{-1}(\operatorname{cosec}\theta) = \theta$ provided that $\theta \in \left[\frac{-\pi}{2}, \frac{\pi}{2}\right] - \{0\}$

14. (i) Let $\theta = \tan^{-1}(-1)$ and $\tan\theta = -1$

$\Rightarrow \theta = -\frac{\pi}{4}$

$\sin\{\tan^{-1}(-1)\} = \sin\left(-\frac{\pi}{4}\right) = \frac{-1}{\sqrt{2}}$

(ii) $\cos^{-1}\left(\sin\frac{\pi}{2}\right) = \cos^{-1}(1) = 0$

15. (i) The range of the $\sin^{-1} x$ is $\left[-\frac{\pi}{2}, \frac{\pi}{2}\right]$

$$\sin^{-1}\left\{\sin\left(\frac{3\pi}{4}\right)\right\} = \sin^{-1}\left\{\sin\left(\pi - \frac{\pi}{4}\right)\right\} = \sin^{-1}\left\{\sin\left(\frac{\pi}{4}\right)\right\} = \frac{\pi}{4}$$

(ii) The range of the $\cot^{-1} x$ is $(0, \pi)$.

$\cot^{-1}\left(\cot\frac{3\pi}{4}\right) = \frac{3\pi}{4}$

(iii) $\cot\left(\frac{37\pi}{6}\right) = \cot\left(\frac{36\pi}{6} + \frac{\pi}{6}\right)$

$$= \cot\left(6\pi + \frac{\pi}{6}\right) = \cot\left(\frac{\pi}{6}\right) = \tan\left(\frac{\pi}{2} - \frac{\pi}{6}\right) = \tan\left(\frac{\pi}{3}\right)$$

$\Rightarrow \tan^{-1}\left\{\cot\left(\frac{37\pi}{6}\right)\right\} = \tan^{-1}\left\{\tan\left(\frac{\pi}{3}\right)\right\} = \frac{\pi}{3}$

(iv)

$$\cos^{-1}\left[\sin\left[\cot^{-1}\left[\tan\left\{\cos^{-1}\left(\sin\frac{\pi}{3}\right)\right\}\right]\right]\right]$$

$$= \cos^{-1}\left[\sin\left[\cot^{-1}\left[\tan\left\{\cos^{-1}\left(\cos\frac{\pi}{6}\right)\right\}\right]\right]\right]$$

$$= \cos^{-1}\left[\sin\left[\cot^{-1}\left[\tan\frac{\pi}{6}\right]\right]\right]$$

$$= \cos^{-1}\left[\sin\left[\cot^{-1}\left(\cot\frac{\pi}{3}\right)\right]\right]$$

$$= \cos^{-1}\left[\sin\frac{\pi}{3}\right]$$

$$= \cos^{-1}\left\{\cos\left(\frac{\pi}{6}\right)\right\} = \frac{\pi}{6}$$

(v) $\tan^{-1}[\cot\{\sin^{-1}(\cos\theta)\}]$

$$= \tan^{-1}\left[\cot\left\{\sin^{-1}\left(\sin\left(\frac{\pi}{2} - \theta\right)\right)\right\}\right]$$

$$= \tan^{-1}\left[\cot\left\{\frac{\pi}{2} - \theta\right\}\right]$$

$$= \tan^{-1}[\tan\theta] = \theta$$

16. (a) Let $y = \sin^{-1}\left(\frac{\sin x + \cos x}{\sqrt{2}}\right)$

$$= \sin^{-1}\left(\frac{1}{\sqrt{2}}\cdot\sin x + \frac{1}{\sqrt{2}}\cdot\cos x\right)$$

$$= \sin^{-1}\left(\sin x\cdot\cos\frac{\pi}{4} + \cos x\cdot\sin\frac{\pi}{4}\right)$$

$$= \sin^{-1}\left\{\sin\left(x + \frac{\pi}{4}\right)\right\}$$

$[\because \sin(A + B) = \sin A\cos B + \cos A\sin B]$

$$= x + \frac{\pi}{4}$$

17. Given, $\cos^{-1}(1 - 2x) - 2\sin^{-1}\sqrt{x}$

Let $x = \sin^2 A$

$$\cos^{-1}(1 - 2x) - 2\sin^{-1}\sqrt{x} = \cos^{-1}(1 - 2\sin^2 A) - 2\sin^{-1}(\sqrt{\sin^2 A})$$

$$= \cos^{-1}(\cos 2A) - 2A = 0$$

18. Given, $\cot^{-1}\frac{\sqrt{a^2 - x^2}}{x} - \sec^{-1}\frac{a}{x}$

Let $x = a\cos A$

$$\cot^{-1}\frac{\sqrt{a^2 - a^2\cos^2 A}}{a\cos A} - \sec^{-1}\frac{a}{a\cos A}$$

$$= \cot^{-1}\frac{\sin A}{\cos A} - \sec^{-1}\frac{1}{\cos A}$$

$$= \cot^{-1}(\tan A) - \sec^{-1}(\sec A)$$

$$= \cot^{-1}\left\{\cot\left(\frac{\pi}{2} - A\right)\right\} - A$$

$$= \frac{\pi}{2} - 2A = \frac{\pi}{2} - 2\cos^{-1}\left(\frac{x}{a}\right)$$

19. Rewrite the given expression

$$\cos^{-1}[x\cdot\sqrt{x} - \sqrt{\{1 - (\sqrt{x})^2\}}\cdot\sqrt{(1 - x^2)}\,]$$

Let $x = \cos A$ and $\sqrt{x} = \cos B$

$$\cos^{-1}[\cos A\cdot\cos B - \sqrt{(1 - \cos^2 B)}\cdot\sqrt{(1 - \cos^2 A)}]$$

$$= \cos^{-1}(\cos A\cdot\cos B - \sin A\cdot\sin B)$$

$$= \cos^{-1}\{\cos(A + B)\} = A + B$$

A and B can be written in the form of x.

$$A + B = \cos^{-1} x + \cos^{-1}\sqrt{x}$$

20. (i) R (ii) $R - (-1, 1)$

21. (d) Given,

$$\cot^{-1}\frac{\{(\sqrt{1 - \cos x}) - (\sqrt{1 + \cos x})\}}{\{(\sqrt{1 - \cos x}) + (\sqrt{1 + \cos x})\}}$$

$$= \cot^{-1}\left(\frac{\sin\frac{x}{2} - \cos\frac{x}{2}}{\sin\frac{x}{2} + \cos\frac{x}{2}}\right)$$

$$= \cot^{-1}\left(\frac{\tan\frac{x}{2} - 1}{\tan\frac{x}{2} + 1}\right)$$

$$= \cot^{-1}\left\{\tan\left(\frac{x}{2} - \frac{\pi}{4}\right)\right\}$$

$$= \cot^{-1}\left\{\cot\left[\frac{\pi}{2} - \left(\frac{x}{2} - \frac{\pi}{4}\right)\right]\right\}$$

$$= \frac{3\pi}{4} - \frac{x}{2}$$

22. Given, $\cot^{-1}\left(\frac{\sqrt{1 + \sin x}}{\sqrt{1 - \sin x}}\right)$

Using the formula

$\cos^2 x + \sin^2 x = 1$

and $\sin 2x = 2\sin x\cdot\cos x$,

$$\cot^{-1}\left(\frac{\sqrt{\cos^2\frac{x}{2} + \sin^2\frac{x}{2} + 2\sin\frac{x}{2}.\cos\frac{x}{2}}}{\sqrt{\cos^2\frac{x}{2} + \sin^2\frac{x}{2} - 2\sin\frac{x}{2}.\cos\frac{x}{2}}}\right)$$

$$= \cot^{-1}\left(\frac{\cos\frac{x}{2} + \sin\frac{x}{2}}{\cos\frac{x}{2} - \sin\frac{x}{2}}\right)$$

Dividing numerator and denominator by $\cos\frac{x}{2}$,

$$= \cot^{-1}\left(\frac{1 + \tan\frac{x}{2}}{1 - \tan\frac{x}{2}}\right)$$

$$= \cot^{-1}\left(\frac{\tan\frac{\pi}{4} + \tan\frac{x}{2}}{1 - \tan\frac{\pi}{4}.\tan\frac{x}{2}}\right)$$

$$= \cot^{-1}\left\{\tan\left(\frac{\pi}{4} + \frac{x}{2}\right)\right\}$$

$$= \cot^{-1}\left[\cot\left\{\frac{\pi}{2} - \left(\frac{\pi}{4} + \frac{x}{2}\right)\right\}\right]$$

$$= \frac{\pi}{4} - \frac{x}{2}$$

Assertion Reason

1. (a) $\sin^{-1}\left(-\frac{1}{2}\right) = \sin^{-1}\left(-\sin\frac{\pi}{6}\right)$

$= \sin^{-1}\left(\sin\left(-\frac{\pi}{6}\right)\right) = -\frac{\pi}{6}$

Hence, both A and R are true and R is the correct explanation of A.

2. (d) $\cos^{-1}\left(\frac{-1}{\sqrt{2}}\right) = \pi - \cos^{-1}\frac{1}{\sqrt{2}}$

$= \pi - \frac{\pi}{4} = \frac{3\pi}{4}$

Hence, A is false and R is true.

3. (b) $\tan^{-1}\left(\tan\frac{3\pi}{4}\right)$

$= \tan^{-1}\left(\tan\left(\pi - \frac{\pi}{4}\right)\right)$

$= \tan^{-1}\left(-\tan\frac{\pi}{4}\right) = -\frac{\pi}{4}$

and range of $\tan^{-1} x$ is $\left(\frac{-\pi}{2}, \frac{\pi}{2}\right)$.

Hence, A is true and R is not the correct explanation of A.

4. (a) $\cos^{-1}\left(\cos\frac{5\pi}{3}\right)$

$= \cos^{-1}\left(\cos\left(2\pi - \frac{\pi}{3}\right)\right)$

$= \cos^{-1}\left(\cos\frac{\pi}{3}\right)$

Hence, both A and R are true R is the correct explanation of A.

5. (c) Hence, A is true and R is false as $\sec^{-1}(-x) = \pi - \sec^{-1}x$, $x \in R - (-1, 1)$.

6. (a) $\cos\left(\sec^{-1}\left(\frac{5}{3}\right)\right)$

$= \cos\left(\cos^{-1}\left(\frac{3}{5}\right)\right) = \frac{3}{5}$

Hence, both A and R are true and R is the correct explanation of A.

7. (d) $\tan^{-1}\sqrt{3} - \sec^{-1}(-2)$

$= \tan^{-1}\left(\tan\frac{\pi}{3}\right) - \{\pi - \sec^{-1}2\}$

$= \frac{\pi}{3} - \pi + \sec^{-1}\left(\sec\frac{\pi}{3}\right)$

$= -\frac{2\pi}{3} + \frac{\pi}{3} = -\frac{\pi}{3}$

Hence, A is false and R is true.

8. (c) $\cos^{-1}\left(\cos\frac{13\pi}{6}\right)$

$= \cos^{-1}\left(\cos\left(2\pi + \frac{\pi}{6}\right)\right)$

$= \cos^{-1}\left(\cos\frac{\pi}{6}\right) = \frac{\pi}{6}$

$\tan^{-1}\left(\tan\frac{5\pi}{6}\right)$

$= \tan^{-1}\left(\tan\left(\pi - \frac{\pi}{6}\right)\right)$

$= \tan^{-1}\left(-\tan\frac{\pi}{6}\right) = -\frac{\pi}{6}$

Hence, A is true and R is false.

9. (d) $\sin\left(\tan^{-1}\frac{a}{b}\right)$

$= \sin\left(\sin^{-1}\frac{a}{\sqrt{a^2+b^2}}\right)$

$= \frac{a}{\sqrt{a^2+b^2}}$

Reason $\tan\left(\cot^{-1}\frac{a}{b}\right)$

$= \tan\left(\tan^{-1}\frac{b}{a}\right) = \frac{b}{a}$

Hence, A is false and R is true.

10. (b) $\sin^{-1}\left(\cos\left(\sin^{-1}\left(\frac{1}{2}\right)\right)\right)$

$= \sin^{-1}\left(\cos\left(\frac{\pi}{6}\right)\right)$

$= \sin^{-1}\left(\frac{\sqrt{3}}{2}\right) = \frac{\pi}{3}$

Reason $\sin^{-1}(\cos x)$

$= \sin^{-1}\left(\sin\left(\frac{\pi}{2} - \pi\right)\right)$

$= \frac{\pi}{2} - x$

Hence, both A is true but R is not correct explanation of A.

Case Based Questions

1. We have,

(i) (d) Now, in ΔABD (right angled)

$\tan\alpha = \frac{BD}{AD}$

$= \frac{45}{15\sqrt{3}}$

$\Rightarrow \tan\alpha = = \sqrt{3} = \tan 60°$

$\Rightarrow \quad \alpha = 60°$

$\Rightarrow \sin\alpha = \sin 60° = \frac{\sqrt{3}}{2}$

$\Rightarrow \quad \alpha = \sin^{-1}\left(\frac{\sqrt{3}}{2}\right)$

(ii) (c) We have, from part (i),

$\alpha = 60°$

$\Rightarrow \cos\alpha = \cos 60° = \frac{1}{2}$

$\Rightarrow \alpha = \cos^{-1}\left(\frac{1}{2}\right)$

(iii) (d) In right ΔBCD, we have

$\tan\beta = \frac{BD}{DC}$

$\Rightarrow \tan\beta = \frac{45}{5\sqrt{3}} = \frac{9}{\sqrt{3}}$

$\Rightarrow \beta = \tan^{-1}(3\sqrt{3})$

(iv) (c) In ΔABC, we have

$\angle ABC + \angle BAC + \angle ACB = 180°$

$\Rightarrow \angle ABC + \alpha + \beta = 180°$

$\Rightarrow \angle ABC + 30° + \tan^{-1}(3\sqrt{3}) = 180°$

[from part (iii) $\beta = \tan^{-1}(\sqrt{3}) = 60°$]

$\Rightarrow \angle ABC = 90° - \tan^{-1}(3\sqrt{3})$

$\Rightarrow \angle ABC = \cot^{-1}(3\sqrt{3})$

(v) (c) Let $\cos^{-1} x = y$

$\Rightarrow \quad x = \cos y$

$-1 \le \cos y \le 1$

$\Rightarrow \quad -1 \le x \le 1$

$\Rightarrow$ Domain $= [-1, 1]$

$0 \le y \le \pi$

$\Rightarrow$ Range $= [0, \pi]$

2. Let $\angle CAB = \alpha$, therefore $\angle DAB = 2\alpha$ and $\angle EAB = 3\alpha$.

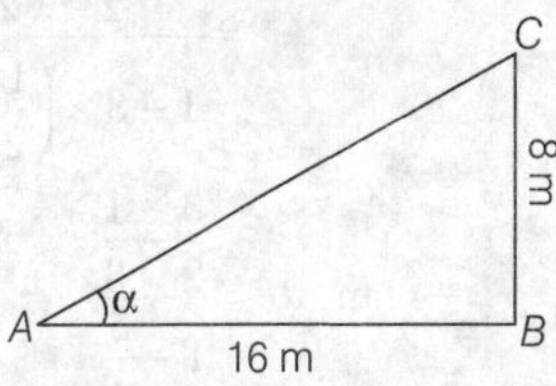

(i) (b) In right ΔABC, we have

$\tan\alpha = \frac{BC}{AB} = \frac{8}{16} = \frac{1}{2}$

$\Rightarrow \alpha = \tan^{-1}\left(\frac{1}{2}\right)$

$\Rightarrow \angle CAB = \tan^{-1}\left(\frac{1}{2}\right)$

(ii) (c) We have, $\tan\alpha = \frac{1}{2}$ [from part (i)]

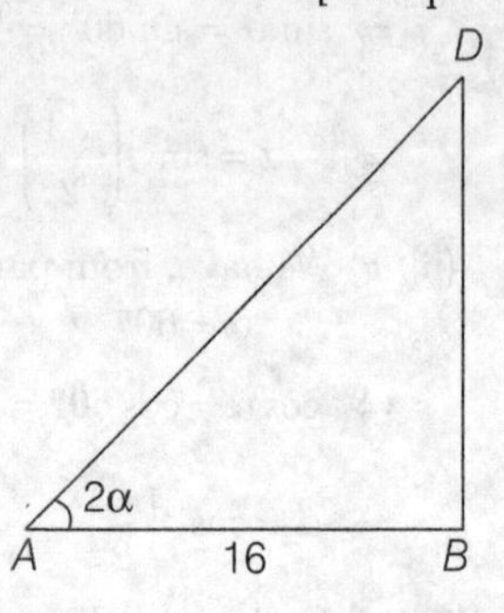

$$\therefore \tan 2\alpha = \frac{2\tan\alpha}{1-\tan^2\alpha} = \frac{2\times\frac{1}{2}}{1-\frac{1}{4}}$$

$$\tan 2\alpha = \frac{1}{\frac{3}{4}} = \frac{4}{3}$$

$$\Rightarrow 2\alpha = \tan^{-1}\left(\frac{4}{3}\right)$$

$$\Rightarrow \angle DAB = \tan^{-1}\left(\frac{4}{3}\right)$$

(iii) (d) We have, $\tan\alpha = \frac{1}{2}$

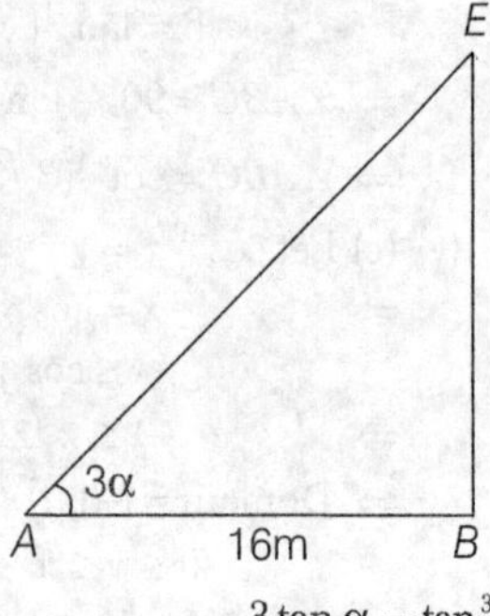

$$\therefore \tan 3\alpha = \frac{3\tan\alpha - \tan^3\alpha}{1-3\tan^2\alpha}$$

$$= \frac{3\times\frac{1}{2}-\left(\frac{1}{2}\right)^3}{1-3\times\left(\frac{1}{2}\right)^2}$$

$$\tan 3\alpha = \frac{\frac{3}{2}-\frac{1}{8}}{1-\frac{3}{4}}$$

$$= \frac{\frac{11}{8}}{\frac{1}{4}} = \frac{11}{8}\times 4 = \frac{11}{2}$$

$$\Rightarrow 3\alpha = \tan^{-1}\left(\frac{11}{2}\right)$$

$$\Rightarrow \angle EAB = \tan^{-1}\left(\frac{11}{2}\right)$$

(iv) (a) In $\angle CA'B = \beta$

We have, in $A'CB$

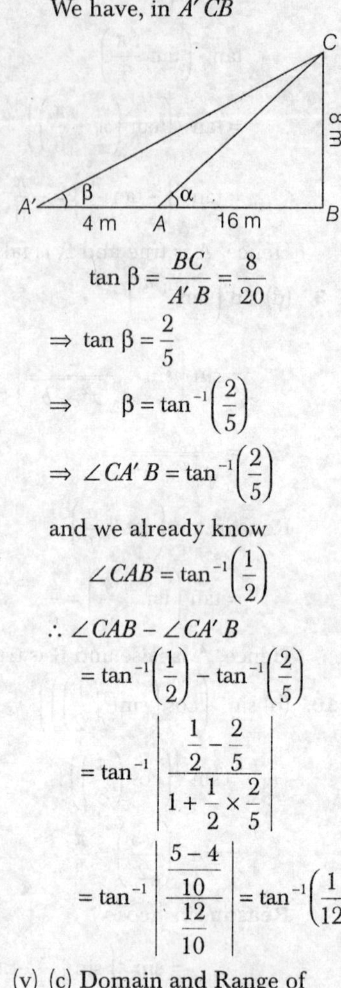

$$\tan\beta = \frac{BC}{A'B} = \frac{8}{20}$$

$$\Rightarrow \tan\beta = \frac{2}{5}$$

$$\Rightarrow \quad \beta = \tan^{-1}\left(\frac{2}{5}\right)$$

$$\Rightarrow \angle CA'B = \tan^{-1}\left(\frac{2}{5}\right)$$

and we already know

$$\angle CAB = \tan^{-1}\left(\frac{1}{2}\right)$$

$$\therefore \angle CAB - \angle CA'B$$

$$= \tan^{-1}\left(\frac{1}{2}\right) - \tan^{-1}\left(\frac{2}{5}\right)$$

$$= \tan^{-1}\left|\frac{\frac{1}{2}-\frac{2}{5}}{1+\frac{1}{2}\times\frac{2}{5}}\right|$$

$$= \tan^{-1}\left|\frac{\frac{5-4}{10}}{\frac{12}{10}}\right| = \tan^{-1}\left(\frac{1}{12}\right)$$

(v) (c) Domain and Range of $\tan^{-1} x$ are respectively $(-\infty, \infty)$ and $\left(-\frac{\pi}{2}, \frac{\pi}{2}\right)$ i.e. $R, \left(-\frac{\pi}{2}, \frac{\pi}{2}\right)$

Competion Connect

1. (i) (False)

Let $\sin^{-1}\frac{1}{x} = \text{cosec}^{-1} x = y$

i.e. $x = \text{cosec}\, y$

$\therefore x \in (-\infty, -1] \cup (1, \infty]$

(ii) (True)

Let $\cos^{-1}\frac{1}{x} = \sec^{-1} x = y$

i.e. $x = \sec y$

$\therefore x \in (-\infty, -1] \cup [1, \infty)$.

(iii) (True)

Let $\tan^{-1}\frac{1}{x} = \cot^{-1} x = y$

i.e. $x = \cot y$

Therefore, $x \in (0, \infty)$

2. (i) $\sin\left\{\frac{\pi}{3} - \sin^{-1}\left(-\frac{1}{2}\right)\right\}$

$$= \sin\left(\frac{\pi}{3} + \sin^{-1}\frac{1}{2}\right)$$

$[\because \sin^{-1}(-\theta) = -\sin^{-1}\theta]$

$$= \sin\left(\frac{\pi}{3}+\frac{\pi}{6}\right) \quad \left[\because \sin\frac{\pi}{6} = \frac{1}{2}\right]$$

$$= \sin\frac{3\pi}{6} = 1$$

(ii) $\cot[\pi - \cot^{-1}(-\sqrt{3})]$

$$= \cot[\pi - (\pi - \cot^{-1}(\sqrt{3}))]$$

$$= \cot[\pi - \pi + \cot^{-1}(\sqrt{3})]$$

$$= \sqrt{3}$$

3. (i) (a) $\cos\left\{\cos^{-1}\left(-\frac{\sqrt{3}}{2}\right) + \frac{\pi}{6}\right\}$

$$= \cos\left(\pi - \cos^{-1}\frac{\sqrt{3}}{2} + \frac{\pi}{6}\right)$$

$$= \cos\left(\pi - \frac{\pi}{6} + \frac{\pi}{6}\right)$$

$$= \cos\pi = -1$$

(ii) (b) Given,

$$\tan\{(\sin^{-1} m + \cos^{-1} m) - \cot^{-1}(1)\}$$

As, $\sin^{-1} x + \cos^{-1} x = \frac{\pi}{2}$

$$\therefore \tan\{(\sin^{-1} m + \cos^{-1} m) - \cot^{-1}(1)\}$$

$$= \tan\left(\frac{\pi}{2} - \frac{\pi}{4}\right)$$

$$= \tan\left(\frac{\pi}{4}\right) = 1$$

(iii) (b) $\alpha \le 4\sin^{-1} x - 3\cos^{-1} x \le \beta$

As, $\sin^{-1} x + \cos^{-1} x = \frac{\pi}{2}$

$$\therefore \alpha \le 4\sin^{-1} x - 3\left(\frac{\pi}{2} - \sin^{-1} x\right) \le \beta$$

$$\alpha \le 7\sin^{-1} x - \frac{3\pi}{2} \le \beta$$

Also, $-\frac{\pi}{2} \le \sin^{-1} x \le \frac{\pi}{2}$

$$-\frac{7\pi}{2} \le 7\sin^{-1} x \le \frac{7\pi}{2}$$

$$-\frac{7\pi}{2} - \frac{3\pi}{2} \le 7\sin^{-1} x - \frac{3\pi}{2} \le \frac{7\pi}{2} - \frac{3\pi}{2}$$

$$-5\pi \le 7\sin^{-1} x - \frac{3\pi}{2} \le 2\pi$$

Hence, $(\alpha, \beta) = (-5\pi, 2\pi)$

(iv) (a) Given, $\sin^{-1} x > \cos^{-1} x$

Using the formula

$\sin^{-1} x + \cos^{-1} x = \frac{\pi}{2}$,

$\sin^{-1} x > \frac{\pi}{2} - \sin^{-1} x$

$2\sin^{-1} x > \frac{\pi}{2}$

$\sin^{-1} x > \frac{\pi}{4}$

$x > \sin\frac{\pi}{4} \Rightarrow x > \frac{1}{\sqrt{2}}$

4. Given, $\cot^{-1} x + \cot^{-1} y = \frac{5\pi}{8}$

As, $\cot^{-1} x = \frac{\pi}{2} - \tan^{-1} x$

$\therefore \left(\frac{\pi}{2} - \tan^{-1} x\right) + \left(\frac{\pi}{2} - \tan^{-1} y\right) = \frac{5\pi}{8}$

$\pi - (\tan^{-1} x + \tan^{-1} y) = \frac{5\pi}{8}$

$\tan^{-1} x + \tan^{-1} y = \pi - \frac{5\pi}{8} = \frac{3\pi}{8}$

5. (True)

LHS $= \frac{7\pi}{30} - \frac{7}{15}\tan^{-1}\frac{21}{20}$

$= \frac{7}{15}\left(\frac{\pi}{2} - \tan^{-1}\frac{21}{20}\right)$

$= \frac{7}{15}\cot^{-1}\frac{21}{20}$

$= \frac{7}{15}\operatorname{cosec}^{-1}\sqrt{1+\left(\frac{21}{20}\right)^2}$

$= \frac{7}{15}\operatorname{cosec}^{-1}\frac{29}{20}$

$= \frac{7}{15}\sin^{-1}\frac{20}{29} =$ RHS

6. Let $y = \sin^{-1} x + \tan^{-1}\frac{1}{x} + \tan^{-1} x$

As, $\tan^{-1}\frac{1}{x} = \cot^{-1} x$,

$\therefore y = \sin^{-1} x + \cot^{-1} x + \tan^{-1} x$

As, $\tan^{-1} x + \cot^{-1} x = \frac{\pi}{2}$

$\therefore \quad y = \sin^{-1} x + \frac{\pi}{2}$

As, $-\frac{\pi}{2} \le \sin^{-1} x \le \frac{\pi}{2}$

$\Rightarrow -\frac{\pi}{2} + \frac{\pi}{2} \le \sin^{-1} x + \frac{\pi}{2} \le \frac{\pi}{2} + \frac{\pi}{2}$

$\Rightarrow 0 \le y \le \pi$

The range of the function

$\sin^{-1} x + \tan^{-1}\frac{1}{x} + \tan^{-1} x$

is $[0, \pi]$.

7. $(\sec^{-1} x)^2 + (\operatorname{cosec}^{-1}\sqrt{2})^2 + 2\sec^{-1} x \cdot \operatorname{cosec}^{-1}\sqrt{2} = \frac{\pi^2}{4}$

$\Rightarrow (\sec^{-1} x + \operatorname{cosec}^{-1}\sqrt{2})^2 = \frac{\pi^2}{4}$

$\Rightarrow \quad \sec^{-1} x + \operatorname{cosec}^{-1}\sqrt{2} = \frac{\pi}{2}$

$\Rightarrow \quad x = \sqrt{2}$

$\left[\because \sec^{-1} x + \operatorname{cosec}^{-1} x = \frac{\pi}{2}\right]$

8. (i) Given, $\cot^{-1}(-1) + \cot^{-1}(-2) + \cot^{-1}(-3)$

Using the formula

$\cot^{-1}(-x) = \pi - \cot^{-1} x$,

$\therefore \pi - \cot^{-1} 1 + \pi - \cot^{-1} 2 + \pi - \cot^{-1} 3$

$= 3\pi - \cot^{-1} 1 - \cot^{-1} 2 - \cot^{-1} 3$

Using the formula

$\cot^{-1} x = \tan^{-1}\frac{1}{x}$,

$\therefore 3\pi - \tan^{-1} 1 - \tan^{-1}\frac{1}{2} - \tan^{-1}\frac{1}{3}$

$= 3\pi - \frac{\pi}{4} - \tan^{-1}\left(\frac{\frac{1}{2}+\frac{1}{3}}{1-\frac{1}{2}.\frac{1}{3}}\right)$

$= 3\pi - \frac{\pi}{4} - \tan^{-1}(1)$

$= 3\pi - \frac{\pi}{4} - \frac{\pi}{4} = \frac{5\pi}{2}$

(ii) $\tan\left[\sin^{-1}\left(\frac{3}{5}\right) + \cot^{-1}\frac{3}{2}\right]$

$= \tan\left[\tan^{-1}\frac{3}{4} + \tan^{-1}\frac{2}{3}\right]$

$= \tan\left[\tan^{-1}\left(\frac{\frac{3}{4}+\frac{2}{3}}{1-\frac{3}{4}.\frac{2}{3}}\right)\right]$

$= \tan\left[\tan^{-1}\frac{17}{6}\right] = \frac{17}{6}$

9. (True)

Given, $\sin^{-1}\left(\frac{8}{17}\right)$ can be written as $\tan^{-1}\left(\frac{8}{15}\right)$

$\sin^{-1}\left(\frac{3}{5}\right)$ can be written as

$\tan^{-1}\left(\frac{3}{4}\right)$

$\therefore \sin^{-1}\left(\frac{8}{17}\right) + \sin^{-1}\left(\frac{3}{5}\right)$

$= \tan^{-1}\left(\frac{8}{15}\right) + \tan^{-1}\left(\frac{3}{4}\right)$

Using the formula

$\tan^{-1} x + \tan^{-1} y = \tan^{-1}\left(\frac{x+y}{1-xy}\right)$,

$\tan^{-1}\left(\frac{8}{15}\right) + \tan^{-1}\left(\frac{3}{4}\right)$

$= \tan^{-1}\left(\frac{\frac{8}{15}+\frac{3}{4}}{1-\frac{8}{15}\times\frac{3}{4}}\right)$

$= \tan^{-1}\left(\frac{32+45}{60-24}\right) = \tan^{-1}\left(\frac{77}{36}\right)$

So, $\tan^{-1}\left(\frac{77}{36}\right)$ can be written as $\sin^{-1}\left(\frac{77}{85}\right)$.

10. Given,

$\sin\left\{\sec^{-1}\left(\frac{17}{8}\right) + \operatorname{cosec}^{-1}\left(\frac{13}{5}\right)\right\}$

$\sec^{-1}\left(\frac{17}{8}\right)$ can be written as

$\tan^{-1}\left(\frac{15}{8}\right)$

$\operatorname{cosec}^{-1}\left(\frac{13}{5}\right)$ can be written as

$\tan^{-1}\left(\frac{5}{12}\right)$

$\therefore \sin\left\{\sec^{-1}\left(\frac{17}{8}\right) + \operatorname{cosec}^{-1}\left(\frac{13}{5}\right)\right\}$

$= \sin\left\{\tan^{-1}\left(\frac{15}{8}\right) + \tan^{-1}\left(\frac{5}{12}\right)\right\}$

$= \sin\left\{\tan^{-1}\left(\frac{\frac{15}{8}+\frac{5}{12}}{1-\frac{15}{8}\times\frac{5}{12}}\right)\right\}$

$= \sin\left\{\tan^{-1}\left(\frac{180+40}{96-75}\right)\right\}$

$= \sin\left\{\tan^{-1}\left(\frac{220}{21}\right)\right\}$

$= \sin\left\{\sin^{-1}\left(\frac{220}{221}\right)\right\} = \frac{220}{221}$

11. (i) Given,

$\cot^{-1}\frac{a}{b} + \cot^{-1}\frac{a+b}{a-b} = \tan^{-1} c$

Using the formula

$\cot^{-1} x = \tan^{-1}\frac{1}{x}$,

$\tan^{-1}\frac{b}{a} + \tan^{-1}\frac{a-b}{a+b} = \tan^{-1} c$

Using the formula

$\tan^{-1} x + \tan^{-1} y = \tan^{-1}\left(\frac{x+y}{1-xy}\right)$,

$$\tan^{-1}\left(\frac{\frac{b}{a}+\left(\frac{a-b}{a+b}\right)}{1-\left(\frac{b}{a}\right)\left(\frac{a-b}{a+b}\right)}\right)=\tan^{-1}c$$

$$\tan^{-1}\left(\frac{ab+b^2+a^2-ab}{a^2+ab-ab+b^2}\right)=\tan^{-1}c$$

$$\tan^{-1}1=\tan^{-1}c$$

$$c=1$$

(ii) $\cot^{-1}\left(\frac{pq+1}{p-q}\right)+\cot^{-1}\left(\frac{qr+1}{q-r}\right)+\cot^{-1}\left[\frac{rp+1}{r-p}\right]$

$=[\cot^{-1}q-\cot^{-1}p]+[\cot^{-1}r-\cot^{-1}q]+[\cot^{-1}p-\cot^{-1}r]=0$

12. (i) (True)

Sum of the interior angles of the triangle is 180°.

$\tan^{-1}2+\tan^{-1}3+\frac{\pi}{4}$

$=\pi+\tan^{-1}\left(\frac{2+3}{1-2\times 3}\right)+\frac{\pi}{4}$

$[\because x\cdot y>1,\text{ where } x=2, y=3]$

$=\pi+\tan^{-1}(-1)+\frac{\pi}{4}$

$=\pi-\tan^{-1}(1)+\frac{\pi}{4}$

$=\pi-\frac{\pi}{4}+\frac{\pi}{4}=\pi$

Therefore, $\tan^{-1}2$, $\tan^{-1}3$ and $\frac{\pi}{4}$ are the three angles of the triangle.

(ii) (True)

$\tan^{-1}\left(\frac{1}{3}\right)+\tan^{-1}\left(\frac{1}{7}\right)+\tan^{-1}\left(\frac{1}{13}\right)+\ldots$

$=\tan^{-1}\left(\frac{1}{1+2}\right)+\tan^{-1}\left(\frac{1}{1+6}\right)+\tan^{-1}\left(\frac{1}{1+12}\right)+\ldots$

$=\tan^{-1}\left(\frac{2-1}{1+2\cdot 1}\right)+\tan^{-1}\left(\frac{3-2}{1+3\cdot 2}\right)+\tan^{-1}\left(\frac{4-3}{1+4.3}\right)+\ldots.+\ldots.+\tan^{-1}\left[\frac{n+1-n}{1+(n+1)\cdot n}\right]$

$=\tan^{-1}(2)-\tan^{-1}(1)+\tan^{-1}(3)-\tan^{-1}(2)+\tan^{-1}(4)-\tan^{-1}(3)+\ldots+\tan^{-1}(n+1)-\tan^{-1}(n)$

$=\tan^{-1}(n+1)-\tan^{-1}(1)$

$=\tan^{-1}\left(\frac{n+1-1}{1+(n+1)\cdot 1}\right)$

$=\tan^{-1}\left(\frac{n}{n+2}\right), n\to\infty$

$=\tan^{-1}(1)=\frac{\pi}{4}$

(iii) (True)

Given,

$\sin^{-1}x-\sin^{-1}\left(\frac{\sqrt{3}x-\sqrt{1-x^2}}{2}\right)$

Let $x=\sin A$

$\therefore \sin^{-1}(\sin A)-\sin^{-1}\left(\frac{\sqrt{3}\sin A}{2}-\frac{\sqrt{1-\sin^2 A}}{2}\right)$

$=A-\sin^{-1}\left(\frac{\sqrt{3}}{2}\cdot\sin A-\frac{1}{2}\cdot\cos A\right)$

$=A-\sin^{-1}\left(\cos\frac{\pi}{6}\cdot\sin A-\sin\frac{\pi}{6}\cdot\cos A\right)$

$=A-\sin^{-1}\left\{\sin\left(A-\frac{\pi}{6}\right)\right\}=\frac{\pi}{6}$

13. (i) $2\tan^{-1}\left(\frac{\sqrt{5}-1}{2}\right)$

$=\tan^{-1}\left\{\frac{\sqrt{5}-1}{1-\frac{(\sqrt{5}-1)^2}{4}}\right\}$

$=\tan^{-1}\left(\frac{4}{2}\right)=\tan^{-1}(2)$

$=\tan\left[2\tan^{-1}\left[\frac{\sqrt{5}-1}{2}\right]\right]$

$=\tan[\tan^{-1}(2)]=2$

(ii) $\tan\left[\frac{1}{2}\cos^{-1}\left(\frac{\sqrt{5}}{3}\right)\right]$

Let $x=\frac{1}{2}\cos^{-1}\left(\frac{\sqrt{5}}{3}\right)$

$\Rightarrow \cos 2x=\frac{\sqrt{5}}{3}$

$\therefore \tan\left[\frac{1}{2}\cos^{-1}\left(\frac{\sqrt{5}}{3}\right)\right]=\tan x$

$=\sqrt{\frac{1-\cos 2x}{1+\cos 2x}}$

$=\sqrt{\frac{1-\frac{\sqrt{5}}{3}}{1+\frac{\sqrt{5}}{3}}}=\sqrt{\frac{3-\sqrt{5}}{3+\sqrt{5}}}$

Rationalizing the factor, we get

$\tan\left[\frac{1}{2}\cos^{-1}\left(\frac{\sqrt{5}}{3}\right)\right]=\frac{3-\sqrt{5}}{2}$

14. (i) (True)

$2\tan^{-1}x=\cos^{-1}\left(\frac{1-x^2}{1+x^2}\right)$

Substituting $x=\tan\theta$, we get

$\Rightarrow 2\tan^{-1}x=2\tan^{-1}(\tan\theta)=2\theta$

$\cos^{-1}\left(\frac{1-x^2}{1+x^2}\right)$

$=\cos^{-1}\left(\frac{1-\tan^2\theta}{1+\tan^2\theta}\right)$

$=\cos^{-1}\left(\frac{\cos^2\theta-\sin^2\theta}{\cos^2\theta+\sin^2\theta}\right)$

$=\cos^{-1}(\cos 2\theta)=2\theta$

$\therefore$ LHS = RHS holds for $x=\tan\theta$

$\because \tan\theta\in(0,\infty)\Rightarrow x\geq 1$

(ii) (False)

x, y and z are in GP

$\Rightarrow \quad y^2=xz \quad \ldots(i)$

$\tan^{-1}x$, $\tan^{-1}y$ and $\tan^{-1}z$ are in AP

$\therefore 2\tan^{-1}y=\tan^{-1}x+\tan^{-1}z \quad \ldots(ii)$

$\tan^{-1}\left(\frac{2y}{1-y^2}\right)=\tan^{-1}\left(\frac{x+z}{1-xz}\right)$

$\frac{2y}{1-y^2}=\frac{x+z}{1-xz}$

$2y=x+z \quad [\because y^2=xz]$

$y=\frac{1}{2}(x+z)$

(iii) (False)

Given,

$2\cot^{-1}5+\tan^{-1}\left(\frac{1}{7}\right)+2\cot^{-1}8$

Using the formula

$\cot^{-1}x=\tan^{-1}\left(\frac{1}{x}\right),$

$2\tan^{-1}\frac{1}{5}+\tan^{-1}\left(\frac{1}{7}\right)+2\tan^{-1}\frac{1}{8}$

$=2\left(\tan^{-1}\frac{1}{5}+\tan^{-1}\frac{1}{8}\right)+\tan^{-1}\frac{1}{7}$

Using the formula

$\tan^{-1}x+\tan^{-1}y=\tan^{-1}\left(\frac{x+y}{1-xy}\right),$

$$2\left\{\tan^{-1}\left(\frac{\frac{1}{5}+\frac{1}{8}}{1-\frac{1}{5}\cdot\frac{1}{8}}\right)\right\}+\tan^{-1}\frac{1}{7}$$

$$=2\left\{\tan^{-1}\left(\frac{13}{39}\right)\right\}+\tan^{-1}\frac{1}{7}$$

$$=2\left\{\tan^{-1}\left(\frac{1}{3}\right)\right\}+\tan^{-1}\frac{1}{7}$$

Using the formula

$$2\tan^{-1}x=\tan^{-1}\left(\frac{2x}{1-x^2}\right),$$

$$\tan^{-1}\left(\frac{2\cdot\frac{1}{3}}{1-\left(\frac{1}{3}\right)^2}\right)+\tan^{-1}\frac{1}{7}$$

$$=\tan^{-1}\left(\frac{6}{8}\right)+\tan^{-1}\left(\frac{1}{7}\right)$$

$$=\tan^{-1}\left(\frac{\frac{3}{4}+\frac{1}{7}}{1-\left(\frac{3}{4}\cdot\frac{1}{7}\right)}\right)$$

$$=\tan^{-1}\left(\frac{25}{25}\right)$$

$$=\frac{\pi}{4}$$

15. (i) Given, $\tan^{-1}\left(\frac{\sqrt{1+\cos x}}{\sqrt{1-\cos x}}\right)=\frac{\pi}{3}$

Using the formula

$1+\cos 2x=2\cos^2 x$

and $1-\cos 2x=2\sin^2 x$,

$$\therefore\quad \tan^{-1}\left(\frac{\sqrt{2\cos^2\frac{x}{2}}}{\sqrt{2\sin^2\frac{x}{2}}}\right)=\frac{\pi}{3}$$

$$\Rightarrow\quad \tan^{-1}\left(\cot\frac{x}{2}\right)=\frac{\pi}{3}$$

$$\Rightarrow \tan^{-1}\left\{\tan\left(\frac{\pi}{2}-\frac{x}{2}\right)\right\}=\frac{\pi}{3}$$

$$\Rightarrow\quad \frac{\pi}{2}-\frac{x}{2}=\frac{\pi}{3}$$

$$\Rightarrow\quad \frac{x}{2}=\frac{\pi}{6}$$

$$\Rightarrow\quad x=\frac{\pi}{3}$$

(ii) Given,

$$\sin^{-1}x-\cos^{-1}x=\sin^{-1}\left(\frac{1}{2}\right)$$

Using the formula

$$\sin^{-1}x+\cos^{-1}x=\frac{\pi}{2},$$

$$\frac{\pi}{2}-\cos^{-1}x-\cos^{-1}x=\frac{\pi}{6}$$

$$\Rightarrow\quad 2\cos^{-1}x=\frac{\pi}{3}$$

$$\Rightarrow\quad x=\cos\frac{\pi}{6}$$

$$\Rightarrow\quad x=\frac{\sqrt{3}}{2}$$

(iii) Given, $3\tan^{-1}x+\cot^{-1}x=\pi$

Using the property

$$\tan^{-1}x+\cot^{-1}x=\frac{\pi}{2},$$

$$\therefore 3\tan^{-1}x+\frac{\pi}{2}-\tan^{-1}x=\pi$$

$$2\tan^{-1}x=\frac{\pi}{2}$$

$$\tan^{-1}x=\frac{\pi}{4}$$

$$\Rightarrow\quad x=1$$

(iv) Given, $(\sin^{-1}x)^2+(\cos^{-1}x)^2=\frac{5\pi^2}{8}$

Adding and subtracting

$2\sin^{-1}x\cdot\cos^{-1}x,$

$$(\sin^{-1}x)^2+(\cos^{-1}x)^2+2\sin^{-1}x\cdot\cos^{-1}x-2\sin^{-1}x\cdot\cos^{-1}x=\frac{5\pi^2}{8}$$

$$(\sin^{-1}x+\cos^{-1}x)^2-2\sin^{-1}x\cdot\cos^{-1}x=\frac{5\pi^2}{8}$$

As, $\sin^{-1}x+\cos^{-1}x=\frac{\pi}{2}$

$$\therefore \frac{\pi^2}{4}-2\sin^{-1}x\cdot\left(\frac{\pi}{2}-\sin^{-1}x\right)=\frac{5\pi^2}{8}$$

$$2(\sin^{-1}x)^2-\pi\sin^{-1}x-\frac{3\pi^2}{8}=0$$

$$16(\sin^{-1}x)^2-8\pi\sin^{-1}x-3\pi^2=0$$

Factorising the result,

$$16(\sin^{-1}x)^2-12\pi\sin^{-1}x+4\pi\sin^{-1}x-3\pi^2=0$$

$$(4\sin^{-1}x-3\pi)(4\sin^{-1}x+\pi)=0$$

$$\sin^{-1}x=\frac{3\pi}{4},-\frac{\pi}{4}$$

As, $-\frac{\pi}{2}\le\sin^{-1}x\le\frac{\pi}{2}$,

$$\sin^{-1}x\ne\frac{3\pi}{4}$$

The value of $\sin^{-1}x$ is $-\frac{\pi}{4}$

$$x=\sin\left(-\frac{\pi}{4}\right)=-\frac{1}{\sqrt{2}}$$

(v) Given,

$$\tan\frac{1}{2}\left(\tan^{-1}\frac{2}{7}+\cot^{-1}y\right)=1$$

$$\frac{1}{2}\left(\tan^{-1}\frac{2}{7}+\cot^{-1}y\right)=\tan^{-1}(1)$$

$$\tan^{-1}\frac{2}{7}+\cot^{-1}y=2\times\frac{\pi}{4}$$

$$\tan^{-1}\frac{2}{7}+\cot^{-1}y=\frac{\pi}{2}$$

Using the property,

$\tan^{-1}x+\cot^{-1}x=\frac{\pi}{2}$, then value of y is $\frac{2}{7}$.

(vi) Given,

$$\tan^{-1}(1+x)+\tan^{-1}(1-x)=\frac{\pi}{2}$$

$$\tan^{-1}\left(\frac{(1+x)+(1-x)}{1-(1+x)(1-x)}\right)=\frac{\pi}{2}$$

$$\tan^{-1}\frac{2}{x^2}=\frac{\pi}{2}$$

$$\frac{2}{x^2}=\infty$$

$$x=0$$

(vii) Given,

$$\sec^{-1}x-\operatorname{cosec}^{-1}x=\frac{\pi}{3}$$

Using the property,

$$\sec^{-1}x+\operatorname{cosec}^{-1}x=\frac{\pi}{2}$$

and adding the above two equations,

$$2\sec^{-1}x=\frac{\pi}{3}+\frac{\pi}{2}$$

$$\sec^{-1}x=\frac{5\pi}{12}$$

$$x=\sec\left(\frac{5\pi}{12}\right)$$

(viii) Given,

$$2\tan^{-1}(\sin x)=\tan^{-1}(2\sec x)$$

Using the formula

$$2\tan^{-1}x=\tan^{-1}\left(\frac{2x}{1-x^2}\right),$$

$$\tan^{-1}\left(\frac{2\sin x}{1-\sin^2 x}\right)=\tan^{-1}\left(\frac{2}{\cos x}\right)$$

$$\frac{2\sin x}{\cos^2 x}=\frac{2}{\cos x}$$

$$\tan x=1\quad x=\frac{\pi}{4}$$

Chapter-3

Matrices

1. (a) The number of elements for a matrix with the order $m \times n$ is equal to mn, where m is the number of rows and n is the number of columns of the matrix.

2. (b) If a matrix has 12 elements, then the possible orders of the matrix are

$1\times 12, 2\times 6, 3\times 4, 4\times 3, 6\times 2, 12\times 1$

Therefore, the possible numbers of order are 6. If a matrix has 7 elements, then the possible orders of the matrix are

$1\times 7, 7\times 1$

Therefore, the possible numbers of order are 2.

If a matrix has 8 elements, then the possible orders of the matrix are

$1\times 8, 2\times 4, 4\times 2, 8\times 1$

Therefore, the possible numbers of order are 4.

If a matrix has 9 elements, then the possible orders of the matrix are

$1\times 9, 3\times 3, 9\times 1$

Therefore, the possible numbers of order are 3.

3. (i) The value of a_{32} is 6.
(ii) The value of a_{31} is 3.
(iii) The value of a_{22} is 5.
(iv) $1+4+8+9=22$
(v) The order of the matrix A is 3×3.

4. (i) 1×1 (ii) 4×1 (iii) 1×4 (iv) 3×2 (v) 3×3 (vi) 2×4

5. (i) The elements of the given matrix is

$$b_{11}=\frac{1-1}{1+1}=0$$
$$b_{12}=\frac{1-2}{2+2}=-\frac{1}{4}$$
$$b_{13}=\frac{1-3}{3+3}=-\frac{1}{3}$$
$$b_{21}=\frac{2-1}{1+1}=\frac{1}{2}$$
$$b_{22}=\frac{2-2}{2+2}=0$$
$$b_{23}=\frac{2-3}{3+3}=-\frac{1}{6}$$

Hence, the given matrix is

$$\begin{bmatrix} 0 & -\frac{1}{4} & -\frac{1}{3} \\ \frac{1}{2} & 0 & -\frac{1}{6} \end{bmatrix}.$$

(ii) The element of the given matrix is

$b_{11}=1, b_{12}=\frac{3}{2}, b_{13}=2$

and $b_{14}=\frac{5}{2}$

$b_{21}=\frac{3}{2}, b_{22}=2, b_{23}=\frac{5}{2}$

and $b_{24}=3$

$b_{31}=2, b_{32}=\frac{5}{2}, b_{33}=3$

and $b_{34}=\frac{7}{2}$

Hence, the given matrix is

$$\begin{bmatrix} 1 & 3/2 & 2 & 5/2 \\ 3/2 & 2 & 5/2 & 3 \\ 2 & 5/2 & 3 & 7/2 \end{bmatrix}.$$

6. (a) **Row matrix** A matrix that contains only one row and any numbers of columns is known as a row matrix.

Therefore, for row matrix,

$$m=1$$

Square matrix A matrix that has an equal number of rows and columns is known as a square matrix.

Therefore, for square matrix,

$$m=n$$

Rectangular matrix A matrix that does not have an equal number of rows and columns is known as a rectangular matrix.

Therefore, for rectangular matrix,

$m \neq n$

Zero matrix A matrix is said to be zero matrix, if all its elements are zero.

i.e. $a_{ij}=0$

Singleton matrix A matrix which has only one element is known as singleton matrix.

Therefore, for singleton matrix,

$$m=n=1$$

7. (i) (True)

Diagonal matrix A matrix that has all elements as 0 except diagonal elements is known as a diagonal matrix.

(ii) (False)

Scalar matrix A matrix that has all elements as 0 except diagonal elements and all diagonal elements are the same is known as a scalar matrix. It is a kind of diagonal matrix where all diagonal elements are the same.

(iii) (False)

Identity Matrix It is a kind of scalar matrix where all the diagonal elements are 1 and all non-diagonal elements are 0. The identity matrix always has an equal number of rows and columns.

(iv) (True)

(v) (True)

A matrix is said to be zero matrix or null matrix, if all elements are zero.

$\begin{bmatrix} 0 & 0 \\ 0 & 0 \end{bmatrix} \begin{bmatrix} 0 & 0 & 0 \\ 0 & 0 & 0 \end{bmatrix}, [0 \quad 0]$ are all zero matrices.

(vi) (True)

Every identity matrix is a scalar matrix because the scalar multiplying factor is 1.

8. (i) Two matrix are equal, if their corresponding elements are equal.

$$x-y=0$$
$$\Rightarrow x=y$$
$$\Rightarrow x+y=4$$
$$\Rightarrow 2x=4$$
$$\Rightarrow x=y=2$$
$$\therefore 2x+z=7$$
$$\Rightarrow 4+z=7$$
$$\Rightarrow z=3$$
$$\therefore 2z+2p=16$$
$$\Rightarrow 6+2p=16$$
$$\Rightarrow p=5$$

(ii) Two matrix are equal, if their corresponding elements are equal

$x+y+z=9$ ...(i)
$x+z=5$ ...(ii)
$y+z=7$ ...(iii)
$x+p=6$ ...(iv)
$z+q=8$ ...(v)
$y-r=2$ ...(vi)

Now, from Eq. (i),

$x+y+z=9$
$\Rightarrow x+(7)=9$ [from Eq. (iii)]
$\Rightarrow x=2$

Now, from Eq. (ii),

$x + z = 5 \Rightarrow z = 5 - 2 = 3$

Similarly, $x + y + z = 9$

$\Rightarrow 2 + y + 3 = 9 \Rightarrow y = 4$

From Eqs. (iv), (v) and (vi), we get

$p = 6 - x = 6 - 2 = 4$

$q = 8 - z = 8 - 3 = 5$

$r = y - 2 = 4 - 2 = 2$

(iii) Two matrix are equal, if their corresponding elements are equal.

$x - y = -1 \quad \ldots(i)$

$2x - y = 0 \quad \ldots(ii)$

$2x + z = 5 \quad \ldots(iii)$

$3z + p = 13 \quad \ldots(iv)$

On subtracting Eq. (i) from Eq. (ii), we get

$x = 1$ and $y = 2$

On putting value of x in Eq. (iii), we get

$z = 3$

On putting value of z in Eq. (iv), we get

$3 \times 3 + p = 13 \Rightarrow p = 4$

Hence, $x = 1$, $y = 2$, $z = 3$ and $p = 4$.

9. (i) $A + B = \begin{bmatrix} 3 & 5 \\ 4 & 8 \end{bmatrix} + \begin{bmatrix} 1 & 3 \\ -2 & 5 \end{bmatrix} = \begin{bmatrix} 4 & 8 \\ 2 & 13 \end{bmatrix}$

(ii) $A + B + C = \begin{bmatrix} 3 & 5 \\ 4 & 8 \end{bmatrix} + \begin{bmatrix} 1 & 3 \\ -2 & 5 \end{bmatrix} + \begin{bmatrix} -1 & 5 \\ 3 & 4 \end{bmatrix} = \begin{bmatrix} 3 & 13 \\ 5 & 17 \end{bmatrix}$

(iii) $A - B = \begin{bmatrix} 3 & 5 \\ 4 & 8 \end{bmatrix} - \begin{bmatrix} 1 & 3 \\ -2 & 5 \end{bmatrix} = \begin{bmatrix} 2 & 2 \\ 6 & 3 \end{bmatrix}$

(iv) $A + B - C = \begin{bmatrix} 3 & 5 \\ 4 & 8 \end{bmatrix} + \begin{bmatrix} 1 & 3 \\ -2 & 5 \end{bmatrix} - \begin{bmatrix} -1 & 5 \\ 3 & 4 \end{bmatrix} = \begin{bmatrix} 5 & 3 \\ -1 & 9 \end{bmatrix}$

10. (i) (b) $X + Y = \begin{bmatrix} 3 & 1 & 3 \\ 2 & 3 & 4 \end{bmatrix} + \begin{bmatrix} -3 & 3 & 0 \\ 2 & 4 & 1 \end{bmatrix}$

$= \begin{bmatrix} 3+(-3) & 1+3 & 3+0 \\ 2+2 & 3+4 & 4+1 \end{bmatrix} = \begin{bmatrix} 0 & 4 & 3 \\ 4 & 7 & 5 \end{bmatrix}$

(ii) (c) $(X + Y) + (X - Y) = \begin{bmatrix} 5 & 2 \\ 0 & 9 \end{bmatrix} + \begin{bmatrix} 3 & 6 \\ 0 & -1 \end{bmatrix}$

$\Rightarrow 2X = \begin{bmatrix} 8 & 8 \\ 0 & 8 \end{bmatrix}$

$\Rightarrow X = \frac{1}{2}\begin{bmatrix} 8 & 8 \\ 0 & 8 \end{bmatrix} = \begin{bmatrix} 4 & 4 \\ 0 & 4 \end{bmatrix}$

Similarly,

$(X + Y) - (X - Y) = \begin{bmatrix} 5-3 & 2-6 \\ 0 & 9+1 \end{bmatrix}$

$\Rightarrow 2Y = \begin{bmatrix} 2 & -4 \\ 0 & 10 \end{bmatrix}$

$\therefore Y = \begin{bmatrix} 1 & -2 \\ 0 & 5 \end{bmatrix}$

11. (i) Given,

$2\begin{bmatrix} 3 & 4 \\ 5 & x \end{bmatrix} + \begin{bmatrix} 1 & y \\ 0 & 1 \end{bmatrix} = \begin{bmatrix} 7 & 0 \\ 10 & 5 \end{bmatrix}$

$\Rightarrow \begin{bmatrix} 6 & 8 \\ 10 & 2x \end{bmatrix} + \begin{bmatrix} 1 & y \\ 0 & 1 \end{bmatrix} = \begin{bmatrix} 7 & 0 \\ 10 & 5 \end{bmatrix}$

$\Rightarrow \begin{bmatrix} 7 & 8+y \\ 10 & 2x+1 \end{bmatrix} = \begin{bmatrix} 7 & 0 \\ 10 & 5 \end{bmatrix}$

On comparing the corresponding element of the matrix, we get

$2x + 1 = 5 \Rightarrow x = 2$

$\Rightarrow 8 + y = 0 \Rightarrow y = -8$

$\Rightarrow x + y = 2 + (-8) = -6$

(ii) $\begin{bmatrix} x & -5 & 3+x \\ 7 & y & 4 \\ y & 4+x & x+2 \end{bmatrix} + \begin{bmatrix} y & 6 & y-2 \\ 4+x & x & 3 \\ x+2 & y & y-2 \end{bmatrix} = \begin{bmatrix} 11 & 1 & 12 \\ 22 & 11 & 7 \\ 13 & 15 & 11 \end{bmatrix}$

$\begin{bmatrix} x+y & 1 & x+y+1 \\ 11+x & x+y & 7 \\ y+x+2 & 4+x+y & x+y \end{bmatrix} = \begin{bmatrix} 11 & 1 & 12 \\ 22 & 11 & 7 \\ 13 & 15 & 11 \end{bmatrix}$

On comparing the corresponding element of the matrix, we get

$11 + x = 22$

$\Rightarrow x = 11$

Now, $x + y = 11$

$\Rightarrow y = 0$

$\therefore x - y = 11 - 0 = 11$

(iii) Given,

$\begin{bmatrix} 2x+4y & 1 \\ 3x-z & 2z \end{bmatrix} = \begin{bmatrix} 26 & 1 \\ 6 & 6 \end{bmatrix}$

$2z = 6$

$\Rightarrow z = 3$

Also, $3x - z = 6$

$\Rightarrow 3x - 3 = 6$

$\Rightarrow 3x = 9$

$\Rightarrow x = 3$

Also, $2x + 4y = 26$

$\Rightarrow 2 \times 3 + 4y = 26$

$\Rightarrow 4y = 20$

$\Rightarrow y = 5$

$\therefore x + y + z = 3 + 5 + 3 = 11$

12. (i) $3C + D$

$= 3\begin{bmatrix} 0 & 6 \\ -4 & 2 \end{bmatrix} + \begin{bmatrix} -2 & 3 \\ 5 & -4 \end{bmatrix} = \begin{bmatrix} 0 & 18 \\ -12 & 6 \end{bmatrix} + \begin{bmatrix} -2 & 3 \\ 5 & -4 \end{bmatrix} = \begin{bmatrix} -2 & 21 \\ -7 & 2 \end{bmatrix}$

(ii) $4A - 3B$

$= 4\begin{bmatrix} 1 & -2 \\ 3 & 4 \end{bmatrix} - 3\begin{bmatrix} 2 & -3 \\ 5 & -1 \end{bmatrix} = \begin{bmatrix} 4 & -8 \\ 12 & 16 \end{bmatrix} - \begin{bmatrix} 6 & -9 \\ 15 & -3 \end{bmatrix} = \begin{bmatrix} -2 & 1 \\ -3 & 19 \end{bmatrix}$

(iii) $3A + 2B - 4C + 2D + 5E$

$= \begin{bmatrix} 3 & -6 \\ 9 & 12 \end{bmatrix} + \begin{bmatrix} 4 & -6 \\ 10 & -2 \end{bmatrix} - \begin{bmatrix} 0 & 24 \\ -16 & 8 \end{bmatrix} + \begin{bmatrix} -4 & 6 \\ 10 & -8 \end{bmatrix} + \begin{bmatrix} 10 & 25 \\ 35 & 15 \end{bmatrix}$

$= \begin{bmatrix} 13 & -5 \\ 80 & 9 \end{bmatrix}$

13. (i) Given, $B=\begin{bmatrix}4 & -7\\0 & 7\end{bmatrix}$

and $5A+B=\begin{bmatrix}4 & 3\\5 & 2\end{bmatrix}$

On substitute the value of matrix B in $5A+B$, we get

$$5A+\begin{bmatrix}4 & -7\\0 & 7\end{bmatrix}=\begin{bmatrix}4 & 3\\5 & 2\end{bmatrix}$$

$$\Rightarrow 5A=\begin{bmatrix}4 & 3\\5 & 2\end{bmatrix}-\begin{bmatrix}4 & -7\\0 & 7\end{bmatrix}$$

$$\Rightarrow 5A=\begin{bmatrix}0 & 10\\5 & -5\end{bmatrix}$$

Then, $A=\begin{bmatrix}0 & 2\\1 & -1\end{bmatrix}$

(ii) Here, $2A-3B+5C=O$

$\Rightarrow 2A=3B-5C$

$\Rightarrow A=\frac{1}{2}[3B-5C]$

$$=\frac{1}{2}\left[3\begin{bmatrix}-2 & 2 & 0\\3 & 1 & 4\end{bmatrix}-5\begin{bmatrix}2 & 0 & -2\\7 & 1 & 6\end{bmatrix}\right]$$

$$=\frac{1}{2}\left[\begin{bmatrix}-6 & 6 & 0\\9 & 3 & 12\end{bmatrix}-\begin{bmatrix}10 & 0 & -10\\35 & 5 & 30\end{bmatrix}\right]$$

$$=\frac{1}{2}\begin{bmatrix}-16 & 6 & 10\\-26 & -2 & -18\end{bmatrix}$$

$$=\begin{bmatrix}-8 & 3 & 5\\-13 & -1 & -9\end{bmatrix}$$

14. (i) $A=\begin{bmatrix}\sin\alpha & -\sin\beta\\\sin\beta & \sin\alpha\end{bmatrix}$

$$=\begin{bmatrix}1 & 0\\0 & 1\end{bmatrix}$$

$\Rightarrow \sin\alpha=1\Rightarrow\alpha=90°$

and $\sin\beta=0\Rightarrow\beta=0°$

(ii) $A=\begin{bmatrix}\alpha+\beta & 2\alpha\\2\beta & 3(\alpha-\beta)\end{bmatrix}$

$B=\begin{bmatrix}5 & -4\beta\\-1 & 3\end{bmatrix}$

$A+2B=15I$

$$\begin{bmatrix}\alpha+\beta+10 & 2\alpha-8\beta\\2\beta-2 & 3\alpha-3\beta+6\end{bmatrix}=\begin{bmatrix}15 & 0\\0 & 15\end{bmatrix}$$

On comparing the corresponding elements of the matrix, we get

$\alpha+\beta+10=15$ ...(i)

$3\alpha-3\beta+6=15$ ...(ii)

On solving Eqs. (i) and (ii), we get

$\alpha=4$ and $\beta=1$

15. (i) (False)

Given,

$$k\begin{bmatrix}5 & 4\\3 & 2\end{bmatrix}-\begin{bmatrix}4 & a\\b & 4\end{bmatrix}=\begin{bmatrix}11 & 7\\6 & 2\end{bmatrix}$$

$$\begin{bmatrix}5k & 4k\\3k & 2k\end{bmatrix}-\begin{bmatrix}4 & a\\b & 4\end{bmatrix}=\begin{bmatrix}11 & 7\\6 & 2\end{bmatrix}$$

$$\begin{bmatrix}5k-4 & 4k-a\\3k-b & 2k-4\end{bmatrix}=\begin{bmatrix}11 & 7\\6 & 2\end{bmatrix}$$

$\Rightarrow 5k-4=11$

$\Rightarrow k=3$

$\Rightarrow 4k-a=7$

$\Rightarrow 4\times3-a=7$

$\Rightarrow a=5$

and $3k-b=6$

$\Rightarrow 3\times3-b=6$

$\Rightarrow b=3$

Hence, $k=b$ and $k\neq a+b$.

(ii) (True)

If $A=[a_{ij}]_{m\times n}$ be a matrix and k, l are scalars, then $(k+l)A=kA+lA$

(iii) (True)

$A=\begin{bmatrix}1 & 0 & 0\\0 & 2 & 0\\0 & 0 & 3\end{bmatrix}$

and $B=\begin{bmatrix}2 & 0 & 0\\0 & 3 & 0\\0 & 0 & 1\end{bmatrix}$

$2A+3B$

$$=2\begin{bmatrix}1 & 0 & 0\\0 & 2 & 0\\0 & 0 & 3\end{bmatrix}+3\begin{bmatrix}2 & 0 & 0\\0 & 3 & 0\\0 & 0 & 1\end{bmatrix}$$

$$=\begin{bmatrix}2 & 0 & 0\\0 & 4 & 0\\0 & 0 & 6\end{bmatrix}+\begin{bmatrix}6 & 0 & 0\\0 & 9 & 0\\0 & 0 & 3\end{bmatrix}$$

$$=\begin{bmatrix}8 & 0 & 0\\0 & 13 & 0\\0 & 0 & 9\end{bmatrix}$$

16. (i) $AB=\begin{bmatrix}1 & -1\\2 & -2\end{bmatrix}\begin{bmatrix}3 & -4\\-1 & 2\end{bmatrix}$

$$=\begin{bmatrix}3+1 & -4-2\\6+2 & -8-4\end{bmatrix}$$

$$=\begin{bmatrix}4 & -6\\8 & -12\end{bmatrix}$$

$$BA=\begin{bmatrix}3 & -4\\-1 & 2\end{bmatrix}\begin{bmatrix}1 & -1\\2 & -2\end{bmatrix}$$

$$=\begin{bmatrix}3-8 & -3+8\\-1+4 & 1-4\end{bmatrix}$$

$$=\begin{bmatrix}-5 & 5\\3 & -3\end{bmatrix}$$

(ii) $A=\begin{bmatrix}2 & -1 & -3\\0 & -4 & 7\end{bmatrix}$

and $B=\begin{bmatrix}2 & 1 & -1 & 4\\0 & -2 & 3 & 5\\-6 & 4 & -2 & 0\end{bmatrix}$

$$AB=\begin{bmatrix}2 & -1 & -3\\0 & -4 & 7\end{bmatrix}\begin{bmatrix}2 & 1 & -1 & 4\\0 & -2 & 3 & 5\\-6 & 4 & -2 & 0\end{bmatrix}$$

$$=\begin{bmatrix}4+0+18 & 2+2-12 & -2-3+6 & 8-5+0\\0+0-42 & 0+8+28 & 0-12-14 & 0-20+0\end{bmatrix}$$

$$=\begin{bmatrix}22 & -8 & 1 & 3\\-42 & 36 & -26 & -20\end{bmatrix}$$

$$BA=\begin{bmatrix}2 & 1 & -1 & 4\\0 & -2 & 3 & 5\\-6 & 4 & -2 & 0\end{bmatrix}\begin{bmatrix}2 & -1 & -3\\0 & -4 & 7\end{bmatrix}$$

If A, B are respectively $m\times n$, $k\times l$ matrices, then both AB and BA are defined, if and only if $n=k$ and $l=m$.

In the given matrices, $n=k=3$ but $l\neq m$ as $l=4$ and $m=2$.

Hence, BA is not defined.

17. (i) $A^2=\begin{bmatrix}3 & 1\\-1 & 2\end{bmatrix}\begin{bmatrix}3 & 1\\-1 & 2\end{bmatrix}=\begin{bmatrix}8 & 5\\-5 & 3\end{bmatrix}$

$\Rightarrow f(A)=A^2-5A+7I$

$$=\begin{bmatrix}8 & 5\\-5 & 3\end{bmatrix}-5\begin{bmatrix}3 & 1\\-1 & 2\end{bmatrix}+7\begin{bmatrix}1 & 0\\0 & 1\end{bmatrix}$$

$$=\begin{bmatrix}8 & 5\\-5 & 3\end{bmatrix}-\begin{bmatrix}15 & 5\\-5 & 10\end{bmatrix}+\begin{bmatrix}7 & 0\\0 & 7\end{bmatrix}$$

$$=\begin{bmatrix}0 & 0\\0 & 0\end{bmatrix}$$

(ii) Given, $f(x) = x^2 - 4x + 2$

and $A = \begin{bmatrix} 1 & 0 \\ -1 & 1 \end{bmatrix}$

$$A^2 = A \cdot A = \begin{bmatrix} 1 & 0 \\ -1 & 1 \end{bmatrix}\begin{bmatrix} 1 & 0 \\ -1 & 1 \end{bmatrix} = \begin{bmatrix} 1 & 0 \\ -2 & 1 \end{bmatrix}$$

$$\Rightarrow f(A) = A^2 - 4A + 2I$$

$$= \begin{bmatrix} 1 & 0 \\ -2 & 1 \end{bmatrix} - 4\begin{bmatrix} 1 & 0 \\ -1 & 1 \end{bmatrix} + 2\begin{bmatrix} 1 & 0 \\ 0 & 1 \end{bmatrix}$$

$$= \begin{bmatrix} 1-4+2 & 0-0+0 \\ -2+4+0 & 1-4+2 \end{bmatrix} = \begin{bmatrix} -1 & 0 \\ 2 & -1 \end{bmatrix}$$

18. Given,

$$A^2 = \begin{bmatrix} 0 & 1 & 2 \\ -1 & 2 & 0 \\ 2 & -1 & -1 \end{bmatrix}\begin{bmatrix} 0 & 1 & 2 \\ -1 & 2 & 0 \\ 2 & -1 & -1 \end{bmatrix} = \begin{bmatrix} 3 & 0 & -2 \\ -2 & 3 & -2 \\ -1 & 1 & 5 \end{bmatrix}$$

$$A^3 = A^2 \cdot A = \begin{bmatrix} 3 & 0 & -2 \\ -2 & 3 & -2 \\ -1 & 1 & 5 \end{bmatrix}\begin{bmatrix} 0 & 1 & 2 \\ -1 & 2 & 0 \\ 2 & -1 & -1 \end{bmatrix} = \begin{bmatrix} -4 & 5 & 8 \\ -7 & 6 & -2 \\ 9 & -4 & -7 \end{bmatrix}$$

19. (i) Given,

$$\begin{bmatrix} 1 & 4 \\ 2 & 3 \end{bmatrix}\begin{bmatrix} 1 & 3 \\ 2 & 4 \end{bmatrix} = \begin{bmatrix} 9 & \lambda \\ 8 & 18 \end{bmatrix}$$

$$\begin{bmatrix} 9 & 19 \\ 8 & 18 \end{bmatrix} = \begin{bmatrix} 9 & \lambda \\ 8 & 18 \end{bmatrix}$$

Hence, $\lambda = 19$

(ii) $A = \begin{bmatrix} 2 & 1 \\ 3 & -2 \end{bmatrix}$

$$A^2 = A \times A = \begin{bmatrix} 2 & 1 \\ 3 & -2 \end{bmatrix}\begin{bmatrix} 2 & 1 \\ 3 & -2 \end{bmatrix} = \begin{bmatrix} 7 & 0 \\ 0 & 7 \end{bmatrix} = 7I$$

Hence, $\lambda = 7$

(iii) Given, $A = \begin{bmatrix} 1 & 2 & 2 \\ 2 & 1 & 2 \\ 2 & 2 & 1 \end{bmatrix}$

$$A^2 = A \cdot A = \begin{bmatrix} 1 & 2 & 2 \\ 2 & 1 & 2 \\ 2 & 2 & 1 \end{bmatrix}\begin{bmatrix} 1 & 2 & 2 \\ 2 & 1 & 2 \\ 2 & 2 & 1 \end{bmatrix} = \begin{bmatrix} 9 & 8 & 8 \\ 8 & 9 & 8 \\ 8 & 8 & 9 \end{bmatrix}$$

Now, $A^2 - 4A$

$$= \begin{bmatrix} 9 & 8 & 8 \\ 8 & 9 & 8 \\ 8 & 8 & 9 \end{bmatrix} - 4\begin{bmatrix} 1 & 2 & 2 \\ 2 & 1 & 2 \\ 2 & 2 & 1 \end{bmatrix} = \begin{bmatrix} 9 & 8 & 8 \\ 8 & 9 & 8 \\ 8 & 8 & 9 \end{bmatrix} - \begin{bmatrix} 4 & 8 & 8 \\ 8 & 4 & 8 \\ 8 & 8 & 4 \end{bmatrix} = \begin{bmatrix} 5 & 0 & 0 \\ 0 & 5 & 0 \\ 0 & 0 & 5 \end{bmatrix} = 5I$$

Hence, $\lambda = 5$

20. (i) $A = a\begin{bmatrix} 1 & 0 & 0 \\ 0 & 1 & 0 \\ 0 & 0 & 1 \end{bmatrix}$

$$A = \begin{bmatrix} a & 0 & 0 \\ 0 & a & 0 \\ 0 & 0 & a \end{bmatrix}$$

$$A^2 = \begin{bmatrix} a & 0 & 0 \\ 0 & a & 0 \\ 0 & 0 & a \end{bmatrix}\begin{bmatrix} a & 0 & 0 \\ 0 & a & 0 \\ 0 & 0 & a \end{bmatrix} = \begin{bmatrix} a^2 & 0 & 0 \\ 0 & a^2 & 0 \\ 0 & 0 & a^2 \end{bmatrix} = a^2 I$$

Hence, $A^n = a^n I$

(ii) $A = \begin{bmatrix} 1 & x \\ 0 & 1 \end{bmatrix}$

$$A^2 = A \cdot A = \begin{bmatrix} 1 & x \\ 0 & 1 \end{bmatrix}\begin{bmatrix} 1 & x \\ 0 & 1 \end{bmatrix} = \begin{bmatrix} 1 & 2x \\ 0 & 1 \end{bmatrix}$$

$$A^3 = A^2 \cdot A = \begin{bmatrix} 1 & 2x \\ 0 & 1 \end{bmatrix}\begin{bmatrix} 1 & x \\ 0 & 1 \end{bmatrix} = \begin{bmatrix} 1 & 3x \\ 0 & 1 \end{bmatrix}$$

Hence, $A^n = \begin{bmatrix} 1 & na \\ 0 & 1 \end{bmatrix}$

21. (i) (a) $A = \begin{bmatrix} 1 & -1 \\ -1 & 1 \end{bmatrix}$

$$A^2 = \begin{bmatrix} 1 & -1 \\ -1 & 1 \end{bmatrix}\begin{bmatrix} 1 & -1 \\ -1 & 1 \end{bmatrix} = \begin{bmatrix} 2 & -2 \\ -2 & 2 \end{bmatrix} = 2\begin{bmatrix} 1 & -1 \\ -1 & 1 \end{bmatrix} = 2A$$

$$\therefore A^2 - 3A = -A$$

(ii) (b) Given, $A = \begin{bmatrix} 1 & 2 & 3 \\ 3 & -2 & 1 \\ 4 & 2 & 1 \end{bmatrix}$

$$A^2 = \begin{bmatrix} 1 & 2 & 3 \\ 3 & -2 & 1 \\ 4 & 2 & 1 \end{bmatrix}\begin{bmatrix} 1 & 2 & 3 \\ 3 & -2 & 1 \\ 4 & 2 & 1 \end{bmatrix} = \begin{bmatrix} 19 & 4 & 8 \\ 1 & 12 & 8 \\ 14 & 6 & 15 \end{bmatrix}$$

$$A^3 = A \cdot A^2 = \begin{bmatrix} 1 & 2 & 3 \\ 3 & -2 & 1 \\ 4 & 2 & 1 \end{bmatrix}\begin{bmatrix} 19 & 4 & 8 \\ 1 & 12 & 8 \\ 14 & 6 & 15 \end{bmatrix} = \begin{bmatrix} 63 & 46 & 69 \\ 69 & -6 & 23 \\ 92 & 46 & 63 \end{bmatrix}$$

Now, $A^3 - 23A$

$$= \begin{bmatrix} 63 & 46 & 69 \\ 69 & -6 & 23 \\ 92 & 46 & 63 \end{bmatrix} - 23\begin{bmatrix} 1 & 2 & 3 \\ 3 & -2 & 1 \\ 4 & 2 & 1 \end{bmatrix}$$

$$= \begin{bmatrix} 63 & 46 & 69 \\ 69 & -6 & 23 \\ 92 & 46 & 63 \end{bmatrix} - \begin{bmatrix} 23 & 46 & 69 \\ 69 & -46 & 23 \\ 92 & 46 & 23 \end{bmatrix} = \begin{bmatrix} 40 & 0 & 0 \\ 0 & 40 & 0 \\ 0 & 0 & 40 \end{bmatrix} = 40\,I$$

(iii) (c) Given,

$$\begin{bmatrix} 1 & x & 1 \end{bmatrix}\begin{bmatrix} 1 & 3 & 2 \\ 2 & 5 & 1 \\ 15 & 3 & 2 \end{bmatrix}\begin{bmatrix} 1 \\ 2 \\ x \end{bmatrix} = O$$

$$\Rightarrow \begin{bmatrix} 16+2x & 6+5x & 4+x \end{bmatrix}\begin{bmatrix} 1 \\ 2 \\ x \end{bmatrix} = O$$

$$\Rightarrow 16 + 2x + 12 + 10x + 4x + x^2 = 0$$

$\Rightarrow \quad x^2 + 16x + 28 = 0$

$\Rightarrow \quad x^2 + 14x + 2x + 28 = 0$

$\Rightarrow x(x + 14) + 2(x + 14) = 0$

$\Rightarrow \quad (x + 14)(x + 2) = 0$

$\therefore \quad x = -14, -2$

(iv) (a) $f(\alpha) = \begin{bmatrix} \cos\alpha & \sin\alpha \\ -\sin\alpha & \cos\alpha \end{bmatrix}$

$f(\beta) = \begin{bmatrix} \cos\beta & \sin\beta \\ -\sin\beta & \cos\beta \end{bmatrix}$

$\Rightarrow f(\alpha)\,f(\beta) = \begin{bmatrix} \cos\alpha & \sin\alpha \\ -\sin\alpha & \cos\alpha \end{bmatrix} \begin{bmatrix} \cos\beta & \sin\beta \\ -\sin\beta & \cos\beta \end{bmatrix}$

$= \begin{bmatrix} \cos\alpha\cos\beta - \sin\alpha\sin\beta & \cos\alpha\sin\beta + \sin\alpha\cos\beta \\ -\sin\alpha\cos\beta - \cos\alpha\sin\beta & -\sin\alpha\sin\beta + \cos\alpha\cos\beta \end{bmatrix}$

$= \begin{bmatrix} \cos(\alpha+\beta) & \sin(\alpha+\beta) \\ -\sin(\alpha+\beta) & \cos(\alpha+\beta) \end{bmatrix}$

$= f(\alpha + \beta)$

(v) (a) $AB = A$

Multiply A from left on both sides, we get

$ABA = A^2$

$A(BA) = A^2$

$AB = A^2 \Rightarrow A = A^2$

Similarly, $B^2 = B$

$A^2 + B^2 - A - B$

$= A + B - A - B$

$= 0$

22. (i) Two matrices A and B are conformable for the product AB, if the number of columns in A is same as the number of rows in B.

And the order of AB is (number of rows in A) $\times$ (number of columns in B)

Hence, the order of product AB is $m \times p$.

(ii) The order of matrix $[1 \quad 5 \quad 4]$ is 1×3.

The order of matrix $\begin{bmatrix} 4 & 5 & 6 \\ 1 & 2 & 3 \\ \alpha & \beta & \gamma \end{bmatrix}$ is 3×3.

The order of matrix $\begin{bmatrix} a \\ b \\ c \end{bmatrix}$ is 3×1.

Hence, the order of matrix $[1 \quad 5 \quad 4] \begin{bmatrix} 4 & 5 & 6 \\ 1 & 2 & 3 \\ \alpha & \beta & \gamma \end{bmatrix} \begin{bmatrix} a \\ b \\ c \end{bmatrix}$ is 1×1.

23. (i) $[6 \quad 3 \quad -4]$

(ii) $\begin{bmatrix} 1 & 3 \\ 3 & 6 \\ 2 & 5 \end{bmatrix}$

(iii) $\begin{bmatrix} 6 & 2 & 8 \\ -5 & 7 & 3 \\ 4 & -6 & -5 \end{bmatrix}$

24. (i) (True)

$A' = \begin{bmatrix} -1 & 5 & 2 \\ 2 & 7 & 1 \\ 3 & 9 & 1 \end{bmatrix}$ and

$B' = \begin{bmatrix} -4 & 1 & 1 \\ 1 & 2 & 3 \\ -5 & 0 & 1 \end{bmatrix}$

$(A + B) = \begin{bmatrix} -5 & 3 & -2 \\ 6 & 9 & 9 \\ 3 & 4 & 2 \end{bmatrix}$

$(A + B)' = \begin{bmatrix} -5 & 6 & 3 \\ 3 & 9 & 4 \\ -2 & 9 & 2 \end{bmatrix}$

$A' + B' = \begin{bmatrix} -1 & 5 & 2 \\ 2 & 7 & 1 \\ 3 & 9 & 1 \end{bmatrix} + \begin{bmatrix} -4 & 1 & 1 \\ 1 & 2 & 3 \\ -5 & 0 & 1 \end{bmatrix} = \begin{bmatrix} -5 & 6 & 3 \\ 3 & 9 & 4 \\ -2 & 9 & 2 \end{bmatrix}$

(ii) (True)

$A = \begin{bmatrix} -1 & 0 \\ 2 & 1 \end{bmatrix}$ and $A' = \begin{bmatrix} -1 & 2 \\ 0 & 1 \end{bmatrix}$

$B = \begin{bmatrix} -1 & 2 \\ 1 & 2 \end{bmatrix}$ and $B' = \begin{bmatrix} -1 & 1 \\ 2 & 2 \end{bmatrix}$

$\Rightarrow (A - B) = \begin{bmatrix} 0 & -2 \\ 1 & -1 \end{bmatrix}$

$\Rightarrow (A - B)' = \begin{bmatrix} 0 & 1 \\ -2 & -1 \end{bmatrix}$

$\therefore \quad A' - B' = \begin{bmatrix} 0 & 1 \\ -2 & -1 \end{bmatrix}$

(iii) (True)

$A + B = \begin{bmatrix} 3 & 4 & 3 \\ -1 & 2 & 4 \end{bmatrix} + \begin{bmatrix} 1 & 2 & 3 \\ 0 & -1 & 2 \end{bmatrix}$

$= \begin{bmatrix} 4 & 6 & 6 \\ -1 & 1 & 6 \end{bmatrix}$

$(A + B)' = \begin{bmatrix} 4 & -1 \\ 6 & 1 \\ 6 & 6 \end{bmatrix}$

$(A + B)' - C' = \begin{bmatrix} 4 & -1 \\ 6 & 1 \\ 6 & 6 \end{bmatrix} - \begin{bmatrix} 1 & 4 \\ 2 & 1 \\ -4 & 3 \end{bmatrix}$

$= \begin{bmatrix} 3 & -5 \\ 4 & 0 \\ 10 & 3 \end{bmatrix}$

(iv) (True)

$AB = \begin{bmatrix} 1 \\ -4 \\ 2 \end{bmatrix} [1 \quad 2 \quad -1]$

$= \begin{bmatrix} 1 & 2 & -1 \\ -4 & -8 & 4 \\ 2 & 4 & -2 \end{bmatrix}$

$(AB)' = \begin{bmatrix} 1 & -4 & 2 \\ 2 & -8 & 4 \\ -1 & 4 & -2 \end{bmatrix}$

$A' = [1 \quad -4 \quad 2]$

and $B' = \begin{bmatrix} 1 \\ 2 \\ -1 \end{bmatrix}$

$B'A' = \begin{bmatrix} 1 \\ 2 \\ -1 \end{bmatrix} [1 \quad -4 \quad 2]$

$= \begin{bmatrix} 1 & -4 & 2 \\ 2 & -8 & 4 \\ -1 & 4 & -2 \end{bmatrix}$

Hence, $(AB)' = B'A'$.

(v) (True)

If $B' = \begin{bmatrix} 1 & 3 & 3 \\ 1 & 4 & 3 \\ 1 & 3 & 4 \end{bmatrix}$,

then $B = \begin{bmatrix} 1 & 1 & 1 \\ 3 & 4 & 3 \\ 3 & 3 & 4 \end{bmatrix}$

$AB = \begin{bmatrix} 5 & 0 & 4 \\ 2 & 3 & 2 \\ 1 & 2 & 1 \end{bmatrix} \begin{bmatrix} 1 & 1 & 1 \\ 3 & 4 & 3 \\ 3 & 3 & 4 \end{bmatrix}$

$= \begin{bmatrix} 17 & 17 & 21 \\ 17 & 20 & 19 \\ 10 & 12 & 11 \end{bmatrix}$

$(AB)' = \begin{bmatrix} 17 & 17 & 10 \\ 17 & 20 & 12 \\ 21 & 19 & 11 \end{bmatrix}$

(vi) (False)

$$A=\begin{bmatrix}1&2&2\\2&1&-2\\a&2&b\end{bmatrix}$$

$AA^T=9I_3$

$$\begin{bmatrix}1&2&2\\2&1&-2\\a&2&b\end{bmatrix}\begin{bmatrix}1&2&a\\2&1&2\\2&-2&b\end{bmatrix}=9\begin{bmatrix}1&0&0\\0&1&0\\0&0&1\end{bmatrix}$$

$\Rightarrow$

$$\begin{bmatrix}9&0&a+4+2b\\0&9&2a+2-2b\\a+4+2b&2a+2-2b&a^2+4+b^2\end{bmatrix}=\begin{bmatrix}9&0&0\\0&9&0\\0&0&9\end{bmatrix}$$

$\Rightarrow a+4+2b=0$

$a+2b=-4$ ...(i)

and $2a+2-2b=0$

$a-b=-1$ ...(ii)

On substracting Eq. (ii) from Eq. (i), we get

$3b=-3$

$b=-1\Rightarrow a-(-1)=-1$

$a+1=-1\Rightarrow a=-2$

Hence, $a+b=-2-1=-3$

25. (i) (d) Let $A=\begin{bmatrix}2&3&0\\a&4&5\\b&c&1\end{bmatrix}$ is symmetric, then $A=A^T$

$$\begin{bmatrix}2&3&0\\a&4&5\\b&c&1\end{bmatrix}=\begin{bmatrix}2&a&b\\3&4&c\\0&5&1\end{bmatrix}$$

$\Rightarrow a=3, b=0, c=5$

Hence, $a+b+c=3+0+5=8$

(ii) (c) As all the diagonal elements of a matrix is zero and $a_{ij}=-a_{ji}$, then given matrix A is skew-symmetric matrix.

(iii) (b) Given, A be a skew-symmetric, then

$A^T=-A$

$(A^3)^T=(AAA)^T$

$=A^TA^TA^T$

$=(-A)(-A)(-A)$

$=-A^3$

Hence, A^3 is a skew-symmetric.

26. Let $A=\begin{bmatrix}0&2&3\\a&b&c\\d&1&0\end{bmatrix}$

If A is skew-symmetric, then

$A^T=-A$

$$\begin{bmatrix}0&a&d\\2&b&1\\3&c&0\end{bmatrix}=-\begin{bmatrix}0&2&3\\a&b&c\\d&1&0\end{bmatrix}$$

$\Rightarrow a=-2, d=-3, b=0, c=-1$

27. (i) (False)

$\because A$ is a symmetric matrix

$\therefore A^T=A$

$(B^TAB)^T=B^TA^T(B^T)^T$

$[\because (ABC)^T=C^TB^TA^T]$

$=B^TA^TB$ $\quad[\because (B^T)^T=B]$

$=B^TAB$

$[\because A$ is a symmetric matrix$]$

Hence, if A is a symmetric matrix, then B^TAB is also a symmetric matrix.

(ii) (True)

We have, $A=\begin{bmatrix}1&2\\3&4\end{bmatrix}$

and $A=P+Q$, where P is a symmetric matrix and Q is a skew-symmetric matrix.

Clearly, $P=\frac{1}{2}(A+A^T)$

$$=\frac{1}{2}\left(\begin{bmatrix}1&2\\3&4\end{bmatrix}+\begin{bmatrix}1&3\\2&4\end{bmatrix}\right)$$

$$=\frac{1}{2}\begin{bmatrix}2&5\\5&8\end{bmatrix}=\begin{bmatrix}1&5/2\\5/2&4\end{bmatrix}$$

28. (i) Let $A=\begin{bmatrix}4&5\\1&2\end{bmatrix}$

We know that

$$A=\frac{1}{2}(A+A')+\frac{1}{2}(A-A')$$

where $\frac{1}{2}(A+A')$ is symmetric matrix and $\frac{1}{2}(A-A')$ is skew-symmetric matrix.

$A'=\begin{bmatrix}4&1\\5&2\end{bmatrix}$

$$\frac{1}{2}(A+A')=\frac{1}{2}\begin{bmatrix}8&6\\6&4\end{bmatrix}=\begin{bmatrix}4&3\\3&2\end{bmatrix}$$

$$\Rightarrow\frac{1}{2}(A-A')=\frac{1}{2}\begin{bmatrix}0&4\\-4&0\end{bmatrix}=\begin{bmatrix}0&2\\-2&0\end{bmatrix}$$

$$\therefore A=\begin{bmatrix}4&3\\3&2\end{bmatrix}+\begin{bmatrix}0&2\\-2&0\end{bmatrix}$$

(ii) Let $A=\begin{bmatrix}2&3&5\\6&-2&1\\2&-1&3\end{bmatrix}$

$A'=\begin{bmatrix}2&6&2\\3&-2&-1\\5&1&3\end{bmatrix}$

$$\frac{1}{2}(A+A')=\frac{1}{2}\begin{bmatrix}4&9&7\\9&-4&0\\7&0&6\end{bmatrix}=\begin{bmatrix}2&\frac{9}{2}&\frac{7}{2}\\\frac{9}{2}&-2&0\\\frac{7}{2}&0&3\end{bmatrix}$$

$$\frac{1}{2}(A-A')=\frac{1}{2}\begin{bmatrix}0&-3&3\\3&0&2\\-3&-2&0\end{bmatrix}=\begin{bmatrix}0&-\frac{3}{2}&\frac{3}{2}\\\frac{3}{2}&0&1\\-\frac{3}{2}&-1&0\end{bmatrix}$$

$$\therefore A=\begin{bmatrix}2&\frac{9}{2}&\frac{7}{2}\\\frac{9}{2}&-2&0\\\frac{7}{2}&0&3\end{bmatrix}+\begin{bmatrix}0&-\frac{3}{2}&\frac{3}{2}\\\frac{3}{2}&0&1\\-\frac{3}{2}&-1&0\end{bmatrix}$$

(iii) Let $A=\begin{bmatrix}1&2&3\\-6&8&3\\-4&6&5\end{bmatrix}$,

$A'=\begin{bmatrix}1&-6&-4\\2&8&6\\3&3&5\end{bmatrix}$

$\frac{1}{2}(A + A')$

$$= \frac{1}{2}\left\{\begin{bmatrix} 1 & 2 & 3 \\ -6 & 8 & 3 \\ -4 & 6 & 5 \end{bmatrix} + \begin{bmatrix} 1 & -6 & -4 \\ 2 & 8 & 6 \\ 3 & 3 & 5 \end{bmatrix}\right\}$$

$$= \frac{1}{2}\begin{bmatrix} 2 & -4 & -1 \\ -4 & 16 & 9 \\ -1 & 9 & 10 \end{bmatrix}$$

$\frac{1}{2}(A - A')$

$$= \frac{1}{2}\left\{\begin{bmatrix} 1 & 2 & 3 \\ -6 & 8 & 3 \\ -4 & 6 & 5 \end{bmatrix} - \begin{bmatrix} 1 & -6 & -4 \\ 2 & 8 & 6 \\ 3 & 3 & 5 \end{bmatrix}\right\}$$

$$= \frac{1}{2}\begin{bmatrix} 0 & 8 & 7 \\ -8 & 0 & -3 \\ -7 & 3 & 0 \end{bmatrix}$$

Hence, $A = \frac{1}{2}\begin{bmatrix} 2 & -4 & -1 \\ -4 & 16 & 9 \\ -1 & 9 & 10 \end{bmatrix} + \frac{1}{2}\begin{bmatrix} 0 & 8 & 7 \\ -8 & 0 & -3 \\ -7 & 3 & 0 \end{bmatrix}$

$$A = \begin{bmatrix} 1 & -2 & \frac{-1}{2} \\ -2 & 8 & \frac{9}{2} \\ -\frac{1}{2} & \frac{9}{2} & 5 \end{bmatrix} + \begin{bmatrix} 0 & 4 & \frac{7}{2} \\ -4 & 0 & -\frac{3}{2} \\ -\frac{7}{2} & \frac{3}{2} & 0 \end{bmatrix}$$

29. $A^2 + 7I = O$

$A^2 = -7I$

$A \cdot A = -7I$

$A \cdot A \cdot A^{-1} = -7IA^{-1}$

$A(A \cdot A^{-1}) = -7(I \cdot A^{-1})$

$A = -7A^{-1}$

$[\because AA^{-1} = I \text{ and } IA^{-1} = A^{-1}]$

Therefore, $A^{-1} = -\frac{1}{7}A$

Assertion-Reason

1. (d) Given, $A = \begin{bmatrix} 0 & 1 \\ 1 & 0 \end{bmatrix}$

We know that $A = \begin{bmatrix} 0 & 1 \\ 1 & 0 \end{bmatrix}$ is not a identity matrix.

$\therefore$ Given Assertion is false.

We know that for identity matrix.

$a_{ij} = 1, \quad \text{if } i = j$

$a_{ij} = 0, \quad \text{if } i \neq j$

Reason is true for identity matrix.

2. (a) Given, Matrix $= \begin{bmatrix} 1 \\ 7 \\ 2 \end{bmatrix}$

We know that the order of column matrix is always $m \times 1$.

$\therefore \begin{bmatrix} 1 \\ 7 \\ 2 \end{bmatrix}$ is column matrix.

$\therefore$ Assertion is true also reason is true and correct explanation of A.

3. (c) Given, matrix $A = [2 \;\; 5 \;\; -1]$

$A' = \begin{bmatrix} 2 \\ 5 \\ -1 \end{bmatrix}$, which is column matrix.

$\therefore$ Given Assertion (A) is true, we know that the transpose of matrix of order $m \times n$ is of order $n \times m$.

$\therefore$ Reason is false.

4. (a) Given, $\begin{bmatrix} xy & 4 \\ z+5 & x+y \end{bmatrix} = \begin{bmatrix} 4 & w \\ 0 & 4 \end{bmatrix}$,

and $x = 2, y = 2, z = -5$ and $w = 4$

On comparing, we get

$z + 5 = 0, \;\; x + y = 4$

$z = -5, \quad x \cdot y = 4$

$w = 4, \quad x = 2$ and $y = 2$

Assertion is true and Reason is true and Reason is correct explanation of Assertion.

5. (c) Given, Matrix $= \begin{bmatrix} 3 & 2 & 2 \\ 2 & 3 & 2 \\ 2 & 2 & 3 \end{bmatrix}$

Let $A = \begin{bmatrix} 3 & 2 & 2 \\ 2 & 3 & 2 \\ 2 & 2 & 3 \end{bmatrix}$

$A' = \begin{bmatrix} 3 & 2 & 2 \\ 2 & 3 & 2 \\ 2 & 2 & 3 \end{bmatrix} = A$

$\because$ A is a symmetric matrix.

$\therefore$ Assertion is true.

We know that A matrix is symmetric if $A' = A$

Given Reason is false.

Assertion is true but Reason is false.

6. (a) Given Matrices,

$A = \begin{bmatrix} 2 & 0 \\ 0 & 3 \end{bmatrix}$ and $B = \begin{bmatrix} 5 & 0 \\ 0 & 0 \end{bmatrix}$

$AB = \begin{bmatrix} 2 & 0 \\ 0 & 3 \end{bmatrix}\begin{bmatrix} 5 & 0 \\ 0 & 0 \end{bmatrix} = \begin{bmatrix} 10 & 0 \\ 0 & 0 \end{bmatrix}$

$BA = \begin{bmatrix} 5 & 0 \\ 0 & 0 \end{bmatrix}\begin{bmatrix} 2 & 0 \\ 0 & 3 \end{bmatrix} = \begin{bmatrix} 10 & 0 \\ 0 & 0 \end{bmatrix}$

$AB = BA$

$(A + B)^2 = (A + B)(A + B)$

$\Rightarrow (A + B)^2 = A^2 + AB + BA + B^2$

$\Rightarrow (A + B)^2 = A^2 + AB + AB + B^2$

$\{\because AB = BA\}$

$\Rightarrow (A + B)^2 = A^2 + 2AB + B^2$

$\therefore$ Assertion is true.

Reason is also true and it is correct explanation of assertion.

7. (b) Given, matrix $A = \begin{bmatrix} 1 & 2 & 4 \\ 6 & 8 & 2 \\ 2 & -2 & 7 \end{bmatrix}$

Let $P = A - A'$

$\Rightarrow P' = (A - A')' = A' - (A')'$

$= -(A - A') = -P$

$A - A'$ is skew-symmetric.

Now, $A = \begin{bmatrix} 1 & 2 & 4 \\ 6 & 8 & 2 \\ 2 & -2 & 7 \end{bmatrix}$

$\Rightarrow A' = \begin{bmatrix} 1 & 6 & 2 \\ 2 & 8 & -2 \\ 4 & 2 & 7 \end{bmatrix}$

$\therefore A - A' = \begin{bmatrix} 0 & -4 & 2 \\ 4 & 0 & 4 \\ -2 & -4 & 0 \end{bmatrix}$

$\Rightarrow \frac{1}{2}(A - A') = \begin{bmatrix} 0 & -2 & 1 \\ 2 & 0 & 2 \\ -1 & -2 & 0 \end{bmatrix}$

which is skew-symmetric matrix.

$\therefore$ Both Assertion and Reason are true but Reason is not the correct explanation of the Assertion.

8. (a) Given, matrices

$A = \begin{bmatrix} -3 & 2 \\ -5 & 4 \end{bmatrix}, B = \begin{bmatrix} 4 & -2 \\ 5 & -3 \end{bmatrix}$

$AB = \begin{bmatrix} -3 & 2 \\ -5 & 4 \end{bmatrix}\begin{bmatrix} 4 & -2 \\ 5 & -3 \end{bmatrix}$

$\Rightarrow AB = \begin{bmatrix} -2 & 0 \\ 0 & -2 \end{bmatrix}$

$BA = \begin{bmatrix} 4 & -2 \\ 5 & -3 \end{bmatrix}\begin{bmatrix} -3 & 2 \\ -5 & 4 \end{bmatrix}$

$\Rightarrow BA = \begin{bmatrix} -2 & 0 \\ 0 & -2 \end{bmatrix}$

$A^nB = BA^n$

Assertion is true and Reason is true, and Reason is the correct explanation of Assertion.

9. (d) An orthogonal matrix A has the property that

$$A^T \cdot A = I$$

where, A^T is the transpose of A and I is the identity matrix.
Similarly, for an orthogonal matrix B.

$$B^T \cdot B = I$$

The Assertion claims that the sum of two orthogonal matrices is always orthogonal. To determine this, consider two orthogonal matrices A and B. For their sum $C = A + B$ to be orthogonal, it must satisfy $C^T \cdot C = I$

$$C = A + B$$

$$C^T = (A + B)^T = A^T + B^T$$

$$C^T \cdot C = (A^T + B^T)(A + B)$$

$$\Rightarrow C^T \cdot C = A^T A + A^T B + B^T A + B^T B$$

$$\Rightarrow I = I + I + A^T B + B^T A \quad [\text{for } C^T C = I]$$

$$\Rightarrow A^T B + B^T A = -I$$

This condition is generally not satisfied for arbitrary orthogonal matrices A and B. Therefore, C is not necessarily orthogonal.
The Assertion is false because the sum of two orthogonal matrices is not necessarily orthogonal.
But the reason correctly states the definition of orthogonal matrices. Two matrices A and B are orthogonal if $A^T A = I$ and $B^T B = I$.
$\therefore$ Reason is true.

10. (a) A Matrix A is symmeric if it is equal to its transpose, $A = A^T$. This means that the elements of A are symmetric about the main diagonal.
The Assertion claims that the transpose of a symmetric matrix is always symmetric. Let's denote a symmetric matrix by A. By definition, $A = A^T$.
Using the property of transpose that the transpose of a matrix returns the original matrix.

$$(A^T)^T = A$$

Since, A is symmetric $A = A^T$.
Taking the transpose of A gives A back. Therefore, the transpose of a symmetric matrix is the matrix itself, which is symmetric.
Assertion is true because the transpose of a symmetric matrix is always symmetric.
The Reason correctly states the definition of a symmetric matrix A is symmetric if $A = A^T$.

Case Based Questions

1. (i) (d) In factory A, number of units of types I, II and III for boys are 80, 70, 65 respectively and number of units of types I, II and III for girls are 80, 75 90 respectively.

$$\therefore P = \begin{matrix} & \text{Boys} & \text{Girls} \\ \text{I} \\ \text{II} \\ \text{III} \end{matrix}\begin{bmatrix} 80 & 80 \\ 70 & 75 \\ 65 & 90 \end{bmatrix}$$

(ii) (a) In factory B, number of units of types I, II and III for boys are 85, 65, 72 respectively and number of units of types I, II and III for girls are 50, 55, 80 respectively.

$$\therefore Q = \begin{matrix} & \text{Boys} & \text{Girls} \\ \text{I} \\ \text{II} \\ \text{III} \end{matrix}\begin{bmatrix} 85 & 50 \\ 65 & 55 \\ 72 & 80 \end{bmatrix}$$

(iii) (c) Let X be the matrix that represent the number of units of each type produced by factory A for boys and Y be the matrix that represent the number of units of each type produced by factory B for boys.

Then, $X = \begin{matrix} \text{I} & \text{II} & \text{III} \\ [80 & 70 & 65] \end{matrix}$

and $Y = \begin{matrix} \text{I} & \text{II} & \text{III} \\ [85 & 65 & 72] \end{matrix}$

Now, required matrix

$$= X + Y$$

$$= [80 \;\; 70 \;\; 65] + [85 \;\; 65 \;\; 72]$$

$$= [165 \;\; 135 \;\; 137]$$

(iv) (a) Required matrix

$$= [80 \;\; 75 \;\; 90] + [50 \;\; 55 \;\; 80]$$

$$= [130 \;\; 130 \;\; 170]$$

2. (i) (a) Let F be the matrix representing the number of family members and R be the matrix representing the requirement of calories and protein for each person. Then,

$$F = \begin{matrix} & \text{Man} & \text{Woman} & \text{Children} \\ \text{Family } A \\ \text{Family } B \end{matrix}\begin{bmatrix} 4 & 4 & 4 \\ 2 & 2 & 2 \end{bmatrix}$$

$$R = \begin{matrix} & \text{Calorie} & \text{Proteins} \\ \text{Man} \\ \text{Woman} \\ \text{Children} \end{matrix}\begin{bmatrix} 2400 & 45 \\ 1900 & 55 \\ 1800 & 33 \end{bmatrix}$$

(ii) (b) The requirement of calories and protein for each of the two families is given by product matrix FR.

$$FR = \begin{bmatrix} 4 & 4 & 4 \\ 2 & 2 & 2 \end{bmatrix}\begin{bmatrix} 2400 & 45 \\ 1900 & 55 \\ 1800 & 33 \end{bmatrix}$$

$$\Rightarrow FR = \begin{bmatrix} 4(2400 + 1900 + 1800) & 4(45 + 55 + 33) \\ 2(2400 + 1900 + 1800) & 2(45 + 55 + 55) \end{bmatrix}$$

$$FR = \begin{matrix} \text{Calories} & \text{Protein} & \\ \end{matrix}\begin{bmatrix} 24400 & 532 \\ 12200 & 266 \end{bmatrix}\begin{matrix} \text{Family } A \\ \text{Family } B \end{matrix}$$

(iii) (c) Requirement of protein for family $B = 266$ grams

(iv) (c) Since, $AB = B \quad \ldots(\text{i})$

$BA = A \quad \ldots(\text{ii})$

$$\therefore A^2 + B^2 = A \cdot A + B \cdot B$$

$$= A(BA) + B(AB) \quad [\text{using Eqs. (i) and (ii)}]$$

$$= (AB)A + (BA)B \quad [\text{Associative law}]$$

$$= BA + AB \quad [\text{using Eqs. (i) and (ii)}]$$

$$= A + B$$

Chapter-4

Determinant

1. (a)
2. True
3. (i) $9\left(\frac{2}{3}\right)-(-1)(-2)=6-2=4$

(ii) $(a+b)\,b-(-a)\,(a-b)$
$= b^2+ab+a^2-ab$
$= a^2+b^2$

(iii) $\sec\theta\cdot(-\sec\theta)-\tan\theta\,(-\tan\theta)$
$=-\sec^2\theta+\tan^2\theta$
$=-(\sec^2\theta-\tan^2\theta)$
$=-1$

(iv) Expanding the determinant along R_1.

$$21\begin{vmatrix}25 & 26\\28 & 29\end{vmatrix}-22\begin{vmatrix}24 & 26\\27 & 29\end{vmatrix}+23\begin{vmatrix}24 & 25\\27 & 28\end{vmatrix}$$
$=21(725-728)-22(696-702)+23(672-675)$
$=-63+132-69=0$

(v) Expanding the determinant along R_1

$$a\begin{vmatrix}c & a\\a & b\end{vmatrix}-b\begin{vmatrix}b & a\\c & b\end{vmatrix}+c\begin{vmatrix}b & c\\c & a\end{vmatrix}$$
$\Rightarrow a[bc-a^2]-b[b^2-ac]+c\,[ab-c^2]$
$\Rightarrow abc-a^3-b^3+abc+abc-c^3$
$\Rightarrow -(a^3+b^3+c^3-3abc)$
$\Rightarrow -(a+b+c)\,(a^2+b^2+c^2-ab-bc-ca)$

(vi) Expanding the determinant along R_1

$$=\sin\theta\begin{vmatrix}\sin\theta & \cos\theta\\1 & \sin\theta\end{vmatrix}-\cos\theta\begin{vmatrix}1 & \cos\theta\\\cos\theta & \sin\theta\end{vmatrix}+1\begin{vmatrix}1 & \sin\theta\\\cos\theta & 1\end{vmatrix}$$
$=\sin\theta(\sin^2\theta-\cos\theta)-\cos\theta(\sin\theta-\cos^2\theta)+1\,(1-\sin\theta\cos\theta)$
$=\sin^3\theta-\sin\theta\cdot\cos\theta-\sin\theta\cdot\cos\theta+\cos^3\theta+1-\sin\theta\cdot\cos\theta$
$=\sin^3\theta+\cos^3\theta+1-3\sin\theta\cdot\cos\theta$

4. (i) (True)

Given, $A=\begin{bmatrix}5 & -2\\6 & 7\end{bmatrix}$
$\Rightarrow |A|=35-(-12)$
$=35+12=47$

(ii) (False)

Given, $A=\begin{bmatrix}1 & 0 & 1\\0 & 2 & 1\\-1 & 0 & 3\end{bmatrix}$
$$\Rightarrow |A|=1\begin{vmatrix}2 & 1\\0 & 3\end{vmatrix}-0+1\begin{vmatrix}0 & 2\\-1 & 0\end{vmatrix}$$
$=(6-0)+2=6+2=8$

5. (i) Given, $\begin{vmatrix}2x & 5\\8 & 1\end{vmatrix}=\begin{vmatrix}6 & 6\\3 & 1\end{vmatrix}$
$\Rightarrow\ 2x-40=6-18$
$\Rightarrow\ 2x=40-12$
$\Rightarrow\ 2x=28$
$\therefore\ x=14$

(ii) Given, $\begin{vmatrix}4 & -3\\2 & 3\end{vmatrix}=\begin{vmatrix}6 & -1\\8 & 9/y\end{vmatrix}$
$\Rightarrow 12-(-6)=6\times\frac{9}{y}-(-8)$
$\Rightarrow\ 12+6=\frac{54}{y}+8$
$\Rightarrow\ 18-8=\frac{54}{y}$
$\therefore\ y=\frac{54}{10}=\frac{27}{5}$

(iii) Given, $\begin{vmatrix}\sin\theta & \sec^2\theta\\1 & \operatorname{cosec}\theta\end{vmatrix}=\begin{vmatrix}\sin\theta & 1\\\sec^2\theta & \sec\theta\end{vmatrix}$
$\Rightarrow \sin\theta\cdot\operatorname{cosec}\theta-\sec^2\theta=\sin\theta\cdot\sec\theta-\sec^2\theta$
$\Rightarrow 1-\sec^2\theta=\tan\theta-\sec^2\theta$
$\Rightarrow\ \tan\theta=1$
$\therefore\ \theta=45°$

6. Given, $\begin{vmatrix}1 & 2 & 2\\2 & a & -1\\3 & 4 & 2a\end{vmatrix}=74$

Expanding along R_1,
$1(2a^2+4)-2(4a+3)+2(8-3a)=74$
$\Rightarrow 2a^2+4-8a-6+16-6a=74$
$\Rightarrow\ 2a^2-14a+14-74=0$
$\Rightarrow\ a^2-7a-30=0$
$\Rightarrow\ a^2-10a+3a-30=0$
$\Rightarrow\ a(a-10)+3(a-10)=0$
$\Rightarrow\ (a-10)\,(a+3)=0$
$\Rightarrow\ a-10=0$ or $a+3=0$
$\therefore\ a=10,-3$

Sum of the value of
$a=10+(-3)=7$

7. (i) Let $\Delta=\begin{vmatrix}x & -3 & 5\\3 & x & -4\\1 & 1 & -2\end{vmatrix}$

Expanding the determinant Δ along R_1,
$\Delta=x(-2x+4)+3(-6+4)+5(3-x)$
$=-2x^2+4x-6+15-5x$
$=-2x^2-x+9$

According to the question,
$\Delta=-1$
$\Rightarrow -2x^2-x+9=-1$
$\Rightarrow\ 2x^2+x-10=0$
$\Rightarrow\ 2x^2+5x-4x-10=0$
$\Rightarrow x(2x+5)-2(2x+5)=0$
$\Rightarrow\ (x-2)\,(2x+5)=0$
$\Rightarrow\ x-2=0$ or $2x+5=0$
$\Rightarrow\ x=2$ or $x=-\frac{5}{2}$

Hence, the positive value of x is 2.

(ii) $\left(-\frac{5}{2}\right)$

(iii) $2+\left(-\frac{5}{2}\right)=-\frac{1}{2}$

8. (i) Area of ΔABC with vertices $A(2,3), B(4,5)$ and $C(8,6)$.
$$=\frac{1}{2}\begin{vmatrix}2 & 3 & 1\\4 & 5 & 1\\8 & 6 & 1\end{vmatrix}$$
$=\frac{1}{2}|2(5-6)-3(4-8)+1(24-40)|$
$=\frac{1}{2}|-2+12-16|=\frac{1}{2}|-6|$
$=3$ sq units

(ii) Area of ΔABC with vertices $A(2,3), B(-1,0), C(2,-4)$
$$=\frac{1}{2}\begin{vmatrix}2 & 3 & 1\\-1 & 0 & 1\\2 & -4 & 1\end{vmatrix}$$
$=\frac{1}{2}|2(4)-3(-1-2)+1(4)|$
$=\frac{1}{2}|8+9+4|=\frac{21}{2}$ sq units

(iii) Area of ΔABC with vertices $A(-5,-1)$, $B(3,-5)$ and $C(5,-2)$

$$=\frac{1}{2}\begin{vmatrix}-5 & -1 & 1\\ 3 & -5 & 1\\ 5 & -2 & 1\end{vmatrix}$$

$$=\frac{1}{2}|-5(-5+2)+1(3-5)+1(-6+25)|$$

$$=\frac{1}{2}|15-2+19|$$

$=16$ sq units

9. From the graph, we have $A(1,1)$, $B(3,2)$ and $C(2,5)$

$$\text{Area of } \Delta ABC=\frac{1}{2}\begin{vmatrix}1 & 1 & 1\\ 3 & 2 & 1\\ 2 & 5 & 1\end{vmatrix}$$

$$=\frac{1}{2}|1(2-5)-1(3-2)+1(15-4)|$$

$$=\frac{1}{2}|-3-1+11|=\frac{7}{2}\text{ sq units}$$

10. (True)

The points (a, a^2-bc), (b, b^2-ca) and (c, c^2-ab) are collinear, if

$$\begin{vmatrix}a & a^2-bc & 1\\ b & b^2-ca & 1\\ c & c^2-ab & 1\end{vmatrix}=0$$

$$\text{Let } \Delta=\begin{vmatrix}a & a^2-bc & 1\\ b & b^2-ca & 1\\ c & c^2-ab & 1\end{vmatrix}$$

Expanding the determinant along C_3 we get

$$(bc^2-ab^2-b^2c+ac^2)-(ac^2-a^2b-a^2c+bc^{2)}+(ab^2-a^2c-a^2b+b^2c)$$

$=0$

11. (i) Given, points $(2,4)$, (λ,λ) and $(1,5)$ are collinear, then

$$\begin{vmatrix}2 & 4 & 1\\ \lambda & \lambda & 1\\ 1 & 5 & 1\end{vmatrix}=0$$

Expanding along R_1,

$$2(\lambda-5)-4(\lambda-1)+1(5\lambda-\lambda)=0$$

$\Rightarrow$ $2\lambda-10-4\lambda+4+4\lambda=0$

$\Rightarrow$ $2\lambda-6=0$

$\therefore$ $\lambda=3$

(ii) Given points $(2,3)$, $(4,\lambda)$ and $(6,-3)$ are collinear, then

$$\begin{vmatrix}2 & 3 & 1\\ 4 & \lambda & 1\\ 6 & -3 & 1\end{vmatrix}=0$$

$\Rightarrow 2(\lambda+3)-3(4-6)+1(-12-6\lambda)=0$

$\Rightarrow 2\lambda+6-12+18-12-6\lambda=0$

$\Rightarrow$ $4\lambda=0$

$\therefore$ $\lambda=0$

(iii) Given points $(1,0)$, $(3,\lambda^2)$ and $(5,9)$ are collinear.

$$\text{Then, } \begin{vmatrix}1 & 0 & 1\\ 3 & \lambda^2 & 1\\ 5 & 9 & 1\end{vmatrix}=0$$

$\Rightarrow 1(\lambda^2-9)-0+1(27-5\lambda^2)=0$

$\Rightarrow$ $\lambda^2-9+27-5\lambda^2=0$

$\Rightarrow$ $4\lambda^2=18$

$\Rightarrow$ $\lambda^2=\frac{18}{4}$

$\Rightarrow$ $\lambda=\pm\frac{3\sqrt{2}}{2}$

12. Area of $\Delta ABC=15$ sq units

$$\frac{1}{2}\begin{vmatrix}-1 & -8 & 1\\ k & k-1 & 1\\ 3 & 2 & 1\end{vmatrix}=\pm 15$$

Expanding the determinant along R_1, we get

$$-1(k-1-2)+8(k-3)+1(2k-3k+3)=\pm 30$$

$\Rightarrow -k+3+8k-24-k+3=\pm 30$

$\Rightarrow$ $6k-18=\pm 30$

$\Rightarrow$ $k-3=\pm 5$

$\Rightarrow$ $k-3=-5$ or $k-3=5$

$\Rightarrow$ $k=-2$ or 8

Hence, the number of possible values of k is 2.

13. The equation of line joining the points $(3,-2)$ and $(7,7)$ is

$$\begin{vmatrix}x & y & 1\\ 3 & -2 & 1\\ 7 & 7 & 1\end{vmatrix}=0$$

Expanding the determinant along R_1, we get

$$x(-2-7)-y(3-7)+1(21+14)=0$$

$-9x+4y+35=0$

or $9x-4y=35$

14. (i) $M_{22}=3$

and $A_{21}=(-1)^{2+1}(-1)=1$

(ii) $M_{31}=\begin{vmatrix}1 & 5\\ 3 & 4\end{vmatrix}=4-15=-11$

$A_{22}=(-1)^{2+2}\begin{vmatrix}2 & 5\\ 7 & 2\end{vmatrix}$

$=4-35=-31$

15. $M_{23}=\begin{vmatrix}1 & 2\\ 2 & 1\end{vmatrix}=1-4=-3$

16. (i) $M_{23}=\begin{vmatrix}1 & 2\\ 9 & 1\end{vmatrix}=-17$

(ii) $M_{31}=\begin{vmatrix}2 & 3\\ 1 & 0\end{vmatrix}=-3$

(iii) $M_{13}=\begin{vmatrix}2 & 1\\ 9 & 1\end{vmatrix}=-7$

17. (c) The element 3 is on second row and second column

$$C_{22}=\begin{vmatrix}1 & 4\\ 1 & 8\end{vmatrix}=8-4=4$$

18. (False) The minor of element 4 is

$$M_{22}=\begin{vmatrix}5 & -8\\ 5 & -8\end{vmatrix}=0$$

The cofactor of element 4 is

$C_{22}=(-1)^{2+2}M_{22}$

$=0$

19. (c) Cofactor of element 1

$=(-1)^{1+1}\begin{vmatrix}-5 & 6\\ 2 & 3\end{vmatrix}$

$=-15-12=-27$

Cofactor of element 8

$=(-1)^{1+2}\begin{vmatrix}0 & 6\\ -1 & 3\end{vmatrix}=-6$

Cofactor of element -1

$=(-1)^{3+1}\begin{vmatrix}8 & 2\\ -5 & 6\end{vmatrix}$

$=48+10=58$

Cofactor of element 3

$=(-1)^{3+3}\begin{vmatrix}1 & 8\\ 0 & -5\end{vmatrix}=-5$

20. Minor of $a_{21}=M_{21}=\begin{vmatrix}2 & -1\\ -1 & 2\end{vmatrix}$

$=4-1=3$

Cofactor of $a_{21}=A_{21}=(-1)^{2+1}M_{21}$

$=-3$

Minor of $a_{22}=M_{22}=\begin{vmatrix}1 & -1\\ 2 & 2\end{vmatrix}$

$=2+2=4$

Cofactor of $a_{22}=A_{22}$

$=(-1)^{2+2}M_{22}$

$=4$

Minor of $a_{32}=M_{32}=\begin{vmatrix}1 & -1\\ 1 & 3\end{vmatrix}$

$=3+1=4$

Cofactor of $a_{32}=A_{32}$

$=(-1)^{3+2}M_{32}$

$=-4$

21. Let $\Delta = \begin{vmatrix} 1 & -1 & 2 \\ 5 & 3 & 8 \\ 1 & 2 & 3 \end{vmatrix}$

$A_{21} = (-1)^{2+1}\begin{vmatrix} -1 & 2 \\ 2 & 3 \end{vmatrix}$

$= -(-3-4) = 7$

$A_{22} = (-1)^{2+2}\begin{vmatrix} 1 & 2 \\ 1 & 3 \end{vmatrix}$

$= 3 - 2 = 1$

$A_{23} = (-1)^{3+2}\begin{vmatrix} 1 & -1 \\ 1 & 2 \end{vmatrix}$

$= -(2+1) = -3$

$\therefore \Delta = a_{21}A_{21} + a_{22}A_{22} + a_{23}A_{23}$

$= 5 \times 7 + 3 \times 1 + 8 \times (-3)$

$= 35 + 3 - 24 = 38 - 24 = 14$

22. (False)

Let $A = \begin{bmatrix} 1 & 2 & 4 \\ 3 & -1 & 0 \\ -7 & 2 & 1 \end{bmatrix}$

Now, $|A| = 1(-1) - 2(3) + 4(6-7)$

$= -1 - 6 + 4(-1)$

$= -1 - 6 - 4$

$= -11 \neq 0$

23. The matrix $\begin{bmatrix} 2 & 4 \\ 8-2x & x+1 \end{bmatrix}$ is singular

$\Rightarrow \begin{vmatrix} 2 & 4 \\ 8-2x & x+1 \end{vmatrix} = 0$

$\Rightarrow 2(x+1) - 4(8-2x) = 0$

$\Rightarrow 2x + 2 - 32 + 8x = 0$

$\Rightarrow 10x - 30 = 0$

$\Rightarrow 10x = 30$

$\therefore x = 3$

24. (i) Let $A = \begin{bmatrix} 1 & 3 \\ 4 & 5 \end{bmatrix}$

Cofactor of $a_{11} = 5$

Cofactor of $a_{12} = -4$

Cofactor of $a_{21} = -3$

Cofactor of $a_{22} = 1$

$\therefore \text{adj } A = \begin{bmatrix} 5 & -4 \\ -3 & 1 \end{bmatrix}^T = \begin{bmatrix} 5 & -3 \\ -4 & 1 \end{bmatrix}$

(ii) Let $A = \begin{bmatrix} a & b^2 \\ -c & 3a \end{bmatrix}$

Cofactor of $a_{11} = 3a$

Cofactor of $a_{12} = c$

Cofactor of $a_{21} = -b^2$

Cofactor of $a_{22} = a$

$\therefore \text{adj } A = \begin{bmatrix} 3a & c \\ -b^2 & a \end{bmatrix}^T = \begin{bmatrix} 3a & -b^2 \\ c & a \end{bmatrix}$

(iii) Let $A = \begin{bmatrix} 1 & 2 & 3 \\ 1 & -1 & 0 \\ 4 & -2 & 3 \end{bmatrix}$

$A_{11} = \begin{vmatrix} -1 & 0 \\ -2 & 3 \end{vmatrix} = -3$

$A_{12} = -\begin{vmatrix} 1 & 0 \\ 4 & 3 \end{vmatrix} = -3$

$A_{13} = \begin{vmatrix} 1 & -1 \\ 4 & -2 \end{vmatrix} = -2 + 4 = 2$

$A_{21} = -\begin{vmatrix} 2 & 3 \\ -2 & 3 \end{vmatrix}$

$= -(6+6) = -12$

$A_{22} = \begin{vmatrix} 1 & 3 \\ 4 & 3 \end{vmatrix} = 3 - 12 = -9$

$A_{23} = -\begin{vmatrix} 1 & 2 \\ 4 & -2 \end{vmatrix}$

$= -(-2-8) = 10$

$A_{31} = \begin{vmatrix} 2 & 3 \\ -1 & 0 \end{vmatrix} = 3$

$A_{32} = -\begin{vmatrix} 1 & 3 \\ 1 & 0 \end{vmatrix} = 3$

$A_{33} = \begin{vmatrix} 1 & 2 \\ 1 & -1 \end{vmatrix}$

$= -1 - 2 = -3$

Therefore,

$\text{adj } A = \begin{bmatrix} -3 & -3 & 2 \\ -12 & -9 & 10 \\ 3 & 3 & -3 \end{bmatrix}^T$

$= \begin{bmatrix} -3 & -12 & 3 \\ -3 & -9 & 3 \\ 2 & 10 & -3 \end{bmatrix}$

(iv) Let $A = \begin{bmatrix} 1 & -1 & 0 \\ 2 & 1 & 4 \\ -3 & 2 & 5 \end{bmatrix}$

$A_{11} = \begin{vmatrix} 1 & 4 \\ 2 & 5 \end{vmatrix} = 5 - 8 = -3$

$A_{12} = -\begin{vmatrix} 2 & 4 \\ -3 & 5 \end{vmatrix} = -(10+12) = -22$

$A_{13} = \begin{vmatrix} 2 & 1 \\ -3 & 2 \end{vmatrix} = 4 + 3 = 7$

$A_{21} = -\begin{vmatrix} -1 & 0 \\ 2 & 5 \end{vmatrix} = -(-5) = 5$

$A_{22} = \begin{vmatrix} 1 & 0 \\ -3 & 5 \end{vmatrix} = 5$

$A_{23} = -\begin{vmatrix} 1 & -1 \\ -3 & 2 \end{vmatrix} = -(2-3) = 1$

$A_{31} = \begin{vmatrix} -1 & 0 \\ 1 & 4 \end{vmatrix} = -4$

$A_{32} = -\begin{vmatrix} 1 & 0 \\ 2 & 4 \end{vmatrix} = -4$

$A_{33} = \begin{vmatrix} 1 & -1 \\ 2 & 1 \end{vmatrix} = 1 + 2 = 3$

Therefore,

$\text{adj } A = \begin{bmatrix} -3 & -22 & 7 \\ 5 & 5 & 1 \\ -4 & -4 & 3 \end{bmatrix}^T$

$= \begin{bmatrix} -3 & 5 & -4 \\ -22 & 5 & -4 \\ 7 & 1 & 3 \end{bmatrix}$

25. (False)

Given, $A = \begin{bmatrix} \tan\theta & -\sec\theta \\ \sec\theta & -\tan\theta \end{bmatrix}$

$\Rightarrow \text{adj } A = \begin{bmatrix} -\tan\theta & \sec\theta \\ -\sec\theta & \tan\theta \end{bmatrix}$

$\therefore |\text{adj } A| = \begin{vmatrix} -\tan\theta & \sec\theta \\ -\sec\theta & \tan\theta \end{vmatrix}$

$= -\tan^2\theta + \sec^2\theta$

$= 1$

26. (b) $|\text{adj } A| = |A|^{n-1} = \Delta^{n-1}$

Hence, determinant of adj $A = \Delta^{n-1}$.

27. (c) Given, $\text{adj } A = \begin{bmatrix} 64 & 0 & 0 \\ 0 & 64 & 0 \\ 0 & 0 & 64 \end{bmatrix}$

$\Rightarrow \text{adj } A = 64\begin{bmatrix} 1 & 0 & 0 \\ 0 & 1 & 0 \\ 0 & 0 & 1 \end{bmatrix}$

$\Rightarrow |\text{adj } A| = (64)^3$

$\Rightarrow |A|^2 = (64)^3$

$\therefore |A| = 512$

28. (True)

Let A be a square matrix of order n, where n is an odd positive integer.

As, A is skew-symmetric matrix,

$A^T = -A$

$\Rightarrow |A^T| = |-A|$

$\Rightarrow |A| = (-1)^n |A|$ $[\because |A^T| = |A|]$

$\Rightarrow |A| = -|A|$

$\Rightarrow 2|A| = 0$

$\therefore |A| = 0$

29. $|A(\text{adj } A)| = |A||\text{adj } A|$
$= |A||A|^{n-1}$
$[\because |\text{adj } A| = |A|^{n-1}]$
$= |A|^n$
$\therefore |A(\text{adj } A)| = 5^3 = 125$

30. Given, $AB = 10I$
$\Rightarrow |AB| = |10I|$
$\Rightarrow |A||B| = 10^3|I|$
$[\because |AB| = |A||B|]$
$\Rightarrow 5|B| = 1000 \quad [\because |I| = 1]$
$\therefore |B| = 200$

31. $A(\text{adj } A) = (\text{adj } A)A = |A| I_n$

$A(\text{adj } A) = |A|\begin{vmatrix} 1 & 0 \\ 0 & 1 \end{vmatrix}$

$\Rightarrow \begin{vmatrix} 7 & 0 \\ 0 & 7 \end{vmatrix} = |A|\begin{vmatrix} 1 & 0 \\ 0 & 1 \end{vmatrix}$

$\Rightarrow 7\begin{vmatrix} 1 & 0 \\ 0 & 1 \end{vmatrix} = |A|\begin{vmatrix} 1 & 0 \\ 0 & 1 \end{vmatrix}$

$\therefore |A| = 7$

32. (c) $A(\text{adj } A) = |A| I_n$

$A(\text{adj } A) = \begin{vmatrix} 3 & 1 \\ 4 & 2 \end{vmatrix}\begin{bmatrix} 1 & 0 \\ 0 & 1 \end{bmatrix}$

$= 2\begin{bmatrix} 1 & 0 \\ 0 & 1 \end{bmatrix} = \begin{bmatrix} 2 & 0 \\ 0 & 2 \end{bmatrix}$

33. If A is a singular matrix of order n, then $|A| = 0$
$A(\text{adj } A) = |A| I_n$
$= 0 \times I_n = O$

Hence, if A is a singular matrix of order n, then $A(\text{adj } A)$ is a zero or null matrix.

34. (True)

Let $A = \begin{bmatrix} a_{11} & a_{12} \\ a_{21} & a_{22} \end{bmatrix}$ be a square matrix of order 2

$\text{adj}(A) = \begin{bmatrix} A_{11} & A_{21} \\ A_{12} & A_{22} \end{bmatrix}$

$A(\text{adj } A) = \begin{bmatrix} a_{11} & a_{12} \\ a_{21} & a_{22} \end{bmatrix}\begin{bmatrix} A_{11} & A_{21} \\ A_{12} & A_{22} \end{bmatrix}$

$= \begin{bmatrix} a_{11}A_{11} + a_{12}A_{12} & a_{11}A_{21} + a_{12}A_{22} \\ a_{21}A_{11} + a_{22}A_{12} & a_{21}A_{21} + a_{22}A_{22} \end{bmatrix}$

$= \begin{bmatrix} |A| & 0 \\ 0 & |A| \end{bmatrix} = |A|\begin{bmatrix} 1 & 0 \\ 0 & 1 \end{bmatrix}$

$= C|A| \text{In}$

Now,

$(\text{adj } A)A = \begin{bmatrix} A_{11} & A_{21} \\ A_{12} & A_{22} \end{bmatrix}\begin{bmatrix} a_{11} & a_{12} \\ a_{21} & a_{22} \end{bmatrix}$

$= \begin{bmatrix} A_{11}a_{11} + A_{21}a_{21} & A_{11}a_{12} + A_{21}a_{22} \\ A_{12}a_{11} + A_{22}a_{21} & A_{12}a_{12} + A_{22}a_{22} \end{bmatrix}$

$= \begin{bmatrix} |A| & 0 \\ 0 & |A| \end{bmatrix} = |A|\begin{bmatrix} 1 & 0 \\ 0 & 1 \end{bmatrix} = |A| \text{In}$

Hence, $A(\text{adj } A) = (\text{adj } A)A = |A| I_n$

35. (True)

Let $I = \begin{bmatrix} 1 & 0 & 0 \\ 0 & 1 & 0 \\ 0 & 0 & 1 \end{bmatrix}$

$\Rightarrow KI = \begin{bmatrix} K & 0 & 0 \\ 0 & K & 0 \\ 0 & 0 & K \end{bmatrix}$

$\text{adj}(KI) = \begin{bmatrix} K^2 & 0 & 0 \\ 0 & K^2 & 0 \\ 0 & 0 & K^2 \end{bmatrix}$

$= K^2\begin{bmatrix} 1 & 0 & 0 \\ 0 & 1 & 0 \\ 0 & 0 & 1 \end{bmatrix} = K^2 I_3$

36. (c) We know that
$|\text{adj}(\text{adj } A)| = |A|^{(n-1)^2}$

Since, $|A| = \begin{vmatrix} 1 & -1 & 1 \\ 0 & 2 & -3 \\ 2 & 1 & 0 \end{vmatrix}$

$= 1(3) + 1(6) + 1(-4) = 5$

Therefore,
$|\text{adj}(\text{adj } A)| = (5)^{(3-1)^2} = 5^4 = 625$
$\Rightarrow |5A| = 5^3|A|$
$= 125 \times 5 = 625$
$\therefore \dfrac{|\text{adj}(\text{adj } A)|}{|5A|} = \dfrac{625}{625} = 1$

37. (True) $|\text{adj } A| = |A|^{n-2}$
If $|A| = 0$, then $|A|^{n-2} = 0$
Hence, $|\text{adj } A| = 0$

38. Let $AB = C$,
where $B = \begin{bmatrix} 3 & 2 \\ 1 & 1 \end{bmatrix}$
and $C = \begin{bmatrix} 4 & 1 \\ -1 & 2 \end{bmatrix}$
$\Rightarrow A = CB^{-1}$
$\because B^{-1} = \dfrac{1}{|B|}\text{adj}(B)$
$= \dfrac{1}{(3-2)}\begin{bmatrix} 1 & -2 \\ -1 & 3 \end{bmatrix}$
$= \begin{bmatrix} 1 & -2 \\ -1 & 3 \end{bmatrix}$
$\therefore A = CB^{-1}$
$= \begin{bmatrix} 4 & 1 \\ -1 & 2 \end{bmatrix}\begin{bmatrix} 1 & -2 \\ -1 & 3 \end{bmatrix}$
$= \begin{bmatrix} 3 & -5 \\ -3 & 8 \end{bmatrix}$

39. $A = \begin{bmatrix} 4 & 1 \\ 5 & 2 \end{bmatrix}$
$\therefore A^{-1} = \dfrac{1}{|A|}\text{adj}(A)$
$\Rightarrow \text{adj}(A) = \begin{bmatrix} 2 & -1 \\ -5 & 4 \end{bmatrix}$
$\therefore |A| = 4 \times 2 - 5 \times 1$
$= 8 - 5$
$= 3$
Hence, $A^{-1} = \dfrac{1}{3}\begin{bmatrix} 2 & -1 \\ -5 & 4 \end{bmatrix}$

40. (i) True
(ii) True
(iii) (False) $A \text{ adj } A = |A| I_n$
$(A \text{ adj } A)^T = [|A| I_n]^T$
$(\text{adj } A)^T \cdot A^T = |A| I_n$ ...(i)
Also, $(\text{adj } A^T) A^T = |A^T| I_n$
$(\text{adj } A^T) A^T = |A| I_n$ ...(ii)
On comparing Eqs. (i) and (ii), we get
$\text{adj } A^T = (\text{adj } A)^T$
(iv) True

41. Given, $A = \begin{bmatrix} 4 & 1 \\ -1 & 3 \end{bmatrix}$

Now, $A^2 = A \cdot A = \begin{bmatrix} 4 & 1 \\ -1 & 3 \end{bmatrix}\begin{bmatrix} 4 & 1 \\ -1 & 3 \end{bmatrix}$

$\Rightarrow A^2 = \begin{bmatrix} 15 & 7 \\ -7 & 8 \end{bmatrix}$

$\therefore A^2 - 5A + 7I$
$= \begin{bmatrix} 15 & 7 \\ -7 & 8 \end{bmatrix} - 5\begin{bmatrix} 4 & 1 \\ -1 & 3 \end{bmatrix} + 7\begin{bmatrix} 1 & 0 \\ 0 & 1 \end{bmatrix}$
$= \begin{bmatrix} 15 - 20 + 7 & 7 - 5 + 0 \\ -7 + 5 + 0 & 8 - 15 + 7 \end{bmatrix}$
$= \begin{bmatrix} 2 & 2 \\ -2 & 0 \end{bmatrix}$

and $A^{-1} = \dfrac{1}{7}(5I - A)$
$= \dfrac{1}{7}\left(5\begin{bmatrix} 1 & 0 \\ 0 & 1 \end{bmatrix} - \begin{bmatrix} 4 & 1 \\ -1 & 3 \end{bmatrix}\right)$
$= \dfrac{1}{7}\left(\begin{bmatrix} 5 & 0 \\ 0 & 5 \end{bmatrix} - \begin{bmatrix} 4 & 1 \\ -1 & 3 \end{bmatrix}\right)$
$= \dfrac{1}{7}\begin{bmatrix} 1 & -1 \\ 1 & 2 \end{bmatrix}$

42. $A=\begin{bmatrix}2 & 7\\-6 & 4\end{bmatrix}$

Therefore,

$$A^2=A\cdot A=\begin{bmatrix}2 & 7\\-6 & 4\end{bmatrix}\begin{bmatrix}2 & 7\\-6 & 4\end{bmatrix}$$

$$\Rightarrow A^2=\begin{bmatrix}-38 & 42\\-36 & -26\end{bmatrix}$$

According to the question,

$$A^2+aA+bI=O$$

$$\Rightarrow \begin{bmatrix}-38 & 42\\-36 & -26\end{bmatrix}+a\begin{bmatrix}2 & 7\\-6 & 4\end{bmatrix}+b\begin{bmatrix}1 & 0\\0 & 1\end{bmatrix}=O$$

$$\Rightarrow \begin{bmatrix}-38+2a+b & 42+7a+0\\-36-6a+0 & -26+4a+b\end{bmatrix}=O$$

$$\Rightarrow 42+7a=0 \Rightarrow a=-6$$

Now, $-38+2a+b=0$

$$\Rightarrow -38+2(-6)+b=0$$

$$\Rightarrow b=50$$

Hence, $a=-6$ and $b=50$

43. Given, $A=\begin{bmatrix}1 & 1 & 1\\1 & 3 & -4\\3 & -1 & 5\end{bmatrix}$

According to the question,

$$A^3-6A^2-5A+11I=O$$

On multiplying by A^{-1}, we get

$$A^3\cdot A^{-1}-6A^2A^{-1}-5A\cdot A^{-1}, +11IA^{-1}=O\cdot A^{-1}$$

$$A^{-1}=\frac{1}{11}[-A^2+6A+5I]$$

Now,

$$A^2=\begin{bmatrix}1 & 1 & 1\\1 & 3 & -4\\3 & -1 & 5\end{bmatrix}\begin{bmatrix}1 & 1 & 1\\1 & 3 & -4\\3 & -1 & 5\end{bmatrix}$$

$$=\begin{bmatrix}1+1+3 & 1+3-1 & 1-4+5\\1+3-12 & 1+9+4 & 1-12-20\\3-1+15 & 3-3-5 & 3+4+25\end{bmatrix}$$

$$=\begin{bmatrix}5 & 3 & 2\\-8 & 14 & -31\\17 & -5 & 32\end{bmatrix}$$

$$A^{-1}=\frac{1}{11}\left[-1\begin{bmatrix}5 & 3 & 2\\-8 & 14 & -31\\17 & -5 & 32\end{bmatrix}+6\begin{bmatrix}1 & 1 & 1\\1 & 3 & -4\\3 & -1 & 5\end{bmatrix}+5\begin{bmatrix}1 & 0 & 0\\0 & 1 & 0\\0 & 0 & 1\end{bmatrix}\right]$$

$$=\frac{1}{11}\begin{bmatrix}-5+6+5 & -3+6+0 & -2+6+0\\8+6+0 & -14+18+5 & 31-24+0\\-17+18+0 & 5-6+0 & -32+30+5\end{bmatrix}$$

$$\therefore A^{-1}=\frac{1}{11}\begin{bmatrix}6 & 3 & 4\\14 & 9 & 7\\1 & -1 & 3\end{bmatrix}$$

44. (i) The given system of equations can be written as

$$\begin{bmatrix}1 & 2 & -3\\2 & 3 & 2\\3 & -3 & -4\end{bmatrix}\begin{bmatrix}x\\y\\z\end{bmatrix}=\begin{bmatrix}-4\\2\\11\end{bmatrix},$$

where $A=\begin{bmatrix}1 & 2 & -3\\2 & 3 & 2\\3 & -3 & -4\end{bmatrix}$,

$$\Rightarrow X=\begin{bmatrix}x\\y\\z\end{bmatrix} \text{ and } B=\begin{bmatrix}-4\\2\\11\end{bmatrix}$$

$$\Rightarrow AX=B \Rightarrow X=A^{-1}B$$

$$\Rightarrow \text{adj } A=\begin{bmatrix}-6 & 17 & 13\\14 & 5 & -8\\-15 & 9 & -1\end{bmatrix}$$

$$\Rightarrow |A|=\begin{vmatrix}1 & 2 & -3\\2 & 3 & 2\\3 & -3 & -4\end{vmatrix}$$

$$=-6+28+45=67$$

$$\therefore X=A^{-1}B$$

$$=\frac{1}{67}\begin{bmatrix}-6 & 17 & 13\\14 & 5 & -8\\-15 & 9 & -1\end{bmatrix}\begin{bmatrix}-4\\2\\11\end{bmatrix}$$

$$=\frac{1}{67}\begin{bmatrix}24+34+143\\-56+10-88\\60+18-11\end{bmatrix}=\begin{bmatrix}3\\-2\\1\end{bmatrix}$$

Hence, $x=3$, $y=-2$, $z=1$.

(ii) Given, system of equation is

$$x-y+2z=7,$$
$$3x+4y-5z=-5$$
and $$2x-y+3z=12$$

In matrix form, it can be written as $AX=B$ ...(i)

where,

$$A=\begin{bmatrix}1 & -1 & 2\\3 & 4 & -5\\2 & -1 & 3\end{bmatrix}, X=\begin{bmatrix}x\\y\\z\end{bmatrix}$$

and $B=\begin{bmatrix}7\\-5\\12\end{bmatrix}$

Here, $|A|=1(12-5)+1(9+10)+2(-3-8)$

$$=1(7)+1(19)+2(-11)=4$$

$$\Rightarrow |A|\neq 0$$

So, A is non-singular and its inverse exists

$$A_{11}=(-1)^2\begin{vmatrix}4 & -5\\-1 & 3\end{vmatrix}=7$$

$$A_{12}=(-1)^3\begin{vmatrix}3 & -5\\2 & 3\end{vmatrix}=-19$$

$$A_{13}=(-1)^4\begin{vmatrix}3 & 4\\2 & -1\end{vmatrix}=-11$$

$$A_{21}=(-1)^3\begin{vmatrix}-1 & 2\\-1 & 3\end{vmatrix}$$

$$=-1(-3+2)=1$$

$$A_{22}=(-1)^4\begin{vmatrix}1 & 2\\2 & 3\end{vmatrix}=-1$$

$$A_{23}=(-1)^5\begin{vmatrix}1 & -1\\2 & -1\end{vmatrix}=-1$$

$$A_{31}=(-1)^4\begin{vmatrix}-1 & 2\\4 & -5\end{vmatrix}=-3$$

$$A_{32}=(-1)^5\begin{vmatrix}1 & 2\\3 & -5\end{vmatrix}=11$$

$$A_{33}=(-1)^6\begin{vmatrix}1 & -1\\3 & 4\end{vmatrix}=7$$

$$\text{adj } A=\begin{bmatrix}7 & 1 & -3\\-19 & -1 & 11\\-11 & -1 & 7\end{bmatrix}$$

$$A^{-1}=\frac{\text{adj}A}{|A|}=\frac{1}{4}\begin{bmatrix}7 & 1 & -3\\-19 & -1 & 11\\-11 & -1 & 7\end{bmatrix}$$

Now, from Eq. (i), we get

$$X=A^{-1}B$$

$$\begin{bmatrix}x\\y\\z\end{bmatrix}=\frac{1}{4}\begin{bmatrix}7 & 1 & -3\\-19 & -1 & 11\\-11 & -1 & 7\end{bmatrix}\begin{bmatrix}7\\-5\\12\end{bmatrix}$$

$$=\frac{1}{4}\begin{bmatrix}49-5-36\\-133+5+132\\-77+5+84\end{bmatrix}$$

$$=\frac{1}{4}\begin{bmatrix}8\\4\\12\end{bmatrix}$$

Hence, $x=2$, $y=1$ and $z=3$.

45. (i) (True)

The given system of equations can be written in matrix form as $AX = B$,

where $A = \begin{bmatrix} 1 & 2 \\ 2 & 3 \end{bmatrix}, X = \begin{bmatrix} x \\ y \end{bmatrix}$

and $B = \begin{bmatrix} 2 \\ 3 \end{bmatrix}$

Now, $|A| = \begin{vmatrix} 1 & 2 \\ 2 & 3 \end{vmatrix} = 1(3) - 2(2)$

$= 3 - 4 = -1 \neq 0$

Since, A is non-singular, so A^{-1} exists.

Hence, the given system of equations is consistent.

(ii) (False)

Given system of equations is

$3x - y = 5$ ...(i)

and $6x - 2y = 3$ ...(ii)

Given equations can be written in matrix form as $AX = B$,

where $A = \begin{bmatrix} 3 & -1 \\ 6 & -2 \end{bmatrix}, X = \begin{bmatrix} x \\ y \end{bmatrix}$

and $B = \begin{bmatrix} 5 \\ 3 \end{bmatrix}$

Now, $|A| = \begin{vmatrix} 3 & -1 \\ 6 & -2 \end{vmatrix} = -6 + 6 = 0$

$\therefore A^{-1}$ does not exist.

Now, $\text{adj}(A) = \begin{bmatrix} -2 & 1 \\ -6 & 3 \end{bmatrix}$

$\left[\because \text{adj}\begin{bmatrix} a & b \\ c & d \end{bmatrix} = \begin{bmatrix} d & -b \\ -c & a \end{bmatrix}\right]$

$\therefore \text{adj}(A)B = \begin{bmatrix} -2 & 1 \\ -6 & 3 \end{bmatrix}\begin{bmatrix} 5 \\ 3 \end{bmatrix}$

$= \begin{bmatrix} -10+3 \\ -30+9 \end{bmatrix} = \begin{bmatrix} -7 \\ -21 \end{bmatrix}$

$\Rightarrow \text{adj}(A)B \neq O$

Hence, equations are inconsistent and have no solution.

(iii) (False) Given system of equations can be written as

$3x - y - 2z = 2,\ 0 \cdot x + 2y - z = -1$ and $3x - 5y + 0 \cdot z = 3$

and its matrix form is $AX = B$, where

$A = \begin{bmatrix} 3 & -1 & -2 \\ 0 & 2 & -1 \\ 3 & -5 & 0 \end{bmatrix}, X = \begin{bmatrix} x \\ y \\ z \end{bmatrix}$

and $B = \begin{bmatrix} 2 \\ -1 \\ 3 \end{bmatrix}$

Here, $|A| = \begin{vmatrix} 3 & -1 & -2 \\ 0 & 2 & -1 \\ 3 & -5 & 0 \end{vmatrix}$

$= 3(0-5) + 1(0+3) - 2(0-6)$

$= -15 + 3 + 12 = 0$

$\therefore A^{-1}$ does not exist.

Consider, the cofactors of elements of $|A|$, i.e.

$A_{11} = (-1)^{1+1}\begin{vmatrix} 2 & -1 \\ -5 & 0 \end{vmatrix}$

$= (0-5) = -5$

$A_{12} = (-1)^{1+2}\begin{vmatrix} 0 & -1 \\ 3 & 0 \end{vmatrix}$

$= -(0+3) = -3$

$A_{13} = (-1)^{1+3}\begin{vmatrix} 0 & 2 \\ 3 & -5 \end{vmatrix}$

$= (0-6) = -6$

$A_{21} = (-1)^{2+1}\begin{vmatrix} -1 & -2 \\ -5 & 0 \end{vmatrix}$

$= -(0-10) = 10$

$A_{22} = (-1)^{2+2}\begin{vmatrix} 3 & -2 \\ 3 & 0 \end{vmatrix}$

$= (0+6) = 6$

$A_{23} = (-1)^{2+3}\begin{vmatrix} 3 & -1 \\ 3 & -5 \end{vmatrix}$

$= -(-15+3) = 12$

$A_{31} = (-1)^{3+1}\begin{vmatrix} -1 & -2 \\ 2 & -1 \end{vmatrix}$

$= (1+4) = 5$

$A_{32} = (-1)^{3+2}\begin{vmatrix} 3 & -2 \\ 0 & -1 \end{vmatrix}$

$= -(-3+0) = 3$

$A_{33} = (-1)^{3+3}\begin{vmatrix} 3 & -1 \\ 0 & 2 \end{vmatrix}$

$= (6+0) = 6$

$\therefore \text{adj}(A) = \begin{bmatrix} A_{11} & A_{12} & A_{13} \\ A_{21} & A_{22} & A_{23} \\ A_{31} & A_{32} & A_{33} \end{bmatrix}^T$

$= \begin{bmatrix} -5 & -3 & -6 \\ 10 & 6 & 12 \\ 5 & 3 & 6 \end{bmatrix}^T = \begin{bmatrix} -5 & 10 & 5 \\ -3 & 6 & 3 \\ -6 & 12 & 6 \end{bmatrix}$

Now,

$\text{adj}(A) \cdot B = \begin{bmatrix} -5 & 10 & 5 \\ -3 & 6 & 3 \\ -6 & 12 & 6 \end{bmatrix}\begin{bmatrix} 2 \\ -1 \\ 3 \end{bmatrix}$

$= \begin{bmatrix} -10-10+15 \\ -6-6+9 \\ -12-12+18 \end{bmatrix}$

$= \begin{bmatrix} -5 \\ -3 \\ -6 \end{bmatrix} \neq O \Rightarrow \text{adj}(A) \cdot B \neq O$

Hence, the given system of linear equations is inconsistent.

46. (i) (False)

The given system of equations $y - z = 1, -x + 2z = -2$ and $x - 2y = 3$ can be written as

$\begin{bmatrix} 0 & 1 & -1 \\ -1 & 0 & 2 \\ 1 & -2 & 0 \end{bmatrix}\begin{bmatrix} x \\ y \\ z \end{bmatrix} = \begin{bmatrix} 1 \\ -2 \\ 3 \end{bmatrix},$

where $A = \begin{bmatrix} 0 & 1 & -1 \\ -1 & 0 & 2 \\ 1 & -2 & 0 \end{bmatrix},$

$X = \begin{bmatrix} x \\ y \\ z \end{bmatrix}$ and $B = \begin{bmatrix} 1 \\ -2 \\ 3 \end{bmatrix}$

$\therefore |A| = \begin{vmatrix} 0 & 1 & -1 \\ -1 & 0 & 2 \\ 1 & -2 & 0 \end{vmatrix}$

Expanding the determinant along R_1,

$= -1\begin{vmatrix} -1 & 2 \\ 1 & 0 \end{vmatrix} - 1\begin{vmatrix} -1 & 0 \\ 1 & -2 \end{vmatrix}$

$= -1(-2) - 1(2) = 2 - 2 = 0$

Hence, the given system of equations has either no solution or infinitely many solution.

(ii) (True)

The given system of equations $x + 3y + 3z = 2,\ x + 4y + 3z = 1$ and $x + 3y + 4z = 2$ can be written as

$\begin{bmatrix} 1 & 3 & 3 \\ 1 & 4 & 3 \\ 1 & 3 & 4 \end{bmatrix}\begin{bmatrix} x \\ y \\ z \end{bmatrix} = \begin{bmatrix} 2 \\ 1 \\ 2 \end{bmatrix},$

where $A = \begin{bmatrix} 1 & 3 & 3 \\ 1 & 4 & 3 \\ 1 & 3 & 4 \end{bmatrix},$

$X = \begin{bmatrix} x \\ y \\ z \end{bmatrix}$ and $B = \begin{bmatrix} 2 \\ 1 \\ 2 \end{bmatrix}$

$\therefore |A| = \begin{vmatrix} 1 & 3 & 3 \\ 1 & 4 & 3 \\ 1 & 3 & 4 \end{vmatrix}$

Expanding the determinant along R_1,

$= 1\begin{vmatrix} 4 & 3 \\ 3 & 4 \end{vmatrix} - 3\begin{vmatrix} 1 & 3 \\ 1 & 4 \end{vmatrix} + 3\begin{vmatrix} 1 & 4 \\ 1 & 3 \end{vmatrix}$

$= 1(16-9) - 3(4-3) + 3(3-4)$

$= 7 - 3 - 3 = 1 \neq 0$

$\Rightarrow \quad |A| \neq 0$

Hence, the given system of equations has unique solution.

47. (False) Given system of linear equations has no solution.

$$\therefore \begin{vmatrix} 1 & 2a & a \\ 1 & 3b & b \\ 1 & 4c & c \end{vmatrix} = 0$$

Expanding along C_3,

$$a(4c - 3b) - b(4c - 2a) + c(3b - 2a) = 0$$

$$\Rightarrow 4ac - 3ab - 4bc + 2ab + 3bc - 2ac = 0$$

$$\Rightarrow 2ac - ab - bc = 0$$

$$\Rightarrow 2ac = ab + bc$$

On dividing by abc,

$$\frac{2ac}{abc} = \frac{bc}{abc} + \frac{ab}{abc} \Rightarrow \frac{2}{b} = \frac{1}{a} + \frac{1}{c}$$

Hence, a, b and c are in HP.

Assertion-Reason

1. (c) Minor of element

$$6 = M_{12} = \begin{vmatrix} 1 & 2 \\ 2 & 1 \end{vmatrix} = 1 - 4 = -3$$

$\therefore$ Given Assertion (A) is true.

Also, we know that minor of an element a_{ij} of a matrix is the determinant obtained by deleting its ith row and jth column.

$\therefore$ Reason is false.

A is true but R is false.

2. (b) Here,

$$|2AB| = 2^3|AB| = 8|A||B| = 8 \times 3 \times -4 = -96$$

$\therefore$ Assertion is true,

$$[\because |kA| = k^n|A| \text{ and } |AB| = |A||B|]$$

Also we know that $|kA| = k^n|A|$ for matrix A of order n.

$\therefore$ Reason is true.

But $|AB| = |A||B|$ is not mentioned in Reason.

$\therefore$ Both A and R are true but R is not the correct explanation of A.

3. (a) Given, $A = \begin{bmatrix} 4 & 1 \\ 3 & 2 \end{bmatrix}$

$$\Rightarrow |A| = \begin{vmatrix} 4 & 1 \\ 3 & 2 \end{vmatrix} = 8 - 3 = 5.$$

We know $A\,(\text{adj } A)\, A = |A|\, I$

$$\therefore A\,(\text{adj } A) = 5I = 5\begin{bmatrix} 1 & 0 \\ 0 & 1 \end{bmatrix} = \begin{bmatrix} 5 & 0 \\ 0 & 5 \end{bmatrix}$$

$\therefore$ Both Assertion and Reason are true and R is the correct explanation of A.

4. (b) Given, $A^{-1} = \frac{1}{5} \text{adj } A$

We know that $A^{-1} = \frac{1}{|A|} \text{adj } A$

$$\therefore |A| = 5$$

Also, $|2A| = 2^2|A|$

$$[\because |kA| = k^n|A|]$$

$$= 4 \times 5 = 20$$

$\therefore$ Given Assertion is true.

Also Reason is true.

Since $|kA| = k^n|A|$ is not mentioned in Reason.

$\therefore$ Reason is not correct explanation of A.

5. (c) Given, Matrix A is singular.

$$\therefore |A| = 0$$

$$\Rightarrow \begin{vmatrix} 2 & 1 & 0 \\ 0 & 1 & 2 \\ 1 & -2 & x \end{vmatrix} = 0$$

$$\Rightarrow 2\begin{vmatrix} 1 & 2 \\ -2 & x \end{vmatrix} - 1\begin{vmatrix} 0 & 2 \\ 1 & x \end{vmatrix} + 0 = 0$$

$$\Rightarrow 2(x + 4) - (0 - 2) = 0$$

$$\Rightarrow 2x + 8 + 2 = 0$$

$$\Rightarrow 2x = -10$$

$$\Rightarrow x = -5$$

$\therefore$ Given, Assertion is true. Also, we know that for singular matrix A, $|A| = 0$

$\therefore$ Given, Reason is false.

6. (d) We know that $(kA)^{-1} \neq \frac{1}{k}(A^{-1})$

$\therefore$ Given Assertion is not true.

Clearly Reason is true.

$\therefore$ A is false and R is true.

7. (a) Given, det (adj A) = 49

$$\Rightarrow |A|^2 = 49$$

$$\Rightarrow |A| = \pm 7$$

$\therefore$ Given Assertion is true. Also, we know that for a square matrix of order n, $|\text{adj } A| = |A|^{n-1}$

$\therefore$ For $n = 3$, $|\text{adj } A| = |A|^2$

$\therefore$ Given Reason is true and R is the correct explanation for given Assertion.

8. (a) Given Assertion is adj (adj A) $= |A|^{n-2} A$

We know that if A is an invertible matrix, then

$$A^{-1} = \frac{\text{adj } A}{|A|}$$

$$\Rightarrow \text{adj } A = A^{-1}|A|$$

$$\therefore A\,(\text{adj } A) = A \cdot A^{-1}|A| = I\,|A| = |A|\, I$$

$$\Rightarrow A\,(\text{adj } A) = |A|\begin{bmatrix} 1\,0\,0\,0 \ldots 0 \\ 0\,1\,0\,0 \ldots 0 \\ 0\,0\,1\,0 \ldots 0 \\ \ldots\ldots\ldots\ldots \\ \ldots\ldots\ldots\ldots \\ 0\,0\,0 \ldots 1 \end{bmatrix}$$

$$\Rightarrow |A\,(\text{adj } A)| = \begin{vmatrix} |A|\,0\,0 \ldots 0 \\ 0\,|A|\,0 \ldots 0 \\ \ldots\ldots\ldots\ldots \\ \ldots\ldots\ldots\ldots \\ \ldots\ldots\ldots\ldots \\ 0\,0 \ldots |A| \end{vmatrix} = |A|^n$$

$$\Rightarrow |A||\text{adj } A| = |A|^n$$

$$\Rightarrow |\text{adj } A| = |A|^{n-1} \quad \ldots\text{(i)}$$

Given Reason is true.

Now, $A^{-1} = \frac{\text{adj } A}{|A|}$

$$\Rightarrow \text{adj } A = A^{-1}|A|$$

On multiplying both sides with $(\text{adj } A)^{-1}$

$$\therefore (\text{adj } A)(\text{adj } A)^{-1} = A^{-1}|A|(\text{adj } A)^{-1}$$

$$\Rightarrow I = A^{-1}|A|(\text{adj } A)^{-1}$$

On multiplying both sides with A

$$\therefore A = |A|(\text{adj } A)^{-1}$$

$$\Rightarrow (\text{adj } A)^{-1} = \frac{A}{|A|} \quad \ldots\text{(ii)}$$

Also $(\text{adj } A)^{-1} = \frac{\text{adj}(\text{adj } A)}{|\text{adj } A|}$

$$\Rightarrow (\text{adj } A)^{-1} \cdot |\text{adj } A| = \text{adj}(\text{adj } A)$$

$$\Rightarrow \frac{A}{|A|} \cdot |A|^{n-1} = \text{adj}(\text{adj } A)$$

[using Eqs. (i) and (ii)]

$$\therefore \text{adj}(\text{adj } A) = |A|^{n-2} \cdot A$$

$\Rightarrow$ Assertion (A) is true.

$\therefore$ Both A and R are true and R is the correct explanation of A.

9. (d) Given Assertion is $|A^2| = 25$

$$\Rightarrow |AA| = 25$$

$$\Rightarrow |A||A| = 25$$

$$\Rightarrow |A|^2 = 25$$

$$\Rightarrow |A| = \pm 5$$

$\therefore$ Given Assertion is false.

Also, $|AB| = |A||B|$

[property of determinant]

$\therefore$ Reason is true.

10. (d) Given, area of triangle,

$$\Delta = \frac{1}{2}\begin{vmatrix} 1 & 1 & 1 \\ 0 & 2 & 1 \\ k & 0 & 1 \end{vmatrix} = \pm 3$$

$$\Rightarrow \frac{1}{2}\left[1\begin{vmatrix}2 & 1\\0 & 1\end{vmatrix} - 1\begin{vmatrix}0 & 1\\k & 1\end{vmatrix} + 1\begin{vmatrix}0 & 2\\k & 0\end{vmatrix}\right] = \pm 3$$

$$\Rightarrow (2-0)-(0-k) + (0-2k) = \pm 6$$

$$\Rightarrow \quad 2 + k - 2k = \pm 6$$

$$\Rightarrow \quad -k = \pm 6 - 2$$

$$\Rightarrow \quad -k = 6-2, -k = -6-2$$

$$\Rightarrow \quad -k = 4, -k = -8$$

$$\Rightarrow \quad k = -4, k = 8$$

$\therefore$ Assertion is false.

Also, Reason is true.

Case Based Questions

1. (i) (c) Area of triangle is given by

$$\left|\frac{1}{2}\begin{vmatrix}x_1 & y_1 & 1\\x_2 & y_2 & 1\\x_3 & y_3 & 1\end{vmatrix}\right|$$

$\therefore$ Required area

$$= \left|\frac{1}{2}\begin{vmatrix}0 & 0 & 1\\2 & \sqrt{2} & 1\\2 & -\sqrt{2} & 1\end{vmatrix}\right|$$

$$= \left|\frac{1}{2}[1(-2\sqrt{2}-2\sqrt{2})]\right|$$

[expanding along R_1]

$= 2\sqrt{2}$ sq units

(ii) (c) Since, a face of the Pyramid consist of 30 smaller equilateral triangles.

$\therefore$ Required area

$$= 30 \times 2\sqrt{2} = 60\sqrt{2} \text{ sq units}$$

(iii) (b) Area of equilateral triangle $= \frac{\sqrt{3}}{4}a^2$

$$\therefore \quad 2\sqrt{2} = \frac{\sqrt{3}}{4}a^2 \Rightarrow a^2 = 8\sqrt{2}$$

(iv) (c) Let the third vertex be (x, y), then we get

$$\frac{1}{2}\begin{vmatrix}2 & 4 & 1\\2 & 6 & 1\\x & y & 1\end{vmatrix} = \pm 2\sqrt{2}$$

$$\Rightarrow \frac{1}{2}[2(6-y) - 4(2-x) + 1 (2y - 6x)] = \pm 2\sqrt{2}$$

$$\Rightarrow 12 - 2y - 8 + 4x + 2y - 6x = \pm 4\sqrt{2}$$

$$\Rightarrow 4 - 2x = \pm 4\sqrt{2}$$

$$\Rightarrow \quad 2 - x = \pm 2\sqrt{2}$$

$$\Rightarrow \quad x = 2 \pm 2\sqrt{2}$$

(v) (c) Area of

$$\Delta ABC = \frac{1}{2}\begin{vmatrix}a & 0 & 1\\0 & b & 1\\1 & 1 & 1\end{vmatrix}$$

$$= \frac{1}{2}[a(b-1) - 0 + 1(0-b)]$$

$$= \frac{1}{2}(ab - a - b) = 0$$

$$\left[\because \frac{1}{a} + \frac{1}{b} = 1 \Rightarrow b + a = ab\right]$$

$\therefore$ Points A, B and C are collinear.

2. Three equations are formed from the given statements.

$$3x + 2y + z = 2200$$

$$4x + y + 3z = 3100$$

and $x + y + z = 1200$

Converting the system of equations in matrix form, we get

$$\begin{bmatrix}3 & 2 & 1\\4 & 1 & 3\\1 & 1 & 1\end{bmatrix}\begin{bmatrix}x\\y\\z\end{bmatrix} = \begin{bmatrix}2200\\3100\\1200\end{bmatrix}$$

i.e. $PX = Q$,

where $P = \begin{bmatrix}3 & 2 & 1\\4 & 1 & 3\\1 & 1 & 1\end{bmatrix}$, $X = \begin{bmatrix}x\\y\\z\end{bmatrix}$

and $Q = \begin{bmatrix}2200\\3100\\1200\end{bmatrix}$

$$|P| = 3(1-3) - 2(4-3) + 1(4-1)$$

$$= -6 - 2 + 3 = -5 \neq 0$$

$\Rightarrow X = P^{-1}Q$, provided P^{-1} exists.

$$\therefore \text{adj } P = \begin{bmatrix}-2 & -1 & 5\\-1 & 2 & -5\\3 & -1 & -5\end{bmatrix}$$

$$\therefore \quad P^{-1} = \frac{1}{|P|}(\text{adj } P)$$

$$= \frac{1}{-5}\begin{bmatrix}-2 & -1 & 5\\-1 & 2 & -5\\3 & -1 & -5\end{bmatrix}$$

$$= \frac{1}{5}\begin{bmatrix}1 & -2 & 5\\-3 & 1 & 5\end{bmatrix}$$

$$\therefore \quad X = \frac{1}{5}\begin{bmatrix}2 & 1 & -5\\1 & -2 & 5\\-3 & 1 & 5\end{bmatrix}\begin{bmatrix}2200\\3100\\1200\end{bmatrix}$$

$$= \frac{1}{5}\begin{bmatrix}4400 + 3100 - 6000\\2200 - 6200 + 6000\\-6600 + 3100 + 6000\end{bmatrix}$$

$$= \begin{bmatrix}300\\400\\500\end{bmatrix}$$

$\Rightarrow x = 300$, $y = 400$ and $z = 500$

Hence, the money awarded for Honesty, Hardwork and Punctuality are ₹ 300, ₹ 400 and ₹ 500, respectively.

(i) (b)

(ii) (d)

(iii) (b)

(iv) (c) If a matrix P is both symmetric and skew-symmetric, then it will be a zero matrix. So, $|P| = 0$.

(v) (a) We have,

$$Q^2 = QQ = Q(PQ)$$

$$= (QP)Q = PQ = Q$$

$$\therefore \; |Q^2| = |Q|$$

Chapter-5

Continuity and Differentiability

1. (i) (Continuous)

Clearly, the function is defined at the given point $x = 1$ and its value is 7.

Then, find the limit of the function at $x = 1$.

Clearly,

$$\lim_{x \to 1} f(x) = \lim_{x \to 1}(2x + 5)$$

$$= 2(1) + 5 = 7$$

Thus, $\lim_{x \to 1} f(x) = f(1)$

So, f is continuous at $x = 1$.

(ii) (Continuous)

Clearly, the function is defined at the given point $x = 5$ and its value is 74.

Then, find the limit of the function at $x = 5$

$$\lim_{x \to 5} f(x) = \lim_{x \to 5}(3x^2 - 1)$$

$$= 3(5)^2 - 1 = 74$$

Thus, $\lim_{x \to 1} f(x) = f(5)$

So, f is continuous at $x = 5$

(iii) (Continuous)

Clearly, the function is defined at the given point at $x = -2$ and its value is 0.

Then, find the limit of the function at $x = -2$

$$\lim_{x\to-2} f(x) = \lim_{x\to-2}\left(\frac{x^2-4}{2x-3}\right)$$
$$= \frac{(-2)^2-4}{2(-2)-3} = 0$$

Thus, $\lim_{x\to-2} f(x) = f(-2)$

So, f is continuous at $x = -2$.

2. (i) Given that

$$f(x) = \begin{cases} \frac{|x|}{x}, & x \neq 0 \\ 1, & x = 0 \end{cases}$$
$$= \begin{cases} \frac{x}{x} = 1, & x > 0 \\ \frac{-x}{x} = -1, & x < 0 \\ 1, & x = 0 \end{cases}$$
$$\left[\because |x| = \begin{cases} x, & x > 0 \\ -x, & x < 0 \end{cases}\right]$$

$\therefore$ (LHL at $x = 0$)
$$= \lim_{x\to0^-} f(x) = \lim_{x\to0^-}(-1) = -1$$

$\therefore$ (RHL at $x = 0$)
$$= \lim_{x\to0^+} f(x) = \lim_{x\to0^+}(1) = 1$$

So,
$$\lim_{x\to0^-} f(x) \neq \lim_{x\to0^+} f(x) = f(0)$$

$\therefore f$ is not continuous at $x = 0$.

(ii) The function is defined at the given point $x = 0$ and its value is 1.

Then, find the limit of the function at $x = 0$.

Clearly,
$$\lim_{x\to0} f(x) = \lim_{x\to0}(x^3 + 3x + 3)$$
$$= 0^3 + 3\cdot0 + 3 = 3$$

Thus, $\lim_{x\to0} f(x) \neq f(0)$

So, f is not continuous at $x = 0$.

3. We observe that

(LHL at $x = 0$)
$$= \lim_{x\to0^-} f(x) = \lim_{h\to0} f(0-h)$$
$$= \lim_{h\to0} f(-h) = \lim_{h\to0}\frac{e^{-1/h}-1}{e^{-1/h}+1}$$
$$= \lim_{h\to0}\frac{\frac{1}{e^{1/h}}-1}{\frac{1}{e^{1/h}}+1}$$

Since, $\lim_{h\to0}\frac{1}{e^{1/h}} = 0$

So, $\lim_{h\to0}\frac{\frac{1}{e^{1/h}}-1}{\frac{1}{e^{1/h}}+1} = \frac{-1}{1} = -1$

and (RHL at $x = 0$)
$$= \lim_{x\to0^+} f(x) = \lim_{h\to0} f(0+h)$$
$$= \lim_{h\to0} f(h) = \lim_{h\to0}\frac{e^{1/h}-1}{e^{1/h}+1}$$
$$= \lim_{h\to0}\frac{1-\frac{1}{e^{1/h}}}{1+\frac{1}{e^{1/h}}} = \frac{1-0}{1+0} = 1$$

So,

(LHL at $x = 0$) $\neq$ (RHL at $x = 0$)

Thus, f is not continuous (discontinuous) at $x = 0$.

4. (False)

Given, $f(x) = 2x - |x|$
$$= \begin{cases} 2x - x, & x \geq 0 \\ 2x - (-x), & x < 0 \end{cases}$$
$$= \begin{cases} x, & x \geq 0 \\ 3x, & x < 0 \end{cases}$$

Now, (LHL at $x = 0$)
$$= \lim_{x\to0^-} f(x)$$
$$= \lim_{x\to0^-}(3x) = 3\cdot0 = 0$$

(RHL at $x = 0$)
$$= \lim_{x\to0^+} f(x) = \lim_{x\to0^+}(x) = 0$$

and $f(0) = 0$

So, $\lim_{x\to0^-} f(x) = \lim_{x\to0^+} f(x) = f(0)$

So, the function f is continuous at $x = 0$.

5. (c) The given function f is,
$$f(x) = \begin{cases} \frac{1}{2} - x, & 0 \leq x < \frac{1}{2} \\ 1, & x = \frac{1}{2} \\ \frac{3}{2} - x, & \frac{1}{2} < x \leq 1 \end{cases}$$

Now, (LHL at $x = \frac{1}{2}$)
$$= \lim_{x\to\left(\frac{1}{2}\right)^-} f(x) = \lim_{x\to\left(\frac{1}{2}\right)^-}\left(\frac{1}{2} - x\right)$$
$$= \frac{1}{2} - \frac{1}{2} = 0$$
$$\left[\because f(x) = \left(\frac{1}{2} - x\right), 0 \leq x < \frac{1}{2}\right]$$

(RHL at $x = \frac{1}{2}$)
$$= \lim_{x\to\left(\frac{1}{2}\right)^+} f(x) = \lim_{x\to\left(\frac{1}{2}\right)^+}\left(\frac{3}{2} - x\right)$$
$$= \frac{3}{2} - \frac{1}{2} = 1$$
$$\left[\because f(x) = \left(\frac{3}{2} - x\right), \frac{1}{2} < x \leq 1\right]$$

Clearly,
$$\lim_{x\to\left(\frac{1}{2}\right)^-} f(x) \neq \lim_{x\to\left(\frac{1}{2}\right)^+} f(x) = f\left(\frac{1}{2}\right)$$

Hence, $f(x)$ is not continuous at $x = \frac{1}{2}$.

So, f is discontinuous at $x = \frac{1}{2}$.

6. (d) Given,
$$f(x) = \begin{cases} \frac{|x^2 - x|}{x^2 - x}, & x \neq 0, 1 \\ 1, & x = 0 \\ -1, & x = 1 \end{cases}$$
$$= \begin{cases} 1, & x > 1 \\ 1, & x \leq 0 \\ -1, & 0 < x \leq 1 \end{cases}$$

Now, for $x = 0$,
$$\lim_{x\to0^-} f(x) = \lim_{x\to0^-}(1) = 1$$

and $\lim_{x\to0^+} f(x) = \lim_{x\to0^+}(-1) = -1$

$\therefore \quad \lim_{x\to0^-} f(x) \neq \lim_{x\to0^+} f(x)$

i.e. f is discontinuous at $x = 0$.

Now, for $x = 1$,
$$\lim_{x\to1^-} f(x) = \lim_{x\to1^-}(-1) = -1$$

and $\lim_{x\to1^+} f(x) = 1$

Thus, $\lim_{x\to1^-} f(x) \neq \lim_{x\to1^+} f(x)$

i.e. f is discontinuous at $x = 1$.

7. (i) (True)

Since, the given function
$$f(x) = \frac{x^3 - a^3}{x - a}\ (x \neq a)$$

is continuous at $x = a$

$\Rightarrow \quad \lim_{x\to a} f(x) = f(a)$

So, $f(a) = \lim_{x\to a}\frac{x^3 - a^3}{x - a}$
$$= 3a^{3-1} = 3a^2$$
$$\left[\text{we know, } \lim_{x\to a}\frac{x^n - a^n}{x - a} = na^{n-1}\right]$$

Thus, the value of $f(a)$ is $3a^2$.

(ii) (False)

Given,
$$f(x) = \frac{(27 - 2x)^{1/3} - 3}{9 - 3(243 + 5x)^{1/5}}$$

is continuous at $x = 0$, then

$\lim_{x\to0} f(x) = f(0)$
$$f(0) = \lim_{x\to0}\frac{(27 - 2x)^{1/3} - 3}{9 - 3(243 + 5x)^{1/5}}$$

$$=\frac{2}{15}\lim_{x\to 0}\frac{\frac{(27-2x)^{1/3}-(27)^{1/3}}{27-2x-27}}{\frac{(243+5x)^{1/5}-(243)^{1/5}}{243+5x-243}}$$

$$=\frac{2}{15}\cdot\left(\frac{1}{3}\right)\cdot\left(\frac{1}{(27)^{2/3}}\right)\cdot(5)\cdot(243)^{4/5}$$

$=2$

Thus, the value of $f(0)$ is 2.

(iii) (False)

Since, the function f is continuous at $x=0$.

So, $\lim_{x\to 0} f(x)=f(0)$

$$\Rightarrow \quad f(0)=\lim_{x\to 0}\frac{2x+3\sin x}{3x+2\sin x}$$

$$\Rightarrow f(0)=\lim_{x\to 0}\frac{2+3\frac{\sin x}{x}}{3+2\frac{\sin x}{x}}$$

$$\Rightarrow f(0)=\frac{2+3\left(\lim_{x\to 0}\frac{\sin x}{x}\right)}{3+2\left(\lim_{x\to 0}\frac{\sin x}{x}\right)}$$

$$=\frac{2+3}{2+3}\left[\because \lim_{x\to 0}\frac{\sin x}{x}=1\right]$$

$$=\frac{5}{5}=1$$

So, the value of $f(0)$ is 1.

(iv) (False)

Since, $f(x)$ is a continuous function at $x=0$

So, $\lim_{x\to 0} f(x)=f(0)$

$$\Rightarrow f(0)=\lim_{x\to 0}\frac{(4^x-1)^2}{\log\left(1+\frac{x^2}{3}\right)}$$

$$=\lim_{x\to 0}\frac{\left(\frac{4^x-1}{x}\right)^2}{\left(\frac{\log\left(1+\frac{x^2}{3}\right)}{\frac{x^2}{3}}\times 3\right)}$$

$$=\frac{(\log_e 4)^2}{\frac{1}{3}}$$

$$\left[\because \lim_{x\to 0}\left(\frac{a^x-1}{x}\right)=\log_e a \text{ and } \lim_{x\to 0}\frac{\log(1+x)}{x}=1\right]$$

$\therefore\ f(0)=3(\log_e 4)^2$

Thus, the value of $f(0)$ is $3(\log_e 4)^2$.

(v) (True)

Since, $f(x)$ is continuous at $x=1$

So, $\lim_{x\to 1} f(x)=f(1)$

$$\Rightarrow f(1)=\lim_{x\to 1}(x-1)\tan\frac{\pi x}{2}$$

$$=\lim_{x\to 1}(x-1)\lim_{x\to 1}\tan\frac{\pi x}{2}=0$$

Thus, the value of $f(1)$ is 0.

(vi) (True)

Since, $f(x)$ is a continuous function at $x=2$

So, $\lim_{x\to 2} f(x)=f(2)$

$$\Rightarrow \quad f(2)=\lim_{x\to 2} f(x)$$

$$=\lim_{x\to 2}\frac{x^3+x^2-16x+20}{(x-2)^2}$$

$$=\lim_{x\to 2}\frac{(x-2)^2(x+5)}{(x-2)^2}$$

$$=\lim_{x\to 2}(x+5)=7$$

Thus, the value of $f(2)$ is 7.

8. Given that $f(x)=\dfrac{1-\cos 6(x-\pi)}{10(x-\pi)^2}$ is continuous at $x=\pi$

So, $\lim_{x\to\pi} f(x)=f(\pi)$

Thus, $f(\pi)=\lim_{x\to\pi} f(x)$

$$=\lim_{x\to\pi}\frac{1-\cos 6(x-\pi)}{10(x-\pi)^2}$$

$$=\lim_{x\to\pi}\frac{2\sin^2 3(x-\pi)}{10(x-\pi)^2}$$

$$=\lim_{x\to\pi}\frac{1}{5}\cdot\left(\frac{\sin 3(x-\pi)}{3(x-\pi)}\right)^2\times 9$$

$$\therefore\ f(\pi)=\frac{9}{5}\cdot 1=\frac{9}{5}$$

Thus, the value of $f(\pi)$ is $\frac{9}{5}$.

9. (True)

We observe that

$$f(x)=\begin{cases}\dfrac{x^2}{2}, & 0\le x\le 1\\ 2x^2-3x+\dfrac{3}{2}, & 1<x\le 2\end{cases}$$

Here, f is defined at all points in real numbers.

Now, (LHL at $x=1$),

$$=\lim_{x\to 1^-} f(x)=\lim_{x\to 1^-}\left(\frac{x^2}{2}\right)=\frac{1}{2}$$

(RHL at $x=1$)

$$=\lim_{x\to 1^+} f(x)$$

$$=\lim_{x\to 1^+}\left(2x^2-3x+\frac{3}{2}\right)$$

$$=2\cdot 1^2-3\cdot 1+\frac{3}{2}=2-\frac{3}{2}=\frac{1}{2}$$

and $f(1)=\frac{1}{2}$

Thus,

$$\lim_{x\to 1^-} f(x)=\lim_{x\to 1^+} f(x)=f(1)$$

Hence, f is continuous at $x=1$.

10. (b) Given that

$$f(x)=\begin{cases}\dfrac{1-\cos 4x}{x^2}, & x<0\\ \dfrac{\sqrt{x}}{\sqrt{16+\sqrt{x}}-4}, & x>0\end{cases}$$

is continuous at $x=0$,

we must have,

$$\lim_{x\to 0^-} f(x)=\lim_{x\to 0^+} f(x)=f(0) \quad \ldots(\text{i})$$

Now, $\lim_{x\to 0^-} f(x)=\lim_{x\to 0^-}\dfrac{1-\cos 4x}{x^2}$

$$=\lim_{x\to 0^-}\frac{2\sin^2 2x}{x^2}$$

$$=\lim_{x\to 0^-} 2\left(\frac{\sin 2x}{2x}\right)^2\cdot 4$$

$$=8\cdot\lim_{x\to 0^-}\left(\frac{\sin 2x}{2x}\right)^2$$

$$=8\cdot 1^2=8$$

and

$$\lim_{x\to 0^+} f(x)=\lim_{x\to 0^+}\frac{\sqrt{x}}{\sqrt{16+\sqrt{x}}-4}\times\frac{\sqrt{16+\sqrt{x}}+4}{\sqrt{16+\sqrt{x}}+4}$$

$$=\lim_{x\to 0^+}\frac{\sqrt{x}}{16+\sqrt{x}-16}\times\sqrt{16+\sqrt{x}}+4$$

$$=\lim_{x\to 0^+}(\sqrt{16+\sqrt{x}}+4)$$

$$=4+4=8$$

From Eq. (i), we get

$f(0)=8$

Thus, the value of $f(0)$ is 8.

11. (a) We observe that

(LHL at $x=0$)

$$=\lim_{x\to 0^-} f(x)=\lim_{h\to 0} f(0-h)$$

$$=\lim_{h\to 0} f(-h)$$

$$=\lim_{h\to 0}\frac{\sin(-h)+(-h)\cos(-h)}{(-h)}$$

$$=\lim_{h\to 0}\frac{\sin h}{h}+\lim_{h\to 0}\cos h$$

$$=1+1=2$$

(RHL at $x=0$)

$= \lim_{x \to 0^+} f(x) = \lim_{h \to 0} f(0+h)$

$= \lim_{h \to 0} f(h)$

$= \lim_{h \to 0} \frac{\sin(h) + h\cos h}{h} = 2$

and $f(0) = 2$

Thus,

$\lim_{x \to 0^-} f(x) = \lim_{x \to 0^+} f(x) = f(0)$

$\therefore$ $f(x)$ is continuous at $x = 0$.

12. (c) The given function is

$$f(x) = \begin{cases} x, & x \le 1 \\ 2, & x > 1 \end{cases}$$

At $x = 0$,

It is evident that f is defined at 0 and its value at 0 is 0

and $\lim_{x \to 0} f(x) = \lim_{x \to 0} (x)$

$= 0 = f(0)$

$\therefore$ f is continuous at $x = 0$

At $x = 1$,

It is evident that f is defined at 1 and its value at 1 is 1.

Now, (LHL at $x = 1$)

$= \lim_{x \to 1^-} f(x) = \lim_{x \to 1^-} (x) = 1$

and (RHL at $x = 1$)

$= \lim_{x \to 1^+} f(x) = \lim_{x \to 1^+} 2 = 2$

and $f(1) = 1$

So, $\lim_{x \to 1^+} f(x) \ne \lim_{x \to 1^-} f(x) = f(1)$

Therefore, f is not continuous at $x = 1$.

Thus, f is continuous at all points in R except $x = 1$

13. (i) (False)

The given function is

$$f(x) = \begin{cases} \frac{x^2 - x - 6}{x - 3}, & x \ne 3 \\ 5, & x = 3 \end{cases}$$

So, $\lim_{x \to 3} f(x) = \lim_{x \to 3} \frac{x^2 - x - 6}{x - 3}$

$= \lim_{x \to 3}$ [illegible]

$= \lim_{x \to 3} (x + 2)$

$= 5 = f(3)$

Thus, $\lim_{x \to 3} f(x) = f(3)$

$\therefore$ f is continuous at $x = 3$

(ii) (True)

The given function is

$$f(x) = |x - 5| = \begin{cases} x - 5, & x \ge 5 \\ 5 - x, & x < 5 \end{cases}$$

This function f is defined at all points of the real line.

Check the continuity at $x = 5$.

$f(5) = (5 - 5) = 0$

and $\lim_{x \to 5^+} f(x) = \lim_{x \to 5^+} x - 5$

$= (5 - 5) = 0$

and $\lim_{x \to 5^-} f(x) = \lim_{x \to 5^-} 5 - x = 0$

$\therefore$ $\lim_{x \to 5^+} f(x) = \lim_{x \to 5^-} f(x) = f(5)$

i.e. f is continuous at $x = 5$

So, f is continuous at all real numbers.

(iii) (False)

The given function is

$$f(x) = \begin{cases} \frac{2(x) + x^2}{x} = 2 + x, & x > 0 \\ \frac{2(-x) + x^2}{x} = -2 + x, & x < 0 \\ 0, & x = 0 \end{cases}$$

Now, (LHL at $x = 0$)

$= \lim_{x \to 0^-} f(x) = \lim_{x \to 0^-} (x - 2) = -2$

(RHL at $x = 0$)

$= \lim_{x \to 0^+} f(x) = \lim_{x \to 0^+} (x + 2) = 2$

and $f(0) = 0$

So,

(LHL at $x = 0$) $\ne$ (RHL at $x = 0$)

$\ne f(0)$

So, f is not continuous at $x = 0$.

(iv) (False)

Given that

$$f(x) = \begin{cases} \frac{e^x - 1}{\log(1 + 2x)}, & x \ne 0 \\ 5, & x = 0 \end{cases}$$

is continuous at $x = 0$.

So, $\lim_{x \to 0} f(x) = f(0)$

$\therefore \lim_{x \to 0} f(x) = \lim_{x \to 0} \frac{e^x - 1}{\log(1 + 2x)}$

$= \lim_{x \to 0} \frac{(e^x - 1)}{\log(1 + 2x)}$ [illegible] $2x$ [illegible]

Thus, the function f is not continuous at $x = 0$.

(v) (False)

Given,

$$f(x) = \begin{cases} \frac{x - a}{x - a} = 1, & x > a \\ \frac{-(x - a)}{x - a} = -1, & x < a \\ 1, & x = a \end{cases}$$

So, (LHL at $x = a$)

$= \lim_{x \to a^-} f(x) = \lim_{x \to a^-} (-1) = -1$

and (RHL at $x = a$)

$= \lim_{x \to a^+} f(x) = \lim_{x \to a^+} (1) = 1$

and $f(a) = 1$

So, $\lim_{x \to a^-} f(x) \ne \lim_{x \to a^+} f(x) = f(1)$

$\therefore f$ is not continuous at $x = a$.

14. (i) Given that

$$f(x) = \begin{cases} x + 3, & x < 1 \\ 0, & x = 1 \\ x - 3, & x > 1 \end{cases}$$

The function f is defined at all points of the real line and f is continuous at $x \ne 1$.

Now, the continuity of $f(x)$ at $x = 1$:

(LHL at $x = 1$) $= \lim_{x \to 1^-} (x + 3)$

$= 1 + 3 = 4$

and (RHL at $x = 1$)

$\lim_{x \to 1^+} (x - 3) = 1 - 3 = -2$

Since, (LHL at $x = 1$)

$\ne$ (RHL at $x = 1$)

So, f is not continuous at $x = 1$ and so, '1' is the only point of discontinuity.

(ii) Check if $\lim_{x \to 0} f(x) = f(0)$, then f is continuous at $x = 0$, otherwise not.

Clearly if $x \ne 0$, then

$f(x) = \frac{x^4 + 2x^3 + 3x^2}{(\tan^{-1} x)^2}$ is continuous.

Now, check continuity at $x = 0$.

So, $\lim_{x \to 0} f(x) = \lim_{x \to 0} \frac{x^4 + 2x^3 + 3x^2}{(\tan^{-1} x)^2}$

$= \lim$ [illegible]

$\left[\because \lim_{x \to 0} \frac{\tan^{-1} x}{x} = 1\right]$

and $f(0) = 5$

So, $\lim_{x \to 0} f(x) \ne f(0)$

So, $x = 0$ is the only point of discontinuity.

(iii) The given function is

$$f(x)=\begin{cases}|x|+3, & x\le -3\\ -2x, & -3<x<3\\ 6x+2, & x\ge 3\end{cases}$$

$$=\begin{cases}3-x, & x\le -3\\ -2x, & -3<x<3\\ 6x+2, & x\ge 3\end{cases}$$

Check continuity at $x=-3$,

$\lim\limits_{x\to -3^-} f(x)=\lim\limits_{x\to -3^-}(3-x)=6$

$\lim\limits_{x\to -3^+} f(x)=\lim\limits_{x\to -3^+}(-2x)=6$

and $f(-3)=6$

Thus,

$\lim\limits_{x\to -3^-} f(x)=\lim\limits_{x\to -3^+} f(x)=f(-3)$

i.e. f is continuous at $x=-3$.

Now, check continuity at $x=3$,

$\lim\limits_{x\to 3^-} f(x)=\lim\limits_{x\to 3^-}(-2x)=-6$

and $\lim\limits_{x\to 3^+} f(x)=\lim\limits_{x\to 3^+}(6x+2)=20$

and $\quad f(3)=20$

Thus, $\lim\limits_{x\to 3^-} f(x)\ne \lim\limits_{x\to 3^+} f(x)$

i.e. f is not continuous at $x=3$

So, $x=3$ is the only point of discontinuity.

(iv) The given function is

$$f(x)=\begin{cases}\dfrac{2x^2+3}{5}, & x\le 1\\ -5x+6, & 1<x<3\\ x-3, & x\ge 3\end{cases}$$

Now, check at $x=1$,

$\lim\limits_{x\to 1^-} f(x)=\lim\limits_{x\to 1^-}\left(\dfrac{2x^2+3}{5}\right)=1$

$\lim\limits_{x\to 1^+} f(x)=\lim\limits_{x\to 1^+}(6-5x)=1$

Thus,

$\lim\limits_{x\to 1^-} f(x)=\lim\limits_{x\to 1^+} f(x)=f(1)$

i.e. f is continuous at $x=1$.

Now, check at $x=3$,

$\lim\limits_{x\to 3^-} f(x)=\lim\limits_{x\to 3^-}(6-5x)=-9$

$\lim\limits_{x\to 3^+} f(x)=\lim\limits_{x\to 3^+}(x-3)=0$

$\therefore \lim\limits_{x\to 3^-} f(x)\ne \lim\limits_{x\to 3^+} f(x)$

i.e. f is not continuous at $x=3$.

Thus, the point of discontinuity of f is $x=3$.

(v) Given, $f(t)=\dfrac{1}{t^2+t-2}$

and $\quad t=\dfrac{1}{x-2}$

Clearly, $t=\dfrac{1}{x-2}$ is discontinuous and undefined at $x=2$.

For $x\ne 2$, then $f(t)=\dfrac{1}{(t+2)(t-1)}$, this is discontinuous at $t=-2$ and $t=1$.

For $t=-2$, $t=\dfrac{1}{x-2}\Rightarrow x=\dfrac{3}{2}$

For $t=1$, $t=\dfrac{1}{x-2}\Rightarrow x=3$

Hence, the point of discontinuity of the function f are 2, $\dfrac{3}{2}$ and 3.

15. (b) We have,

$$f(x)=\begin{cases}\dfrac{\log(1+3x)}{e^{2x}-1}, & x>0\\ \dfrac{3}{2}, & x=0\\ \dfrac{\sin 3x}{\tan 2x}, & x<0\end{cases}$$

Now, (LHL at $x=0$)

$$=\lim_{x\to 0^-} f(x)=\lim_{x\to 0^-}\frac{\sin 3x}{\tan 2x}$$

$$=\lim_{x\to 0^-}\frac{\dfrac{\sin 3x}{3x}\times(3x)}{\dfrac{\tan 2x}{2x}(2x)}$$

$$\Rightarrow \frac{3}{2}\lim_{x\to 0^-}\frac{\dfrac{\sin 3x}{3x}}{\dfrac{\tan 2x}{2x}}=\frac{3}{2}$$

$$\left[\because \lim_{x\to 0}\frac{\sin x}{x}=1 \text{ and } \lim_{x\to 0}\frac{\tan x}{x}=1\right]$$

and (RHL at $x=0$)

$$\lim_{x\to 0^+}\frac{\log(1+3x)}{e^{2x}-1}$$

$$=\lim_{x\to 0^+}\frac{\left(\dfrac{\log(1+3x)}{3x}\right)(3x)}{\left(\dfrac{e^{2x}-1}{2x}\right)(2x)}$$

$$=\frac{3}{2}\lim_{x\to 0^+}\frac{\dfrac{\log(1+3x)}{3x}}{\dfrac{e^{2x}-1}{2x}}$$

$$=\frac{3}{2}\cdot 1=\frac{3}{2}$$

$$\left[\because \lim_{x\to 0}\frac{\log(1+x)}{x}=1 \text{ and } \lim_{x\to 0}\frac{e^x-1}{x}=1\right]$$

So, (LHL at $x=0$) $=$ (RHL at $x=0$) $=f(0)$

Thus, f is continuous at $x=0$.

16. (a) The given function is

$$f(x)=\begin{cases}3, & 1\le x\le 2\\ 4, & 2<x<3\\ 5, & 3\le x\le 5\end{cases}$$

Check continuity at $x=2$,

$\lim\limits_{x\to 2^+} f(x)=4$ and $\lim\limits_{x\to 2^-} f(x)=3$

$\therefore$ Thus, $\lim\limits_{x\to 2^+} f(x)\ne \lim\limits_{x\to 2^-} f(x)$

Check continuity at $x=3$,

$\lim\limits_{x\to 3^+} f(x)=5$ and $\lim\limits_{x\to 3^-} f(x)=4$

So, $\lim\limits_{x\to 3^+} f(x)\ne \lim\limits_{x\to 3^-} f(x)$

Thus, clearly from above the given function is discontinuous at $x=2$ and 3 and at all other points f is continuous.

17. (a) We observe that

$$f(x)=\begin{cases}\dfrac{x-|x|}{x}, & x\ne 0\\ 1, & x=0\end{cases}$$

$$=\begin{cases}0, & x>0\\ 2, & x<0\\ 1, & x=0\end{cases}$$

Thus, (RHL at $x=0$)

$=\lim\limits_{x\to 0^+} f(x)=0$

(LHL at $x=0$)

$=\lim\limits_{x\to 0^-} f(x)=\lim\limits_{x\to 0^-}(2)=2$

and $f(0)=1$

So,

$\lim\limits_{x\to 0^-} f(x)\ne \lim\limits_{x\to 0^+} f(x)\ne f(0)$

$\therefore f$ is discontinuous at $x=0$.

18. (True)

The given function is $f(x)=x-[x]$, it is evident that f is defined at all integral points.

Let n be an int...

Then, (LHL at $x=n$)

$=\lim\limits_{x\to n^-} f(x)=\lim\limits_{x\to n^-}(x-[x])$

$=\lim\limits_{x\to n^-} x-\lim\limits_{x\to n^-}[x]$

$=n-(n-1)=1$

and (RHL at $x=n$)

$=\lim\limits_{x\to n^+} f(x)=\lim\limits_{x\to n^+}(x-[x])$

$=n-n=0$

and $f(n)=n-[n]=n-n=0$

Thus,
$\lim_{x\to n^-} f(x) \neq \lim_{x\to n^+} f(x) = f(n)$

Hence, f is discontinuous at all integral points.

19. The given function $f(x) = \dfrac{1}{\log|x|}$ is not continuous at $x = -1, 0, 1$ because at $x = -1$, 0 and 1 points f is not defined.

So, the set of points at which f is not continuous is 0, – 1 and 1.

20. (c) The given function is

$$f(x) = \begin{cases} x^{10} - 1, & x \leq 1 \\ x^5, & x > 1 \end{cases}$$

The given function f is defined at all points of the real line.

Check the continuity at $x = 1$.

(LHL at $x = 1$)

$= \lim_{x\to 1^-} f(x) = \lim_{x\to 1^-}(x^{10} - 1) = 0$

(RHL at $x = 1$)

$\lim_{x\to 1^+} f(x) = \lim_{x\to 1^+} x^5 = 1$

$\therefore \lim_{x\to 1^-} f(x) \neq \lim_{x\to 1^+} f(x)$

Hence, f is not continuous at $x = 1$

Thus, 1 is the only point of discontinuity of f.

Next, the given fucntion is

$$g(x) = \begin{cases} x + 5, & x \leq 1 \\ x - 5, & x > 1 \end{cases}$$

The given function is defined at all points and continuous at all points $x < 1$ and $x > 1$.

Now, check only at $x = 1$,

$\lim_{x\to 1^-} g(x) = \lim_{x\to 1^-}(x + 5) = 6$

$\lim_{x\to 1^+} g(x) = \lim_{x\to 1^+}(x - 5) = -4$

$\therefore \lim_{x\to 1^-} g(x) \neq \lim_{x\to 1^+} g(x)$

Thus, g is not continuous at $x = 1$, so $x = 1$ is only the point of discontinuity of g.

Hence, statement I is true but statement II false.

21. (c) The given function is

$$f(x) = \frac{4 + x^2}{4x - x^3}$$

This function is discontinuous if

$4x - x^3 = 0$

$\Rightarrow \quad x(4 - x^2) = 0$

$\Rightarrow \quad x = 0, \pm 2$

If $x = 0$, 2 and -2, then the above function fails its continuity property. So, the function f is discontinuous at exactly 3 points.

22. (False)

We have, $f(x) = |x| - |x + 1|$

$$= \begin{cases} -x + x + 1, & x < -1 \\ -x - x - 1, & -1 \leq x < 0 \\ x - (x + 1), & x \geq 0 \end{cases}$$

$$= \begin{cases} 1, & x < -1 \\ -2x - 1, & -1 \leq x < 0 \\ -1, & x \geq 0 \end{cases}$$

Clearly, $f(x)$ is continuous for all x satisfying $x < -1$, $-1 < x < 0$ and $x > 0$.

Now, check the continuity at $x = -1$ and $x = 0$

At $x = -1$,

$\lim_{x\to -1^-} f(x) = \lim_{x\to -1^-} 1 = 1$

and $\lim_{x\to -1^+} f(x) = 1$ and $f(-1) = 1$

Thus,

$\lim_{x\to -1^-} f(x) = \lim_{x\to -1^+} f(x) = f(-1)$ i.e. f is continuous at $x = -1$.

Now, check at $x = 0$,

$\lim_{x\to 0^+} f(x) = \lim_{x\to 0^+}(-1) = -1$

and $\lim_{x\to 0^-} f(x) = \lim_{x\to 0^-}(-2x - 1)$

$= -1$

and $f(0) = -1$

$\therefore \lim_{x\to 0^-} f(x) = \lim_{x\to 0^+} f(x) = f(0)$

Thus, f is continuous at $x = 0$.

Hence, the function $f(x)$ is continuous everywhere.

23. (c) The given function is

$$f(x) = \begin{cases} x^2 \sin\dfrac{1}{x^2}, & x \neq 0 \\ 0, & x = 0 \end{cases}$$

Clearly, f is continuous at $x \neq 0$.

Now, $\lim_{x\to 0} f(x) = \lim_{x\to 0} x^2 \sin\dfrac{1}{x^2}$

$= (\lim_{x\to 0} x^2) \times \left(\lim_{x\to 0} \sin\dfrac{1}{x^2}\right)$

$= 0 \times$ (an oscillating number between -1 and 1)

$= 0 = f(0)$

So, $f(x)$ is continuous at $x = 0$.

Hence, f is continuous everywhere, so no point of discontinuity.

24. When $x < 0$, then $f(x) = \dfrac{\sin 2x}{x}$

We know that $\sin 2x$ as well as x both are everywhere continuous.

So, the quotient function $\dfrac{\sin 2x}{x}$ is continuous at every $x < 0$.

When $x > 0$, then $f(x) = x + 2$ this is a polynomial function, which is continuous at every $x > 0$.

Now, check continuity at $x = 0$,

$\lim_{x\to 0^+} f(x) = \lim_{x\to 0^+}(x + 2) = 2$

and $\lim_{x\to 0^-} f(x) = \lim_{x\to 0^-} \dfrac{\sin 2x}{x}$

$= 2 \lim_{x\to 0^-} \dfrac{\sin 2x}{2x}$

$= 2 \cdot 1 = 2$

and $\quad f(0) = 2$

Thus,

$\lim_{x\to 0^+} f(x) = \lim_{x\to 0^-} f(x) = f(0)$

So, $f(x)$ is also continuous at $x = 0$.

Hence, f is continuous everywhere ($x \in R$).

25. (False)

The given function is

$$f(x) = \begin{cases} \sin x - \cos x, & x \neq 0 \\ -1, & x = 0 \end{cases}$$

The given function f is defined at all the points of the real line.

Case I When $x \neq 0$, then $f(x) = \sin x - \cos x$, is continuous everywhere for all points $x \neq 0$

Case II When $x = 0$, then

$f(0) = -1$

and

$\lim_{x\to 0^+} f(x) = \lim_{x\to 0^+}(\sin x - \cos x)$

$= -1$

and

$\lim_{x\to 0^-} f(x) = \lim_{x\to 0^-}(\sin x - \cos x)$

$= -1$

$\therefore \lim_{x\to 0^-} f(x) = \lim_{x\to 0^+} f(x) = f(0)$

i.e. f is continuous at $x = 0$

From the above case (I) and case (II), we get f is continuous at every point of the real line.

So, the function has no point of discontinuity.

26. (a) **Statement I**

The given function is

$$f(x) = |1 - x + |x||$$

Let $g(x) = 1 - x + |x|$

and $h(x) = |x|$

be two functions defined on R.

Then,

$$(hog)(x) = h\{g(x)\} = h(1 - x + |x|)$$
$$= |1 - x + |x||$$
$$= f(x)\ \forall\ x \in R$$

Since, $(1 - x)$ is a polynomial function and $|x|$ is a modulus function.

Hence, these are continuous on R.

So, $g(x) = 1 - x + |x|$ is also continuous everywhere.

and $h(x) = |x|$ is also continuous everywhere.

Hence, $f = hog$ is continuous everywhere

So, statement I is true.

Statement II

Given, $f(x) = \sqrt{|x| - x}$

$$= \begin{cases} \sqrt{x - x} = 0, & x \geq 0 \\ \sqrt{-x - x} = \sqrt{-2x}, & x < 0 \end{cases}$$

For, $x \geq 0$, we have, $f(x) = 0$, being a constant function, it is continuous everywhere.

For $x < 0$, we have, $f(x) = \sqrt{-2x}$, we know, square root of a function is continuous in its domain.

So, $f(x) = \sqrt{-2x}$ is continuous for all $x < 0$.

Now, check at $x = 0$,

$$\lim_{x \to 0^-} f(x) = \lim_{x \to 0^-} \sqrt{-2x} = 0$$

and $\lim_{x \to 0^+} f(x) = \lim_{x \to 0^+} (0) = 0$

and $f(0) = 0$

Thus,

$$\lim_{x \to 0^-} f(x) = \lim_{x \to 0^+} f(x) = f(0)$$

i.e. $f(x)$ is continuous at $x = 0$.

Hence, $f(x)$ is everywhere continuous.

So, statement II is also true.

27. (i) (True)

Given function $f(x) = \cos(x^2)$

This function f is defined for every real number and f can be written as the composition of two functions as $f = goh$,

where $g(x) = \cos x$ and $h(x) = x^2$

$$[\because goh(x) = g\{h(x)\} = g(x^2)$$
$$= \cos(x^2) = f(x)]$$

We know, $\cos x$ and x^2 both are everywhere continuous.

So, the composition function $\cos(x^2)$ is continuous everywhere.

(ii) (True)

The given function $f(x) = |\cos x|$

This function defined for every real number and f can be written as the composition of two functions as $f = goh$,

where $g(x) = |x|$

and $h(x) = \cos x$

$$[\because goh(x) = g\{h(x)\} = g(\cos x)$$
$$= |\cos x| = f(x)]$$

We know, $\cos x$ and $|x|$ both functions are continuous everywhere.

So, the composition function $|\cos x|$ is continuous everywhere.

28. (c) **Statement I**

Let c be any real number.

Then, $\lim_{x \to c^-} f(x) = \lim_{x \to c^-} \sin|x|$

$$= \lim_{h \to 0} \sin|c - h| = \sin|c|$$

and $\lim_{x \to c^+} f(x) = \lim_{x \to c^+} \sin|x|$

$$= \lim_{h \to 0} \sin|c + h| = \sin|c|$$

and $f(c) = \sin|c|$

$$\therefore \lim_{x \to c^-} f(x) = \lim_{x \to c^+} f(x) = f(c)$$

i.e. $f(x)$ is continuous at $x = c$.

Since, c is any real number.

Then, $f(x)$ is continuous everywhere.

Statement II

Clearly, $g(x)$ is discontinuous and undefined at $x = -2$.

So, for $x \neq -2$, we have

$$g\{g(x)\} = g\left(\frac{1}{x+2}\right) = \frac{1}{\frac{1}{x+2} + 2}$$
$$= \frac{x+2}{2x+5}$$

Therefore, we observe that, $g\{g(x)\}$ is discontinuous and undefined at $x = -\frac{5}{2}$.

So, the point of discontinuity of $g\{g(x)\}$ are -2 and $-\frac{5}{2}$.

Hence, statement I is true but statement II is false.

29. (d) Given, $f(x) = 2x$ and $g(x) = \frac{x^2}{2} + 1$ both of the functions is continuous for all $x \in R$.

Then, $f(x) + g(x)$, $f(x) - g(x)$ and $f(x) \cdot g(x)$ all of the functions are continuous for all $x \in R$.

But only $\frac{g(x)}{f(x)}$ function is discontinuous and if $f(x) = 0$, then $\frac{g(x)}{f(x)}$ has discontinuity points.

Then, the required discontinuous function is $\frac{g(x)}{f(x)}$.

30. (i) Given that

$$f(x) = \begin{cases} \frac{x^2 - 2x - 3}{x - 3}, & x \neq 3 \\ k, & x = 3 \end{cases}$$

Since, f is continuous at $x = 3$,

then $\lim_{x \to 3} f(x) = f(3)$ ...(i)

i.e. $\lim_{x \to 3} \frac{x^2 - 2x - 3}{x - 3}$

$$= \lim_{x \to 3} \frac{(x-3)(x+1)}{(x-3)}$$
$$= \lim_{x \to 3} (x+1) = 4$$

and $f(3) = k$

Thus, from Eq. (i), we get

$$k = 4$$

Hence, the value of k is 4.

(ii) Since, $f(x)$ is a continuous at $x = 0$

So, $\lim_{x \to 0} f(x) = f(0)$

$$\Rightarrow k = \lim_{x \to 0} \frac{1 - \cos 2x}{4x^2}$$
$$= \lim_{x \to 0} \frac{2 \cdot \sin^2 x}{4x^2}$$
$$[\because 1 - \cos 2x = 2\sin^2 x]$$
$$= \frac{1}{2} \lim_{x \to 0} \left(\frac{\sin x}{x}\right)^2 = \frac{1}{2} \cdot 1^2 = \frac{1}{2}$$
$$\left[\because \lim_{x \to 0} \frac{\sin x}{x} = 1\right]$$

Thus, the value of k is $\frac{1}{2}$.

(iii) The given function $f(x)$ is continuous at $x = 0$

So, $\lim_{x \to 0^+} f(x) = \lim_{x \to 0^-} f(x) = f(0)$

$$\Rightarrow \lim_{x \to 0^-} f(x) = f(0)$$

$\Rightarrow \quad k(0-0) = \cos(0)$

$\Rightarrow \quad 0 = 1$, not possible

So, for no value of k, the given function is continuous at $x = 0$.

(iv) Since, $f(x)$ is continuous at $x = 0$

So, $\lim_{x \to 0} f(x) = f(0) = k$

$$\Rightarrow \lim_{x \to 0} \left\{ \frac{\log(1+2x) - \log(1-3x)}{x} \right\} = k$$

$$\Rightarrow \lim_{x \to 0} \left\{ \frac{\log(1+2x)}{x} - \frac{\log(1-3x)}{x} \right\} = k$$

$$\Rightarrow \lim_{x \to 0} \left\{ \frac{\log(1+2x)}{x} \right\} - \lim_{x \to 0} \left\{ \frac{\log(1-3x)}{x} \right\} = k$$

$$\Rightarrow 2 \lim_{x \to 0} \frac{\log(1+2x)}{2x} + 3 \lim_{x \to 0} \left\{ \frac{\log(1-3x)}{-3x} \right\} = k$$

$$\Rightarrow \quad 2 \cdot 1 + 3 \cdot 1 = k$$

$$\therefore \quad k = 5$$

$$\left[\because \lim_{x \to 0} \frac{\log(1+x)}{x} = 1 \right]$$

Thus, the value of k is 5.

(v) For $f(x)$ to be continuous at $x = \frac{\pi}{4}$.

We must have,

$$\lim_{x \to \pi/4} f(x) = f\left(\frac{\pi}{4}\right)$$

$$\Rightarrow \quad f\left(\frac{\pi}{4}\right) = \lim_{x \to \pi/4} f(x)$$

$$\Rightarrow k = \lim_{x \to \pi/4} \frac{\sqrt{2}\left(\cos x - \frac{1}{\sqrt{2}}\right)}{\cot x - 1}$$

$$\Rightarrow k = \lim_{x \to \pi/4} \frac{\sqrt{2}\left(\cos x - \cos\frac{\pi}{4}\right)}{\cot x - \cot\frac{\pi}{4}}$$

$$\left[\because \cos\frac{\pi}{4} = \frac{1}{\sqrt{2}} \text{ and } \cot\frac{\pi}{4} = 1 \right]$$

$$\Rightarrow k = \lim_{x \to \pi/4} \frac{-\sqrt{2}\left[2\sin\left(\frac{x}{2} - \frac{\pi}{8}\right) \sin\left(\frac{x}{2} + \frac{\pi}{8}\right)\right]}{\left[\cos x \cdot \sin\frac{\pi}{4} - \sin x \cdot \cos\frac{\pi}{4}\right]} \times \sin x \sin\frac{\pi}{4}$$

$$\Rightarrow k = -2\sqrt{2} \lim_{x \to \pi/4} \frac{\sin\left(\frac{x}{2} - \frac{\pi}{8}\right) \sin\left(\frac{x}{2} + \frac{\pi}{8}\right)}{-\sin\left(x - \frac{\pi}{4}\right)} \times \sin x \sin\frac{\pi}{4}$$

$$\Rightarrow k = -2\sqrt{2} \lim_{x \to \pi/4} \frac{\sin\left(\frac{x}{2} - \frac{\pi}{8}\right) \sin\left(\frac{x}{2} + \frac{\pi}{8}\right)}{-2\sin\left(\frac{x}{2} - \frac{\pi}{8}\right) \cos\left(\frac{x}{2} - \frac{\pi}{8}\right)} \times \sin x \sin\frac{\pi}{4}$$

$$[\because \sin 2\theta = 2\sin\theta\cos\theta]$$

$$= \sqrt{2} \lim_{x \to \pi/4} \frac{\sin\left(\frac{x}{2} + \frac{\pi}{8}\right)}{\cos\left(\frac{x}{2} - \frac{\pi}{8}\right)} \times \sin x \sin\frac{\pi}{4}$$

$$= \sqrt{2} \frac{\sin\left(\frac{\pi}{8} + \frac{\pi}{8}\right)}{\cos\left(\frac{\pi}{8} - \frac{\pi}{8}\right)} \times \sin\frac{\pi}{4} \cdot \sin\frac{\pi}{4}$$

$$= \sqrt{2} \cdot \frac{\sin\left(\frac{\pi}{4}\right)}{\cos(0)} \times \left(\sin\frac{\pi}{4}\right)^2$$

$$= \sqrt{2} \cdot \frac{1}{\sqrt{2}} \cdot \frac{1}{2} = \frac{1}{2}$$

Thus, the value of k is $\frac{1}{2}$.

(vi) The given function is

$$f(x) = \begin{cases} \frac{1-\cos 2x}{2x^2}, & x < 0 \\ k, & x = 0 \\ \frac{x}{|x|}, & x > 0 \end{cases}$$

is continuous at $x = 0$.

i.e. $\lim_{x \to 0^+} f(x) = \lim_{x \to 0^-} f(x) = f(0)$ ...(i)

So, $\lim_{x \to 0^+} f(x) = \lim_{x \to 0^+} \frac{x}{x} = 1$

and $\lim_{x \to 0^-} f(x) = \lim_{x \to 0^-} \frac{1-\cos 2x}{2x^2}$

$$= \lim_{x \to 0^-} \frac{2\sin^2 x}{2x^2} = \lim_{x \to 0^-} \left(\frac{\sin x}{x}\right)^2$$

$= 1$

Thus, from Eq. (i), we get

$k = 1$

So, the value of k is 1.

31. The given function,

$$f(x) = \begin{cases} ax+1, & x \le 3 \\ bx+3, & x > 3 \end{cases}$$

is continuous at $x = 3$.

So, $\lim_{x \to 3^+} f(x) = \lim_{x \to 3^-} f(x) = f(3)$

So, $\lim_{x \to 3^+} f(x) = f(3)$

$\Rightarrow \lim_{x \to 3^+} (bx+3) = 3a+1$

$\Rightarrow \quad 3b + 3 = 3a + 1$

$\Rightarrow \quad 3a - 3b = 2$

Thus, the required relation between 'a' and 'b' is $3a - 3b = 2$.

32. (True)

Since, $f(x) = \begin{cases} 2x+1, & x < 2 \\ a, & x = 2 \text{ is} \\ 3x-1, & x > 2 \end{cases}$

continuous at $x = 2$

So, $\lim_{x \to 2^-} f(x) = \lim_{x \to 2^+} f(x) = f(2)$ ...(i)

Now, $\lim_{x \to 2^-} f(x) = \lim_{x \to 2^-} (2x+1) = 5$

and $\lim_{x \to 2^+} f(x) = \lim_{x \to 2^+} (3x-1) = 5$

and $\quad f(2) = a$

Thus, from Eq. (i), we get

$a = 5$

33. (d) Since, $f(x) = \begin{cases} -2x^2 + a, & x < 0 \\ 2x^2 + a, & x \ge 0 \end{cases}$

is continuous at $x = 0$, then

$\lim_{x \to 0^-} f(x) = \lim_{x \to 0^+} f(x) = f(0)$

Now,

$\lim_{x \to 0^-} f(x) = \lim_{x \to 0^-} (-2x^2 + a) = a$

and

$\lim_{x \to 0^+} f(x) = \lim_{x \to 0^+} (2x^2 + a) = a$

and $f(0) = a$

Thus, from above we conclude that

$\lim_{x \to 0^-} f(x) = \lim_{x \to 0^+} f(x) = f(0)$

So, the value of a can be any real number.

34. (b) (LHL at $x = 1$)

$= \lim_{x \to 1^-} f(x)$

$= \lim_{x \to 1^-} (5ax - 2b) = (5a - 2b)$

and (RHL at $x = 1$)

$= \lim_{x \to 1^+} f(x) = \lim_{x \to 1^+} (3ax + b)$

$= (3a + b)$

and $f(1) = 11$

Since, f is continuous at $x=1$

So, $\lim_{x\to 1^-} f(x) = \lim_{x\to 1^+} f(x) = f(1)$

$\Rightarrow \quad 5a-2b = 3a+b = 11$

So, $\quad 5a-2b=11$ and $3a+b=11$

Solving these two equations, we get $a=3$ and $b=2$

So, $a+b=3+2=5>a$

and $\quad a+b>b$

and $a-b=3-2=1<a$

and $\quad a-b<b$

So, $a+b<a$ is false relation

$a-b<b$ is true relation

$f(1)=11$ [given]

$a+b=5$

35. We observe that

(LHD at $x=1$)

$$= \lim_{h\to 0}\frac{f(1-h)-f(1)}{(1-h)-1}$$

$$= \lim_{h\to 0}\frac{(1-h)^2-1^2}{-h}$$

$$= \lim_{h\to 0}\frac{-2h+h^2}{-h}$$

$$= \lim_{h\to 0}(2-h)=2$$

and (RHD at $x=1$)

$$= \lim_{h\to 0}\frac{f(1+h)-f(1)}{(1+h)-1}$$

$$= \lim_{h\to 0}\frac{(1+h)^2-1^2}{h}$$

$$= \lim_{h\to 0}\frac{2h+h^2}{h}=2$$

$\therefore$ (LHD at $x=1$)

= (RHD at $x=1$) = 2

So, $f(x)$ is differentiable at $x=1$ and $f'(1)=2$.

Hence, the value of $f'(1)$ is 2.

36. (b) Clearly, $f(x)$ being a polynomial function, is everywhere differentiable.

Thus, the derivative of f at x is given by

$$f'(x) = \lim_{h\to 0}\frac{f(x+h)-f(x)}{h}$$

$$= \lim_{h\to 0}\frac{[(x+h)^2-6(x+h)+9] - [x^2-6x+9]}{h}$$

$$= \lim_{h\to 0}\frac{2xh-6h+h^2}{h}$$

$\therefore f'(x)=2x-6$

Now, $f'(2x)=2(2x)-6=4x-6$

$f'(2x)-f'(x)=2x$

and $f'(5)-3f'(2)=4+6=10$

and $f'(8)-1=10-1=9$

37. (True)

Since, f is differentiable at $x=a$

Therefore, $\lim_{x\to a}\frac{f(x)-f(a)}{x-a}$ exist finitely, say $\{=f'(a)\}$

Now, $\lim_{x\to a}\frac{x^2f(a)-a^2f(x)}{x-a}$

$$= \lim_{x\to a}\frac{x^2f(a)-a^2f(x)-a^2f(a)+a^2f(a)}{x-a}$$

$$= \lim_{x\to a}\frac{(x^2-a^2)f(a)-a^2\{f(x)-f(a)\}}{(x-a)}$$

$$= \lim_{x\to a}\left\{\frac{(x^2-a^2)f(a)}{(x-a)} - a^2\left(\frac{f(x)-f(a)}{x-a}\right)\right\}$$

$$= 2af(a)-f'(a)\cdot a^2$$

38. (c) We have,

$$f(x)=|x-1|+|x+1| = \begin{cases}-2x, & x<-1\\ 2, & -1\le x<1\\ 2x, & x\ge 1\end{cases}$$

Differentiability at $x=-1$, we observe that

(LHD at $x=-1$)

$$= \lim_{x\to -1^-}\frac{f(x)-f(-1)}{x-(-1)}$$

$$= \lim_{x\to -1^-}\frac{(-2x)-2}{x+1}=-2$$

(RHD at $x=-1$)

$$= \lim_{x\to -1^+}\frac{f(x)-f(-1)}{x+1}$$

$$= \lim_{x\to -1^+}\frac{2-2}{x+1}=0$$

$\therefore$ (LHD at $x=-1$)

$\neq$ (RHD at $x=-1$)

So, $f(x)$ is non-differentiable at $x=-1$.

Differentiability at $x=1$, we observe that

(LHD at $x=1$)

$$= \lim_{x\to 1^-}\frac{f(x)-f(1)}{x-1}$$

$$= \lim_{x\to 1^-}\frac{2-2}{x-1}=0$$

(RHD at $x=1$)

$$= \lim_{x\to 1^+}\frac{f(x)-f(1)}{x-1}$$

$$= \lim_{x\to 1^+}\frac{2x-2}{x-1}=2$$

$\therefore$ (LHD at $x=1$)

$\neq$ (RHD at $x=1$)

So, $f(x)$ is non-differentiable at $x=1$.

Hence, $f(x)$ is non-differentiable at $x=1$ and $x=-1$.

39. (a) The given function is

$$f(x)=x|x| = \begin{cases}-x^2, & x<0\\ 0, & x=0\\ x^2, & x>0\end{cases}$$

Clearly, x^2 and $-x^2$ both polynomial functions and we know, they are differentiable.

The only possible point is non-differentiable at $x=0$

(LHD at $x=0$)

$$= \lim_{x\to 0^-}\frac{f(x)-f(0)}{x-0}$$

$$= \lim_{h\to 0}\frac{f(0-h)-f(0)}{-h}$$

$$= \lim_{h\to 0}\frac{-(-h)^2-0}{-h}=0$$

(RHD at $x=0$)

$$= \lim_{x\to 0^+}\frac{f(x)-f(0)}{x-0}$$

$$= \lim_{h\to 0}\frac{f(0+h)-f(0)}{h}$$

$$= \lim_{h\to 0}\frac{h^2-0}{h}=0$$

$\therefore$ LHD = RHD

So, f is differentiable at $x=0$.

Hence, f is differentiable for all $x\in(-\infty,\infty)$.

40. We observe that

$$f(x)=|x|^3 = \begin{cases}-x^3, & x<0\\ x^3, & x\ge 0\end{cases}$$

(LHD at $x=0$)

$$\lim_{x\to 0^-}\frac{f(x)-f(0)}{x-0}$$

$$= \lim_{h\to 0}\frac{f(0-h)-f(0)}{-h}$$

$$= \lim_{h\to 0}\frac{h^3}{-h}=0$$

(RHD at $x=0$)

$$\lim_{x\to 0^+}\frac{f(x)-f(0)}{x-0}$$

$$= \lim_{h \to 0} \frac{f(0+h) - f(0)}{h}$$

$$= \lim_{h \to 0} \frac{h^3}{h} = 0$$

Thus, $\lim_{x \to 0^-} \frac{f(x) - f(0)}{x - 0}$

$$= \lim_{x \to 0^+} \frac{f(x) - f(0)}{x - 0} = f'(0)$$

$\therefore \quad f'(0) = 0$

Thus, the value of $f'(0)$ is 0.

41. (True)

Given that

$$f(x) = \begin{cases} a + bx + x^4 c, & x \geq 0 \\ a - bx + cx^4, & x < 0 \end{cases}$$ is

differentiable at $x = 0$

So, $\lim_{x \to 0^-} \frac{f(x) - f(0)}{x - 0}$

$$= \lim_{x \to 0^+} \frac{f(x) - f(0)}{x - 0}$$

$$\Rightarrow \lim_{h \to 0} \frac{f(0-h) - f(0)}{-h} = \lim_{h \to 0} \frac{f(0+h) - f(0)}{h}$$

$$\Rightarrow \lim_{h \to 0} \frac{a + bh + ch^4 - a}{-h} = \lim_{h \to 0} \frac{(a + bh + ch^4) - a}{h}$$

$$\Rightarrow \lim_{h \to 0}(-b - ch^3) = \lim_{h \to 0}(b + ch^3)$$

$$\Rightarrow \quad -b = b \Rightarrow b = 0$$

$\therefore f(x)$ is differentiable at $x = 0$ if $b = 0$.

42. (b) The given function is

$$f(x) = |\sin x|$$

To find whether the function is differentiable or not, we can make a graph of the function and look for the pointed edges, not smooth edges, if there are multiple slopes present which makes the function non-differentiable.

The graph of $|\sin x|$ is

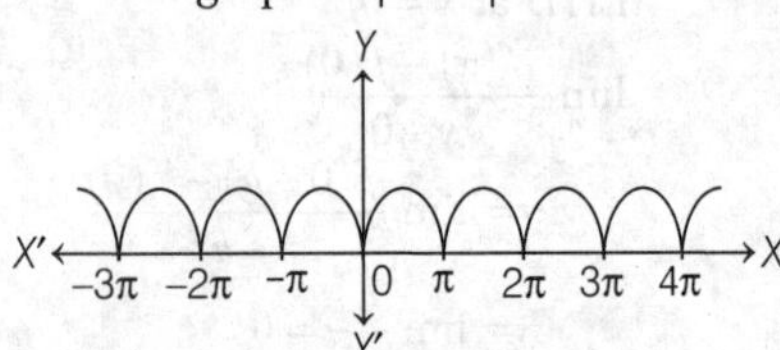

From the above graph $y = |\sin x|$, we can see at every integral multiple of π there is a pointed edges which shows multiple slopes which makes the function non-differentiable.

Thus, $f(x)$ is non-differentiable at $x = n\pi, n \in Z$ and clearly, $f(x)$ is continuous everywhere.

43. (True)

$$f(x) = e^{|x|} = \begin{cases} e^x, & x \geq 0 \\ e^{-x}, & x < 0 \end{cases}$$

Now, for differentiability at $x = 0$

$$\text{LHD} = \lim_{x \to 0^-} \frac{f(x) - f(0)}{x - 0}$$

$$= \lim_{h \to 0} \frac{f(0-h) - f(0)}{-h}$$

$$= \lim_{h \to 0} \frac{e^h - 1}{-h} = -1 \quad \left[\because \lim_{x \to 0} \frac{e^x - 1}{x} = 1\right]$$

$$\text{RHD} = \lim_{x \to 0^+} \frac{f(x) - f(0)}{x - 0}$$

$$= \lim_{h \to 0} \frac{f(0+h) - f(0)}{h - 0}$$

$$= \lim_{h \to 0} \frac{f(h) - f(0)}{h}$$

$$= \lim_{h \to 0} \frac{e^h - 1}{h} = 1$$

$\therefore$ LHD $\neq$ RHD

i.e. f is non-differentiable at $x = 1$.

44. (d) Given that

$$f(x) = \begin{cases} \frac{1}{1 + e^{1/x}}, & x \neq 0 \\ 0, & x = 0 \end{cases}$$

checking continuity at $x = 0$,

$$\lim_{h \to 0} f(0-h) = \lim_{h \to 0} \frac{1}{1 + e^{-1/h}}$$

$$= \frac{1}{1+0} = 1$$

and $\lim_{h \to 0} f(0+h) = \lim_{h \to 0} \frac{1}{1 + e^{1/h}}$

$$= \lim_{h \to 0} \frac{e^{-1/h}}{e^{-1/h} + 1}$$

$$= \frac{0}{1} = 0$$

Since,

$$\lim_{h \to 0} f(0-h) \neq \lim_{h \to 0} f(0+h).$$

Therefore, $f(x)$ is not continuous and hence not differentiable at $x = 0$.

45. (False)

$$\text{LHL} = \lim_{x \to 1^-} f(x)$$

$$= \lim_{h \to 0} 3^{(1-h)} = 3$$

$$\text{RHL} = \lim_{x \to 1^+} f(x)$$

$$= \lim_{h \to 0} 4 - (1 + h)$$

$$= 3$$

$$f(1) = 3$$

Here, LHL = RHL = $f(1)$

Hence, $f(x)$ is continuous at $x = 1$.

$$f'(x) = \begin{cases} 3^x \log 3 & -1 < x < 1 \\ -1 & 1 < x < 4 \end{cases}$$

$$\lim_{x \to 1^-} f'(x) = \lim_{x \to 1^-} 3^x \log 3$$

$$= 3 \log 3$$

$$\lim_{x \to 1^+} f'(x) = \lim_{x \to 1^+}(-1)$$

$$= -1$$

LHL $\neq$ RHL

$\therefore$ It is non-differentiable at $x = 1$.

46. (i) Let $y = (x + 3)^2 \cdot (x + 4)^3 \cdot (x + 5)^4$

Now, differentiating both sides w.r.t. x, we get

$$\frac{dy}{dx} = \left[\frac{d}{dx}(x + 3)^2\right] \cdot (x + 4)^3 \cdot (x + 5)^4 + (x + 3)^2 \left[\frac{d}{dx}(x + 4)^3\right](x + 5)^4 + (x + 3)^2 (x + 4)^3 \cdot \left[\frac{d}{dx} \cdot (x + 5)^4\right]$$

$$= 2(x + 3) \cdot (x + 4)^3 \cdot (x + 5)^4 + 3(x + 3)^2 (x + 4)^2 (x + 5)^4 + 4(x + 3)^2 (x + 4)^3 (x + 5)^3$$

Now, at $x = -3$,

$$\frac{dy}{dx} = 0$$

(ii) Let $y = \tan(x^2 + 3)$

$v = x^2 + 3$ and $y = \tan v$

$$\frac{dy}{dx} = \frac{dy}{dv} \cdot \frac{dv}{dx}$$

$$\frac{dy}{dx} = \sec^2 v \cdot 2x$$

$$\frac{dy}{dx} = \sec^2(x^2 + 3) \cdot 2x$$

(iii) Let $y = \sin(\cos x)$

$v = \cos x$ and $y = \sin v$

$$\frac{dy}{dx} = \frac{dy}{dv} \cdot \frac{dv}{dx} = \cos v \cdot (-\sin x)$$

$$\frac{dy}{dx} = -[\cos(\cos x)](\sin x)$$

(iv) Let $y = \sin x^3 \cdot \sin^2(x^4)$

$$\frac{dy}{dx} = \left[\frac{d}{dx}(\sin x^3)\right] \cdot \sin^2 x^4 + \sin x^3 \left[\frac{d}{dx}(\sin^2 x^4)\right]$$

$$\frac{dy}{dx} = \cos x^3 \cdot (3x^2) \cdot \sin^2 x^4 + \sin x^3 \, [2 \sin x^4 \cdot \cos x^4 (4x^3)]$$

$$\frac{dy}{dx} = 3x^2 \cdot \sin^2 x^4 \cdot \cos x^3 + 8x^3 \cdot \sin x^3 \cdot \sin x^4 \cdot \cos x^4$$

47. (False)

Given, $y = (x^2 + x + 1)^4$, putting $x^2 + x + 1 = u$, we get

$$y = u^4 \text{ and } \frac{du}{dx} = 2x + 1$$

$$\Rightarrow \quad \frac{dy}{du} = 4u^3$$

Now, $\frac{dy}{dx} = \frac{dy}{du} \cdot \frac{du}{dx}$

$$= 4 \cdot u^3 \cdot (2x + 1)$$

$$= 4\,(x^2 + x + 1)^3 \cdot (2x + 1)$$

At $x = -\frac{1}{2}$.

$$\frac{dy}{dx} = 0$$

48. (d) Given, $y = \log(\sec x + \tan x)$

Put $u = \sec x + \tan x$, we get

$y = \log u$

and $u = \sec x + \tan x$

$\therefore \quad \frac{dy}{du} = \frac{1}{u}$

and $\frac{du}{dx} = \sec x \cdot \tan x + \sec^2 x$

$$\therefore \quad \frac{dy}{dx} = \frac{dy}{du} \cdot \frac{du}{dx}$$

$$= \frac{1}{u} \times (\sec x \cdot \tan x + \sec^2 x)$$

$$= \sec x$$

At $x = \frac{\pi}{3}$, $\frac{dy}{dx} = \sec\frac{\pi}{3}$

$$= \frac{1}{\cos\frac{\pi}{3}} = \frac{1}{1/2} = 2$$

49. (c) Given, $y = f(x^2)$

and $f'(x) = e^{\sqrt{x}}$

$$\frac{dy}{dx} = f'(x^2) \cdot \frac{d}{dx}(x^2)$$

$$= f'(x^2) \cdot 2x$$

$$\frac{dy}{dx} = e^x \cdot 2x = 2xe^x$$

$$[\because f'(x) = e^{\sqrt{x}} \Rightarrow f'(x^2) = e^x]$$

50. Given, $y = \sqrt{\log\left\{\sin\left(\frac{x^2}{4} - 1\right)\right\}}$

Put $\frac{x^2}{4} - 1 = v$, we get

$$\sin\left(\frac{x^2}{4} - 1\right) = \sin v = u$$

$$\log\left\{\sin\left(\frac{x^2}{4} - 1\right)\right\} = \log u = w$$

$\therefore \; y = \sqrt{w}$, $w = \log u$,

$u = \sin v$, $v = \frac{x^2}{4} - 1$

$$\Rightarrow \quad \frac{dy}{dw} = \frac{1}{2\sqrt{w}}, \; \frac{dw}{du} = \frac{1}{u},$$

$$\frac{du}{dv} = \cos v, \; \frac{dv}{dx} = \frac{x}{2}$$

Now, $\frac{dy}{dx} = \frac{dy}{dw} \cdot \frac{dw}{du} \cdot \frac{du}{dv} \cdot \frac{dv}{dx}$

$$= \left(\frac{1}{2\sqrt{w}}\right) \cdot \left(\frac{1}{u}\right) \cdot (\cos v) \cdot \left(\frac{x}{2}\right)$$

$$= \frac{x}{2} \frac{\cos v}{2u\sqrt{\log u}}$$

$$= \frac{x}{4} \cdot \frac{\cos\left(\frac{x^2}{4} - 1\right)}{\sin\left(\frac{x^2}{4} - 1\right)\sqrt{\log\left(\sin\left(\frac{x^2}{4} - 1\right)\right)}}$$

$$\therefore \frac{dy}{dx} = \frac{x \cdot \cot\left(\frac{x^2}{4} - 1\right)}{4 \cdot \sqrt{\log\left\{\sin\left(\frac{x^2}{4} - 1\right)\right\}}}$$

This is required answer.

51. (a) Given, $y = e^{ax}\cos(bx + c)$

Let $u = e^{ax}$, $v = \cos(bx + c)$

and $w = bx + c$

Thus, $\frac{du}{dx} = ae^{ax}$, $\frac{dv}{dw} = -\sin w$

and $\frac{dw}{dx} = b$

So, $\frac{dv}{dx} = -b \cdot \sin w = -b \cdot \sin(bx + c)$

Thus, $y = u \cdot v$

Using product rule,

$$\frac{dy}{dx} = u \cdot \frac{dv}{dx} + v \cdot \frac{du}{dx}$$

$$= e^{ax}\{-b \cdot \sin(bx + c)\} + (ae^{ax}) \cdot (\cos(bx + c))$$

$$= e^{ax}\{a\cos(bx + c) - b\sin(bx + c)\}$$

52. Given, $y = x^x \cdot e^{2(x+3)}$

$$= e^{x \log x} \cdot e^{2(x+3)}$$

$$\Rightarrow \quad y = e^{x \log x + 2(x+3)}$$

$$[e^a \cdot e^b = e^{a+b}]$$

Now, differentiating both sides w.r.t. x, we get

$$\frac{dy}{dx} = e^{x \log x + 2(x+3)} \cdot \frac{d}{dx}\{x \cdot \log x + 2(x + 3)\}$$

$$= e^{x \log x} \cdot e^{2(x+3)} \left\{\frac{d}{dx}(x \cdot \log x) + \frac{d}{dx}(2x + 6)\right\}$$

$$= x^x \cdot e^{2(x+3)} \cdot \left\{x \cdot \frac{1}{x} + \log x + 2\right\}$$

$$\therefore \frac{dy}{dx} = x^x \cdot e^{2(x+3)}\{3 + \log x\}$$

At $x = 1$, $\frac{dy}{dx} = (1)^1 e^{2(1+3)} \cdot \{3 + \log 1\}$

$$= e^8 \cdot 3 = 3e^8$$

Thus, the value of $\left.\frac{dy}{dx}\right|_{x=1}$ is $3e^8$.

53. Given, $y = \cos x^3 \cdot \sin^2(x^5) = u \cdot v$

where $u = \cos x^3$

and $v = \sin^2(x^5)$

Let $p = x^3$, then $u = \cos p$

and $q = \sin(x^5)$, then $v = q^2$

and $q = \sin(x^5) = \sin(s)$,

where $s = x^5$

Now differentiating,

$$\frac{dy}{dx} = u\frac{dv}{dx} + v \cdot \frac{du}{dx} \quad \text{...(i)}$$

and $\frac{du}{dp} = -\sin p$ and $\frac{dp}{dx} = 3x^2$

$\frac{dq}{ds} = \cos s$, $\frac{ds}{dx} = 5x^4$ and $\frac{dv}{dq} = 2q$

$$\therefore \frac{dv}{dx} = \frac{dv}{dq} \cdot \frac{dq}{ds} \cdot \frac{ds}{dx}$$

$$= 2q \cdot \cos s \cdot 5x^4$$

$$= 2\sin(x^5) \cdot \cos s \cdot 5x^4$$

$$\therefore \frac{dv}{dx} = 10\sin(x^5)\cos(x^5) \cdot x^4$$

and $\frac{du}{dx} = \frac{du}{dp} \cdot \frac{dp}{dx} = (-3x^2)\sin(x^3)$

From Eq. (i),

$$\frac{dy}{dx} = (\cos x^3)[10x^4 \sin(x^5) \cos(x^5)] + (\sin^2(x^5)) \cdot [(-3x^2) \sin(x^3)]$$

This is required answer.

54. (d) Given, $y = \dfrac{\sin(ax+b)}{\cos(cx+d)}$

$= \dfrac{u}{v}$ (say)

$u = \sin(ax+b)$

$v = \cos(cx+d)$

where, $u = \sin p$ and $p = ax + b$ (say)

and $v = \cos q$ and $q = cx + d$ (say)

Now, $y = \dfrac{u}{v}$

$\Rightarrow \dfrac{dy}{dx} = \dfrac{u' \cdot v - u \cdot v'}{v^2}$ ...(i)

$\therefore \dfrac{du}{dx} = \dfrac{du}{dp} \cdot \dfrac{dp}{dx} = (\cos p) \cdot (a)$

$\dfrac{dv}{dx} = \dfrac{dv}{dq} \cdot \dfrac{dq}{dx} = (-\sin q)(c)$

Thus, from Eq. (i), we get

$$\frac{dy}{dx} = \frac{a\cos(ax+b)\cdot\cos(cx+d) - \sin(ax+b)(-c)\sin(cx+d)}{\cos^2(cx+d)}$$

$$= \frac{a\cos(ax+b)\cdot\cos(cx+d) + c\sin(ax+b)\cdot\sin(cx+d)}{\cos^2(cx+d)}$$

55. (i) Given, $x\sqrt{1+y} + y\sqrt{1+x} = 0$

$\Rightarrow x\sqrt{1+y} = -y\sqrt{1+x}$

$\Rightarrow x^2(1+y) = y^2(1+x)$ [squaring both sides]

$\Rightarrow x^2 - y^2 = y^2x - x^2y$

$\Rightarrow (x+y)(x-y) = -xy(x-y)$

$\Rightarrow (x+y) = -xy$ $[\because x - y \neq 0]$

$\Rightarrow y = -\dfrac{x}{1+x}$

$\Rightarrow \dfrac{dy}{dx} = -\left[\dfrac{(1+x)\cdot 1 - 1\cdot(x)}{(1+x)^2}\right]$

$= -\dfrac{1}{(1+x)^2}$

Thus, the value of $\dfrac{dy}{dx}$ is $-\dfrac{1}{(1+x)^2}$.

(ii) Given, $\sin y = x\sin(a+y)$

Differentiating both sides w.r.t. x, we get

$\dfrac{d}{dx}(\sin y) = \dfrac{d}{dx}\{x\sin(a+y)\}$

$\Rightarrow \cos y \cdot \dfrac{dy}{dx} = \sin(a+y) + x\cos(a+y)\dfrac{d}{dx}(a+y)$

$\Rightarrow \cos y \cdot \dfrac{dy}{dx} - x\cos(a+y)\dfrac{dy}{dx} = \sin(a+y)$

$\Rightarrow \left\{\cos y - \dfrac{\sin y}{\sin(a+y)} \cdot \cos(a+y)\right\}\dfrac{dy}{dx} = \sin(a+y)$

$\Rightarrow \left\{\dfrac{\sin(a+y)\cdot\cos y - \sin y\cos(a+y)}{\sin(a+y)}\right\}\dfrac{dy}{dx} = \sin(a+y)$

$\Rightarrow \dfrac{\sin a}{\sin(a+y)}\dfrac{dy}{dx} = \sin(a+y)$

$[\because \sin(A-B) = \sin A\cos B - \cos A\sin B]$

$\Rightarrow \dfrac{dy}{dx} = \dfrac{\sin^2(a+y)}{\sin a}$

(iii) Given,

$4x + 3y = \log(4x - 3y)$

We have to find $\dfrac{dy}{dx}$ by using given condition, so by differentiating both sides w.r.t. x, we get

$\dfrac{d}{dx}(4x+3y) = \dfrac{d}{dx}\{\log(4x-3y)\}$

$\Rightarrow 4 + 3\dfrac{dy}{dx} = \dfrac{1}{4x-3y}\left[4 - 3\dfrac{dy}{dx}\right]$

$\Rightarrow \left(3 + \dfrac{3}{4x-3y}\right)\dfrac{dy}{dx} = \dfrac{4}{4x-3y} - 4$

$\Rightarrow \left(\dfrac{12x - 9y + 3}{4x-3y}\right)\dfrac{dy}{dx} = \left(\dfrac{4 - 16x + 12y}{4x-3y}\right)$

$\Rightarrow \dfrac{dy}{dx} = \dfrac{4(1-4x+3y)}{3(4x-3y+1)}$

(iv) Given, $y = \sin^{-1}\left(\dfrac{2x}{1+x^2}\right)$

Put $x = \tan\theta$, we get

$y = \sin^{-1}\left(\dfrac{2\tan\theta}{1+\tan^2\theta}\right)$

$= \sin^{-1}(\sin 2\theta)$

Since, $1 < x < \infty$

$\Rightarrow 1 < \tan\theta < \infty$

$\Rightarrow \dfrac{\pi}{4} < \theta < \dfrac{\pi}{2} \Rightarrow \dfrac{\pi}{2} < 2\theta < \pi$

$\Rightarrow 0 < \pi - 2\theta < \dfrac{\pi}{2}$

Thus, $y = \sin^{-1}(\sin 2\theta)$

$= \sin^{-1}\{\sin(\pi - 2\theta)\}$

$= \pi - 2\theta = \pi - 2\tan^{-1} x$ $[\because \theta = \tan^{-1} x]$

$\therefore \dfrac{dy}{dx} = -\dfrac{2}{1+x^2}$

(v) Given, $y = \tan^{-1}\left\{\sqrt{\dfrac{1-\cos x}{1+\cos x}}\right\}$

$= \tan^{-1}\left\{\sqrt{\dfrac{2\sin^2\frac{x}{2}}{2\cos^2\frac{x}{2}}}\right\}$

$= \tan^{-1}\left|\tan\dfrac{x}{2}\right|$

$= \begin{cases} \tan^{-1}\left(\tan\dfrac{x}{2}\right), & \text{if } \tan\dfrac{x}{2} \geq 0 \\ \tan^{-1}\left(-\tan\dfrac{x}{2}\right), & \text{if } \tan\dfrac{x}{2} < 0 \end{cases}$

$\therefore y = \begin{cases} \dfrac{x}{2}, & 0 \leq x < \pi \\ -\dfrac{x}{2}, & -\pi < x < 0 \end{cases}$

Differentiating both sides w.r.t. x, we get

$\dfrac{dy}{dx} = \begin{cases} \dfrac{1}{2}, & 0 < x < \pi \\ -\dfrac{1}{2}, & -\pi < x < 0 \end{cases}$

56. (i) (True)

Given, $x^2 + 2xy + y^3 = 100$

Differentiating both sides w.r.t. x, we get

$\dfrac{d}{dx}(x^2) + \dfrac{d}{dx}(2xy) + \dfrac{d}{dx}(y^3) = \dfrac{d}{dx}(100)$

$\Rightarrow 2x + 2\left[x\dfrac{dy}{dx} + y\right] + 3y^2\dfrac{dy}{dx} = 0$

$\Rightarrow \dfrac{dy}{dx}(2x + 3y^2) + (2x + 2y) = 0$

$\Rightarrow \dfrac{dy}{dx} = \dfrac{-2(x+y)}{(2x+3y^2)}$

(ii) (False)

Given, $\sin^2 y + \cos xy = k$

Differentiating both sides w.r.t. x, we get

$\dfrac{d}{dx}(\sin^2 y) + \dfrac{d}{dx}(\cos xy) = \dfrac{d}{dx}(k)$

$\Rightarrow 2\sin y \cdot \cos y \cdot \dfrac{dy}{dx} - \sin(xy)\left[x\dfrac{dy}{dx} + y\right] = 0$

$$\Rightarrow \frac{dy}{dx}[\sin 2y - x\sin xy] = y\cdot\sin(xy)$$

$$\therefore \frac{dy}{dx} = \frac{y\sin(xy)}{\sin 2y - x\sin xy}$$

Now, $$\left.\frac{dy}{dx}\right|_{\left(1,\frac{\pi}{4}\right)} = \frac{\frac{\pi}{4}\sin\left(\frac{\pi}{4}\right)}{\sin\frac{\pi}{2} - 1\cdot\sin\frac{\pi}{4}}$$

$$= \frac{\frac{\pi}{4}\cdot\frac{1}{\sqrt{2}}}{1-\frac{1}{\sqrt{2}}} = \frac{\pi}{4(\sqrt{2}-1)}$$

(iii) (True)

If $e^{x-y} = \log\left(\frac{x}{y}\right)$

We have to find $\frac{dy}{dx}$ of it, so by differentiating the equation on both sides w.r.t. x, we get

$$e^{x-y}\left\{1-\frac{dy}{dx}\right\} = \frac{1}{x} - \frac{1}{y}\frac{dy}{dx}$$

$$\Rightarrow \left\{e^{x-y} - \frac{1}{y}\right\}\frac{dy}{dx} = \left(e^{x-y} - \frac{1}{x}\right)$$

$$\Rightarrow \left\{\frac{y\cdot e^{x-y}-1}{y}\right\}\cdot\frac{dy}{dx} = \left(\frac{xe^{x-y}-1}{x}\right)$$

$$\Rightarrow \frac{dy}{dx} = \frac{\frac{(x\cdot e^{x-y}-1)}{x}}{\frac{(y\cdot e^{x-y}-1)}{y}}$$

$$= \frac{y}{x}\frac{(x\cdot e^{x-y}-1)}{(y\cdot e^{x-y}-1)}$$

(iv) (True)

Given, $e^x + e^y = e^{x+y}$

On differentiating both sides w.r.t. x, we get

$$e^x + e^y\cdot\frac{dy}{dx} = e^{x+y}\left(1+\frac{dy}{dx}\right)$$

$$\Rightarrow \{e^y - e^{x+y}\}\frac{dy}{dx} = (e^{x+y} - e^x)$$

$$\Rightarrow \frac{dy}{dx} = \frac{e^{x+y}-e^x}{e^y - e^{x+y}}$$

$$\Rightarrow \frac{dy}{dx} = \frac{e^x + e^y - e^x}{e^y - e^x - e^y}$$

$$\Rightarrow \frac{dy}{dx} = -e^{y-x}$$

$$\Rightarrow \frac{dy}{dx} + e^{y-x} = 0$$

(v) (True)

Given, $xy^2 = 1$

We have to find $\frac{dy}{dx}$ of it, so by differentiating the equation on both sides w.r.t. x, we get

$$\frac{d}{dx}\{xy^2\} = \frac{d}{dx}(1)$$

$$\Rightarrow x\left\{2y\frac{dy}{dx}\right\} + y^2 = 0$$

$$\Rightarrow \frac{dy}{dx} = \frac{-y^2}{2xy} = -\frac{y^2}{2\left(\frac{1}{y}\right)}$$

$$[\because xy^2 = 1]$$

$$\therefore \frac{dy}{dx} = -\frac{y^3}{2}$$

57. (a) Given,

$$\log\sqrt{x^2+y^2} = \tan^{-1}\left(\frac{y}{x}\right)$$

$$\Rightarrow \log(x^2+y^2) = 2\tan^{-1}\left(\frac{y}{x}\right)$$

On differentiating both sides w.r.t. x, we get

$$\frac{2x+2y\frac{dy}{dx}}{x^2+y^2} = \frac{2}{1+\frac{y^2}{x^2}}\left(\frac{x\frac{dy}{dx}-y}{x^2}\right)$$

$$\Rightarrow \frac{2\left(x+y\frac{dy}{dx}\right)}{x^2+y^2} = \frac{2x^2}{x^2+y^2}\left(\frac{x\frac{dy}{dx}-y}{x^2}\right)$$

$$\Rightarrow x + y\frac{dy}{dx} = x\frac{dy}{dx} - y$$

$$\Rightarrow \frac{dy}{dx}(y-x) = -y-x$$

$$\Rightarrow \frac{dy}{dx} = \frac{x+y}{x-y}$$

58. (i) (True)

Let $y = \tan^{-1}x$,

then $x = \tan y$

On differentiating both sides w.r.t. x, we get

$$1 = \sec^2 y\frac{dy}{dx}$$

$$\Rightarrow \frac{dy}{dx} = \frac{1}{\sec^2 y} = \frac{1}{\tan^2 y + 1}$$

$$= \frac{1}{1+(\tan(\tan^{-1}x))^2} = \frac{1}{1+x^2}$$

(ii) (False)

Given, $y = \sin^{-1}\left(\frac{1-x^2}{1+x^2}\right)$, $0 < x < 1$

Put $x = \tan\theta$, then

$$y = \sin^{-1}\left(\frac{1-\tan^2\theta}{1+\tan^2\theta}\right)$$

$$= \sin^{-1}(\cos 2\theta)$$

$$= \sin^{-1}\left(\sin\left(\frac{\pi}{2}-2\theta\right)\right)$$

$$= \frac{\pi}{2} - 2\theta$$

$$\Rightarrow y = \frac{\pi}{2} - 2\tan^{-1}x$$

$$\therefore \frac{dy}{dx} = \frac{-2}{1+x^2}$$

(iii) (False)

Given, $y = \sec^{-1}\left(\frac{1}{2x^2-1}\right)$,

$$0 < x < \frac{1}{\sqrt{2}}$$

Let $x = \cos\theta$, then

$$y = \sec^{-1}\left(\frac{1}{2\cos^2\theta - 1}\right)$$

$$= \sec^{-1}\left(\frac{1}{\cos 2\theta}\right)$$

$$[\because \cos 2\theta = 2\cos^2\theta - 1]$$

$$= \sec^{-1}(\sec 2\theta) = 2\theta$$

$$= 2\cos^{-1}x$$

$$\therefore \frac{dy}{dx} = \frac{-2}{\sqrt{1-x^2}}$$

(iv) (True)

Given, $y = \tan^{-1}\left(\frac{3x-x^3}{1-3x^2}\right)$

Put $x = \tan\theta$, then

$$y = \tan^{-1}\left(\frac{3\tan\theta - \tan^3\theta}{1-3\tan^2\theta}\right)$$

$$= \tan^{-1}(\tan 3\theta) = 3\theta$$

If $-\frac{1}{\sqrt{3}} < x < \frac{1}{\sqrt{3}}$, then

$$-\frac{1}{\sqrt{3}} < \tan\theta < \frac{1}{\sqrt{3}}$$

$$\Rightarrow -\frac{\pi}{6} < \theta < \frac{\pi}{6}$$

$$\Rightarrow -\frac{\pi}{2} < 3\theta < \frac{\pi}{2}$$

$$\therefore y = 3\tan^{-1}x \Rightarrow \frac{dy}{dx} = \frac{3}{1+x^2}$$

(v) (True)

Given, $y = \cos^{-1}(2x\sqrt{1-x^2})$,

$$-\frac{1}{\sqrt{2}} < x < \frac{1}{\sqrt{2}}$$

Put $x = \sin\theta$, we get

$$y = \cos^{-1}(2\sin\theta\cos\theta)$$

$$= \cos^{-1}(\sin 2\theta)$$

$$= \cos^{-1}\left\{\cos\left(\frac{\pi}{2}-2\theta\right)\right\}$$

$$y = \frac{\pi}{2} - 2\theta$$

$\because -\frac{1}{\sqrt{2}} < x < \frac{1}{\sqrt{2}}$

$\Rightarrow -\frac{1}{\sqrt{2}} < \sin\theta < \frac{1}{\sqrt{2}}$

$\Rightarrow -\frac{\pi}{4} < \theta < \frac{\pi}{4}$

$\Rightarrow -\frac{\pi}{2} < 2\theta < \frac{\pi}{2}$

$\Rightarrow 0 < \frac{\pi}{2} - 2\theta < \pi$

$\therefore y = \frac{\pi}{2} - 2\sin^{-1} x$

$\Rightarrow \frac{dy}{dx} = -\frac{2}{\sqrt{1-x^2}}$

59. (b) Given,

$y = \sin^{-1} x + \sin^{-1}\sqrt{1-x^2}, 0 < x < 1$

Put $x = \sin\theta$,

$\therefore y = \sin^{-1}(\sin\theta) + \sin^{-1}\sqrt{1-\sin^2\theta}$

$= \theta + \frac{\pi}{2} - \theta$

$[\because 0 < x < 1 \Rightarrow 0 < \sin\theta < 1$

$\Rightarrow 0 < \theta < \sin^{-1}(1) \Rightarrow 0 < \theta < \frac{\pi}{2}$

$\Rightarrow 0 < \frac{\pi}{2} - \theta < \frac{\pi}{2}]$

$\therefore \frac{dy}{dx} = 0$

Thus, the value of $\frac{dy}{dx}$ is 0.

60. Given,

$y = \tan^{-1}\left(\frac{a\cos x - b\sin x}{b\cos x + a\sin x}\right)$

Then, $y = \tan^{-1}\left(\frac{\frac{a}{b} - \tan x}{1 + \frac{a}{b}\tan x}\right)$

[dividing numerator and denominator by $b\cos x$]

$= \tan^{-1}\left(\frac{\tan p - \tan x}{1 + \tan p \cdot \tan x}\right)$ [let $\frac{a}{b} = \tan p$]

$= \tan^{-1}\{\tan(p - x)\}$

$= p - x$

$\therefore y = \tan^{-1}\left(\frac{a}{b}\right) - x$ $\left[\because p = \tan^{-1}\left(\frac{a}{b}\right)\right]$

$\therefore \frac{dy}{dx} = -1$

Thus, $\frac{dy}{dx}(0, 1) = -1$.

61. (a) Given,

$y = \sin^{-1}\left(\frac{2x}{1+x^2}\right) + \cos^{-1}\left(\frac{1-x^2}{1+x^2}\right)$

Put $x = \tan\theta$, we get

$y = \sin^{-1}\left(\frac{2\tan\theta}{1+\tan^2\theta}\right) + \cos^{-1}\left(\frac{1-\tan^2\theta}{1+\tan^2\theta}\right)$

$= \sin^{-1}(\sin 2\theta) + \cos^{-1}(\cos 2\theta)$

Since, $0 < x < 1$

$\Rightarrow 0 < \tan\theta < 1$

$\Rightarrow 0 < \theta < \frac{\pi}{4} \Rightarrow 0 < 2\theta < \frac{\pi}{2}$

$\therefore y = 2\theta + 2\theta = 4\theta$

$= 4\tan^{-1} x [\because \theta = \tan^{-1} x]$

Thus, $\frac{dy}{dx} = \frac{4}{1+x^2}$.

62. (i) Let $y = e^x \cdot \sin x$

$\frac{dy}{dx} = e^x \frac{d}{dx}(\sin x) + \sin x \frac{d}{dx}(e^x)$

$\frac{dy}{dx} = e^x \cos x + e^x \sin x$

$= e^x(\sin x + \cos x)$

(ii) Let $y = 3e^x + 4\sin x \cdot e^x$

$\frac{dy}{dx} = 3\frac{d}{dx}e^x + 4\left[\frac{d}{dx}(\sin x)\right]\cdot e^x + 4\sin x \frac{d}{dx}(e^x)$

$= 3e^x + 4e^x\cos x + 4e^x \sin x$

$= 3e^x + 4e^x(\sin x + \cos x)$

$= e^x(3 + 4\sin x + 4\cos x)$

(iii) Let $y = \cos e^x$

Put $e^x = u$ and $y = \cos u$

$\frac{dy}{dx} = \frac{dy}{du}\cdot\frac{du}{dx}$

$= -\sin u \cdot e^x = -(\sin e^x)\cdot e^x$

(iv) Let $y = \sin(\log x)$

Now, differentiating both sides w.r.t. x using chain rule,

$\frac{dy}{dx} = \cos(\log x)\cdot\frac{d}{dx}(\log x)$

$= \cos(\log x)\cdot\frac{1}{x} = \frac{\cos(\log x)}{x}$

(v) Let $y = \log(\cos e^x)$

Now, differentiating both sides w.r.t. x, we get

$\frac{dy}{dx} = \frac{d}{dx}\{\log(\cos e^x)\}$

$= \frac{1}{\cos(e^x)}\cdot\frac{d}{dx}\{\cos(e^x)\}$

$= \frac{1}{\cos(e^x)}\{-\sin(e^x)\}\cdot\frac{d}{dx}(e^x)$

$= -\tan(e^x)\cdot e^x$

Thus, the value of $\frac{dy}{dx}$ is $-e^x\tan(e^x)$.

63. Let $y = \sqrt{\frac{(x+3)(x^3+4)}{(2x^2+3x+9)}}$

Taking logarithm on both sides, we get

$\log y = \frac{1}{2}[\log(x+3) + \log(x^3+4) - \log(2x^2+3x+9)]$

Now, differentiating both sides w.r.t. x, we get

$\frac{1}{y}\frac{dy}{dx} = \frac{1}{2}\left[\frac{1}{x+3} + \frac{3x^2}{x^3+4} - \frac{4x+3}{2x^2+3x+9}\right]$

$\Rightarrow \frac{dy}{dx} = \frac{1}{2}\sqrt{\frac{(x+3)(x^3+4)}{(2x^2+3x+9)}}\left[\frac{1}{x+3} + \frac{3x^2}{x^3+4} - \frac{4x+3}{2x^2+3x+9}\right]$

64. (i) (True)

Given, $y = \sin\{\tan^{-1}(e^x)\}$

$\Rightarrow \frac{dy}{dx} = \frac{d}{dx}\{\sin(\tan^{-1} e^x)\}$

$= \cos(\tan^{-1} e^x)\cdot\frac{d}{dx}\{\tan^{-1}(e^x)\}$

$= \cos(\tan^{-1} e^x)\cdot\frac{1}{1+(e^x)^2}\cdot\frac{d}{dx}(e^x)$

$\therefore \frac{dy}{dx} = \frac{e^x\cos\{\tan^{-1}(e^x)\}}{1+e^{2x}}$

(ii) (True)

Given, $y = x^{\sqrt{x}}$,

then $y = e^{\sqrt{x}\log x}$

Differentiating both sides w.r.t. x, we get

$\frac{dy}{dx} = e^{\sqrt{x}\log x}\cdot\frac{d}{dx}(\sqrt{x}\log x)$

$= x^{\sqrt{x}}\left\{\sqrt{x}\cdot\frac{d}{dx}(\log x) + \left(\frac{d}{dx}(\sqrt{x})\right)\log x\right\}$

$\therefore \frac{dy}{dx} = x^{\sqrt{x}}\left\{\frac{1}{\sqrt{x}} + \frac{\log x}{2\sqrt{x}}\right\}$

At $x = 1$, $\frac{dy}{dx} = 1$

Thus, the value of $\left(\frac{dy}{dx}\right)_{x=1}$ is 1.

(iii) (True)

Given, $y = x^{\sin x} \cdot (x > 0)$

Taking log on both sides, we get

$$\log y = \sin x \cdot \log x$$

$$\Rightarrow \frac{1}{y} \cdot \frac{dy}{dx} = \sin x \left[\frac{d}{dx}(\log x)\right] + \left[\frac{d}{dx}(\sin x)\right] \cdot \log x$$

$$= (\sin x) \cdot \frac{1}{x} + \cos x \cdot \log x$$

$$\Rightarrow \frac{dy}{dx} = \left[\frac{\sin x}{x} + \cos x \cdot \log x\right] \cdot y$$

$$\Rightarrow \frac{dy}{dx} = x^{\sin x - 1} \cdot \sin x + x^{\sin x} \cdot \cos x \cdot \log x$$

(iv) (True)

Given, $y = e^x + x^x + a^x + x^a$

$\therefore \quad y = e^x + e^{x \log x} + a^x + x^a$

Now, differentiating both sides w.r.t. x, we get

$$\frac{dy}{dx} = \frac{d}{dx}(a^x) + \frac{d}{dx}(e^x) + \frac{d}{dx}(e^{x \log x}) + \frac{d}{dx}(x^a)$$

$$= a^x \log a + e^x + e^{x \log x}\left\{x\frac{1}{x} + \log x\right\} + ax^{a-1}$$

$$\therefore \frac{dy}{dx} = a^x \cdot \log a + e^x + x^x(1 + \log x) + ax^{a-1}$$

$$\therefore \left(\frac{dy}{dx}\right)_{x=a} = a^a \cdot \log a + e^a + a^a(1 + \log a) + a \cdot a^{a-1}$$

$$= e^a + 2a^a(1 + \log a)$$

(v) (False)

Given, $x^{13}y^7 = (x+y)^{20}$

Taking log on both sides, we get

$$\log(x^{13}y^7) = \log(x+y)^{20}$$

$$\Rightarrow 13 \log x + 7 \log y = 20 \log(x+y)$$

$$\Rightarrow 13\frac{d}{dx}(\log x) + 7\frac{d}{dx}(\log y) = 20\frac{d}{dx}\{\log(x+y)\}$$

$$\Rightarrow \frac{13}{x} + \frac{7}{y} \cdot \frac{dy}{dx} = 20\frac{1}{x+y}\left(1 + \frac{dy}{dx}\right)$$

$$\Rightarrow \left(\frac{7}{y} - \frac{20}{x+y}\right)\frac{dy}{dx} = \frac{20}{x+y} - \frac{13}{x}$$

$$= \frac{20x - 13x - 13y}{x(x+y)}$$

$$\Rightarrow \frac{7x + 7y - 20y}{y(x+y)} \frac{dy}{dx} = \frac{(7x - 13y)}{x(x+y)}$$

$$\Rightarrow \frac{dy}{dx} = \frac{y}{x} \cdot \frac{(7x - 13y)}{(7x - 13y)} = \frac{y}{x}$$

$$\therefore \quad x\frac{dy}{dx} - y = 0,$$

this relation holds.

(vi) (False)

Given, $y = x^{\log x} + (\log x)^x$

Let $u = (x)^{\log x}$ and $v = (\log x)^x$

$\therefore \quad y = u + v$

$$\Rightarrow \quad \frac{dy}{dx} = \frac{du}{dx} + \frac{dv}{dx} \qquad \ldots(i)$$

Now, $u = (x)^{\log x}$

$$\log u = (\log x) \cdot (\log x) = (\log x)^2$$

On differentiating both sides w.r.t. x, we get

$$\frac{1}{u} \cdot \frac{du}{dx} = 2 \cdot (\log x) \cdot \frac{d}{dx}(\log x)$$

$$\Rightarrow \quad \frac{du}{dx} = \frac{2}{x}(\log x) \cdot u$$

$$= \frac{2}{x} \cdot \log x \cdot x^{(\log x)}$$

$$= 2 \cdot x^{\log x - 1} \cdot \log x$$

$$\therefore \quad \frac{du}{dx} = 2 \cdot x^{\log x - 1} \cdot \log x$$

and $\quad v = (\log x)^x$

$$\log v = x \log(\log x)$$

On differentiating both sides w.r.t. x, we get

$$\frac{1}{v} \cdot \frac{dv}{dx} = \left[\frac{d}{dx}(x)\right] \cdot \log\{\log(x)\} + x \cdot \frac{d}{dx}\{\log(\log x)\}$$

$$= \log(\log x) + x \cdot \frac{1}{\log x} \cdot \frac{1}{x}$$

$$= \log(\log x) + \frac{1}{\log x}$$

$$\Rightarrow \frac{dv}{dx} = (\log x)^x \left[\frac{\log(\log x) \cdot \log x + 1}{\log x}\right]$$

$$\therefore \frac{dv}{dx} = (\log x)^{x-1} \cdot \{1 + \log x \cdot \log(\log x)\}$$

From Eq. (i), we get

$$\frac{dy}{dx} = 2x^{\log x - 1} \log x + (\log x)^{x-1} \{1 + \log x \cdot \log(\log x)\}$$

At $x = 1, \dfrac{dy}{dx} = 0 < \dfrac{3}{2}$

65. Given, $y = (\sin x)^x + \sin^{-1}(\sqrt{x})$

Then, $y = e^{x \log \sin x} + \sin^{-1}(\sqrt{x})$

On differentiating both sides w.r.t. x, we get

$$\frac{dy}{dx} = e^{x \log \sin x} \cdot \frac{d}{dx}(x \log \sin x) + \frac{d}{dx}(\sin^{-1}\sqrt{x})$$

$$= (\sin x)^x\{x \cot x + \log \sin x\} + \frac{1}{\sqrt{1-x}}\frac{1}{2\sqrt{x}}$$

$$\therefore \frac{dy}{dx} = (\sin x)^x\{x \cot x + \log \sin x\} + \frac{1}{2\sqrt{x - x^2}}$$

At $x = \dfrac{\pi}{2}, \dfrac{dy}{dx} = \left(\sin\dfrac{\pi}{2}\right)^{\pi/2}$

$$\left\{\frac{\pi}{2}\cot\frac{\pi}{2} + \log \sin\frac{\pi}{2}\right\} + \frac{1}{2\sqrt{\frac{\pi}{2} - \frac{\pi^2}{4}}}$$

$$= (1)^{\pi/2}\{0\} + \frac{2}{2\sqrt{2\pi - \pi^2}}$$

$$\left.\frac{dy}{dx}\right|_{x=\frac{\pi}{2}} = \frac{1}{\sqrt{2\pi - \pi^2}}$$

This is required answer.

66. Given, $y = \log_5(\log_5 x)$

Put $u = \log_5 x$,

$\therefore \quad y = \log_5 u$ and $u = \log_5 x$

$$\frac{dy}{du} = \frac{1}{u \log_e 5}$$

and $\quad \dfrac{du}{dx} = \dfrac{1}{x \log_e 5}$

Now,

$$\frac{dy}{dx} = \frac{dy}{du} \cdot \frac{du}{dx} = \frac{1}{u \log_e 5} \cdot \frac{1}{x \log_e 5}$$

$$= \frac{1}{\log_5 x \cdot \log_e 5 \cdot x \cdot \log_e 5}$$

$[\because u = \log_5 x]$

$$\therefore \frac{dy}{dx} = \frac{1}{x(\log_5 x) \cdot (\log_e 5)^2}$$

Thus, the value of $\dfrac{dy}{dx}$ is

$$\frac{1}{x \cdot (\log_5 x) \cdot (\log_e 5)^2}$$

67. (False)

Given, $y = \log \tan\left(\dfrac{\pi}{4} + \dfrac{x}{2}\right)$

Putting $\dfrac{\pi}{4} + \dfrac{x}{2} = v$, then

$$\tan\left(\frac{\pi}{4} + \frac{x}{2}\right) = \tan v = u \qquad \text{(say)}$$

we get $y = \log u$, $u = \tan v$

and $v = \frac{\pi}{4} + \frac{x}{2}$

On differentiating, we get

$\frac{dy}{du} = \frac{1}{u}$, $\frac{du}{dv} = \sec^2 v$ and $\frac{dv}{dx} = \frac{1}{2}$

Now, $\frac{dy}{dx} = \frac{dy}{du} \cdot \frac{du}{dv} \cdot \frac{dv}{dx}$

$= \frac{1}{u} \cdot \sec^2 v \cdot \frac{1}{2}$

$= \frac{1}{\tan v} \cdot \sec^2 v \cdot \frac{1}{2}$

$= \frac{1}{2 \sin v \cos v} = \frac{1}{\sin 2v}$

$= \frac{1}{\sin\left(\frac{\pi}{2} + x\right)} = \sec x$

$\therefore \left.\frac{dy}{dx}\right|_{\left(x=\frac{\pi}{4}\right)} = \sqrt{2}$

68. (False)

Given,

$y = \log\left\{\frac{a + b \sin x}{a - b \sin x}\right\}$

$\therefore y = \log(a + b \sin x) - \log(a - b \sin x)$

Put $u = \log(a + b \sin x)$

$v = \log(a - b \sin x)$

$p = a + b \sin x$

and $q = a - b \sin x$

Thus, $y = u - v$

$\therefore \frac{dy}{dx} = \frac{du}{dx} - \frac{dv}{dx}$ ...(i)

Now, $u = \log p$

and $p = a + b \sin x$

$\therefore \frac{du}{dp} = \frac{1}{p}$ and $\frac{dp}{dx} = b \cos x$

$\therefore \frac{du}{dx} = \frac{b \cos x}{a + b \sin x}$

and similarly, $\frac{dv}{dx} = \frac{-b \cos x}{a - b \sin x}$

From Eq. (i), we get

$\frac{dy}{dx} = \frac{b \cos x}{a + b \sin x} + \frac{b \cos x}{a - b \sin x}$

$= b \cos x\left[\frac{1}{a + b \sin x} + \frac{1}{a - b \sin x}\right]$

$= \frac{b \cos x \cdot 2a}{a^2 - b^2 \sin^2 x} = \frac{2ab \cos x}{a^2 - b^2 \sin x}$

Now, $\left.\frac{dy}{dx}\right|_{x=\frac{\pi}{2}} = \frac{2ab \cos\frac{\pi}{2}}{a^2 - b^2 \sin\frac{\pi}{2}} = 0$

69. (d) Given, $x + y = e^{1/xy}$

$\Rightarrow \log(x + y) = \frac{1}{xy}$

$\Rightarrow xy \log(x + y) = 1$

By using triple product rule,

$\frac{d}{dx}(u, v, w) = \frac{du}{dx} \cdot v \cdot w + u \frac{dv}{dx} \cdot w + u \cdot v \frac{dw}{dx}$

Applying above rule,

$1 \cdot y \cdot \log(x + y) + x \cdot \frac{dy}{dx} \cdot \log(x + y) + \frac{xy}{x + y}\left(1 + \frac{dy}{dx}\right) = 0$

$\Rightarrow \frac{y}{xy} + \frac{x}{xy} \cdot \frac{dy}{dx} + \frac{xy}{(x + y)}\left(1 + \frac{dy}{dx}\right) = 0$

$\left[\because \log(x + y) = \frac{1}{xy}\right]$

$\Rightarrow \frac{x^2 y + x + y}{(x + y)x} + \frac{dy}{dx}\left\{\frac{y^2 x + x + y}{(x + y)y}\right\} = 0$

$\Rightarrow \frac{dy}{dx} = -\frac{\frac{(x^2 y + x + y)}{(x + y)x}}{\frac{(y^2 x + x + y)}{(x + y) \cdot y}}$

$= -\frac{y(x^2 y + x + y)}{x(xy^2 + x + y)}$

$\therefore \frac{dy}{dx} = -\frac{y}{x} \cdot \frac{(x + y + x^2 y)}{(x + y + xy^2)}$

70. (i) Given $x = at^3$ and $y = 2at$

$\frac{dx}{dt} = 3at^2$ and $\frac{dy}{dt} = 2a$

$\frac{dy}{dx} = \frac{dy/dt}{dx/dt}$

$\frac{dy}{dx} = \frac{2a}{3at^2} = \frac{2}{3t^2}$

(ii) Given, $x = a(t - \sin t)$ and $y = a(1 - \cos t)$

On differentiating both sides w.r.t. t, we get

$\frac{dx}{dt} = a(1 - \cos t)$ and $\frac{dy}{dt} = a \sin t$

$\therefore \frac{dy}{dx} = \frac{dy}{dt}\Big/\frac{dx}{dt} = \frac{a \sin t}{a(1 - \cos t)}$

$= \frac{2 \sin\frac{t}{2} \cos\frac{t}{2}}{2 \sin^2\frac{t}{2}} = \cot\frac{t}{2}$

(iii) We have, $x = \sqrt{a^{\sin^{-1} t}}$

and $y = \sqrt{a^{\cos^{-1} t}}$

$\frac{dx}{dt} = \frac{1}{2}(a^{\sin^{-1} t})^{-1/2} \frac{d}{dt}(a^{\sin^{-1} t})$

$= \frac{1}{2}(a^{\sin^{-1} t})^{-1/2} \cdot (a^{\sin^{-1} t} \log_e a) \cdot \frac{d}{dt}(\sin^{-1} t)$

$= \frac{1}{2}(a^{\sin^{-1} t})^{1/2} \cdot (\log_e a) \frac{1}{\sqrt{1 - t^2}}$

$= \frac{x \log_e a}{2\sqrt{1 - t^2}}$

and $\frac{dy}{dt} = \frac{1}{2}(a^{\cos^{-1} t})^{-1/2} \cdot \frac{d}{dt}(a^{\cos^{-1} t})$

$= \frac{1}{2}(a \cos^{-1} t)^{-1/2} \cdot (a \cos^{-1} t \cdot \log_e a) \cdot \frac{d}{dt}(\cos^{-1} t)$

$= \frac{1}{2}(a^{\cos^{-1} t})^{1/2} \cdot \frac{(-1) \cdot \log_e a}{\sqrt{1 - t^2}}$

$= \frac{-y \log_e a}{2\sqrt{1 - t^2}}$

$\therefore \frac{dy}{dx} = \frac{dy/dt}{dx/dt} = -\frac{y}{x}$

(iv) Given, $y = \sin(2\cos^{-1} t)$

and $x = \cos(2 \sin^{-1} t)$

$\Rightarrow \sin^{-1} y = 2\cos^{-1} t$

and $\cos^{-1} x = 2 \sin^{-1} t$

$\Rightarrow \cos^{-1} x + \sin^{-1} y = 2(\cos^{-1} t + \sin^{-1} t)$

$= 2\frac{\pi}{2} = \pi$

$\left[\because \sin^{-1} t + \cos^{-1} t = \frac{\pi}{2}\right]$

On differentiating both sides w.r.t. x, we get

$-\frac{1}{\sqrt{1 - x^2}} + \frac{1}{\sqrt{1 - y^2}} \frac{dy}{dx} = 0$

$\Rightarrow \frac{dy}{dx} = \frac{\sqrt{1 - y^2}}{\sqrt{1 - x^2}} = \sqrt{\frac{1 - y^2}{1 - x^2}}$

Thus, the value of $\frac{dy}{dx}$ is $\sqrt{\frac{1 - y^2}{1 - x^2}}$.

(v) Given, $x = e^{\cos 2t}$ and $y = e^{\sin 2t}$

On differentiating both sides w.r.t. t using chain rule,

$\frac{dx}{dt} = e^{\cos 2t} \cdot \frac{d}{dt}(\cos 2t)$

$= -2 \sin 2t \cdot e^{\cos 2t}$

$= -2(\log y) \cdot x = -2x \log y$

and $\frac{dy}{dt} = e^{\sin 2t} \cdot \frac{d}{dt}(\sin 2t)$

$$= 2\cos 2t \cdot e^{\sin 2t} = 2\cdot(\log x)\cdot y$$
$$= 2y\log x$$

Now, $\frac{dy}{dx} = \frac{dy/dt}{dx/dt} = \frac{2y\log x}{-2x\log y}$

$$= -\frac{y\log x}{x\log y}$$

71. (b) Given, $x = 2\cos t - \cos 2t$

$\Rightarrow \frac{dx}{dt} = -2\sin t + 2\sin 2t$

$= 2(\sin 2t - \sin t)$

and $y = 2\sin t - \sin 2t$

$\Rightarrow \frac{dy}{dt} = 2(\cos t - \cos 2t)$

$\therefore \frac{dy}{dx} = \frac{dy/dt}{dx/dt}$

$\Rightarrow \frac{dy}{dx} = \frac{\cos t - \cos 2t}{\sin 2t - \sin t}$

$$= \frac{2\sin\frac{3t}{2}\cdot\sin\left(\frac{t}{2}\right)}{2\cos\frac{3t}{2}\cdot\sin\left(\frac{t}{2}\right)}$$

$\therefore \frac{dy}{dx} = \tan\left(\frac{3t}{2}\right)$

Now, at $t = \frac{\pi}{6}$,

$$\frac{dy}{dx} = \tan\left(\frac{3}{2}\cdot\frac{\pi}{6}\right) = \tan\left(\frac{\pi}{4}\right) = 1$$

72. (i) (True)

Given, $x = \cos t$ and $y = \sin t$

$\frac{dx}{dt} = -\sin t$ and $\frac{dy}{dt} = \cos t$

$\therefore \frac{dy}{dx} = -\cot t$

At $t = \frac{2\pi}{3}$, $\frac{dy}{dx} = -\cot\left(\frac{2\pi}{3}\right)$

$$= -\cot\left(\pi - \frac{\pi}{3}\right) = \cot\frac{\pi}{3} = \frac{1}{\sqrt{3}}$$

(ii) (True)

Given, $x = \sin^{-1}\left(\frac{2t}{1+t^2}\right)$

and $y = \tan^{-1}\left(\frac{2t}{1-t^2}\right), -1 < t < 1$

Put $t = \tan\theta$, then

$x = \sin^{-1}\left(\frac{2\tan\theta}{1+\tan^2\theta}\right)$

$= \sin^{-1}(\sin 2\theta) = 2\theta = 2\tan^{-1} t$

$\therefore \frac{dx}{dt} = \frac{2}{1+t^2}$

and $y = \tan^{-1}\left(\frac{2\tan\theta}{1-\tan^2\theta}\right)$

$= \tan^{-1}(\tan 2\theta) = 2\theta = 2\tan^{-1} t$

$\therefore \frac{dy}{dt} = \frac{2}{1+t^2}$

$\therefore \frac{dy}{dx} = \frac{dy/dt}{dx/dt} = \frac{2/1+t^2}{2/1+t^2} = 1$

(iii) (True)

Given, $x = e^t\left(t + \frac{1}{t}\right)$

and $y = e^{-t}\left(t - \frac{1}{t}\right)$

Now, differentiating both sides w.r.t. t, we get

$\frac{dx}{dt} = e^t\left(1 - \frac{1}{t^2}\right) + \left(t + \frac{1}{t}\right)e^t$

$= e^t\left(1 - \frac{1}{t^2} + t + \frac{1}{t}\right)$

$= e^t\left(\frac{t^2 - 1 + t^3 + t}{t^2}\right)$

and $\frac{dy}{dt} = e^{-t}\left(1 + \frac{1}{t^2}\right) + \left(t - \frac{1}{t}\right)(-e^{-t})$

$= e^{-t}\left(1 + \frac{1}{t^2} - t + \frac{1}{t}\right)$

$= e^{-t}\left(\frac{t^2 + 1 - t^3 + t}{t^2}\right)$

Now,

$\frac{dy}{dx} = \frac{dy/dt}{dx/dt} = e^{-2t}\left(\frac{-t^3 + t^2 + t + 1}{t^3 + t^2 + t - 1}\right)$

At $t = 1$, $\frac{dy}{dx} = e^{-2}\left(\frac{2}{2}\right) = \frac{1}{e^2}$

Thus, the value of $\frac{dy}{dx}$ is $\frac{1}{e^2}$.

(iv) (True)

Given, $x = a\cos^3 t$

and $y = a\sin^3 t$

$\frac{dx}{dt} = 3a\cos^2 t(-\sin t)$

and $\frac{dy}{dt} = 3a\sin^2 t(\cos t)$

$\therefore \frac{dy}{dx} = -\frac{3a\sin^2 t\cos t}{3a\cos^2 t\sin t}$

$= -\frac{\sin t}{\cos t} = -\tan t$

$\therefore \sqrt{1 + \left(\frac{dy}{dx}\right)^2} = \sqrt{1 + \tan^2 t}$

$= \sqrt{\sec^2 t} = |\sec t|$

73. (i) Let $y = x^3 + \sin x$

On differentiating both sides w.r.t. x, we get

$$\frac{dy}{dx} = 3x^2 + \cos x$$

Again, differentiating both sides w.r.t. x, we get

$$\frac{d}{dx}\left(\frac{dy}{dx}\right) = 6x + (-\sin x)$$

$$\frac{d^2y}{dx^2} = 6x - \sin x$$

(ii) Let $y = \cos(\log x)$

On differentiating both sides w.r.t. x, we get

$$\frac{dy}{dx} = -\sin(\log x) \times \frac{1}{x}$$

On differentiating both sides w.r.t. x, we get

$\frac{d^2y}{dx^2} =$

$$-\left[\frac{x\frac{d}{dx}[\sin(\log x)] - \sin(\log x).\frac{d}{dx}(x)}{x^2}\right]$$

$$= -\left[\frac{\frac{x\cos(\log x)}{x} - \sin(\log x)}{x^2}\right]$$

$$\frac{d^2y}{dx^2} = \left[\frac{\sin(\log x) - \cos(\log x)}{x^2}\right]$$

(iii) Let $y = \sin^{-1} x$

$$\frac{dy}{dx} = \frac{1}{\sqrt{1-x^2}}$$

On differentiating both sides w.r.t. x, we get

$$\frac{d^2y}{dx^2} = \frac{0 - \frac{1}{2\sqrt{1-x^2}}(-2x)}{(\sqrt{1-x^2})^2}$$

$$\frac{d^2y}{dx^2} = \frac{-x}{\sqrt{1-x^2}\,(\sqrt{1-x^2})^2}$$

$$\frac{d^2y}{dx^2} = -\frac{x}{(\sqrt{1-x^2})^3} = \frac{-x}{(1-x^2)^{3/2}}$$

(iv) We have, $e^y(x+1) = 1$

$\Rightarrow e^y = \frac{1}{x+1}$

$\Rightarrow y\log_e e = \log\left(\frac{1}{x+1}\right)$

$\Rightarrow y = -\log(x+1)$

$\Rightarrow y(x) = -\log(x+1)$

On differentiating both sides w.r.t. x, we get

$$\frac{dy}{dx} = -\frac{1}{x+1} \text{ and } \frac{d^2y}{dx^2} = \frac{1}{(x+1)^2}$$

Thus, the value of $\frac{d^2y}{dx^2}$ is $\frac{1}{(x+1)^2}$.

74. (True)

Given,

$y = A\cos(\log x) + B\sin(\log x)$

On differentiating both sides w.r.t. x, we get

$$\frac{dy}{dx} = -A\sin(\log x)\frac{1}{x} + B\cdot\cos(\log x)\cdot\frac{1}{x}$$

$$\Rightarrow x\frac{dy}{dx} = -A\sin(\log x) + B\cos(\log x)$$

Again, differentiating both sides, we get

$$x\frac{d^2y}{dx^2} + \frac{dy}{dx} = -\frac{A}{x}\cos(\log x) - \frac{B}{x}\sin(\log x)$$

$$\Rightarrow x^2\frac{d^2y}{dx^2} + x\frac{dy}{dx} = -A\cos(\log x) - B\sin(\log x) = -y$$

Thus, $x^2\dfrac{d^2y}{dx^2} + x\dfrac{dy}{dx} + y = 0$

75. (a) Given, $f(x)$ is polynomial, so it is infinitely many times differentiable.

So, now $y = f(e^x)$ (say)

$$\frac{dy}{dx} = \frac{d}{dx}\{f(e^x)\} = f'(e^x)\frac{d}{dx}(e^x) = e^x f'(e^x)$$

and

$$\frac{d^2y}{dx^2} = e^x\cdot f''(e^x)\cdot e^x + e^x\cdot f'(e^x)$$

$$\therefore \frac{d^2y}{dx^2} = f''(e^x)\cdot e^{2x} + f'(e^x)\cdot e^x$$

76. Given,

$x(t) = f(t)\cos t - f'(t)\sin t$

Then, $\dfrac{dx}{dt} = f'(t)\cos t - f(t)\sin t - f''(t)\sin t - f'(t)\cos t$

$\therefore \quad \dfrac{dx}{dt} = -f(t)\sin t - f''(t)\sin t$

and $y(t) = f(t)\sin t + f'(t)\cos t$

Then,

$$\frac{dy}{dt} = f'(t)\sin t + f(t)\cos t + f''(t)\cos t - f'(t)\sin t = f(t)\cos t + f''(t)\cos t$$

Now, $\left(\dfrac{dx}{dt}\right)^2 + \left(\dfrac{dy}{dt}\right)^2$

$$= (-f(t)\sin t - f''(t)\sin t)^2 + (f(t)\cos t + f''(t)\cos t)^2 = \{f(t) + f''(t)\}^2$$

This is required answer.

77. (b) Given, $y = x\log\left(\dfrac{x}{a+bx}\right)$

$$\Rightarrow \frac{y}{x} = \log x - \log(a+bx) \quad \left[\because \log\left(\frac{p}{q}\right) = \log p - \log q\right]$$

On differentiating both sides w.r.t. x, we get

$$\frac{x\dfrac{dy}{dx} - y}{x^2} = \frac{1}{x} - \frac{1}{a+bx}\cdot\frac{d}{dx}(a+bx) = \frac{1}{x} - \frac{b}{a+bx}$$

$$\Rightarrow x\frac{dy}{dx} - y = x^2\left\{\frac{1}{x} - \frac{b}{a+bx}\right\} = x - \frac{bx^2}{a+bx} = \frac{ax}{a+bx} \quad \ldots(i)$$

Again, differentiating both sides, we get

$$x\frac{d^2y}{dx^2} + \frac{dy}{dx} - \frac{dy}{dx} = \frac{a(a+bx) - ax\cdot b}{(a+bx)^2}$$

$$\Rightarrow x\frac{d^2y}{dx^2} + 0 = \frac{a^2}{(a+bx)^2}$$

$$\Rightarrow x^2\left\{x\frac{d^2y}{dx^2}\right\} = \frac{a^2x^2}{(a+bx)^2} = \left(x\frac{dy}{dx} - y\right)^2 \quad \text{[from Eq. (i)]}$$

$$\Rightarrow \quad x^3\frac{d^2y}{dx^2} = \left(x\frac{dy}{dx} - y\right)^2$$

78. (i) (True)

Given, $y = e^{a\cos^{-1}x}$

On differentiating both sides w.r.t. x, we get

$$\frac{dy}{dx} = e^{a\cos^{-1}x}\left(-\frac{a}{\sqrt{1-x^2}}\right)$$

$$\Rightarrow \quad \sqrt{1-x^2}\,\frac{dy}{dx} = -ae^{a\cos^{-1}x}$$

$$\Rightarrow (1-x^2)\left(\frac{dy}{dx}\right)^2 = a^2(e^{a\cos^{-1}x})^2 = a^2y^2$$

Again, on differentiating both sides, we get

$$(1-x^2)2\left(\frac{dy}{dx}\right)\left(\frac{d^2y}{dx^2}\right) - 2x\left(\frac{dy}{dx}\right)^2 = 2a^2y\frac{dy}{dx}$$

$$\Rightarrow (1-x^2)\frac{d^2y}{dx^2} - x\frac{dy}{dx} - a^2y = 0 \quad \left[\because \frac{dy}{dx} \neq 0\right]$$

(ii) (True)

Given, $x = \tan\left(\dfrac{1}{a}\log y\right)$

$\Rightarrow \quad a\tan^{-1}x = \log y$

Now, differentiating both sides w.r.t. x, we get

$$\frac{a}{1+x^2} = \frac{1}{y}\frac{dy}{dx} \Rightarrow (1+x^2)\frac{dy}{dx} = ay$$

Again, differentiating, we get

$$(1+x^2)\frac{d^2y}{dx^2} + (2x-a)\frac{dy}{dx} = 0$$

(iii) (False)

We have,

$$(x-a)^2 + (y-b)^2 = c^2 \quad \ldots(i)$$

Differentiating both sides w.r.t. x, we get

$$2(x-a) + 2(y-b)\frac{dy}{dx} = 0$$

$$\Rightarrow \quad (x-a) + (y-b)\frac{dy}{dx} = 0 \quad \ldots(ii)$$

Again, differentiating w.r.t. x, we get

$$1 + (y-b)\frac{d^2y}{dx^2} + \left(\frac{dy}{dx}\right)^2 = 0$$

$$\Rightarrow \frac{d^2y}{dx^2} = -\frac{\left\{1 + \left(\dfrac{dy}{dx}\right)^2\right\}}{(y-b)} \quad \ldots(iii)$$

From Eq. (ii), we get

$$\frac{dy}{dx} = -\left(\frac{x-a}{y-b}\right)$$

$$1 + \left(\frac{dy}{dx}\right)^2 = 1 + \frac{(x-a)^2}{(y-b)^2} = \frac{(x-a)^2 + (y-b)^2}{(y-b)^2} = \frac{c^2}{(y-b)^2} \quad \ldots(iv)$$

$$\Rightarrow \left\{1 + \left(\frac{dy}{dx}\right)^2\right\}^{3/2} = \frac{c^3}{(y-b)^3} \quad \ldots(v)$$

From Eqs. (iii) and (iv), we get

$$\frac{d^2y}{dx^2} = -\frac{c^2/(y-b)^2}{(y-b)} = -\frac{c^2}{(y-b)^3} \quad \ldots(vi)$$

From Eqs. (v) and (vi), we get

$$\frac{\left\{1 + \left(\dfrac{dy}{dx}\right)^2\right\}^{3/2}}{\left(\dfrac{d^2y}{dx^2}\right)} = \frac{c^3/(y-b)^3}{-c^2/(y-b)^3} = -c$$

79. (a) Given, $y^2 = ax^2 + bx + c$

On differentiating both sides w.r.t. x, we get

$$2y\frac{dy}{dx} = 2ax + b$$

$$\Rightarrow 2\left\{\left(\frac{dy}{dx}\right)^2 + y\frac{d^2y}{dx^2}\right\} = 2a$$

$$\Rightarrow y\frac{d^2y}{dx^2} + \left(\frac{dy}{dx}\right)^2 = a$$

$$\Rightarrow y^3\frac{d^2y}{dx^2} + \left(y\frac{dy}{dx}\right)^2 = ay^2$$

$$\Rightarrow y^3\frac{d^2y}{dx^2} + \frac{(2ax+b)^2}{4} = a(ax^2 + bx + c)$$

$$\Rightarrow y^3\frac{d^2y}{dx^2} = a^2x^2 + abx + ac - \frac{(2ax+b)^2}{4}$$

$$= \frac{4a^2x^2 + 4abx + 4ac - 4a^2x^2 - 4abx - b^2}{4}$$

$$\Rightarrow y^3\frac{d^2y}{dx^2} = \frac{4ac - b^2}{4} = \text{(constant)}$$

80. (True)

Let $u = \tan^{-1}\left(\frac{\sqrt{1+x^2}-1}{x}\right)$

and $v = \tan^{-1} x$

Put $x = \tan\theta$, we get

$$u = \tan^{-1}\left(\frac{\sqrt{1+\tan^2\theta}-1}{\tan\theta}\right)$$

$$= \tan^{-1}\left(\frac{\sec\theta - 1}{\tan\theta}\right)$$

$$= \tan^{-1}\left(\frac{1-\cos\theta}{\sin\theta}\right)$$

$$= \tan^{-1}\left(\tan\frac{\theta}{2}\right) = \frac{\theta}{2} = \frac{\tan^{-1}x}{2}$$

Thus, $u = \frac{1}{2}\tan^{-1} x$

and $v = \tan^{-1} x$

$$\frac{du}{dx} = \frac{1}{2(1+x^2)} \text{ and } \frac{dv}{dx} = \frac{1}{1+x^2}$$

Hence, $\frac{du}{dv} = \frac{du/dx}{dv/dx}$

$$= \frac{1}{2(1+x^2)}\cdot(1+x^2) = \frac{1}{2}$$

81. (b) Let

$$u = \tan^{-1}\left\{\frac{\sqrt{1+x^2}-\sqrt{1-x^2}}{\sqrt{1+x^2}+\sqrt{1-x^2}}\right\}$$

and $v = \cos^{-1} x^2$

Put $x^2 = \cos\theta$, we get

$$u = \tan^{-1}\left\{\frac{\sqrt{1+\cos\theta}-\sqrt{1-\cos\theta}}{\sqrt{1+\cos\theta}+\sqrt{1-\cos\theta}}\right\}$$

$$= \tan^{-1}\left\{\frac{\sqrt{2\cos^2\frac{\theta}{2}}-\sqrt{2\sin^2\frac{\theta}{2}}}{\sqrt{2\cos^2\frac{\theta}{2}}+\sqrt{2\sin^2\frac{\theta}{2}}}\right\}$$

$$= \tan^{-1}\left\{\frac{\cos\frac{\theta}{2}-\sin\frac{\theta}{2}}{\cos\frac{\theta}{2}+\sin\frac{\theta}{2}}\right\}$$

$$= \tan^{-1}\left\{\frac{1-\tan\frac{\theta}{2}}{1+\tan\frac{\theta}{2}}\right\}$$

$$= \tan^{-1}\left\{\tan\left(\frac{\pi}{4}-\frac{\theta}{2}\right)\right\}$$

$$\therefore u = \frac{\pi}{4} - \frac{\theta}{2} = \frac{\pi}{4} - \frac{1}{2}\cos^{-1} x^2$$

$$\frac{du}{dx} = \frac{x}{\sqrt{1-x^4}}$$

and $v = \cos^{-1} x^2$

$$\Rightarrow \frac{dv}{dx} = \frac{-1\times 2x}{\sqrt{1-x^4}}$$

Thus, $\frac{du}{dv} = \frac{du/dx}{dv/dx} = -\frac{1}{2}$

82. Let $u = \tan^{-1}\left(\frac{2x}{1-x^2}\right)$

and $v = \sin^{-1}\left(\frac{2x}{1+x^2}\right)$

Now, put $x = \tan\theta$, we get

$$u = \tan^{-1}\left(\frac{2\tan\theta}{1-\tan^2\theta}\right)$$

$$= \tan^{-1}(\tan 2\theta) = 2\theta$$

and $v = \sin^{-1}\left(\frac{2\tan\theta}{1+\tan^2\theta}\right)$

$$= \sin^{-1}(\sin 2\theta) = 2\theta$$

Since, $-1 < x < 1$

$$\Rightarrow -1 < \tan\theta < 1$$

$$\Rightarrow -\frac{\pi}{4} < \theta < \frac{\pi}{4}$$

$$\Rightarrow -\frac{\pi}{2} < 2\theta < \frac{\pi}{2}$$

Thus, $u = 2\tan^{-1} x$

and $v = 2\tan^{-1} x$

$$\therefore \frac{du}{dx} = \frac{2}{1+x^2}$$

and $\frac{dv}{dx} = \frac{2}{1+x^2}$

$$\frac{du}{dv} = \frac{du/dx}{dv/dx} = 1$$

Hence, the required value of differentiation is 1.

83. (d) Let $u = \tan^{-1}\left(\frac{\sqrt{1-x^2}}{x}\right)$

and $v = \cos^{-1}(2x\sqrt{1-x^2})$

Taking $x = \sin\theta$, then

$$\frac{1}{\sqrt{2}} < x < 1$$

$$\Rightarrow \frac{1}{\sqrt{2}} < \sin\theta < 1$$

$$\Rightarrow \frac{\pi}{4} < \theta < \frac{\pi}{2}$$

Now, $u = \tan^{-1}\left(\frac{\sqrt{1-x^2}}{x}\right)$

$$= \tan^{-1}\left(\frac{\sqrt{1-\sin^2\theta}}{\sin\theta}\right)$$

$$= \tan^{-1}(\cot\theta)$$

$$= \tan^{-1}\left[\tan\left(\frac{\pi}{2}-\theta\right)\right]$$

Since, $\frac{\pi}{4} < \theta < \frac{\pi}{2}$

$$\Rightarrow 0 < \frac{\pi}{2} - \theta < \frac{\pi}{4}$$

Thus, $u = \frac{\pi}{2} - \theta = \frac{\pi}{2} - \sin^{-1} x$

$[\because \theta = \sin^{-1} x]$

$$\frac{du}{dx} = -\frac{1}{\sqrt{1-x^2}}$$

and $v = \cos^{-1}(2x\sqrt{1-x^2})$

$$= \frac{\pi}{2} - \sin^{-1}(2x\sqrt{1-x^2})$$

$$= \frac{\pi}{2} - \sin^{-1}(\sin 2\theta)$$

$$= \frac{\pi}{2} - (\pi - 2\theta)$$

$$= 2\theta - \frac{\pi}{2}$$

$$\therefore v = -\frac{\pi}{2} + 2\sin^{-1} x$$

$[\because \theta = \sin^{-1} x]$

Thus, $\frac{dv}{dx} = \frac{2}{\sqrt{1-x^2}}$

Hence, $\frac{du}{dv} = \frac{du/dx}{dv/dx}$

$$= \frac{\frac{-1}{\sqrt{1-x^2}}}{\frac{2}{\sqrt{1-x^2}}} = -\frac{1}{2}$$

84. (i) (True)

Take $u = \sin^2 x$ and $v = e^{\cos x}$

On differentiating both sides w.r.t. x by chain rule, we get

$$\frac{du}{dx} = 2\sin x \cdot \cos x$$

and $\frac{dv}{dx} = e^{\cos x}(-\sin x)$

$$\therefore \quad \frac{du}{dv} = \frac{du/dx}{dv/dx} = \frac{2\sin x \cdot \cos x}{e^{\cos x}(-\sin x)}$$

$$= 2e^{-\cos x}(-\cos x)$$

$$= -2e^{-\cos x}\cos x$$

Thus, the required differentiate value is $(-2e^{-\cos x}\cos x)$.

(ii) (True)

Let $u = \tan^{-1}\left(\frac{\sqrt{1+x^2}-1}{x}\right)$

and $v = \sin^{-1}\left(\frac{2x}{1+x^2}\right)$

Let $x = \tan\theta$, then

$$u = \tan^{-1}\left(\frac{\sqrt{1+\tan^2\theta}-1}{\tan\theta}\right)$$

$$= \tan^{-1}\left(\frac{\sec\theta - 1}{\tan\theta}\right)$$

$$= \tan^{-1}\left(\frac{1-\cos\theta}{\sin\theta}\right)$$

$$= \tan^{-1}\left(\frac{2\sin^2\frac{\theta}{2}}{2\sin\frac{\theta}{2}\cos\frac{\theta}{2}}\right)$$

$$= \tan^{-1}\left(\tan\frac{\theta}{2}\right)$$

Since, $-1 < x < 1$

$\Rightarrow \quad -1 < \tan\theta < 1$

$\Rightarrow \quad -\frac{\pi}{4} < \theta < \frac{\pi}{4} \Rightarrow -\frac{\pi}{8} < \frac{\theta}{2} < \frac{\pi}{8}$

Thus, $u = \tan^{-1}\left(\tan\frac{\theta}{2}\right)$

$$= \frac{\theta}{2} = \frac{\tan^{-1}x}{2}$$

$[\because \theta = \tan^{-1}x]$

$$\therefore \quad \frac{du}{dx} = \frac{1}{2(1+x^2)}$$

Again, $v = \sin^{-1}\left(\frac{2x}{1+x^2}\right)$

$$= \sin^{-1}\left(\frac{2\tan\theta}{1+\tan^2\theta}\right) = \sin^{-1}(\sin 2\theta)$$

$$= 2\theta = 2\tan^{-1}x$$

$$\therefore \frac{dv}{dx} = \frac{2}{1+x^2}$$

Hence, $\frac{du}{dv} = \frac{du/dx}{dv/dx}$

$$= \frac{\frac{1}{2(1+x^2)}}{2/(1+x^2)} = \frac{1}{4}$$

Assertion-Reason

1. (d) For $x < 0$,

$$\frac{d}{dx}(\ln|-x|) = \frac{d}{dx}(\ln x)$$

$[\because \text{ for } x < 0, |x| = -x]$

$$= \frac{1}{x}$$

$\therefore$ Assertion is false.

2. (c) We have, $y = \log_{10} x + \log_e y$

$$\Rightarrow \quad y = \frac{\log x}{\log 10} \times \frac{\log e}{\log e} + \frac{\log y}{\log e}$$

So, $\frac{dy}{dx} = \frac{\log_{10} e}{x} + \frac{1}{y}\frac{dy}{dx}$

$$\Rightarrow \quad \frac{dy}{dx}\left(1 - \frac{1}{y}\right) = \frac{\log_{10} e}{x}$$

$$\Rightarrow \quad \frac{dy}{dx} = \frac{\log_{10} e}{x}\left(\frac{y}{y-1}\right)$$

$\therefore$ Assertion is true.

Also, $\frac{d}{dx}(\log_{10} x) = \frac{\log_{10} e}{x}$

$\therefore$ Reason is false.

3. (d) We know that a function $f(x)$ is continuous at point $x = a$ if $\lim_{x \to a} f(x) = f(a)$.

$\Rightarrow \quad \lim_{x \to 2} f(x) = f(2)$

$\Rightarrow \quad \lim_{h \to 0}(2(2-h)-1)$

$= \lim_{h \to 0}((2+h)+1) = k$

$\Rightarrow \quad 4 - 0 - 1 = 2 + 0 + 1 = k$

$\Rightarrow \quad k = 3$

$\therefore$ Assertion is false.

4. (b) Here, $|x| = \begin{cases} x, & x \geq 0 \\ -x, & x < 0 \end{cases}$

and $|x-1| = \begin{cases} x-1, & x \geq 1 \\ -(x-1), & x < 1 \end{cases}$

$$\therefore \quad f(x) = |x| + |x-1|$$

$$= \begin{cases} 1-2x, & x < 0 \\ 1, & 0 \leq x < 1 \\ 2x-1, & x \geq 1 \end{cases}$$

At $x = 0$, $f(0) = 1$

$$\text{RHL} = \lim_{x \to 0^+} f(x) = \lim_{h \to 0} f(0+h)$$

$$= \lim_{h \to 0} 1 = 1$$

$$\text{LHL} = \lim_{x \to 0^-} f(x) = \lim_{h \to 0} f(0-h)$$

$$= \lim_{h \to 0} 1 = 1$$

$\therefore$ RHL $= f(0) =$ LHL

$\because f(x)$ is continuous at $x = 0$

Similarly, $f(x)$ is continuous at $x = 1$

Let us check the differentiability at $x = 0$,

For differentiability, LHD (at $x = 0$) = RHD (at $x = 0$)

At $x = 0$

$$\text{LHD} = \lim_{x \to 0^-} \frac{f(x) - f(0)}{x - 0}$$

$$= \lim_{x \to 0^-} \frac{2x+1-1}{x-0}$$

$$= \lim_{x \to 0^-} \frac{2x}{x} = 2$$

$$\text{RHD} = \lim_{x \to 0^+} \frac{f(x) - f(0)}{x - 0}$$

$$= \lim_{x \to 0^+} \frac{1-1}{x} = 0$$

$\because$ LDH $\neq$ RHD

$\therefore f(x)$ is not differentiable at $x = 0$

Similarly, $f(x)$ is not differentiable at $x = 1$.

$\therefore$ Assertion is true.

5. (b) We have, $y = \log(\sin e^x)$

$$\frac{dy}{dx} = \frac{1}{\sin e^x}\cos(e^x) \cdot e^x$$

$$= e^x \cot(e^x)$$

6. (d) We have, $x = a\sin\theta$,

$y = a\cos\theta$

So, $\frac{dx}{d\theta} = a\cos\theta$, $\frac{dy}{d\theta} = -\sin\theta$

$$\Rightarrow \quad \frac{dy}{dx} = \frac{\frac{dy}{d\theta}}{\frac{dx}{d\theta}} = \frac{-a\sin\theta}{a\cos\theta} = -\tan\theta$$

So, $\frac{d^2y}{dx^2} = \frac{d}{dx}\left(\frac{dy}{dx}\right)$

$$= \frac{d}{d\theta}\left(\frac{dy}{dx}\right)\frac{d\theta}{dx}$$

$$= -\sec^2\theta \cdot \frac{1}{a\cos\theta}$$

$$= -\frac{1}{a}\sec^3\theta$$

$\therefore$ Assertion is false.

7. (b) We have, $\sin y = x \sin(a + y)$

$\Rightarrow \quad x = \dfrac{\sin y}{\sin(a+y)}$

$$\text{So,} \quad \frac{dx}{dy} = \frac{\cos y \sin(a+y) - \sin y \cos(a+y)}{\sin^2(a+y)}$$

$$= \frac{\sin(a+y-y)}{\sin^2(a+y)} = \frac{\sin a}{\sin^2(a+y)}$$

$$\Rightarrow \frac{dy}{dx} = \frac{\sin^2(a+y)}{\sin a}$$

8. (b) $\dfrac{d}{dx}(e^{\cos x})$

$$= \frac{d}{dx}(e^{\cos x}) \cdot \frac{d}{dx}(\cos x)$$

$$= e^{\cos x}(-\sin x)$$

$$\frac{d}{dx}(e^x) = e^x$$

9. (c) We know that
If $f(a) = \lim\limits_{x \to a} f(x)$, then $f(x)$ is continuous at $x = a$, while both hand limit must exist. If $f(x)$ is continuous at a point, then it is not necessary that $\dfrac{1}{f(x)}$ is also continuous at that point.
e.g. $f(x) = x$ is continuous at $x = 0$ but $f(x) = \dfrac{1}{x}$ is not continuous at $x = 0$.

10. (a) $f(x) = [x]$ is not continuous when x is an integer. So, $f(x)$ is not continuous at $x = 2$.
A differential function is always continuous. Since, $f(x) = [x]$ is not continuous at $x = 2$, it is also not differentiable at $x = 2$.

Case Based

1. (i) (c) Let

$$y = \sqrt{\sin\sqrt{x}} = (\sin\sqrt{x})^{\frac{1}{2}}$$

On differentiating both sides w.r.t. x, we get

$$\frac{dy}{dx} = \frac{d}{dx}(\sin\sqrt{x})^{\frac{1}{2}}$$

$$= \frac{1}{2}(\sin\sqrt{x})^{\frac{1}{2}-1} \frac{d}{dx}(\sin\sqrt{x})$$

$$= \frac{1}{2}(\sin\sqrt{x})^{\frac{-1}{2}} \cos\sqrt{x} \, \frac{d}{dx}(\sqrt{x})$$

$$= \frac{1}{2\sqrt{\sin\sqrt{x}}} \cos\sqrt{x} \cdot \frac{1}{2\sqrt{x}}$$

$$= \frac{\cos\sqrt{x}}{4\sqrt{\sin\sqrt{x}}}$$

(ii) (b) Let $y = \cos(x^3)$
On differentiating both sides w.r.t. x, we get

$$\frac{dy}{dx} = -\sin x^3 (3x^2) = -3x^2 \sin x^3$$

(iii) (a) Let $y = \ln(\sin x - \cot x)$
On differentiating both sides w.r.t. x, we get

$$\frac{dy}{dx} = \frac{d}{dx}(\ln(\sin x - \cot x))$$

$$= \frac{1}{(\sin x - \cot x)} \frac{d}{dx}(\sin x - \cot x)$$

$$= \frac{1}{(\sin x - \cot x)}(\cos x + \operatorname{cosec}^2 x)$$

$$= \frac{\cos x + \operatorname{cosec}^2 x}{\sin x - \cot x}$$

2. (i) (b) Given,

$$x^3 + x^2 y + xy^2 + y^3 = 81$$

$$\Rightarrow 3x^2 + x^2\frac{dy}{dx} + 2xy + 2xy\frac{dy}{dx} + y^2 + 3y^2\frac{dy}{dx} = 0$$

$$\Rightarrow (x^2 + 2xy + 3y^2)\frac{dy}{dx} = -3x^2 - 2xy - y^2$$

$$\Rightarrow \frac{dy}{dx} = \frac{-(3x^2 + 2xy + y^2)}{x^2 + 2xy + 3y^2}$$

(ii) (c) Given, $x^y = e^{x-y}$
On taking log both sides, we get

$$\Rightarrow y \cdot \log x = x - y$$

$$\Rightarrow y \times \frac{1}{x} + \log x \cdot \frac{dy}{dx} = 1 - \frac{dy}{dx}$$

$$\Rightarrow \frac{dy}{dx}(\log x + 1) = 1 - \frac{y}{x}$$

$$\Rightarrow \frac{dy}{dx} = \frac{x - y}{x(1 + \log x)}$$

(iii) (d) $\sin^2 x + \cos^2 y = 1$

$$\Rightarrow 2\sin x \cdot \cos x + 2\cos y\left(-\sin y \cdot \frac{dy}{dx}\right) = 0$$

$$\Rightarrow \frac{dy}{dx} = \frac{-\sin 2x}{-\sin 2y} \Rightarrow \frac{dy}{dx} = \frac{\sin 2x}{\sin 2y}$$

Competition Connect

1. (True)

$$\text{We have, } y = \begin{vmatrix} f(x) & g(x) & h(x) \\ l & m & n \\ a & b & c \end{vmatrix}$$

$$\frac{dy}{dx} = \begin{vmatrix} \frac{d}{dx}\{f(x)\} & \frac{d}{dx}\{g(x)\} & \frac{d}{dx}\{h(x)\} \\ l & m & n \\ a & b & c \end{vmatrix} + \begin{vmatrix} f(x) & g(x) & h(x) \\ \frac{d}{dx}(l) & \frac{d}{dx}(m) & \frac{d}{dx}(n) \\ a & b & c \end{vmatrix} + \begin{vmatrix} f(x) & g(x) & h(x) \\ l & m & n \\ \frac{d}{dx}(a) & \frac{d}{dx}(b) & \frac{d}{dx}(c) \end{vmatrix}$$

$$= \begin{vmatrix} f'(x) & g'(x) & h'(x) \\ l & m & n \\ a & b & c \end{vmatrix} + \begin{vmatrix} f(x) & g(x) & h(x) \\ 0 & 0 & 0 \\ a & b & c \end{vmatrix} + \begin{vmatrix} f(x) & g(x) & h(x) \\ l & m & n \\ 0 & 0 & 0 \end{vmatrix}$$

$$\therefore \frac{dy}{dx} = \begin{vmatrix} f'(x) & g'(x) & h'(x) \\ l & m & n \\ a & b & c \end{vmatrix} + 0 + 0$$

$$\Rightarrow \frac{dy}{dx} = \begin{vmatrix} f'(x) & g'(x) & h'(x) \\ l & m & n \\ a & b & c \end{vmatrix}$$

2. (b) Since, $f(x)$, $g(x)$ and $h(x)$ all are polynomial of dgree 2, then

$$f(x) = a_1 x^2 + a_2 x + a_3$$
$$g(x) = b_1 x^2 + b_2 x + b_3$$
$$\text{and } h(x) = c_1 x^2 + c_2 x + c_3$$
$$f'(x) = 2a_1 x + a_2$$
$$g'(x) = 2b_1 x + b_2$$
$$\text{and } h'(x) = 2c_1 x + c_2$$
$$f''(x) = 2a_1, \; g''(x) = 2b_1$$
$$\text{and } h''(x) = 2c_1$$
$$f'''(x) = 0, \; g'''(x) = 0, \; h'''(x) = 0$$

Now, given

$$\phi(x) = \begin{vmatrix} f(x) & g(x) & h(x) \\ f'(x) & g'(x) & h'(x) \\ f''(x) & g''(x) & h''(x) \end{vmatrix}$$

$$\phi'(x) = \begin{vmatrix} f'(x) & g'(x) & h'(x) \\ f'(x) & g'(x) & h'(x) \\ f''(x) & g''(x) & h''(x) \end{vmatrix} + \begin{vmatrix} f(x) & g(x) & h(x) \\ f''(x) & g''(x) & h''(x) \\ f''(x) & g''(x) & h''(x) \end{vmatrix} + \begin{vmatrix} f(x) & g(x) & h(x) \\ f'(x) & g'(x) & h'(x) \\ f'''(x) & g'''(x) & h'''(x) \end{vmatrix}$$

$$\phi'(x) = 0$$

$\Rightarrow \phi(x)$ is a constant polynomial.

Chapter-6

Application of Derivatives

1. (i) Let r be the radius, V be the volume and S be the surface area of the sphere.

Then, $V = \frac{4}{3}\pi r^3$ and $S = 4\pi r^2$

Now, find $\frac{dV}{dS}$,

Since, $V = \frac{4}{3}\pi r^3$ and $S = 4\pi r^2$

$\therefore \quad \frac{dV}{dr} = 4\pi r^2$ and $\frac{dS}{dr} = 8\pi r$

$$\frac{dV}{dS} = \frac{dV/dr}{dS/dr} = \frac{4\pi r^2}{8\pi r} = \frac{r}{2}$$

(ii) Let x be the side of cube, V be the volume of cube and S be the surface area of cube.

$\therefore V = x^3$ and $S = 6x^2$

$\frac{dV}{dx} = 3x^2$ and $\frac{dS}{dx} = 12x$

Now, $\frac{dV}{dS} = \frac{dV/dx}{dS/dx} = \frac{3x^2}{12x} = \frac{x}{4}$

2. (i) (False)

Given, $r = 2.2$ cm

Then, we know the area of a circle, $A = \pi r^2$

$\therefore$ The rate of change of the area with respect to radius is given by

$$\frac{dA}{dr} = \frac{d}{dr}(\pi r^2) = 2\pi r$$

Since, $r = 2.2$ cm

$\therefore \quad \frac{dA}{dr} = 2\pi(2.2) = 4.4\pi$

Thus, the rate of change of area of a circle w.r.t. radius is 4.4 π.

(ii) (True)

Given, $x = 4$ cm

We know that area of equilateral triangle, $A = \frac{\sqrt{3}}{4}x^2$

$\therefore \quad \frac{dA}{dx} = \frac{\sqrt{3}}{4}(2x) = \frac{\sqrt{3}}{2}x$

$\Rightarrow \left(\frac{dA}{dx}\right)_{x=4} = \frac{\sqrt{3}}{2} \times 4$

$= 2\sqrt{3}$ cm

Hence, the rate of change of area of equilateral triangle with respect to side is $2\sqrt{3}$ cm.

(iii) (True)

Given, $x = 5$ cm

We know that area of square,

$$A = x^2$$

$$\frac{dA}{dx} = 2x$$

$\Rightarrow \left(\frac{dA}{dx}\right)_{x=5} = 2 \times 5 = 10$

$\therefore$ Rate of change of area of square with respect to side of square is 10 cm.

3. (d) The area of a circle with radius r is πr^2 i.e. $A = \pi r^2$

Therefore, the rate of change of area A with respect to time t is

$$\frac{dA}{dt} = \frac{d}{dt}(\pi r^2) = \frac{d}{dr}(\pi r^2)\frac{dr}{dt}$$

$= (2\pi r)\cdot\frac{dr}{dt}$ [by chain rule]

Since, $\frac{dr}{dt} = 5$ cm/s

Hence, $\frac{dA}{dt} = (2\pi r)\cdot 5 = 10\pi r$

So, when $r = 9$ cm

Then, $\frac{dA}{dt} = 10\pi(9) = 90\pi$ cm^2/s

4. (True)

Let r be the radius and V be the volume of the balloon.

Then, $V = \frac{4}{3}\pi r^3 \Rightarrow \frac{dV}{dr} = 4\pi r^2$

When $r = 7$, then $\frac{dV}{dr} = 4\pi(7)^2$

$= 196\pi$ cm^2

Thus, the volume is increasing with respect to its radius at the rate 196π cm^2, when the radius is 7 cm.

5. Let the length of edge and the volume of the cube respectively be x and V, then $V = x^3$

Now, $\frac{dV}{dt} = \frac{d}{dt}(x^3) = 3x^2\frac{dx}{dt}$

Given, $\frac{dx}{dt} = 3$ cm/s

Thus, $\frac{dV}{dt} = 3x^2(3) = 9x^2$

When $x = 9$ cm, then

$$\frac{dV}{dt} = 9(9)^2 = 729 \text{ cm}^3/\text{s}$$

Hence, the volume of the cube is increasing at the rate of 729 cm^3/s.

6. (d) Let x be the length of a side, V be the volume and S be the surface area of the cube.

Then, $V = x^3$ and $S = 6x^2$

$\Rightarrow \quad \frac{dV}{dt} = 9$ cm^3/s

$\therefore \quad \frac{dV}{dt} = \frac{d}{dt}(x^3) = 3x^2\cdot\frac{dx}{dt}$

$\therefore \quad 9 = 3x^2\cdot\frac{dx}{dt}$

$\Rightarrow \quad \frac{dx}{dt} = \frac{3}{x^2}$ ...(i)

Now, $\frac{dS}{dt} = \frac{d}{dt}(6x^2)$

$= \frac{d}{dx}(6x^2)\cdot\frac{dx}{dt} = \frac{36}{x}$

Thus, $\frac{dS}{dt} = \frac{36}{x}$

When $x = 9$ cm, then

$\frac{dS}{dt} = \frac{36}{9}$ cm^2/s

$= 4$ cm^2/s

7. (True)

Let m be the slope of the curve at xy arbitrary point (x, y) on it.

Then, $m = \frac{dy}{dx}$ ...(i)

Given, $y = 5x - 2x^3$

$\Rightarrow \quad \frac{dy}{dx} = 5 - 6x^2$

$\therefore \quad m = 5 - 6x^2$ [from Eq. (i)]

Given, $\frac{dx}{dt} = 2$ units/s

and we have to find $\frac{dm}{dt}$, when $x = 3$

Thus, $m = 5 - 6x^2$

$\Rightarrow \quad \frac{dm}{dt} = -12x\frac{dx}{dt}$

At $x = 3$,

$\frac{dm}{dt} = -12\cdot(3)\cdot(2)$

$= -72$ units/s

Thus, the slope of the curve is decreasing at the rate of 72 units/s.

8. (b) Let A_1 and A_2 denote the area of squares of sides a and b, respectively.

Then, $A_1 = a^2$ and $A_2 = b^2$

$\Rightarrow \quad A_1 = a^2$ and $A_2 = (a + a^2)^2$

[$\because b = a + a^2$

$$\therefore \quad \frac{dA_1}{da} = 2a$$

and $\dfrac{dA_2}{da} = 2(a + a^2) \cdot (1 + 2a)$

Now, $\dfrac{dA_2}{dA_1} = \dfrac{dA_2 / da}{dA_1 / da}$

$$= \frac{2(a + a^2)(1 + 2a)}{2a}$$

$$= (1 + a)(1 + 2a)$$

$$= 1 + 3a + 2a^2$$

9. (a) Let A be the area and P be the perimeter of the rectangle at any time t.

Then, $P = 2(x + y)$ and $A = xy$

It is given $\dfrac{dx}{dt} = -2$ cm/s

and $\dfrac{dy}{dt} = 2$ cm/s

For Statement I

Given, $P = 2(x + y)$

$$\Rightarrow \frac{dP}{dt} = 2\left(\frac{dx}{dt} + \frac{dy}{dt}\right)$$

$$= 2(-2 + 2) = 0 \text{ cm/s}$$

Thus, the rate of change of the perimeter remains constant.

For Statement II

Given, $A = xy$

$$\Rightarrow \frac{dA}{dt} = \frac{d}{dt}(xy)$$

$$= x\left(\frac{dy}{dt}\right) + y \cdot \left(\frac{dx}{dt}\right)$$

$$\Rightarrow \frac{dA}{dt} = (12) \cdot (2) + (5) \cdot (-2)$$

$$= 14 \text{ cm}^2/\text{s}$$

Thus, the rate of change of area of rectangle is 14 cm^2/s.

10. (True)

Let α be the semi-vertical angle of the water tank of the form of cone.

Then, $\alpha = \tan^{-1}\left(\dfrac{1}{3}\right)$

$$\Rightarrow \tan \alpha = \frac{1}{3}$$

$$\Rightarrow \frac{r}{h} = \frac{1}{3} \Rightarrow r = \frac{h}{3}$$

Let V be the volume of water in water tank.

Then, $\dfrac{dV}{dt} = 7$ m^3/s

We have to find $\dfrac{dh}{dt}$, when $h = 4$ m

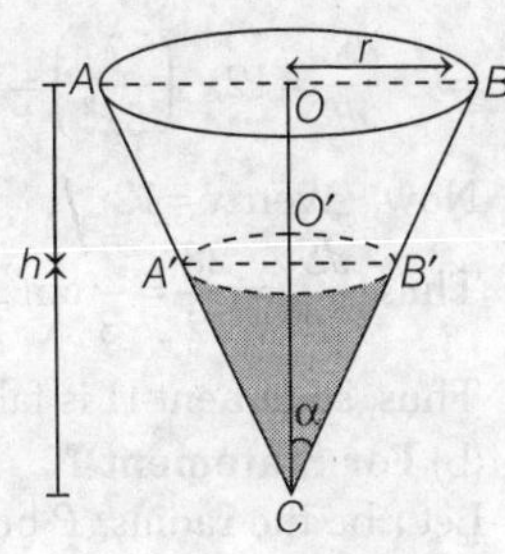

Now, $V = \dfrac{\pi}{3} r^2 h = \dfrac{1}{3}\pi\left(\dfrac{h}{3}\right)^2 \cdot h$

$$= \frac{1}{3} \cdot \frac{\pi}{9} h^3 = \frac{\pi h^3}{27}$$

$$\Rightarrow V = \frac{\pi h^3}{27}$$

$$\Rightarrow \frac{dV}{dt} = \frac{\pi}{27} \cdot 3h^2 \frac{dh}{dt}$$

$$\Rightarrow 7 = \frac{\pi}{27} \cdot 3 \cdot 4^2 \cdot \frac{dh}{dt}$$

$$\Rightarrow \frac{dh}{dt} = \frac{7 \times 27}{3 \times 16 \times \pi}$$

$$= \frac{7 \times 27 \times 7}{3 \times 16 \times 22} = \frac{441}{352} \text{ m/s}$$

11. (a) Let AB be the position of the ladder at any time t such that

$$OA = x \text{ and } OB = y$$

Then, $OA^2 + OB^2 = AB^2$

$$\Rightarrow x^2 + y^2 = 10^2$$

$$\Rightarrow x^2 + y^2 = 100 \quad \ldots\text{(i)}$$

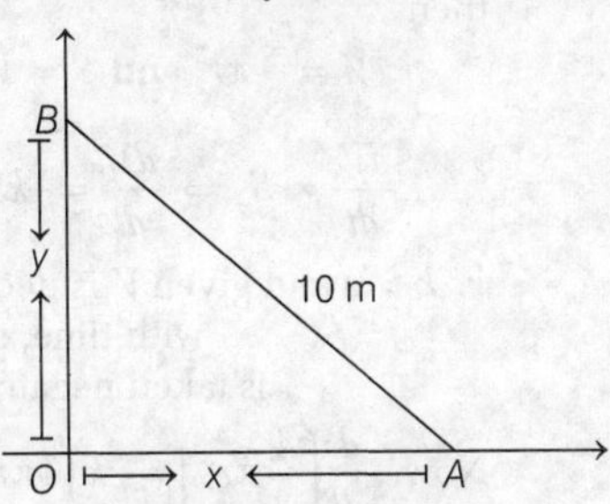

It is given that the bottom of the ladder is pulled along the ground away from the wall at the rate of 2 m/s.

$$\therefore \quad \frac{dx}{dt} = 2 \text{ m/s}$$

Now, $x^2 + y^2 = 100$

Differentiating both sides w.r.t. t, we get

$$2x\frac{dx}{dt} + 2y\frac{dy}{dt} = 0$$

$$\Rightarrow 2 \cdot x \cdot (2) + 2y\frac{dy}{dt} = 0 \quad \left[\because \frac{dx}{dt} = 2\right]$$

$$\Rightarrow \frac{dy}{dt} = -\frac{2x}{y} \quad \ldots\text{(ii)}$$

Putting $x = 6$ in Eq. (i), we get

$$y = \sqrt{100 - 36} = 8$$

Putting $x = 6$ and $y = 8$ in Eq. (ii), we get

$$\frac{dy}{dt} = -\frac{3}{2} \text{ m/s}$$

Hence, the rate of decrease in the height of the ladder on the wall is $\dfrac{3}{2}$ m/s.

12. (True)

Let r be the radius and h be the height and V be the volume of the sand-cone at any time t.

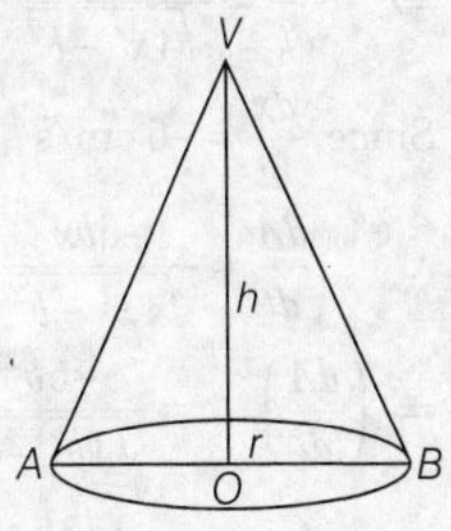

Then, $V = \dfrac{1}{3}\pi r^2 h$

Since, $r = 6h$, then

$$V = \frac{1}{3}\pi(6h)^2 \cdot h$$

$$= 12\pi h^3$$

$$\therefore \quad \frac{dV}{dt} = 36\pi h^2\left(\frac{dh}{dt}\right)$$

Since, $\dfrac{dV}{dt} = 12$ [given]

$$\therefore \quad 12 = 36\pi h^2\left(\frac{dh}{dt}\right)$$

$$\therefore \quad \frac{dh}{dt} = \frac{1}{3\pi h^2}$$

Now, at $h = 4$,

$$\frac{dh}{dt} = \frac{1}{3\pi(4)^2} = \frac{1}{48\pi}$$

13. (False)

Let length of each equal side be x cm and area of triangle be A at any time t.

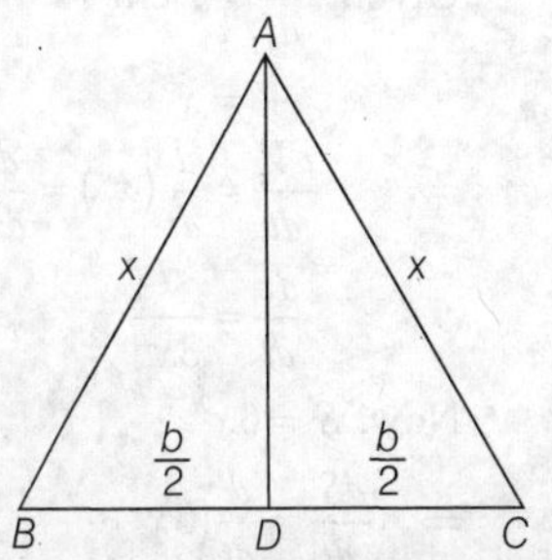

Then, $A = \frac{1}{2}(AD \times BC)$

$\Rightarrow \quad A = \frac{1}{2} \times \sqrt{x^2 - \frac{b^2}{4}} \times b$

$\Rightarrow \quad A = \frac{b}{4}\sqrt{4x^2 - b^2}$

$\Rightarrow \quad \frac{dA}{dt} = \frac{d}{dt}\left\{\frac{b}{4}\sqrt{4x^2 - b}\right\}$

$= \frac{d}{dx}\left\{\frac{b}{4}\sqrt{4x^2 - b}\right\} \cdot \frac{dx}{dt}$

$= \frac{b}{8\sqrt{4x^2 - b^2}} \cdot (8x) \cdot \frac{dx}{dt}$

$\Rightarrow \quad \frac{dA}{dt} = \frac{bx}{\sqrt{4x^2 - b^2}} \cdot \frac{dx}{dt}$

Since, $\frac{dx}{dt} = -6$ cm/s

$\therefore \quad \frac{dA}{dt} = \frac{-6bx}{\sqrt{4x^2 - b^2}}$

$\Rightarrow \left(\frac{dA}{dt}\right)_{x=b} = \frac{-6b^2}{\sqrt{4b^2 - b^2}} = \frac{-6b^2}{\sqrt{3}b}$

$= -2\sqrt{3}b$ cm²/s

Hence, the area is decreasing by $2\sqrt{3}b$ cm²/s.

14. (c) **For Statement I**

Let x be the length of each edge of the cube, S be its surface area and V be its volume at any time t.

Then, $V = x^3$ and $S = 6x^2$

and $\frac{dV}{dt} = k$ (say constant)

Given, $V = x^3$

$\Rightarrow \quad \frac{dV}{dt} = 3x^2 \frac{dx}{dt}$

$\Rightarrow \quad \frac{dx}{dt} = \frac{k}{3x^2}$ and $S = 6x^2$

$\Rightarrow \quad \frac{dS}{dt} = 12x \cdot \frac{dx}{dt} \Rightarrow \frac{dS}{dt} = \frac{4k}{x}$

$\therefore \quad \frac{dS}{dt} \propto \frac{1}{x}$

$\therefore$ Statement I is true.

For Statement II

Given, $\frac{dV}{dt} = 7$ cm³/s

$V = x^3$

$\Rightarrow \quad \frac{dV}{dt} = \frac{d}{dt}(x^3) = \frac{d}{dx}(x^3)\frac{dx}{dt}$

$\therefore \quad \frac{dx}{dt} = \frac{7}{3x^2}$

Now, $S = 6x^2$

$\Rightarrow \quad \frac{dS}{dt} = \frac{d}{dt}(6x^2)$

$\Rightarrow \quad \frac{dS}{dt} = 12x \cdot \left(\frac{7}{3x^2}\right) = \frac{28}{x}$

Now, given $x = 12$

Thus, $\frac{dS}{dt} = \frac{28}{12} = \frac{7}{3}$ cm²/s

Thus, statement II is false.

15. (b) **For Statement I**

Let r be the radius, P be the perimeter and A be the area of the circle at any time t.

Then, $A = \pi r^2$ and $P = 2\pi r$

Given, $\frac{dA}{dt} = k$ (say constant)

Now, $A = \pi r^2$ and $P = 2\pi r$

$\Rightarrow \quad A = \frac{P^2}{4\pi}$

$\therefore \quad \frac{dA}{dt} = \frac{1}{4\pi} \cdot 2P\frac{dP}{dt}$

$\therefore \quad k = \frac{1}{2\pi}(2\pi r) \cdot \frac{dP}{dt}$

$\left[\because \frac{dA}{dt} = k \text{ and } P = 2\pi r\right]$

$\Rightarrow \quad \frac{dP}{dt} = \frac{k}{r}$

Statement I is correct.

For Statement II

Let V, S and r denote the volume, surface area and radius of the salt ball at any instant t, then

$V = \frac{4}{3}\pi r^3$ and $S = 4\pi r^2$

$\frac{dV}{dt} \propto S \Rightarrow \frac{dV}{dt} = -kS$

[$\because k > 0$ and given V is decreasing with time, so there is taken negative sign]

Now, $\frac{d}{dt}\left(\frac{4}{3}\pi r^3\right) = -k(4\pi r^2)$

$\therefore \quad \frac{dr}{dt} = -k$

$\Rightarrow r$ decreases with a constant rate.

Hence, Statement II is correct.

16. (True)

Since, the marginal cost is the rate of change of total cost with respect to the output.

$\therefore$ Marginal cost (MC) $= \frac{d}{dx}\{C(x)\}$

$= \frac{d}{dx}(0.005x^3 - 0.02x^2 + 30x + 5000)$

$= 0.005(3x^2) - 0.02(2x) + 30$

When $x = 3$, then

Marginal cost

$= 0.005 \cdot 3 \cdot 3^2 - 0.02 \cdot 2 \cdot 3 + 30$

$= 0.135 - 0.12 + 30$

$= 30.015$

$= 30.02$ (nearly)

17. (a) Since, the marginal revenue is the rate of change of total revenue with respect to the numbers of units sold.

$\therefore$ Marginal revenue

$= \frac{dR}{dx} = \frac{d}{dx}(13x^2 + 26x + 15)$

$= 26x + 26$

When $x = 7$, then

Marginal revenue

$= 26 \times 7 + 26 = 182 + 26$

$= 208$

18. (i) (True)

Let $x_1, x_2 \in [0, \infty)$ such that $x_1 < x_2$.

Then, $x_1 < x_2 \Rightarrow x_1^2 < x_1 x_2$ [multiplying both sides by x_1]

and $x_1 < x_2 \Rightarrow x_1 x_2 < x_2^2$ [multiplying both sides by x_2]

Thus, from above,

$x_1^2 < x_1 x_2 < x_2^2$

$\therefore \quad x_1 < x_2 \Rightarrow x_1^2 < x_2^2$

$\Rightarrow f(x_1) < f(x_2) \ \forall \ x_1, x_2 \in [0, \infty)$

Hence, by the definition of strictly increasing function $f(x)$ is strictly increasing on $[0, \infty)$.

(ii) (True)

Let x_1 and x_2 be any two numbers in R.

Then, $x_1 < x_2$

$\Rightarrow \quad 7x_1 < 7x_2 \Rightarrow 7x_1 - 3 < 7x_2 - 3$

$\Rightarrow f(x_1) < f(x_2)$

Thus, by definition of strictly increasing function, $f(x)$ is strictly increasing, hence increasing.

Thus, f is increasing function on R.

(iii) (True)

Let $x_1, x_2 \in R$ such that $x_1 < x_2$.

Then, $x_1 < x_2 \Rightarrow -3x_1 > -3x_2$

$\Rightarrow \quad -3x_1 + 4 > -3x_2 + 4$

$\Rightarrow \quad f(x_1) > f(x_2)$

Thus, $x_1 < x_2$

$\Rightarrow f(x_1) > f(x_2) \ \forall \ x_1, x_2 \in R$

So, $f(x)$ is strictly decreasing function on R.

(iv) (True)

$f(x)=x^2$ is strictly increasing on $[0, \infty)$ and strictly decreasing on $(-\infty, 0]$. Then, from above, it is clear that $f(x)=x^2$ is neither strictly increasing nor strictly decreasing on R.

19. (b) **For Statement I**

When $0<a<1$, for any $x_1, x_2 \in (0, \infty)$.

Then, $x_1 > x_2 \Rightarrow \log_a x_1 < \log_a x_2$

$\Rightarrow f(x_1) < f(x_2)$

So, $f(x)$ is decreasing on $(0, \infty)$.

For Statement II

When $a>1$, for any $x_1, x_2 \in (0, \infty)$

Then, $x_1 > x_2$

$\Rightarrow \log_a x_1 > \log_a x_2$

$\Rightarrow f(x_1) > f(x_2)$

So, $f(x)$ is increasing on $(0, \infty)$.

20. (a) **For Statement I**

Let $x_1, x_2 \in R$ such that $x_1 < x_2$.

Then, $x_1 < x_2 \Rightarrow a^{x_1} < a^{x_2}$

[$\because a>1$, so $x_1 < x_2 \Rightarrow a^{x_1} < a^{x_2}$]

$\Rightarrow \quad f(x_1) < f(x_2)$

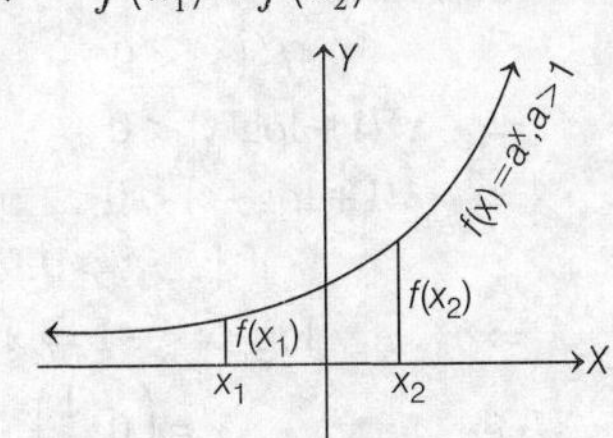

Hence, $f(x)=a^x$ is strictly increasing function on R if $a>1$.

For Statement II

Let $x_1, x_2 \in R$ such that $x_1 < x_2$.

Then, $x_1 < x_2 \Rightarrow a^{x_1} > a^{x_2}$

$\Rightarrow f(x_1) > f(x_2)\ \forall\ x_1, x_2 \in R$

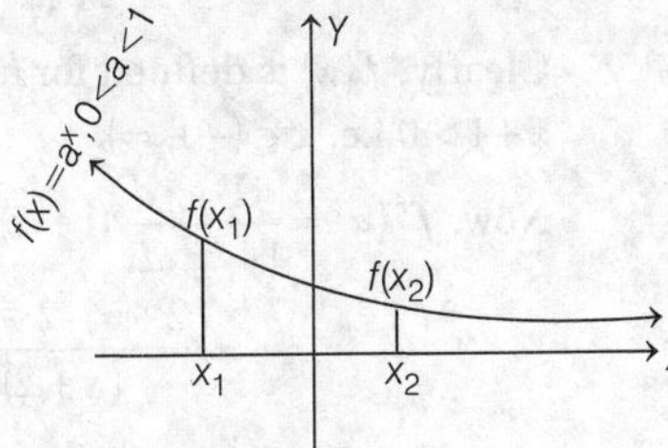

Hence, $f(x)=a^x$ is strictly decreasing function on R if $0<a<1$.

21. (i) Given,

$$f(x)=x^3-3x^2+4x,\ x \in R$$

$$\therefore f'(x)=3x^2-6x+4$$

$$=3(x^2-2x+1)+1$$

$$=3(x-1)^2+1>0,$$

in any interval of R.

Therefore, the function f is increasing on R.

(ii) Given,

$$f(x)=2x^3-9x^2+12x+25$$

$$\therefore f'(x)=6x^2-18x+12$$

$$=6(x^2-3x+2)$$

$$=6(x-1)(x-2)$$

Since, the function $f(x)$ is increasing, so we must have

$$f'(x)>0$$

$\Rightarrow 6(x-1)(x-2)>0$

$\Rightarrow (x-1)(x-2)>0$

$\Rightarrow \quad x<1$ or $x>2$

$\Rightarrow x \in (-\infty, 1) \cup (2, \infty)$

So, $f(x)$ is increasing on $(-\infty, 1) \cup (2, \infty)$.

(iii) Given, $f(x)=\dfrac{4x^2+1}{x}=4x+\dfrac{1}{x}$

$$\therefore \quad f'(x)=4-\frac{1}{x^2}$$

For, $f(x)$ to be decreasing, we must have

$$f'(x)<0$$

$\Rightarrow \quad 4-\dfrac{1}{x^2}<0$

$\Rightarrow \quad 4x^2-1<0$

$\Rightarrow (2x+1)(2x-1)<0$

$\Rightarrow \quad -\dfrac{1}{2}<x<\dfrac{1}{2}$

$\therefore \quad x \in \left(-\dfrac{1}{2}, \dfrac{1}{2}\right)$

But domain $(f)=R-\{0\}$

So, $f(x)$ is decreasing on $\left(-\dfrac{1}{2}, 0\right) \cup \left(0, \dfrac{1}{2}\right)$.

(iv) We have, $f(x)=\dfrac{x}{2}+\dfrac{2}{x}$

$$f'(x)=\frac{1}{2}-\frac{2}{x^2}$$

$f(x)$ will be increasing, if $f'(x)>0$

$\therefore \dfrac{1}{2}-\dfrac{2}{x^2}>0 \Rightarrow \dfrac{x^2-4}{2x^2}>0$

$\Rightarrow x^2-4>0\quad [\because x^2>0, \forall\ x \in R]$

$\Rightarrow (x+2)(x-2)>0$

$\Rightarrow \quad x<-2$ or $x>2$

So, $f(x)$ is increasing on $(-\infty, -2) \cup (2, \infty)$.

22. (a) We have,

$$f(x)=(x+1)^3(x-3)^3$$

$$f'(x)=\left\{3(x+1)^2\frac{d}{dx}(x+1)\right\}\cdot(x-3)^3 + (x+1)^3\left\{3(x-3)^2\cdot\frac{d}{dx}(x-3)\right\}$$

$$=6(x+1)^2(x-3)^2(x-1)$$

For Statement I

For $f(x)$ to be increasing, we must have,

$$f'(x)>0$$

$\Rightarrow 6(x+1)^2(x-3)^2(x-1)>0$

$\Rightarrow \quad x-1>0$ and $x \neq -1, 1, 3$

$\Rightarrow \quad x>1$ and $x \neq -1, 1, 3$

$\Rightarrow \quad x \in (1, 3) \cup (3, \infty)$

For Statement II

For $f(x)$ is to be decreasing, we must have,

$$f'(x)<0$$

$\Rightarrow 6(x+1)^2(x-3)^2(x-1)<0$

$\Rightarrow \quad x-1<0$ and $x \neq -1, 1, 3$

$\Rightarrow \quad x<1$ and $x \neq -1, 1, 3$

$\Rightarrow \quad x \in (-\infty, -1) \cup (-1, 1)$

So, $f(x)$ is decreasing on $(-\infty, -1) \cup (-1, 1)$.

23. (True)

We have, $f(x)=\cos\left(2x+\dfrac{\pi}{4}\right)$

$$f'(x)=-2\sin\left(2x+\frac{\pi}{4}\right)$$

Now, $x \in \left(\dfrac{3\pi}{8}, \dfrac{7\pi}{8}\right)$

$\Rightarrow \quad \dfrac{3\pi}{8}<x<\dfrac{7\pi}{8}$

$\Rightarrow \quad \dfrac{3\pi}{4}<2x<\dfrac{7\pi}{4}$

$\Rightarrow \quad \dfrac{3\pi}{4}+\dfrac{\pi}{4}<2x+\dfrac{\pi}{4}<\dfrac{7\pi}{4}+\dfrac{\pi}{4}$

$\Rightarrow \quad \pi<\left(2x+\dfrac{\pi}{4}\right)<2\pi$

$\therefore \sin\left(2x+\dfrac{\pi}{4}\right)<0$

[$\because$ sine function is negative in third and fourth quadrants]

$\Rightarrow \quad -2\sin\left(2x+\dfrac{\pi}{4}\right)>0$

$\Rightarrow \quad f'(x)>0$

$\therefore f(x)$ is increasing on $\left(\dfrac{3\pi}{8}, \dfrac{7\pi}{8}\right)$.

24. (i) Given, $f(x) = \sin 3x - \cos 3x$

$\Rightarrow \quad f'(x) = 3(\cos 3x + \sin 3x)$

$\Rightarrow f'(x)$

$= 3\sqrt{2}\left(\frac{1}{\sqrt{2}}\cos 3x + \frac{1}{\sqrt{2}}\sin 3x\right)$

$= 3\sqrt{2}\left(\cos 3x \cdot \sin\frac{\pi}{4} + \cos\frac{\pi}{4}\cdot \sin 3x\right)$

$\therefore f'(x) = 3\sqrt{2}\cdot \sin\left(3x + \frac{\pi}{4}\right)$

Since, $0 < x < \pi$

$\Rightarrow \quad 0 < 3x < 3\pi$

$\Rightarrow 0 + \frac{\pi}{4} < 3x + \frac{\pi}{4} < 3\pi + \frac{\pi}{4}$

$\Rightarrow \quad \frac{\pi}{4} < \left(3x + \frac{\pi}{4}\right) < \frac{13\pi}{4}$

For $f(x)$ to be increasing, we must have

$$f'(x) > 0$$

$\Rightarrow \quad 3\sqrt{2}\sin\left(3x + \frac{\pi}{4}\right) > 0$

$\Rightarrow \quad \sin\left(3x + \frac{\pi}{4}\right) > 0$

$\Rightarrow \quad \frac{\pi}{4} < 3x + \frac{\pi}{4} < \pi$

or $\quad 2\pi < 3x + \frac{\pi}{4} < 3\pi$

$\Rightarrow \quad 0 < 3x < \frac{3\pi}{4}$

or $\quad \frac{7\pi}{4} < 3x < \frac{11\pi}{4}$

$\Rightarrow \quad 0 < x < \frac{\pi}{4}$

or $\quad \frac{7\pi}{12} < x < \frac{11\pi}{12}$

$\therefore \quad x \in \left(0, \frac{\pi}{4}\right) \cup \left(\frac{7\pi}{12}, \frac{11\pi}{12}\right)$

$\therefore f(x)$ is strictly increasing on the interval $\left(0, \frac{\pi}{4}\right) \cup \left(\frac{7\pi}{12}, \frac{11\pi}{12}\right)$.

(ii) We have,

$f(x) = \tan^{-1}(\sin x + \cos x)$

$f'(x) = \frac{1}{1 + (\sin x + \cos x)^2}(\cos x - \sin x)$

$\Rightarrow f'(x) = \frac{\cos x(1 - \tan x)}{1 + (\sin x + \cos x)^2}$

For increasing, $f'(x) > 0$

$\therefore \quad \frac{\cos x(1 - \tan x)}{1 + (\sin x + \cos x)^2} > 0$

$\cos x > 0, \frac{1}{1 + (\sin x + \cos x)^2} > 0$

and $1 - \tan x > 0$ in $\left(0, \frac{\pi}{4}\right)$

$\therefore f'(x) > 0$ in $\left(0, \frac{\pi}{4}\right)$

$f(x)$ is increasing in $\left(0, \frac{\pi}{4}\right)$.

But $(1 - \tan x) < 0$ in $\left(\frac{\pi}{4}, \frac{\pi}{2}\right)$.

So, $f'(x) < 0$ in $\left(\frac{\pi}{4}, \frac{\pi}{2}\right)$

Hence, $f(x)$ is decreasing in $\left(\frac{\pi}{4}, \frac{\pi}{2}\right)$.

$\therefore f(x)$ is increasing in $\left(0, \frac{\pi}{4}\right)$

and decreasing in $\left(\frac{\pi}{4}, \frac{\pi}{2}\right)$.

(iii) We have, $f(x) = \log\cos x$

$$f'(x) = -\tan x$$

For increasing or decreasing

$f'(x) > 0$ or $f'(x) < 0$

$\therefore$ For increasing, $f'(x) > 0$

$$-\tan x > 0$$

$\Rightarrow \tan x < 0$ in $\left(-\frac{\pi}{2}, 0\right)$

and $\tan x > 0$ in $\left(0, \frac{\pi}{2}\right)$

$\therefore f(x)$ is increasing in $\left(-\frac{\pi}{2}, 0\right)$

and decreasing in $\left(0, \frac{\pi}{2}\right)$.

(iv) We have,

$f(x) = \frac{4\sin x - 2x - x\cos x}{2 + \cos x}$

$\Rightarrow f(x) = \frac{4\sin x}{2 + \cos x} - \frac{x(2 + \cos x)}{2 + \cos x}$

$\Rightarrow f(x) = \frac{4\sin x}{2 + \cos x} - x$

$\Rightarrow f'(x) = \frac{(2 + \cos x)(4\cos x) - 4\sin x(-\sin x)}{(2 + \cos x)^2} - 1$

$\Rightarrow f'(x) = \frac{8\cos x + 4\cos^2 x + 4\sin^2 x}{(2 + \cos x)^2} - 1$

$\Rightarrow$

$f'(x) = \frac{4 + 8\cos x - (2 + \cos x)^2}{(2 + \cos x)^2}$

$\Rightarrow f'(x) = \frac{\cos x(4 - \cos x)}{(2 + \cos x)^2}$

Now, $f'(x) = 0$

$\Rightarrow \quad \cos x = 0 \quad [\because \cos x \neq 4]$

or $\quad x = \frac{\pi}{2}, \frac{3\pi}{2}$

$\cos x > 0$

for $x \in \left(0, \frac{\pi}{2}\right) \cup \left(\frac{3\pi}{2}, 2\pi\right)$

and $\cos x < 0$

for $x \in \left(\frac{\pi}{2}, \frac{3\pi}{2}\right)$

Thus, $f(x)$ is increasing for $x \in \left(0, \frac{\pi}{2}\right) \cup \left(\frac{3\pi}{2}, 2\pi\right)$

and $f(x)$ is decreasing for $x \in \left(\frac{\pi}{2}, \frac{3\pi}{2}\right)$.

(v) Clearly, $f(x) = x^x$ is defined for $x > 0$

Now, $f(x) = x^x = e^{x\log x}$

$\therefore \quad f'(x) = e^{x\log x}\cdot\frac{d}{dx}(x\log x)$

$$= x^x\cdot(1 + \log_e x)$$

For $f(x)$ to be decreasing, we must have

$$f'(x) < 0$$

$\Rightarrow \quad x^x(1 + \log x) < 0$

$\Rightarrow \quad (1 + \log_e x) < 0$

$[\because x^x > 0 \text{ for } x > 0]$

$\Rightarrow \quad \log_e x < -1 \Rightarrow x < e^{-1}$

i.e. $\quad x \in \left(0, \frac{1}{e}\right)$

Thus, $f(x)$ is decreasing on $\left(0, \frac{1}{e}\right)$.

25. (i) (True)

We have,

$$f(x) = \log(1 + x) - \frac{2x}{2 + x}$$

Clearly, $f(x)$ is defined for all $x + 1 > 0$ i.e. $x \in (-1, \infty)$.

Now, $f'(x) = \frac{1}{1 + x}\cdot\frac{d}{dx}(1 + x) - \frac{(2 + x)\cdot 2 - 2x(1)}{(x + 2)^2}$

$= \frac{1}{1 + x} - \frac{4}{(2 + x)^2}$

$= \left(\frac{x}{2 + x}\right)^2\cdot\frac{1}{1 + x}$

For $f(x)$ to be increasing, we must have $f'(x) > 0$

$\Rightarrow \left(\frac{x}{2+x}\right)^2 \cdot \frac{1}{1+x} > 0$

$= \frac{1}{1+x} > 0$ and $x \neq 0$

$\left[\text{since} \left(\frac{x}{2+x}\right)^2 > 0 \ \forall \ x \neq 0\right]$

$\Rightarrow \ x > -1$ and $x \neq 0$

$\therefore \ x \in (-1, 0) \cup (0, \infty)$

(ii) (True)

$f(x) = \log \sin x$

$\Rightarrow \ f'(x) = \frac{1}{\sin x} \cdot \cos x = \cot x$

Given, $x \in \left(0, \frac{\pi}{2}\right)$ in this range

$\cot x > 0$, so $f'(x) > 0$

Thus, $f(x)$ is increasing

on $\left(0, \frac{\pi}{2}\right)$.

(iii) (True)

$f(x) = \cos^2 x$

$\Rightarrow \quad f'(x) = 2\cos x(-\sin x)$

$= -\sin 2x$

Since, $0 < x < \frac{\pi}{2}$

$\Rightarrow \quad 0 < 2x < \pi \Rightarrow \sin 2x > 0$

$\therefore f'(x) = -\sin 2x < 0$

$\forall \ x \in \left(0, \frac{\pi}{2}\right)$

Thus, $f(x)$ is decreasing

on $\left(0, \frac{\pi}{2}\right)$.

(iv) (True)

We have,

$f(x) = \sqrt{3} \sin x - \cos x - 2ax + b$

$\Rightarrow f'(x) = \sqrt{3}\cos x + \sin x - 2a$

$\Rightarrow f'(x) = 2\left(\frac{\sqrt{3}}{2}\cos x + \frac{1}{2}\sin x\right) - 2a$

$= 2\left[\sin\frac{\pi}{3}\cos x + \cos\frac{\pi}{3} \cdot \sin x\right] - 2a$

$= 2\left[\sin\left(x + \frac{\pi}{3}\right)\right] - 2a$

$= 2\left\{\sin\left(x + \frac{\pi}{3}\right) - a\right\}$

Since, $\sin\left(x + \frac{\pi}{3}\right) \leq 1$

and $a \geq 1 \ \forall \ x \in R$

So, $f'(x) < 0 \quad \forall \ x \in R$

Hence, $f(x)$ is decreasing on R.

26. (i) (b)

(a) Let $f(x) = \sin x$

$\Rightarrow f'(x) = \cos x$

Now, $x \in \left(0, \frac{\pi}{2}\right)$

$\Rightarrow \cos x > 0 \Rightarrow f'(x) > 0$

$\therefore f(x)$ is increasing on $\left(0, \frac{\pi}{2}\right)$.

(b) Let $f(x) = \cos 2x$, then

$f'(x) = -2\sin 2x$

Now, $x \in \left(0, \frac{\pi}{2}\right)$

$\Rightarrow \quad 0 < x < \frac{\pi}{2}$

$\Rightarrow \quad 0 < 2x < \pi$

$\Rightarrow \quad \sin 2x > 0$

$\therefore f'(x) = -2\sin 2x < 0$

in $x \in \left(0, \frac{\pi}{2}\right)$

Thus, $f(x)$ is decreasing

on $\left(0, \frac{\pi}{2}\right)$.

(c) Let $f(x) = \tan x$, then

$f'(x) = \sec^2 x$

Now, $x \in \left(0, \frac{\pi}{2}\right) \Rightarrow \sec^2 x > 0$

$\Rightarrow \quad f'(x) > 0$

So, $f(x)$ is increasing

on $\left(0, \frac{\pi}{2}\right)$.

(d) Let $f(x) = \cos 3x$, then

$f'(x) = -3\sin 3x$

Now, $x \in \left(0, \frac{\pi}{2}\right)$

$\Rightarrow 0 < x < \frac{\pi}{2} \Rightarrow 0 < 3x < \frac{3\pi}{2}$

$\therefore \sin 3x$ can be positive as well as negative.

So, $f'(x) = -3\sin 3x$ can be positive as well as negative.

So, $f(x)$ is neither increasing nor decreasing on $\left(0, \frac{\pi}{2}\right)$.

(ii) (b) Given,

$f(x) = x - e^x + \tan\left(\frac{2\pi}{7}\right)$

$\Rightarrow \quad f'(x) = 1 - e^x$

Since, f is increasing,

So, $\quad f'(x) > 0 \Rightarrow 1 - e^x > 0$

$\Rightarrow \quad e^x < 1 \Rightarrow x < 0$

i.e. $\quad x \in (-\infty, 0)$

27. (d) Given,

$f(x) = \log_e(x^3 + \sqrt{x^6 + 1})$

$\therefore \quad f'(x) = \frac{1}{(x^6+1)^{1/2} + x^3} \left[3x^2 + \frac{6x^5}{2(x^6+1)^{1/2}}\right]$

$= \frac{3x^2}{\sqrt{x^6+1}} > 0$

Thus, $f'(x) > 0$ i.e. function is strictly increasing.

$f(x) = \log(x^3 + \sqrt{x^6+1}) \quad \ldots(i)$

$f(-x) = \log(-x^3 + \sqrt{x^6+1}) \ldots(ii)$

Adding Eqs. (i) and (ii), we get

$f(x) + f(-x) = \log(x^3 + \sqrt{x^6+1}) + \log(-x^3 + \sqrt{x^6+1})$

$= \log(x^3 + \sqrt{x^6+1})(-x^3 + \sqrt{x^6+1})$

$= \log(x^6 + 1 - x^6) = \log 1 = 0$

$\Rightarrow \quad f(-x) = -f(x)$

i.e. odd function.

Hence, $f(x)$ is odd and strictly increasing function.

28. Since, it is given that $f(x)$ is increasing on R.

Therefore, $f'(x) > 0 \ \forall \ x \in R$

$\Rightarrow 3kx^2 - 18kx + 9 > 0 \quad \forall \ x \in R$

$\Rightarrow \quad kx^2 - 6kx + 3 > 0 \quad \forall \ x \in R$

$\Rightarrow \quad k > 0$ and $36k^2 - 12k < 0$

$[\because ax^2 + bx + c > 0 \ \forall x \in R \Rightarrow a > 0$ and $D < 0]$

$\Rightarrow \quad k > 0$ and $k(3k - 1) < 0$

$\therefore \ 3k - 1 < 0 \Rightarrow k < \frac{1}{3}$

$\Rightarrow \quad k \in \left(0, \frac{1}{3}\right)$

Hence, $f(x)$ is increasing on R if $k \in \left(0, \frac{1}{3}\right)$.

29. We have,

$f(x) = (k+2)x^3 - 3kx^2 + 9kx - 1$

$\Rightarrow f'(x) = 3(k+2)x^2 - 6kx + 9k$

Since, $f(x)$ is decreasing $\forall \ x \in R$

$\therefore \quad f'(x) < 0$

$\Rightarrow 3(k+2)x^2 - 6kx + 9k < 0$

$\Rightarrow (k+2)x^2 - 2kx + 3k < 0$

$\Rightarrow \quad k + 2 < 0$

and $4k^2 - 4(k+2)(3k) < 0$

$[\because ax^2 + bx + c < 0, \forall \ x \in R \Rightarrow a < 0, D < 0]$

$\Rightarrow k < -2$ and $k^2 - 3k^2 - 6k < 0$

$\Rightarrow k < -2$ and $-2k(k+3) < 0$

Now, $-2k(k+3) < 0$

$\Rightarrow \quad k(k+3) > 0$

$\Rightarrow \quad k < -3$ or $k > 0$

$\Rightarrow \quad k \in (-\infty, -3) \cup (0, \infty)$

$\therefore \quad k < -2$ and $-2k(k+3) < 0$

$\Rightarrow \quad k \in (-\infty, -2)$

and $\quad k \in (-\infty, -3) \cup (0, \infty)$

$\Rightarrow \quad k \in (-\infty, -2)$

30. We have, $f(x) = \sin x - kx + c$

$$f'(x) = \cos x - k$$

Since, $f(x)$ is decreasing, $\forall x \in R$.

$\therefore \quad f'(x) < 0$

$\Rightarrow \quad \cos x - k < 0 \Rightarrow k > \cos x$

$\Rightarrow \quad k > 1 \quad [\because \cos x \le 1]$

31. We have,

$f(x) = \sqrt{3}\sin x - \cos x - 2kx + b$

$\Rightarrow f'(x) = \sqrt{3}\cos x + \sin x - 2k$

Since, $f(x)$ is decreasing, $\forall x \in R$.

$\therefore \quad f'(x) < 0$

$\Rightarrow \sqrt{3}\cos x + \sin x - 2k < 0$

$\Rightarrow k > \frac{\sqrt{3}}{2}\cos x + \frac{\sin x}{2}$

$\Rightarrow k > \sin\left(\frac{\pi}{3} + x\right)$

$\Rightarrow k > 1 \quad \left[\because \sin\left(\frac{\pi}{3} + x\right) \le 1\right]$

32. (i) Given,

$f(x) = -|x-1| + 5 \ \forall x \in R$

Clearly, $|x-1| \ge 0 \ \forall x \in R$

$\Rightarrow \quad -|x-1| \le 0 \ \forall x \in R$

$\Rightarrow -|x-1| + 5 \le 5 \ \forall x \in R$

$\Rightarrow \quad f(x) \le 5 \ \forall x \in R$

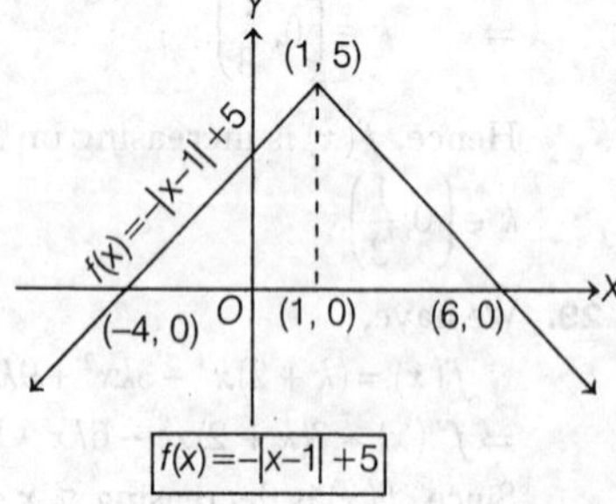

Now, $f(x) = 5$

$\Rightarrow \quad -|x-1| + 5 = 5 \Rightarrow x = 1$

$\therefore f(x)$ attains the maximum value 5 at $x = 1$.

$\therefore$ The required maximum value of $f(x) = -|x-1| + 5$ is 5.

Clearly from graph,

Minimum value does not exist.

(ii) The given function,

$f(x) = \sin 3x + 4,\ x \in \left(-\frac{\pi}{2}, \frac{\pi}{2}\right)$.

f(x)=sin3x+4

Clearly, $-1 \le \sin 3x \le 1$

$\Rightarrow -1 + 4 \le \sin 3x + 4 \le 1 + 4$

$\Rightarrow \quad 3 \le f(x) \le 5$

Thus, the maximum value of $f(x)$ is 5 and the minimum value of $f(x)$ is 3.

(iii) Given function,

$f(x) = 4x^2 - 4x + 4$

$\Rightarrow f(x) = 4(x^2 - x + 1)$

$\Rightarrow f(x) = 4\left(x^2 - x + \frac{1}{4} + 1 - \frac{1}{4}\right)$

$\Rightarrow f(x) = 4\left(x - \frac{1}{2}\right)^2 + 4\left(\frac{3}{4}\right)$

$\Rightarrow f(x) = 4\left(x - \frac{1}{2}\right)^2 + 3$

Clearly, $4\left(x - \frac{1}{2}\right)^2 \ge 0,\ \forall x \in R$

$\Rightarrow 4\left(x - \frac{1}{2}\right)^2 + 3 \ge 3,\ \forall x \in R$

Thus, minimum value of $f(x)$ is 3.

The maximum value of $f(x)$ does not exist.

33. (i) (False)

Given, $f(x) = |x+2|,\ \forall x \in R$

Clearly, $|x+2| \ge 0,\ \forall x \in R$

$\Rightarrow \quad f(x) \ge 0,\ \forall x \in R$

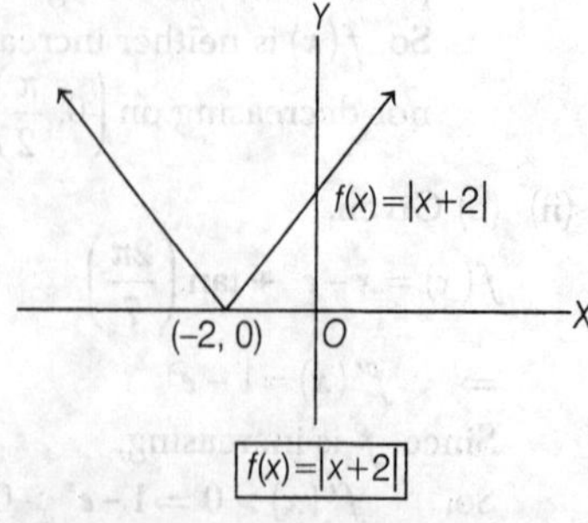

So, the maximum value of $f(x)$ does not exist, so $f(x)$ does not have the maximum value. (but minimum value of $f(x)$ is 0 and attains at $x = -2$).

(ii) (True)

The given function is

$$f(x) = -(x-1)^2 + 10\ \forall x \in R$$

It can be observed that

$(x-1)^2 \ge 0 \ \ \forall x \in R$

$-(x-1)^2 \le 0$

$\therefore -(x-1)^2 + 10 \le 10 \ \ \forall x \in R$

Thus, the maximum value of f is 10 and attains $x = 1$.

(iii) (True)

The given function is

$$g(x) = |\sin 2x + 3|$$

We know that $-1 \le \sin 2x \le 1$

$\therefore \ -1 + 3 \le \sin 2x + 3 \le 1 + 3$

$\Rightarrow \quad 2 \le |\sin 2x + 3| \le 4$

Hence, the maximum value of f is 4 and the minimum value of f is 2.

$\therefore$ Maximum value > Minimum value

34. (i) We have,

$f(x) = (x-1)(x+2)^2$

$\Rightarrow \quad f'(x) = (x+2)^2 + 2(x-1)(x+2)$

$\Rightarrow f'(x) = (x+2)(x+2+2x-2)$

$\Rightarrow f'(x) = (x+2)(3x)$

For local maxima or local minima, putting $f'(x) = 0$, we get

$$3x(x+2) = 0$$

$\Rightarrow \quad x = 0, -2$

$-\infty \quad + \quad -2 \quad - \quad 0 \quad + \quad \infty$

$f'(x)$ changes sign from positive to negative as x passes through -2.

So, $x = -2$ is a point of local maxima.

The local maximum value of $f(x)$ at $x = -2$ is

$f(-2) = (-2-1)(-2+2)^2 = 0$

and $f'(x)$ changes sign from negative to positive as x passes through 0.

So, $x = 0$ is a point of local minima.

The local minimum value of $f(x)$ at $x = 0$ is

$f(0) = (0-1)(0+2)^2 = -4$

(ii) We have, $f(x) = \sin x - \cos x$

$$f'(x) = \cos x + \sin x$$

For maxima or minima, putting $f'(x) = 0$, we get

$$\cos x + \sin x = 0$$

$$\Rightarrow \tan x = -1$$

$$\Rightarrow x = \frac{3\pi}{4}, \frac{7\pi}{4} \quad [\because 0 < x < 2\pi]$$

(Sign diagram: + on $(0, 3\pi/4)$, − on $(3\pi/4, 7\pi/4)$, + on $(7\pi/4, 2\pi)$)

$f'(x)$ changes sign from positive to negative as x passes through $\frac{3\pi}{4}$.

So, $x = \frac{3\pi}{4}$ is a point of local maxima.

The local maximum value of $f(x)$ at $x = \frac{3\pi}{4}$ is

$$f\left(\frac{3\pi}{4}\right) = \sin\left(\frac{3\pi}{4}\right) - \cos\left(\frac{3\pi}{4}\right)$$

$$= \frac{1}{\sqrt{2}} + \frac{1}{\sqrt{2}} = \sqrt{2}$$

and $f'(x)$ changes sign from negative to positive as x passes through $\frac{7\pi}{4}$.

So, $x = \frac{7\pi}{4}$ is a point of local minima.

The local minimum value of $f(x)$ at $x = \frac{7\pi}{4}$ is

$$f\left(\frac{7\pi}{4}\right) = \sin\left(\frac{7\pi}{4}\right) - \cos\left(\frac{7\pi}{4}\right)$$

$$= -\frac{1}{\sqrt{2}} - \frac{1}{\sqrt{2}} = -\sqrt{2}$$

(iii) We have, $f(x) = x\sqrt{1-x}$

$$\Rightarrow f'(x) = \sqrt{1-x} - \frac{x}{2\sqrt{1-x}}$$

$$\Rightarrow f'(x) = \frac{2(1-x) - x}{2\sqrt{1-x}}$$

$$= \frac{2-3x}{2\sqrt{1-x}}$$

For maxima or minima, putting $f'(x) = 0$, we get

$$\frac{2-3x}{2\sqrt{1-x}} = 0 \Rightarrow x = \frac{2}{3}$$

(Sign diagram: + before 2/3, − after 2/3)

$f'(x)$ changes from positive to negative as x passes through $\frac{2}{3}$.

So, $x = \frac{2}{3}$ is point of local maxima.

The local maximum value of $f(x)$ at $x = \frac{2}{3}$ is

$$f\left(\frac{2}{3}\right) = \frac{2}{3}\sqrt{1 - \frac{2}{3}} = \frac{2\sqrt{3}}{9}$$

(iv) We have, $f(x) = \sin^4 x + \cos^4 x$

$$\Rightarrow f'(x) = 4\sin^3 x \cos x - 4\cos^3 x \sin x$$

$$= 4\sin x \cos x(\sin^2 x - \cos^2 x)$$

$$= 2\sin 2x(-\cos 2x)$$

$$= -\sin 4x$$

For maxima or minima, putting $f'(x) = 0$, we get

$$-\sin 4x = 0$$

$$\Rightarrow x = \frac{\pi}{4} \quad \left[\because 0 < x < \frac{\pi}{2}\right]$$

$f'(x)$ changes sign from negative to positive as x passes through $\frac{\pi}{4}$.

(Sign diagram: − before π/4, + after π/4)

So, $x = \frac{\pi}{4}$ is a point of local minima.

The local minimum value of $f(x)$ at $x = \frac{\pi}{4}$ is

$$f\left(\frac{\pi}{4}\right) = \sin^4\left(\frac{\pi}{4}\right) + \cos^4\left(\frac{\pi}{4}\right)$$

$$= \frac{1}{4} + \frac{1}{4} = \frac{1}{2}$$

35. We have,

$$f(x) = 2x^3 - 6x^2 + 6x + 5$$

$$\therefore f'(x) = 6x^2 - 12x + 6$$

$$= 6(x^2 - 2x + 1)$$

$$= 6(x-1)^2$$

For critical points of f,

$$f'(x) = 0 \Rightarrow x = 1$$

Now, we have to examine whether these point has point of inflexion or not.

Clearly, $f'(x) \geq 0 \ \forall \ x \in R$

So, by the first derivative test, the point $x = 1$ is neither point of local maxima nor point of local minima.

$\therefore x = 1$ is a point of inflexion.

36. (i) We have,

$$f(x) = x^3 - 6x^2 + 9x + 15$$

$$f'(x) = 3x^2 - 12x + 9$$

$$f'(x) = 3(x^2 - 4x + 3)$$

$$= 3(x-1)(x-3)$$

For maxima or minima, putting $f'(x) = 0$, we get

$$3(x-1)(x-3) = 0 \Rightarrow x = 1, 3$$

Now, $f''(x) = 3[(x-1) + (x-3)]$

$$= 3(2x - 4)$$

At $x = 1$, $f''(1) = 3(2-4) = -6 < 0$

So, $x = 1$ is a point of local maxima.

The local maximum value of $f(x)$ at $x = 1$ is

$$f(1) = 1 - 6 + 9 + 15 = 19$$

At $x = 3$,

$$f''(3) = 3(6-4) = 6 > 0$$

So, $x = 3$ is a point of local minima.

The local minimum value of $f(x)$ at $x = 3$ is

$$f(3) = 27 - 54 + 27 + 15 = 15$$

(ii) We have, $f(x) = \sin 2x - x$

$$f'(x) = 2\cos 2x - 1$$

For maxima or minima, putting $f'(x) = 0$, we get

$$2\cos 2x - 1 = 0 \Rightarrow \cos 2x = \frac{1}{2}$$

$$\Rightarrow 2x = -\frac{\pi}{3} \text{ or } 2x = \frac{\pi}{3}$$

$$\left[\because -\frac{\pi}{2} < x < \frac{\pi}{2}\right]$$

$$\Rightarrow x = -\frac{\pi}{6}, \frac{\pi}{6}$$

Now, $f''(x) = -4\sin 2x$

At $x = -\frac{\pi}{6}$,

$$f''\left(-\frac{\pi}{6}\right) = -4\sin\left(-\frac{\pi}{3}\right)$$

$$= -4 \times \left(-\frac{\sqrt{3}}{2}\right) = 2\sqrt{3} > 0$$

So, $x = -\frac{\pi}{6}$ is a point of local minima.

The local minimum value of $f(x)$ at $x = -\frac{\pi}{6}$ is

$$f\left(-\frac{\pi}{6}\right) = \sin\left(-\frac{\pi}{3}\right) + \frac{\pi}{6}$$

$$= -\frac{\sqrt{3}}{2} + \frac{\pi}{6}$$

At $x = \frac{\pi}{6}$,

$$f''\left(\frac{\pi}{6}\right) = -4\sin\left(\frac{\pi}{3}\right) = -2\sqrt{3} < 0$$

So, $x = \frac{\pi}{6}$ is a point of local maxima.

The local maximum value of $f(x)$ at $x = \frac{\pi}{6}$ is

$$f\left(\frac{\pi}{6}\right) = \sin\left(\frac{\pi}{3}\right) - \frac{\pi}{6} = \frac{\sqrt{3}}{2} - \frac{\pi}{6}$$

(iii) We have, $f(x) = (x-1)(x-2)^2$

$$f'(x) = (x-2)^2 + 2(x-2)(x-1)$$
$$= (x-2)(3x-4)$$

For maxima or minima, putting $f'(x) = 0$, we get

$$(x-2)(3x-4) = 0$$
$$\Rightarrow \quad x = 2, \frac{4}{3}$$

Now, $f''(x) = (3x-4) + (x-2)3$
$$= 6x - 10$$

At $x = 2$,
$$f''(2) = 12 - 10 = 2 > 0$$

$\therefore$ $x = 2$ is a point of local minima.

The local minimum value of $f(x)$ at $x = 2$ is $f(2) = 0$

At $x = \frac{4}{3}$,

$$f''(4/3) = 6 \times \frac{4}{3} - 10 = -2 < 0$$

$\therefore x = \frac{4}{3}$ is point of local maxima.

The local maximum value of $f(x)$ at $x = \frac{4}{3}$ is

$$f\left(\frac{4}{3}\right) = \left(\frac{4}{3} - 1\right)\left(\frac{4}{3} - 2\right)^2 = \frac{4}{27}$$

(iv) We have, $f(x) = x^3 - 2ax^2 + a^2x$

$$\Rightarrow \quad f'(x) = 3x^2 - 4ax + a^2$$
$$= (x-a)(3x-a)$$

For local maxima or local minima, putting $f'(x) = 0$, we get

$$(x-a)(3x-a) = 0 \Rightarrow x = a, \frac{a}{3}$$

Now, $f''(x) = 6x - 4a$

At $x = a$,

$$f''(a) = 6a - 4a = 2a > 0$$
$$[\because a > 0]$$

$\therefore$ $x = a$ is a point of local minima.

The local minimum value of $f(x)$ at $x = a$ is

$$f(a) = a^3 - 2a^3 + a^3 = 0$$

At $x = \frac{a}{3}$,

$$f''\left(\frac{a}{3}\right) = 6\left(\frac{a}{3}\right) - 4a = -2a < 0$$
$$[\because a > 0]$$

$\therefore x = \frac{a}{3}$ is a point of local maxima.

The local maximum value of $f(x)$ at $x = \frac{a}{3}$ is

$$f\left(\frac{a}{3}\right) = \left(\frac{a}{3}\right)^3 - 2a\left(\frac{a}{3}\right)^2 + a^2\left(\frac{a}{3}\right)$$
$$= \frac{a^3}{27} - \frac{2a^3}{9} + \frac{a^3}{3} = \frac{4a^3}{27}$$

37. We observe that $f(x)$ is defined $\forall\, x \neq 0$.

Now, $f(x) = a\log|x| + bx^2 + x$

$$\Rightarrow \quad f'(x) = \frac{a}{x} + 2bx + 1$$

It is given that $f(x)$ has extreme value at $x = -1$ and $x = 2$, then

$$f'(-1) = 0 \text{ and } f'(2) = 0$$
$$\Rightarrow -a - 2b + 1 = 0$$

and $\frac{a}{2} + 4b + 1 = 0$

Now, solve these two equations, we get

$$a = 2 \text{ and } b = -\frac{1}{2}$$

Thus, $a + b = 2 - \frac{1}{2} = \frac{3}{2}$

$\therefore$ The value of $(a+b)$ is $\frac{3}{2}$.

38. (i) (True)

Let $y = \left(\frac{1}{x}\right)^x = x^{-x}$

Taking log on both sides,

$$\log y = -x\log x$$
$$\Rightarrow \quad \frac{1}{y}\frac{dy}{dx} = -(1 + \log x)$$
$$\Rightarrow \quad \frac{dy}{dx} = -y(1 + \log x)$$
$$\Rightarrow \quad \frac{d^2y}{dx^2} = -\frac{dy}{dx}(1 + \log x) - \frac{y}{x}$$
$$= y(1 + \log x)^2 - \frac{y}{x}$$
$$\Rightarrow \quad \frac{d^2y}{dx^2} = x^{-x}(1 + \log x)^2 - x^{-x-1}$$

At the point of local maxima and local minima, we must have

$$\frac{dy}{dx} = 0$$
$$\Rightarrow -y(1 + \log x) = 0$$
$$\Rightarrow \quad 1 + \log x = 0$$
$$\Rightarrow \quad \log x = -1$$
$$\therefore \quad x = \frac{1}{e}$$

Now, $\left.\frac{d^2y}{dx^2}\right|_{x=\frac{1}{e}} = \left(\frac{1}{e}\right)^{-1/e}\left(1 + \log\frac{1}{e}\right)^2 - \left(\frac{1}{e}\right)^{-\frac{1}{e}-1}$

$$= (e^{-1})^{-1/e}(1 - \log e)^2 - (e^{-1})^{-\frac{1}{e}-1}$$
$$= -e^{e^{-1}+1} < 0$$

So, $x = \frac{1}{e}$ is a point of local maxima.

The local maximum value of $\left(\frac{1}{x}\right)^x$ is $e^{1/e}$.

(ii) (True)

The given function, $f(x) = \frac{\log x}{x}$

Then, $f'(x) = \frac{x\left(\frac{1}{x}\right) - \log x}{x^2}$

$$= \frac{1 - \log x}{x^2}$$

Now, $f'(x) = 0 \Rightarrow 1 - \log x = 0$

$$\Rightarrow \quad \log x = 1 \Rightarrow x = e$$

Now,

$$f''(x) = \frac{x^2\left(-\frac{1}{x}\right) - (1 - \log x)\cdot(2x)}{x^4}$$
$$= \frac{-x - 2x(1 - \log x)}{x^4}$$
$$= \frac{-3 + 2\log x}{x^3}$$
$$f''(x)|_{x=e} = \frac{-3 + 2\log e}{e^3} = -\frac{1}{e^3} < 0$$

Therefore, by the 2nd derivative test, f is maximum at $x = e$ and the maximum value is

$$f(e) = \frac{\log e}{e} = \frac{1}{e}$$

(iii) (True)

Given, $f(x) = \sin x + \sqrt{3}\cos x$

$$f'(x) = \cos x - \sqrt{3}\sin x$$

and $f''(x) = -\sin x - \sqrt{3}\cos x$

Now, $f'(x) = 0$

$\Rightarrow \cos x - \sqrt{3}\sin x = 0$

$\Rightarrow \quad \cot x = \sqrt{3} = \cot\frac{\pi}{6}$

$\therefore \quad x = \frac{\pi}{6}$

Now, $f''\left(\frac{\pi}{6}\right) = -\sin\frac{\pi}{6} - \sqrt{3}\cos\frac{\pi}{6}$

$= -\frac{1}{2} - \frac{3}{2} = -2 < 0$

Hence, by the 2nd derivative test, $f(x)$ has maximum value at $x = \frac{\pi}{6}$.

39. (i) We have,

$f(x) = 2x^3 - 24x + 107$

$\Rightarrow \quad f'(x) = 6x^2 - 24$

Now, $f'(x) = 0 \Rightarrow 6x^2 - 24 = 0$

$\Rightarrow \quad x = \pm 2$

But $x = -2 \notin [1, 3]$, so $x = 2$ is the only stationary point.

Now, compute the value of $f(x)$ at $x = 1, 2, 3$

$\therefore f(1) = 2 - 24 + 107 = 85$

$f(2) = 16 - 48 + 107 = 75$

$f(3) = 54 - 72 + 107 = 89$

$\therefore$ Maximum value is 89 and minimum value is 75.

(ii) We have, $f(x) = \left(\frac{1}{2} - x\right)^2 + x^3$

$f'(x) = -2\left(\frac{1}{2} - x\right) + 3x^2$

$= 3x^2 + 2x - 1$

Now, $\quad f'(x) = 0$

$\Rightarrow 3x^2 + 2x - 1 = 0$

$\Rightarrow (3x - 1)(x + 1) = 0$

$\Rightarrow \quad x = \frac{1}{3}, -1$

Now, compute the value of $f(x)$ at $x = -2, -1, \frac{1}{3}, \frac{5}{2}$

$\therefore f(-2) = \left(\frac{1}{2} + 2\right)^2 + (-2)^3$

$= \frac{25}{4} - 8 = -\frac{7}{4}$

$f(-1) = \left(\frac{1}{2} + 1\right)^2 + (-1)^3$

$= \frac{9}{4} - 1 = \frac{5}{4}$

$f\left(\frac{1}{3}\right) = \left(\frac{1}{2} - \frac{1}{3}\right)^2 + \left(\frac{1}{3}\right)^3$

$= \frac{1}{36} + \frac{1}{27} = \frac{7}{108}$

$f\left(\frac{5}{2}\right) = \left(\frac{1}{2} - \frac{5}{2}\right)^2 + \left(\frac{5}{2}\right)^3 = \frac{157}{8}$

$\therefore$ Maximum value $= \frac{157}{8}$

and minimum value $= -\frac{7}{4}$.

(iii) We have, $f(x) = \cos^2 x + \sin x$

$f'(x) = -2\cos x \sin x + \cos x$

Now, $f'(x) = 0$

$\Rightarrow \cos x(-2\sin x + 1) = 0$

$\Rightarrow \cos x = 0$ or $\sin x = \frac{1}{2}$

$\Rightarrow x = \frac{\pi}{2}$ or $x = \frac{\pi}{6}, \frac{5\pi}{6}$

Now, compute the value of $f(x)$ at $x = 0, \frac{\pi}{6}, \frac{\pi}{2}, \frac{5\pi}{6}, \pi$

$f(0) = \cos^2 0 + \sin 0 = 1$

$f\left(\frac{\pi}{6}\right) = \cos^2\left(\frac{\pi}{6}\right) + \sin\left(\frac{\pi}{6}\right)$

$= \frac{3}{4} + \frac{1}{2} = \frac{5}{4}$

$f\left(\frac{\pi}{2}\right) = \cos^2\left(\frac{\pi}{2}\right) + \sin\left(\frac{\pi}{2}\right)$

$= 0 + 1 = 1$

$f\left(\frac{5\pi}{6}\right) = \cos^2\left(\frac{5\pi}{6}\right) + \sin\left(\frac{5\pi}{6}\right)$

$= \frac{3}{4} + \frac{1}{2} = \frac{5}{4}$

$f(\pi) = \cos^2\pi + \sin\pi = 1 + 0 = 1$

So, absolute maximum value is $\frac{5}{4}$ and absolute minimum value is 1.

(iv) We have,

$f(x) = 3x^4 - 8x^3 + 12x^2 - 48x + 1$

$f'(x) = 12x^3 - 24x^2 + 24x - 48$

$f'(x) = 12(x^3 - 2x^2 + 2x - 4)$

$f'(x) = 12(x - 2)(x^2 + 2)$

Now, $f'(x) = 0$

$\Rightarrow 12(x - 2)(x^2 + 2) = 0 \Rightarrow x = 2$

or $\quad x^2 + 2 \neq 0$

Now, compute the value of $f(x)$ at $x = 1, 2, 4$

$\therefore f(1) = 3 - 8 + 12 - 48 + 1 = -40$

$f(2) = 48 - 64 + 48 - 96 + 1 = -63$

$f(4) = 768 - 512 + 192 - 192 + 1$

$= 257$

So, the absolute maximum value is 257 and the absolute minimum value is -63.

40. (True)

Let one of the number be x and then other number is $(15 - x)$.

Let $S(x)$ denotes sum of the squares of these numbers.

Then, $S(x) = x^2 + (15 - x)^2$

$= 2x^2 - 30x + 225$

$\therefore \quad S'(x) = 4x - 30$

$\therefore \quad S''(x) = 4$

Now, $S'(x) = 0$

$\Rightarrow \quad x = \frac{15}{2}$

Also, $S''\left(\frac{15}{2}\right) = 4 > 0$

Therefore, by 2nd derivative test, $x = \frac{15}{2}$ is the point of local minima of S.

Hence, the sum of squares of numbers is minimum, when numbers are $\frac{15}{2}$ and $\left(15 - \frac{15}{2}\right) = \frac{15}{2}$.

41. (c) Let $P = xy^3$ and given that $x + y = 60$, therefore

$P = (60 - y) \cdot y^3$

$= 60y^3 - y^4$

$\therefore \quad \frac{dP}{dy} = 180y^2 - 4y^3$

and $\frac{d^2P}{dy^2} = 360y - 12y^2$

The critical points of P are given by $\frac{dP}{dy} = 0$,

So, $\quad \frac{dP}{dy} = 0$

$\Rightarrow 180y^2 - 4y^3 = 0$

$\Rightarrow \quad y^2(y - 45) = 0$

$\Rightarrow \quad y = 0, 45$

$y = 0$ is impossible, so

$y = 45$

$\therefore \quad \left(\frac{d^2P}{dy^2}\right)\Bigg|_{y=45} = -8100 < 0$

So, P is maximum when $y = 45$.

Putting $y = 45$ in $x + y = 60$, we obtain

$x = 15$

Hence, xy^3 is maximum when $x = 15$ and $y = 45$.

Thus, the relation between x and y is $x < y$.

42. Let the required numbers be x and y.

Then, $xy = 256$ [given] ...(i)

Let $S = x + y$, then

$$S = x + \frac{256}{x}$$

$$\Rightarrow \frac{dS}{dx} = 1 - \frac{256}{x^2} \text{ and } \frac{d^2S}{dx^2} = \frac{512}{x^3}$$

The critical points of S are given by $\frac{dS}{dx} = 0$,

$$\therefore 1 - \frac{256}{x^2} = 0$$

$$\Rightarrow x^2 = 256 \Rightarrow x = 16$$

Now, $\left.\frac{d^2S}{dx^2}\right|_{x=16} = \frac{1}{8} > 0$

Thus, S is minimum when $x = 16$, putting $x = 16$ in Eq. (i), we get

$$y = 16$$

Hence, those required numbers are both equal to 16.

43. (d) Let $P = ax + by$, where $xy = c^2$

Then, $P = ax + \frac{bc^2}{x}$

$$\left[\because xy = c^2 \Rightarrow y = \frac{c^2}{x}\right]$$

$$\Rightarrow \frac{dP}{dx} = a - \frac{bc^2}{x^2} \text{ and } \frac{d^2P}{dx^2} = \frac{2bc^2}{x^3}$$

The critical points of P are given by $\frac{dP}{dx} = 0$

$$\therefore \frac{dP}{dx} = 0 \Rightarrow a - \frac{bc^2}{x^2} = 0$$

$$\Rightarrow x^2 = \frac{bc^2}{a} \Rightarrow x = \pm\sqrt{\frac{b}{a}}\,c$$

At $x = \sqrt{\frac{b}{a}}\,c$, then

$$\frac{d^2P}{dx^2} = 2bc^2\left(\sqrt{\frac{a}{b}} \cdot \frac{1}{c}\right)^3$$

$$= \frac{2a}{c}\sqrt{\frac{a}{b}} > 0$$

So, P is minimum at $x = \sqrt{\frac{b}{a}}\,c$

Thus, the minimum value of P is given by

$$P = a\sqrt{\frac{b}{a}}\,c + \frac{bc^2}{c}\sqrt{\frac{a}{b}}$$

$$= c\sqrt{ab} + c\sqrt{ab} = 2\sqrt{ab}\,c$$

Thus, the minimum value of $ax + by$, where $xy = c^2$ is $2\sqrt{ab}\,c$.

44. (True)

Let $ABCD$ be a rectangle inscribed in a given circle with centre O and radius a.

Let $AB = 2x$ and $BC = 2y$.

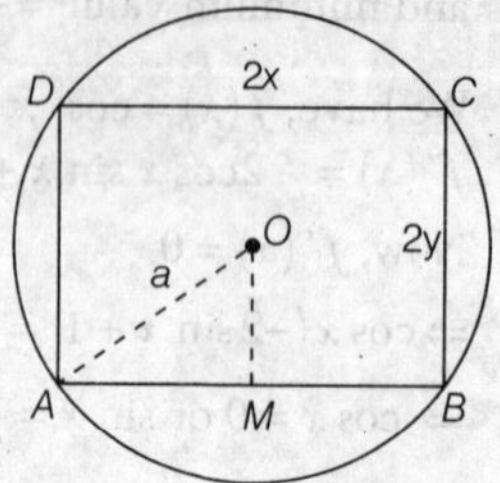

Applying Pythagoras theorem in right ΔOAM, we obtain

$$OA^2 = OM^2 + AM^2 = x^2 + y^2$$

$$\therefore a^2 = x^2 + y^2$$

$$\Rightarrow y = \sqrt{a^2 - x^2} \quad \text{...(i)}$$

Let A be the area of the rectangle $ABCD$, then

$$A = 4xy = 4x\sqrt{a^2 - x^2}$$

[using Eq.(i)]

$$\Rightarrow \frac{dA}{dx} = 4\left\{\sqrt{a^2 - x^2} - \frac{x^2}{\sqrt{a^2 - x^2}}\right\}$$

$$= 4\left\{\frac{a^2 - 2x^2}{\sqrt{a^2 - x^2}}\right\}$$

$$\therefore \frac{d^2A}{dx^2} = 4\frac{d}{dx}\{(a^2 - 2x^2)(a^2 - x^2)^{-1/2}\}$$

$$= 4\left\{\frac{-4x}{\sqrt{a^2 - x^2}} + \frac{x(a^2 - 2x^2)}{(a^2 - x^2)^{3/2}}\right\}$$

Now, the critical points of A are given by $\frac{dA}{dx} = 0$,

then $4\left\{\frac{a^2 - 2x^2}{\sqrt{a^2 - x^2}}\right\} = 0$

$$\Rightarrow x = \frac{a}{\sqrt{2}}$$

Now, $\left.\frac{d^2A}{dx^2}\right|_{x = \frac{a}{\sqrt{2}}} = -16 < 0$

Thus, A is maximum when $x = \frac{a}{\sqrt{2}}$.

On putting $x = \frac{a}{\sqrt{2}}$ in Eq. (i),

we get

$$y = \frac{a}{\sqrt{2}}$$

$$\therefore x = \frac{a}{\sqrt{2}} \text{ and } y = \frac{a}{\sqrt{2}}$$

$$\Rightarrow 2x = 2y = \sqrt{2}\,a$$

$\therefore AB = BC$ i.e. $ABCD$ is a square.

45. (d) **For Statement I**

Let ACB be a right angled triangle with base $BC = x$ and hypotenuse $AB = y$ such that $x + y = k$, k be any constant.

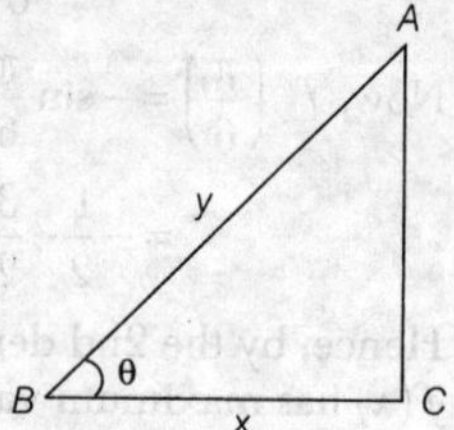

Let θ be the angle between the base and hypotenuse.

Let A be the area of the triangle.

Then,

$$A = \frac{1}{2}BC \cdot AC = \frac{1}{2}x\sqrt{y^2 - x^2}$$

$$\therefore A^2 = \frac{x^2}{4}(y^2 - x^2)$$

$$\Rightarrow A^2 = \frac{x^2}{4}\{(k - x)^2 - x^2\}$$

$[\because x + y = k]$

$$\Rightarrow A^2 = \frac{x^2k^2 - 2kx^3}{4} \quad \text{...(i)}$$

On differentiating both sides w.r.t. x, we get

$$2A\frac{dA}{dx} = \frac{2k^2x - 6kx^2}{4} \quad \text{...(ii)}$$

$$\Rightarrow \frac{dA}{dx} = \frac{k^2x - 3kx^2}{4A}$$

Now, $\frac{dA}{dx} = 0 \Rightarrow x = \frac{k}{3}$

On differentiating Eq. (ii) w.r.t. x, we get

$$2\left(\frac{dA}{dx}\right)^2 + 2A\frac{d^2A}{dx^2} = \frac{2k^2 - 12kx}{4} \quad \text{...(iii)}$$

When $x = \frac{k}{3}$ and $\frac{dA}{dx} = 0$, put these in Eq. (iii), we get

$$\frac{d^2A}{dx^2} = -\frac{k^2}{4A} < 0$$

Thus, A is maximum when

$$x = \frac{k}{3}$$

On putting $x = \frac{k}{3}$ in $x + y = k$

we obtain $y = \frac{2k}{3}$

In ΔABC, $\cos\theta = \frac{1}{2} = \cos\frac{\pi}{3}$

$$\therefore \theta = \frac{\pi}{3}$$

For Statement II

Let the length, width and height of the open tank be x, x and y units, respectively.

Then, the volume is x^2y and the total surface area $x^2 + 4xy$.

It is given that tank can hold a given quantity of water. This means that its volume is constant.

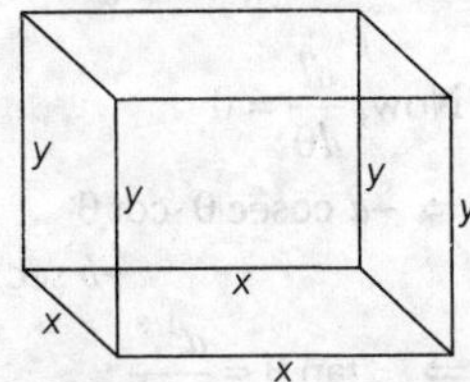

Let it is V.

Then, $V = x^2y$ ...(i)

Let S be denote the surface area.

Then, $S = x^2 + 4xy$ ...(ii)

We have to minimise S to reduce the cost of the material.

Now, $S = x^2 + \frac{4V}{x}$

$\therefore \quad \frac{dS}{dx} = 2x - \frac{4V}{x^2}$

and $\frac{d^2S}{dx^2} = 2 + \frac{8V}{x^3}$

Now, $\frac{dS}{dx} = 0 \Rightarrow 2x - \frac{4V}{x^2} = 0$

$\Rightarrow 2x^3 = 4x^2y \Rightarrow x = 2y$

Clearly, $\frac{d^2S}{dx^2} = 2 + \frac{8V}{x^3} > 0 \; \forall x$

Hence, the cost of the material will be least when depth of the tank (y) is half of its width $\left(\frac{x}{2}\right)$.

46. (True)

Let r be the radius, l be the slant height and h be the height of the cone ABC of given surface area S.

Then, $S = \pi r^2 + \pi rl$

$\Rightarrow \quad l = \frac{S - \pi r^2}{\pi r}$ ...(i)

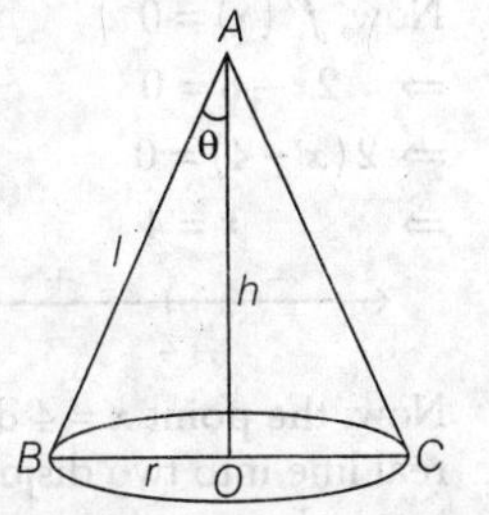

Let V be the volume of the cone.

Then, $V = \frac{1}{3}\pi r^2 h$

$\Rightarrow V^2 = \frac{1}{9}\pi^2 r^4 h^2 = \frac{1}{9}\pi^2 r^4 (l^2 - r^2)$

$\Rightarrow V^2 = \frac{\pi^2}{9} r^4 \left\{\frac{(S - \pi r^2)^2}{(\pi r)^2} - r^2\right\}$

$= \frac{1}{9}(S^2 r^2 - 2\pi S r^4)$

Let $P = V^2$.

Then, V is maximum or minimum according as P is maximum or minimum.

Now, $P = \frac{1}{9} S (Sr^2 - 2\pi r^4)$

Since, S is constant.

$\frac{dP}{dr} = \frac{1}{9} S(2Sr - 8\pi r^3)$

$\therefore \quad \frac{d^2P}{dr^2} = \frac{S}{9}(2S - 24\pi r^2)$

Now, $\frac{dP}{dr} = 0 \Rightarrow r^2 = \frac{S}{4\pi}$

Now, $\left.\frac{d^2P}{dr^2}\right|_{r^2 = \frac{S}{4\pi}} = -\frac{4S^2}{9} < 0$

$\therefore$ P is maximum when $r^2 = \frac{S}{4\pi}$

i.e. $S = 4\pi r^2$.

Hence, V is maximum when

$S = 4\pi r^2$

Now, $S = 4\pi r^2$

$\Rightarrow \quad \pi rl + \pi r^2 = 4\pi r^2 \Rightarrow l = 3r$

$\therefore \quad \sin\theta = \frac{r}{l} = \frac{1}{3}$

$\therefore \quad \theta = \sin^{-1}\left(\frac{1}{3}\right)$

Hence, V is maximum when

$\theta = \sin^{-1}\left(\frac{1}{3}\right)$

47. (a) Let $ABCD$ be the given trapezium such that $AD = DC = BC = 10$ cm.

Draw DP and CQ perpendicular from D and C, respectively on AB.

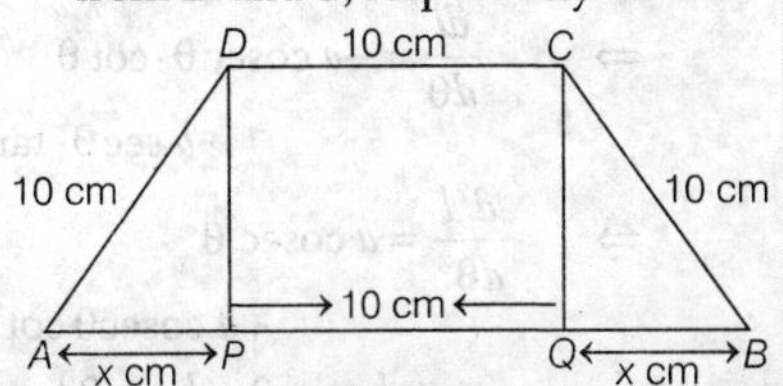

Clearly, $\Delta APD \cong \Delta BQC$

Let $AP = x$ cm and then

$BQ = x$ cm

Applying Pythagoras theorem,

$DP = QC = \sqrt{100 - x^2}$

Let A be the area of trapezium $ABCD$. Then,

$\therefore \quad A = (10 + x)\sqrt{100 - x^2}$ ...(i)

$\therefore \quad \frac{dA}{dx} = \frac{100 - 10x - 2x^2}{\sqrt{100 - x^2}}$

$\Rightarrow \frac{d^2A}{dx^2} = \frac{2x^3 - 300x - 1000}{(100 - x^2)^{3/2}}$

Now, $\frac{dA}{dx} = 0$

$\Rightarrow \quad 100 - 10x - 2x^2 = 0$

$\Rightarrow \quad (x + 10)(x - 5) = 0 \Rightarrow x = 5$

$\therefore \quad \left.\frac{d^2A}{dx^2}\right|_{x=5} = -\frac{30}{\sqrt{75}} < 0$

Thus, the area of trapezium is maximum when $x = 5$.

On putting $x = 5$ in Eq. (i), we get

$A = (10 + 5)\sqrt{100 - 25}$

$= 75\sqrt{3}$ cm^2

48. (True)

Let VAB be a cone of the greatest volume inscribed in a sphere of radius R. It is obvious that for maximum volume the axis of the cone must be along a diameter of the sphere.

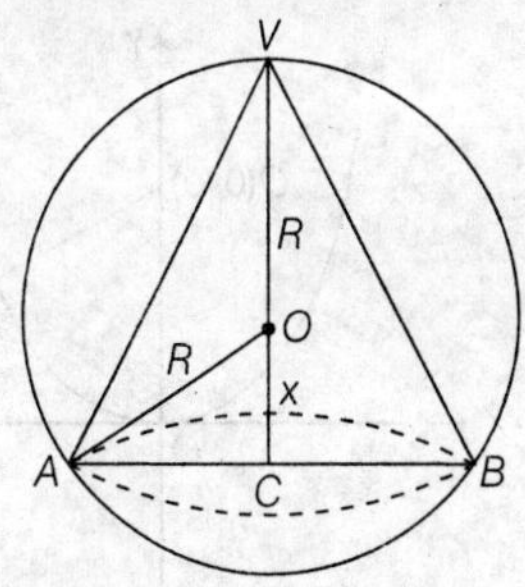

Let VC be the axis of the cone and O be the centre of the sphere such that $OC = x$.

Then, $VC = VO + OC = R + x$

= Height of the cone

Applying Pythagoras theorem in ΔACO, we get

$AC^2 = R^2 - x^2$

Let V be the volume of the cone.

Then, $V = \frac{1}{3}\pi(AC)^2 \cdot (VC)$

$$= \frac{1}{3}\pi(R^2 - x^2)(R + x) \quad \ldots(i)$$

$$\therefore \quad \frac{dV}{dx} = \frac{1}{3}\pi(R^2 - 2Rx - 3x^2)$$

and $\frac{d^2V}{dx^2} = \frac{1}{3}\pi(-2R - 6x)$

Now, $\frac{dV}{dx} = 0 \Rightarrow x = \frac{R}{3}$

On putting $x = \frac{R}{3}$ in $\frac{d^2V}{dx^2}$, then

$$\frac{d^2V}{dx^2} = -\frac{4R\pi}{3} < 0$$

Thus, V is maximum when $x = \frac{R}{3}$.

On putting $x = \frac{R}{3}$ in Eq. (i),

we obtain

$$V = \frac{1}{3}\pi\left(R^2 - \frac{R^2}{9}\right)\left(R + \frac{R}{3}\right)$$

$$= \frac{32\pi R^3}{81} = \frac{8}{27}\left(\frac{4}{3}\pi R^3\right)$$

$$= \frac{8}{27} \text{ [volume of the sphere]}$$

Hence, volume of cone

$$= \frac{8}{27} \times \text{[volume of sphere]}$$

49. Let $P(x, y)$ be any point on the parabola and $Q(0, c)$ be the given point.

Then, $PQ^2 = x^2 + (y - c)^2 \quad \ldots(i)$

$= x^4 - x^2(2c - 1) + c^2 \quad \ldots(ii)$

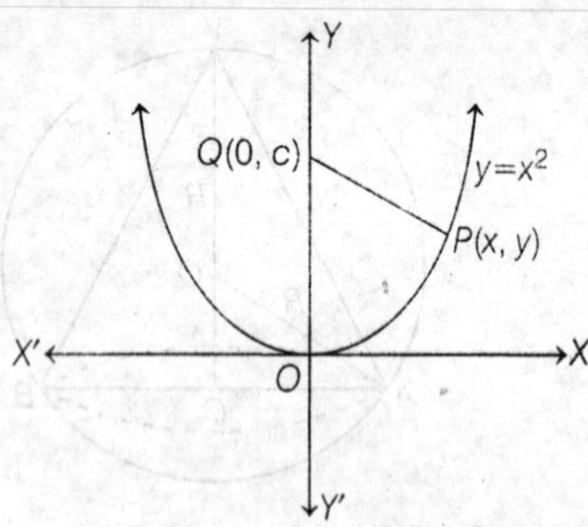

Clearly, PQ will be minimum when PQ^2 is minimum.

Let $D = PQ^2$.

Then, $D = x^4 - x^2(2c - 1) + c^2$.

$$\therefore \quad \frac{dD}{dx} = 4x^3 - 2x(2c - 1)$$

and $\frac{d^2D}{dx^2} = 12x^2 - 2(2c - 1)$

Now, for the critical points of D are given by $\frac{dD}{dx} = 0$

Thus, $\frac{dD}{dx} = 0$

$\Rightarrow x\{4x^2 - 2(2c - 1)\} = 0$

$\therefore \quad x = 0,\ x = \pm\sqrt{\frac{2c - 1}{2}}$

Clearly,

$$\left.\frac{d^2D}{dx^2}\right|_{x = \pm\sqrt{\frac{2c-1}{2}}} = 12\left(\pm\sqrt{\frac{2c - 1}{2}}\right)^2 - 2(2c - 1)$$

$$= (2c - 1) > 0$$

Thus, D is minimum at

$$x = \pm\sqrt{\frac{2c - 1}{2}}.$$

Hence, PQ is minimum at

$$x = \pm\sqrt{\frac{2c - 1}{2}}.$$

Now, putting $x = \pm\sqrt{\frac{2c - 1}{2}}$ in Eq. (i), we get

$$\therefore PQ^2 = \left(\pm\sqrt{\frac{2c - 1}{2}}\right)^2 + \left\{\left(\pm\sqrt{\frac{2c - 1}{2}}\right)^2 - c\right\}^2$$

$$= \frac{4c - 1}{4}$$

$$\therefore \quad PQ = \frac{\sqrt{4c - 1}}{2}$$

50. (c) Let AOB be a right triangle with hypotenuse AB such that a point C on AB is at distance a and b from OA and OB, respectively.

In ΔAQC and ΔCPB, we get

$$\sin\theta = \frac{a}{AC} \text{ and } \cos\theta = \frac{b}{BC}$$

$\therefore \quad AC = a \operatorname{cosec}\theta$

and $\quad BC = b \sec\theta$

Let l be the length of hypotenuse AB, then

$$l = AC + BC$$

$$\Rightarrow \quad \frac{dl}{d\theta} = -a \operatorname{cosec}\theta \cdot \cot\theta + b\sec\theta \cdot \tan\theta$$

$$\Rightarrow \quad \frac{d^2l}{d\theta^2} = a\operatorname{cosec}^3\theta + a\operatorname{cosec}\theta\cot^2\theta + b\sec^3\theta + b\sec\theta\tan^2\theta$$

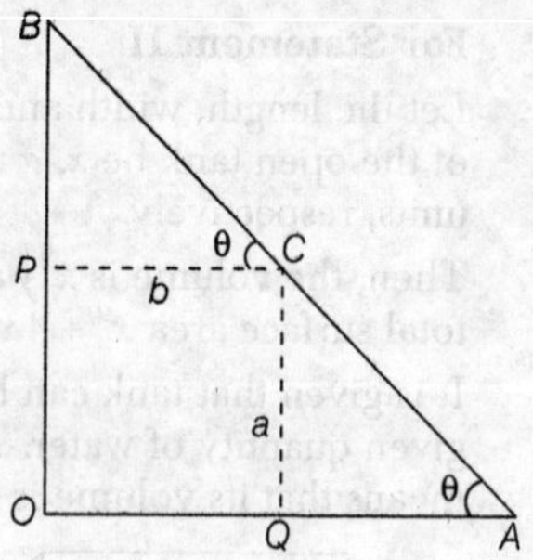

Now, $\frac{dl}{d\theta} = 0$

$\Rightarrow -a\operatorname{cosec}\theta \cdot \cot\theta + b\sec\theta \cdot \tan\theta = 0$

$\Rightarrow \quad \tan\theta = \frac{a^{1/3}}{b}$

$\therefore \quad \sin\theta = \frac{a^{1/3}}{\sqrt{a^{2/3} + b^{2/3}}}$

and $\cos\theta = \frac{b^{1/3}}{\sqrt{a^{2/3} + b^{2/3}}}$

Clearly, $\frac{d^2l}{d\theta^2} > 0$ for $\tan\theta = \left(\frac{a}{b}\right)^{1/3}$

Thus, l is minimum when

$$\theta = \tan^{-1}\left(\frac{a}{b}\right)^{1/3}.$$

The minimum value of l is given by,

$$l = a\operatorname{cosec}\theta + b\sec\theta$$

$$\therefore \quad l = (a^{2/3} + b^{2/3})^{3/2}$$

Hence, the minimum length of hypotenuse is $(a^{2/3} + b^{2/3})^{3/2}$.

Assertion-Reason

1. (a) Given, $f(x) = 5 + \frac{6}{x},\ x \neq 0$

$\Rightarrow f'(x) = 0 - \frac{6}{x^2},\ x \neq 0$

Since, $x^2 > 0$

$\therefore f'(x) < 0$

$\Rightarrow f(x)$ is decreasing function.

2. (b) We have, $f(x) = x^2 - 8x + 15$

$\Rightarrow f'(x) = 2x - 8$

Now, $f'(x) = 0$

$\Rightarrow \quad 2x - 8 = 0$

$\Rightarrow 2(x - 4) = 0$

$\Rightarrow \quad x = 4$

(Number line: $-$ to the left of 4, $+$ to the right of 4)

Now, the point $x = 4$ divides the real line into two disjoint intervals, namely $(-\infty, 4)$ and $(4, \infty)$.

In the interval $(4, \infty)$,
$f'(x) = 2x - 8 > 0$, so the function $f(x)$ is strictly increasing in this interval.

In the interval $(-\infty, 4)$,
$f'(x) = 2x - 8 < 0$, so the function $f(x)$ is strictly decreasing in this interval.

3. (a) Given, $f(x) = \log \sin x$

$$\Rightarrow f'(x) = \frac{1}{\sin x} \cdot \cos x = \cot x$$

For increasing function, $f'(x) > 0$

$\Rightarrow \cot x > 0$

We know that tan x is positive in first quadrant.

3. (b) Let $f(x) = \dfrac{e^x + e^{-x}}{2}$

$$\Rightarrow \quad f'(x) = \frac{e^x - e^{-x}}{2}$$

$$= \frac{1}{2}\left(e^x - \frac{1}{e^x}\right)$$

$$= \frac{1}{2}\left(\frac{e^{2x} - 1}{e^x}\right) \quad \ldots(\text{i})$$

Now, for $x \ge 0$, we have

$$2x \ge 0$$

$$\Rightarrow \quad e^{2x} \ge e^0$$

[$\because e^x$ is an increasing function]

$\Rightarrow e^{2x} \ge 1$

Also, for $x \ge 0$

$\Rightarrow e^x \ge 1$

$\therefore$ From Eq. (i), we get

$$f'(x) = \frac{1}{2}\left(\frac{e^{2x} - 1}{e^x}\right) \ge 0$$

So, $f(x)$ is an increasing function on $[0, \infty)$.

Let $g(x) = \dfrac{e^x - e^{-x}}{2}$

$$\Rightarrow g'(x) = \frac{e^x + e^{-x}}{2} > 0$$

[$\because e^x$ and e^{-x} both are greater than zero in $(-\infty, \infty)$]

$\therefore g(x)$ is an increasing function on $(-\infty, \infty)$.

5. (c) Given,

$$f(x) = -x^3 + 6x^2 - 9x + 10$$

$$\Rightarrow f'(x) = -3x^2 + 12x - 9$$

$$= 3(-x^2 + 4x - 3)$$

For critical points,

$f'(x) = 0$

$\Rightarrow x^2 - 4x + 3 = 0$

$\Rightarrow (x - 1)(x - 3) = 0$

$\Rightarrow x = 1, 3$

At $x = 1$,

$$f''(x) = -6x + 12$$
$$= -6(1) + 12 = 6 > 0$$

At $x = 3$,

$$f''(x) = -6x + 12$$
$$= -6(3) + 12 = -6 < 0$$

$\therefore f(x)$ has maximum at $x = 3$.

So, maximum value of $f(x)$, at $x = 3$

$$f(3) = -(3)^2 - 9(3) + 10 = 10$$

6. (d) Given, $f(x) = \sin x$

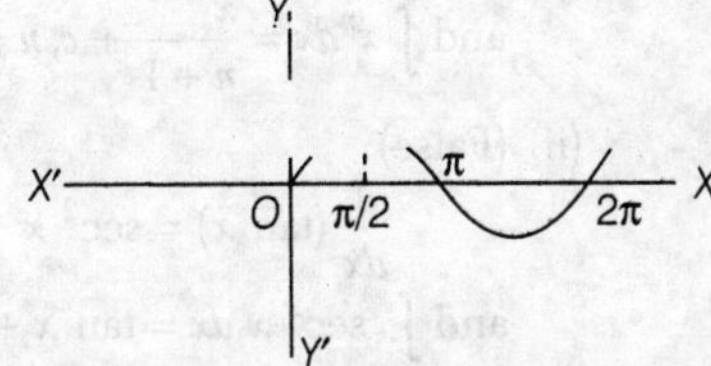

From the graph of sin x, we observe that $f(x)$ increases on the interval $\left(0, \dfrac{\pi}{2}\right)$.

$\therefore$ A is false.

Given, function $f(x) = \cos x$

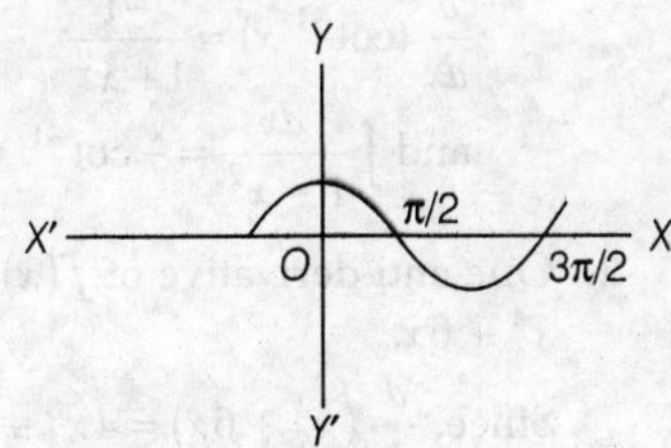

From the graph of cos x, we observe that $f(x)$ decreases on the interval $\left(0, \dfrac{\pi}{2}\right)$.

$\therefore$ R is true.

7. (b) Given, $f(x) = x^3 - 3x + 3$

$$\Rightarrow \quad f'(x) = 3x^2 - 3$$

For critical points, $f'(x) = 0$

$\Rightarrow 3x^2 - 3 = 0$

$\Rightarrow x^2 - 1 = 0$

$\Rightarrow \quad x^2 = 1$

$\Rightarrow \quad x = \pm 1$

Also, $f''(x) = 6x$

At $x = 1$,

$f''(1) = 6 > 0$

At $x = -1$,

$f''(-1) = -6 < 0$

$\therefore f(x)$ has local maxima at $x = -1$

Also, we know that for local minima,

$f''(x) > 0$

8. (b) We have,

$$f(x) = 2x^3 - 9x^2 + 12x - 3$$

$$\Rightarrow f'(x) = 6x^2 - 18x + 12$$

For increasing function, $f'(x) \ge 0$

$\therefore 6x^2 - 18x + 12 \ge 0$

$\Rightarrow 6(x - 2)(x - 1) \ge 0$

$\Rightarrow x \le 1$ and $x \ge 2$

$\therefore f(x)$ is increasing outside the interval $(1, 2)$.

Now, $f'(x) < 0$

$\Rightarrow 6(x - 2)(x - 1) < 0$

$\Rightarrow 1 < x < 2$

9. (d) Let x and y be two numbers such that

$x + y = 24$ and $P = xy$

So, $P = x(24 - x) = 24x - x^2$

$\Rightarrow P'(x) = 24 - 2x$

For critical points, $P'(x) = 0$

$\Rightarrow \quad 24 - 2x = 0$

$\Rightarrow \quad 2x = 24$

$\Rightarrow \quad x = 12$

At $x = 12$,

$P''(x) = -2 < 0$

So, $x = 12$

and $y = 24 - 12 = 12$

$\therefore$ The two numbers are 12 and 12.

Hence, A is false.

Also, we know that a function $f(x)$ minimum at $x = a$, if $f'(a) = 0$ and $f''(a) \ge 0$.

10. (b) We have $y = [x(x - 2)]^2$

$$= [x^2 - 2x]^2$$

$$\Rightarrow \frac{dy}{dx} = 2(x^2 - 2x)(2x - 2)$$

$$= 4x(x - 1)(x - 2)$$

On equating $\dfrac{dy}{dx} = 0$, we get

$4x(x - 1)(x - 2) = 0$

$\Rightarrow \quad x = 0, 1, 2$

−	+	−	+
0	1	2	

$\therefore$ Intervals are $(-\infty, 0)$, $(0, 1)$, $(1, 2)$, $(2, \infty)$.

Since, $\dfrac{dy}{dx} > 0$ in $(0, 1)$ or $(2, \infty)$

$\therefore f(x)$ is increasing in $(0, 1) \cup (2, \infty)$.

Case Based Questions

1. (i) (c) We have, $y = 4x - \frac{1}{2}x^2$

To find the rate of growth,

$$\frac{dy}{dx} = \frac{d}{dx}\left(4x - \frac{1}{2}x^2\right)$$
$$= 4 - \frac{2x}{2} = 4 - x$$

(ii) (a) We have, $\frac{dy}{dx} = 4 - x$ [from part (i)]

To find the number of days, find the critical point.

So, $\frac{dy}{dx} = 0$

$\Rightarrow 4 - x = 0 \Rightarrow x = 4$

$\therefore$ If will take 4 days for the plant to grow to maximum height.

(iii) (d) We have, $y = 4x - \frac{1}{2}x^2$

and $x = 4$ [from part (i)]

$\therefore \quad y = 4 \times 4 - \frac{1}{2}(4)^2$
$$= 16 - 8 = 8$$

$\therefore$ The maximum height of the plant is 8 cm.

2. (i) Let y be the length of rectangular garden and x be the breadth of the rectangular garden.

We need to fence the other three sides excluding the side of the brick wall.

$\therefore$ Perimeter = 200

$\Rightarrow \quad 2x + y = 200$

$\therefore$ The relation represent the total amount of fencing wire is $2x + y = 200$.

(ii) Area of the garden as a function of x can be represented as $A(x) = x \cdot y$

$= x(200 - 2x) = 200x - 2x^2$ [from (i)]

(iii) We have, $A(x) = 200x - 2x^2$

$$\Rightarrow \frac{dA}{dx} = \frac{d}{dx}(200x - 2x^2)$$
$$= 200 - 4x$$

For the area to be maximum,

$$\frac{dA(x)}{dx} = 0$$

$\Rightarrow 200 - 4x = 0$

$\Rightarrow \quad 4x = 200 \Rightarrow x = 50$

$\therefore$ The area will be maximum when x is 50 ft.

(iv) Maximum area of the garden, is at $x = 50$

$\therefore A(50) = 200(50) - 2(50)^2$
$$= 10000 - 5000$$
$$= 5000$$

$\therefore$ The maximum area if 5000 sq. ft.

Chapter-7

Integrals

1. (i) (False)

We know, $\frac{d}{dx}\left(\frac{x^{n+1}}{n+1}\right) = x^n$

and $\int x^n dx = \frac{x^{n+1}}{n+1} + c, n \neq -1$

(ii) (False)

$\frac{d}{dx}(\tan x) = \sec^2 x$

and $\int \sec^2 x \, dx = \tan x + C$

(iii) (True)

$\frac{d}{dx}(\sin^{-1} x) = \frac{1}{\sqrt{1 - x^2}}$

and $\int \frac{dx}{\sqrt{1 - x^2}} = \sin^{-1} x + C$

(iv) (False)

$\frac{d}{dx}(\cot^{-1} x) = \frac{-1}{1 + x^2}$

and $\int \frac{dx}{1 + x^2} = -\cot^{-1} x + C$

2. One anti-derivative of $f(x)$ is $x^4 + 6x$.

Since, $\frac{d}{dx}(x^4 + 6x) = 4x^3 + 6$

Therefore, the anti-derivative F is given by

$$F(x) = x^4 + 6x + C,$$

where c is constant.

Given, $F(0) = 3$, then

$$3 = 0 + 0 + c \Rightarrow C = 3$$

Hence, required anti-derivative is $x^4 + 6x + 3$ of function $f(x) = 4x^3 + 6$.

3. (i) Let $I = \int x^3\left(1 + \frac{1}{x^2}\right) dx$

$$I = \int x^3 \, dx + \int x \, dx$$
$$= \frac{x^4}{4} + \frac{x^2}{2} + C$$

(ii) Let $I = \int (ax^3 + bx^2 + C) \, dx$

$$I = a\int x^3 dx + b\int x^2 dx + C\int dx$$
$$I = \frac{ax^4}{4} + \frac{bx^3}{3} + Cx + C_1$$

(iii) We have,

$$\int\left(x^{3/2} + 2e^x - \frac{1}{x}\right) dx$$
$$= \int x^{3/2} \, dx + 2\int e^x \, dx - \int \frac{dx}{x}$$
$$= \frac{x^{3/2+1}}{\frac{3}{2}+1} + 2e^x - \log|x| + C$$
$$= \frac{2}{5}x^{5/2} + 2e^x - \log|x| + C$$

(iv) Let $I = \int (\sin x - \cos x + x) \, dx$

$$= \int \sin x \, dx - \int \cos x \, dx + \int x \, dx$$
$$= -\cos x - \sin x + \frac{x^2}{2} + C$$

(v) Let $I = \int \sec^2(7 + x) \, dx$

$$= \tan(7 + x) + C$$

Thus, the required integral value is $\tan(7 + x) + C$.

(vi) Given,

$$\int \operatorname{cosec} x(\operatorname{cosec} x + \cot x) \, dx$$
$$= \int \operatorname{cosec}^2 x \, dx + \int \operatorname{cosec} x \cdot \cot x \, dx$$
$$= -\cot x - \operatorname{cosec} x + C$$

(vii) Let $I = \int (\cos x + \sin x) \, dx$

$$I = \int \cos x \, dx + \int \sin x \, dx$$
$$= \sin x - \cos x + C$$

(viii) Let $I = \int (\sin x - 4e^x) dx$

$$= \int \sin x \, dx - \int 4e^x \, dx$$
$$= -\cos x - 4e^x + C$$

(ix) Let $I = \int (e^x + \cos x) dx$

$$= \int e^x \, dx + \int \cos x \, dx$$
$$= e^x + \sin x + C$$

(x) Let

$$I = \int \left\{(x + 3)^5 + \frac{1}{(x - 5)^3} + \frac{1}{\sqrt{x - 4}} + \sqrt{x + 2}\right\} dx$$
$$= \int (x + 3)^5 \, dx + \int \frac{dx}{(x - 5)^3} + \int \frac{dx}{(x - 4)^{1/2}} + \int (x + 2)^{1/2} dx$$
$$= \frac{(x + 3)^6}{6} + \frac{(x - 5)^{-2}}{-2} + \frac{(x - 4)^{1/2}}{\frac{1}{2}} + \frac{(x + 2)^{3/2}}{\frac{3}{2}} + C$$

$\therefore I = \frac{1}{6}(x+3)^6 - \frac{1}{2}(x-5)^{-2} + 2(x-4)^{1/2} + \frac{2}{3}(x+2)^{3/2} + C$

4. (i) (True)

Let $I = \int \left(\sqrt{x} - \frac{1}{\sqrt{x}}\right)^2 dx$

$= \int \left(x + \frac{1}{x} - 2\right) dx$

$= \frac{x^2}{2} + \log|x| - 2x + C$

(ii) (True)

Let $I = \int \sqrt{x}(3x^2 + 2x + 3)\, dx$

$= 3\int x^{5/2}\, dx + 2\int x^{3/2}\, dx + 3\int x^{1/2}\, dx$

$= \frac{6}{7}x^{7/2} + \frac{4}{5}x^{5/2} + 2x^{3/2} + C$

(iii) (True)

Let $I = \int \frac{x^3 - x^2 + x - 1}{(x-1)} dx$

$= \int \frac{x^2(x-1) + 1(x-1)}{(x-1)} dx$

$= \int (x^2 + 1)\, dx$

$= \frac{x^3}{3} + x + C$

(iv) (True)

Let $I = \int \{x^2 + e^{\log x} + e^x\}\, dx$

$= \int x^2 dx + \int x\, dx + \int e^x dx$

$\therefore I = \frac{x^3}{3} + \frac{x^2}{2} + \frac{e^x}{\log(e)} + C$

(v) (False)

Let $I = \int \frac{x^5 + x^{-2} + 2}{x^2} dx$

$= \int x^3\, dx + \int x^{-4}\, dx + 2\int x^{-2}\, dx$

$= \frac{x^4}{4} - \frac{x^{-3}}{3} - \frac{2}{x} + C$

(vi) (False)

Let $I = \int \frac{5\cos^3 x + 6\sin^3 x}{2\sin^2 x \cos^2 x} dx$

$= \frac{5}{2}\int \operatorname{cosec} x \cot x\, dx + 3\int \sec x \tan x\, dx$

$= -\frac{5}{2}\operatorname{cosec} x + 3\sec x + C$

5. Given, $\int \sqrt{1 - \sin 2x}\, dx$

$= \int \sqrt{\sin^2 x + \cos^2 x - 2\sin x \cos x}\, dx$

$= \int \sqrt{(\sin x - \cos x)^2}\, dx$

$= \int |\sin x - \cos x|\, dx$

$= \int \sin x\, dx - \int \cos x\, dx \quad \left[\because \frac{\pi}{4} < x < \frac{\pi}{2}\right]$

$= -\cos x - \sin x + C$

Thus, the required integral value is $-(\cos x + \sin x) + C$.

6. Given, $I = \int \tan^{-1}\left(\sqrt{\frac{1-\sin x}{1+\sin x}}\right) dx$

$= \int \tan^{-1}\left(\sqrt{\frac{\left(\cos\frac{x}{2} - \sin\frac{x}{2}\right)^2}{\left(\cos\frac{x}{2} + \sin\frac{x}{2}\right)^2}}\right) dx$

$= \int \tan^{-1}\left(\frac{\cos\frac{x}{2} - \sin\frac{x}{2}}{\cos\frac{x}{2} + \sin\frac{x}{2}}\right) dx$

$= \int \tan^{-1}\left(\frac{1 - \tan\frac{x}{2}}{1 + \tan\frac{x}{2}}\right) dx$

$= \int \tan^{-1}\tan\left(\frac{\pi}{4} - \frac{x}{2}\right) dx$

$= \int \left(\frac{\pi}{4} - \frac{x}{2}\right) dx$

$= \frac{\pi x}{4} - \frac{x^2}{4} + C$

$\therefore I = \frac{\pi x}{4} - \frac{x^2}{4} + C$

This is required answer.

7. (a) A. Given,

$\int \tan^{-1}(\sec x + \tan x)\, dx$ (say I)

$\therefore I = \int \tan^{-1}(\sec x + \tan x)\, dx$

$= \int \tan^{-1}\left(\frac{1}{\cos x} + \frac{\sin x}{\cos x}\right) dx$

$= \int \tan^{-1}\left(\frac{1 + \sin x}{\cos x}\right) dx$

$= \int \tan^{-1}\left(\frac{\sin^2\frac{x}{2} + \cos^2\frac{x}{2} + 2\sin\frac{x}{2}\cos\frac{x}{2}}{\cos^2\frac{x}{2} - \sin^2\frac{x}{2}}\right) dx$

$= \int \tan^{-1}\left(\frac{\left(\sin\frac{x}{2} + \cos\frac{x}{2}\right)^2}{\left(\cos\frac{x}{2} + \sin\frac{x}{2}\right)\left(\cos\frac{x}{2} - \sin\frac{x}{2}\right)}\right) dx$

$= \int \tan^{-1}\left(\frac{\sin\frac{x}{2} + \cos\frac{x}{2}}{\cos\frac{x}{2} - \sin\frac{x}{2}}\right) dx$

$= \int \tan^{-1}\left(\frac{\tan\frac{\pi}{4} + \tan\frac{x}{2}}{1 - \tan\frac{\pi}{4}\cdot\tan\frac{x}{2}}\right) dx$

$= \int \tan^{-1}\tan\left(\frac{\pi}{4} + \frac{x}{2}\right) dx$

$= \int \left(\frac{\pi}{4} + \frac{x}{2}\right) dx = \frac{\pi x}{4} + \frac{x^2}{4} + C$

Thus, $\int \tan^{-1}(\sec x + \tan x)\, dx$

$= \frac{\pi x}{4} + \frac{x^2}{4} + C$

B. Let $I = \int \left(\frac{x}{m} + \frac{m}{x} + x^m + m^x\right) dx$

$= \frac{1}{m}\int x\, dx + m\int \frac{dx}{x} + \int x^m\, dx + \int m^x\, dx$

$= \frac{x^2}{2m} + m\log x + \frac{x^{m+1}}{m+1} + \frac{m^x}{\log_e m} + C$

$\because \int \left(\frac{x}{m} + \frac{m}{x} + x^m + m^x\right) dx$

$= \frac{x^2}{2m} + m\log x + \frac{x^{m+1}}{m+1} + \frac{m^x}{\log_e m} + C$

C. Let $I = \int \frac{2 - 3\sin x}{\cos^2 x} dx$

$= 2\int \sec^2 x\, dx - 3\int \sec x \tan x\, dx$

$= 2\tan x - 3\sec x + C$

$\therefore \int \frac{2 - 3\sin x}{\cos^2 x} dx = 2\tan x - 3\sec x + C$

D. We have,

$f'(x) = 3x^2 - \frac{2}{x^3}.$

We know, $f(x) = \int f'(x)\, dx$

$$= \int \left(3x^2 - \frac{2}{x^3}\right) dx$$

$$\therefore \quad f(x) = x^3 + \frac{1}{x^2} + C$$

Since, $f(1) = 0$, then

$$0 = 1 + 1 + C \Rightarrow C = -2$$

Thus, $f(x) = x^3 + \frac{1}{x^2} - 2$

8. (i) $1 + x^5 = t$

(ii) $3 + 2x^3 = t$

(iii) $x^2 = t$

(iv) $mx = t$

(v) $x^3 + 1 = t$

(vi) $x^2 + 3 = t$

9. To find $\int \frac{1}{4x} dx$

Let $I = \int \frac{1}{4x} dx$

Robert $I = \frac{1}{4}\int \frac{1}{x} dx = \frac{1}{4} \ln|x| + C$ ...(i)

Roy $I = \int \frac{1}{(4x)} \cdot dx$

Let $4x = z \Rightarrow dx = \frac{dz}{4}$

$$I = \int \frac{1}{z} \cdot \frac{dz}{4} = \frac{1}{4} \ln|z| + C$$

$$= \frac{1}{4} \ln|4x| + C \quad \text{...(ii)}$$

Eq. (ii) can also be written as

$$I = \frac{1}{4} \ln|x \times 4| + C$$

$$= \frac{1}{4} \ln|x| + \frac{1}{4} \ln|4| + C$$

$$= \frac{1}{4} \ln|x| + C_1 \quad \text{...(iii)}$$

$$\left[\because C_1 = \frac{1}{4} \ln|4| + C\right]$$

Hence, robert got the correct answer.

10. (i) Let $I = \int \frac{3x^2}{2 + x^3} dx$

Put $2 + x^3 = t \Rightarrow 3x^2 dx = dt$

$$\therefore \quad I = \int \frac{dt}{t} = \log|t| + C$$

$$= \log|2 + x^3| + C$$

(ii) Let $I = \int \frac{(1 + \log x)}{x} dx$

Put $1 + \log x = t \Rightarrow \frac{1}{x} dx = dt$

$$\therefore I = \int t\, dt = \frac{t^2}{2} + C$$

$$= \frac{(1 + \log x)^2}{2} + C$$

(iii) Let $I = \int \cos x \cos(\sin x)\, dx$

Put $\sin x = t \Rightarrow \cos x\, dx = dt$

$$\therefore I = \int \cos t\, dt = \sin t + C$$

$$= \sin(\sin x) + C$$

11. Let $I = \int \{f(ax + b)\}^n \cdot f'(ax + b)\, dx, n \neq -1$

Let $f(ax + b) = z \therefore \int \text{cosec } x\, dx$

$\Rightarrow f'(ax + b) \cdot a\, dx = dz$

$$\therefore I = \int z^n \frac{dz}{a} = \frac{1}{a} \frac{z^{n+1}}{n+1} + C$$

$$= \frac{1}{a} \cdot \frac{\{f(ax + b)\}^{n+1}}{n+1} + C, \quad n \neq -1$$

Thus, $\int \{f(ax + b)\}^n f'(ax + b)\, dx$

$$= \frac{\{f(ax + b)\}^{n+1}}{a(n+1)} + c, n \neq -1$$

12. (c) Let $I = \int 2^{2^{2^x}} \cdot 2^{2^x} \cdot 2^x\, dx$

Let $2^{2^{2^x}} = z \therefore \int \tan x\, dx$

$$\Rightarrow 2^{2^{2^x}} \cdot 2^{2^x} \cdot 2^x (\log 2)^3 \cdot dx = dz$$

$$\therefore 2^{2^{2^x}} \cdot 2^{2^x} \cdot 2^x\, dx = \frac{dz}{(\log_e 2)^3}$$

Then,

$$I = \int \frac{dz}{(\log_e 2)^3} = \frac{1}{(\log_e 2)^3} z + C$$

$$= \frac{2^{2^{2^x}}}{(\log_e 2)^3} + C$$

13. (i) (Incorrect)

$$\int \cot x\, dx = \int \frac{\cos x}{\sin x} dx.$$

Let $\sin x = z$

$\Rightarrow \cos x\, dx = dz$

$$\therefore \int \cot x\, dx = \int \frac{dz}{z}$$

$$= \log|z| + C$$

$$= \log|\sin x| + C$$

(ii) (Incorrect)

$\int \sec x\, dx$

$$= \int \frac{\sec x (\sec x + \tan x)}{(\sec x + \tan x)} dx$$

Let $\sec x + \tan x = z$

$\Rightarrow \sec x (\sec x + \tan x)\, dx = dz$

$$\therefore \int \sec x\, dx = \int \frac{dz}{z}$$

$$= \log|z| + C$$

$$= \log|\sec x + \tan x| + C$$

(iii) (Correct)

$\int \text{cosec } x\, dx$

$$= \int \frac{\text{cosec} x (\text{cosec} x + \cot x)}{(\text{cosec } x + \cot x)} dx$$

Let $\text{cosec } x + \cot x = z$

$\Rightarrow -\text{cosec} x (\text{cosec} x + \cot x)\, dx = dz$

$$= \int \frac{-dz}{z} = -\log z + C$$

$$= -\log|\text{cosec } x + \cot x| + C$$

$$= \log|\text{cosec } x - \cot x| + C$$

$\therefore \int \text{cosec } x\, dx$

$$= \log|\text{cosec } x - \cot x| + C$$

(iv) (Incorrect)

$$\int \tan x\, dx = \int \frac{\sin x}{\cos x} dx$$

Let $\cos x = z$

$\Rightarrow -\sin x\, dx = dz$

$\therefore \sin x\, dx = -dz$

$$= \int \frac{-dz}{z}$$

$$= -\log|z| + C$$

$$= -\log|\cos x| + C$$

$$= \log|\sec x| + C$$

$$\therefore \int \tan x\, dx = \log|\sec x| + C$$

14. (i) (True)

Let $I = \int \frac{dx}{\sqrt{3x + 4} - \sqrt{3x + 1}}$

$$= \int \frac{(\sqrt{3x+4} + \sqrt{3x+1})\, dx}{(\sqrt{3x+4} - \sqrt{3x+1})(\sqrt{3x+4} + \sqrt{3x+1})}$$

$$= \frac{1}{3} \int \sqrt{3x + 4}\, dx + \frac{1}{3} \int \sqrt{3x + 1}\, dx$$

Let $3x + 4 = p$ and $3x + 1 = q$

$\Rightarrow \quad 3\,dx = dp$ and $3\,dx = dq$

$$= \frac{1}{3} \int \frac{\sqrt{p}}{3} dp + \frac{1}{3} \int \frac{\sqrt{q}\, dq}{3}$$

$$= \frac{2}{27} [(3x + 4)^{3/2} + (3x + 1)^{3/2}] + C$$

$$\therefore \int \frac{dx}{\sqrt{3x + 4} - \sqrt{3x + 1}}$$

$$= \frac{2}{27} [(3x + 4)^{3/2} + (3x + 1)^{3/2}] + C$$

(ii) (True)

Let $I = \int \tan^2 (2x - 3)\, dx$

Let $2x - 3 = z$

$\Rightarrow \quad 2\, dx = dz$

$\therefore dx = \dfrac{dz}{2}$

$\Rightarrow I = \int \tan^2 z \cdot \dfrac{dz}{2}$

$= \dfrac{1}{2} \int (\sec^2 z - 1)\, dz$

$= \dfrac{1}{2} [\tan z - z] + C$

$= \dfrac{1}{2} \tan(2x - 3) - x + \left(c + \dfrac{3}{2}\right)$

$\therefore \int \tan^2 (2x - 3)\, dx$

$= \dfrac{1}{2} \tan(2x - 3) - x + C_1,$

where $c_1 = c + \dfrac{3}{2}$

(iii) (True)

Let $I = \int \dfrac{dx}{x(1 + \log x)}$

Let $1 + \log x = z$

$\therefore \quad \dfrac{dx}{x} = dz$

$I = \int \dfrac{dz}{z} = \log |z| + C$

$= \log |1 + \log x| + C$

$\therefore \int \dfrac{dx}{x(1 + \log x)}$

$= \log |1 + \log x| + C$

(iv) (False)

Let

$I = \int (4x + 2) \sqrt{(x^2 + x + 1)}\, dx$

$= 2 \int (2x + 1) \sqrt{x^2 + x + 1}\, dx$

Let $x^2 + x + 1 = z$

$\Rightarrow (2x + 1)\, dx = dz$

$I = 2 \int \sqrt{z}\, dz$

$= 2 \cdot \dfrac{z^{3/2}}{3/2} + C$

$= \dfrac{4}{3} z^{3/2} + C$

$= \dfrac{4}{3} (x^2 + x + 1)^{3/2} + C$

$\therefore \int (4x + 2) \sqrt{(x^2 + x + 1)}\, dx$

$= \dfrac{4}{3} (x^2 + x + 1)^{3/2} + C$

(v) (True)

Let $I = \int \dfrac{dx}{x(\log x)^m}$

Let $\log x = z \Rightarrow \dfrac{dx}{x} = dz$

$\therefore I = \int \dfrac{dz}{z^m} = \int z^{-m}\, dz$

$= \dfrac{z^{1-m}}{1 - m} + C = \dfrac{(\log x)^{1-m}}{1 - m} + C$

Thus,

$\int \dfrac{dx}{x(\log x)^m} = \dfrac{(\log x)^{1-m}}{1 - m} + C$

15. (b) A. Let $I = \int \dfrac{e^{\tan^{-1} x}}{1 + x^2}\, dx$

Let $\tan^{-1} x = z$

$\Rightarrow \dfrac{1}{1 + x^2}\, dx = dz$

$\therefore I = \int e^z dz = e^z + C$

$= e^{\tan^{-1} x} + C$

Hence,

$\int \dfrac{e^{\tan^{-1} x}}{1 + x^2}\, dx = e^{\tan^{-1} x} + C$

B. $\int \dfrac{dx}{\cos^2 x(1 - \tan x)^2}$

$= \int \dfrac{\sec^2 x\, dx}{(1 - \tan x)^2}$

Let $1 - \tan x = z$

$0 - \sec^2 x dx = dz$

$\Rightarrow \quad \sec^2 x dx = -dz$

$-\int \dfrac{dz}{z^2} = -\dfrac{z^{-2+1}}{-2+1} + C$

$= -\dfrac{z^{-1}}{-1} + C = \dfrac{1}{z} + C$

$= \dfrac{1}{(1 - \tan x)} + C$

C. $\int \dfrac{(1 + \log x)^2}{x}\, dx$

Let $1 + \log x = z \Rightarrow \dfrac{1}{x}\, dx = dz$

$\therefore \int \dfrac{(1 + \log x)^2}{x}\, dx$

$= \int z^2 \cdot dz = \dfrac{z^3}{3} + C$

$= \dfrac{1}{3} (1 + \log x)^3 + C$

$\Rightarrow \int \dfrac{(1 + \log x)^2}{x}\, dx$

$= \dfrac{1}{3} (1 + \log x)^3 + C$

D. $\int \dfrac{\sqrt{\tan x}}{\sin x \cdot \cos x}\, dx$

$= \int \dfrac{\sqrt{\tan x} \cdot \cos x}{\sin x \cdot \cos^2 x}\, dx$

$= \int \dfrac{\sqrt{\tan x}}{\tan x \cdot \cos^2 x}\, dx$

$= \int \dfrac{\sec^2 x\, dx}{\sqrt{\tan x}}$

Let $\tan x = z$

$\Rightarrow \sec^2 x\, dx = dz$

$\therefore \int \dfrac{\sqrt{\tan x}}{\sin x \cdot \cos x}\, dx$

$= \int \dfrac{dz}{\sqrt{z}} = \int z^{-1/2}\, dz$

$= \dfrac{z^{1/2}}{1/2} + C$

$= 2\sqrt{\tan x} + C$

16. (True)

Let $I = \int \dfrac{x^3 \sin (\tan^{-1} x^4)}{1 + x^8}\, dx$

Let $x^4 = z \Rightarrow 4x^3\, dx = dz$

$\therefore \quad I = \int \dfrac{\sin (\tan^{-1} z)}{1 + z^2} \dfrac{dz}{4}$

$= \dfrac{1}{4} \int \dfrac{\sin (\tan^{-1} z)}{1 + z^2}\, dz$

Let $\tan^{-1} z = t \Rightarrow \dfrac{dz}{1 + z^2} = dt$

$\therefore I = \int \dfrac{\sin t}{4}\, dt = -\dfrac{1}{4} \cos t + C$

$= -\dfrac{1}{4} \cos (\tan^{-1} z) + C$

$\Rightarrow I = -\dfrac{1}{4} \cos \{\tan^{-1}(x^4)\} + C$

Thus, $\int \dfrac{x^3 \sin(\tan^{-1} x^4)}{1 + x^8}\, dx$

$= -\dfrac{1}{4} \cos\{\tan^{-1}(x^4)\} + C$

17. Let $I = \int \dfrac{(10x^9 + 10^x \cdot \log_e 10)}{x^{10} + 10^x}\, dx$

Let $10^x + x^{10} = z$

$\Rightarrow (10x^9 + 10^x \cdot \log_e 10)\, dx = dz$

$\therefore \quad I = \int \dfrac{dz}{z} = \log |z| + C$

$= \log |10^x + x^{10}| + C$

$\therefore \int \dfrac{(10x^9 + 10^x \cdot \log_e 10)}{10^x + x^{10}}\, dx$

$= \log |10^x + x^{10}| + C$

18. (i) Let $I = \int \frac{e^{2x} - e^{-2x}}{e^{2x} + e^{-2x}} dx$

Let $e^{2x} + e^{-2x} = z$

$\Rightarrow 2(e^{2x} - e^{-2x})\, dx = dz$

$\therefore I = \int \frac{dz}{2z} = \frac{1}{2} \log |z| + C$

$= \frac{1}{2} \log |e^{2x} + e^{-2x}| + C$

$\therefore \int \frac{e^{2x} - e^{-2x}}{e^{2x} + e^{-2x}} dx = \frac{1}{2} \log |e^{2x} + e^{-2x}| + C$

(ii) Let $I = \int \frac{e^{2x} - 1}{e^{2x} + 1} dx$

$= \int \frac{e^{x} - e^{-x}}{e^{x} + e^{-x}} dx$

[multiplying numerator and denominator by e^{-x}]

Let $e^x + e^{-x} = z$

$\Rightarrow (e^x - e^{-x})\, dx = dz$

$\therefore I = \int \frac{e^{2x} - 1}{e^{2x} + 1} dx$

$= \int \frac{dz}{z} = \log |z| + C$

$= \log |e^x + e^{-x}| + C$

$\therefore \int \frac{e^{2x} - 1}{e^{2x} + 1} dx = \log|e^x + e^{-x}| + C$

(iii) Given integral is

$\int \frac{x^2}{(3x^3 + 2)^3} dx$

Let $3x^3 + 2 = z$

$\Rightarrow 9x^2\, dx = dz \Rightarrow x^2\, dx = \frac{dz}{9}$

$\int \frac{x^2}{(3x^3 + 2)^3} dx = \int \frac{dz}{9 \cdot z^3}$

$= -\frac{1}{18} \frac{1}{(3x^3 + 2)^2} + C$

(iv) Integral (say I)

$= \int \frac{8x + 13}{\sqrt{4x + 7}} dx$

$= 2 \int \frac{4x + \frac{13}{2}}{\sqrt{4x + 7}} dx$

$= 2 \int \frac{4x + 7 - \frac{1}{2}}{\sqrt{4x + 7}} dx$

$\therefore \int \frac{8x + 13}{\sqrt{4x + 7}} dx$

$= \frac{1}{3} (4x + 7)^{3/2} - \frac{1}{2} (4x + 7)^{1/2} + C$

(v) Let $I = \int (7x - 2) \sqrt{3x + 2}\, dx$

$\therefore \int (7x - 2) \sqrt{3x + 2}\, dx$

$= 7 \int \left(x - \frac{2}{7}\right) \sqrt{3x + 2}\, dx$

$= \frac{7}{3} \int \left(3x + 2 - 2 - \frac{6}{7}\right) \sqrt{3x + 2}\, dx$

$= \frac{7}{3} \int (3x + 2)^{3/2}\, dx - \frac{20}{3} \int \sqrt{3x + 2}\, dx$

$= \frac{14}{45} (3x + 2)^{5/2} - \frac{40}{27} (3x + 2)^{3/2} + C$

(vi) Let $I = \int \frac{\sin x\, dx}{(1 + \cos x)^2}$

Let $1 + \cos x = z$

$\Rightarrow -\sin x\, dx = dz$

$I = \int \frac{(-dz)}{z^2} = \frac{1}{z} + C$

$= \frac{1}{1 + \cos x} + C$

$\therefore \int \frac{\sin x}{(1 + \cos x)^2} dx = \frac{1}{1 + \cos x} + C$

19. Let $I = \int \sin^3 x \cos^2 x\, dx$

$= \int \sin^2 x \cdot \sin x \cdot \cos^2 x\, dx$

$= \int (1 - \cos^2 x) \cdot \cos^2 x \cdot \sin x\, dx$

Let $\cos x = z$

$\Rightarrow -\sin x\, dx = dz$

$\therefore \quad I = \int (1 - z^2) z^2 \cdot (-dz)$

$= -\int (z^2 - z^4)\, dz$

$= -\left[\frac{z^3}{3} - \frac{z^5}{5}\right] + C$

$= \frac{z^5}{5} - \frac{z^3}{3} + C$

$= \frac{\cos^5 x}{5} - \frac{\cos^3 x}{3} + C$

Thus, $\int \sin^3 x \cos^2 x\, dx = \frac{\cos^5 x}{5} - \frac{\cos^3 x}{3} + C$

20. (d) Given, $\int \frac{\sin x - x \cos x}{x(x + \sin x)} dx$ (say I)

$\therefore I = \int \frac{\sin x - x \cos x}{x(x + \sin x)} dx$

$\Rightarrow I = \int \frac{(x + \sin x) - x - x \cos x}{x(x + \sin x)} dx$

$\Rightarrow I = \int \frac{dx}{x} - \int \frac{(1 + \cos x)\, dx}{x + \sin x}$

$\Rightarrow I = \log|x| - \log|x + \sin x| + C$

$\Rightarrow I = \log \left| \frac{x}{x + \sin x} \right| + C$

21. (a) Let $I = \int \frac{dx}{1 + \tan x}$

$= \int \frac{(\cos x)\, dx}{\cos x + \sin x}$

$= \frac{1}{2} \int \frac{(\cos x + \sin x + \cos x - \sin x)}{\cos x + \sin x} dx$

$= \frac{1}{2} \int \frac{\cos x + \sin x}{\cos x + \sin x} dx + \frac{1}{2} \int \frac{\cos x - \sin x}{\cos x + \sin x} dx$

$\therefore I = \frac{1}{2} \int dx + \frac{1}{2} \int \frac{\cos x - \sin x}{\cos x + \sin x} dx$ ...(i)

Now consider, $\int \frac{\cos x - \sin x}{\cos x + \sin x} dx$

Let $\cos x + \sin x = z$

$\Rightarrow (-\sin x + \cos x)\, dx = dz$

Thus, $\int \frac{(\cos x - \sin x)}{\cos x + \sin x} dx$

$= \int \frac{dz}{z} = \log |z| + c_1$

$= \log|\cos x + \sin x| + c_1$

Now, from Eq. (i), we get

$\int \frac{dx}{1 + \tan x}$

$= \frac{x}{2} + \frac{1}{2} \log|\cos x + \sin x| + c_1 + c_2$

$= \frac{x}{2} + \frac{1}{2} \log|\cos x + \sin x| + C$

[$\because C = c_1 + c_2$ take]

22. (False)

Let $I = \int \frac{8^{1 + x} + 4^{1 - x}}{2^x} dx$

$= \int \frac{2^{3x + 3} + 2^{2 - 2x}}{2^x} dx$

$= \int 2^{3 + 2x}\, dx + \int 2^{2 - 3x}\, dx$

$= \frac{2^{2x + 3}}{2 \log 2} + \frac{2^{2 - 3x}}{(-3) \log 2} + C$

$= \frac{2^{2x + 3}}{2 \log 2} - \frac{2^{2 - 3x}}{3 \log 2} + C$

$\therefore \int \frac{8^{1 + x} + 4^{1 - x}}{2^x} dx$

$= \frac{2^{2x + 3}}{2 \cdot \log 2} - \frac{2^{2 - 3x}}{3 \log 2} + C$

23. (i) Let $I = \int \frac{e^x\, dx}{(1+e^x)^2}$

Let $1 + e^x = z$

$\Rightarrow \quad e^x\, dx = dz$

$\therefore I = \int \frac{dz}{z^2} = -\frac{1}{z} + C$

$= -\frac{1}{1+e^x} + C$

(ii) Let $I = \int x^{2x}(1 + \log x)\, dx$

Let $x^x = z$

$\Rightarrow \quad e^{x \log x} = z$

$\Rightarrow e^{x\log x}(1 + \log x)\, dx = dz$

$\Rightarrow \quad x^x(1 + \log x)\, dx = dz$

$\therefore \; I = \int x^{2x}(1 + \log x)\, dx$

$= \int x^x \cdot x^x(1 + \log x)\, dx$

$= \int z \cdot dz$

$= \frac{z^2}{2} + c = \frac{x^{2x}}{2} + C$

24. (i) Let $\quad I = \int \frac{\sin x}{1 + \cos x}\, dx$

$= \int \frac{2\sin\frac{x}{2}\cos\frac{x}{2}}{2\cos^2\frac{x}{2}}\, dx$

$= \int \tan\frac{x}{2}\, dx$

Let $\frac{x}{2} = z \Rightarrow dx = 2\, dz$

$I = \int \tan z (2\, dz)$

$= 2\int \tan z\, dz$

$= 2\log|\sec z| + C$

$= 2\log\left|\sec\frac{x}{2}\right| + C$

$\therefore \int \frac{\sin x}{\cos x + 1}\, dx$

$= 2\log\left|\sec\frac{x}{2}\right| + C$

(ii) Let $I = \int \sin 2x \cdot \cos 3x\, dx$

$= \frac{1}{2}\int 2\sin 2x \cdot \cos 3x\, dx$

$= \frac{1}{2}\int [\sin 5x - \sin x]\, dx$

$= \frac{1}{2}\left[\frac{\cos 5x}{-5} - \frac{\cos x}{-1}\right] + C$

$\therefore \int \sin 2x \cdot \cos 3x\, dx$

$= -\frac{\cos 5x}{10} + \frac{1}{2}\cos x + C$

(iii) Let $I = \int \sin^2 x \cos^2 x\, dx$

$= \frac{1}{4}\int 4\sin^2 x \cos^2 x\, dx$

$= \frac{1}{4}\int (2\sin x \cos x)^2\, dx$

$= \frac{1}{4}\int \sin^2 2x\, dx$

$= \frac{1}{8}\int 2\sin^2 2x\, dx$

$= \frac{1}{8}\int (1 - \cos 4x)\, dx$

$= \frac{1}{8}\left[x - \frac{\sin 4x}{4}\right] + C$

$\therefore \int \sin^2 x \cdot \cos^2 x\, dx$

$= \frac{1}{8}\left[x - \frac{\sin 4x}{4}\right] + C$

(iv) Let $I = \int \sin^2(2x + 5)\, dx$

Let $2x + 5 = p \Rightarrow 2dx = dp$

$\therefore I = \int \sin^2 p \cdot \left(\frac{dp}{2}\right)$

$= \frac{1}{4}\int 2\sin^2 p\, dp$

$= \frac{1}{4}\int (1 - \cos 2p)\, dp$

$\therefore I = \frac{p}{4} - \frac{\sin 2p}{8} + c_1$

$\therefore I = \frac{(2x+5)}{4}$

$- \frac{1}{8}\sin 2(2x + 5) + c_1$

$= \frac{x}{2} - \frac{1}{8}\sin(4x + 10) + C$

$\left[\because c = c_1 + \frac{5}{4}\right]$

$\therefore \int \sin^2(2x + 5)\, dx$

$= \frac{x}{2} - \frac{1}{8}\sin(4x + 10) + C$

(v) $\int (\sin^4 x + \cos^4 x)\, dx$

$= \int \sin^4 x\, dx + \int \cos^4 x\, dx$

$\therefore \int (\sin^4 x + \cos^4 x)\, dx$

$= \int [(\sin^2 x + \cos^2 x)^2$

$-2\sin^2 x \cdot \cos^2 x]\, dx$

$= \int \left[1 - \frac{1}{2}\sin^2 2x\right] dx$

$= \int \frac{4 - 2\sin^2 2x}{4}\, dx$

$= \int \left[\frac{3}{4} + \frac{\cos 4x}{4}\right] dx$

$= \frac{3x}{4} + \frac{\sin 4x}{16} + C$

25. **To show** $\cos^4 x = \frac{1}{8}\cos(4x) + \frac{1}{2}\cos(2x) + \frac{3}{8}$

Using identity,

$\cos^2\theta = \frac{1}{2} + \frac{1}{2}\cos(2\theta)$

$\text{LHS} = \cos^4 x$

$= (\cos^2 x)^2$

$= \left(\frac{1}{2} + \frac{1}{2}\cos 2x\right)^2$

$= \frac{1}{4} + \frac{1}{4}\cos^2 2x + \frac{1}{2}\cos 2x$

$= \frac{1}{4} + \frac{1}{4}\left(\frac{1}{2} + \frac{1}{2}\cos 4x\right) + \frac{1}{2}\cos 2x$

$= \frac{1}{4} + \frac{1}{8} + \frac{1}{8}\cos 4x + \frac{1}{2}\cos 2x$

$= \frac{3}{8} + \frac{1}{8}\cos 4x + \frac{1}{2}\cos 2x$

= RHS

Let $I = \int \cos^4 x\, dx$

$= \int \left[\frac{1}{8}\cos 4x + \frac{1}{2}\cos 2x + \frac{3}{8}\right] dx$

$= \frac{1}{8}\cdot\frac{\sin 4x}{4} + \frac{1}{2}\cdot\frac{\sin 2x}{2} + \frac{3}{8}\cdot x + C$

$= \frac{\sin 4x}{32} + \frac{\sin 2x}{4} + \frac{3}{8}\cdot x + C$

26. (True)

Let $\quad I = \int \frac{\cos 2x}{(\cos x + \sin x)^2}\, dx$

$\Rightarrow \quad I = \int \frac{\cos 2x}{1 + \sin 2x}\, dx$

Let $1 + \sin 2x = z$

$\Rightarrow 2\cos 2x\, dx = dz$

$I = \int \frac{dz}{2(z)} = \frac{1}{2}\log|z| + C$

$= \frac{1}{2}\log|1 + \sin 2x| + C$

27. (b) Given, $\int \frac{\sin x}{\sin(x + a)}\, dx = I$ (say)

$\therefore \; I = \int \frac{\sin x}{\sin(x + a)}\, dx$

Let $x + a = z \Rightarrow dx = dz$

$\therefore x = z - a$

$I = \int \frac{\sin(z - a)}{\sin z}\, dz$

$= \int \frac{\sin z \cdot \cos a - \cos z \cdot \sin a}{\sin z}\, dz$

$= \int (\cos a)\, dz - \sin a \int \frac{\cos z}{\sin z}\, dz$

$= \cos a \cdot z - \sin a \int \cot z \, dz + c_1$
$= \cos a \cdot (x + a) - \sin a \log |\sin (x + a)| + c_1 + c_2$
$= (x + a) \cos a - \sin a \log \sin |(x + a)| + c_1 + c_2$
$= x \cos a - \sin a \log |\sin (x + a)| + C$

where $c = a \cos a + c_1 + c_2$

$\therefore \int \frac{\sin x}{\sin (x + a)} dx = x \cos a - \sin a \cdot \log |\sin (x + a)| + C$

28. (d) Given,

$I = \int \sin x \cdot \sin 2x \cdot \sin 3x \, dx$

$= \frac{1}{2} \int \sin x \, (2 \sin 2x \sin 3x) \, dx$

$= \frac{1}{2} \int \sin x \, [\cos x - \cos 5x] \, dx$

$= \frac{1}{2} \int \sin x \cos x \, dx - \frac{1}{2} \int \sin x \cos 5x \, dx$

$= \frac{1}{4} \int 2 \sin x \cos x \, dx - \frac{1}{4} \int 2 \sin x \cos 5x \, dx$

$= \frac{1}{4} \int \sin 2x \, dx - \frac{1}{4} \int (\sin 6x - \sin 4x) \, dx$

$= -\frac{1}{4} \frac{\cos 2x}{2} - \frac{1}{4} \left[\frac{-\cos 6x}{6} + \frac{\cos 4x}{4} \right] + C$

$\therefore \int \sin x \cdot \sin 2x \cdot \sin 3x \, dx = \frac{1}{4} \left[\frac{\cos 4x}{4} - \frac{\cos 2x}{2} + \frac{\cos 6x}{6} \right] + C$

29. (False)

Given, $\int \frac{\cos 5x + \cos 4x}{1 - 2 \cos 3x} dx$

$I = \int \frac{2 \cos \frac{9x}{2} \cos \frac{x}{2}}{1 - 2\left(2 \cos^2 \frac{3x}{2} - 1\right)} dx$

$= -\int \frac{2 \cos \frac{9x}{2} \cos \frac{x}{2}}{4 \cos^2 \frac{3x}{2} - 3} dx$

$I = -\int \frac{2 \cos \frac{9x}{2} \cos \frac{x}{2} \cos \frac{3x}{2}}{4 \cos^3 \frac{3x}{2} - 3 \cos \frac{3x}{2}} dx$

$= -\int \frac{2 \cos \frac{9x}{2} \cos \frac{x}{2} \cos \frac{3x}{2}}{\cos 3\left(\frac{3x}{2}\right)} dx$

$= -\int 2 \cos \frac{3x}{2} \cdot \cos \frac{x}{2} \, dx$

$= -\int (\cos 2x + \cos x) \, dx$

$\therefore \int \frac{\cos 5x + \cos 4x}{1 - 2 \cos 3x} dx = -\left(\frac{\sin 2x}{2} + \sin x \right) + C$

30. Given, $\int \sqrt{\frac{1 - \cos 2x}{1 + \cos 2x}} dx$

$= \int \sqrt{\frac{2 \sin^2 x}{2 \cos^2 x}} dx = \int \frac{\sin x}{\cos x} dx$

$= \int \tan x \, dx = \log |\sec x| + C$

$\therefore \int \sqrt{\frac{1 - \cos 2x}{1 + \cos 2x}} dx = \log |\sec x| + C$

This is required answer.

31. (a) Given,

$\int \frac{\sin 2x}{a^2 \sin^2 x + b^2 \cos^2 x} dx$

Let $a^2 \sin^2 x + b^2 \cos^2 x = z$

$\therefore (a^2 - b^2) \sin 2x \, dx = dz$

$\Rightarrow \sin 2x \, dx = \frac{dz}{a^2 - b^2}$

$\therefore \int \frac{\sin 2x}{a^2 \sin^2 x + b^2 \cos^2 x} dx$

$= \int \frac{dz}{(a^2 - b^2) z} = \frac{1}{a^2 - b^2} \int \frac{dz}{z}$

$= \frac{1}{a^2 b^2} \log |z| + c$

$= \frac{1}{a^2 - b^2} \log |a^2 \sin^2 x + b^2 \cos^2 x| + C$

$\therefore \int \frac{\sin 2x}{a^2 \sin^2 x + b^2 \cos^2 x} dx = \frac{1}{a^2 - b^2} \log |a^2 \sin^2 x + b^2 \cos^2 x| + C$

32. (True)

Let $I = \int \frac{\sin 2x}{\sin \left(x - \frac{\pi}{6}\right) \sin \left(x + \frac{\pi}{6}\right)} dx$

$= \int \frac{\sin \left\{ \left(x - \frac{\pi}{6}\right) + \left(x + \frac{\pi}{6}\right) \right\}}{\sin \left(x - \frac{\pi}{6}\right) \sin \left(x + \frac{\pi}{6}\right)} dx$

$= \int \frac{\sin \left(x - \frac{\pi}{6}\right) \cdot \cos \left(x + \frac{\pi}{6}\right) + \cos \left(x - \frac{\pi}{6}\right) \cdot \sin \left(x + \frac{\pi}{6}\right)}{\sin \left(x - \frac{\pi}{6}\right) \cdot \sin \left(x + \frac{\pi}{6}\right)} dx$

$= \int \cot \left(x + \frac{\pi}{6}\right) dx + \int \cot \left(x - \frac{\pi}{6}\right) dx$

$= \log \left| \sin \left(x + \frac{\pi}{6}\right) \right| + \log \left| \sin \left(x - \frac{\pi}{6}\right) \right| + C$

$\therefore \int \frac{\sin 2x}{\sin \left(x - \frac{\pi}{6}\right) \sin \left(x + \frac{\pi}{6}\right)} dx = \log \left| \sin \left(x + \frac{\pi}{6}\right) \right| + \log \left| \sin \left(x - \frac{\pi}{6}\right) \right| + C$

33. Let $I = \int \frac{\sin (x - \alpha)}{\sin (x + \alpha)} dx$

$= \int \frac{\sin (x + \alpha - 2\alpha)}{\sin (x + \alpha)} dx$

$= \int \frac{\sin (x + \alpha) \cdot \cos 2\alpha - \cos (x + \alpha) \sin 2\alpha}{\sin (x + \alpha)} dx$

$= \int \cos 2\alpha \cdot dx - \sin 2\alpha \int \cot (x + \alpha) \, dx$

$= \cos 2\alpha \cdot \int dx - \sin 2\alpha \int \cot (x + \alpha) \, dx$

$\Rightarrow I = x \cdot \cos 2\alpha - \sin 2\alpha \cdot \log |\sin (x + \alpha)| + C$

Hence, $\int \frac{\sin (x - \alpha)}{\sin (x + \alpha)} dx = x \cdot \cos 2\alpha - \sin 2\alpha \cdot \log |\sin (x + \alpha)| + C$

This is required answer.

34. (False)

Let $I = \int \frac{\cos^3 x}{\sin^2 x + \sin x} dx$

$= \int \frac{\cos^2 x}{\sin x \, (1 + \sin x)} \cdot \cos x \, dx$

$= \int \frac{(1 - \sin^2 x)}{\sin x \cdot (1 + \sin x)} \cdot \cos x \, dx$

$= \int \frac{1 - \sin x}{\sin x} \cdot \cos x \, dx$

Let $\sin x = z \Rightarrow \cos x \, dx = dz$

$\therefore I = \int \frac{1 - z}{z} dz = \int \left(\frac{1}{z} - 1 \right) dz$

$= \log |z| - z + c$

$= \log |\sin x| - \sin x + C$

35. Let $I = \int \sec^4 x \, dx$

$= \int \sec^2 x \cdot \sec^2 x \, dx$

$= \int (1 + \tan^2 x) \sec^2 x \, dx$

Let $\tan x = z \Rightarrow \sec^2 x \, dx = dz$

$\therefore \; I = \int (1 + z^2) \, dz = z + \dfrac{z^3}{3} + C$

$= (\tan x) + \dfrac{1}{3}(\tan^3 x) + C$

$\therefore \int \sec^4 x \, dx = \tan x + \dfrac{1}{3}\tan^3 x + C$

This is required answer.

36. (i) (False)

Given,

$I = \int \dfrac{dx}{x^2 - a^2}$

$= \int \dfrac{1}{(x+a)(x-a)} \, dx$

$= \dfrac{1}{2a} \int \dfrac{(x+a)-(x-a)}{(x+a)(x-a)} \, dx$

$= \dfrac{1}{2a} [\log|x - a| - \log|x + a|] + C$

$\therefore \int \dfrac{dx}{x^2 - a^2} = \dfrac{1}{2a} \log\left|\dfrac{x-a}{x+a}\right| + C$

(ii) (False)

Given, $\int \dfrac{dx}{x^2 + a^2}$

Let $x = a \tan\theta$

$\Rightarrow dx = a \sec^2\theta \, d\theta$

$\int \dfrac{dx}{x^2 + a^2} = \int \dfrac{a \sec^2\theta d\theta}{a^2(1 + \tan^2\theta)}$

$= \dfrac{1}{a} \int d\theta = \dfrac{\theta}{a}$

$\therefore \int \dfrac{dx}{x^2 + a^2} = \dfrac{1}{a} \tan^{-1}\left(\dfrac{x}{a}\right) + C$

(iii) (False)

Given, $\int \dfrac{dx}{\sqrt{x^2 + a^2}}$

Let $x = a \tan\theta$

$\Rightarrow dx = a \sec^2\theta \, d\theta$

$\therefore \int \dfrac{dx}{\sqrt{x^2 + a^2}}$

$= \int \dfrac{a \sec^2\theta \, d\theta}{\sqrt{a^2 \tan^2\theta + a^2}}$

$= \int \sec\theta \, d\theta$

$= \log|(\sec\theta + \tan\theta)| + c_1$

$= \log\left|\dfrac{x}{a} + \sqrt{\dfrac{x^2}{a^2} + 1}\right| + c_1$

Then, $\int \dfrac{dx}{\sqrt{x^2 + a^2}}$

$= \log|x + \sqrt{x^2 + a^2}| + C$

(iv) (True)

Given, $\int \dfrac{dx}{\sqrt{a^2 - x^2}}$

Let $x = a \sin\theta$

$\Rightarrow dx = a \cos\theta \, d\theta$

$\Rightarrow \int \dfrac{a \cos\theta \, d\theta}{a \cdot \cos\theta} = \int d\theta = \theta + C$

Thus, $\int \dfrac{dx}{\sqrt{a^2 - x^2}}$

$= \sin^{-1}\left(\dfrac{x}{a}\right) + C$

37. (i) Let $I = \int \dfrac{dx}{9x^2 - 4}$

$= \dfrac{1}{9} \int \dfrac{dx}{x^2 - \dfrac{4}{9}}$

$= \dfrac{1}{9} \int \dfrac{dx}{(x)^2 - (2/3)^2}$

$= \dfrac{1}{9} \cdot \dfrac{1}{2 \cdot \left(\dfrac{2}{3}\right)} \log\left|\dfrac{x - \dfrac{2}{3}}{x + \dfrac{2}{3}}\right| + C$

$= \dfrac{1}{12} \log\left|\dfrac{3x - 2}{3x + 2}\right| + C$

$\therefore \int \dfrac{dx}{9x^2 - 4}$

$= \dfrac{1}{12} \log\left|\dfrac{3x-2}{3x+2}\right| + C,$

where C is a constant.

(ii) Let $I = \int \dfrac{dx}{\sqrt{2x - x^2}}$

$= \int \dfrac{dx}{\sqrt{1 - (x-1)^2}}$

Let $(x - 1) = t \Rightarrow dx = dt$

$\therefore I = \int \dfrac{dt}{\sqrt{1 - t^2}} = \sin^{-1}(t) + C$

$= \sin^{-1}(x - 1) + C$

$\therefore \int \dfrac{dx}{\sqrt{2x - x^2}}$

$= \sin^{-1}(x - 1) + C$

(iii) Let $I = \int \dfrac{dx}{\sqrt{16x^2 + 25}}$

$= \int \dfrac{dx}{\sqrt{(4x)^2 + 5^2}}$

$= \dfrac{1}{4} \int \dfrac{dx}{\sqrt{x^2 + (5/4)^2}}$

$= \dfrac{1}{4} \cdot \log\left|x + \sqrt{x^2 + \left(\dfrac{5}{4}\right)^2}\right| + C_1$

$= \dfrac{1}{4} \cdot \log\left|\dfrac{4x + \sqrt{16x^2 + 25}}{4}\right| + C_1$

$= \dfrac{1}{4} \cdot \log|4x + \sqrt{16x^2 + 25}| + C,$

where $c = c_1 - \dfrac{1}{4} \log 4.$

Thus, $\int \dfrac{dx}{\sqrt{16x^2 + 25}}$

$= \dfrac{1}{4} \log|4x + \sqrt{16x^2 + 25}| + C$

(iv) Let $I = \int \dfrac{dx}{\sqrt{9 - 25x^2}}$

$= \dfrac{1}{5} \int \dfrac{dx}{\sqrt{\dfrac{9}{25} - x^2}}$

$= \dfrac{1}{5} \int \dfrac{dx}{\sqrt{\left(\dfrac{3}{5}\right)^2 - x^2}}$

$= \dfrac{1}{5} \cdot \sin^{-1}\left(\dfrac{x}{3/5}\right)$

$= \dfrac{1}{5} \sin^{-1}\left(\dfrac{5x}{3}\right) + C$

Thus, $\int \dfrac{dx}{\sqrt{9 - 25x^2}}$

$= \dfrac{1}{5} \sin^{-1}\left(\dfrac{5x}{3}\right) + C$

38. (i) (False)

Let $I = \int \dfrac{3x^2}{x^6 + 1} \, dx$

$= \int \dfrac{3x^2 \, dx}{(x^3)^2 + 1}$

Let $x^3 = z \Rightarrow 3x^2 dx = dz$

$\therefore I = \int \dfrac{dz}{z^2 + 1}$

$= \tan^{-1}(z) + C$

$= \tan^{-1}(x^3) + C$

(ii) (True)

Let $I = \int \frac{dx}{a^2x^2 - b^2}$

$= \frac{1}{a^2} \int \frac{dx}{x^2 - \left(\frac{b}{a}\right)^2}$

$\therefore \quad I = \frac{1}{2ab} \log \left| \frac{ax - b}{ax + b} \right| + C$

(iii) (False)

Let $I = \int \frac{dx}{\sqrt{(2 - x)^2 + 1}}$

Let $2 - x = z$

$\Rightarrow \quad -dx = dz$

$\Rightarrow \quad dx = -dz$

$\therefore I = \int \frac{-dz}{\sqrt{z^2 + 1}}$

$= -\log |z + \sqrt{z^2 + 1}| + C$

$= -\log |(2 - x) + \sqrt{(2 - x)^2 + 1}| + C$

39. Let $I = \int \frac{dx}{2x^2 + x - 1}$

$= \frac{1}{2} \int \frac{dx}{x^2 + \frac{x}{2} - \frac{1}{2}}$

$= \frac{1}{2} \int \frac{dx}{x^2 + \frac{x}{2} + \left(\frac{1}{4}\right)^2 - \left(\frac{1}{4}\right)^2 - \frac{1}{2}}$

$= \frac{1}{2} \int \frac{dx}{x^2 + \frac{x}{2} + \left(\frac{1}{4}\right)^2 - \left(\frac{3}{4}\right)^2}$

$= \frac{1}{2} \int \frac{dx}{\left(x + \frac{1}{4}\right)^2 - \left(\frac{3}{4}\right)^2}$

$= \frac{1}{2} \cdot \frac{1}{2 \cdot \left(\frac{3}{4}\right)} \log \left| \frac{x + \frac{1}{4} - \frac{3}{4}}{x + \frac{1}{4} + \frac{3}{4}} \right| + C$

$= \frac{1}{3} \log \left| \frac{x - \frac{1}{2}}{x + 1} \right| + C$

$= \frac{1}{3} \log \left| \frac{2x - 1}{2(x + 1)} \right| + C$

$\therefore \int \frac{dx}{2x^2 + x - 1} = \frac{1}{3} \log \left| \frac{2x - 1}{2(x + 1)} \right| + C$

This is required answer.

40. (d) Let $I = \int \frac{dx}{x^2 + 4x + 8}$

$= \int \frac{dx}{x^2 + 4x + 4 + 4}$

$= \int \frac{dx}{(x + 2)^2 + 2^2}$

$= \frac{1}{2} \tan^{-1} \left(\frac{x + 2}{2} \right) + C$

$\therefore \int \frac{dx}{x^2 + 4x + 8} = \frac{1}{2} \tan^{-1} \left(\frac{x + 2}{2} \right) + C$

41. (True)

Let $I = \int \frac{dx}{\sqrt{5x^2 - 2x}}$

$= \int \frac{dx}{\sqrt{5\left(x^2 - \frac{2}{5}x\right)}}$

$= \int \frac{1}{\sqrt{5}} \frac{1}{\sqrt{\left(x - \frac{1}{5}\right)^2 - \left(\frac{1}{5}\right)^2}} dx$

Let $\left(x - \frac{1}{5}\right) = z \Rightarrow dx = dz$

$I = \int \frac{1}{\sqrt{5}} \frac{dz}{\sqrt{z^2 - \left(\frac{1}{5}\right)^2}}$

$= \frac{1}{\sqrt{5}} \int \frac{dz}{\sqrt{z^2 - \left(\frac{1}{5}\right)^2}}$

$= \frac{1}{\sqrt{5}} \log \left| z + \sqrt{z^2 - \left(\frac{1}{5}\right)^2} \right| + C$

$= \frac{1}{\sqrt{5}} \log \left| \left(x - \frac{1}{5}\right) + \sqrt{\left(x - \frac{1}{5}\right)^2 - \left(\frac{1}{5}\right)^2} \right| + C$

$= \frac{1}{\sqrt{5}} \log \left| \left(x - \frac{1}{5}\right) + \sqrt{x^2 - \frac{2x}{5}} \right| + C$

$\therefore \int \frac{dx}{\sqrt{5x^2 - 2x}} = \frac{1}{\sqrt{5}} \log \left| \left(x - \frac{1}{5}\right) + \sqrt{x^2 - \frac{2x}{5}} \right| + C$

42. (b) Let

$I = \int \frac{dx}{x\{6(\log x)^2 + 7 \log x + 2\}}$

Let $\log x = z \Rightarrow \frac{dx}{x} = dz$

$\therefore I = \int \frac{dz}{6z^2 + 7z + 2}$

$= \int \frac{dz}{6\left(z^2 + \frac{7}{6}z + \frac{1}{3}\right)}$

$= \frac{1}{6} \int \frac{dz}{\left(z + \frac{7}{12}\right)^2 + \frac{1}{3} - \frac{49}{144}}$

$= \frac{1}{6} \int \frac{dz}{\left(z + \frac{7}{12}\right)^2 - \left(\frac{1}{12}\right)^2}$

$= \frac{1}{6 \times 2 \cdot \left(\frac{1}{12}\right)} \log \left| \frac{z + \frac{7}{12} - \frac{1}{12}}{z + \frac{7}{12} + \frac{1}{12}} \right| + c_1$

$= \log \left| \frac{2z + 1}{3z + 2} \right| + C,$

where $c = c_1 + \log \frac{3}{2}$

$I = \log \left| \frac{2 \log x + 1}{3 \log x + 2} \right| + C$

Thus,

$\int \frac{dx}{x\{6(\log x)^2 + 7(\log x) + 2\}} = \log \left| \frac{2 \log x + 1}{3 \log x + 2} \right| + C$

43. Let $I = \int \frac{\sin x + \cos x}{9 + 16 \sin 2x} dx$

$= \int \frac{\sin x + \cos x}{9 + 16[1 - (\sin x - \cos x)^2]} dx$

$= \int \frac{(\sin x + \cos x)}{25 - 16 (\sin x - \cos x)^2} dx$

Let $\sin x - \cos x = z$

$\Rightarrow (\cos x + \sin x)\, dx = dz$

$\therefore I = \int \frac{dz}{25 - 16z^2}$

$= \frac{1}{16} \int \frac{dz}{\left(\frac{5}{4}\right)^2 - z^2}$

$= \frac{1}{16} \cdot \frac{1}{2 \cdot \frac{5}{4}} \log \left| \frac{\frac{5}{4} + z}{\frac{5}{4} - z} \right| + C$

$= \frac{1}{40} \log \left| \frac{5 + 4(\sin x - \cos x)}{5 - 4(\sin x - \cos x)} \right| + C$

44. (i) (True)

Let $I=\int \frac{dx}{\sqrt{9+8x-x^2}}$

$=\int \frac{dx}{\sqrt{-(x^2-8x-9)}}$

$=\int \frac{dx}{\sqrt{-(x^2-8x+16-25)}}$

$=\int \frac{dx}{\sqrt{-\{(x-4)^2-(5)^2\}}}$

$=\int \frac{dx}{\sqrt{(5)^2-(x-4)^2}}$

$\therefore \quad I=\int \frac{dx}{\sqrt{(5)^2-(x-4)^2}}$

$=\sin^{-1}\left(\frac{x-4}{5}\right)+C$

Then, $\int \frac{dx}{\sqrt{9+8x-x^2}}$

$=\sin^{-1}\left(\frac{x-4}{5}\right)+C$

(ii) (True)

Let $I=\int \frac{dx}{\sqrt{2x^2+3x-2}}$

$=\frac{1}{\sqrt{2}}\int \frac{dx}{\sqrt{x^2+\frac{3}{2}x-1}}$

$=\frac{1}{\sqrt{2}}\int \frac{dx}{\sqrt{\left(x+\frac{3}{4}\right)^2-\frac{9}{16}-1}}$

$=\frac{1}{\sqrt{2}}\int \frac{dx}{\sqrt{\left(x+\frac{3}{4}\right)^2-\left(\frac{5}{4}\right)^2}}$

$=\frac{1}{\sqrt{2}}\log\left|\left(x+\frac{3}{4}\right)+\sqrt{x^2+\frac{3}{2}x-1}\right|+C$

Thus, $\int \frac{dx}{\sqrt{2x^2+3x-2}}$

$=\frac{1}{\sqrt{2}}\log\left|\left(x+\frac{3}{4}\right)+\sqrt{x^2+\frac{3}{2}x-1}\right|+C$

(iii) (True)

Let $I=\int \frac{\sec^2 x\,dx}{\sqrt{\tan^2 x+4}}$

Let $\tan x=z \Rightarrow \sec^2 x\,dx=dz$

$\therefore \quad I=\int \frac{dz}{\sqrt{z^2+4}}$

$=\log|z+\sqrt{z^2+4}|+c$

$=\log|\tan x+\sqrt{\tan^2 x+4}|+C$

Thus, $\int \frac{\sec^2 x\,dx}{\sqrt{\tan^2 x+4}}$

$=\log|\tan x+\sqrt{\tan^2 x+4}|+C$

45. Let $I=\int \frac{e^x\,dx}{\sqrt{5-4e^x-e^{2x}}}$

$=\int \frac{e^x\,dx}{\sqrt{5-4e^x-(e^x)^2}}$

Let $e^x=z$, then $e^x dx=dz$

$\therefore \quad I=\int \frac{dz}{\sqrt{5-4z-z^2}}$

$=\int \frac{dz}{\sqrt{-(z^2+4z-5)}}$

$=\int \frac{dz}{\sqrt{-\{(z+2)^2-3^2\}}}$

$=\int \frac{dz}{\sqrt{(3)^2-(z+2)^2}}$

$=\sin^{-1}\left(\frac{z+2}{3}\right)+C$

$\therefore I=\sin^{-1}\left(\frac{e^x+2}{3}\right)+C$

Thus, $\int \frac{e^x\,dx}{\sqrt{5-4e^x-e^{2x}}}$

$=\sin^{-1}\left(\frac{e^x+2}{3}\right)+C$

46. (c) Let $I=\int \frac{\sin 2x\cdot\cos 2x}{\sqrt{9-\cos^4 2x}}\,dx$

$=\int \frac{\sin 2x\cdot\cos 2x}{\sqrt{(3)^2-(\cos^2 2x)^2}}\,dx$

Let $\cos^2 2x=z$

$\Rightarrow -4\cos 2x\cdot\sin 2x\,dx=dz$

$\therefore \cos 2x\cdot\sin 2x\,dx=-\frac{dz}{4}$

$\therefore I=\int \frac{-dz}{4\sqrt{3^2-z^2}}$

$=-\frac{1}{4}\sin^{-1}\left(\frac{z}{3}\right)+C$

$=-\frac{1}{4}\sin^{-1}\left(\frac{\cos^2 2x}{3}\right)+C$

Thus, $\int \frac{\sin 2x\cos 2x}{\sqrt{9-\cos^4 2x}}\,dx$

$=-\frac{1}{4}\sin^{-1}\left(\frac{\cos^2 2x}{3}\right)+C$

47. (True)

Let $I=\int \frac{dx}{\sqrt{1-e^{2x}}}=\int \frac{e^{-x}dx}{\sqrt{e^{-2x}-1}}$

$=\int \frac{e^{-x}\,dx}{\sqrt{(e^{-x})^2-1}}$

Let $\quad e^{-x}=z \Rightarrow -e^{-x}\,dx=dz$

$\therefore e^{-x}\,dx=-dz$

$\therefore I=\int \frac{-dz}{\sqrt{z^2-1}}=-\int \frac{dz}{\sqrt{z^2-1}}$

$=-\log|z+\sqrt{z^2-1}|+C$

$=-\log|e^{-x}+\sqrt{e^{-2x}-1}|+C$

$=\log|e^{-x}-\sqrt{e^{-2x}-1}|+C$

48. Let $I=\int \frac{(4x+1)}{x^2+3x+2}\,dx$

Let $(4x+1)$

$=\lambda\frac{d}{dx}(x^2+3x+2)+\mu$

$=\lambda(2x+3)+\mu$

Comparing coefficient of like power of 'x', we get

$2\lambda=4$ and $3\lambda+\mu=1$

$\Rightarrow \lambda=2$ and $\mu=-5$

$\therefore I=\int \frac{(4x+1)}{x^2+3x+2}\,dx$

$=\int \frac{2(2x+3)-5}{x^2+3x+2}\,dx$

$\Rightarrow I=2\int \frac{(2x+3)\,dx}{x^2+3x+2}-5\int \frac{dx}{x^2+3x+2}$

$\Rightarrow I=2\log|x^2+3x+2|-5\int \frac{dx}{x^2+3x+\left(\frac{9}{4}\right)-\frac{9}{4}+2}$

$\Rightarrow I=2\log|x^2+3x+2|-5\int \frac{dx}{\left(x+\frac{3}{2}\right)^2-\left(\frac{1}{2}\right)^2}$

$\Rightarrow I=2\log|x^2+3x+2|-5\frac{1}{2\cdot\left(\frac{1}{2}\right)}\log\left|\frac{x+\frac{3}{2}-\frac{1}{2}}{x+\frac{3}{2}+\frac{1}{2}}\right|$

$\Rightarrow I=2\log|x^2+3x+2|-5\cdot\log\left|\frac{x+1}{x+2}\right|+C$

$\therefore \int \frac{(4x+1)\,dx}{x^2+3x+2}$

$=2\log|x^2+3x+2|-5\log\left|\frac{x+1}{x+2}\right|+C$

This is required answer.

49. (b) Let $(2x+3)$

$$= \lambda \frac{d}{dx}(x^2+4x+1)+\mu$$
$$= \lambda(2x+4)+\mu$$

Comparing the coefficient of like power of x, we get

$$2\lambda = 2 \text{ and } 4\lambda + \mu = 3$$
$$\Rightarrow \quad \lambda = 1 \text{ and } \mu = -1$$
$$\therefore I = \int \frac{2x+3}{\sqrt{x^2+4x+1}}\,dx$$
$$= \int \frac{(2x+4)-1}{\sqrt{x^2+4x+1}}\,dx$$
$$= \int \frac{(2x+4)\,dx}{\sqrt{x^2+4x+1}} - \int \frac{dx}{\sqrt{x^2+4x+1}}$$
$$= \int \frac{(2x+4)\,dx}{\sqrt{x^2+4x+1}} - \int \frac{dx}{\sqrt{(x+2)^2-(\sqrt{3})^2}}$$
$$= 2\sqrt{x^2+4x+1} - \log|x + 2 + \sqrt{x^2+4x+1}| + C$$

Thus, $\int \frac{2x+3}{\sqrt{x^2+4x+1}}\,dx$

$$= 2\sqrt{x^2+4x+1} - \log|(x+2) + \sqrt{x^2+4x+1}| + C$$

50. Let $I = \int \frac{x^2+5x+3}{x^2+3x+2}\,dx$

$$= \int \left(1 + \frac{2x+1}{x^2+3x+2}\right) dx$$
$$= \int 1\cdot dx + \int \frac{2x+1}{x^2+3x+2}\,dx$$

Let

$$(2x+1) = \lambda \frac{d}{dx}(x^2+3x+2)+\mu$$
$$= \lambda(2x+3)+\mu$$

Equating both sides the power of 'x', we get

$$\lambda = 1 \text{ and } \mu = -2$$

Thus, $I = \int dx + \int \frac{(2x+3)-2}{x^2+3x+2}\,dx$

$$\Rightarrow I = x + \int \frac{(2x+3)}{x^2+3x+2}\,dx - 2\int \frac{dx}{x^2+3x+2}$$
$$\Rightarrow I = x + \log|x^2+3x+2| - 2\int \frac{dx}{\left(x+\frac{3}{2}\right)^2 - \left(\frac{1}{2}\right)^2}$$
$$\Rightarrow I = x + \log|x^2+3x+2| - 2\cdot\frac{1}{2\cdot\left(\frac{1}{2}\right)} \log\left|\frac{x+\frac{3}{2}-\frac{1}{2}}{x+\frac{3}{2}+\frac{1}{2}}\right| + C$$

Thus, $\int \frac{x^2+5x+3}{x^2+3x+2}\,dx$

$$= x + \log|x^2+3x+2| - 2\log\left|\frac{x+1}{x+2}\right| + C$$

This is required answer.

51. (i) (False)

Let

$$I = \int \frac{(3\sin x - 2)\cos x}{5-\cos^2 x - 4\sin x}\,dx$$
$$= \int \frac{(3\sin x - 2)\cos x}{4+\sin^2 x - 4\sin x}\,dx$$

Let $\sin x = t \Rightarrow \cos x\,dx = dt$

$$\therefore I = \int \frac{(3t-2)\,dt}{4+t^2-4t}$$
$$= \int \frac{(3t-2)\,dt}{t^2-4t+4}$$

Let $(3t-2)$

$$= \mu \frac{d}{dt}(t^2-4t+4)+\lambda$$
$$= \mu(2t-4)+\lambda$$

Then, $\mu = \frac{3}{2}$ and $\lambda = 4$

$$\Rightarrow I = \int \frac{\frac{3}{2}(2t-4)+4}{t^2-4t+4}\,dt$$
$$= \frac{3}{2}\int \frac{2t-4}{t^2-4t+4}\,dt + 4\int \frac{dt}{t^2-4t+4}$$
$$= \frac{3}{2}\log|t^2-4t+4| + \int \frac{4\,dt}{(t-2)^2}$$
$$\therefore \int \frac{(3\sin x-2)\cos x}{5-\cos^2 x - 4\sin x}\,dx$$
$$= 3\log|\sin x - 2| + \frac{4}{2-\sin x} + C$$

(ii) (False)

Let $I = \int \frac{3x+5}{x^2+3x-18}\,dx$

Let $3x+5$

$$= \lambda\left\{\frac{d}{dx}(x^2+3x-18)\right\}+\mu$$
$$= \lambda(2x+3)+\mu$$
$$\lambda = \frac{3}{2}$$

and $\mu + 3\lambda = 5$

$$\Rightarrow \mu = 5 - \frac{9}{2} = \frac{1}{2}$$

Then, $I = \int \frac{\frac{3}{2}(2x+3)+\frac{1}{2}}{x^2+3x-18}\,dx$

$$\Rightarrow I = \frac{3}{2}\int \frac{(2x+3)\,dx}{x^2+3x-18} + \frac{1}{2}\int \frac{dx}{x^2+3x-18}$$
$$\Rightarrow I = \frac{3}{2}\log|x^2+3x-18| + \frac{1}{2}\int \frac{dx}{\left(x+\frac{3}{2}\right)^2 - \left(\frac{9}{2}\right)^2}$$
$$\therefore \int \frac{3x+5}{x^2+3x-18}\,dx$$
$$= \frac{3}{2}\log|x^2+3x-18| + \frac{1}{18}\log\left|\frac{x-3}{x+6}\right| + C$$

(iii) (True)

Let $I = \int \frac{x^3+1}{x^3-x}\,dx$

$$= \int \frac{(x^3-x)+(1+x)}{x^3-x}\,dx$$
$$\therefore I = \int dx + \int \frac{(x+1)}{x(x^2-1)}\,dx$$
$$\therefore \int \frac{x^3+1}{x^3-x}\,dx = x + \log\left|\frac{x-1}{x}\right| + C$$

52. (a)

53. (i) Let

$$I = \int \frac{\cos\theta}{(2+\sin\theta)(3+4\sin\theta)}\,d\theta$$

On putting $\sin\theta = t$

$$\Rightarrow \quad \cos\theta\,d\theta = dt$$
$$\therefore I = \int \frac{dt}{(2+t)(3+4t)}$$

Let $\frac{1}{(2+t)(3+4t)}$

$$= \frac{A}{(2+t)} + \frac{B}{(3+4t)}$$

$\therefore\ 1 = A(3+4t) + B(2+t)$

On solving, we get

$$A = -\frac{1}{5} \text{ and } B = \frac{4}{5}$$

Then, $\frac{1}{(2+t)(3+4t)}$

$$= -\frac{1}{5}\frac{1}{(2+t)} + \frac{4}{5}\cdot\frac{1}{(3+4t)}$$

Thus, $I = \int \frac{dt}{(2+t)(3+4t)}$

$$= -\frac{1}{5}\int\frac{dt}{(2+t)} + \frac{4}{5}\int\frac{dt}{(3+4t)}$$

$$= -\frac{1}{5}\log|2+t| + \frac{4}{5}\cdot\frac{1}{4}\log|3+4t| + C$$

$$= \frac{1}{5}\log\left|\frac{3+4t}{2+t}\right| + C$$

$$= \frac{1}{5}\log\left|\frac{3+4\sin\theta}{2+\sin\theta}\right| + C$$

Hence, $\int \frac{\cos\theta\, d\theta}{(2+\sin\theta)(3+4\sin\theta)}$

$$= \frac{1}{5}\log\left|\frac{3+4\sin\theta}{2+\sin\theta}\right| + C$$

(ii) Let $I = \int \frac{(3x-1)}{(x+2)^2}\,dx$

Let $\frac{3x-1}{(x+2)^2} = \frac{A}{(x+2)} + \frac{B}{(x+2)^2}$

$\therefore\ (3x-1) = A(x+2) + B$

Equating coefficient of x and constant term, we get

$$A = 3 \text{ and } B = -7$$

$$\therefore \frac{3x-1}{(x+2)^2} = \frac{3}{(x+2)} - \frac{7}{(x+2)^2}$$

$$\Rightarrow \int \frac{3x-1}{(x+2)^2}\,dx = 3\int\frac{dx}{(x+2)} - 7\int\frac{dx}{(x+2)^2}$$

$$= 3\log|x+2| + 7\left(\frac{1}{x+2}\right) + C$$

$$\therefore \int\frac{(3x-1)\,dx}{(x+2)^2} = 3\log|x+2| + \frac{7}{x+2} + C$$

(iii) Let $\frac{x}{(x-1)^2(x+2)}$

$$= \frac{A}{(x-1)} + \frac{B}{(x-1)^2} + \frac{C}{(x+2)}$$

$\therefore\ x = A(x-1)(x+2) + B(x+2) + C(x-1)^2$

Equating the coefficient of x^2, x and constant terms, we get

$A + C = 0,\ A + B - 2C = 1$

and $-2A + 2B + C = 0$

On solving these equations

$$A = \frac{2}{9}, B = \frac{1}{3} \text{ and } C = -\frac{2}{9}$$

$$\therefore \frac{x}{(x-1)^2(x+2)} = \frac{2}{9(x-1)} + \frac{1}{3(x-1)^2} - \frac{2}{9(x+2)}$$

$$\Rightarrow \int\frac{x}{(x-1)^2(x+2)}\,dx = \frac{2}{9}\int\frac{dx}{x-1} + \frac{1}{3}\int\frac{dx}{(x-1)^2} - \frac{2}{9}\int\frac{dx}{(x+2)}$$

$$= \frac{2}{9}\log|x-1| - \frac{1}{3}\frac{1}{x-1} - \frac{2}{9}\log|x+2| + C$$

$$= \frac{2}{9}\log\left|\frac{x-1}{x+2}\right| - \frac{1}{3}\frac{1}{(x-1)} + C$$

$$\therefore \int\frac{x\,dx}{(x-1)^2(x+2)} = \frac{2}{9}\log\left|\frac{x-1}{x+2}\right| - \frac{1}{3}\frac{1}{(x-1)} + C$$

(iv) Let $\frac{x^2+1}{(x-1)^2(x+3)}$

$$= \frac{A}{(x-1)} + \frac{B}{(x-1)^2} + \frac{C}{(x+3)}$$

On putting $x^2 + 1 = C(x-1)^2 + B(x+3) + A(x-1)(x+3)$

Equating the coefficient of x^2, x and constant terms, we get

$$A = \frac{3}{8}, B = \frac{1}{2} \text{ and } C = \frac{5}{8}$$

$$\therefore \frac{x^2+1}{(x-1)^2(x+3)} = \frac{3}{8}\frac{1}{(x-1)} + \frac{1}{2}\frac{1}{(x-1)^2} + \frac{5}{8}\frac{1}{(x+3)}$$

$$\Rightarrow \int\frac{(x^2+1)\,dx}{(x-1)^2(x+3)} = \frac{3}{8}\int\frac{dx}{(x-1)} + \frac{1}{2}\int\frac{dx}{(x-1)^2} + \frac{5}{8}\int\frac{dx}{(x+3)}$$

$$= \frac{3}{8}\log|x-1| - \frac{1}{2}\frac{1}{(x-1)} + \frac{5}{8}\log|x+3| + C$$

$$\therefore \int\frac{(x^2+1)\,dx}{(x-1)^2(x+3)} = \frac{3}{8}\log|x-1| - \frac{1}{2}\frac{1}{(x-1)} + \frac{5}{8}\log|x+3| + C$$

(v) Let $\frac{8}{(x+2)(x^2+4)}$

$$= \frac{A}{(x+2)} + \frac{Bx+C}{(x^2+4)}$$

Then,

$8 = A(x^2+4) + (Bx+C)(x+2)$

Equating both sides the coefficient of x, x^2 and constant term, we get

$$A = 1, B = -1 \text{ and } C = 2$$

Thus, $\frac{8}{(x+2)(x^2+4)}$

$$= \frac{1}{x+2} + \frac{-x+2}{x^2+4}$$

$$\int\frac{8\,dx}{(x+2)(x^2+4)} = \int\frac{dx}{(x+2)} + \int\frac{-x+2}{x^2+4}\,dx$$

$$= \int\frac{dx}{(x+2)} - \frac{1}{2}\int\frac{2x\,dx}{x^2+4} + 2\int\frac{dx}{x^2+4}$$

$$= \log|x+2| - \frac{1}{2}\log|x^2+4| + 2\tan^{-1}\left(\frac{x}{2}\right) + C$$

Thus, $\int\frac{8\,dx}{(x+2)(x^2+4)}$

$$= \log|x+2| - \frac{1}{2}\log|x^2+4| + 2\tan^{-1}\left(\frac{x}{2}\right) + C$$

54. (a) $\dfrac{2x-3}{(x^2-1)(2x+3)}$

$$=\frac{2x-3}{(x-1)(x+1)(2x+3)}$$

Let $\dfrac{2x-3}{(x^2-1)(2x+3)}$

$$=\frac{A}{(x+1)}+\frac{B}{(x-1)}+\frac{C}{(2x+3)}$$

Then, $(2x-3)=A(x-1)(2x+3)$
$+B(x+1)(2x+3)$
$+C(x+1)(x-1)$

$\therefore (2x-3)=(2A+2B+C)x^2$
$+(A+5B)x$
$+(-3A+3B-C)$

Equating the coefficient of x^2, x and constant terms, we get

$2A+2B+C=0$, $A+5B=2$

and $-3A+3B-C=-3$

Then, $A=\dfrac{5}{2}$, $B=-\dfrac{1}{10}$

and $C=\dfrac{-24}{5}$

$$\therefore \frac{(2x-3)}{(x+1)(x-1)(2x+3)}=\frac{5}{2(x+1)}-\frac{1}{10(x-1)}-\frac{24}{5(2x+3)}$$

$$\Rightarrow \int\frac{(2x-3)\,dx}{(x+1)(x-1)(2x+3)}=\frac{5}{2}\int\frac{dx}{x+1}-\frac{1}{10}\int\frac{dx}{x-1}-\frac{24}{5}\int\frac{dx}{2x+3}$$

$$=\frac{5}{2}\log|x+1|-\frac{1}{10}\log|x-1|-\frac{24}{10}\log|2x+3|+C$$

Thus, $\displaystyle\int\frac{(2x-3)\,dx}{(x+1)(x-1)(2x+3)}$

$$=\frac{5}{2}\log|x+1|-\frac{12}{5}\log|2x+3|-\frac{1}{10}\log|x-1|+C$$

55. (True)

Let $\dfrac{2}{(1-x)(1+x^2)}$

$$=\frac{A}{1-x}+\frac{Bx+C}{1+x^2}$$

Then,

$$2=A(1+x^2)+(Bx+C)(1-x)$$

$\Rightarrow 2=(A-B)x^2+(B-C)x$
$+(A+C)$

Equating both sides the coefficient of x^2, x and constant terms, we get

$$A-B=0,\ B-C=0$$

and $A+C=2$

Then, $A=1$, $B=1$ and $C=1$.

Thus,

$$\frac{2}{(1-x)(1+x^2)}=\frac{1}{(1-x)}+\frac{x+1}{(1+x^2)}$$

$$=\frac{1}{(1-x)}+\frac{1}{2}\frac{2x}{x^2+1}+\frac{1}{x^2+1}$$

$$\therefore \int\frac{2\,dx}{(1-x)(x^2+1)}=\int\frac{dx}{(1-x)}+\frac{1}{2}\int\frac{2x}{(1+x^2)}dx+\int\frac{dx}{(1+x^2)}$$

$$=-\log|1-x|+\frac{1}{2}\log|1+x^2|+\tan^{-1}x+C$$

$$=\frac{1}{2}\log|x^2+1|-\log|1-x|+\tan^{-1}x+C$$

Hence, $\displaystyle\int\frac{2\,dx}{(1-x)(x^2+1)}$

$$=\frac{1}{2}\log|x^2+1|-\log|1-x|+\tan^{-1}x+C$$

56. (b) Let $x^2=y$, then

$$\frac{x^2}{(x^2+1)(x^2+4)}=\frac{y}{(y+1)(y+4)}$$

Now, let

$$\frac{y}{(y+1)(y+4)}=\frac{A}{(y+1)}+\frac{B}{(y+4)}$$

$\therefore y=A(y+4)+B(y+1)$

Equating both sides the power of y, we get

$$A=-\frac{1}{3}\text{ and }B=\frac{4}{3}$$

$$\therefore \frac{y}{(y+1)(y+4)}=-\frac{1}{3(y+1)}+\frac{4}{3(y+4)}$$

$$\Rightarrow \int\frac{x^2}{(x^2+1)(x^2+4)}dx=-\frac{1}{3}\int\frac{dx}{(x^2+1)}+\frac{4}{3}\int\frac{dx}{(x^2+4)}+C$$

$$=-\frac{1}{3}\tan^{-1}x+\frac{2}{3}\tan^{-1}\left(\frac{x}{2}\right)+C$$

57. Given, $\displaystyle\int\frac{(3\sin\phi-2)\cos\phi}{5-\cos^2\phi-4\sin\phi}\,d\phi$

Let $\sin\phi=y \Rightarrow dy=\cos\phi\,d\phi$

$$=\int\frac{(3y-2)\,dy}{5-(1-y^2)-4y}$$

$$=\int\frac{3y-2}{(y-2)^2}dy=I\text{ (say)}$$

Thus, $\dfrac{3y-2}{(y-2)^2}=\dfrac{A}{(y-2)}+\dfrac{B}{(y-2)^2}$

$\Rightarrow (3y-2)=A(y-2)+B$

Comparing the coefficient of y and constant term, we get

$$A=3\text{ and }B=4$$

Then, $\dfrac{(3y-2)}{(y-2)^2}=\dfrac{3}{(y-2)}+\dfrac{4}{(y-2)^2}$

Integrating both sides,

$$\int\frac{3y-2}{(y-2)^2}dy=3\int\frac{dy}{(y-2)}+4\int\frac{dy}{(y-2)^2}$$

$$=3\log|y-2|+4\left(-\frac{1}{y-2}\right)+C$$

$$=3\log|\sin\phi-2|-\frac{4}{\sin\phi-2}+C$$

Thus, $\displaystyle\int\frac{(3\sin\phi-2)\cos\phi}{5-\cos^2\phi-4\sin\phi}d\phi$

$$=3\log|\sin\phi-2|+\frac{4}{2-\sin\phi}+C$$

58. (True)

$$\frac{(x^2+1)(x^2+2)}{(x^2+3)(x^2+4)}=\frac{x^4+3x^2+2}{x^4+7x^2+12}$$

$$=\frac{(x^4+7x^2+12)-4x^2-10}{x^4+7x^2+12}$$

$$=1-\frac{(4x^2+10)}{x^4+7x^2+12}$$

Now,

$$\frac{4x^2+10}{x^4+7x^2+12}=\frac{4x^2+10}{(x^2+3)(x^2+4)}$$

$$\frac{4x^2+10}{(x^2+3)(x^2+4)}=\frac{Ax+B}{(x^2+3)}+\frac{Cx+D}{(x^2+4)}$$

$\Rightarrow (4x^2+10)=(Ax+B)(x^2+4)$
$+(Cx+D)(x^2+3)$

Equating coefficient of x^2, x and constant term, we get

$A=0$, $B=-2$, $C=0$ and $D=6$

$\therefore \int \frac{(x^2+1)(x^2+2)}{(x^2+3)(x^2+4)} dx$

$= \int \left(1 + \frac{2}{x^2+3} - \frac{6}{x^2+4}\right) dx$

$= x + \frac{2}{\sqrt{3}} \tan^{-1}\left(\frac{x}{\sqrt{3}}\right) - 3\tan^{-1}\left(\frac{x}{2}\right) + C$

Hence, $\int \frac{(x^2+1)(x^2+2)}{(x^2+3)(x^2+4)} dx$

$= x + \frac{2}{\sqrt{3}} \tan^{-1}\left(\frac{x}{\sqrt{3}}\right) - 3\tan^{-1}\left(\frac{x}{2}\right) + C$

59. (i) Given, $I = \int x^n \cdot \log x \, dx$

Using integration by parts,

$I = \log x \int x^n \, dx - \int \left[\frac{d}{dx}(\log x) \cdot \int x^n \, dx\right] dx + C$

$\Rightarrow \quad I = \frac{x^{n+1}}{n+1} \cdot \log x - \int \frac{1}{x} \cdot \frac{x^{n+1}}{n+1} dx + C$

$\Rightarrow \quad I = \frac{x^{n+1}}{n+1} \cdot \log x - \frac{1}{n+1} \int x^n dx + C$

$\Rightarrow \quad I = \frac{x^{n+1}}{n+1} \cdot \log x - \frac{1}{(n+1)^2} \cdot x^{n+1} + C$

Hence,

$\int x^n \cdot \log x \, dx = \frac{x^{n+1}}{n+1} \cdot \log x - \frac{1}{(n+1)^2} \cdot x^{n+1} + C$

(ii) Taking first function as $\log x$ and second function as x.

$I = \int x \cdot \log x \, dx$

$\Rightarrow I = \log x \cdot \{\int x \, dx\} - \int \left\{\frac{d}{dx}(\log x) \cdot \int x \, dx\right\} dx$

$\Rightarrow I = \frac{x^2 \log x}{2} - \int \frac{1}{x} \cdot \left(\frac{x^2}{2}\right) dx + C$

$\Rightarrow I = \frac{x^2 \log x}{2} - \frac{x^2}{4} + C$

$\therefore \int x \log x \, dx = \frac{x^2 \log x}{2} - \frac{x^2}{4} + C$

(iii) Let $I = \int (x+1) \log x \, dx$

Using integration by parts, we get

$\therefore I = \log x \cdot \int (x+1) \, dx - \int \left[\frac{d}{dx}(\log x) \cdot \int (x+1) dx\right] dx + C$

$\Rightarrow I = \left(\frac{x^2}{2} + x\right) \cdot \log x - \int \frac{1}{x} \cdot \left(\frac{x^2}{2} + x\right) dx + C$

$\Rightarrow I = \left(x + \frac{x^2}{2}\right) \cdot \log x - \int \left(\frac{x}{2} + 1\right) dx + C$

$\Rightarrow I = \left(x + \frac{x^2}{2}\right) \cdot \log x - \left(\frac{x^2}{4} + x\right) + C$

Then, $\int (x+1) \cdot \log x \, dx$

$= \left(x + \frac{x^2}{2}\right) \cdot \log x - \left(x + \frac{x^2}{4}\right) + C$

(iv) Let $I = \int x^3 \cdot \cos x^2 \, dx$

Let $x^2 = z \Rightarrow 2x \, dx = dz$

$\Rightarrow x \, dx = \frac{dz}{2}$

$\therefore I = \int x^2 \cdot \cos x^2 \cdot (x \, dx)$

$= \int z \cdot \cos z \frac{dz}{2} = \frac{1}{2} \int z \cos z \, dz$

$= \frac{1}{2} [z \cdot \int \cos z \, dz - \int \left\{\frac{d}{dz}(z) \cdot \int \cos z \, dz\right\} dz] + C$

[using integration by parts]

$= \frac{1}{2} [z \sin z + \cos z] + C$

$\therefore I = \frac{1}{2} [x^2 \cdot \sin x^2 + \cos x^2] + C$

Hence, $\int x^3 \cdot \cos x^2 \, dx$

$= \frac{1}{2} [x^2 \cdot \sin x^2 + \cos x^2] + C$

(v) Let $I = \int e^x \cdot \sin x \, dx$ ...(i)

Using integrating by parts, we get

$\therefore I = e^x \cdot \int \sin x \, dx - \int \left[\frac{d}{dx}(e^x) \cdot \int \sin x \, dx\right] dx + C$

$\Rightarrow I = e^x \cdot (-\cos x) + \int e^x \cdot \cos x \, dx + C$

$\Rightarrow I = -e^x \cdot \cos x + [e^x \int \cos x \, dx - \int \left\{\frac{d}{dx}(e^x) \cdot \int \cos x \, dx\right\} dx] + C$

$\Rightarrow I = -e^x \cdot \cos x + [e^x \cdot \sin x - \int e^x \cdot \sin x \, dx] + C$

$\Rightarrow I = -e^x \cdot \cos x + e^x \sin x - I + C$

[from Eq. (i)]

Then, $2I = e^x(\sin x - \cos x) + C$

$\therefore I = \frac{e^x}{2}(\sin x - \cos x) + \frac{C}{2}$

$= \frac{e^x}{2}(\sin x - \cos x) + c_1$

Thus, $\int e^x \cdot \sin x \, dx$

$= \frac{e^x}{2}(\sin x - \cos x) + c_1$

(vi) Taking x^2 as a first function and e^x as a second function,

$I = \int x^2 \cdot e^x \, dx$

$\Rightarrow I = x^2 \cdot \int e^x \, dx - \int \left[\frac{d}{dx}(x^2) \cdot \int e^x \, dx\right] dx + C$

$\Rightarrow I = x^2 \cdot e^x - [\int 2x \cdot e^x \, dx] + C$

$\therefore I = x^2 e^x - 2 \int x \cdot e^x \, dx + C$

$\Rightarrow I = x^2 e^x - 2 \left[x \int e^x \, dx - \int \left[\frac{d}{dx}(x) \cdot \int e^x \, dx\right] dx\right] + C$

$\Rightarrow I = x^2 e^x - 2[x e^x - e^x] + C$

$\Rightarrow I = x^2 e^x - 2x e^x + 2e^x + C$

Thus,

$\int x^2 e^x \, dx = x^2 e^x - 2x e^x + 2e^x + C$

(vii) Let $\tan^{-1} x = \theta$

$\Rightarrow x = \tan \theta$ and $dx = \sec^2 \theta \, d\theta$

Let $I = \int \tan^{-1} x \, dx = \int \theta \sec^2 \theta \, d\theta$

Taking θ as the first function and $\sec^2 \theta$ as the second function,

$I = \theta (\int \sec^2 \theta \, d\theta) - \int [1 \cdot \int \sec^2 \theta \, d\theta] \, d\theta + C$

$\Rightarrow I = \theta \cdot \tan \theta - \int \tan \theta \, d\theta + C$

$\Rightarrow I = \theta \cdot \tan \theta + \log |\cos \theta| + C$

$\Rightarrow I = \tan^{-1} x \cdot x + \log \left|\frac{1}{\sqrt{1+x^2}}\right| + C$

Thus, $\int \tan^{-1} x \cdot dx = x \tan^{-1} x - \frac{1}{2} \log |1 + x^2| + C$

60. (b) Let $I = \int x \cdot \tan^{-1} x \, dx$

Taking $\tan^{-1} x$ as a first function and x as a second function,

$$I = \int x \cdot \tan^{-1} x \, dx$$

$$\Rightarrow I = \tan^{-1} x \cdot \int x \, dx - \int \left[\frac{d}{dx} (\tan^{-1} x) \cdot \int [x \, dx] \right] dx + C$$

$$\Rightarrow I = \frac{x^2 \cdot \tan^{-1} x}{2} - \int \left(\frac{1}{1+x^2} \cdot \frac{x^2}{2} \right) dx + C$$

$$\therefore I = \frac{1}{2}(x^2 \cdot \tan^{-1} x - x + \tan^{-1} x) + C$$

61. (i) (True)

Let $I = \int x^3 \cdot e^x \, dx$

Taking x^3 as the first function and e^x as the second function,

$$I = x^3 \cdot e^x - \int 3x^2 \cdot e^x \, dx$$

$$= x^3 \cdot e^x - 3 \int x^2 \cdot e^x \, dx$$

$$I = x^3 e^x - 3 [x^2 e^x - \int 2x e^x dx] + C$$

$$I = x^3 e^x - 3[x^2 e^x - 2\int x e^x dx] + C$$

$$I = x^3 e^x - 3x^2 e^x + 6\int x e^x dx + C$$

$$I = x^3 e^x - 3x^2 e^x + 6[x e^x - \int e^x dx] + C$$

$$I = x^3 e^x - 3x^2 e^x + 6x e^x - 6e^x + C$$

$$\therefore \int x^3 \cdot e^x \, dx = (x^3 - 3x^2 + 6x - 6)\, e^x + C$$

(ii) (True)

Let $I = \int \frac{x \cos^{-1} x}{\sqrt{1-x^2}} dx$

Let $\cos^{-1} x = z \Rightarrow x = \cos z$

and $\frac{1}{\sqrt{1-x^2}} dx = -dz$

$$\therefore I = -\int z \cdot \cos z \, dz$$

Taking z as the first function and $\cos z$ as the second function,

$$I = -\int z \cdot \cos z \, dz$$

$$I = -[z \sin z - \int \sin z \, dz] + C$$

$$I = -z \sin z - \cos z + C$$

$$\therefore \int \frac{x \cos^{-1} x}{\sqrt{1-x^2}} dx = -(x + \cos^{-1} x \cdot \sqrt{1-x^2} + C)$$

62. (a) Let $I = \int e^x \left(\frac{1}{x} - \frac{1}{x^2} \right) dx$

Then, the given integrand is of the form $e^x [f(x) + f'(x)]$,

where $f(x) = \frac{1}{x}$

and $f'(x) = -\frac{1}{x^2}$

Therefore,

$$I = \int e^x \left(\frac{1}{x} - \frac{1}{x^2} \right) dx = \frac{e^x}{x} + C$$

$$[\because \int \{f(x) + f'(x)\} \cdot e^x \, dx = e^x \cdot f(x) + C]$$

63. Let $f(x) = \frac{d}{dx}(e^x \sin x)$

$$= e^x \cdot \cos x + e^x \sin x$$

$$= e^x (\cos x + \sin x)$$

Let $I = \int e^x (\sin x + \cos x) \, dx$

Then, given integrand is of the form $e^x [f(x) + f'(x)]$,

where $f(x) = \sin x$

and $f'(x) = \cos x$

Therefore,

$$I = e^x f(x) = e^x \sin x$$

64. Let $I = \int \frac{(x^2+1)\, e^x}{(x+1)^2} dx$

$$= \int \frac{e^x [x^2 - 1 + 1 + 1]}{(x+1)^2} dx$$

$$= \int e^x \left[\frac{x^2 - 1}{(x+1)^2} + \frac{2}{(x+1)^2} \right] dx$$

$$\Rightarrow I = \int e^x \left[\frac{x-1}{x+1} + \frac{2}{(x+1)^2} \right] dx \quad \ldots \text{(i)}$$

Let $f(x) = \frac{x-1}{x+1}$

and $g(x) = \frac{2}{(x+1)^2}$

Now, Eq. (i) is of the form $\int e^x \{f(x) + f'(x)\} \, dx$

Therefore, $I = e^x \cdot \left(\frac{x-1}{x+1} \right) + C$

$$\therefore \int \frac{(x^2+1)}{(x+1)^2} e^x \, dx = e^x \cdot \left(\frac{x-1}{x+1} \right) + C$$

65. (True)

Let $I = \int e^x \left(\frac{2 + \sin 2x}{1 + \cos 2x} \right) dx$

$$\Rightarrow I = \int e^x \left(\frac{2 + 2 \sin x \cdot \cos x}{2 \cos^2 x} \right) dx$$

$$\Rightarrow I = \int e^x (\sec^2 x + \tan x) \, dx$$

$$\Rightarrow I = \int e^x (\tan x + \sec^2 x) \, dx$$

Thus, the given integral is of the form $\int e^x \{f(x) + f'(x)\} \, dx$

Hence, $I = e^x \cdot \tan x + C$

$$\therefore \int e^x \left(\frac{2 + \sin 2x}{1 + \cos 2x} \right) dx = e^x \cdot \tan x + C$$

66. (a) A. Let $I = \int e^x \frac{x}{(x+1)^2} dx$

$$= \int e^x \cdot \frac{(x+1) - 1}{(x+1)^2} dx$$

$$= \int e^x \left[\frac{1}{x+1} - \frac{1}{(x+1)^2} \right] dx$$

$$= \frac{e^x}{x+1} + C$$

B. Let $I = \int \left\{ \frac{1}{\log x} - \frac{1}{(\log x)^2} \right\} dx$

Let $\log x = z$

$\Rightarrow \quad x = e^z$

$\Rightarrow \quad dx = e^z \cdot dz$

$$= \int \left(\frac{1}{z} - \frac{1}{z^2} \right) e^z \, dz$$

$$= \frac{e^z}{z} + c = \frac{x}{\log x} + C$$

$$\therefore \int \left\{ \frac{1}{\log x} - \frac{1}{(\log x)^2} \right\} dx = \frac{x}{\log x} + C$$

C. Let $I = \int e^{2x} \left(\frac{1 + \sin 2x}{1 + \cos 2x} \right) dx$

Let $2x = t$

$\Rightarrow \quad dx = \frac{dt}{2}$

$$\therefore I = \frac{1}{2} \int e^t \left\{ \frac{1 + \sin t}{1 + \cos t} \right\} dt$$

$$= \frac{1}{2} \int e^t \left\{ \frac{1 + 2 \sin \frac{t}{2} \cos \frac{t}{2}}{2 \cos^2 \frac{t}{2}} \right\} dt$$

$= \frac{1}{2}\int e^t \left\{\frac{1}{2}\sec^2\frac{t}{2} + \tan\frac{t}{2}\right\} dt$

$= \frac{1}{2}e^t \tan\frac{t}{2} + C$

Then, $I = \frac{e^{2x}}{2}\cdot \tan x + C$

Hence, $\int e^{2x}\cdot\left(\frac{1+\sin 2x}{1+\cos 2x}\right) dx$

$= \frac{e^{2x}}{2}\cdot \tan x + C$

D. Let $I = \int \sin^{-1}\left(\frac{2x}{1+x^2}\right) dx$

$\Rightarrow I = 2\int \tan^{-1} x\, dx$

$\therefore \int \sin^{-1}\frac{2x}{1+x^2}\, dx$

$= 2x\tan^{-1} x - \log|1+x^2| + C$

67. (i) (True)

Let $I = \int \sqrt{x^2+2x+5}\, dx$

$= \int \sqrt{(x+1)^2+4}\, dx$

Let $(x+1) = z \Rightarrow dx = dz$

$\therefore I = \int \sqrt{z^2+4}\, dz$

Hence, $I = \int \sqrt{z^2+2^2}\, dz$

$\Rightarrow I = \frac{z\sqrt{z^2+4}}{2} + \frac{4}{2}\log|z+\sqrt{z^2+4}| + C$

$\Rightarrow I = \frac{(x+1)\sqrt{x^2+2x+5}}{2} + 2\log|(x+1) + \sqrt{x^2+2x+5}| + C$

Hence, $\int \sqrt{x^2+2x+5}\, dx$

$= \frac{(x+1)\sqrt{x^2+2x+5}}{2} + 2\log|(x+1) + \sqrt{x^2+2x+5}| + C$

(ii) (True)

Let $I = \int \sqrt{3-2x-x^2}\, dx$

$= \int \sqrt{4-(x+1)^2}\, dx$

Let $(x+1) = z \Rightarrow dx = dz$

$\therefore I = \int \sqrt{4-z^2}\, dz$

$= \int \sqrt{2^2-z^2}\, dz$

Thus, $\int \sqrt{3-2x-x^2}\, dx$

$= \frac{(x+1)\sqrt{3-2x-x^2}}{2} + 2\sin^{-1}\left(\frac{x+1}{2}\right) + C$

(iii) (True)

Let $I = \int \frac{\sqrt{16+(\log x)^2}}{x}\, dx$

Let $\log x = z \Rightarrow \frac{dx}{x} = dz$

$\therefore I = \int \sqrt{16+z^2}\, dz$

$= \int \sqrt{4^2+z^2}\, dz$

$\Rightarrow I = \frac{z\sqrt{4^2+z^2}}{2} + 8\log|z + \sqrt{4^2+z^2}| + C$

Thus, $\int \frac{\sqrt{16+(\log x)^2}}{x}\, dx$

$= \frac{\log x\sqrt{16+(\log x)^2}}{2} + 8\log|\log x + \sqrt{16+(\log x)^2}| + C$

(iv) (True)

Let $I = \int \sqrt{x^2-8x+7}\, dx$

$= \int \sqrt{(x^2-8x+16)-9}\, dx$

$\Rightarrow I = \int \sqrt{(x-4)^2-3^2}\, dx$

Thus, $\int \sqrt{x^2-8x+7}\, dx$

$= \frac{(x-4)\sqrt{x^2-8x+7}}{2} - \frac{9}{2}\log|(x-4) + \sqrt{x^2-8x+7}| + C$

(v) (True)

Let $I = \int \cos x\sqrt{4-\sin^2 x}\, dx$

Let $\sin x = z$

$\Rightarrow \cos x\, dx = dz$

$\therefore I = \int \sqrt{4-z^2}\, dz$

$= \sqrt{2^2-z^2}\, dz$

Thus, $\int \cos x\sqrt{4-\sin^2 x}\, dx$

$= \frac{\sin x\sqrt{4-\sin^2 x}}{2} + 2\sin^{-1}\left(\frac{\sin x}{2}\right) + C$

68. Let $I = \int \sqrt{4x^2+9}\, dx$

Then, $I = 2\int \sqrt{x^2+\frac{9}{4}}\, dx$

$= 2\int \sqrt{x^2+\left(\frac{3}{2}\right)^2}\, dx$

$\Rightarrow I = 2\left\{\frac{x\sqrt{x^2+\frac{9}{4}}}{2} + \frac{9}{8}\log|2x+\sqrt{4x^2+9}|\right\} + C$

$\Rightarrow I = \{\frac{x}{2}\sqrt{4x^2+9} + \frac{9}{4}\log|2x+\sqrt{4x^2+9}|\} + C$

Thus, $\int \sqrt{4x^2+9}\, dx$

$= \frac{x}{2}\sqrt{4x^2+9} + \frac{9}{4}\log|2x+\sqrt{4x^2+9}| + C$

69. Let $I = \int \sqrt{x^2-2x}\, dx$

$= \int \sqrt{(x-1)^2-1^2}\, dx$

Then, $I = \int \sqrt{(x-1)^2-1^2}\, dx$

Hence, $\int \sqrt{x^2-2x}\, dx$

$= \frac{(x-1)\sqrt{x^2-2x}}{2} - \frac{1}{2}\log|(x-1) + \sqrt{(x^2-2x)}| + C$

This is required answer.

70. Let $I = \int \sqrt{(x-3)(5-x)}\, dx$

$\Rightarrow I = \int \sqrt{-x^2+8x-15}\, dx$

$\Rightarrow I = \int \sqrt{1^2-(x-4)^2}\, dx$

Then, $\int \sqrt{(x-3)(5-x)}\, dx$

$= \frac{(x-4)\sqrt{(x-3)(5-x)}}{2} + \frac{1}{2}\sin^{-1}(x-4) + C$

71. (i) Let $I = \int_4^5 e^x\, dx$

Consider, $\int e^x\, dx = e^x = F(x)$ (say)

Now, using second fundamental theorem of calculus,

$I = F(5) - F(4)$

$\Rightarrow \int_4^5 e^x\, dx = e^5 - e^4$

(ii) Let $I = \int_1^2 (4x^3 - 5x^2 + 6x + 9)\, dx$

$\therefore \int (4x^3 - 5x^2 + 6x + 9)\, dx$

$= x^4 - \frac{5x^3}{3} + 3x^2 + 9x$

$= F(x)$ (say)

$I = F(2) - F(1)$

$= \left\{2^4 - \frac{5(2)^3}{3} + 3\cdot(2)^2 + 9\cdot 2\right\}$

$- \left\{(1)^4 - \frac{5(1)^3}{3} + 3(1)^2 + 9(1)\right\}$

$= \left\{16 - \frac{40}{3} + 12 + 18\right\}$

$- \left\{1 - \frac{5}{3} + 3 + 9\right\}$

Hence,

$\int_1^2 (4x^3 - 5x^2 + 6x + 9)\, dx = \frac{64}{3}$

(iii) Using partial fraction, we get

$\frac{x}{(x+1)(x+2)} = \frac{-1}{x+1} + \frac{2}{x+2}$

So, $\int \frac{x\, dx}{(x+1)(x+2)}$

$= -\log|x+1| + 2\log|x+2|$

$= F(x)$ (say)

We have, $I = F(2) - F(1)$

$= [-\log 3 + 2\log 4]$

$- [-\log 2 + 2\log 3]$

$= \log\left(\frac{32}{27}\right)$

Hence,

$\int_1^2 \frac{x\, dx}{(x+1)(x+2)} = \log\left(\frac{32}{27}\right)$

(iv) Let $I = \int_0^{\pi/2} \cos 2x\, dx$

Consider,

$\int \cos 2x\, dx = \frac{\sin 2x}{2} = F(x)$ (say)

$I = F\left(\frac{\pi}{2}\right) - F(0)$

$\therefore \int_0^{\pi/2} \cos 2x\, dx = 0$

(v) Let $I = \int_0^{\pi/4} \sin^3 2x \cdot \cos 2x\, dx$

Consider, $\int \sin^3 2x \cos 2x\, dx$

On putting $\sin 2x = z$,

$\Rightarrow 2\cos 2x\, dx = dz$

$\Rightarrow \cos 2x\, dx = \frac{1}{2} dz$

So, $\int \sin^3 2x \cdot \cos 2x\, dx$

$= \frac{1}{2}\int z^3\, dz = \frac{z^4}{8}$

$= \frac{\sin^4 2x}{8} = F(x)$ (say)

$I = F\left(\frac{\pi}{4}\right) - F(0)$

$\therefore \int_0^{\pi/4} \sin^3 2x \cdot \cos 2x\, dx = \frac{1}{8}$

72. (i) (False)

Let $I = \int_0^1 \frac{dx}{\sqrt{1-x^2}}$.

Consider, $\int \frac{dx}{\sqrt{1-x^2}} = \sin^{-1} x$

$= F(x)$ (say)

Using second fundamental theorem of calculus, we get

$I = F(1) - F(0)$

$= \sin^{-1}(1) - \sin^{-1}(0)$

$= \frac{\pi}{2} - 0 = \frac{\pi}{2}$

Then, $\int_0^1 \frac{dx}{\sqrt{1-x^2}} = \frac{\pi}{2}$

(ii) (True)

Let $I = \int_0^{\pi/2} \cos^2 x\, dx$

Consider,

$\int \cos^2 x\, dx = \int \frac{1}{2}(1 + \cos 2x)\, dx$

$= \frac{x}{2} + \frac{\sin 2x}{4} = F(x)$

$I = F\left(\frac{\pi}{2}\right) - F(0)$

$\therefore \int_0^{\pi/2} \cos^2 x\, dx = \frac{\pi}{4}$

(iii) (True)

Let $I = \int_0^1 \frac{2x+3}{5x^2+1}\, dx$

Consider, $\int \frac{2x+3}{5x^2+1}\, dx$

$= \frac{1}{5}\int \frac{10x+15}{5x^2+1}\, dx$

$= \frac{1}{5}\int \frac{10x\, dx}{5x^2+1} + \frac{3}{5}\int \frac{dx}{x^2 + \left(\frac{1}{\sqrt{5}}\right)^2}$

$\therefore \int \frac{2x+3}{5x^2+1}\, dx$

$= \frac{1}{5}\log(5x^2+1)$

$+ \frac{3}{\sqrt{5}}\tan^{-1}(\sqrt{5}x)$

$= F(x)$ (say)

$I = F(1) - F(0)$

$= \left\{\frac{1}{5}\log 6 + \frac{3}{\sqrt{5}}\tan^{-1}\sqrt{5}\right\} - 0$

Thus, $\int_0^1 \frac{2x+3}{5x^2+1}\, dx$

$= \frac{1}{5}\log 6 + \frac{3}{\sqrt{5}}\tan^{-1}\sqrt{5}$

73. (a) Let $I = \int_0^{\pi/4} (\sec^2 x + x^3 + 2)\, dx$

Consider, $\int (\sec^2 x + x^3 + 2)\, dx$

$= \int \sec^2 x\, dx + \int x^3\, dx + 2\int dx$

$= \tan x + \frac{x^4}{4} + 2x = F(x)$

$I = F\left(\frac{\pi}{4}\right) - F(0)$

Thus, $\int_0^{\pi/4} (\sec^2 x + x^3 + 2)\, dx$

$= 1 + \frac{\pi}{2} + \frac{\pi^4}{1024}$

74. Let $I = \int_0^1 \left(xe^x + \sin\frac{\pi x}{4}\right) dx$

Consider, $\int \left(xe^x + \sin\frac{\pi x}{4}\right) dx$

$= \int xe^x\, dx + \int \sin\frac{\pi x}{4}\, dx$

$= xe^x - e^x - \frac{4}{\pi}\cos\frac{\pi x}{4}$

$= F(x)$ (say)

Using second fundamental theorem of calculus, we get

$I = F(1) - F(0)$

$= \left\{e - e - \frac{4}{\pi}\cos\frac{\pi}{4}\right\}$

$- \left\{0\cdot e^0 - e^0 - \frac{4}{\pi}\cos 0\right\}$

$\therefore I = 1 + \frac{4}{\pi} - \frac{2\sqrt{2}}{\pi}$

Hence, $\int_0^1 \left(xe^x + \sin\frac{\pi x}{4}\right) dx$

$= 1 + \frac{4}{\pi} - \frac{2\sqrt{2}}{\pi}$

75. (c) Let $I = \int_0^{2/3} \frac{dx}{4+9x^2}$

Consider,

$\int \frac{dx}{4+9x^2} = \frac{1}{9}\int \frac{dx}{x^2 + \left(\frac{2}{3}\right)^2}$

$= \frac{1}{6}\tan^{-1}\left(\frac{3x}{2}\right) = F(x)$ (say)

Using second fundamental theorem of calculus, we get

$\int_0^{2/3} \frac{dx}{4+9x^2} = F\left(\frac{2}{3}\right) - F(0)$

$$= \frac{1}{6}\tan^{-1}\left(\frac{2}{3}\cdot\frac{3}{2}\right) - \frac{1}{6}\tan^{-1}(0)$$

$$= \frac{1}{6}\tan^{-1}(1) - 0 = \frac{\pi}{4}\cdot\frac{1}{6} = \frac{\pi}{24}$$

Thus, $\int_0^{2/3} \frac{dx}{4+9x^2} = \frac{\pi}{24}$

76. (i) Let $I = \int_0^1 \frac{\tan^{-1} x}{1+x^2}\,dx$

Let $\tan^{-1} x = z \Rightarrow \frac{dx}{1+x^2} = dz$

When $x = 0$, then $z = 0$

and when $x = 1$, then $z = \frac{\pi}{4}$

$$\therefore I = \int_0^{\pi/4} z\cdot dz = \left(\frac{z^2}{2}\right)_0^{\pi/4}$$

$$= \frac{\pi^2}{2\cdot 4^2} = \frac{\pi^2}{32}$$

Hence, $\int_0^1 \frac{\tan^{-1} x}{1+x^2}\,dx = \frac{\pi^2}{32}$

(ii) Let $I = \int_0^{\pi/2} \sqrt{\sin\phi}\cos^4\phi\cos\phi\, d\phi$

$$= \int_0^{\pi/2} \sqrt{\sin\phi}\,(1-\sin^2\phi)^2\cdot\cos\phi\, d\phi$$

Let $\sin\phi = z \Rightarrow \cos\phi\, d\phi = dz$

When $\phi = 0 \Rightarrow z = 0$

and $\phi = \frac{\pi}{2} \Rightarrow z = 1$

Then, $I = \int_0^1 \sqrt{z}\,(1-z^2)^2\cdot dz$

$$= \int_0^1 (z^{1/2} + z^{9/2} - 2z^{5/2})\,dz$$

$$= \left(\frac{z^{3/2}}{3/2}\right)_0^1 + \left(\frac{z^{11/2}}{11/2}\right)_0^1 - 2\left(\frac{z^{7/2}}{7/2}\right)_0^1$$

Hence,

$$\int_0^{\pi/2} \sqrt{\sin\phi}\cdot\cos^5\phi\, d\phi = \frac{64}{231}$$

(iii) Consider,

$I = \int_0^1 \sin^{-1}\left(\frac{2x}{1+x^2}\right)dx$

Let $x = \tan\theta \Rightarrow dx = \sec^2\theta\, d\theta$

x	0	1
θ	0	$\frac{\pi}{4}$

Thus, $I = \int_0^{\pi/4} \sin^{-1}\left(\frac{2\tan\theta}{1+\tan^2\theta}\right)\sec^2\theta\, d\theta$

$$= 2\int_0^{\pi/4} \theta\sec^2\theta\, d\theta$$

$$I = 2\left[\theta\int\sec^2\theta\, d\theta - \int\left(\frac{d}{d\theta}(\theta)\cdot\int\sec^2\theta\, d\theta\right)d\theta\right]_0^{\pi/4}$$

$$= 2\,[\theta\tan\theta - \int\tan\theta\, d\theta]_0^{\pi/4}$$

$$= 2\left[\frac{\pi}{4} + \log\left(\frac{1}{\sqrt{2}}\right) - \log 1\right]$$

Hence,

$$\int_0^1 \sin^{-1}\left(\frac{2x}{1+x^2}\right)dx = \frac{\pi}{2} - \log 2$$

(iv) Let $I = \int_0^{\pi/2} \frac{\sin x}{1+\cos^2 x}\,dx$

Put $\cos x = t \Rightarrow -\sin x\, dx = dt$

When $x = 0$, then $t = 1$

and when $x = \frac{\pi}{2}$, then $t = 0$

Thus, $I = \int_1^0 \frac{-dt}{1+t^2}$

$$= \int_0^1 \frac{dt}{1+t^2} = (\tan^{-1} t)_0^1$$

$$= \left(\frac{\pi}{4}\right) = \frac{\pi}{4}$$

Hence, $\int_0^{\pi/2} \frac{\sin x}{1+\cos^2 x}\,dx = \frac{\pi}{4}$

77. (a) Given, $\int_1^a (3x^2 + 2x + 1)\,dx = 11$

$\Rightarrow \quad (x^3 + x^2 + x)_1^a = 11$

$\Rightarrow \quad a^3 + a^2 + a = 11 + 3$

$\Rightarrow \quad a^3 + a^2 + a - 14 = 0$

$\Rightarrow (a-2)(a^2 + 3a + 7) = 0$

Since, $a^2 + 3a + 7 \neq 0,\ \forall\, a \in R$

Then, $a - 2 = 0 \Rightarrow a = 2$

Thus, the value of a is 2.

78. Let $I = \int_0^{\pi/2} \cos^3 x\, dx$

$$= \frac{1}{4}\int_0^{\pi/2} 4\cos^3 x\, dx$$

$$= \frac{1}{4}\int_0^{\pi/2} [\cos 3x + 3\cos x]\,dx$$

$$= \frac{1}{4}\left[\frac{\sin 3x}{3} + 3\sin x\right]_0^{\pi/2}$$

$$= \frac{1}{4}\left[\frac{\sin\frac{3\pi}{2}}{3} + 3\sin\frac{\pi}{2}\right]$$

$$= \frac{1}{4}\left(-\frac{1}{3} + 3\right) = \frac{2}{3}$$

Hence, $I = \frac{2}{3}$

$\therefore \int_0^{\pi/2} \cos^3 x\, dx = \frac{2}{3}$

79. (i) (True)

Let $I = \int_0^{\pi/4} \sin 3x\cdot\sin 2x\, dx$

$$\Rightarrow I = \frac{1}{2}\int_0^{\pi/4} 2\sin 3x\cdot\sin 2x\, dx$$

$$\Rightarrow I = \frac{1}{2}\int_0^{\pi/4} [\cos x - \cos 5x]\,dx$$

$$\Rightarrow I = \frac{1}{2}\left[\sin x - \frac{\sin 5x}{5}\right]_0^{\pi/4}$$

$$= \frac{1}{2}\left[\sin\frac{\pi}{4} - \frac{\sin\frac{5\pi}{4}}{5}\right]$$

$$\Rightarrow I = \frac{1}{2}\left[\frac{1}{\sqrt{2}} + \frac{1}{5\sqrt{2}}\right] = \frac{3\sqrt{2}}{10}$$

Hence, $\int_0^{\pi/4} \sin 3x\cdot\sin 2x\, dx = \frac{3\sqrt{2}}{10}$

(ii) (True)

Let $I = \int_0^4 \frac{dx}{\sqrt{x^2 + 2x + 3}}$

$$= \int_0^4 \frac{dx}{\sqrt{(x+1)^2 + (\sqrt{2})^2}}$$

$$\Rightarrow I = [\log|(x+1) + \sqrt{(x+1)^2 + 2}|]_0^4$$

$$\therefore \int_0^4 \frac{dx}{\sqrt{x^2 + 2x + 3}} = \log\left(\frac{5+3\sqrt{3}}{1+\sqrt{3}}\right)$$

(iii) (True)

$$I = \int_{-1}^1 \frac{dx}{x^2 + 2x + 5}$$

$$= \int_{-1}^1 \frac{dx}{(x+1)^2 + 4}$$

$$= \int_{-1}^1 \frac{dx}{(x+1)^2 + 2^2}$$

Let $x + 1 = t$

$\Rightarrow \quad dx = dt$

When $x = -1$, then $t = 0$

and when $x = 1$, then $t = 2$

$$\therefore \quad I = \int_0^2 \frac{dt}{t^2 + 2^2}$$

$$= \frac{1}{2}\left(\tan^{-1}\frac{t}{2}\right)_0^2$$

Thus, $\int_{-1}^1 \frac{dx}{x^2 + 2x + 5} = \frac{\pi}{8}$

80. Let $I = \int_1^2 \frac{5x^2}{x^2+4x+3}\,dx$

$$= 5\int_1^2 \frac{x^2\,dx}{x^2+4x+3}$$

$$= 5\int_1^2 \left(1 - \frac{4x+3}{x^2+4x+3}\right) dx$$

$$\therefore I = \int_1^2 5\,dx - 5\int_1^2 \frac{(4x+3)}{x^2+4x+3}\,dx$$

$$\Rightarrow I = 5 - 5\int_1^2 \left[\frac{2(2x+4)}{x^2+4x+3} - \frac{5}{x^2+4x+3}\right] dx$$

$$\Rightarrow I = 5 - 10(\log 15 - \log 8) + 25\cdot\frac{1}{2}\left[\log\left|\frac{x+1}{x+3}\right|_1^2\right]$$

Thus, $\int_1^2 \frac{5x^2\,dx}{x^2+4x+3}$

$$= 5 - 10\log\left(\frac{15}{8}\right) + \frac{25}{2}\log\left(\frac{6}{5}\right)$$

81. (a) We have, $f(x) = a + bx + cx^2$

$$\therefore f(0) = a,\ f\left(\frac{1}{2}\right) = a + \frac{b}{2} + \frac{C}{4}$$

and $f(1) = a + b + c$

$$\Rightarrow \frac{1}{6}\left\{f(0) + 4f\left(\frac{1}{2}\right) + f(1)\right\}$$

$$= \frac{1}{6}(6a + 3b + 2c) \quad \ldots\text{(i)}$$

Now,

$$\int_0^1 f(x)\,dx = \int_0^1 (a + bx + cx^2)\,dx$$

$$= \left[ax + \frac{bx^2}{2} + \frac{cx^3}{3}\right]_0^1$$

$$= \frac{1}{6}(6a + 3b + 2c) \quad \ldots\text{(ii)}$$

From Eq. (i) and (ii), we get

$$\int_0^1 f(x)\,dx = \frac{1}{6}\left\{f(0) + 4f\left(\frac{1}{2}\right) + f(1)\right\}$$

82. (True)

Let $I = \int_{\pi/6}^{\pi/3} \frac{\cos x + \sin x}{\sqrt{\sin 2x}}\,dx$

$$= \int_{\pi/6}^{\pi/3} \frac{(\cos x + \sin x)}{\sqrt{1 - (\cos x - \sin x)^2}}\,dx$$

Let $\cos x - \sin x = t$, then

$$-(\cos x + \sin x)\,dx = dt$$

Also, $x = \frac{\pi}{6}$

$$\Rightarrow t = \cos\frac{\pi}{6} - \sin\frac{\pi}{6} = \frac{\sqrt{3}-1}{2}$$

and $x = \frac{\pi}{3} \Rightarrow t = \frac{1-\sqrt{3}}{2}$

$$\therefore I = \int_{\frac{\sqrt{3}-1}{2}}^{\frac{1-\sqrt{3}}{2}} \frac{-1}{\sqrt{1-t^2}}\,dt$$

$$= -(\sin^{-1} t)_{\frac{\sqrt{3}-1}{2}}^{\frac{1-\sqrt{3}}{2}}$$

Thus, $I = \int_{\pi/6}^{\pi/3} \frac{\cos x + \sin x}{\sqrt{\sin 2x}}\,dx$

$$= 2\sin^{-1}\frac{\sqrt{3}-1}{2}$$

83. Let $I = \int_0^1 x(\tan^{-1} x)^2\,dx$

Then, $I = \left[(\tan^{-1} x)^2 \frac{x^2}{2}\right]_0^1 - \int_0^1 2\tan^{-1} x \cdot \frac{1}{1+x^2}\cdot\frac{x^2}{2}\,dx$

$$\Rightarrow I = \left\{\frac{1}{2}(\tan^{-1} 1)^2 - 0\right\} - \int_0^1 \frac{x^2}{1+x^2}\tan^{-1} x\,dx$$

$$\Rightarrow I = \frac{\pi^2}{32} - \int_0^1 \tan^{-1} x\,dx + \int_0^1 \frac{\tan^{-1} x}{1+x^2}\,dx$$

$$\Rightarrow I = \frac{\pi^2}{32} - \int_0^1 \tan^{-1} x\,dx + \left[\frac{1}{2}(\tan^{-1} x)^2\right]_0^1$$

$$\Rightarrow I = \frac{\pi^2}{16} - \left(\frac{\pi}{4}\right) + \frac{1}{2}[\log(1+x^2)]_0^1$$

Hence, $\int_0^1 (\tan^{-1} x)^2 \cdot x\,dx$

$$= \frac{\pi^2}{16} - \frac{\pi}{4} + \frac{1}{2}\log 2$$

84. (i) Let

$$I = \int_{-3}^{2} [-2f(x) + 5g(x)]\,dx$$

$$I = -2\int_{-3}^{2} f(x)\,dx + 5\int_{-3}^{2} g(x)\,dx$$

$$I = -2(5) + 5(-2)$$

$$I = -10 - 10 = -20$$

(ii) Let $I = \int_2^{-3} f(x)\,dx$

$$= -\int_{-3}^{2} f(x)\,dx = -5$$

(iii) Let $I = \int_{-3}^{1} [2f(x) + 3g(x)]\,dx$

$$I = 2\int_{-3}^{1} f(x)\,dx + 3\int_{-3}^{1} g(x)\,dx$$

$$I = 2(0) + 3(4) = 12$$

(iv) Let $I = \int_1^{-3} g(x)\,dx$

$$= -\int_{-3}^{1} g(x)\,dx = -4$$

85. Given, $\int_1^3 f(x)\,dx = 4$

and $\int_1^6 f(x)\,dx = -8$

We know,

$$\int_a^b f(x)\,dx = \int_a^c f(x)\,dx + \int_c^b f(x)\,dx$$

$$\therefore \int_1^6 f(x)\,dx = \int_1^3 f(x)\,dx + \int_3^6 f(x)\,dx$$

$$\Rightarrow -8 = 4 + \int_3^6 f(x)\,dx$$

$$\Rightarrow \int_3^6 f(x)\,dx = -12$$

86. Using additive identity of integration, we obtain

$$\therefore I = \int_1^4 f(x)\,dx$$

$$= \int_1^2 f(x)\,dx + \int_2^4 f(x)\,dx$$

$$= \int_1^2 (2x+8)\,dx + \int_2^4 6x\,dx$$

[using the definition of $f(x)$]

$$= (x^2 + 8x)_1^2 + (3x^2)_2^4$$

$$= (20 - 9) + (48 - 12) = 47$$

Thus, $\int_1^4 f(x)\,dx = 47$

87. (True)

Let $I = \int_{-1}^{2} |x^3 - x|\,dx$

Let $f(x) = x^3 - x = x(x+1)(x-1)$

We observe that

$$|f(x)| = \begin{cases} f(x), & x \in (-1, 0) \cup (1, 2) \\ -f(x), & x \in (0, 1) \end{cases}$$

$$\Rightarrow |x^3 - x| = \begin{cases} x^3 - x, & x \in (-1, 0) \cup (1, 2) \\ -(x^3 - x), & x \in (0, 1) \end{cases}$$

Now, $I = \int_{-1}^{2} |x^3 - x|\,dx$

$$= \int_{-1}^{0} |x^3 - x|\,dx + \int_0^1 |x^3 - x|\,dx + \int_1^2 |x^3 - x|\,dx$$

$$= \int_{-1}^{0} (x^3 - x)\,dx - \int_0^1 (x^3 - x)\,dx + \int_1^2 (x^3 - x)\,dx$$

$$= -\left(\frac{1}{4} - \frac{1}{2}\right) - \left(\frac{1}{4} - \frac{1}{2}\right) + \left(\frac{16}{4} - \frac{4}{2}\right) - \left(\frac{1}{4} - \frac{1}{2}\right)$$

$$= \frac{11}{4}$$

88. We have,

$$I = \int_0^{\pi/2} |\cos 2x|\, dx$$

So, $\int_0^{\pi/4} (\cos 2x)\, dx + \int_{\pi/4}^{\pi/2} -(\cos 2x)\, dx$

$$= \left(\frac{\sin 2x}{2}\right)_0^{\pi/4} + \left(\frac{-\sin 2x}{2}\right)_{\pi/4}^{\pi/2}$$

Thus, $\int_0^{\pi/2} |\cos 2x|\, dx = 1$

89. (b) Let $I = \int_2^8 |x-5|\, dx$

Since,

$$|x-5| = \begin{cases} (x-5), & x \in (5, 8) \\ -(x-5), & x \in (2, 5) \end{cases}$$

Using additive identity property, we get

$$\int_2^8 |x-5|\, dx = \int_2^5 -(x-5)\, dx + \int_5^8 (x-5)\, dx$$

$$= -\left(\frac{x^2}{2} - 5x\right)_2^5 + \left(\frac{x^2}{2} - 5x\right)_5^8$$

$$= 9$$

90. Let $I = \int_1^4 \{|x-1| + |x-2| + |x-4|\}\, dx$

$$\Rightarrow I = \int_1^2 (x - 1 - x + 2 - x + 4)\, dx + \int_2^4 (x - 1 + x - 2 - x + 4)\, dx$$

$$\Rightarrow I = \int_1^2 (5-x)\, dx + \int_2^4 (x+1)\, dx$$

$$\Rightarrow I = \left[5x - \frac{x^2}{2}\right]_1^2 + \left[\frac{x^2}{2} + x\right]_2^4$$

$$= \frac{23}{2}$$

Hence, the value of

$$\int_1^4 \{|x-1| + |x-2| + |x-4|\}\, dx = \frac{23}{2}$$

91. (True)

Let $I = \int_a^b \frac{f(x)}{f(x) + f(a+b-x)}\, dx$ ...(i)

Then,

$$I = \int_a^b \frac{f(a+b-x)}{f(a+b-x) + f\{a+b-(a+b-x)\}}\, dx$$

$$= \int_a^b \frac{f(a+b-x)}{f(a+b-x) + f(x)}\, dx \quad \text{...(ii)}$$

On adding Eqs. (i) and (ii), we get

$$2I = \int_a^b \frac{f(x) + f(a+b-x)}{f(x) + f(a+b-x)}\, dx$$

$$= \int_a^b dx = (b-a)$$

$$\therefore I = \frac{b-a}{2}$$

Hence, $\int_a^b \frac{f(x)}{f(x) + f(a+b-x)}\, dx = \frac{b-a}{2}$

92. (b) Let $I = \int_{\pi/6}^{\pi/3} \frac{dx}{1 + \sqrt{\cot x}}$

$$= \int_{\pi/6}^{\pi/3} \frac{\sqrt{\sin x}}{\sqrt{\sin x} + \sqrt{\cos x}}\, dx \quad \text{...(i)}$$

Then, $I = \int_{\pi/6}^{\pi/3} \frac{\sqrt{\sin\left(\frac{\pi}{2} - x\right)}}{\sqrt{\sin\left(\frac{\pi}{2} - x\right)} + \sqrt{\cos\left(\frac{\pi}{2} - x\right)}}\, dx$

$$= \int_{\pi/6}^{\pi/3} \frac{\sqrt{\cos x}}{\sqrt{\cos x} + \sqrt{\sin x}}\, dx \quad \text{...(ii)}$$

On adding Eqs. (i) and (ii), we get

$$2I = \int_{\pi/6}^{\pi/3} \frac{\sqrt{\sin x} + \sqrt{\cos x}}{\sqrt{\sin x} + \sqrt{\cos x}}\, dx$$

$$= \left(\frac{\pi}{3} - \frac{\pi}{6}\right) = \frac{\pi}{6}$$

Hence, $I = \frac{\pi}{12}$

Thus, $\int_{\pi/6}^{\pi/3} \frac{dx}{1 + \sqrt{\cot x}} = \frac{\pi}{12}$

93. Let $I = \int_0^{2\pi} \frac{e^{\sin x}}{e^{\sin x} + e^{-\sin x}}\, dx$ ...(i)

By property

$$\int_a^b f(x)\, dx = \int_a^b f(a+b-x)\, dx,$$

$$I = \int_0^{2\pi} \frac{e^{\sin(2\pi - x)}}{e^{\sin(2\pi - x)} + e^{-\sin(2\pi - x)}}\, dx$$

$$\therefore I = \int_0^{2\pi} \frac{e^{-\sin x}}{e^{-\sin x} + e^{\sin x}}\, dx \quad \text{...(ii)}$$

On adding Eqs. (i) and (ii), we get

$$2I = \int_0^{2\pi} 1\, dx$$

$$\therefore \quad I = \pi$$

Thus, $\int_0^{2\pi} \frac{e^{\sin x}}{e^{\sin x} + e^{-\sin x}}\, dx = \pi$

94. Let $I = \int_{-a}^{a} \frac{dx}{1 + a^x}$

By integration property, we know

$$\int_{-m}^{m} f(x)\, dx = \int_0^m f(x)\, dx + \int_0^m f(-x)\, dx$$

Thus, $I = \int_0^a \frac{dx}{1 + a^x} + \int_0^a \frac{dx}{1 + a^{-x}}$

$$= \int_0^a \frac{dx}{1 + a^x} + \int_0^a \frac{a^x}{1 + a^x}\, dx$$

Now, $I = \int_0^a \frac{1 + a^x}{1 + a^x}\, dx = \int_0^a 1\, dx = a$

Hence, $\int_{-a}^{a} \frac{dx}{1 + a^x} = a$

95. (a) Let $I = \int_0^7 \frac{\sqrt[3]{x}}{\sqrt[3]{x} + \sqrt[3]{7-x}}\, dx$ ...(i)

We know,

$$\int_a^b f(x)\, dx = \int_a^b f(a+b-x)\, dx$$

Then, $I = \int_0^7 \frac{\sqrt[3]{7-x}}{\sqrt[3]{x} + \sqrt[3]{7-x}}$ ...(ii)

On adding Eqs. (i) and (ii), we get

$$2I = \int_0^7 \frac{\sqrt[3]{x} + \sqrt[3]{7-x}}{\sqrt[3]{x} + \sqrt[3]{7-x}}\, dx$$

$$= \int_0^7 dx = 7$$

$$\therefore \quad I = \frac{7}{2}$$

Thus, $\int_0^7 \frac{\sqrt[3]{x}}{\sqrt[3]{x} + \sqrt[3]{7-x}}\, dx = \frac{7}{2}$

96. Let $I = \int_0^{\pi/2} \frac{\sin x}{\sin x + \cos x}\, dx$ ...(i)

Using $\int_0^a f(x)\, dx = \int_0^a f(a-x)\, dx$,

$$I = \int_0^{\pi/2} \frac{\sin\left(\frac{\pi}{2} - x\right)}{\sin\left(\frac{\pi}{2} - x\right) + \cos\left(\frac{\pi}{2} - x\right)}\, dx$$

$$= \int_0^{\pi/2} \frac{\cos x\, dx}{\cos x + \sin x} \quad \text{...(ii)}$$

On adding Eqs. (i) and (ii), we get

$$2I = \int_0^{\pi/2} \frac{\sin x}{\sin x + \cos x}\, dx + \int_0^{\pi/2} \frac{\cos x\, dx}{\cos x + \sin x}$$

$$= \frac{\pi}{2}$$

$$\Rightarrow I = \frac{\pi}{4}$$

$$\therefore \int_0^{\pi/2} \frac{\sin x\, dx}{\sin x + \cos x} = \frac{\pi}{4}$$

97. (True)

Let $I = \int_0^{\pi/4} \log(1 + \tan x)\, dx$

Then,

$$I = \int_0^{\pi/4} \log\left\{1 + \tan\left(\frac{\pi}{4} - x\right)\right\} dx$$

$$\left[\text{using } \int_0^a f(x)\, dx = \int_0^a f(a - x)\, dx\right]$$

$$\Rightarrow I = \int_0^{\pi/4} \log \left\{1 + \frac{\tan\frac{\pi}{4} - \tan x}{1 + \tan\frac{\pi}{4} \cdot \tan x}\right\} dx$$

$$\Rightarrow \quad I = \int_0^{\pi/4} \log\left\{\frac{2}{1 + \tan x}\right\} dx$$

$$\Rightarrow \quad I = \int_0^{\pi/4} \log 2\, dx - \int_0^{\pi/4} \log(1 + \tan x)\, dx$$

$$\Rightarrow 2I = \log 2 \cdot \frac{\pi}{4} \Rightarrow I = \frac{\pi}{8} \cdot \log 2$$

Thus, $\int_0^{\pi/4} \log(1 + \tan x)\, dx = \frac{\pi}{8} \cdot \log 2$

98. Let $I = \int_0^{\pi/2} \sin 2x \cdot \log \tan x\, dx$ ...(i)

$$\Rightarrow \quad I = \int_0^{\pi/2} \sin 2\left(\frac{\pi}{2} - x\right) \log \tan\left(\frac{\pi}{2} - x\right) dx$$

$$\Rightarrow I = \int_0^{\pi/2} \sin 2x \cdot \log \cot x\, dx \quad \text{...(ii)}$$

On adding Eqs. (i) and (ii), we get

$$2I = \int_0^{\pi/2} \sin 2x \{\log \cot x + \log \tan x\}\, dx$$

$$= \int_0^{\pi/2} \sin 2x \log 1\, dx = 0$$

$\therefore I = 0$

Thus, $\int_0^{\pi/2} \sin 2x \cdot \log \tan x\, dx = 0$

99. (a) Let $I = \int_0^{\pi/2} \frac{\sin^2 x\, dx}{\sin x + \cos x}$ ...(i)

Then,

$$I = \int_0^{\pi/2} \frac{\sin^2\left(\frac{\pi}{2} - x\right)}{\sin\left(\frac{\pi}{2} - x\right) + \cos\left(\frac{\pi}{2} - x\right)} dx$$

$$\Rightarrow I = \int_0^{\pi/2} \frac{\cos^2 x}{\sin x + \cos x} dx \quad \text{...(ii)}$$

On adding Eqs. (i) and (ii), we get

$$2I = \int_0^{\pi/2} \frac{\sin^2 x\, dx}{\sin x + \cos x} + \int_0^{\pi/2} \frac{\cos^2 x}{\cos x + \sin x} dx$$

$$\Rightarrow 2I = \int_0^{\pi/2} \frac{dx}{\sin x + \cos x}$$

$$\Rightarrow 2I = \frac{1}{\sqrt{2}} \int_0^{\pi/2} \frac{dx}{\frac{1}{\sqrt{2}} \sin x + \frac{1}{\sqrt{2}} \cos x}$$

$$\Rightarrow 2I = \frac{1}{\sqrt{2}} \int_0^{\pi/2} \frac{dx}{\sin\left(x + \frac{\pi}{4}\right)}$$

$$= \frac{1}{\sqrt{2}} \int_0^{\pi/2} \operatorname{cosec}\left(x + \frac{\pi}{4}\right) dx$$

$$\Rightarrow 2I = \frac{1}{\sqrt{2}} \left[\log\left\{\operatorname{cosec}\left(x + \frac{\pi}{4}\right) - \cot\left(x + \frac{\pi}{4}\right)\right\}\right]_0^{\pi/2}$$

$$= \frac{1}{\sqrt{2}} \left[\log\left(\operatorname{cosec}\frac{3\pi}{4} - \cot\frac{3\pi}{4}\right) - \log\left(\operatorname{cosec}\frac{\pi}{4} - \cot\frac{\pi}{4}\right)\right]$$

$$= \frac{1}{\sqrt{2}} \log\left(\frac{\sqrt{2} + 1}{\sqrt{2} - 1}\right)$$

$$= \frac{1}{\sqrt{2}} \log(\sqrt{2} - 1)^{-2}$$

$$= -\sqrt{2} \log(\sqrt{2} - 1)$$

$$\Rightarrow I = \frac{-1}{\sqrt{2}} \log(\sqrt{2} - 1)$$

100. Let $I = \int_0^{2\pi} \frac{dx}{1 + e^{\sin x}}$

Using $\int_0^{2a} f(x)\, dx = \int_0^a \{f(x) + f(2a - x)\}\, dx$

$$I = \int_0^{\pi} \left\{\frac{1}{1 + e^{\sin x}} + \frac{1}{1 + e^{\sin(2\pi - x)}}\right\} dx$$

$$= \int_0^{\pi} \left\{\frac{1 + e^{\sin x}}{1 + e^{\sin x}}\right\} dx$$

$= \pi$

Thus, $\int_0^{2\pi} \frac{dx}{1 + e^{\sin x}} = \pi$

101. (a) Let $I = \int_0^{\pi} \frac{x\, dx}{a^2 \cos^2 x + b^2 \sin^2 x}$ ...(i)

$$\therefore I = \int_0^{\pi} \frac{(\pi - x)\, dx}{a^2 \cos^2 x + b^2 \sin^2 x} \quad \text{...(ii)}$$

On adding Eqs. (i) and (ii), we get

$$2I = \int_0^{\pi} \frac{\pi\, dx}{a^2 \cos^2 x + b^2 \sin^2 x}$$

$$= \pi \int_0^{\pi} \frac{dx}{a^2 \cos^2 x + b^2 \sin^2 x}$$

Using $\int_0^{2a} f(x)\, dx = \int_0^a \{f(x) + f(2a - x)\}\, dx$, we obtain

$$2I = \pi \int_0^{\pi/2} \left\{\frac{1}{a^2 \cos^2 x + b^2 \sin^2 x} + \frac{1}{a^2 \cos^2(\pi - x) + b^2 \sin^2(\pi - x)}\right\} dx$$

$$\Rightarrow \; 2I = 2\pi \int_0^{\pi/2} \frac{1}{a^2 \cos^2 x + b^2 \sin^2 x} dx$$

$$\Rightarrow I = \pi \int_0^{\pi/2} \frac{\sec^2 x\, dx}{a^2 + b^2 \tan^2 x}$$

$$= \frac{\pi}{ab} \left[\tan^{-1}\left(\frac{b \tan x}{a}\right)\right]_0^{\pi/2}$$

Thus, $\int_0^{\pi} \frac{x}{a^2 \cos^2 x + b^2 \sin^2 x} dx = \frac{\pi^2}{2ab}$

102. (True)

Let $f(x) = \cos^5 x$

Then, $f(2\pi - x) = \{\cos(2\pi - x)\}^5 = \cos^5 x$

Thus,

$$\int_0^{2\pi} \cos^5 x\, dx = 2\int_0^{\pi} \cos^5 x\, dx$$

Now, let $I = 2\int_0^{\pi} \cos^5 x\, dx$ ...(i)

$$I = 2\int_0^{\pi} \cos^5(\pi - x)\, dx$$

$$I = -2\int_0^{\pi} \cos^5 x\, dx \quad \text{...(ii)}$$

On adding Eqs. (i) and (ii), we get

$2I = 0$

$\Rightarrow \quad I = 0$

Thus, $\int_0^{2\pi} \cos^5 x\, dx = 0$

103. Let $$I = \int_0^{2\pi} \frac{x \sin^{2n} x}{\sin^{2n} x + \cos^{2n} x} dx \quad \ldots(i)$$

Using $\int_0^a f(x)\, dx = \int_0^a f(a - x)\, dx$,

$$I = \int_0^{2\pi} \frac{(2\pi - x) \sin^{2n} x}{\sin^{2n} x + \cos^{2n} x} dx \quad \ldots(ii)$$

On adding Eqs. (i) and (ii), we get

$$2I = \int_0^{2\pi} \frac{x \sin^{2n} x}{\sin^{2n} x + \cos^{2n} x} dx + \int_0^{2\pi} \frac{(2\pi - x) \sin^{2n} x}{\sin^{2n} x + \cos^{2n} x} dx$$

$$\Rightarrow \quad 2I = 2\pi \int_0^{2\pi} \frac{\sin^{2n} x}{\cos^{2n} x + \sin^{2n} x} dx$$

$$\Rightarrow \quad I = 4\pi \int_0^{\pi/2} \frac{\sin^{2n} x}{\cos^{2n} x + \sin^{2n} x} dx \quad \ldots(iii)$$

$$\Rightarrow \quad I = 4\pi \int_0^{\pi/2} \frac{\cos^{2n} x}{\cos^{2n} x + \sin^{2n} x} dx \quad \ldots(iv)$$

On adding Eqs. (iii) and (iv), we get

$$2I = 4\pi \int_0^{\pi/2} \frac{\sin^{2n} x + \cos^{2n} x}{\sin^{2n} x + \cos^{2n} x} dx$$

$$= 2\pi^2$$

$$\therefore \quad I = \pi^2$$

Hence, $\int_0^{2\pi} \frac{x \sin^{2n} x}{\sin^{2n} x + \cos^{2n} x} dx = \pi^2$

104. (False)

Given, $I = \int_{-\pi/2}^{\pi/2} \sin^7 x\, dx$

Since, $f(x) = \sin^7 x$

$\therefore \quad f(-x) = \sin^7(-x)$

$= (-\sin x)^7 = -\sin^7 x = -f(x)$

Since, $f(x)$ is odd function.

Thus, by property, $I = 0$

$\therefore \quad \int_{-\pi/2}^{\pi/2} \sin^7 x\, dx = 0$

105. Let $I = \int_{-1}^{1} \sin^5 x \cos^4 x\, dx$

Let $f(x) = \sin^5 x \cos^4 x\, dx$

$\therefore f(-x) = \sin^5(-x) \cos^4(-x)$

$= -\sin^5 x \cdot \cos^4 x = -f(x)$

Thus, f is odd function.

Hence, $\int_{-1}^{1} \sin^5 x \cos^4 x\, dx = 0$

106. (b) Let $$I = \int_{-1}^{1} \frac{x^3 + |x| + 1}{x^2 + 2|x| + 1} dx$$

$$I = \int_{-1}^{1} \frac{x^3}{(|x| + 1)^2} dx + \int_{-1}^{1} \frac{|x| + 1}{(|x| + 1)^2} dx$$

Since, $\frac{x^3}{(|x| + 1)^2}$ is odd function and $\frac{|x| + 1}{(|x| + 1)^2}$ is even function.

$$\Rightarrow \quad I = 0 + 2\int_0^1 \frac{|x| + 1}{(|x| + 1)^2} dx$$

$$= 2\{\log(x + 1)\}_0^1$$

$$\therefore \quad I = 2 \log 2$$

Hence, $\int_{-1}^{1} \frac{x^3 + |x| + 1}{x^2 + 2|x| + 1} dx$

$= 2 \log 2$

107. Let $f(x) = |\sin x|$

Then, $f(-x) = |\sin(-x)| = |-\sin x|$

$= |\sin x| = f(x)$

$$\therefore \quad I = \int_{-\pi/2}^{\pi/2} |\sin x|\, dx = 2\int_0^{\pi/2} \sin x\, dx$$

$$= 2[-\cos x]_0^{\pi/2} = 2$$

Thus, the value of $\int_{-\pi/2}^{\pi/2} |\sin x|\, dx = 2$

108. (True)

Let $I = \int_{-\pi/2}^{\pi/2} \sin^2 x\, dx$

Since, $f(x) = \sin^2 x$

$f(-x) = \sin^2(-x)$

$= (-\sin x)^2 = \sin^2 x = f(x)$

i.e. $f(x)$ is even function.

So, $I = \int_{-\pi/2}^{\pi/2} \sin^2 x\, dx$

$$= 2\int_0^{\pi/2} \sin^2 x\, dx = \left(x - \frac{\sin 2x}{2}\right)_0^{\pi/2}$$

$$\therefore \quad \int_{-\pi/2}^{\pi/2} \sin^2 x\, dx = \frac{\pi}{2}$$

Assertion Reason

1. (a) $\int \frac{dx}{x^2 + a^2} = \frac{1}{a} \tan^{-1}\left(\frac{x}{a}\right) + C$

This is standard integral and hence R is true.

$$\int \frac{dx}{x^2 + 2x + 3} = \int \frac{dx}{(x + 1)^2 + (\sqrt{2})^2}$$

$$= \frac{1}{\sqrt{2}} \tan^{-1}\left(\frac{x + 1}{\sqrt{2}}\right) + C$$

2. (d) $\int e^x[f(x) + f'(x)]dx = \int e^x f(x)dx + \int e^x f'(x)dx$

$$= f(x)e^x - \int f'(x)e^x dx + \int f'(x)e^x dx = e^x f(x) + C$$

Hence, reason is true.

$$\int e^x(\sin x - \cos x)dx = e^x(-\cos x) + C$$

$$= -e^x \cos x + C \quad \left[\because \frac{d}{dx}(-\cos x) = \sin x\right]$$

Hence, assertion is false.

3. (a) Let $\quad y = x^x$

On taking log both sides, we get

$$\Rightarrow \quad \log y = x \log x$$

On differentiating w.r.t. x, we get

$$\Rightarrow \quad \frac{1}{y}\frac{dy}{dx} = x\left(\frac{1}{x}\right) + \log x(1)$$

$$\frac{dy}{dx} = y(1+\log x) = x^x(1+\log x)$$

Hence, reason is true.

Since, $\frac{d}{dx}(x^x) = x^x(1+\log x)$

$$\int x^x(1+\log x)dx = x^x + C$$

Using the concept of anti-derivative, assertion is true. reason is the correct explanation for assertion.

4. (c) Since, $\int x^n dx = \frac{x^{n+1}}{n+1} + C$

$$\int x^2 dx = \frac{x^{2+1}}{2+1} + c = \frac{x^3}{3} + C$$

$\therefore$ Assertion is true.

$\int e^{x^2} dx$ is a function which can not be integrated

$\therefore$ Reason is false.

5. (a) Let $I = \int_0^{\pi/2} \frac{\sin x}{\sin x + \cos x} dx$ ... (i)

$$\int_0^a f(x)\,dx = \int_0^a f(a-x)\,dx$$

$$\therefore \quad I = \int_0^{\pi/2} \frac{\sin\left(\frac{\pi}{2}-x\right)dx}{\sin\left(\frac{\pi}{2}-x\right)+\cos\left(\frac{\pi}{2}-x\right)}$$

$$I = \int \frac{\cos x}{\cos x + \sin x} dx \quad \text{... (ii)}$$

On adding Eqs. (i) and (ii), we get

$$\Rightarrow \quad 2I = \int_0^{\pi/2} \frac{\sin x + \cos x}{\sin x + \cos x} dx = \int_0^{\pi/2} 1\,dx = [x]_0^{\pi/2} = \frac{\pi}{2}$$

$$\therefore \quad I = \frac{\pi}{4}$$

Hence, reason is true.

From Eq. (ii), assertion is also true.

6. (c) Let $f(x) = x^3 + 5$

$$f(-x) = (-x)^3 + 5 = -x^3 + 5$$

$f(x)$ is neither even or odd. Hence, reason is false.

$$\int_{-3}^{3} x^3 dx = 0 \qquad [\because x^3 \text{ is odd}]$$

$$\int_{-3}^{3} 5dx = 5[x]_{-3}^{3} = 30$$

$$\therefore \int_{-3}^{3} (x^3+5)\,dx = 0 + 30 = 30$$

Hence, assertion is true.

7. (a) $\int \frac{dx}{x^2+a^2} = \frac{1}{a}\tan^{-1}\left(\frac{x}{a}\right) + C$

This is a standard integral and hence true. So, reason is true.

$$\int_0^{x^2} \frac{dt}{t^2+4} = \left[\frac{1}{2}\tan^{-1}\left(\frac{t}{2}\right)\right]_0^{x^2} = \frac{1}{2}\tan^{-1}\left(\frac{x^2}{2}\right)$$

$$\frac{d}{dx}\left[\int_0^{x^2} \frac{dt}{t^2+4}\right] = \frac{d}{dx}\left[\frac{1}{2}\tan^{-1}\left(\frac{x^2}{2}\right)\right]$$

$$= \frac{1}{2} \times \frac{1}{1+\frac{x^4}{4}} \times \frac{2x}{2} = \frac{x}{2} \times \frac{4}{4+x^4} = \frac{2x}{4+x^4}$$

Hence, assertion is true and reason is the correct explanation for assertion.

8. (d) $\int_{-a}^{a} f(x)\,dx = \begin{cases} 2\int_0^a f(x)\,dx, & \text{if } f(x) \text{ is an even function i.e. } (-x) = f(x) \\ 0, & \text{if } f(x) \text{ is an odd function i.e. } f(-x) = -f(x) \end{cases}$

This is a property of the definite integrals and hence reason is true.

$$\int_{-1}^{1} (x^3 + \sin x + 2)dx = \int_{-1}^{1} (x^3 + \sin x)\,dx + \int_{-1}^{1} 2dx$$

$\downarrow$ Odd function $\qquad \downarrow$ Even function

$$= 0 + 2[x]_{-1}^{1} = 2 \times 2 = 4$$

Hence, assertion is false.

9. (a) Let $f(x) = \log\left(\frac{1+x}{1-x}\right) \Rightarrow f(-x) = \log\left(\frac{1-x}{1+x}\right)$

$$= \log(1-x) - \log(1+x)$$

$$= -\log\left(\frac{1+x}{1-x}\right) = -f(x)$$

$\therefore f(x)$ is an odd function $\Rightarrow \int_{-2}^{2} \log\left(\frac{1+x}{1-x}\right) dx = 0$

10. (a) Let $f(x) = \tan x \Rightarrow f'(x) = \sec^2 x$

$$\therefore \int e^x(\tan x + \sec^2 x)dx = e^x \tan x + C$$

Case Based

1. (i) (a) This is of form $\int_{-a}^{a} f(x)dx$

$$f(x) = x^{99}$$

$$f(-x) = (-x)^{99} = -x^{99}$$

Thus, $f(-x) = -f(x)$

Using the property

$$\int_{-a}^{a} f(x)dx = 0,$$

if f is an odd function i.e. if $f(-x) = -f(x)$.

$$\int_{-1}^{1} x^{99}\,dx = 0$$

(ii) (b) This is of form $\int_{-a}^{a} f(x)dx$

$f(x) = x\cos x$

$f(-x) = (-x)\cos(-x)$

$= -x\cos x$

Thus, $f(-x) = -f(x)$

Using the property

$\int_{-a}^{a} f(x)dx = 0,$

if f is an odd function i.e. if $f(-x) = -f(x)$

$\int_{-\pi}^{\pi} x\cos x\, dx = 0.$

(iii) (b) This is of form $\int_{-a}^{a} f(x)dx$

$f(x) = \sin^3 x$

$f(-x) = \sin^3(-x)$

$= (-\sin x)^3 = -\sin^3 x$

Thus, $f(-x) = -f(x)$

Using the property

$\int_{-a}^{a} f(x)dx = 0$

if f is an odd function i.e. if $f(-x) = -f(x)$

$\int_{\frac{-\pi}{2}}^{\frac{\pi}{2}} \sin^3 x\, dx = 0.$

(iv) (c) This is of form $\int_{-a}^{a} f(x)dx$

$f(x) = x\sin x$

$f(-x) = (-x)\sin(-x)$

$= -x \times -\sin x = \text{Sin}x$

Thus, $f(-x) = f(x)$

Using the property

$\int_{-a}^{a} f(x)dx = 2\int_{0}^{a} f(x)\, dx$

If f is an even function i.e. if $f(-x) = f(x)$

Therefore,

$\int_{-\pi}^{\pi} x\sin x\, dx = 2\int_{0}^{\pi} x\sin x\, dx$

Let $I = 2\int_{0}^{\pi} x\sin x\, dx$ ... (i)

Using the property

$\int_{0}^{a} f(x)dx = \int_{0}^{a} f(a-x)\, dx$

$I = 2\int_{0}^{\pi} (\pi - x)\sin(\pi - x)\, dx$

$I = 2\int_{0}^{\pi} (\pi - x)\sin x\, dx$

$I = 2\int_{0}^{\pi} \pi \sin x\, dx$

$- 2\int_{0}^{\pi} x\sin x\, dx$ ... (ii)

On adding Eqs. (i) and (ii), we get

$I + I = 2\int_{0}^{\pi} x\sin x\, dx + 2$

$\int_{0}^{\pi} \pi\sin x\, dx - 2\int_{0}^{\pi} x\sin x\, dx$

$2I = 2\int_{0}^{\pi} \pi\sin x\, dx$

$I = \int_{0}^{\pi} \pi\sin x\, dx$

$I = \pi\int_{0}^{\pi} \sin x\, dx$

$I = \pi\,[-\cos x]_{0}^{\pi}$

$I = \pi\,[-\cos\pi - (-\cos 0)]$

$I = \pi[-\cos\pi + \cos 0]$

$I = \pi[-(-1) + 1]$

$I = \pi\,[1 + 1]$

$I = 2\pi$

(v) (c) This is of form $\int_{-a}^{a} f(x)\, dx$

$f(x) = \tan x\sec^2 x$

$f(-x) = \tan(-x)\sec^2(-x)$

$= -\tan x\sec^2 x$

Thus, $f(-x) = -f(x)$

Using the property

$\int_{-a}^{a} f(x)\, dx = 0,$

if f is an odd function i.e., if $f(-x) = -f(x)$

$\int_{-\pi}^{\pi} \tan x\sec^2 x\, dx = 0.$

2. $\int e^x[f(x) + f'(x)]\, dx$

$= \int e^x f(x)\, dx + \int e^x f'(x)dx$

Using the integration by parts

$= f(x)\int e^x\, dx - \int f'(x)e^x dx$

$+ \int f'(x)e^x dx$

$= f(x)e^x - \int f'(x)e^x dx$

$+ \int f'(x)e^x dx$

$= e^x f(x) + C$

Based on the above information, answer the following questions.

(i) (b) $\int e^x(\sin x + \cos x)\, dx$

It is of form

$\int e^x(f(x) + f'(x))\, dx$

$= e^x f(x) + C$

On putting $f(x) = \sin x$

$\therefore f'(x) = \cos x$

Thus, $\int e^x(\sin x + \cos x)\, dx$

$= e^x\sin x + C$

(ii) (b) $\int e^x\left(\frac{x-1}{x^2}\right) dx$

$= \int e^x\left(\frac{x}{x^2} - \frac{1}{x^2}\right)dx$

$= \int e^x\left(\frac{1}{x} - \frac{1}{x^2}\right)dx$

It is of form

$\int e^x(f(x) + f'(x))dx$

$= e^x f(x) + C$

On putting $f(x) = \frac{1}{x}$

$\therefore f'(x) = \frac{-1}{x^2}$

Thus, $\int e^x\left(\frac{1}{x} - \frac{1}{x^2}\right)dx = \frac{e^x}{x} + C$

(iii) (a) $\int e^x(1+x)dx = \int e^x(x+1)dx$

It is of form

$\int e^x(f(x) + f'(x))dx$

$= e^x f(x) + C$

On putting $f(x) = x$

$\therefore f'(x) = 1$

Thus,

$\int e^x(x+1)dx = e^x \times x + C.$

(iv) (a) $\int_{0}^{\pi} e^x(\tan x + \sec^2 x)\, dx$

It is of form

$\int e^x(f(x) + f'(x))dx$

$= e^x f(x) + C$

On putting $f(x) = \tan x$

$\therefore f'(x) = \sec^2 x$

Thus, $\int_{0}^{\pi} e^x(\tan x + \sec^2 x)\, dx$

$= [e^x \tan x]_{0}^{\pi}$

$= [e^x\tan\pi - e^x\tan 0]$

$= [e^x \times 0 - e^x \times 0]$

$= 0 - 0 = 0$

(v) (d) $\int e^x\left(\frac{x}{(1+x)^2}\right) dx$

$= \int e^x\left(\frac{1+x-1}{(1+x)^2}\right) dx$

$= \int e^x\left(\frac{1+x}{(1+x)^2} - \frac{1}{(1+x)^2}\right) dx$

$= \int e^x\left(\frac{1}{(1+x)} - \frac{1}{(1+x)^2}\right) dx$

It is of form

$\int e^x(f(x) + f'(x))dx$

$= e^x f(x) + C$

On putting $f(x) = \frac{1}{(1+x)}$

$\therefore f'(x) = \frac{-1}{(1+x)^2}$

Thus,

$\int e^x\left(\frac{1}{(1+x)} - \frac{1}{(1+x)^2}\right) dx$

$= \frac{e^x}{(1+x)} + C$

Chapter-8

Application of Integrals

1. Required area
= Area of shaded region $ABCD$

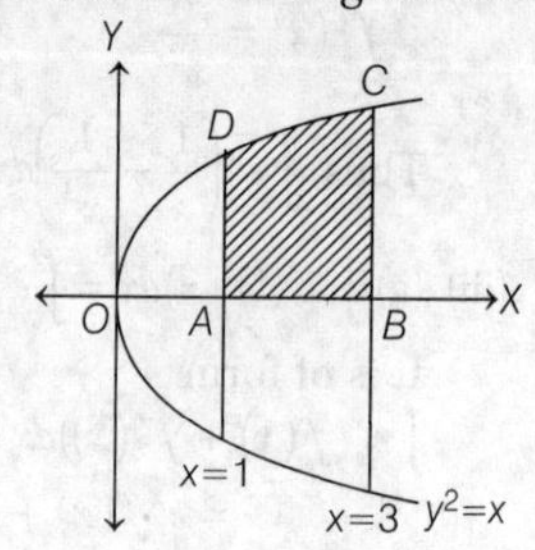

$= \int_1^3 y\, dx = \int_1^3 \sqrt{x}\, dx = \frac{2}{3}[x^{3/2}]_1^3$

$= \frac{2}{3}[3^{3/2} - 1]$ sq units

2. Required area
= Area of shaded region $ABCD$

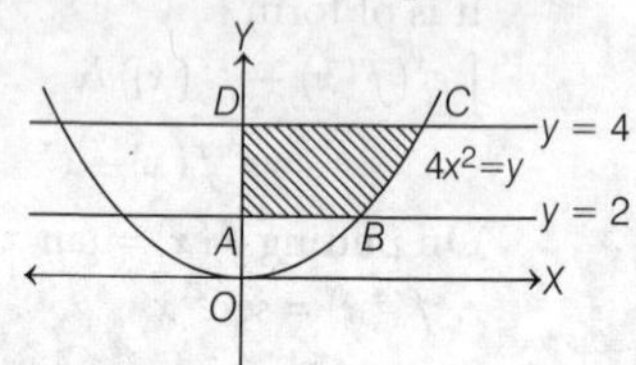

$= \int_2^4 x\, dy = \frac{1}{2}\int_2^4 \sqrt{y}\, dy$

$= \frac{1}{2}\cdot\frac{2}{3}[y^{3/2}]_2^4$

$= \frac{1}{3}[8 - 2\sqrt{2}]$ sq units

3. (a) The required area
= Area of OAB

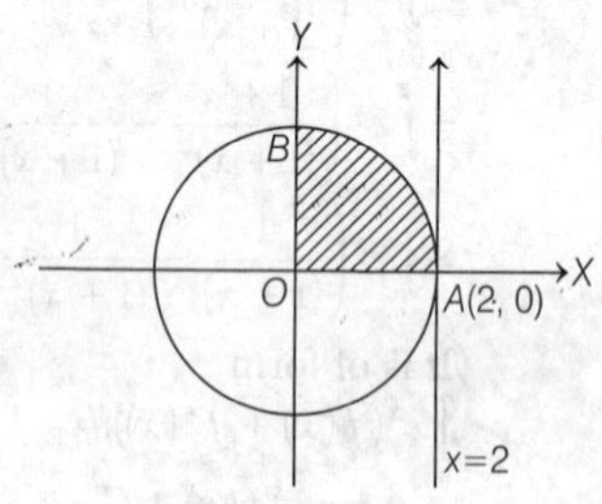

$= \int_0^2 y\, dx = \int_0^2 \sqrt{4 - x^2}\, dx$

$= \left[\frac{x\sqrt{4-x^2}}{2} + \frac{4}{2}\sin^{-1}\frac{x}{2}\right]_0^2$

$= 2\left(\frac{\pi}{2}\right) = \pi$

Thus, the required area is π sq units.

4. Required area (OAB)
= Area of ΔOAC + Area of ABC

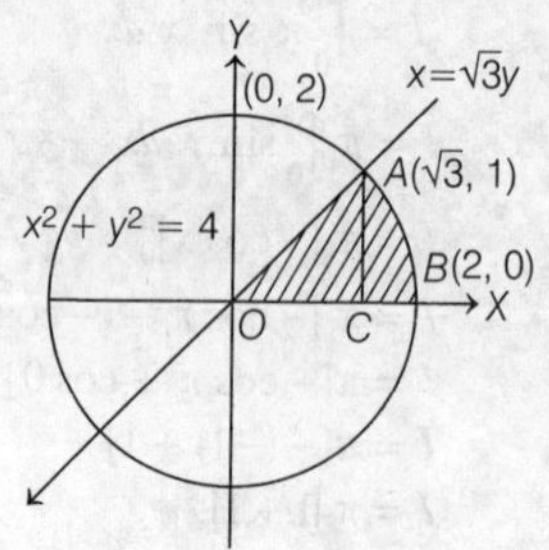

Now, area of
$\Delta OAC = \frac{1}{2} OC \cdot AC = \frac{1}{2}\cdot\sqrt{3}\cdot 1 = \frac{\sqrt{3}}{2}$

and area of ABC

$= \int_{\sqrt{3}}^2 y\, dx = \int_{\sqrt{3}}^2 \sqrt{4 - x^2}\, dx$

$= \left[\frac{x\sqrt{4-x^2}}{2} + \frac{4}{2}\sin^{-1}\left(\frac{x}{2}\right)\right]_{\sqrt{3}}^2$

$= \left[2\cdot\frac{\pi}{2} - \frac{\sqrt{3}}{2}\sqrt{4-3} - 2\sin^{-1}\left(\frac{\sqrt{3}}{2}\right)\right]$

$= \left[\pi - \frac{\sqrt{3}}{2} - 2\sin^{-1}\left(\frac{\sqrt{3}}{2}\right)\right]$

$= \left[\pi - \frac{2\pi}{3} - \frac{\sqrt{3}}{2}\right] = \left(\frac{\pi}{3} - \frac{\sqrt{3}}{2}\right)$

Now, area of

$OAB = \left(\frac{\sqrt{3}}{2}\right) + \left(\frac{\pi}{3} - \frac{\sqrt{3}}{2}\right)$

$= \frac{\pi}{3}$ sq units

5. (a) The required area (A) is given by

$A = \int_0^2 y\, dx$

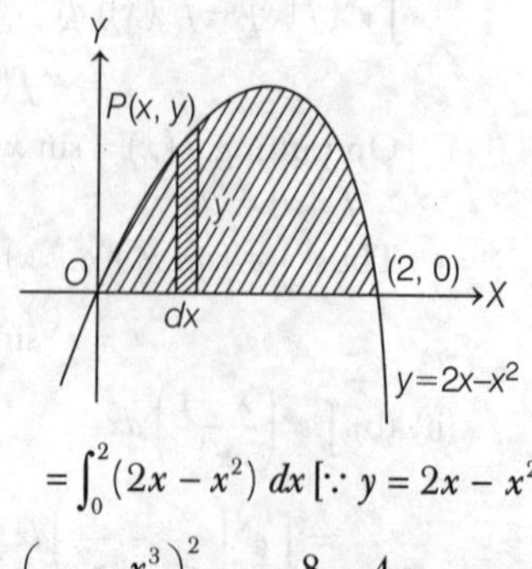

$= \int_0^2 (2x - x^2)\, dx\ [\because y = 2x - x^2]$

$= \left(x^2 - \frac{x^3}{3}\right)_0^2 = 4 - \frac{8}{3} = \frac{4}{3}$ sq units

6. The equation $y^2 = 16x$ represents a parabola with vertex at the origin and axis of symmetry along the positive direction of X-axis.

Clearly, $x = 4$ is the line parallel to Y-axis. The region is the shaded portion shown in the figure.

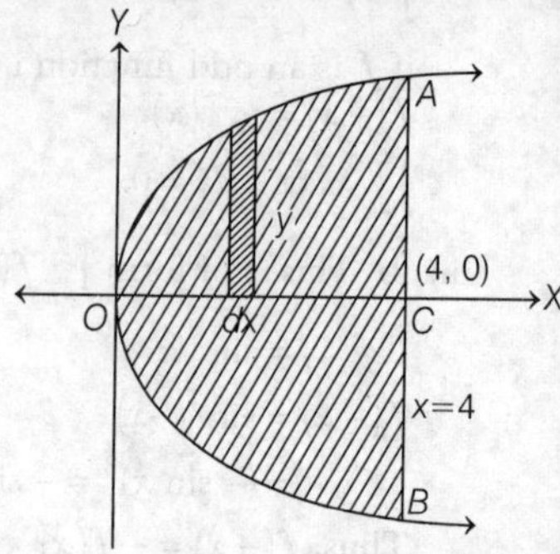

Since, $y^2 = 16x$ is symmetrical about X-axis.

$\therefore$ Required area

$= 2$ (area $OCAO$)

$= 2\int_0^4 y\, dx$

$= 2\int_0^4 \sqrt{16x}\, dx$

$= 2\cdot 4\int_0^4 \sqrt{x}\, dx$

$= 8\cdot\left[\frac{x^{3/2}}{3/2}\right]_0^4$

$= 8\left[\frac{2}{3}\cdot x^{3/2}\right]_0^4$

$= \frac{16}{3}(4)^{3/2}$

$= \frac{128}{3}$ sq units

7. (a) The required area
= Area of the region $OABO$
+ Area of the region $BCDB$
+ Area of the region $DEFD$

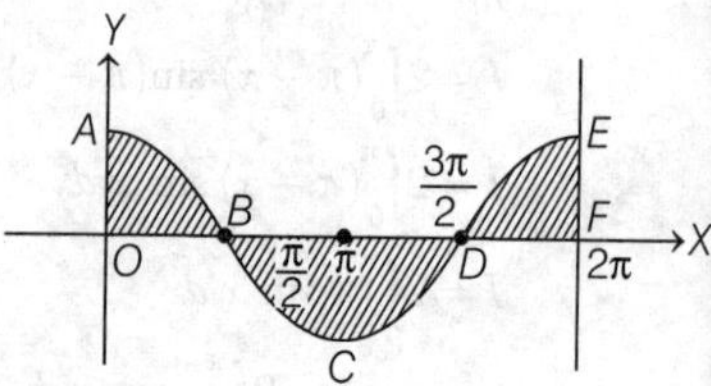

Thus, we have the required area,

$= \int_0^{\pi/2} \cos x\, dx$

$+ \left|\int_{\pi/2}^{3\pi/2} \cos x\, dx\right| + \int_{3\pi/2}^{2\pi} \cos x\, dx$

$= [\sin x]_0^{\pi/2} + |[\sin x]_{\pi/2}^{3\pi/2}| + [\sin x]_{\frac{3\pi}{2}}^{2\pi}$

$= 1 + 2 + 1$

$= 4$ sq units

8. Clearly, $2y = -x + 8$ represents a straight line cutting X and Y-axes at (8, 0) and (0, 4), respectively.

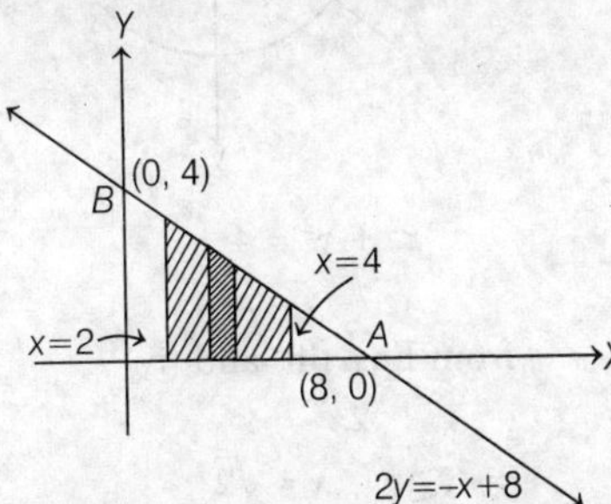

Also, $x = 2$ and $x = 4$ are straight lines parallel to Y-axis as shown in the given figure. To find the area of the shaded portion.

Thus, the required area is

$$= \int_2^4 y\, dx = \int_2^4 \left(\frac{-x+8}{2}\right) dx$$

$$= \frac{1}{2}\left[-\frac{x^2}{2} + 8x\right]_2^4$$

$$= \frac{1}{2}\left[\left(\frac{-16}{2} + 32\right) - \left(-\frac{4}{2} + 16\right)\right]$$

$= 5$ sq units

9. (True)

The graph of $y = 2^{kx}$, $x = 0$ and $x = 2$ are shown in figure and the region bounded by these curve in first quadrant is shaded in this figure.

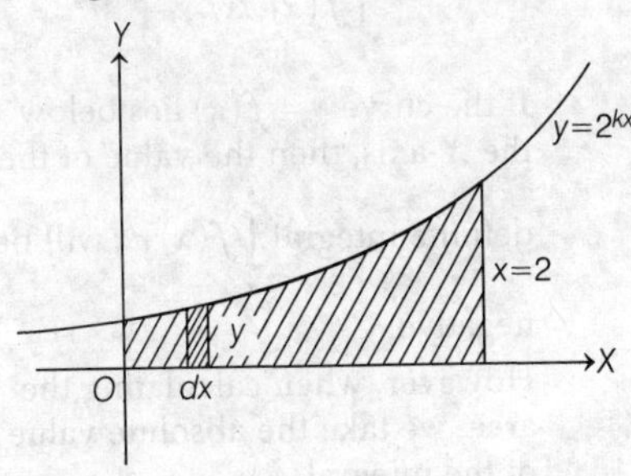

Thus, the area of the shaded region is $\int_0^2 y\, dx$

But it is given that the area of the shaded region is $\frac{3}{\log_e 2}$.

Then, $\int_0^2 y\, dx = \frac{3}{\log_e 2}$

$$\Rightarrow \int_0^2 2^{kx}\, dx = \frac{3}{\log_e 2}$$

$$\Rightarrow \left[\frac{2^{kx}}{k \log_e 2}\right]_0^2 = \frac{3}{\log_e 2}$$

$$\Rightarrow \frac{2^{2k} - 1}{k \log_e 2} = \frac{3}{\log_e 2}$$

$$\Rightarrow \frac{4^k - 1}{k} = 3 \quad \dots(i)$$

Clearly, $k = 1$ satisfies the Eq. (i),

Hence, $k = 1$.

10. Since, the line $x = a$ divides the area bounded by the parabola and $x = 4$ into two equal parts.

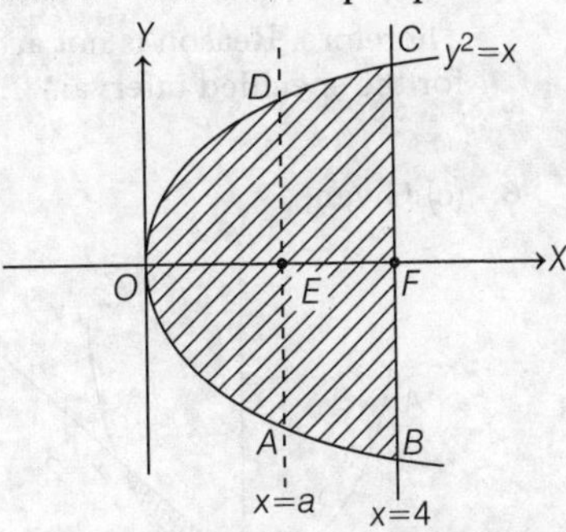

Therefore, area (OAD)

$= \text{Area}(ABCD)$

We observed that the given area is symmetrical about X-axis.

Hence, area (OED)

$= \text{Area}(EFCD)$

$$\Rightarrow \int_0^a y\, dx = \int_a^4 y\, dx$$

$$\Rightarrow \int_0^a \sqrt{x}\, dx = \int_a^4 \sqrt{x}\, dx \quad [\because y^2 = x]$$

Thus, $\frac{2}{3} a^{3/2} = \frac{2}{3}[8 - a^{3/2}]$

$$\Rightarrow 2(a)^{3/2} = 8 \Rightarrow a = (4)^{2/3}$$

11. (True)

The required region is the shaded region $ABCD$, whose area

$$= \int_1^4 x\, dy = \int_1^4 \frac{\sqrt{y}}{2}\, dy$$

$$= \frac{1}{2}\left[\frac{y^{3/2}}{3/2}\right]_1^4 = \frac{1}{3}\{(4)^{3/2} - 1\}$$

$$= \frac{1}{3}\{8 - 1\} = \frac{7}{3}$$

Thus, the required area of the shaded region is $\frac{7}{3}$ sq units.

Assertion-Reason

1. (a) Given, $y^2 = 4x$ and $y = x$

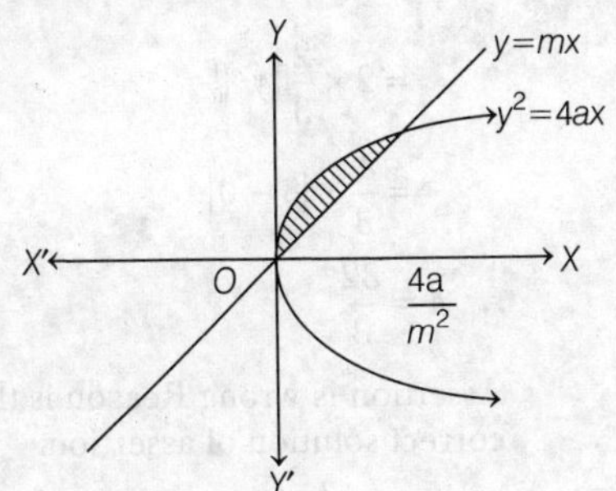

$$\text{Area} = \int_0^{\frac{4a}{m^2}} (\sqrt{4ax} - mx)\, dx$$

$$\Rightarrow \text{Area} = \left[\frac{2}{3} \times 2a^{\frac{1}{2}} x^{\frac{3}{2}} - m\frac{x^2}{2}\right]_0^{\frac{4a}{m^2}}$$

$$\Rightarrow \text{Area} = \frac{8a^2}{3m^3} \quad \text{(Reason is true)}$$

Assertion is true by inspection.

So, Assertion and Reason are true Reason explains Assertion.

2. (a) Given, $x^2 + y^2 = a^2$

$$\Rightarrow x = \sqrt{a^2 - y^2}$$

$$\text{Area of circle} = 4\int_0^a x\, dy$$

$$= 4\int_0^a \sqrt{a^2 - y^2}\, dy$$

$$= 4\left[\frac{y}{2}\sqrt{a^2 - y^2} + \frac{a^2}{2}\sin^{-1}\frac{y}{a}\right]_0^a$$

$$= 4\left[\left(\frac{a}{2} \times 0 + \frac{a^2}{a} \cdot \sin^{-1} 1\right) - 0\right]$$

$$= 4 \cdot \frac{a^2}{2} \cdot \frac{\pi}{2}$$

$\therefore$ Area of circle $= \pi a^2$

The area enclosed by circle

$= \pi a^2$

Assertion and Reason both are true, Reason is the correct explanation of Assertion.

3. (d) Since, the given curve represented by the equation $y = x^2$ is a parabola symmetrical about Y-axis only, therefore from the figure, the required area of the region $AOBA$ is given by

$$A = 2\int_0^4 x\,dy$$

$$= 2\int_0^4 \sqrt{y}\,dy$$

$$= 2 \times \frac{2}{3}[y^{\frac{3}{2}}]_0^4$$

$$= \frac{4}{3} \times [8 - 0]$$

$$\therefore \quad A = \frac{32}{3}$$

Assertion is wrong Reason is the correct solution of assertion.

4. (a) Given, $\int_a^b f(x)\,dx$

This is true. The area under the curve $y = f(x)$ from $x = a$ to $x = b$ is indeed given by the definite integral $\int_a^b f(x)\,dx$.

So, Assertion is true.

Now, The reason is also true.

The definite integral $\int_a^b f(x)\,dx$ can be interpreted as the sum of the areas of infinitesimally small rectangles under the curve from $x = a$ to $x = b$.

Since, both the Assertion and the Reason are true and Reason correctly explains the Assertion.

5. (c) Given,

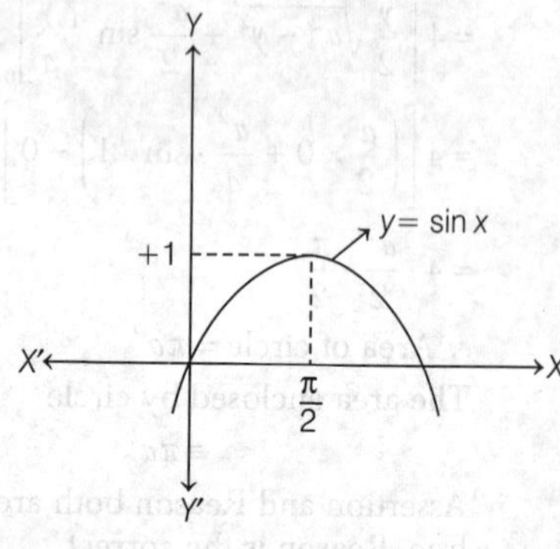

Let $A = \int_0^{\pi} \sin x\,dx$

$$= [-\cos x]_0^{\pi}$$

$$= -(\cos \pi - \cos 0)$$

$$= -(-1 - 1) = 2$$

$\therefore$ Assertion is true.

Now, the function $f(x) = \sin x$ indeed has a maximum value of 1 and a minimum value of −1.

However, with the interval $[0, \pi]$, the minimum value of $\sin x$ is 0 at $(x = 0)$ and $(x = \pi)$ and the maximum value is 1 at $\left(x = \frac{\pi}{2}\right)$.

Therefore, Reason is not accurate for the specified interval.

6. (c) Given,

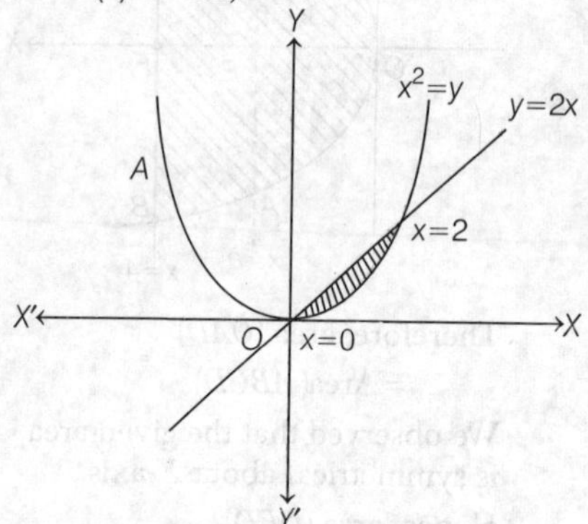

Equation of parabola

$x^2 = y$ and $y = 2x$

$$x^2 = y \quad \ldots(i)$$

$$2x = y \quad \ldots(ii)$$

From Eqs. (i) and (ii), we get

$$x^2 = 2x$$

$$\Rightarrow x(x - 2) = 0$$

$$x = 0, 2$$

$$A = \int_0^2 2x\,dx - \int_0^2 x^2\,dx$$

$$= \left[2 \times \frac{x^2}{2}\right]_0^2 - \left[\frac{x^3}{3}\right]_0^2$$

$$= 4 - \frac{8}{3}$$

$$= \frac{4}{3}$$

Now, given equation of circle

$x^2 + y^2 = 4$ and $y = x$ and $y = 0$

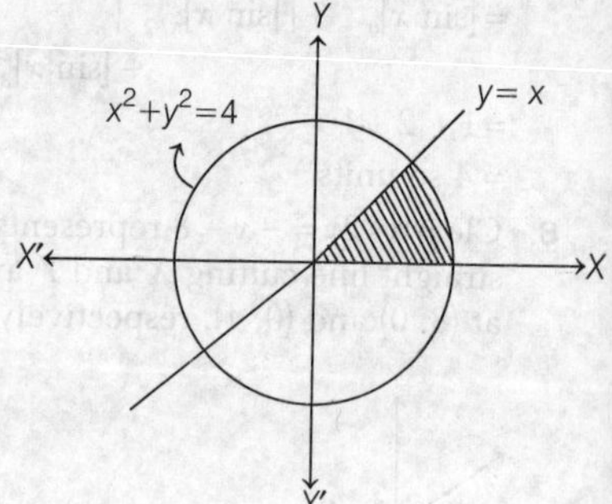

$$x^2 + y^2 = 4 \quad \ldots(iii)$$

$$y = x \quad \ldots(iv)$$

from Eqs. (iii) and (iv)

$$2x^2 = 4$$

$$\Rightarrow \quad x = \sqrt{2}$$

$$\text{Area} = \int_0^{\sqrt{2}} x\,dx + \int_{\sqrt{2}}^{2} \sqrt{2^2 - x^2}\,dx$$

$$= \left[\frac{x^2}{2}\right]_0^{\sqrt{2}} + \left[\frac{x\sqrt{4 - x^2}}{2} + \frac{4}{2}\sin^{-1}\left(\frac{x}{2}\right)\right]_{\sqrt{2}}^{2}$$

$$= 1 - 0 + 0 + 2 \times \frac{\pi}{2} - 1 - 2 \times \frac{\pi}{4}$$

$$= \frac{\pi}{2}$$

$\therefore$ Reason is false and Assertion is true.

7. (c) Here, the Assertion is true. The area under the curve $y = f(x)$ between $x = a$ and $x = b$ is indeed given by the definite integral

$$\int_a^b f(x)\,dx$$

If the curve $y = f(x)$ lies below the X-axis, then the value of the definite integral $\int_a^b f(x)\,dx$ will be negative.

However, when calculating the area, we take the absolute value of the integral.

Therefore, when the integral gives the signed area, then the actual bounded area (considering it as a positive value) left $\int_a^b f(x)\,dx$, $\int_a^b f(x)\,dx$ right.

Hence, Assertion is true in the context of finding the area under the curve and Reason is false because it does not account for taking the absolute value when the curve lies below the X-axis.

8. (b) Given,

$$y^2 = 4ax \qquad \ldots(i)$$

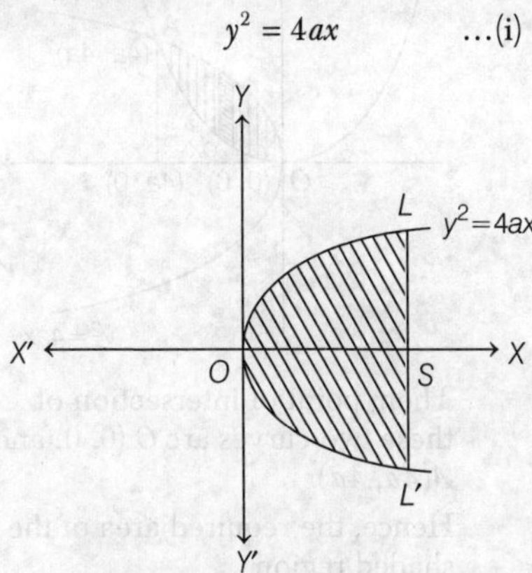

Let O be the vertex, S be the focus and LL' be the latus rectum of parabola.

The equation of latus rectum is $x = a$.

Also, we know that parabola is symmetric about X-axis.

$\therefore$ Required area

$$= 2 \text{ (area of } OSLO)$$

$$\therefore \text{ Area} = 2\int_0^a y\,dx$$

$$= 2\int_0^a 2\sqrt{a}\sqrt{x}\,dx$$

$$= 2 \cdot 2\sqrt{a}\int_0^a \sqrt{x}\,dx$$

$$= 4\sqrt{a} \cdot \frac{2}{3}[x^{\frac{3}{2}}]_0^a$$

$$= \frac{8}{3}\sqrt{a} \cdot a^{\frac{3}{2}}$$

$$\Rightarrow \text{ Area} = \frac{8}{3}a^2 \text{ sq units}$$

$\therefore$ Assertion is true.

Now, $x^2 = 4ay$

$$\Rightarrow \quad x = 2\sqrt{a} \cdot \sqrt{y}$$

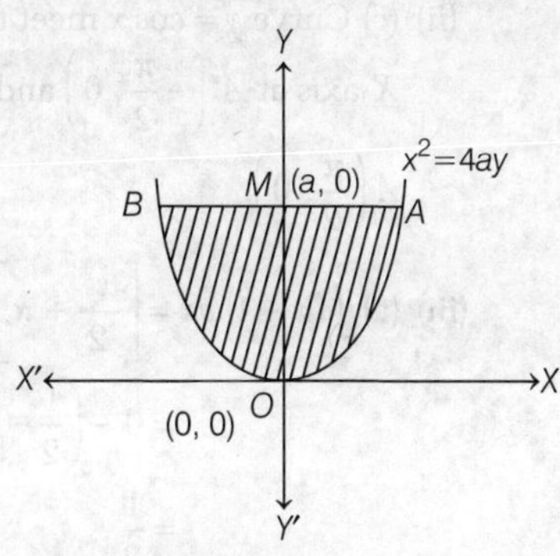

$$\text{Area of } OABO = 2\int_0^a 2\sqrt{a} \cdot \sqrt{y}\,dy$$

$$= 2 \cdot 2\sqrt{a}\int_0^a \sqrt{y}\,dy$$

$$= 4\sqrt{a}\left[\frac{y^{\frac{3}{2}}}{\frac{3}{2}}\right]_0^a$$

$$= 4\sqrt{a} \cdot \frac{2}{3}(a^{\frac{3}{2}})$$

$$= \frac{8}{3}a^2$$

Both Assertion and Reason are correct and Reason is not the correct explanation of Assertion.

9. (a) Given, equation of parabola

$$y^2 = 4x \text{ and } x = 1, x = 4 \text{ and}$$

$$y^2 = 4x$$

$$\Rightarrow \quad y = 2\sqrt{x}$$

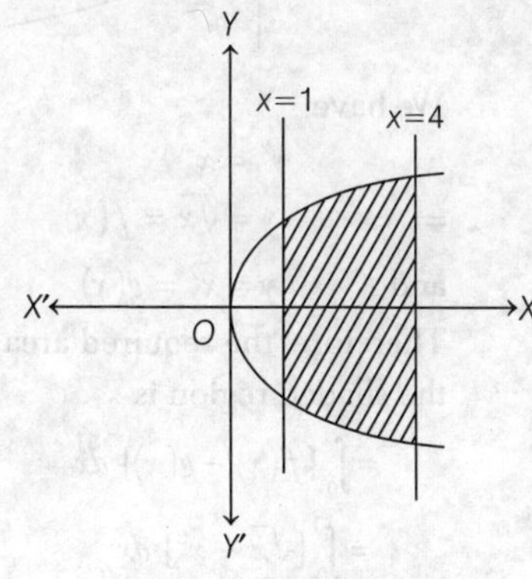

$$\text{Required Area} = 2\int_1^4 \sqrt{x}\,dx$$

$$= 2 \cdot \frac{2}{3}[x^{\frac{3}{2}}]_1^4$$

$$= \frac{4}{3}(4^{\frac{3}{2}} - 1^{\frac{3}{2}})$$

$$\Rightarrow \text{ Area} = \frac{28}{3} \text{ sq units.}$$

$\therefore$ Assertion is true.

Now, Reason is also true and it is the correct explanation of Assertion.

10. (c) Given, $y = \sin x$, $y = \cos x$, $0 \le x \le \frac{\pi}{2}$

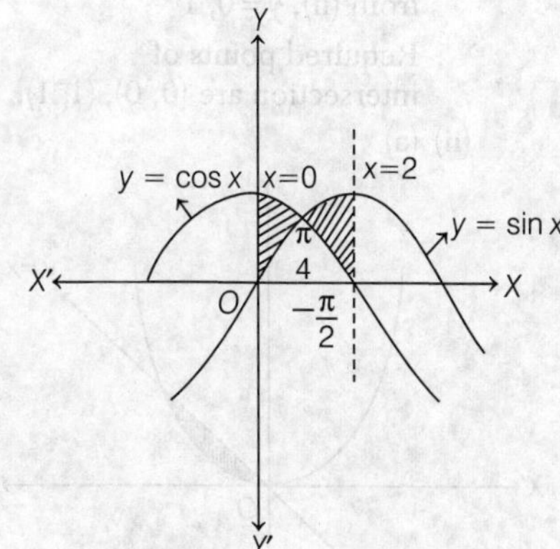

Required Area

$$= 2\int_0^{\frac{\pi}{4}} (\cos x - \sin x)\,dx$$

$$= 2\,[\sin x + \cos x]_0^{\frac{\pi}{4}}$$

$$= 2\left[\frac{1}{\sqrt{2}} + \frac{1}{\sqrt{2}} - 0 - 1\right]$$

$$\Rightarrow \text{ Area} = 2(\sqrt{2} - 1) \text{ sq units}$$

$\therefore$ Assertion is true.

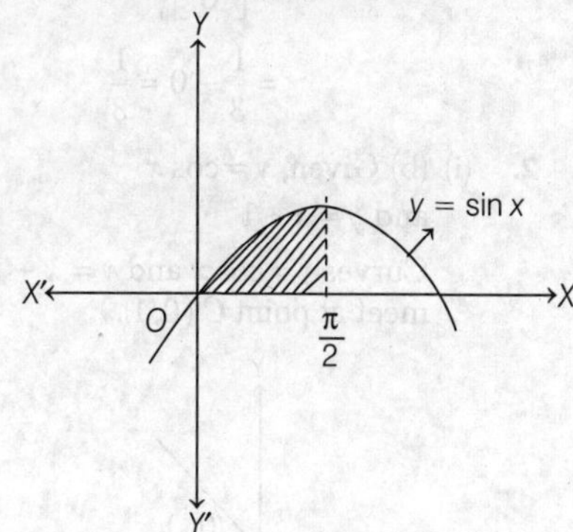

$$\text{Now, Area} = \int_0^{\frac{\pi}{2}} \sin x\,dx$$

$$= [-\cos x]_0^{\frac{\pi}{2}} = -0 + 1$$

$\Rightarrow$ Area = 1

$\therefore$ Reason is false.

Case Based Questions

1. (i) (b) Given, $x^2 = y$ ...(i)
and $x = y$ ...(ii)
from Eqs. (i) and (ii), we get
$x^2 = x$
$\Rightarrow x^2 - x = 0$
$\Rightarrow x(x-1) = 0$
$x = 0, 1$
from (ii), $y = 0, 1$
Required points of intersection are (0, 0), (1, 1).
(ii) (a)

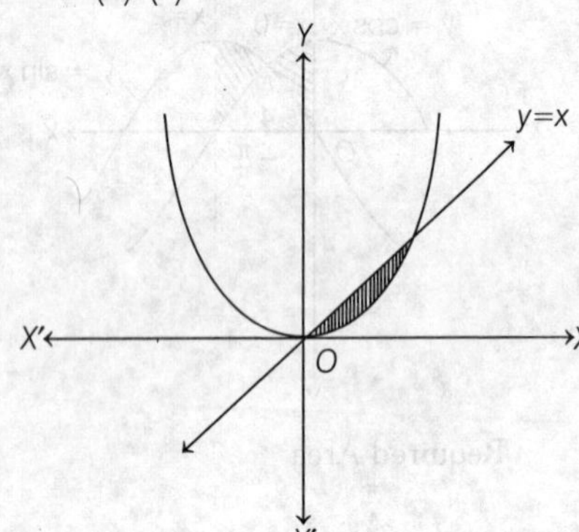

(iii) (c) $\int_0^1 x\,dx = \left[\frac{x^2}{2}\right]_0^1$
$= \frac{1}{2} - 0 = \frac{1}{2}$
(iv) (b) $\int_0^1 x^2\,dx = \left[\frac{x^3}{3}\right]_0^1$
$= \frac{1}{3} - 0 = \frac{1}{3}$

2. (i) (b) Given, $y = \cos x$
and $y = x + 1$
Curves $y = \cos x$ and $y = x + 1$ meet at point $C(0, 1)$.

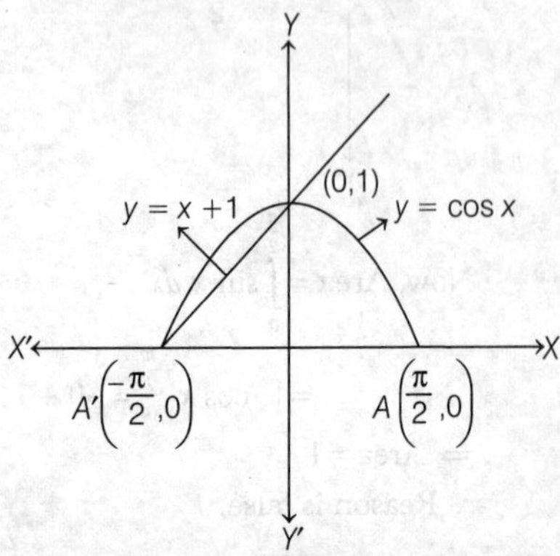

(ii) (c) Curve $y = \cos x$ meet the X-axis at $A'\left(-\frac{\pi}{2}, 0\right)$ and $A\left(\frac{\pi}{2}, 0\right)$.
(iii) (a) $\int_{-1}^{0} (x+1)\,dx = \left[\frac{x^2}{2} + x\right]_{-1}^{0}$
$= 0 - \left(\frac{1}{2} - 1\right)$
$= \frac{1}{2}$
(iv) (d) $\int_0^{\frac{\pi}{2}} \cos x\,dx = [\sin x]_0^{\frac{\pi}{2}}$
$= \sin\frac{\pi}{2} - \sin 0 = 1$

Competition Connect

1. (True)
The point of intersection of these two parabolas are $O(0, 0)$ and $A(1, 1)$ as shown in the given figure.

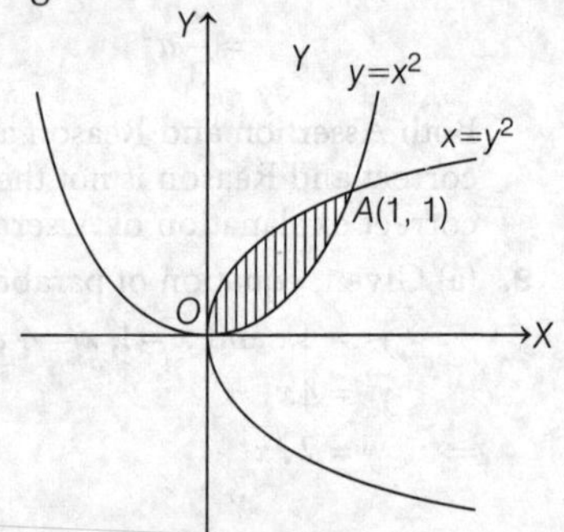

We have,
$y^2 = x$
$\Rightarrow y = \sqrt{x} = f(x)$
and $y = x^2 = g(x)$
Therefore, the required area of the shaded region is
$= \int_0^1 \{f(x) - g(x)\}\,dx$
$= \int_0^1 \{\sqrt{x} - x^2\}\,dx$
$= \left[\frac{2}{3}x^{3/2} - \frac{x^3}{3}\right]_0^1$
$= \frac{2}{3} - \frac{1}{3}$
$= \frac{1}{3}$ sq unit

2. (b) The given equation of the curves are
$y^2 = 4ax$ ...(i)
and $x^2 = 4ay$ ...(ii)

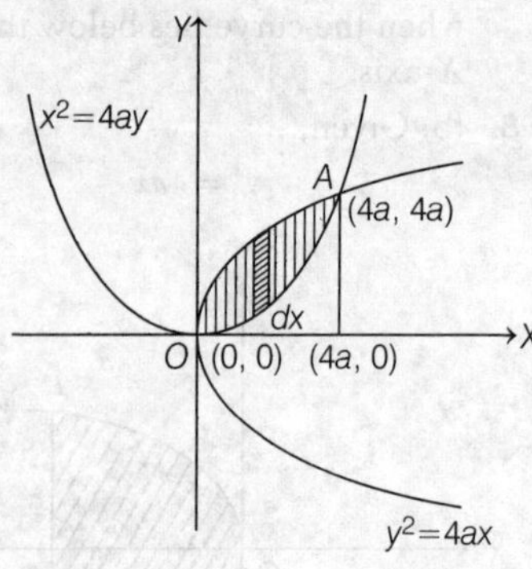

Then, point of intersection of these two curves are $O(0, 0)$ and $A(4a, 4a)$.
Hence, the required area of the shaded region
$= \int_0^{4a} |f(x) - g(x)|\,dx$
[where $y = 2\sqrt{ax} = f(x)$ and $y = \frac{x^2}{4a} = g(x)$ and $f(x) \geq g(x)$]
$= \int_0^{4a} \{f(x) - g(x)\}\,dx$
$= \int_0^{4a} \left\{2\sqrt{ax} - \frac{x^2}{4a}\right\} dx$
$= \left[\frac{4\sqrt{a}}{3}x^{3/2} - \frac{x^3}{12a}\right]_0^{4a}$
$= \frac{4\sqrt{a}\cdot(4a)^{\frac{3}{2}}}{3} - \frac{(4a)^3}{12a}$
$= \frac{32a^2}{3} - \frac{16a^2}{3}$
$= \frac{16a^2}{3}$ sq units

3. The point of intersection of these two curves are $O(0,0)$ and $B(4, 4)$ above the X-axis.

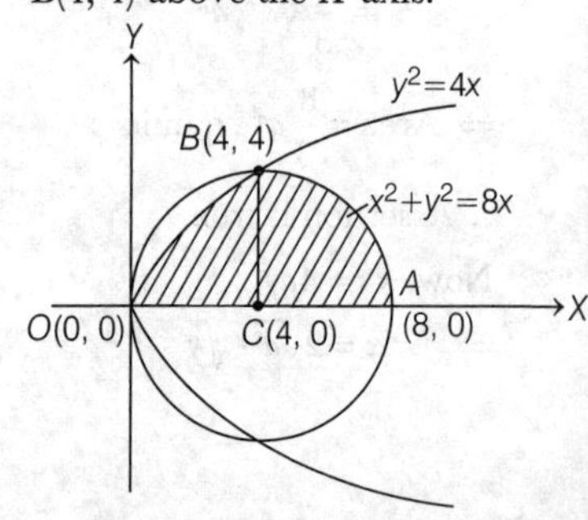

Therefore, the required area of the shaded region

= (area of the region $OBCO$)

+ (area of the region $BCAB$)

$$= \int_0^4 y\,dx + \int_4^8 y\,dx$$

$$= \int_0^4 2\sqrt{x}\,dx + \int_4^8 \sqrt{4^2 - (x-4)^2}\,dx$$

$$= \frac{32}{3} + \int_0^4 \sqrt{4^2 - z^2}\,dz,$$

where $x - 4 = z$

and $x \to 4$

$\Rightarrow z \to 0$ and $x \to 8 \Rightarrow z \to 4$

$$= \frac{32}{3} + \left[\frac{z\sqrt{4^2 - z^2}}{2} + \frac{1}{2}\cdot 4^2 \cdot \sin^{-1}\frac{z}{4}\right]_0^4$$

$$= \frac{32}{3} + \left[\frac{4}{2}\cdot 0 + \frac{1}{2}\cdot 4^2 \cdot \sin^{-1}(1)\right]$$

$$= \frac{32}{3} + 8\cdot\frac{\pi}{2}$$

$$= \frac{32}{3} + 4\pi$$

$$= \frac{4}{3}(8 + 3\pi) \text{ sq units}$$

4. (i) (True)

Vertices of the triangle are $A(0, 1)$, $B(4, 13)$ and $C(4, 9)$

Area of ΔACB = area of $OLBAO$ − area of $OLCA$

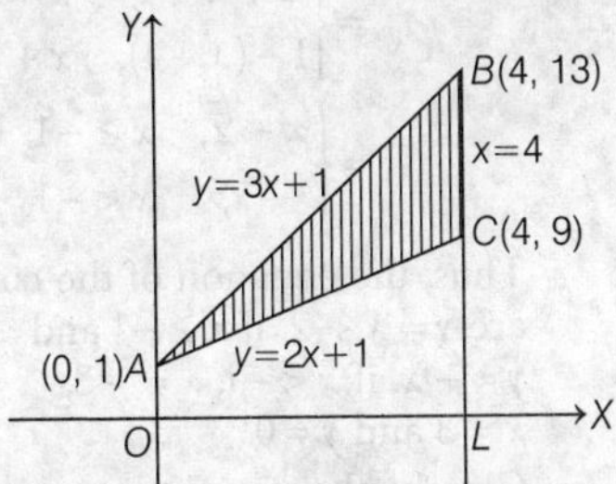

$$= \int_0^4 (3x+1)\,dx - \int_0^4 (2x+1)\,dx$$

$$= \left[\frac{3x^2}{2} + x\right]_0^4 - [x^2 + x]_0^4$$

$$= (24 + 4) - (16 + 4)$$

$= 8$ sq units

Thus, the area is 8 sq units.

(ii) (False)

Now, Area of $ACBA$

= Area of $OACBO$

− Area of $OABO$

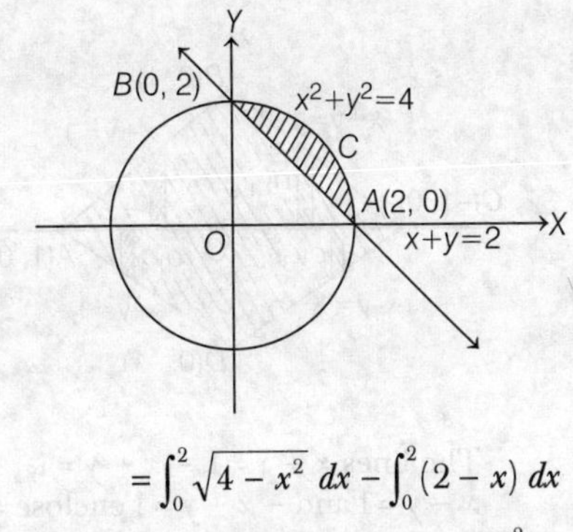

$$= \int_0^2 \sqrt{4 - x^2}\,dx - \int_0^2 (2 - x)\,dx$$

$$= \left[\frac{x\sqrt{4 - x^2}}{2} + \frac{4}{2}\sin^{-1}\frac{x}{2}\right]_0^2 - \left[2x - \frac{x^2}{2}\right]_0^2$$

$$= \left[2\cdot\frac{\pi}{2}\right] - [4 - 2] = \pi - 2$$

Hence, the required area is $(\pi - 2)$ sq units.

(iii) (True)

Let $A(1, 0)$, $B(2, 2)$ and $C(3, 1)$ be the vertices of a ΔABC.

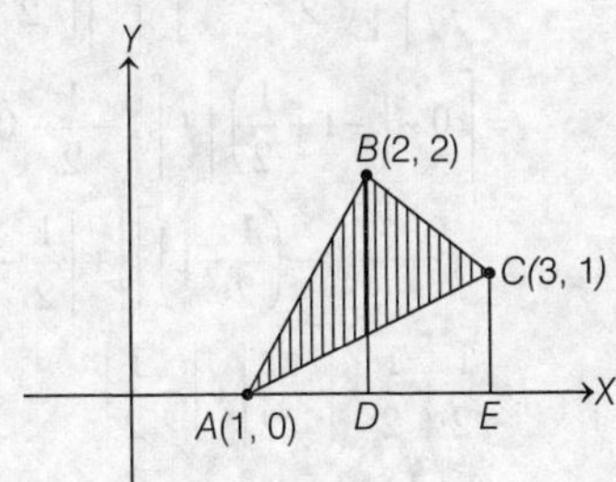

Then, Area of ΔABC

= Area of ΔABD

+ Area of trapezium $BDEC$

− Area of ΔAEC

Now, equations of sides AB, BC and CA are given by

$y = 2(x-1)$, $y = 4 - x$ and

$y = \frac{1}{2}(x-1)$, respectively.

Hence, area of ΔABC

$$= \int_1^2 2(x-1)\,dx + \int_2^3 (4-x)\,dx - \int_1^3 \frac{x-1}{2}\,dx$$

$$= 2\left[\frac{x^2}{2} - x\right]_1^2 + \left[4x - \frac{x^2}{2}\right]_2^3 - \frac{1}{2}\left[\frac{x^2}{2} - x\right]_1^3$$

$$= 2\left[\left(\frac{2^2}{2} - 2\right) - \left(\frac{1}{2} - 1\right)\right] + \left[\left(4\cdot 3 - \frac{3^2}{2}\right) - \left(4\cdot 2 - \frac{2^2}{2}\right)\right] - \frac{1}{2}\left[\left(\frac{3^2}{2} - 3\right) - \left(\frac{1}{2} - 1\right)\right]$$

$$= \frac{3}{2}$$

Thus, the required area is $\frac{3}{2}$ sq units.

5. (a) The equation of the circle is

$x^2 + y^2 = 4$

Differentiating both sides w.r.t. x, we get

$$2x + 2y\frac{dy}{dx} = 0$$

$$\Rightarrow \quad \frac{dy}{dx} = -\frac{x}{y}$$

$$\Rightarrow \quad \left(\frac{dy}{dx}\right)_{(1, \sqrt{3})} = \frac{-1}{\sqrt{3}}$$

So, the equations of tangent and normal to the circle $x^2 + y^2 = 4$ at $(1, \sqrt{3})$ are

$$(y - \sqrt{3}) = \left(\frac{dy}{dx}\right)_{(1, \sqrt{3})}(x - 1)$$

and $(y - \sqrt{3}) = -\dfrac{1}{\left(\frac{dy}{dx}\right)_{(1, \sqrt{3})}}(x - 1)$

$$\Rightarrow \quad (y - \sqrt{3}) = \frac{-1}{\sqrt{3}}(x - 1)$$

and $(y - \sqrt{3}) = \sqrt{3}(x - 1)$

$$\Rightarrow \quad x + \sqrt{3}y = 4$$

and $\quad y = \sqrt{3}x$

So, the triangular region bounded by the positive X-axis, tangent and normal to the circle is the shaded region. A its area (say).

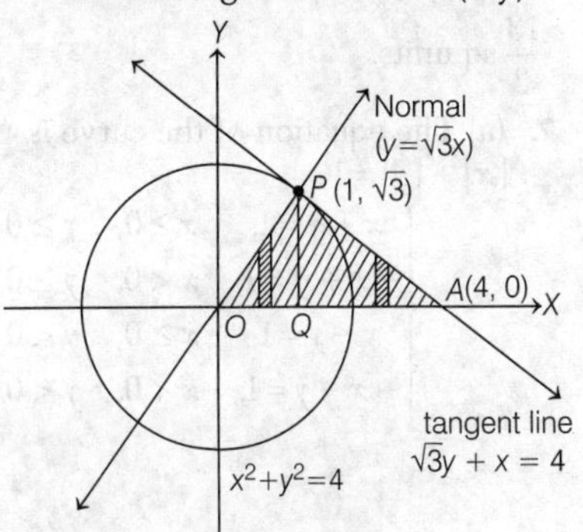

$\therefore$ A = Area of the region $OAPO$
= Area of the region $OPQO$
+ Area of the region $PQAP$

$$= \int_0^1 \sqrt{3}\, x\, dx + \int_1^4 \frac{4-x}{\sqrt{3}}\, dx$$

$$= \left(\frac{\sqrt{3}}{2} + \frac{3\sqrt{3}}{2}\right)$$

$= 2\sqrt{3}$ sq units

6. (a) As shown in this figure, the line $y = 3x + 2$ meets X-axis at $x = -\frac{2}{3}$ and its graph lies below X-axis for $x \in \left(-1, -\frac{2}{3}\right)$ and above X-axis for $x \in \left(-\frac{2}{3}, 1\right)$.

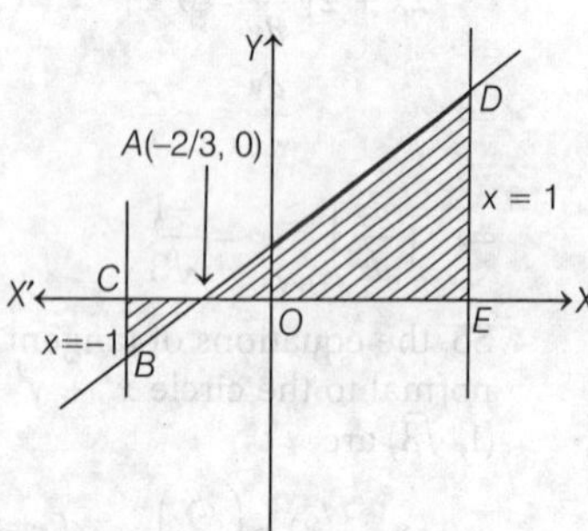

The required area
= Area of region $ACBA$
+ Area of region $ADEA$

$$= \left|\int_{-1}^{-2/3} (3x+2)\, dx\right| + \int_{-2/3}^{1} (3x+2)\, dx$$

$$= \left|\left[\frac{3x^2}{2} + 2x\right]_{-1}^{-\frac{2}{3}}\right| + \left[\frac{3x^2}{2} + 2x\right]_{-\frac{2}{3}}^{1}$$

$$= \frac{1}{6} + \frac{25}{6}$$

$$= \frac{13}{3}$$

Hence, the required area is $\frac{13}{3}$ sq units.

7. (a) The equation of the curve is $|x| + |y| = 1$

$$\begin{cases} x + y = 1, & x \ge 0, \quad y \ge 0 \\ -x + y = 1, & x < 0, \quad y \ge 0 \\ x - y = 1, & x \ge 0, \quad y < 0 \\ -x - y = 1, & x < 0, \quad y < 0 \end{cases}$$

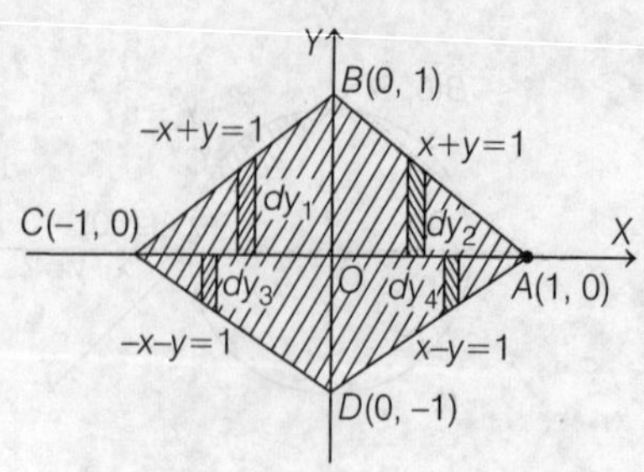

The lines $x + y = 1$, $-x + y = 1$, $x - y = 1$ and $-x - y = 1$ enclose a square shown in above figure.

The area A bounded by the square is given by

A = Area $COBC$ + Area $OABO$
+ Area $CODC$ + Area $ODAO$

$$= \int_{-1}^{0} (1+x)\, dx + \int_0^1 (1-x)\, dx + \left|\int_{-1}^{0} -(x+1)\, dx\right| + \left|\int_0^1 (x-1)\, dx\right|$$

$$= \left[x + \frac{x^2}{2}\right]_{-1}^{0} + \left[x - \frac{x^2}{2}\right]_0^1 + \left|-\left[\left(\frac{x^2}{2} + x\right)\right]_{-1}^{0}\right| + \left|\left[\frac{x^2}{2} - x\right]_0^1\right|$$

$$= \left[0 - \left(-1 + \frac{1}{2}\right)\right] + \left[1 - \frac{1}{2} - 0\right] + \left|-\left[0 - \left(\frac{1}{2} - 1\right)\right]\right| + \left|\frac{1}{2} - 1 - 0\right|$$

$$= \frac{1}{2} + \frac{1}{2} + \left|-\frac{1}{2}\right| + \left|-\frac{1}{2}\right|$$

$= 1 + 1 = 2$

8. (b) Let $R = \{(x, y);\, x^2 \le y \le x\}$

Then, $R = \{(x, y);\, x^2 \le y\} \cap \{(x, y);\, y \le x\}$
$= R_1 \cap R_2$

where $R_1 = \{(x, y);\, x^2 \le y\}$
and $R_2 = \{(x, y);\, y \le x\}$

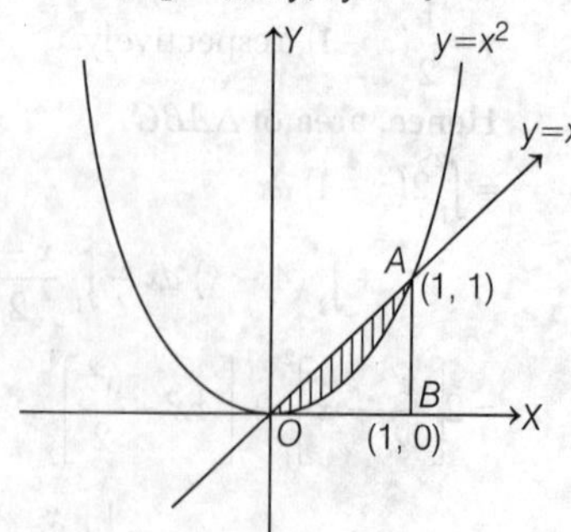

Region R_1 $x^2 = y$ represents a parabola with vertex at (0, 0), positive direction of Y-axis as its axis and it opens upwards. The region R_1 represented by $x^2 \le y$ is the interior of the parabola.

Region R_2 The region R_2 represented by $y \le x$ is the region lying below the line $y = x$.

Hence, the required region R is the shaded region shown in the figure.

Then, solving $y = x^2$ and $y = x$, we get the point of intersection as $O(0, 0)$ and $A(1, 1)$.

Then, the required area,

$$A = \int_0^1 \{f(x) - g(x)\}\, dx$$

$[\because f(x) = x \text{ and } g(x) = x^2]$

$$= \int_0^1 (x - x^2)\, dx$$

$$= \left[\frac{x^2}{2} - \frac{x^3}{3}\right]_0^1$$

$$= \frac{1}{2} - \frac{1}{3} = \frac{1}{6}$$

Thus, the required area is $\frac{1}{6}$ sq units.

9. We have, $y = 1 + |x + 1|$

$$= \begin{cases} 1 + x + 1, & x + 1 \ge 0 \\ 1 - (x+1), & x + 1 < 0 \end{cases}$$

$$= \begin{cases} x + 2, & x \ge -1 \\ -x, & x < -1 \end{cases}$$

Thus, the equation of the curves are $y = x + 2$, if $x \ge -1$ and $y = -x$, if $x < -1$, $x = -3$, $x = 3$ and $y = 0$.

Clearly, the straight line $y = x + 2$ cutting X and Y-axes at $(-2, 0)$ and $(0, 2)$, respectively.

So, $y = x + 2$, if $x > -1$ represents that part of the line which is on the right side of $x = -1$ and equation $y = -x$, if $x < -1$ represents that part of the line passing through the origin and making angle of 135° with X-axis which is on the left side of $x = -1$ and $x = -3$, $x = 3$ both lines are parallel to Y-axis.

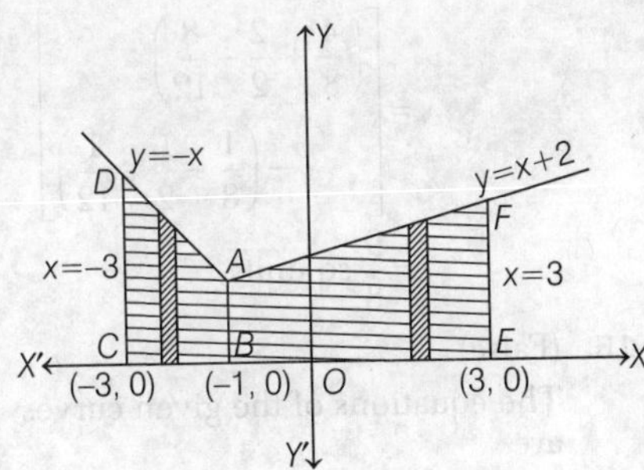

Thus, the required area is equal to (area of $ABCD$ + area of $ABEF$)

Area of

$$ABCD = \int_{-3}^{-1} y\, dx = \int_{-3}^{-1} (-x)\, dx$$

$$= -\left[\frac{x^2}{2}\right]_{-3}^{-1}$$

$$= -\left(\frac{1}{2} - \frac{9}{2}\right)$$

$$= 4 \text{ sq units}$$

Area of

$$ABEF = \int_{-1}^{3} y\, dx$$

$$= \int_{-1}^{3} (x+2)\, dx$$

$$= \left[\frac{x^2}{2} + 2x\right]_{-1}^{3}$$

$$= \left(\frac{9}{2} + 6\right) - \left(\frac{1}{2} - 2\right)$$

$$= \frac{9}{2} - \frac{1}{2} + 8$$

$$= 4 + 8$$

$$= 12 \text{ sq units}$$

$\therefore$ Required area

$$= \text{Area } ABCD + \text{Area } ABEF$$

$$= 4 + 12 = 16 \text{ sq units}$$

10. (b) Let $R = \{(x, y) ; x^2 + y^2 \le 1$ $\{1 \le x + y\}$

Then, $R = \{(x, y) ; x^2 + y^2 \le 1\}$ $\cap \{(x, y) ; x + y \ge 1\}$ $= R_1 \cap R_2$

where $R_1 = \{(x, y); x^2 + y^2 \le 1\}$

and $R_2 = \{(x, y); x + y \ge 1\}$

Region R_1 Clearly, $x^2 + y^2 = 1$ represents a circle with centre (0, 0) and radius unity.

Since, $x^2 + y^2 \le 1$, so, region R_1 represents the interior of the circle $x^2 + y^2 = 1$.

Region R_2 Since, $x + y = 1$ represents a straight line, which cuts X and Y-axes at (1, 0) and (0, 1), respectively. This line divides (x, y) plane in two parts represented by $x + y \le 1$ and $x + y \ge 1$.

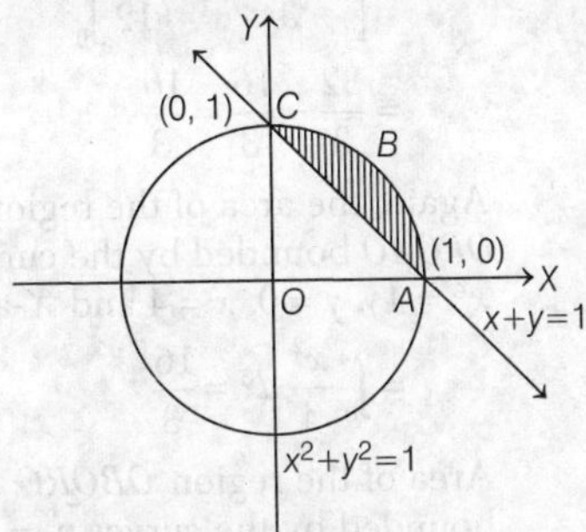

Since, (0, 0) does not satisfies the inequality $x + y \ge 1$.

So, the region R_2 is the above line $x + y = 1$.

Hence, region R is the shaded region as shown in the figure.

Hence, the required area of the shaded region is

$$\int_0^1 |f(x) - g(x)|\, dx$$

$$= \int_0^1 \{f(x) - g(x)\}\, dx$$

where $f(x) = \sqrt{1 - x^2}$,

$g(x) = 1 - x$ and $f(x) > g(x)$

$$= \int_0^1 \{\sqrt{1 - x^2} - (1 - x)\}\, dx$$

$$= \left[\frac{x\sqrt{1 - x^2}}{2} + \frac{1}{2}\sin^{-1}(x)\right]_0^1 - \left[x - \frac{x^2}{2}\right]_0^1$$

$$= \left[\frac{1}{2}\sin^{-1}(1)\right] - \left(\frac{1}{2}\right)$$

$$= \frac{\pi}{4} - \frac{1}{2}$$

Thus, the required area is $\left(\frac{\pi}{4} - \frac{1}{2}\right)$ sq units.

11. (a) The points of intersection of the curves $y^2 = 4x$ and $4x^2 + 4y^2 = 9$ are

$$A\left(\frac{1}{2}, -\sqrt{2}\right) \text{ and } C\left(\frac{1}{2}, \sqrt{2}\right).$$

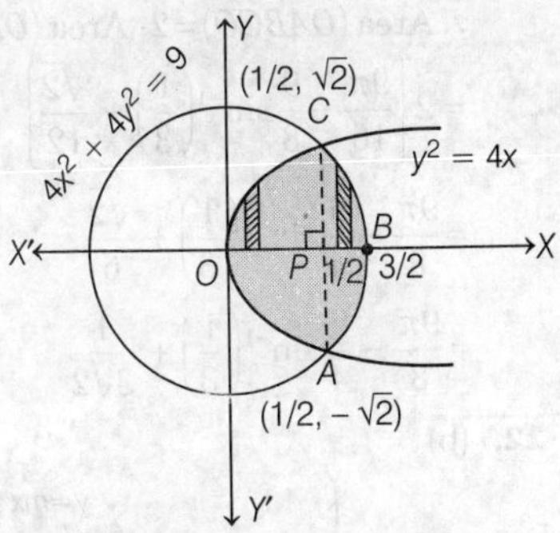

The required area is $OABCO$.

Area $OABCO$ is symmetrical about X-axis.

So, area $(OABCO)$

$$= 2 \times \text{area } (OBCO)$$

Thus, Area $(OBCO)$

$$= \text{Area } (OPC) + \text{Area } (PBC)$$

$$= \int_0^{1/2} 2\sqrt{x}\, dx + \int_{1/2}^{3/2} \frac{1}{2}\sqrt{9 - 4x^2}\, dx$$

$$= \int_0^{1/2} 2\sqrt{x}\, dx + \int_{1/2}^{3/2} \frac{\sqrt{(3)^2 - (2x)^2}}{2}\, dx$$

Let $2x = t$

$$\Rightarrow \quad dx = \frac{dt}{2}$$

When $x = \frac{3}{2}$, then $t = 3$

and when $x = \frac{1}{2}$, then $t = 1$

Thus, area $(OBCO)$

$$= \int_0^{1/2} 2\sqrt{x}\, dx + \frac{1}{4}\int_1^3 \sqrt{(3)^2 - (t)^2}\, dt$$

$$= 2\cdot\left[\frac{x^{3/2}}{3/2}\right]_0^{1/2} + \frac{1}{4}\left[\frac{t\sqrt{9 - t^2}}{2} + \frac{9}{2}\sin^{-1}\left(\frac{t}{3}\right)\right]_1^3$$

$$= 2\left[\frac{2}{3}\left(\frac{1}{2}\right)^{3/2}\right] + \frac{1}{4}\left[\left\{\frac{9}{2}\sin^{-1}(1)\right\} - \left\{\frac{\sqrt{8}}{2} + \frac{9}{2}\sin^{-1}\left(\frac{1}{3}\right)\right\}\right]$$

$$= \frac{\sqrt{2}}{3} + \frac{9\pi}{16} - \frac{\sqrt{2}}{4} - \frac{9}{8}\sin^{-1}\left(\frac{1}{3}\right)$$

$$\therefore \text{ Area } (OBCO) = \frac{9\pi}{16} - \frac{9}{8}\sin^{-1}\left(\frac{1}{3}\right) + \frac{\sqrt{2}}{12}$$

$\therefore$ Area $(OABCO) = 2 \cdot$ Area $(OBCO)$

$$= 2\left\{\frac{9\pi}{16} - \frac{9}{8}\sin^{-1}\left(\frac{1}{3}\right) + \frac{\sqrt{2}}{12}\right\}$$

$$= \frac{9\pi}{8} - \frac{9}{4}\sin^{-1}\left(\frac{1}{3}\right) + \frac{\sqrt{2}}{6}$$

$$= \frac{9\pi}{8} - \frac{9}{4}\sin^{-1}\left(\frac{1}{3}\right) + \frac{1}{3\sqrt{2}}$$

12. (b)

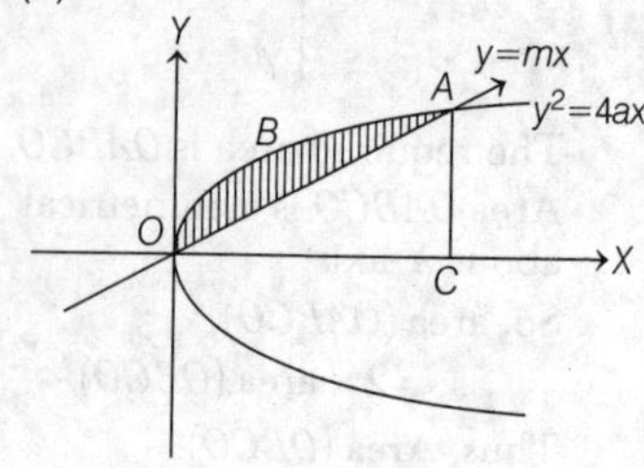

Equation of curves are

$y^2 = 4ax$ and $y = mx$

The point of intersection of the curves are (0,0) and $\left(\frac{4a}{m^2}, \frac{4a}{m}\right)$.

Now, the required region is the shaded region $OABO$, whose area = (area of the region $OCABO$) − (area of OCA)

$$= \int_0^{4a/m^2} 2\sqrt{ax}\, dx - \int_0^{4a/m^2} mx\, dx$$

$$= 2\sqrt{a}\left[\frac{x^{3/2}}{3/2}\right]_0^{4a/m^2} - m\left[\frac{x^2}{2}\right]_0^{4a/m^2}$$

$$= \frac{4\sqrt{a}}{3}\left\{\frac{4a}{m^2}\right\}^{3/2} - \frac{m}{2}\left\{\left(\frac{4a}{m^2}\right)^2\right\}$$

$$= \frac{32a^2}{3m^3} - \frac{m}{2}\left(\frac{16a^2}{m^4}\right)$$

$$= \frac{32a^2}{3m^3} - \frac{8a^2}{m^3}$$

$$= \frac{8a^2}{3m^3}$$

13. (True)

The point of intersection of the parabolas $y^2 = 4x$ and $x^2 = 4y$ are (0, 0) and (4, 4).

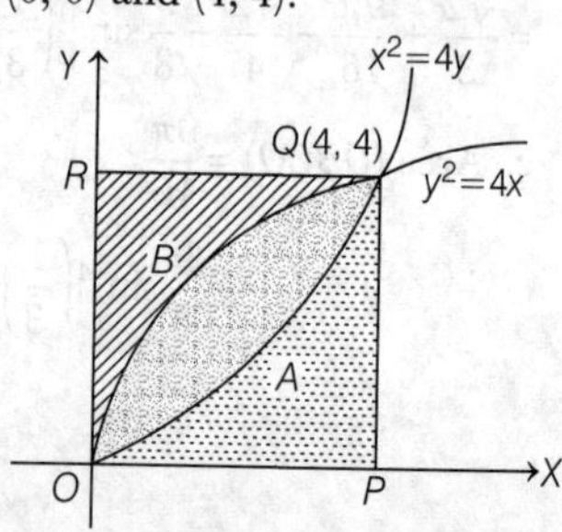

The area of the region $OAQBO$ bounded by the curves $y^2 = 4x$ and $x^2 = 4y$

$$= \int_0^4 \left\{2\sqrt{x} - \frac{x^2}{4}\right\} dx$$

$$= \left[2\cdot\frac{2}{3}x^{3/2} - \frac{x^3}{12}\right]_0^4$$

$$= \frac{32}{3} - \frac{16}{3} = \frac{16}{3} \qquad \ldots\text{(i)}$$

Again, the area of the region $OPQAO$ bounded by the curves $x^2 = 4y$, $y = 0$, $x = 4$ and X-axis

$$= \int_0^4 \frac{x^2}{4} dx = \frac{16}{3} \qquad \ldots\text{(ii)}$$

Area of the region $OBQRO$ bounded by the curves $y^2 = 4x$, $x = 0$, $y = 4$ and Y-axis

$$= \int_0^4 \frac{y^2}{4} dy = \left[\frac{y^3}{12}\right]_0^4 = \frac{16}{3} \qquad \ldots\text{(iii)}$$

From Eqs. (i), (ii) and (iii), we conclude that the area of the region $OAQBO$ = Area of the region $OPQAO$ = Area of the region $OBQRO$.

i.e. the area bounded by the parabolas $y^2 = 4x$ and $x^2 = 4y$ divides the area of the square in three equal parts.

14. The equation of the curves are $x^2 = 4y$ and $x = 4y - 2$

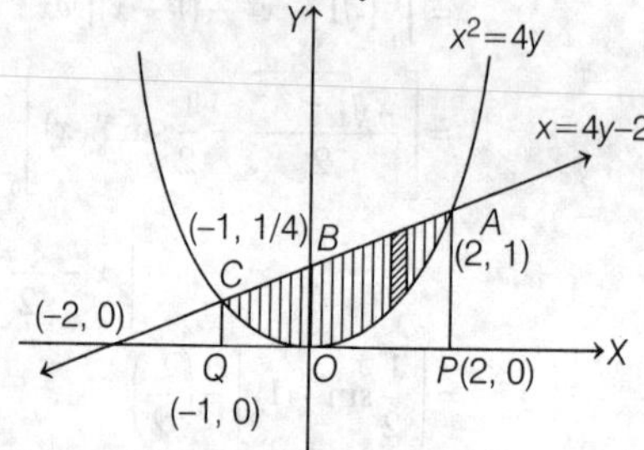

The point of intersection are $A(2, 1)$ and $C(-1, 1/4)$.

Hence, the area of $OABCO$

$$= \int_{-1}^{2} \{f(x) - g(x)\}\, dx$$

where $y = \frac{x^2}{4} = g(x)$

and $y = \frac{x+2}{4} = f(x)$

$$= \int_{-1}^{2} \left\{\frac{x+2}{4} - \frac{x^2}{4}\right\} dx$$

$$= \left[\frac{x^2}{8} + \frac{x}{2} - \frac{x^3}{12}\right]_{-1}^{2}$$

$$= \left[\left(\frac{4}{8} + \frac{2}{2} - \frac{8}{12}\right) - \left(\frac{1}{8} - \frac{1}{2} + \frac{1}{12}\right)\right]$$

$$= \frac{9}{8} \text{ sq units}$$

15. (False)

The equations of the given curves are

$$\frac{x^2}{a^2} + \frac{y^2}{b^2} = 1 \qquad \ldots\text{(i)}$$

and $\frac{x}{a} + \frac{y}{b} = 1 \qquad \ldots$(ii)

Clearly, $\frac{x^2}{a^2} + \frac{y^2}{b^2} = 1$ represents an ellipse as shown in figure and $\frac{x}{a} + \frac{y}{b} = 1$ is the equation of a straight line cutting X and Y-axes at $(a, 0)$ and $(0, b)$, respectively. The smaller region bounded by these two curves is the shaded region given in the figure.

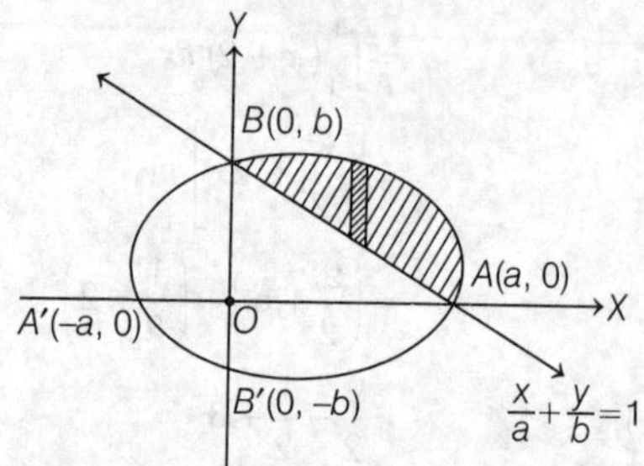

Thus, the required area,

$$A = \int_0^a \{f(x) - g(x)\}\, dx,$$

where $f(x) > g(x)$

Also, $f(x) = \frac{b}{a}\sqrt{a^2 - x^2}$

and $g(x) = \frac{b}{a}(a - x)$

$$= \int_0^a \left\{\frac{b}{a}\sqrt{a^2 - x^2} - \frac{b}{a}(a - x)\right\} dx$$

$$= \frac{b}{a}\left[\int_0^a \sqrt{a^2 - x^2}\, dx - \int_0^a (a - x)\, dx\right]$$

$$= \frac{b}{a}\left[\frac{x\sqrt{a^2 - x^2}}{2} + \frac{a^2}{2}\cdot\sin^{-1}\left(\frac{x}{a}\right)\right]_0^a - \left[ax - \frac{x^2}{2}\right]_0^a$$

$$= \frac{b}{a}\left\{\frac{a^2}{2}\cdot\frac{\pi}{2} - \frac{a^2}{2}\right\}$$

$$= \frac{ab}{2}\left(\frac{\pi}{2} - 1\right) \text{ sq units}$$

16. (b) Given, equation of the ellipse $9x^2 + y^2 = 36$ can be expressed as $\frac{x^2}{4} + \frac{y^2}{36} = 1$.

Since, $A(2, 0)$ and $B(0, 6)$, thus the equation of the chord AB is

$$(y - 0) = \frac{6 - 0}{0 - 2}(x - 2)$$

$$\Rightarrow \quad y = -3(x - 2)$$

$$\Rightarrow y + 3x = 6$$

Thus, the area of the shaded region as shown in the figure

$$= 3\int_0^2 \sqrt{4 - x^2}\, dx - \int_0^2 (6 - 3x)\, dx$$

$$= 3\left[\frac{x\sqrt{4 - x^2}}{2} + \frac{4}{2}\sin^{-1}\frac{x}{2}\right]_0^2 - \left[6x - \frac{3x^2}{2}\right]_0^2$$

$$= 3[2\sin^{-1}(1)] - \left(12 - \frac{12}{2}\right)$$

$$= 3\pi - 6 \text{ sq units}$$

17. (b) Clearly, $y = ax^2$ and $x = ay^2$ intersect at $O(0, 0)$ and $A\left(\frac{1}{a}, \frac{1}{a}\right)$.

Then, the shaded region is the region enclosed by two parabolas.

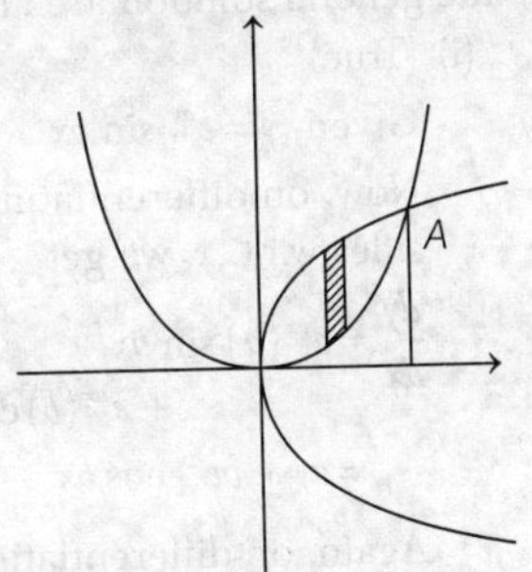

Thus, the required region

$$= \int_0^{1/a} |f(x) - g(x)|\, dx$$

$$= \int_0^{1/a} (\sqrt{x/a} - ax^2)\, dx$$

$$\left[\because f(x) = \sqrt{\frac{x}{a}},\ g(x) = ax^2 \text{ and } f(x) > g(x)\right]$$

$$= \left[\frac{2}{3\sqrt{a}}x^{3/2} - \frac{a}{3}x^3\right]_0^{1/a}$$

$$= \left(\frac{2}{3\sqrt{a}}\cdot\frac{1}{a^{3/2}} - \frac{a}{3}\cdot\frac{1}{a^3}\right)$$

$$= \frac{2}{3a^2} - \frac{1}{3a^2}$$

$$= \frac{1}{3a^2}$$

Since, $\int_0^{1/a} |f(x) - g(x)|\, dx = 1$

$$\Rightarrow \quad \frac{1}{3a^2} = 1$$

$$\Rightarrow \quad a = \frac{1}{\sqrt{3}}$$

Thus, the value of a is $\frac{1}{\sqrt{3}}$.

18. (True)

The graph of $y = \sin x$ and $y = \cos x$ are shown in the figure. These two curves intersect at point A. The point of intersection is $x = \frac{\pi}{4}$.

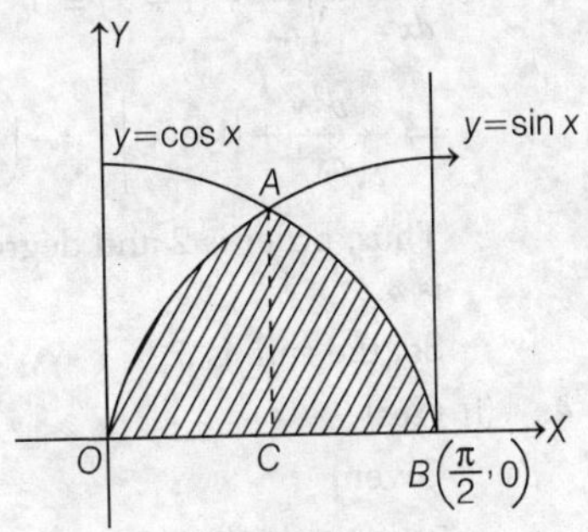

The required region is the shaded region shown in the figure $OCBAO$.

Thus, area (A) = Area OAC + AreaACB

$$= \int_0^{\pi/4} f(x)\, dx + \int_{\pi/4}^{\pi/2} g(x)\, dx$$

$$= \int_0^{\pi/4} \sin x\, dx + \int_{\pi/4}^{\pi/2} \cos x\, dx$$

$$\left[\because \begin{array}{l} y = \sin x = f(x) \\ y = \cos x = g(x) \end{array}\right]$$

$$= [-\cos x]_0^{\pi/4} + [\sin x]_{\pi/4}^{\pi/2}$$

$$= \left(-\frac{1}{\sqrt{2}} + 1\right) + \left(1 - \frac{1}{\sqrt{2}}\right)$$

$$= (2 - \sqrt{2}) \text{ sq units}$$

Thus the area of the region is $(2 - \sqrt{2})$ sq units.

19. Let $y = 2^x$ and $y = 2x - x^2$ be two curves, whose point of intersection with $x = 0$ and $x = 2$ are $B(2, 0)$, $C(2, 4)$, $D(0, 1)$ and $O(0, 0)$.

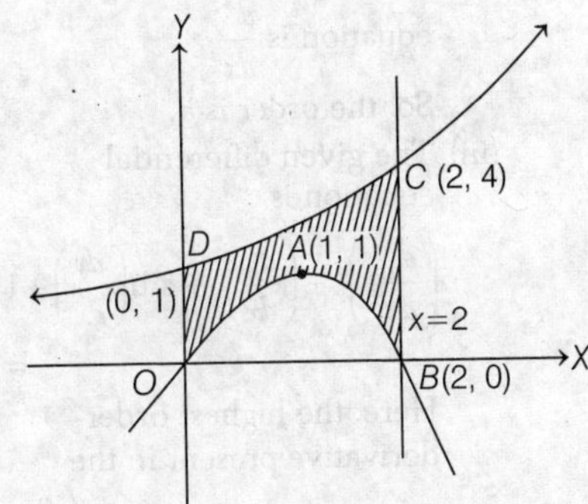

$$= \int_0^2 \{f(x) - g(x)\}\, dx$$

where $f(x) = 2^x$ and $g(x) = 2x - x^2$

$$= \int_0^2 (2^x - 2x + x^2)\, dx$$

$$= \left[\frac{2^x}{\log 2} - x^2 + \frac{x^3}{3}\right]_0^2$$

$$= \frac{4}{\log 2} - 4 + \frac{8}{3} - \frac{1}{\log 2}$$

$$= \left(\frac{3}{\log 2} - \frac{4}{3}\right)$$

Chapter-9

Differential Equations

1. (i) Given,

$$xy\frac{d^2y}{dx^2} + \sin\left(\frac{x}{y}\right) = 0$$

The highest order derivative present in the differential equation is $\frac{d^2y}{dx^2}$.

So, the order is 2.

(ii) Given,

$$xy\frac{d^3y}{dx^3} + x\left(\frac{dy}{dx}\right)^2 - y\frac{dy}{dx} + y = 0$$

The highest order derivative present in the differential equation is $\frac{d^3y}{dx^3}$.

So, the order is 3.

(iii) The given differential equation is

$$\left(\frac{d^2y}{dx^2}\right)^3 + \left(\frac{dy}{dx}\right)^2 + \sin\left(\frac{dy}{dx}\right) + 1 = 0$$

Here, the highest order derivative present in the differential equation is $\frac{d^2y}{dx^2}$.

So, the order is 2.

(iv) Given, $e^{dy/dx} + \frac{d^2y}{dx^2} = 0$

The highest order derivative present in the differential equation is $\frac{d^2y}{dx^2}$.

So, the order is 2.

(v) Given, $\frac{d^2y}{dx^2} + \sin\left(\frac{dy}{dx}\right) = 0$

The highest order derivative present in the differential equation is $\frac{d^2y}{dx^2}$.

So, the order is 2.

2. (i) The power of highest order derivative of equation is 2. Therefore, degree is 2.

(ii) The given differential equation is

$$\frac{d^2y}{dx^2} + \log y = \cos 3x$$

Here, highest power of highest order derivative of $\frac{d^2y}{dx^2}$ is 1.

So, its degree is 1.

(iii) In this differential equation, $\sin\left(\frac{dy}{dx}\right)$ term present.

So, this is not radical free.

So, its degree is not defined.

3. (i) The given differential equation is

$$\left(\frac{d^2y}{dx^2}\right)^5 + \frac{4\left(\frac{d^2y}{dx^2}\right)^3}{\left(\frac{d^3y}{dx^3}\right)} + \left(\frac{d^3y}{dx^3}\right) = x$$

$$\Rightarrow \left(\frac{d^3y}{dx^3}\right)^2 + \left(\frac{d^3y}{dx^3}\right)\left(\frac{d^2y}{dx^2}\right)^5 + 4\left(\frac{d^2y}{dx^2}\right)^3 = x\left(\frac{d^3y}{dx^3}\right)$$

So, order is $(p) = 3$ and degree is $(q) = 2$

So, $p + q = 3 + 2 = 5$

(ii) Given,

$$\frac{d^2y}{dx^2} + \sqrt[3]{\frac{dy}{dx}} + (1 + x) = 0$$

$$\Rightarrow \left\{\frac{d^2y}{dx^2} + (1 + x)\right\}^3 = -\left(\frac{dy}{dx}\right)$$

Thus, order is 2 and degree is 3.

So, the sum is 5.

4. (i) (Yes)

Given,

$$\left[1 + \left(\frac{dy}{dx}\right)^3\right]^{2/3} = 4\left(\frac{d^3y}{dx^3}\right)$$

$$\Rightarrow \left[1 + \left(\frac{dy}{dx}\right)^3\right]^2 = 4^3\left(\frac{d^3y}{dx^3}\right)^3$$

So, order is 3 and degree is 3.

$\therefore$ Order = Degree

(ii) (No)

Given, $\frac{d^2y}{dx^2} + 8\left(\frac{dy}{dx}\right)^3 + 5y = e^x + 2x + 7$

has order 2 and degree 1.

So, order $\neq$ degree

(iii) (No)

Given,

$$5\left(\frac{d^3y}{dx^3}\right)^4 + 8\left(1 + \frac{dy}{dx}\right)^3 + 5y = x^7$$

has order 3 and degree 4.

So, order $\neq$ degree

(iv) (No)

Given,

$\left(y - x^2\frac{dy}{dx}\right)^2 = 1 + \left(\frac{dy}{dx}\right)^2$ has order 1 and degree 2.

So, order $\neq$ degree.

5. (c) Given,

$$\left[1 + \left(\frac{dy}{dx}\right)^2\right]^{2/3} = \frac{d^2y}{dx^2}$$

$$\Rightarrow \left[1 + \left(\frac{dy}{dx}\right)^2\right]^2 = \left(\frac{d^2y}{dx^2}\right)^3$$

So, order $n = 2$ and degree $m = 3$

$\therefore \quad m > n$

and $\frac{m + n}{m - n} = \frac{3 + 2}{3 - 2} = 5 > \frac{5}{2}$

6. We know, if a differential equation has n order, then its number of arbitrary constant in the general solution are also n.

7. (i) (True)

Given, $y = e^{ax}\sin bx \quad \ldots(i)$

Now, on differentiating both sides w.r.t. x, we get

$$\frac{dy}{dx} = e^{ax}(a)\sin bx + e^{ax}(b)\cos bx$$

$$= ay + be^{ax}\cos bx \quad \ldots(ii)$$

Again, on differentiating, we get

$$\frac{d^2y}{dx^2} = a\frac{dy}{dx} + be^{ax}(a)\cos bx - b^2e^{ax}\sin bx$$

$$= a\frac{dy}{dx} + a\frac{dy}{dx} - a^2y - b^2y$$

[using Eqs. (i) and (ii)]

$$\therefore \frac{d^2y}{dx^2} = 2a\frac{dy}{dx} - a^2y - b^2y$$

$$\Rightarrow \frac{d^2y}{dx^2} - 2a\frac{dy}{dx} + a^2y = -b^2y$$

(ii) (False)

Given differential equation,

$$\frac{d^2y}{dx^2} - x^2 \frac{dy}{dx} + xy = x \quad \ldots(i)$$

On putting $y = x$ in Eq. (i), we get

$$\text{LHS} = \frac{d^2x}{dx^2} - x^2 \frac{dx}{dx} + x \cdot x$$

$$= 0 - x^2 + x^2 = 0$$

But, RHS = x [given]

$\therefore$ LHS $\neq$ RHS

[$\because x \neq 0$ always]

(iii) (False)

Given,

$$y = (c_1 + c_2)\cos(x + c_3) - c_4 e^{x + c_5}$$

On differentiating both sides w.r.t. x, we get

$$\frac{dy}{dx} = -(c_1 + c_2)\sin(x + c_3) - c_4 e^{x + c_5}$$

$$\Rightarrow \frac{d^2y}{dx^2} = -(c_1 + c_2)\cos(x + c_3) - c_4 e^{x + c_5}$$

$$= -y - c_4 e^{x + c_5} - c_4 e^{x + c_5}$$

$$= -y - 2c_4 e^{x + c_5}$$

$$\Rightarrow \frac{d^3y}{dx^3} = -\frac{dy}{dx} - 2(c_4 e^{x + c_5})$$

$$= \frac{-dy}{dx} + \left(\frac{d^2y}{dx^2} + y\right)$$

$$\therefore \frac{d^3y}{dx^3} = \frac{d^2y}{dx^2} - \frac{dy}{dx} + y$$

Hence, the differential equation is,

$$\frac{d^3y}{dx^3} - \frac{d^2y}{dx^2} + \frac{dy}{dx} - y = 0$$

So, order of above differential equation is 3.

8. (i) Given differential equation is $\cos y \log(\sec x + \tan x)\, dx$

$= \cos x \log(\sec y + \tan y)\, dy$

Separating the variables and integrating both sides, we get

$$\int \sec x \cdot \log(\sec x + \tan x)\, dx$$

$$= \int \sec y \cdot \log(\sec y + \tan y)\, dy$$

Let $\log(\sec x + \tan x) = z$

$\Rightarrow \sec x\, dx = dz$

$$\Rightarrow \int z\, dz = \int \sec y \cdot \log(\sec y + \tan y)\, dy$$

$$\Rightarrow \frac{z^2}{2} = \int \sec y \cdot \log(\sec y + \tan y)\, dy$$

$$\Rightarrow \frac{[\log(\sec x + \tan x)]^2}{2} = \frac{[\log(\sec y + \tan y)]^2}{2} + C$$

This is required solution.

(ii) Given differential equation is

$$\frac{dy}{dx} = \sqrt{y - x}$$

On putting $y - x = v^2$

$$\Rightarrow \frac{dy}{dx} - 1 = 2v \frac{dv}{dx}$$

Thus, the above differential equation gives,

$$1 + 2v \frac{dv}{dx} = v$$

Separating the variables and integrating both sides, we get

$$\int \frac{2v}{v - 1}\, dv = \int dx$$

$$\Rightarrow \int \frac{2v - 2 + 2}{v - 1}\, dv = \int dx$$

$$\Rightarrow 2\int dv + 2\int \frac{dv}{v - 1} = \int dx$$

$$\Rightarrow 2v + 2\log(v - 1) = x + C$$

$$\Rightarrow 2\sqrt{y - x} + 2\log(\sqrt{y - x} - 1) = x + C$$

(iii) The given differential equation is

$$\frac{dy}{dx} = \frac{y^2 - y - 2}{x^2 + 2x - 3}$$

$$\Rightarrow \frac{dy}{y^2 - y - 2} = \frac{dx}{x^2 + 2x - 3}$$

On integrating both sides, we get

$$\int \frac{dy}{y^2 - y - 2} = \int \frac{dx}{x^2 + 2x - 3}$$

$$\Rightarrow \int \frac{dy}{(y - 2)(y + 1)} = \int \frac{dx}{(x + 3)(x - 1)}$$

$$\Rightarrow \frac{1}{3}\int \left(\frac{1}{y - 2} - \frac{1}{y + 1}\right) dy = \frac{1}{4}\int \left(\frac{1}{x - 1} - \frac{1}{x + 3}\right) dx$$

$$\Rightarrow \frac{1}{3}\log\left|\frac{y - 2}{y + 1}\right| = \frac{1}{4}\log\left|\frac{x - 1}{x + 3}\right| + \frac{C}{12}$$

$$\Rightarrow 4\log\left|\frac{y - 2}{y + 1}\right| = 3\log\left|\frac{x - 1}{x + 3}\right| + C$$

This is required solution.

(iv) Given differential equation is

$$\frac{dy}{dx} = \cos(x + y) \quad \ldots(i)$$

Let $x + y = z$

$$\Rightarrow 1 + \frac{dy}{dx} = \frac{dz}{dx}$$

So, from Eq. (i), we get

$$\frac{dz}{dx} - 1 = \cos z$$

$$\Rightarrow \frac{dz}{dx} = 1 + \cos z = 2\cos^2 \frac{z}{2}$$

$$\Rightarrow \sec^2 \frac{z}{2}\, dz = 2dx$$

On integrating both sides, we get

$$\int \sec^2 \frac{z}{2}\, dz = 2\int dx$$

$$\Rightarrow 2\tan \frac{z}{2} = 2x + 2C$$

$$\Rightarrow \tan\left(\frac{x + y}{2}\right) = x + C$$

[putting $z = x + y$]

$$\Rightarrow (x + y) = 2\tan^{-1}(x + C)$$

[C is an arbitrary constant]

This is required solution.

(v) Given differential equation is

$$\frac{dy}{dx} = \frac{x\log x^2 + x}{\sin y + y\cos y} \quad \ldots(i)$$

Now, separating the variables and integrating both sides, we get

$$\int (\sin y + y\cos y)\, dy = \int (x\log x^2 + x)\, dx$$

$$\Rightarrow -\cos y + y\sin y + \cos y = \frac{x^2}{2}\log x^2 - \int \frac{x^2}{2} \cdot \frac{1}{x^2} \cdot 2x\, dx + \int x\, dx + C$$

$\Rightarrow y\sin y = \frac{x^2}{2}\cdot 2\cdot \log x$

$- \int x\,dx + \int x\,dx + C$

$\Rightarrow y\sin y = x^2 \cdot \log x + C,$

where C is an arbitrary constant.

This is required solution.

9. (i) Given, $\frac{dy}{dx} = y\sin 2x$

$\Rightarrow \quad \frac{dy}{y} = \sin 2x\,dx$

$\Rightarrow \quad \int \frac{dy}{y} = \int \sin 2x\,dx$

[integrate both sides]

$\Rightarrow \quad \log y = -\frac{\cos 2x}{2} + C$

Now, $y(0) = 1$, then

$0 = -\frac{1}{2} + C$

$\Rightarrow \quad C = \frac{1}{2}$

$\Rightarrow \quad \log y = \frac{1-\cos 2x}{2}$

$= \frac{2\sin^2 x}{2} = \sin^2 x$

$\Rightarrow \quad y = e^{\sin^2 x}$

So, this is particular solution.

(ii) Given, $\frac{dy}{dx} = e^{-2y}$

$\Rightarrow \quad e^{2y}dy = dx$

On integrating both sides, we get

$\int e^{2y}dy = \int dx$

$\Rightarrow \quad \frac{e^{2y}}{2} = x + C$

On putting $y = 0$, when $x = 5$, then

$C = -\frac{9}{2}$

$\Rightarrow \quad \frac{e^{2y}}{2} = x - \frac{9}{2}$

Now, when $y = 3$

$\Rightarrow \quad x = \frac{e^6 + 9}{2}$

(iii) Given, $\quad \frac{dy}{dx} = \left(\frac{y}{x}\right)^{1/3}$

$\Rightarrow \quad \frac{dy}{y^{1/3}} = \frac{dx}{x^{1/3}}$

$\Rightarrow \quad \int y^{-1/3}dy = \int x^{-1/3}dx$

[integrate both sides]

$\Rightarrow \quad \frac{y^{-\frac{1}{3}+1}}{-1/3+1} = \frac{x^{-\frac{1}{3}+1}}{-\frac{1}{3}+1} + \frac{c}{-\frac{1}{3}+1}$

$\Rightarrow \quad y^{2/3} = x^{2/3} + c,$

This is general solution.

If $y(1) = -1$

$\Rightarrow (-1)^{2/3} = (1)^{2/3} + C$

$\Rightarrow C = 0$

$\Rightarrow y^{2/3} = x^{2/3} \Rightarrow y = x,$

This is particular solution.

10. (False)

Given differential equation is

$\frac{dy}{dx} = 1 + y^2$

$\Rightarrow \quad \int \frac{dy}{1+y^2} = \int dx$

[integrate both sides]

$\Rightarrow \quad \tan^{-1} y = x + C$

At $x = 0$, $y = 0$, then $C = 0$

At $x = \pi$, $y = 0$, then $C = -\pi$

So, $\tan^{-1} y = x \Rightarrow y = \tan x$

or $\tan^{-1} y = x - \pi$

$\Rightarrow \quad y = -\tan(\pi - x) = \tan x$

Therefore, the solution is $y = \tan x$.

But $\tan x$ is not a continuous function in $(0, \pi)$.

Hence, continuously differentiable solution in $(0, \pi)$ of the differential equation does not exist.

11. (a) Given differential equation is

$x\sqrt{x^2-1}\,dy - y\sqrt{y^2-1}\,dx = 0$

$\Rightarrow \frac{dx}{x\sqrt{x^2-1}} = \frac{dy}{y\sqrt{y^2-1}}$

$\Rightarrow \int \frac{dy}{y\sqrt{y^2-1}} = \int \frac{dx}{x\sqrt{x^2-1}}$

[integrate both sides]

$\Rightarrow \quad \sec^{-1} y = \sec^{-1} x + c$

$\left[\because \sec^{-1} x = \int \frac{dx}{x\sqrt{x^2-1}}\right]$

Given, $\quad y(2) = \frac{2}{\sqrt{3}}$

$\Rightarrow \sec^{-1}\left(\frac{2}{\sqrt{3}}\right) = \sec^{-1} 2 + c$

$\Rightarrow \quad \frac{\pi}{6} = \frac{\pi}{3} + c$

$\Rightarrow \quad c = \frac{\pi}{6} - \frac{\pi}{3} = -\frac{\pi}{6}$

$\Rightarrow \quad \sec^{-1} y = \sec^{-1} x - \frac{\pi}{6}$

$\Rightarrow y(x) = \sec\left(\sec^{-1} x - \frac{\pi}{6}\right)$

12. (i) Given, $\frac{dy}{dx} = 1 + x + y + xy$

$= (1 + x) + y(1 + x)$

$= (1 + x)(1 + y)$

$\Rightarrow \quad \frac{dy}{1+y} = (1 + x)\,dx$

On integrating both sides, we get

$\int \frac{dy}{1+y} = \int (1 + x)\,dx$

$\Rightarrow \log(1 + y) = x + \frac{x^2}{2} + \log C$

$\Rightarrow \quad (1 + y) = ce^{x + \frac{x^2}{2}}$

$\Rightarrow \quad y(x) = ce^{x + \frac{x^2}{2}} - 1$

Given condition, $y(-1) = 0$, then

$0 = ce^{-1/2} - 1$

$\Rightarrow \quad C = e^{1/2}$

$\therefore \quad y(x) = e^{1/2}\cdot e^{x + \frac{x^2}{2}} - 1$

$= e^{\frac{(x+1)^2}{2}} - 1$

This is required answer.

(ii) The given differential equation is,

$ydx + (1 + x^2)\tan^{-1} x\,dy = 0$

On integrating both sides, we get

$\Rightarrow \int \frac{dx}{(1+x^2)\tan^{-1} x} + \int \frac{dy}{y} = 0$

$\Rightarrow \log(\tan^{-1} x) + \log y = \log C$

$\Rightarrow \quad y\tan^{-1} x = C,$

where C is an arbitrary constant.

So, $y = \frac{C}{\tan^{-1} x}$ and $y(1) = 1$

$\Rightarrow C = \frac{\pi}{4}$

So, $y = \frac{\left(\frac{\pi}{4}\right)}{\tan^{-1} x}$

$$\Rightarrow y(-1) = \frac{\frac{\pi}{4}}{\tan^{-1}(-1)}$$

$$= \frac{\pi/4}{-\pi/4} = -1$$

So, the required solution is $y(-1) = -1$.

(iii) Given, $\frac{dy}{dx} = 1 + x + y^2 + xy^2$

$$= (1 + x) + y^2(1 + x)$$

$$= (1 + x)(1 + y^2)$$

$$\Rightarrow \frac{dy}{1 + y^2} = (1 + x)\, dx$$

On integrating both sides, we get

$$\int \frac{dy}{1 + y^2} = \int (1 + x)\, dx$$

$$\Rightarrow \tan^{-1} y = x + \frac{x^2}{2} + C$$

On putting $y(0) = 0$, we get

$$C = 0$$

Then, $\tan^{-1} y = \left(\frac{x^2}{2} + x\right)$

$$\Rightarrow \quad y(x) = \tan\left(\frac{x^2}{2} + x\right)$$

$$\Rightarrow \quad y(\pi) = \tan\left(\frac{\pi^2}{2} + \pi\right)$$

So, the required answer is $\tan\left(\pi + \frac{\pi^2}{2}\right)$.

(iv) Given differential equation is

$$\left(\frac{2 + \sin x}{1 + y}\right)\frac{dy}{dx} = -\cos x$$

$$\Rightarrow \frac{\cos x}{2 + \sin x}\, dx + \frac{dy}{y + 1} = 0$$

On integrating both sides, we get

$$\int \frac{\cos x}{2 + \sin x}\, dx + \int \frac{dy}{y + 1} = 0$$

$$\Rightarrow \log(2 + \sin x) + \log(y + 1) = \log C$$

$$\Rightarrow (y + 1)(2 + \sin x) = C$$

On putting $y(0) = 1$

$$\Rightarrow \quad c = 2 \cdot 2 = 4$$

$$\therefore y = \frac{4}{\sin x + 2} - 1 = \frac{2 - \sin x}{2 + \sin x}$$

$$\therefore y\left(\frac{\pi}{2}\right) = \frac{2 - \sin\frac{\pi}{2}}{2 + \sin\frac{\pi}{2}}$$

$$= \frac{2 - 1}{2 + 1} = \frac{1}{3}$$

13. (i) (c) Given, differential equation is

$$xdy - ydx = 0$$

$$\Rightarrow \quad -\frac{dx}{x} + \frac{1}{y}\, dy = 0$$

$$\Rightarrow \quad \int \frac{dx}{x} = \int \frac{dy}{y}$$

[integrate both sides]

$$\Rightarrow \quad \log x = \log y + \log C$$

$$\Rightarrow \quad x = Cy$$

It is a straight line passing through (0, 0).

(ii) (a) We know that the slope of the tangent to the curve is given by $\frac{dy}{dx}$.

So, $\quad \frac{dy}{dx} = \frac{2x}{y^2} \quad \quad \ldots(i)$

Separating the variables, Eq. (i) can be written as

$$y^2 dy = 2x\, dx$$

Taking integration both sides, we get

$$\int y^2 dy = \int 2x\, dx + C,$$

where C is an arbitrary constant.

$$\Rightarrow \quad \frac{y^3}{3} = x^2 + C$$

When $x = -2$, $y = 3$, then

$$C = 5$$

So, $y^3 = 3x^2 + 15$

Now, when $x = 4$,

then $y^3 = 48 + 15 = 63$

$$y = \sqrt[3]{63}$$

(iii) (a) Given differential equation is

$$\frac{dV(t)}{dt} = -K(T - t)$$

$$\Rightarrow \int dV(t) = \int -K(T - t)dt$$

[integrate both sides]

$$\Rightarrow \quad V(t) = -KTt + \frac{Kt^2}{2} + c$$

At $t = 0$,

$$V(0) = P,$$

then $\quad C = P$

So, $V(t) = -KtT + \frac{Kt^2}{2} + P$

Now, $t = T$

$$\therefore V(T) = -KT^2 + \frac{KT^2}{2} + P$$

$$= P - \frac{KT^2}{2}$$

(iv) (a) Let P be the principal at any time t. According to the given problem,

$$\frac{dP}{dt} = \left(\frac{10}{100}\right) \times P$$

$$\Rightarrow \quad \frac{dP}{dt} = \frac{P}{10}$$

$$\Rightarrow \quad \frac{dP}{P} = \frac{1}{10}\, dt \quad \quad \ldots(i)$$

[using method of separating of the variables]

Now, taking integration on both sides, we get

$$\log P = \frac{t}{10} + \log C$$

$$\Rightarrow \quad P = Ce^{t/10} \quad \quad \ldots(ii)$$

Now, $P = 100$, when $t = 0$

Submitting values of P and t in Eq. (ii), we get

$$C = 100$$

$$\therefore \quad P = 100\, e^{t/10} \quad \ldots(iii)$$

So, let t yr the time required to double the principal.

Then,

$$200 = 100\, e^{t/10}$$

$$\Rightarrow \quad 2 = e^{t/10}$$

$$\Rightarrow \log 2 = \frac{t}{10}$$

$$\Rightarrow \quad t = 10 \log_e 2$$

The required time is $10 \log_e 2$.

14. (i) Given, $\frac{dP}{dt} = \frac{t+2P}{t-P}$

$F(t, P) = \frac{t+2P}{t-P}$

$F(\lambda t, \lambda P) = \frac{\lambda(t+2P)}{\lambda(t-P)}$

$= \lambda^{\circ} \cdot F(t, P)$

$F(t, P)$ is a homogeneous function of zero degree.

It is homogeneous.

(ii) Given, $\frac{dy}{dx} = \frac{5y(\log x - \log y)}{x}$

$F(x, y) = \frac{5y}{x} \log \frac{x}{y}$

$F(\lambda x, \lambda y) = 5\frac{\lambda y}{\lambda x} \log \frac{\lambda x}{\lambda y}$

$= \lambda^{\circ}\left[5\frac{y}{x} \log \frac{x}{y}\right]$

It is homogenous equation of zero degree.

(iii) The given differential equation can be written as

$$\frac{dy}{dx} = \frac{y\cos\left(\frac{y}{x}\right) + x}{x\cos\left(\frac{y}{x}\right)}$$

So, $F(x, y) = \frac{y\cos\left(\frac{y}{x}\right) + x}{x\cos\left(\frac{y}{x}\right)}$

Replacing x by λx and y by λy, so we get

$$F(\lambda x, \lambda y) = \frac{\lambda\left[y\cos\left(\frac{y}{x}\right) + x\right]}{\lambda\left(x\cos\frac{y}{x}\right)}$$

$= \lambda^0[F(x, y)]$

So, it is homogeneous function of zero degree.

15. (i) Given, $\frac{dy}{dx} = \frac{y\sin\frac{y}{x} - 1}{x\sin\frac{y}{x}}$

On putting $\frac{y}{x} = v$

$\Rightarrow \quad \frac{dy}{dx} = x\frac{dv}{dx} + v$

$\therefore \quad x\frac{dv}{dx} + v = \frac{(v\sin v - 1)}{\sin v}$

$= v - \operatorname{cosec} v$

$\Rightarrow \quad x\frac{dv}{dx} = -\operatorname{cosec} v$

$\Rightarrow \quad -\sin v \, dv = \frac{dx}{x}$

$\Rightarrow -\int \sin v \, dv = \int \frac{dx}{x}$

[integrate both sides]

$\Rightarrow \quad \cos v = \log x + C$

$\Rightarrow \cos\left(\frac{y}{x}\right) = \log x + C$

(ii) Given differential equation is

$$(1 + e^{x/y})\, dx + e^{x/y}\left(1 - \frac{x}{y}\right) dy = 0$$

$\therefore \quad \frac{dy}{dx} = \frac{-(1+e^{x/y})}{e^{x/y}\left(1 - \frac{x}{y}\right)}$

$\Rightarrow \frac{dx}{dy} = -\frac{e^{x/y}\left(1 - \frac{x}{y}\right)}{1 + e^{x/y}}$

Let $\frac{x}{y} = v \Rightarrow \frac{dx}{dy} = v + y.\frac{dv}{dy}$

$\therefore v + y\frac{dv}{dy} = -\frac{e^v(1-v)}{1+e^v}$

$\Rightarrow \quad y\frac{dv}{dy} = -\frac{e^v(1-v)}{1+e^v} - v$

$= \frac{-e^v + ve^v - v - ve^v}{1+e^v}$

$\Rightarrow \quad y\frac{dv}{dy} + \frac{e^v + v}{1+e^v} = 0$

$\Rightarrow \int \frac{1+e^v}{v+e^v}\, dv + \int \frac{dy}{y} = 0$

[take integration both sides]

$\Rightarrow \log(v + e^v) + \log y = \log C$

$\Rightarrow \quad y(v + e^v) = C$

$\Rightarrow \quad y\left(\frac{x}{y} + e^{x/y}\right) = C$

$\Rightarrow \quad x + ye^{x/y} = C$

So, this is required answer.

(iii) Given equation

$$\frac{dy}{dx} = \frac{x+y}{x-y}$$

It is homogeneous equation, so putting $y = vx$ and $\frac{dy}{dx} = v + x\frac{dv}{dx}$, we get

$v + x\frac{dv}{dx} = \frac{x + vx}{x - vx} = \frac{1+v}{1-v}$

$\Rightarrow \quad x\frac{dv}{dx} = \frac{1+v^2}{1-v}$

$\Rightarrow \int \frac{1-v}{1+v^2}\, dv = \int \frac{dx}{x}$

[take integration both sides]

$\Rightarrow \int \frac{dv}{1+v^2} - \int \frac{v}{1+v^2}\, dv = \int \frac{dx}{x}$

$\Rightarrow \tan^{-1} v - \frac{1}{2}\log(1+v^2)$

$= \log x + \log C$

On substituting $v = \frac{y}{x}$, we get

$\Rightarrow \tan^{-1}\left(\frac{y}{x}\right) = \frac{1}{2}\log\left(1 + \frac{y^2}{x^2}\right)$

$+ \log x + \log C$

$= \log\left(\frac{(x^2+y^2)^{1/2}}{x}.x\right) + \log C$

$= \log[C(x^2+y^2)^{1/2}]$

$\Rightarrow C\cdot(x^2+y^2)^{1/2} = e^{\tan^{-1}\left(\frac{y}{x}\right)}$

So, this is required solution.

(iv) Given differential equation is

$x\, dy - y dx = (x^2+y^2)^{1/2} dx$

$\Rightarrow xdy = ydx + (x^2+y^2)^{1/2} dx$

$\Rightarrow \quad \frac{dy}{dx} = \frac{y + \sqrt{x^2+y^2}}{x}$

It is homogeneous equation, so putting $y = vx$ and $\frac{dy}{dx} = v + x\frac{dv}{dx}$, we get

$v + x\frac{dv}{dx} = \frac{vx + \sqrt{x^2 + v^2x^2}}{x}$

$= v + \sqrt{1+v^2}$

$\Rightarrow \int \frac{dv}{\sqrt{1+v^2}} = \int \frac{dx}{x}$

[take integration both sides]

$\Rightarrow \log|v + \sqrt{1+v^2}|$

$= \log x + \log C$

$\Rightarrow \log\left|\frac{y}{x} + \sqrt{1 + \frac{y^2}{x^2}}\right| = \log Cx$

$\Rightarrow \log|y + \sqrt{x^2+y^2}|$

$= \log Cx^2$

$\Rightarrow y + \sqrt{x^2+y^2} = Cx^2$,

which is required solution.

(v) The given differential equation is

$$\frac{dy}{dx} = -\frac{(x+y-1)}{(2x+2y-3)}$$

Let $x + y = t \Rightarrow 1 + \frac{dy}{dx} = \frac{dt}{dx}$

$\therefore \frac{dt}{dx} - 1 = \frac{t-1}{2t-3}$

$\Rightarrow \frac{dt}{dx} = -\frac{t-1}{2t-3} + 1$

$\Rightarrow \frac{dt}{dx} = \frac{t-2}{2t-3}$

$\Rightarrow \int \frac{2t-3}{t-2} dt = \int dx$

[integrate both sides]

$\Rightarrow \int \frac{2t-4}{t-2} dt + \int \frac{dt}{t-2} = \int dx$

$\Rightarrow 2t + \log(t-2) = x + C$

$\Rightarrow 2y + 2x + \log(x+y-2) = x + C$

$\Rightarrow 2y + x + \log(x+y-2) = C$

This is required answer.

(vi) Given differential equation is

$x(x-y)\,dy + y^2 dx = 0$

$\Rightarrow \frac{dy}{dx} = \frac{y^2}{x(y-x)}$

Let $y = vx$, then $\frac{dy}{dx} = v + x\frac{dv}{dx}$

$\Rightarrow v + x\frac{dv}{dx} = \frac{v^2x^2}{x^2(v-1)} = \frac{v^2}{v-1}$

$\Rightarrow x\frac{dv}{dx} = \frac{v^2}{v-1} - v = \frac{v}{v-1}$

$\Rightarrow \int \frac{(v-1)}{v} dv = \int \frac{dx}{x}$

[integrate both sides]

$\Rightarrow v - \log v = \log x + \log C$

$\Rightarrow v = \log(vx) + \log C$

$\Rightarrow \frac{y}{x} = \log(yC)$

$\Rightarrow Cy = e^{y/x}$

$\Rightarrow y(x) = C' e^{y/x}$ $\left[\text{where, } C' = \frac{1}{C}\right]$

This is required solution.

(vii) Given, differential equation is

$x^2\frac{dy}{dx} = x^2 + xy + y^2$

$\Rightarrow \frac{dy}{dx} = 1 + \left(\frac{y}{x}\right) + \left(\frac{y}{x}\right)^2$

Let $\frac{y}{x} = v \Rightarrow \frac{dy}{dx} = v + x\frac{dv}{dx}$

So, $v + x\frac{dv}{dx} = 1 + v + v^2$

$\Rightarrow \frac{dv}{1+v^2} = \frac{dx}{x}$

On integrating both sides, we get

$\tan^{-1} v = \log x + C$

$\Rightarrow \tan^{-1}\left(\frac{y}{x}\right) = \log x + C$

This is required solution.

(viii) Given differential equation is

$x\frac{dy}{dx} = y - x\cos^2\frac{y}{x}$

$\Rightarrow \frac{dy}{dx} = \frac{y}{x} - \cos^2\left(\frac{y}{x}\right)$

On putting $y = vx$, we get

$\Rightarrow \frac{dy}{dx} = v + x\frac{dv}{dx}$

$\therefore v + x\frac{dv}{dx} = v - \cos^2 v$

$\Rightarrow x\frac{dv}{dx} = -\cos^2 v$

$\Rightarrow \int \sec^2 v\, dv = -\int \frac{dx}{x} + C$

[integrate both sides]

$\Rightarrow \tan v + \log x = C$

$\Rightarrow \tan\left(\frac{y}{x}\right) + \log x = C$

Now, $y(1) = \frac{\pi}{4}$, then $C = 1$

So, $\tan\left(\frac{y}{x}\right) + \log x = 1$

16. (i) (True)

Given, differential equation is

$x^2 dy + (xy + y^2)dx = 0$

$\Rightarrow \frac{dy}{dx} = -\frac{(xy+y^2)}{x^2}$ ...(i)

This is homogeneous differential equation and let us take $y = vx$

$\Rightarrow \frac{dy}{dx} = v + x\cdot\frac{dv}{dx}$

From Eq. (i), we get

$v + x\cdot\frac{dv}{dx} = \frac{-(vx^2 + v^2x^2)}{x^2}$

$= -v - v^2$

$\Rightarrow x\frac{dv}{dx} = -v^2 - 2v$

$= -v(v+2)$

$\Rightarrow \frac{dv}{v(v+2)} = -\frac{dx}{x}$

$\Rightarrow \frac{1}{2}\left[\frac{2}{v(v+2)}\right] dv = -\frac{dx}{x}$

$\Rightarrow \frac{1}{2}\left[\frac{(v+2)-v}{v(v+2)}\right] dv = -\frac{dx}{x}$

$\Rightarrow \frac{1}{2}\left[\frac{1}{v} - \frac{1}{v+2}\right] dv = -\frac{dx}{x}$

$\Rightarrow \frac{1}{2}[\log v - \log(v+2)]$

$= -\log x + \log c_1$

[integrate both sides]

$\Rightarrow \frac{1}{2}\log\left(\frac{v}{v+2}\right) = \log\left(\frac{c_1}{x}\right)$

$\Rightarrow \left(\frac{v}{v+2}\right) = \frac{c_1^2}{x^2}$

$\Rightarrow \frac{y/x}{y/x+2} = \frac{c_1^2}{x^2}$

$\Rightarrow \frac{y}{2x+y} = \frac{c_1^2}{x^2}$

$\Rightarrow x^2y = C(y + 2x)$ ...(ii)

where $C = c_1^2$

This is required general solution.

(ii) (True)

Now, on putting $x = 1$ and $y = 1$, we get

$\frac{1}{1+2} = C \Rightarrow C = \frac{1}{3}$

So, from Eq. (ii),

$x^2y = \frac{1}{3}(y + 2x)$

$\Rightarrow y + 2x = 3x^2y$

This is particular solution.

17. (i) The slope of the tangent at (x, y) to a curve passing through the point $(2, 1)$ is

$\frac{x^2+y^2}{2xy}$

So, $\frac{dy}{dx} = \frac{x^2+y^2}{2xy}$

Let $y = vx$

$\Rightarrow \frac{dy}{dx} = v + x\cdot\frac{dv}{dx}$

So, $v + x\cdot\frac{dv}{dx} = \frac{x^2 + v^2x^2}{2vx^2}$

$= \frac{1+v^2}{2v}$

$\Rightarrow \frac{2v}{1-v^2} dv = \frac{dx}{x}$

On integrating both sides, we get

$-\log(1-v^2)=\log x+\log C$

$\Rightarrow -\log\left(1-\frac{y^2}{x^2}\right)=\log x+\log C$

Curve is passing through (2, 1)

$\therefore -\log\left(1-\frac{1}{4}\right)=\log 2+\log C$

$\Rightarrow \quad C=\frac{2}{3}$

Thus, $\log\left(\frac{x^2}{-y^2+x^2}\right)=\log\frac{2x}{3}$

$\Rightarrow \quad 2(x^2-y^2)=3x$

(ii) $\because \frac{dy}{dx}=\frac{y}{x}-\cos^2\left(\frac{y}{x}\right)$

Put $\quad y=vx$

$\Rightarrow \frac{dy}{dx}=v+x\frac{dv}{dx}$

$\therefore \; v+x\frac{dv}{dx}=v-\cos^2 v$

$\Rightarrow \quad \frac{dv}{\cos^2 v}=-\frac{dx}{x}$

On integrating both sides, we get

$\tan v=-\log x+\log C$

$\Rightarrow \tan\left(\frac{y}{x}\right)=-\log x+\log C$

Curve is passing through $\left(1,\frac{\pi}{4}\right)$

$\therefore \log c=1=\log e \Rightarrow C=e$

So, $\tan\left(\frac{y}{x}\right)=\log\left(\frac{e}{x}\right)$

$\Rightarrow y=x\tan^{-1}\left[\log\left(\frac{e}{x}\right)\right]$

18. (i) We know, a differential equation in which the dependent variable and its differential coefficient occur only in the first degree and are not multiplied together is called a linear differential equation.

Hence, $y\frac{dy}{dx}+4x^2=0$ is non linear differential equation.

(ii) Non linear differential equation.

(iii) Linear differential equation.

(iv) Non linear differential equation.

(v) $\left(\frac{d^2y}{dx^2}\right)^2+x^2\left(\frac{dy}{dx}\right)=0$ is non linear differential equation.

(vi) $x^2\frac{d^2y}{dx^2}+x\frac{dy}{dx}+y=0$ is non linear differential equation.

(vii) $y=\frac{dy}{dx}+\sqrt[3]{1+\left(\frac{dy}{dx}\right)^2}$

$\Rightarrow \left(y-\frac{dy}{dx}\right)^3=\left(\frac{dy}{dx}\right)^2+1$

This is non linear differential equation.

19. (i) The given differential equation is

$(1+x^2)\frac{dy}{dx}+y=e^{\tan^{-1}x}$

$\Rightarrow \frac{dy}{dx}+\frac{1}{1+x^2}y=\frac{e^{\tan^{-1}x}}{1+x^2}$

Here, $P=\frac{1}{1+x^2}$

and $\quad Q=\frac{e^{\tan^{-1}x}}{1+x^2}$

$\therefore$ IF $=e^{\int\frac{1}{1+x^2}dx}=e^{\tan^{-1}x}$

(ii) Given,

$x\,dy+(2x^2y-y-ax^3)dx=0$

$\Rightarrow \frac{dy}{dx}+\frac{(2x^2-1)}{x}y=ax^2$

Here, $P=\frac{2x^2-1}{x}=2x-\frac{1}{x}$

and $\quad Q=ax^2$

$\therefore$ IF $=e^{\int\left(2x-\frac{1}{x}\right)dx}$

$=e^{x^2-\log_e x}$

(iii) Given,

$\frac{dy}{dx}+y\tan x+\sec x=0$

Here, $P=\tan x$

and $\quad Q=-\sec x$

$\therefore$ IF $=e^{\int Pdx}=c^{\int\tan x\,dx}$

$=e^{\log|\sec x|}$

$=\sec x$

$\therefore$ Required answer is $\sec x$.

(iv) The given differential equation is

$x\frac{dy}{dx}+y\cdot\log x=xe^x\cdot x^{-\frac{1}{2}\log x}, \quad x>0$

$\Rightarrow \frac{dy}{dx}+\frac{\log x}{x}y=e^x x^{-\frac{1}{2}\log x}$

Here, $P=\frac{\log x}{x}$

So, IF $=e^{\int Pdx}=e^{\int\frac{\log x}{x}dx}$

$=e^{\frac{(\log x)^2}{2}}$

IF $=(\sqrt{e})^{(\log x)^2}$

At $x=2$, IF $=(\sqrt{e})^{(\log 2)^2}$

20. (i) Given, $dy+2xy\,dx=2e^{-x^2}dx$

$\Rightarrow \quad \frac{dy}{dx}+2xy=2e^{-x^2}$

Here, $P=2x$ and $Q=2e^{-x^2}$

and this is linear equation in y.

So, IF $=e^{\int 2x\,dx}=e^{x^2}$

The solution is

$y\cdot(\text{IF})=\int Q\cdot(\text{IF})\,dx+C$

$y\cdot e^{x^2}=\int(2e^{-x^2})e^{x^2}dx+C$

$\therefore y\cdot e^{x^2}=2x+c$

(ii) Given, $\frac{dy}{dx}=\frac{1}{1+x+y}$

$\Rightarrow \quad \frac{dx}{dy}=1+x+y$

$\Rightarrow \quad \frac{dx}{dy}-x=1+y$

It is a linear equation in x.

Here, $P=-1$ and $Q=1+y$

So, IF $=e^{\int Pdy}=e^{\int(-1)\,dy}=e^{-y}$

Hence, the solution is

$xe^{-y}=\int(1+y)e^{-y}dy+C$

$=\int e^{-y}dy+\int ye^{-y}dy+C$

$=-e^{-y}+[-ye^{-y}+\int e^{-y}dy]+C$

$=-e^{-y}-ye^{-y}-e^{-y}+C$

$\Rightarrow xe^{-y}=-ye^{-y}-2e^{-y}+C$

$\Rightarrow \quad x=-y-2+Ce^y$

$\Rightarrow \quad x=Ce^y-y-2,$

where C is an arbitrary constant.

Thus, the required solution is $x = Ce^y - y - 2$

(iii) Given differential equation is

$$\frac{dy}{dx} + 2y\cot x = 3x^2\text{cosec}^2 x$$

This is linear differential equation in y.

Here, $P = 2\cot x$

and $Q = 3x^2\text{cosec}^2 x$

$$\therefore \text{IF} = e^{\int 2\cot x\,dx} = e^{2\log \sin x}$$

$$= \sin^2 x$$

The solution is

$$y\cdot(\text{IF}) = \int Q\cdot(\text{IF})\,dx + C$$

$$\Rightarrow y\cdot \sin^2 x$$

$$= \int 3x^2\text{cosec}^2 x\cdot \sin^2 x\,dx + C$$

$$= \int 3x^2\,dx + C$$

i.e. $\sin^2 x\cdot y(x) = x^3 + C$,

where C is an arbitrary constant.

(iv) The given differential equation is

$$\frac{dy}{dx} + \frac{1}{x}y = x^3$$

$$\therefore \quad \text{IF} = e^{\int \frac{1}{x}dx} = e^{\log x} = x$$

The solution is

$$y(x)\cdot x = \int x^3\cdot x\,dx + C$$

$$\Rightarrow \quad y(x)\cdot x = \int x^4\,dx + C$$

$$\Rightarrow \quad y(x)\cdot x = \frac{x^5}{5} + C$$

$$\Rightarrow \quad y(x) = \frac{x^4}{5} + \frac{C}{x}$$

This is required solution.

(v) The given differential equation is

$$\frac{dy}{dx} + 3y = e^{-2x}$$

This is compared to

$$\frac{dy}{dx} + Py = Q,$$

where $P = 3$ and $Q = e^{-2x}$

$$\therefore \text{IF} = e^{\int Pdx} = e^{\int 3dx} = e^{3x}$$

The solution is

$$y\cdot(\text{IF}) = \int (Q\cdot \text{IF})\cdot dx + C$$

$$\Rightarrow y\cdot e^{3x} = \int (e^{-2x}\cdot e^{3x})\,dx + C$$

$$\Rightarrow y\cdot e^{3x} = e^{x} + C$$

$$\Rightarrow \quad y(x) = e^{-2x} + Ce^{-3x},$$

where C is an arbitrary constant.

(vi) The given differential equation is

$$\frac{dy}{dx} + 2y = xe^{4x}$$

This is first order linear equation in y.

Here, $P = 2$ and $Q = xe^{4x}$

$$\therefore \text{IF} = e^{\int Pdx} = e^{\int 2dx} = e^{2x}$$

The solution of the differential equation is

$$y\cdot e^{2x} = \int e^{2x}.(xe^{4x})dx + C$$

$$= \int xe^{6x}dx + C$$

$$\Rightarrow y\cdot e^{2x} = \left[x\frac{e^{6x}}{6} - \frac{1}{36}e^{6x}\right] + C$$

Thus,

$$y\,.\,e^{2x} = \left[\frac{xe^{6x}}{6} - \frac{1}{36}e^{6x}\right] + C$$

$$\Rightarrow \quad y(x) = \frac{xe^{4x}}{6} - \frac{e^{4x}}{36} + Ce^{-2x}$$

21. (i) (c) Given,

$$\frac{dy}{dx} + Py = Q\,y^n, (n > 1)$$

$$\Rightarrow \quad y^{-n}\frac{dy}{dx} + Py^{1-n} = Q$$

Let $y^{1-n} = z$

$$(1-n)\,y^{-n}\frac{dy}{dx} = \frac{dz}{dx}$$

$$\Rightarrow \quad \frac{1}{(1-n)}\frac{dz}{dx} + Pz = Q$$

$$\Rightarrow \quad \frac{dz}{dx} + P(1-n)z = Q(1-n)$$

This is linear equation in z.

(ii) (c) Given differential equation is

$$\frac{dy}{dx} - (\tan x)\,y = 2x\sec x$$

Here, $P = -\tan x$

and $Q = 2x\sec x$

$$\therefore \text{IF} = e^{\int Pdx} = e^{\int -\tan x\,dx}$$

$$= e^{-\log|\sec x|} = \cos x$$

The solution is $y\cdot\cos x$

$$= \int 2x\cdot \sec x\cdot \cos x\,dx + C$$

$$= \int 2x\,dx + C$$

$$\Rightarrow y\cdot\cos x = x^2 + C$$

Given, $y(0) = 0$

$$\Rightarrow \quad 0 = 0 + C \Rightarrow C = 0$$

Thus, $y(x) = x^2\sec x$

$$y'(x) = 2x\sec x + x^2\cdot\sec x\cdot\tan x$$

Now, check by option,

(a) $y\left(\frac{\pi}{3}\right) = \frac{\pi^2}{9}\,.\,\sec\left(\frac{\pi}{3}\right) = \frac{2\pi^2}{9}$

(b) $y'\left(\frac{\pi}{3}\right) = \frac{2\pi}{3}\times 2 + \frac{\pi^2}{9}\cdot 2\cdot\sqrt{3}$

$$= \frac{4\pi}{3} + \frac{2\sqrt{3}\pi^2}{9}$$

(c) $y\left(\frac{\pi}{4}\right) = \frac{\pi^2}{8\sqrt{2}}$

(d) $y'\left(\frac{\pi}{4}\right) = \frac{9\pi^2}{8\sqrt{2}}$

(iii) (c) The given differential equation is

$$x^3\frac{dy}{dx} + 4x^2\tan y = e^x\sec y$$

$$\Rightarrow \cos y\frac{dy}{dx} + \frac{4}{x}\sin y = \frac{e^x}{x^3}$$

Let $\sin y = z \Rightarrow \cos y\frac{dy}{dx} = \frac{dz}{dx}$

$$\therefore \quad \frac{dz}{dx} + \frac{4}{x}\,.\,z = \frac{e^x}{x^3}$$

This is a linear equation of z.

So, $\quad \text{IF} = e^{\int \frac{4}{x}dx} = x^4$

The solution is

$$z\,.\,x^4 = \int x^4.\frac{e^x}{x^3}dx$$

$$= \int x.e^x dx$$

$$= xe^x - e^x + C$$

$$\Rightarrow (\sin y)x^4 = xe^x - e^x + C$$

If $y(1) = 0$, then $C = 0$

So, $(\sin y)\, x^4 = xe^x - e^x$

$= (x-1)\, e^x$

$\therefore \sin y = x^{-4}(x-1)e^x$

$\sin y = e^x(x-1)x^{-4}$

This is required solution.

22. The given equation can be written as $\dfrac{dy}{dx} = y\dfrac{\phi'(x)}{\phi(x)} - \dfrac{y^2}{\phi(x)}$

$\Rightarrow \dfrac{dy}{dx} - y.\dfrac{\phi'(x)}{\phi(x)} = -\dfrac{y^2}{\phi(x)}$

$\Rightarrow -\dfrac{1}{y^2}\dfrac{dy}{dx} + \dfrac{1}{y}\dfrac{\phi'(x)}{\phi(x)} = \dfrac{1}{\phi(x)}$

Let $\dfrac{1}{y} = z$, then

$-\dfrac{1}{y^2}.\dfrac{dy}{dx} = \dfrac{dz}{dx}$

$\therefore \dfrac{dz}{dx} + z\dfrac{\phi'(x)}{\phi(x)} = \dfrac{1}{\phi(x)}$

This is a linear equation of z.

Here, $P = \dfrac{\phi'(x)}{\phi(x)}$ and $Q = \dfrac{1}{\phi(x)}$

So, $\text{IF} = e^{\int P\,dx} = e^{\int \frac{\phi'(x)}{\phi(x)}dx}$

$= e^{\log \phi(x)} = \phi(x)$

$\therefore$ Hence, solution is

$\phi(x)\,.\,z = \int \phi(x)\,.\dfrac{1}{\phi(x)}\,dx + C$

$\Rightarrow \phi(x)\,.\,\dfrac{1}{y} = x + C$

$\Rightarrow \quad y(x) = \dfrac{\phi(x)}{x+C}$

Here, $y(0) = 2$ and $\phi(0) = 1$

$\Rightarrow \quad 2 = \dfrac{1}{C}$

$\Rightarrow \quad C = \dfrac{1}{2}$

$\therefore \; y(x) = \dfrac{\phi(x)}{x + \frac{1}{2}} = \dfrac{2\phi(x)}{2x+1}$

Thus, the required solution is

$y(x) = \dfrac{2\phi(x)}{2x+1}$.

23. (c) Given equation is

$6\int_1^x f(t)\,dt = 3x\,f(x) - x^3 - 5,$

$\forall x \geq 1$

On differentiating this integral equation and applying Leibnitz's rule, we get

$6f(x) = 3f(x) + 3f'(x)\cdot x - 3x^2$

$\Rightarrow 3xf'(x) - 3f(x) - 3x^2 = 0$

$\Rightarrow f'(x) - \dfrac{1}{x}f(x) = x$

This is linear differential equation of first order in $f(x)$.

$\therefore \text{IF} = e^{\int -\frac{1}{x}dx} = \dfrac{1}{x}$

Solution is,

$f(x)\cdot\dfrac{1}{x} = \int x\cdot\dfrac{1}{x}\,dx + C$

$= \int 1\cdot dx + C$

$\Rightarrow \; f(x) = (x+c)x = x^2 + Cx$

On putting $x = 1$ and $f(x) = 2$

$\Rightarrow \quad 2 = 1 + C \Rightarrow C = 1$

$\Rightarrow f(x) = x^2 + x$

$\therefore \; f(2) = 2^2 + 2 = 6$

24. Given,

$y'(x) + P'(x)\,y(x) = P(x)\cdot P'(x),$

$y(0) = 0$

$\Rightarrow \dfrac{d}{dx}y(x) + P'(x)y(x)$

$= P(x)\cdot P'(x)$

This is linear differential equation of first order in $y(x)$.

Now, $\text{IF} = e^{\int P'(x)\,dx} = e^{P(x)}$

The solution is

$y(x)\cdot e^{P(x)} = \int e^{P(x)}\cdot P(x)\cdot P'(x)\,dx$

Let $P(x) = t$

$\Rightarrow P'(x)dx = dt$

$= \int e^t\cdot t\cdot dt$

$= e^t(t-1) + C$

$\Rightarrow y(x)\cdot e^{P(x)} = e^{P(x)}\{P(x) - 1\} + C$

$\Rightarrow \quad y(x) = P(x) - 1 + Ce^{-P(x)}$

Now, $P(0) = 0$ and $y(0) = 0$

$\Rightarrow \quad 0 = P(0) - 1 + Ce^{-P(0)}$

$\Rightarrow \quad C = 1$

$\Rightarrow \quad y(x) = P(x) - 1 + e^{-P(x)}$

$\Rightarrow \quad y(3) = P(3) - 1 + e^{-P(3)}$

$= (0-1) + 1 = 0$

$\therefore \quad y(3) = 0$

This is required answer.

25. (b) Given equation is

$Y - y = m(X - x)$

y-intercept $(X = 0)$

$\Rightarrow \quad Y = y - mx$

Given, $y - mx = x^3$

On differentiating w.r.t. x, we get

$\dfrac{dy}{dx} - m = 3x^2$

$\Rightarrow \quad x\dfrac{dy}{dx} - mx = 3x^3$

$\Rightarrow x\dfrac{dy}{dx} + x^3 - y = 3x^3$

$\Rightarrow \quad x\dfrac{dy}{dx} - y = 2x^3$

$\Rightarrow \quad \dfrac{dy}{dx} - \dfrac{y}{x} = 2x^2$

This is linear equation in y.

So, $\text{IF} = e^{\int -\frac{1}{x}dx} = \dfrac{1}{x}$

Thus, the solution is

$y.\dfrac{1}{x} = \int 2x^2.\dfrac{1}{x}\,dx + C$

$\dfrac{y}{x} = x^2 + C$

$\Rightarrow \quad y = x^3 + Cx$

At $f(1) = 1$,

$y = 1,\; x = 1$, then $C = 0$

$\therefore \quad f(2) = (2)^3 + 2(0) = 8$

26. (True)

Let $f(x, y)$ be curve and (x, y) be a point on the curve.

We know that slope of the tangent to the curve at (x, y) is $\dfrac{dy}{dx}$.

So, $\dfrac{dy}{dx} + 5 = x + y$

$\Rightarrow \quad \dfrac{dy}{dx} = x + y - 5$

$\Rightarrow \quad \dfrac{dy}{dx} - y = x - 5$

This equation is compared to $\dfrac{dy}{dx} + Py = Q$,

where $P = -1$ and $Q = x - 5$

So, $\text{IF} = e^{\int(-1)\,dx} = e^{-x}$

The solution is,

$y\cdot e^{-x} = \int e^{-x}(x-5)\,dx + C$

$= \int x\,e^{-x}dx - 5\int e^{-x}\,dx + C$

$= (-\,xe^{-x}) + \int e^{-x}dx - 5\int e^{-x}dx + C$

$= -\,xe^{-x} + 4e^{-x} + C$

$\Rightarrow y(x)\,.\,e^{-x} = (4-x)e^{-x} + C,$

where C is an arbitrary constant.

$\Rightarrow y(x) = (4-x) + Ce^x$

Assertion-Reason

1. (a) Given differential equation

$\dfrac{dy}{dx} + 3y = \cos x$

Here, the order of the higher derivative is 1.

$\therefore$ The order of the given differential equation is 1.

2. (a) Given differential equation is

$$\left(\frac{dy}{dx}\right)^2 = \frac{x^6 - y^6}{(x^2 + y^2)\,xy}$$

The given differential equation has first order derivative which is free from radical and fraction with power equal to 2.

$\therefore$ The degree of the given differential equation is 2.

3. (b) Given differential equation

$$\sqrt{\frac{d^2y}{dx^2}} = \sqrt{\frac{dy}{dx} + 5}$$

On squaring both sides, we get

$$\frac{d^2y}{dx^2} = \frac{dy}{dx} + 5$$

Here, the highest order is 2 and its power is 1.

$\therefore$ Order is 2 and degree is 1.

We have, differential equation

$$\left(\frac{dx}{dy}\right)^3 + 2y^{\frac{1}{2}} = x$$

$$\Rightarrow \left(\frac{1}{\frac{dy}{dx}}\right)^3 + 2\sqrt{y} = x$$

$$\Rightarrow 1 + 2\sqrt{y}\left(\frac{dy}{dx}\right)^3 = x$$

$$\Rightarrow 1 + 2\sqrt{y}\left(\frac{dy}{dx}\right)^3 = x\left(\frac{dy}{dx}\right)^3$$

Hence, highest order is 1 and its power is 3.

$\therefore$ Order is 1 and degree is 3.

4. (a) Given differential equation

$$\frac{dy}{dx} + x^2y = 5$$

Here, $P = x^2$ and $Q = 5$

So, the given differential equation is of the form $\frac{dy}{dx} + Py = Q$

$\therefore$ It is a first order linear differential equation.

5. (a) Given differential equation

$$\frac{d^2y}{dx^2} + 3\left(\frac{dy}{dx}\right)^2 = x^2 \log\left(\frac{d^2y}{dx^2}\right)$$

Here, the differential equation is not a polynomial in terms of its derivatives.

$\therefore$ The degree is not defined.

6. (a) We have, $x + y = \tan^{-1} y$

On differentiating w.r.t. x, we get

$$1 + \frac{dy}{dx} = \frac{1}{1 + y^2}\frac{dy}{dx}$$

$$\Rightarrow 1 + y^2 + (1 + y^2)\frac{dy}{dx} = \frac{dy}{dx}$$

$$\Rightarrow 1 + y^2 + (1 + y^2 - 1)\frac{dy}{dx} = 0$$

$$\Rightarrow 1 + y^2 + y^2\frac{dy}{dx} = 0$$

$\therefore$ $x + y = \tan^{-1} y$ is the solution of the differential equation

$$y^2\frac{dy}{dx} + y^2 + 1 = 0.$$

7. (d) The given differential equation $\frac{dy}{dx} = \frac{\sin y}{\sin x}$ cannot be written in the form

$$\frac{dy}{dx} = f\left(\frac{y}{x}\right)$$

$\therefore$ It is not a homogeneous differential equation of order 0.

8. (c) Given differential equation

$$(x + y)\frac{dy}{dx} = 1 \Rightarrow \frac{dx}{dy} - y = x$$

$$\therefore \text{IF} = e^{\int P dy} = e^{\int -dy} = e^{-y}$$

Hence, A is true and R is false.

9. (b) Given differential equation is

$$(x + 2)\frac{dy}{dx} = x^2 + 5x - 3$$

$$\Rightarrow \quad dy = \frac{x^2 + 5x - 3}{(x + 2)}dx$$

[separate the variables]

On integrating both sides, we get

$$\int dy = \int \frac{x^2 + 5x - 3}{(x + 2)}dx$$

$$\Rightarrow y = \int\left\{(x + 3) - \frac{9}{(x + 2)}\right\}dx$$

[divide $(x^2 + 5x - 3)$ by $(x + 2)$]

$$\Rightarrow y = \frac{x^2}{2} + 3x - 9\log|x + 2| + C$$

which is the required general solution. Also, we know that the number of arbitrary constant in the general solution is equal to the order of the differential equation.

10. (d) We have,

$$y = C_1e^{x + C_2} + C_3e^{x + C_4}$$

$$\Rightarrow \quad y = (C_1e^{C_2} + C_3e^{C_4})\,e^x$$

$$\Rightarrow \quad y = \lambda e^x$$

[where $\lambda = C_1e^{C_2} + C_3e^{C_4}$]

On differentiating w.r.t. x, we get

$$\frac{dy}{dx} = \lambda e^x \Rightarrow \frac{dy}{dx} = y$$

$\therefore$ Order of the differential equation is 1.

Case Based Questions

1. (i) (b) Given at any time t the thermometer reading be T°F and the outside temperature be S°F. Then, we have

$$\frac{dT}{dt} \propto (T - S) \Rightarrow \frac{dT}{dt} = -\lambda(T - S)$$

(ii) (c) We have, $\frac{dT}{dt} = -\lambda(T - S)$

$$\Rightarrow \quad \frac{dT}{T - S} = -\lambda dt$$

On integrating both sides, we get

$$\int\frac{dT}{T - S} = \int -\lambda\, dt$$

$$\Rightarrow \quad \log(T - S) = -\lambda t + C$$

(iii) (d) We have,

$\log(T - S) = -\lambda t + C$

Since, at $t = 0, T = 80$°F

$\therefore \log(80 - S) = -\lambda(0) + C$

$\Rightarrow C = \log(80 - S)$

2. (i) Given differential equation can be written as

$$\frac{dy}{dx} + \frac{\cos x}{1 + \sin x}y = \frac{-x}{1 + \sin x}$$

Compare it with $\frac{dy}{dx} + Py = Q$, we get

$$P = \frac{\cos x}{1 + \sin x} \text{ and } Q = \frac{-x}{1 + \sin x}$$

(ii) $\text{IF} = e^{\int P dx} = e^{\int \frac{\cos x}{1 + \sin x}dx}$

Put $1 + \sin x = t \Rightarrow \cos x\, dx = dt$

$$\therefore \text{IF} = e^{\int \frac{1}{t}dt} = e^{\log t} = t = 1 + \sin x$$

(iii) Solution of given differential equation is given by

$$y\,(\text{IF}) = \int Q \cdot (\text{IF})\,dx + C$$

$$\Rightarrow y(1 + \sin x) = \int \frac{-x}{1 + \sin x} \cdot (1 + \sin x)\,dx + C$$

$$\Rightarrow y(1 + \sin x) = -\frac{x^2}{2} + C$$

(iv) We have, $y(0) = 1$ i.e. $x = 0, y = 1$

$\therefore 1 \cdot (1 + \sin(0)) = C \Rightarrow C = 1$

$$\therefore y(1 + \sin x) = -\frac{x^2}{2} + 1$$

$$\Rightarrow y(1 + \sin x) = \frac{2 - x^2}{2}$$

$$\therefore y = \frac{2 - x^2}{2(1 + \sin x)}$$

Chapter-10

Vector Algebra

1. (i) Volume is scalar.
(ii) Time is scalar.
(iii) Force is vector.
(iv) Speed is scalar.
(v) Velocity is vector.

2. (c)

3. (i) Given, $\vec{a} = \frac{1}{\sqrt{3}}\hat{i} + \frac{1}{\sqrt{3}}\hat{j} - \frac{1}{\sqrt{3}}\hat{k}$

$\Rightarrow \quad \vec{a} = x\hat{i} + y\hat{j} + z\hat{k}$

$\Rightarrow \quad |\vec{a}| = \sqrt{x^2 + y^2 + z^2}$

$\Rightarrow |\vec{a}| = \sqrt{\left(\frac{1}{\sqrt{3}}\right)^2 + \left(\frac{1}{\sqrt{3}}\right)^2 + \left(-\frac{1}{\sqrt{3}}\right)^2}$

$= \sqrt{\frac{1}{3} + \frac{1}{3} + \frac{1}{3}} = \sqrt{\frac{3}{3}} = 1$

(ii) Given, $\vec{a} = \sqrt{5}\,\hat{i} - \frac{1}{\sqrt{5}}\hat{j} - 2\hat{k}$

$\Rightarrow |\vec{a}| = \sqrt{(\sqrt{5})^2 + \left(-\frac{1}{\sqrt{5}}\right)^2 + (-2)^2}$

$= \sqrt{5 + \frac{1}{5} + 4} = \sqrt{\frac{45+1}{5}} = \sqrt{\frac{46}{5}}$

(iii) Given, $\vec{a} = 2\sqrt{2}\,\hat{i} + 3\hat{j} + 1\hat{k}$

$\Rightarrow |\vec{a}| = \sqrt{(2\sqrt{2})^2 + 3^2 + 1^2}$

$= \sqrt{8 + 9 + 1} = \sqrt{18}$

$= 3\sqrt{2}$

4. (b) Given,

$\vec{a} = \hat{i} + \hat{j} - 2\hat{k} = (x\hat{i} + y\hat{j} + z\hat{k})$

Here, $x = 1$, $y = 1$ and $z = -2$

Direction ratios $= (1, 1, -2)$

$\vec{r} = |\vec{a}| = \sqrt{1^2 + 1^2 + (-2)^2}$

$= \sqrt{1 + 1 + 4} = \sqrt{6}$

Direction cosines $= \left(\frac{x}{r}, \frac{y}{r}, \frac{z}{r}\right)$

$= \left(\frac{1}{\sqrt{6}}, \frac{1}{\sqrt{6}}, -\frac{2}{\sqrt{6}}\right)$

5. (a) $\frac{\vec{r}}{r} = \frac{x}{r}\hat{i} + \frac{y}{r}\hat{j} + \frac{z}{r}\hat{k}$

$= \cos\alpha\hat{i} + \cos\beta\hat{j} + \cos\gamma\hat{k}$

$\cos\alpha = \frac{x}{r}$, $\cos\beta = \frac{y}{r}$ and $\cos\gamma = \frac{z}{r}$

$\Rightarrow (\cos\alpha, \cos\beta, \cos\gamma)$

are direction cosines

$\Rightarrow \cos^2\alpha + \cos^2\beta + \cos^2\gamma = 1$

6. (b)

7. (i) (True)

$\overrightarrow{OA}$ and $\overrightarrow{OB}$ have the same initial point O.

(ii) (True)

$\vec{a}$ and $-\vec{a}$ are parallel to the same line.

(iii) (False)

Let $\vec{a} = \hat{i}$ and $\vec{b} = 2\hat{i}$

$\vec{a}$ and $\vec{b}$ are collinear but the magnitudes are not same.

i.e. $|\vec{a}| \neq |\vec{b}|$

(iv) (False)

Let $\vec{a} = \hat{i}$ and $\vec{b} = \hat{j}$

$|\vec{a}| = |\vec{b}| = 1$

But $\vec{a}$ and $\vec{b}$ are not collinear.

(v) (False)

Let $\vec{a} = \hat{i}$ and $\vec{b} = -\hat{i}$

$|\vec{a}| = |\vec{b}| = 1$

$\vec{a}$ and $\vec{b}$ are two collinear vectors having same magnitude but they are not equal

i.e. $|\vec{a}| \neq |\vec{b}|$

8. (a) **9.** (a)

10. (b) Using triangle law,

$\overrightarrow{AC} = \overrightarrow{AB} + \overrightarrow{BC} = \vec{a} + \vec{b}$

$\overrightarrow{AC'} = \overrightarrow{AB} + \overrightarrow{BC'}$

$= \overrightarrow{AB} - \overrightarrow{BC} = \vec{a} - \vec{b}$

11. (i) (True)

$\overrightarrow{AB} + \overrightarrow{BC} - \overrightarrow{AC}$

$= \overrightarrow{AB} + \overrightarrow{BC} - (\overrightarrow{AB} + \overrightarrow{BC}) = 0$

(ii) (True)

$\overrightarrow{AB} + \overrightarrow{BC} + \overrightarrow{CA}$

$= \overrightarrow{AB} + \overrightarrow{BC} - \overrightarrow{AC} = 0$

(iii) (False)

$\overrightarrow{AB} + \overrightarrow{BC} - \overrightarrow{CA}$

$= \overrightarrow{AB} + \overrightarrow{BC} + \overrightarrow{AC}$

$= \overrightarrow{AB} + \overrightarrow{BC} + \overrightarrow{AB} + \overrightarrow{BC}$

$= 2(\overrightarrow{AB} + \overrightarrow{BC}) \neq 0$

(iv) (True)

$\overrightarrow{AB} - \overrightarrow{CB} + \overrightarrow{CA}$

$= \overrightarrow{AB} - (-\overrightarrow{BC}) + (-\overrightarrow{AC})$

$= \overrightarrow{AB} + \overrightarrow{BC} - \overrightarrow{AC} = 0$

12. Given, $\vec{a} = 2\hat{i} - 4\hat{j} + \hat{k}$

(i) $\frac{1}{2}\vec{a} = \frac{1}{2}(2\hat{i} - 4\hat{j} + \hat{k})$

$= \hat{i} - 2\hat{j} + \frac{1}{2}\hat{k}$

(ii) $3\vec{a} = 3(2\hat{i} - 4\hat{j} + \hat{k})$

$= 6\hat{i} - 12\hat{j} + 3\hat{k}$

(iii) $-\frac{1}{4}\vec{a} = -\frac{1}{4}(2\hat{i} - 4\hat{j} + \hat{k})$

$= -\frac{1}{2}\hat{i} + \hat{j} - \frac{1}{4}\hat{k}$

13. True

14. (No) because their corresponding components are distinct.

15. (b) Let $\vec{a} = x(\hat{i} + \hat{j} + \hat{k})$

$= x\hat{i} + x\hat{j} + x\hat{k}$

Since, $\vec{a}$ is a unit vector.

$\therefore \quad |\vec{a}| = 1$

$\Rightarrow \sqrt{x^2 + x^2 + x^2} = 1$

$\Rightarrow \quad \sqrt{3x^2} = 1$

$\Rightarrow \quad \sqrt{3}x = \pm 1$

$\Rightarrow \quad x = \pm\frac{1}{\sqrt{3}}$

16. (True)

Let $\vec{a} = 5\hat{i} - \hat{j} + 2\hat{k}$

$|\vec{a}| = \sqrt{25 + 1 + 4} = \sqrt{30}$

Unit vector $= \frac{\vec{a}}{|\vec{a}|} = \frac{5\hat{i} - \hat{j} + 2\hat{k}}{\sqrt{30}}$

The vector in the direction of vector $5\hat{i} - \hat{j} + 2\hat{k}$ that has magnitude 8 units

$= 8 \cdot \frac{5\hat{i} - \hat{j} + 2\hat{k}}{\sqrt{30}}$

17. Given $\vec{a} = 2\hat{i} + 2\hat{j} - 5\hat{k}$

and $\vec{b} = 2\hat{i} + \hat{j} + 3\hat{k}$

$\vec{a} + \vec{b} = 4\hat{i} + 3\hat{j} - 2\hat{k}$

$|\vec{a} + \vec{b}| = \sqrt{16 + 9 + 4} = \sqrt{29}$

Unit vector in the direction of

$\vec{a} + \vec{b} = \frac{(\vec{a} + \vec{b})}{|\vec{a} + \vec{b}|}$

$= \frac{4\hat{i} + 3\hat{j} - 2\hat{k}}{\sqrt{29}}$

18. (i) x, y and z (ii) $x\hat{i}$, $y\hat{j}$ and $z\hat{k}$

19. (b) Let $P(x_1, y_1) = (2, 1)$

and $Q(x_2, y_2) = (-5, 7)$

$$\overrightarrow{PQ} = (x_2 - x_1)\hat{i} + (y_2 - y_1)\hat{j}$$
$$= (-5-2)\hat{i} + (7-1)\hat{j}$$
$$= -7\hat{i} + 6\hat{j}$$

Scalar components are $-7, 6$ and vector components are $-7\hat{i}$, $6\hat{j}$.

20. Given, $P = (1, 2, 3)$

$$\Rightarrow \quad \overrightarrow{OP} = \hat{i} + 2\hat{j} + 3\hat{k}$$

and $Q = (4, 5, 6)$

$$\Rightarrow \quad \overrightarrow{OQ} = 4\hat{i} + 5\hat{j} + 6\hat{k}$$
$$\overrightarrow{PQ} = (4-1)\hat{i} + (5-2)\hat{j} + (6-3)\hat{k}$$
$$= 3\hat{i} + 3\hat{j} + 3\hat{k}$$
$$|\overrightarrow{PQ}| = 3\sqrt{3}$$
$$\therefore \text{ Unit vector} = \frac{\overrightarrow{PQ}}{|\overrightarrow{PQ}|}$$
$$= \frac{1}{3\sqrt{3}}(3\hat{i} + 3\hat{j} + 3\hat{k})$$
$$= \frac{1}{\sqrt{3}}(\hat{i} + \hat{j} + \hat{k})$$

21. $P(2, 3, 0) = (x_1, y_1, z_1)$ and $Q(-1, -2, -4) = (x_2, y_2, z_2)$

$$\overrightarrow{PQ} = (x_2 - x_1)\hat{i} + (y_2 - y_1)\hat{j} + (z_2 - z_1)\hat{k}$$
$$= (-1-2)\hat{i} + (-2-3)\hat{j} + (-4-0)\hat{k}$$
$$= -3\hat{i} - 5\hat{j} - 4\hat{k}$$

22. (c) Given points are $A(1, 2, -3)$ and $B(-1, -2, 1)$

$$\Rightarrow x_1 = 1 \text{ and } x_2 = -1$$
$$\Rightarrow y_1 = 2 \text{ and } y_2 = -2$$
$$\Rightarrow z_1 = -3 \text{ and } z_2 = 1$$
$$\overrightarrow{AB} = (x_2 - x_1)\hat{i} + (y_2 - y_1)\hat{j} + (z_2 - z_1)\hat{k}$$
$$= -2\hat{i} - 4\hat{j} + 4\hat{k}$$
$$|\overrightarrow{AB}| = \sqrt{(-2)^2 + (-4)^2 + 4^2}$$
$$= \sqrt{36} = 6$$
$$\hat{AB} = \frac{\overrightarrow{AB}}{|\overrightarrow{AB}|} = \frac{-2\hat{i} - 4\hat{j} + 4\hat{k}}{6}$$
$$= -\frac{1}{3}\hat{i} - \frac{2}{3}\hat{j} + \frac{2}{3}\hat{k}$$

$\therefore$ Direction cosines of AB are $\left(-\frac{1}{3}, -\frac{2}{3}, \frac{2}{3}\right)$.

23. (c)

24. Let B divides AC in the ratio $\lambda : 1$, then

$$\overrightarrow{OB} = \frac{\lambda(\overrightarrow{OC}) + 1\cdot(\overrightarrow{OA})}{\lambda + 1},$$

where $\overrightarrow{OA} = \hat{i} - 2\hat{j} - 8\hat{k}$

$$\overrightarrow{OB} = 5\hat{i} - 2\hat{k}$$
$$\overrightarrow{OC} = 11\hat{i} + 3\hat{j} + 7\hat{k}$$
$$\Rightarrow 5\hat{i} - 2\hat{k} = \frac{\lambda(11\hat{i} + 3\hat{j} + 7\hat{k}) + (\hat{i} - 2\hat{j} - 8\hat{k})}{\lambda + 1}$$
$$\Rightarrow 5(\lambda+1)\hat{i} - 2(\lambda+1)\hat{k} = (11\lambda+1)\hat{i} + (3\lambda-2)\hat{j} + (7\lambda-8)\hat{k}$$

On comparing the components, we get

$$0 = 3\lambda - 2$$
$$\Rightarrow \quad 3\lambda = 2$$
$$\Rightarrow \quad \frac{\lambda}{1} = \frac{2}{3}$$

5. Given points are $P(2, 3, 4)$ and $Q(4, 1, -2)$.

$$\overrightarrow{OP} = 2\hat{i} + 3\hat{j} + 4\hat{k}$$

and $\overrightarrow{OQ} = 4\hat{i} + \hat{j} - 2\hat{k}$

Position vector of the mid-point of the vector joining the points P and $Q = \dfrac{\overrightarrow{OP} + \overrightarrow{OQ}}{2}$

$$= \frac{6\hat{i} + 4\hat{j} + 2\hat{k}}{2}$$
$$= 3\hat{i} + 2\hat{j} + \hat{k}$$

26. (c) Given, $\overrightarrow{OP} = 3\vec{a} - 2\vec{b}$

and $\overrightarrow{OQ} = \vec{a} + \vec{b}$

$$m : n = 2 : 1$$
$$\overrightarrow{OR} = \frac{m(\overrightarrow{OQ}) + n(\overrightarrow{OP})}{m + n}$$
$$= \frac{2(\vec{a} + \vec{b}) + 1(3\vec{a} - 2\vec{b})}{2+1}$$
$$= \frac{2\vec{a} + 2\vec{b} + 3\vec{a} - 2\vec{b}}{3}$$
$$= \frac{5\vec{a}}{3}$$

27. (b) Given, $\overrightarrow{OA} = 2\vec{a} + \vec{b}$

and $\overrightarrow{OB} = \vec{a} - 3\vec{b}$

$$m : n = 1 : 2$$

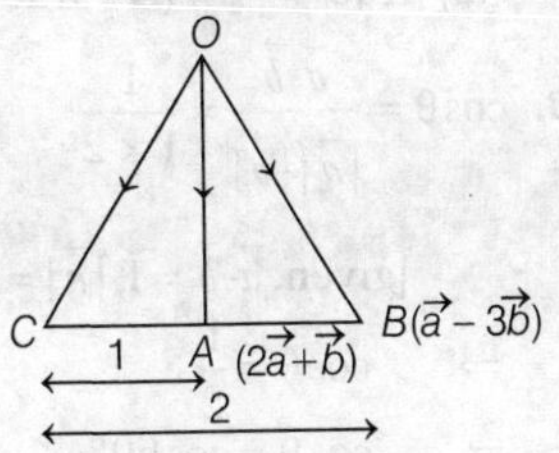

$$\overrightarrow{OC} = \frac{m(\overrightarrow{OB}) - n(\overrightarrow{OA})}{m - n}$$
$$= \frac{1(\vec{a} - 3\vec{b}) - 2(2\vec{a} + \vec{b})}{1-2}$$
$$= \frac{\vec{a} - 3\vec{b} - 4\vec{a} - 2\vec{b}}{-1}$$
$$= 3\vec{a} + 5\vec{b}$$

28. (b) Given, $\vec{a}\cdot\vec{b} \ge 0$

$$\Rightarrow |\vec{a}||\vec{b}|\cos\theta \ge 0$$
$$\Rightarrow \quad \cos\theta \ge 0 \Rightarrow 0 \le \theta \le \frac{\pi}{2}$$

29. (a) $\cos\theta = 0 \Rightarrow \theta = \dfrac{\pi}{2}$

30. (i) $\vec{a} + \lambda\vec{b} = (2-\lambda)\hat{i} + (2+2\lambda)\hat{j} + (3+\lambda)\hat{k}$

Since, $(\vec{a} + \lambda\vec{b}) \perp \vec{c}$

So, $(\vec{a} + \lambda\vec{b})\cdot\vec{c} = 0$

$$\Rightarrow 3(2-\lambda) + 2 + 2\lambda = 0$$
$$\Rightarrow \quad 6 - 3\lambda + 2 + 2\lambda = 0$$
$$\Rightarrow \quad 8 - \lambda = 0 \Rightarrow \lambda = 8$$

(ii) Let $\vec{d} = x\hat{i} + y\hat{j} + z\hat{k}$

Since, $\vec{d}$ is perpendicular to $\vec{a}$ and $\vec{b}$.

So, $\vec{d}\cdot\vec{a} = 0$

$$\Rightarrow \quad x + 4y + 2z = 0 \qquad \text{...(i)}$$
$$\vec{d}\cdot\vec{b} = 0$$
$$\Rightarrow \quad 3x - 2y + 7z = 0 \qquad \text{...(ii)}$$
$$\vec{c}\cdot\vec{d} = 15$$
$$\Rightarrow \quad 2x - y + 4z = 15 \qquad \text{...(iii)}$$

On solving Eqs. (i), (ii) and (iii), we get

$$x = \frac{160}{3}, y = -\frac{5}{3}, z = -\frac{70}{3}$$
$$\therefore \vec{d} = \frac{160}{3}\hat{i} - \frac{5}{3}\hat{j} - \frac{70}{3}\hat{k}$$
$$= \frac{1}{3}(160\hat{i} - 5\hat{j} - 70\hat{k})$$

31. (b) Using $\vec{a}\cdot\vec{b} = |\vec{a}||\vec{b}|\cos\theta$

32. (i) True (ii) False
(iii) True (iv) True

33. $\cos\theta = \dfrac{\vec{a}\cdot\vec{b}}{|\vec{a}||\vec{b}|} = \dfrac{1}{1\times 2}$

[given, $\vec{a}\cdot\vec{b} = 1, |\vec{a}| = 1, |\vec{b}| = 2$]

$\Rightarrow \quad \cos\theta = \dfrac{1}{2}$

$\Rightarrow \quad \cos\theta = \cos 60°$

$\Rightarrow \quad \theta = \dfrac{\pi}{3}$

34. $\cos\theta = \dfrac{\vec{a}\cdot\vec{b}}{|\vec{a}||\vec{b}|}$

$= \dfrac{1-1-1}{\sqrt{1+1+1}\,\sqrt{1+1+1}}$

$= \dfrac{-1}{\sqrt{3}\times\sqrt{3}} = \dfrac{-1}{3}$

$\therefore \quad \theta = \cos^{-1}\left(\dfrac{-1}{3}\right)$

$\Rightarrow \theta = \pi - \cos^{-1}\left(\dfrac{1}{3}\right)$

35. (a) $|\vec{a}-\vec{b}|^2 = |\vec{a}|^2 + |\vec{b}|^2 - 2(\vec{a}\cdot\vec{b})$

$= 4 + 9 - 8 = 5$

36. (False)

Given, $A\,(1, 2, 3)$, $B\,(-1, 0, 0)$ and $C\,(0, 1, 2)$

$\overrightarrow{AB} = (-1-1)\hat{i} + (0-2)\hat{j} + (0-3)\hat{k}$

$= -2\hat{i} - 2\hat{j} - 3\hat{k}$

$\overrightarrow{BC} = (0+1)\hat{i} + (1-0)\hat{j} + (2-0)\hat{k}$

$= \hat{i} + \hat{j} + 2\hat{k}$

Let $\angle ABC = \theta$

$\cos\theta = \dfrac{|\overrightarrow{AB}\cdot\overrightarrow{BC}|}{|\overrightarrow{AB}||\overrightarrow{BC}|}$

$= \dfrac{-2-2-6}{\sqrt{17}\cdot\sqrt{6}}$

$= -\dfrac{10}{\sqrt{102}}$

$\Rightarrow \theta = \cos^{-1}\left(\dfrac{-10}{\sqrt{102}}\right)$

37. (i) Given, $(\vec{a}+\vec{b})\cdot(\vec{a}-\vec{b}) = 8$

$\Rightarrow \vec{a}\cdot\vec{a} - \vec{a}\cdot\vec{b} + \vec{b}\cdot\vec{a} - \vec{b}\cdot\vec{b} = 8$

$\Rightarrow \quad |\vec{a}|^2 - |\vec{b}|^2 = 8$

$\Rightarrow \quad [8|\vec{b}|]^2 - |\vec{b}|^2 = 8$

$\Rightarrow \quad 64|\vec{b}|^2 - |\vec{b}|^2 = 8$

$\Rightarrow \quad 63|\vec{b}|^2 = 8$

$\Rightarrow \quad |\vec{b}|^2 = \dfrac{8}{63}$

$\Rightarrow \quad |\vec{b}| = \dfrac{2\sqrt{2}}{3\sqrt{7}}$

$\therefore |\vec{a}| = 8|\vec{b}| = \dfrac{8\times 2\sqrt{2}}{3\sqrt{7}} = \dfrac{16\sqrt{2}}{3\sqrt{7}}$

(ii) Given, $(\vec{a}+\vec{b})\cdot(\vec{a}-\vec{b}) = 2$

$\Rightarrow \quad |\vec{a}|^2 - |\vec{b}|^2 = 2$

$\Rightarrow \left[\dfrac{7}{2}|\vec{b}|\right]^2 - |\vec{b}|^2 = 2$

$\left[\because |\vec{a}| = \dfrac{7}{2}|\vec{b}|\right]$

$\Rightarrow \quad \dfrac{49}{4}|\vec{b}|^2 - |\vec{b}|^2 = 2$

$\Rightarrow |\vec{b}|^2 \times \left(\dfrac{49}{4} - 1\right) = 2$

$\Rightarrow \quad |\vec{b}|^2\left(\dfrac{45}{4}\right) = 2$

$\Rightarrow \quad |\vec{b}|^2 = \dfrac{8}{45}$

$\Rightarrow \quad |\vec{b}| = \dfrac{2\sqrt{2}}{3\sqrt{5}}$

$\therefore \quad |\vec{a}| = \dfrac{7}{2}\cdot\dfrac{2\sqrt{2}}{3\sqrt{5}} = \dfrac{7\sqrt{2}}{3\sqrt{5}}$

(iii) Given, $(\vec{a}+\vec{b})\cdot(\vec{a}-\vec{b}) = 1$

$\Rightarrow \quad |\vec{a}|^2 - |\vec{b}|^2 = 1$

$\Rightarrow \quad |\vec{a}|^2 - \left(\dfrac{1}{\sqrt{5}}|\vec{a}|\right)^2 = 1$

$\Rightarrow \quad |\vec{a}|^2 - \dfrac{1}{5}|\vec{a}|^2 = 1$

$\Rightarrow \quad 4|\vec{a}|^2 = 5$

$\Rightarrow \quad |\vec{a}|^2 = \dfrac{5}{4}$

$\Rightarrow \quad |\vec{a}| = \dfrac{\sqrt{5}}{2}$

38. $|\vec{a}\cdot\vec{b}| \le |\vec{a}||\vec{b}|$

$\Rightarrow |\vec{a}|\,|\vec{b}|\cos\theta \le |\vec{a}||\vec{b}|$

$\Rightarrow \cos\theta \le 1$ (true)

39. $\overrightarrow{AB} = \vec{b} - \vec{a} = -\hat{i} - 2\hat{j} - 6\hat{k}$

$\overrightarrow{BC} = \vec{c} - \vec{b} = 2\hat{i} - \hat{j} + \hat{k}$

$\overrightarrow{CA} = \vec{a} - \vec{c} = -\hat{i} + 3\hat{j} + 5\hat{k}$

We know, A, B and C are the vertices of a triangle.

$\Rightarrow \overrightarrow{BC}\cdot\overrightarrow{CA} = (2\hat{i} - \hat{j} + \hat{k})\cdot(-\hat{i} + 3\hat{j} + 5\hat{k})$

$= 0$

$\Rightarrow \quad \overrightarrow{BC} \perp \overrightarrow{CA}$

$\therefore \quad \angle BCA = \dfrac{\pi}{2}$

$\Rightarrow$ The points A, B and C are the vertices of right angle triangle.

40. (c) Given,

$\vec{a}\cdot(\vec{b}+\vec{c}) = 0$

$\Rightarrow \quad \vec{a}\cdot\vec{b} + \vec{a}\cdot\vec{c} = 0 \quad$ ...(i)

$\vec{b}\cdot(\vec{c}+\vec{a}) = 0$

$\Rightarrow \quad \vec{b}\cdot\vec{c} + \vec{b}\cdot\vec{a} = 0 \quad$ ...(ii)

$\vec{c}\cdot(\vec{a}+\vec{b}) = 0$

$\Rightarrow \quad \vec{c}\cdot\vec{a} + \vec{c}\cdot\vec{b} = 0 \quad$ ...(iii)

On adding Eqs. (i), (ii) and (iii), we get

$2(\vec{a}\cdot\vec{b} + \vec{b}\cdot\vec{c} + \vec{c}\cdot\vec{a}) = 0,$

then $|\vec{a}+\vec{b}+\vec{c}|^2$

$= |\vec{a}|^2 + |\vec{b}|^2 + |\vec{c}|^2 + 0$

$= 9 + 16 + 25 = 50$

$\Rightarrow |\vec{a}+\vec{b}+\vec{c}| = \sqrt{50}$

$= 5\sqrt{2}$

41. (a) Let $\vec{\beta}_1 = \lambda\vec{\alpha}$

$= 3\lambda\hat{i} - \lambda\hat{j}$

Given, $\vec{\beta}_1 + \vec{\beta}_2 = \vec{\beta}$

$\vec{\beta}_2 = \vec{\beta} - \vec{\beta}_1$

$= (2-3\lambda)\hat{i} + (1+\lambda)\hat{j} - 3\hat{k}$

Since, $\vec{\beta}_2$ is perpendicular to $\vec{\alpha}$

So, $\vec{\alpha}\cdot\vec{\beta}_2 = 0$

$\Rightarrow 3(2-3\lambda) - (1+\lambda) = 0$

On solving,

$\lambda = \dfrac{1}{2}$

$\therefore \quad \vec{\beta}_1 = \dfrac{3}{2}\hat{i} - \dfrac{1}{2}\hat{j}$

and $\quad \vec{\beta}_2 = \dfrac{1}{2}\hat{i} + \dfrac{3}{2}\hat{j} - 3\hat{k}$

42. (False)
We have, $\overrightarrow{OA} = -2\hat{i} + 3\hat{j} + 5\hat{k}$
$\overrightarrow{OB} = \hat{i} + 2\hat{j} + 3\hat{k}$
and $\overrightarrow{OC} = 7\hat{i} - \hat{k}$
$\overrightarrow{AB} = \overrightarrow{OB} - \overrightarrow{OA} = 3\hat{i} - \hat{j} - 2\hat{k}$,
$\overrightarrow{BC} = \overrightarrow{OC} - \overrightarrow{OB} = 6\hat{i} - 2\hat{j} - 4\hat{k}$,
$\overrightarrow{AC} = \overrightarrow{OC} - \overrightarrow{OA} = 9\hat{i} - 3\hat{j} - 6\hat{k}$
$|\overrightarrow{AB}| = \sqrt{14}$, $|\overrightarrow{BC}| = 2\sqrt{14}$
and $|\overrightarrow{AC}| = 3\sqrt{14}$
$|\overrightarrow{AC}| = |\overrightarrow{AB}| + |\overrightarrow{BC}|$
Hence, points A, B and C are collinear.

43. (b)

44. Projection of the vector $\vec{a}$ on the line l is given by $\vec{a} \cdot \hat{P}$ or $\dfrac{\vec{a} \cdot \vec{P}}{|\vec{P}|}$
or $|\vec{a}| \cos\theta$
(i) $\dfrac{\pi}{2}, \dfrac{3\pi}{2}$ (ii) 0, π

45. (a) Along X-axis, i is the unit vector
$$\cos\alpha = \frac{\vec{a} \cdot i}{|\vec{a}||\hat{i}|}$$
$$\cos\alpha = \frac{\vec{a}_1}{|\vec{a}| \cdot 1} \Rightarrow \vec{a}_1 = |\vec{a}| \cos\alpha$$
Similarly, $\vec{a}_2 = |\vec{a}| \cos\beta$
and $\vec{a}_3 = |\vec{a}| \cos\gamma$

46. (c) $\vec{a} = x\hat{i} + y\hat{j} + z\hat{k}$ and $|\vec{a}| = 1$
$$\cos\frac{\pi}{3} = \frac{\vec{a} \cdot \hat{i}}{|\vec{a}| \cdot |\hat{i}|}$$
$$\Rightarrow \frac{1}{2} = \frac{x}{1} \Rightarrow x = \frac{1}{2}$$
Similarly, $y = \dfrac{1}{\sqrt{2}}$ and $z = \dfrac{1}{2}$

47. (i) Projection formula is $\dfrac{\vec{a} \cdot \vec{b}}{|\vec{b}|}$,
where $\vec{a} = \hat{i} + 3\hat{j} + 7\hat{k}$
and $\vec{b} = 7\hat{i} - \hat{j} + 8\hat{k}$
$\therefore$ Required projection
$$= \frac{7 - 3 + 56}{\sqrt{114}} = \frac{60}{\sqrt{114}}$$

(ii) Let $\vec{a} = \hat{i} - \hat{j}$ and $\vec{b} = \hat{i} + \hat{j}$
Projection of $\vec{a}$ on
$$\vec{b} = \frac{\vec{a} \cdot \vec{b}}{|\vec{b}|} = \frac{1 - 1}{\sqrt{1+1}} = 0$$

48. $\dfrac{\pm(\vec{a} \times \vec{b})}{|\vec{a} \times \vec{b}|}$

49. (d)

50. (c) We know, $\sin\theta = \dfrac{|\vec{a} \times \vec{b}|}{|\vec{a}||\vec{b}|}$
$$\Rightarrow \sin\theta = 1 \Rightarrow \theta = \frac{\pi}{2}$$

51. (b) Given, $\vec{a} \times \vec{b}$ is a unit vector
$$\Rightarrow |\vec{a} \times \vec{b}| = 1$$
$$\Rightarrow |\vec{a}||\vec{b}| \sin\theta = 1$$
$$\Rightarrow 3 \times \frac{\sqrt{2}}{3} \sin\theta = 1$$
$$\sin\theta = \frac{1}{\sqrt{2}} \Rightarrow \theta = \frac{\pi}{4}$$

52. (c)

53. (i) Given, $\vec{a} = \hat{i} - 7\hat{j} + 7\hat{k}$
and $\vec{b} = 3\hat{i} - 2\hat{j} + 2\hat{k}$
$$\vec{a} \times \vec{b} = \begin{vmatrix} \hat{i} & \hat{j} & \hat{k} \\ 1 & -7 & 7 \\ 3 & -2 & 2 \end{vmatrix} = 19\hat{j} + 19\hat{k}$$
$$\Rightarrow |\vec{a} \times \vec{b}| = \sqrt{19^2 + 19^2} = 19\sqrt{2}$$

(ii) Given, $\vec{a} = 2\hat{i} - 2\hat{j} + 0\hat{k}$
and $\vec{b} = \hat{i} - \hat{j} + \hat{k}$
$$\Rightarrow \vec{a} \times \vec{b} = \begin{vmatrix} \hat{i} & \hat{j} & \hat{k} \\ 2 & -2 & 0 \\ 1 & -1 & 1 \end{vmatrix}$$
$$= \hat{i}(-2) - \hat{j}(2) + \hat{k}(-2 + 2)$$
$$= -2\hat{i} - 2\hat{j}$$
$$\therefore |\vec{a} \times \vec{b}| = \sqrt{(-2)^2 + (-2)^2}$$
$$= \sqrt{4 + 4} = 2\sqrt{2}$$

(iii) Given, $\vec{a} = \hat{i}$ and $\vec{b} = \hat{k}$
$$\Rightarrow \vec{a} \times \vec{b} = \begin{vmatrix} \hat{i} & \hat{j} & \hat{k} \\ 1 & 0 & 0 \\ 0 & 0 & 1 \end{vmatrix}$$
$$= \hat{i} \times 0 - \hat{j}(1) + \hat{k} \times 0 = -\hat{j}$$
$$\Rightarrow |\vec{a} \times \vec{b}| = \sqrt{(-1)^2} = 1$$

(iv) Given, $\vec{a} = 2\sqrt{2}\,\hat{i} + \sqrt{2}\,\hat{j}$
and $\vec{b} = \hat{i} - 2\sqrt{2}\hat{j} + \hat{k}$
$$\vec{a} \times \vec{b} = \begin{vmatrix} \hat{i} & \hat{j} & \hat{k} \\ 2\sqrt{2} & \sqrt{2} & 0 \\ 1 & -2\sqrt{2} & 1 \end{vmatrix}$$
$$= \hat{i}\,(\sqrt{2}) - \hat{j}(2\sqrt{2}) + \hat{k}\,(-8 - \sqrt{2})$$
$$= \sqrt{2}\,\hat{i} - 2\sqrt{2}\,\hat{j} - \hat{k}\,(8 + \sqrt{2})$$
$$\Rightarrow |\vec{a} \times \vec{b}| = \sqrt{(\sqrt{2})^2 + (-2\sqrt{2})^2 + [-(8 + \sqrt{2})]^2}$$
$$= \sqrt{2 + 8 + 64 + 2 + 16\sqrt{2}}$$
$$= \sqrt{76 + 16\sqrt{2}} = 2\sqrt{19 + 4\sqrt{2}}$$

54. (c) Given, $\vec{a} = 3\hat{i} + 2\hat{j} + 2\hat{k}$
and $\vec{b} = \hat{i} + 2\hat{j} - 2\hat{k}$
$\vec{a} + \vec{b} = 4\hat{i} + 4\hat{j}$
$\vec{a} - \vec{b} = 2\hat{i} + 4\hat{k}$
Let c be the unit vector.
According to the question,
$$\vec{c} = (\vec{a} + \vec{b}) \times (\vec{a} - \vec{b})$$
$$= \begin{vmatrix} \hat{i} & \hat{j} & \hat{k} \\ 4 & 4 & 0 \\ 2 & 0 & 4 \end{vmatrix}$$
$$= \hat{i}(16) - \hat{j}\,(16) + \hat{k}(-8)$$
$$\vec{c} = 16\hat{i} - 16\hat{j} - 8\hat{k}$$
$$\Rightarrow |\vec{c}| = \sqrt{(16)^2 + (16)^2 + (-8)^2}$$
$$= \sqrt{512 + 64} = \sqrt{576} = 24$$
Hence, the required vector
$$= \pm\frac{\vec{c}}{|\vec{c}|} = \pm\frac{8}{24}(2\hat{i} - 2\hat{j} - \hat{k})$$
$$= \pm\frac{1}{3}(2\hat{i} - 2\hat{j} - \hat{k})$$

55. (a)

56. (i) We have, $\overrightarrow{AB} = \hat{j} + 2\hat{k}$
and $\overrightarrow{AC} = \hat{i} + 2\hat{j}$
$$\overrightarrow{AB} \times \overrightarrow{AC} = \begin{vmatrix} \hat{i} & \hat{j} & \hat{k} \\ 0 & 1 & 2 \\ 1 & 2 & 0 \end{vmatrix}$$
$$= -4\hat{i} + 2\hat{j} - \hat{k}$$
Now, $|\overrightarrow{AB} \times \overrightarrow{AC}| = \sqrt{16 + 4 + 1}$
$$= \sqrt{21}$$
$\therefore$ Area of a triangle
$$= \frac{1}{2}|\overrightarrow{AB} \times \overrightarrow{AC}|$$
$$= \frac{\sqrt{21}}{2} \text{ sq units}$$

(ii) We have,

$$\overrightarrow{AB} = \hat{j} \text{ and } \overrightarrow{AC} = -\hat{k}$$

$$\overrightarrow{AB} \times \overrightarrow{AC} = \begin{vmatrix} \hat{i} & \hat{j} & \hat{k} \\ 0 & 1 & 0 \\ 0 & 0 & -1 \end{vmatrix}$$

$$= \hat{i}(-1) = -\hat{i}$$

$$\Rightarrow |\overrightarrow{AB} \times \overrightarrow{AC}| = \sqrt{(-1)^2} = 1$$

$\therefore$ Area of a triangle

$$= \frac{1}{2}|\overrightarrow{AB} \times \overrightarrow{AC}|$$

$$= \frac{1}{2} \text{ sq unit}$$

(iii) We have,

$$\overrightarrow{AB} = -3\hat{i} - \hat{j} + 2\hat{k}$$

and $\overrightarrow{AC} = -\hat{i} + \hat{k}$

$$\overrightarrow{AB} \times \overrightarrow{AC} = \begin{vmatrix} \hat{i} & \hat{j} & \hat{k} \\ -3 & -1 & 2 \\ -1 & 0 & 1 \end{vmatrix}$$

$$= \hat{i}(-1) - \hat{j}(-3+2) + \hat{k}(0-1)$$

$$= -\hat{i} + \hat{j} - \hat{k}$$

$$\Rightarrow |\overrightarrow{AB} \times \overrightarrow{AC}|$$

$$= \sqrt{(-1)^2 + (1)^2 + (-1)^2}$$

$$= \sqrt{1+1+1}$$

$$= \sqrt{3} \text{ sq units}$$

57. (a)

58. We have,

$$\vec{a} = \hat{i} - \hat{j} + 3\hat{k}$$

and $\vec{b} = 2\hat{i} - 7\hat{j} + \hat{k}$

$$\Rightarrow \vec{a} \times \vec{b} = \begin{vmatrix} \hat{i} & \hat{j} & \hat{k} \\ 1 & -1 & 3 \\ 2 & -7 & 1 \end{vmatrix}$$

$$= \hat{i}(-1+21) - \hat{j}(1-6) + \hat{k}(-7+2)$$

$$= 20\hat{i} + 5\hat{j} - 5\hat{k}$$

Now, $|\vec{a} \times \vec{b}| = \sqrt{400+25+25}$

$$= \sqrt{450} = 15\sqrt{2}$$

$\therefore$ The required area

$$= |\vec{a} \times \vec{b}|$$

$$= 15\sqrt{2} \text{ sq units}$$

59. (b) Given, $(2\hat{i} + 6\hat{j} + 27\hat{k}) \times (\hat{i} + \lambda\hat{j} + \mu\hat{k}) = \vec{0}$

$$\begin{vmatrix} \hat{i} & \hat{j} & \hat{k} \\ 2 & 6 & 27 \\ 1 & \lambda & \mu \end{vmatrix} = \vec{0}$$

$$\hat{i}(6\mu - 27\lambda) - \hat{j}(2\mu - 27) + \hat{k}(2\lambda - 6) = 0\hat{i} + 0\hat{j} + 0\hat{k}$$

On comparing both sides, we get

$$6\mu - 27\lambda = 0$$

$$\Rightarrow \quad 2\mu - 27 = 0$$

$$\Rightarrow \quad \mu = \frac{27}{2}$$

and $2\lambda - 6 = 0$

$$\therefore \quad \lambda = \frac{6}{2} = 3$$

Assertion-Reason

1. (b) Given, $\vec{a} = 3\hat{i} - \hat{j} + 2\hat{k}$

$$\vec{b} = \hat{i} + 7\hat{j} + 2\hat{k}$$

$$\vec{a} \cdot \vec{b} = (3\hat{i} - \hat{j} + 2\hat{k}) \cdot (\hat{i} + 7\hat{j} + 2\hat{k})$$

$$\Rightarrow \vec{a} \cdot \vec{b} = 3 - 7 + 4$$

$$\Rightarrow \vec{a} \cdot \vec{b} = 0$$

$$\because \vec{a} \cdot \vec{b} = 0$$

$$\therefore \vec{a} \perp \vec{b}$$

Assertion is true.

Now,

$\because \vec{a} \times \vec{b} = 0$

$\therefore \vec{a} \,||\, \vec{b}$

$\therefore$ Reason is true.

Both Assertion and Reason are true but Reason is not correct explanation of Assertion.

2. (c) Given, $\vec{a} = 2\hat{i} + 2\hat{j} + \hat{k}$

and $\vec{b} = \hat{i} + 3\hat{j} - \hat{k}$

$$\text{Projection of } \vec{a} \text{ along } \vec{b} = \frac{\vec{a} \cdot \vec{b}}{|\vec{b}|}$$

$$= \frac{(2\hat{i} + 2\hat{j} + \hat{k}) \cdot (\hat{i} + 3\hat{j} - \hat{k})}{\sqrt{1+9+1}}$$

$$= \frac{2+6-1}{\sqrt{11}}$$

$$= \frac{7}{\sqrt{11}} = \frac{7}{\sqrt{11}} \times \frac{\sqrt{11}}{\sqrt{11}}$$

$$\Rightarrow \text{Projection of } \vec{a} \text{ along } \vec{b} = \frac{7\sqrt{11}}{11}$$

$\therefore$ Assertion is true.

Now, Reason,

$$\text{Projection of } \vec{p} \text{ along } \vec{q} = \frac{\vec{p} \cdot \vec{q}}{|\vec{q}|}$$

Reason is false.

Assertion is true and Reason is false.

3. (d) Given, $\vec{a} = x\hat{i} + \hat{j} + 3\hat{k}$

and $\vec{b} = 2\hat{i} + 3\hat{j} - y\hat{k}$ and $\vec{a} \,||\, \vec{b}$,

$$x = \frac{2}{3}, y = -\frac{9}{2}$$

$$\frac{x}{2} = \frac{1}{3} = \frac{3}{-y}$$

$$x = \frac{2}{3}$$

and $y = \frac{-9}{1} = -9$

Assertion is false.

Now,

$\because \vec{a} = a_1\hat{i} + a_2\hat{j} + a_3\hat{k}$

$\vec{b} = b_1\hat{i} + b_2\hat{j} + b_3\hat{k}$ are parallel.

$$\therefore \frac{a_1}{b_1} = \frac{a_2}{b_2} = \frac{a_3}{b_3}$$

$\therefore$ Reason is true.

4. (d) Given, $\vec{a} = \hat{i} + \hat{j} + 2\hat{k}$

and $\vec{b} = 2\hat{i} - \hat{j} - \hat{k}$

$$\text{Area of triangle} = \frac{1}{2}|\vec{a} \times \vec{b}|$$

$$\Rightarrow \Delta = \frac{1}{2}|(\hat{i} + \hat{j} + 2\hat{k}) \times (2\hat{i} - \hat{j} - \hat{k})|$$

$$= \frac{1}{2}\begin{vmatrix} \hat{i} & \hat{j} & \hat{k} \\ 1 & 1 & 2 \\ 2 & -1 & -1 \end{vmatrix}$$

$$= \frac{1}{2}(\hat{i} + 5\hat{j} - 3\hat{k})$$

$$\Delta = \frac{1}{2}|\hat{i} + 5\hat{j} - 3\hat{k}|$$

$$\Delta = \frac{1}{2}\sqrt{1+25+9}$$

$$\Delta = \frac{\sqrt{35}}{2}$$

Assertion is false.

Area of parallelogram with sides $\vec{a}$ and $\vec{b}$ will be $|\vec{a} \times \vec{b}|$.

$\therefore$ Assertion is false and Reason is true.

5. (d) Given vector,

$\vec{a} = 3\hat{i} + \hat{j} - \hat{k},$

$\vec{b} = 2\hat{i} + \hat{j} + \hat{k}$

$\vec{c} = \vec{a} + \vec{b}$

$= 5\hat{i} + 2\hat{j}$

$\vec{d} = \vec{b} - \vec{a}$

$= -\hat{i} + 2\hat{k}$

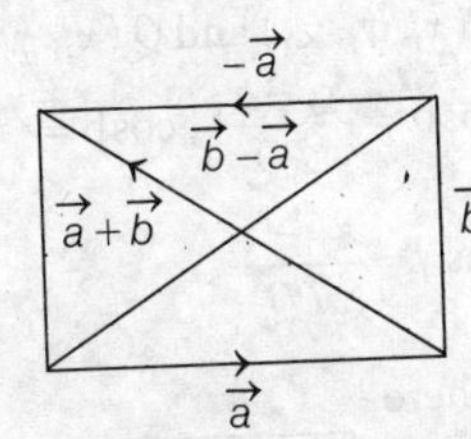

$$\cos\theta = \frac{\vec{c}\cdot\vec{d}}{|\vec{c}|\,|\vec{d}|}$$

$$= \left(\frac{-5+0-0}{\sqrt{29}\,\sqrt{5}}\right)$$

$$\neq \cos\frac{\pi}{3}$$

$\because \cos\frac{\pi}{3}$

Assertion is false.

Now, $\vec{a}$ and $\vec{b}$ are perpendicular

$\therefore \vec{a}\cdot\vec{b} = 0$

$\therefore$ Reason is true.

6. (c) Given points $A(2\vec{a} + \vec{b})$

$B(3\vec{a} + 2\vec{b})$

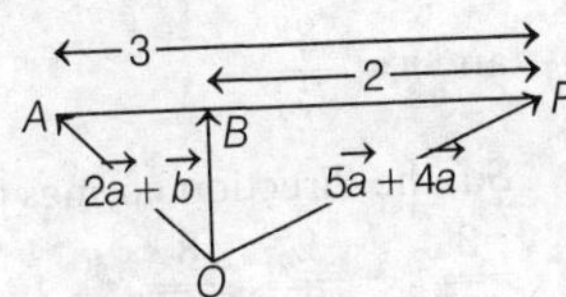

$$\vec{p} = \frac{3(3\vec{a} + 2\vec{b}) - 2(2\vec{a} + \vec{b})}{3-2}$$

$\Rightarrow \vec{p} = 5\vec{a} + 4\vec{b}$

$\therefore$ Assertion is true.

Now, mid-point between A and P

$$\frac{2\vec{a} + \vec{b} + 5\vec{a} + 4\vec{b}}{2} = \frac{7\vec{a} + 5\vec{b}}{2}$$

$\therefore$ Reason is false.

Assertion is true but reason is false.

7. (a) Given, $|\vec{a}| = |\vec{b}| = |\vec{c}| = 1$

and $\vec{a} + \vec{b} + \vec{c} = 0$

$\vec{a} + \vec{b} + \vec{c} = 0$

$\Rightarrow \vec{a}^2 + \vec{b}^2 + \vec{c}^2 + 2(\vec{a}\cdot\vec{b} + \vec{b}\cdot\vec{c} + \vec{c}\cdot\vec{a}) = 0$

$\Rightarrow 1 + 1 + 1 + 2(\vec{a}\cdot\vec{b} + \vec{b}\cdot\vec{c} + \vec{c}\cdot\vec{a}) = 0$

$\Rightarrow 3 + 2(\vec{a}\cdot\vec{b} + \vec{b}\cdot\vec{c} + \vec{c}\cdot\vec{a}) = 0$

$\Rightarrow \vec{a}\cdot\vec{b} + \vec{b}\cdot\vec{c} + \vec{c}\cdot\vec{a} = -\frac{3}{2}$

Assertion is correct and obtained with the help of given Reason which means Reason is also correct with correct explanation of Assertion.

8. (d) A physical quantity is said to be a vector quantity if it has both magnitude and direction. So, the reason statement is true. But the assertion statement is false. If the magnitude of displacement is zero, even then the displacement is termed as a vector quantity.

9. (c) **Explanation for the Assertion** The vectors having the same direction but different magnitude is known as parallel or like vectors.

$\therefore$ Assertion is true.

Explanation for the Reason Vector quantity has magnitude as well as specific direction.

$\therefore$ Reason is false.

10. (a) Given, $\vec{a}_1 = x\hat{i} - \hat{j} + \hat{k}$

and $\vec{a}_2 = \hat{i} + y\hat{j} + z\hat{k}$ are collinear.

$\because a_1$ and a_2 are collinear.

$\therefore \quad \frac{x}{1} = \frac{-1}{y} = \frac{1}{z} = \lambda \quad$ (say)

This gives $x = \lambda,\ y = -\frac{1}{\lambda},\ z = \frac{1}{\lambda}$

Then, unit vector parallel to vector $x\hat{i} + y\hat{j} + z\hat{k}$ will be

$$= \frac{\pm\left((\lambda)\,\hat{i} - \left(\frac{1}{\lambda}\right)\hat{j} + \left(\frac{1}{\lambda}\right)\hat{k}\right)}{\sqrt{\lambda^2 + \left(-\frac{1}{\lambda}\right)^2 + \left(\frac{1}{\lambda}\right)^2}}$$

$$= \pm\frac{(\lambda^2\hat{i} - \hat{j} + \hat{k})\,\lambda}{\lambda\sqrt{\lambda^4 + 2}}$$

$$= \pm\frac{(\lambda^2\hat{i} - \hat{j} + \hat{k})}{\sqrt{\lambda^4 + 2}}$$

Take, $\lambda = 1$, we get

$$\frac{\pm(\hat{i} - \hat{j} + \hat{k})}{\sqrt{3}}$$

$\therefore$ Assertion and Reason are true and Reason is the correct explanation of Assertion.

Case Based Questions

1. Here, $|\vec{F}_1| = \sqrt{(4)^2 + (0)^2} = 4$ KN

$|\vec{F}_2| = \sqrt{(-2)^2 + (4)^2} = \sqrt{20}$ KN

$|\vec{F}_3| = \sqrt{(-3)^2 + (-3)^2} = \sqrt{18}$ KN

(i) (a) Since, $\sqrt{20}$ is larger.

So, team B will win the game.

(ii) (b) Let $\vec{F}$ be the combined force

$\therefore \vec{F} = \vec{F}_1 + \vec{F}_2 + \vec{F}_3$

$\Rightarrow \vec{F} = (4\hat{i} + 0\hat{j}) + (-3\hat{i} - 3\hat{j}) + (-2\hat{i} + 4\hat{j})$

$\Rightarrow \vec{F} = -\hat{i} + \hat{j}$

$\Rightarrow |\vec{F}| = \sqrt{(-1)^2 + (1)^2}$

$= \sqrt{2} = 1.4$ KN

(iii) (c) We have,

$\vec{F} = -\hat{i} + \hat{j}$

$\therefore \theta = \tan^{-1}\left(\frac{F_y}{F_x}\right)$

$= \tan^{-1}\left(\frac{1}{-1}\right)$

$= \frac{3\pi}{4}$ radian

$= \frac{3}{4} \times 3.14$ radian

$= 2.355$

$= 2.4$ radian

(iv) (a) Magnitude of force of Team $B = \sqrt{20}$ KN

$= 2\sqrt{5}$ KN

2. (i) (c) Let OAB be a triangle such that

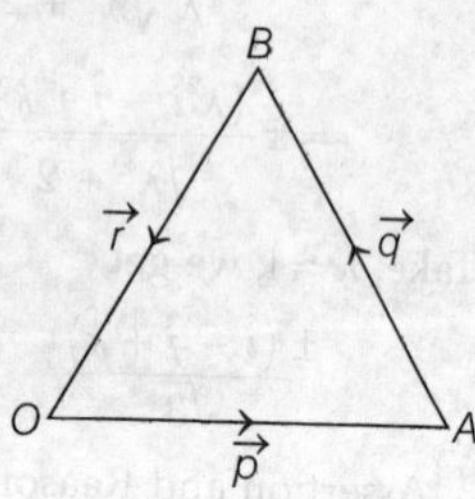

$\vec{AO} = -\vec{p}, \vec{AB} = \vec{q}, \vec{BO} = \vec{r}$

Now, $\vec{q} + \vec{r} = \vec{AB} + \vec{BO}$

$= \vec{AO} = -\vec{p}$

(ii) (c) From triangle law of vector add.

$\vec{AC} + \vec{BD} = \vec{AB} + \vec{BC} + \vec{BC} + \vec{CD}$

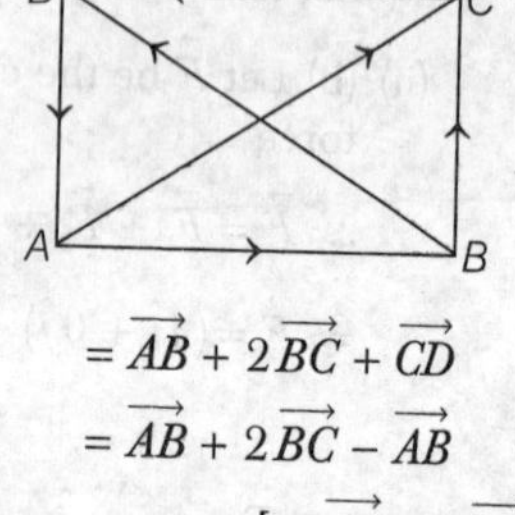

$= \vec{AB} + 2\vec{BC} + \vec{CD}$

$= \vec{AB} + 2\vec{BC} - \vec{AB}$

$[\because \vec{AB} = -\vec{CD}]$

$= 2\vec{BC}$

(iii) (b) In ΔABC, $\vec{AC} = 2\vec{a} + 2\vec{b}$ ...(i)

and in ΔABD,

$2\vec{b} = 2\vec{a} + \vec{BD}$ ...(ii)

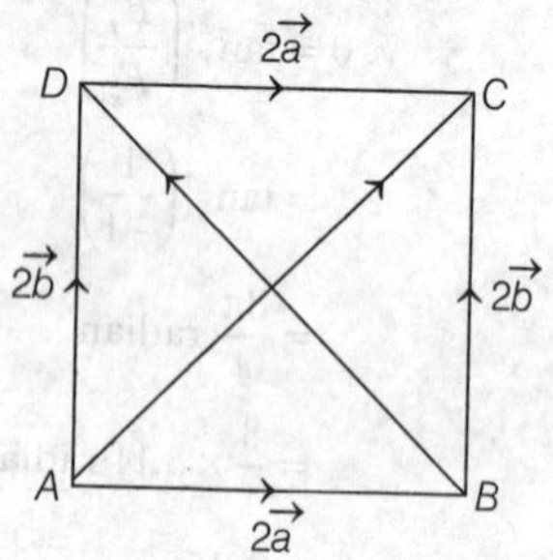

On adding Eqs. (i) and (ii), we get

$\vec{AC} + 2\vec{b} = 4\vec{a} + \vec{BD} + 2\vec{b}$

$\Rightarrow \vec{AC} - \vec{BD} = 4\vec{a}$

(iv) (d) In ΔABC,

$\vec{BA} + \vec{AC} = \vec{BC}$ ...(i)

In ΔBCD,

$\vec{BC} + \vec{CD} = \vec{BD}$ ...(ii)

From Eqs. (i) and (ii), we get

$\vec{BA} + \vec{AC} = \vec{BD} - \vec{CD}$

$\vec{BA} + \vec{CD} = \vec{BD} - \vec{AC}$

$= \vec{BD} + \vec{CA}$

Chapter-11

Three Dimensional Geometry

1. $l^2 + m^2 + n^2 = 1$

or $\cos^2\alpha + \cos^2\beta + \cos^2\gamma = 1$

2. $\sin^2\alpha + \sin^2\beta + \sin^2\gamma$

$= 1 - \cos^2\alpha + 1 - \cos^2\beta + 1 - \cos^2\gamma$

$= 3 - (\cos^2\alpha + \cos^2\beta + \cos^2\gamma)$

$= 3 - 1 = 2$

Therefore,

$\sin^2\alpha + \sin^2\beta + \sin^2\gamma = 2$

3. (i) The direction cosines of a line is given by

$l = \cos\alpha, m = \cos\beta, n = \cos\gamma$

Then, $l = \cos 90°, m = \cos 60°,$

$n = \cos 30° \Rightarrow l = 0,$

$m = \frac{1}{2}, n = \frac{\sqrt{3}}{2}$

So, the direction cosines are

$0, \frac{1}{2}, \frac{\sqrt{3}}{2}.$

(ii) Direction cosines are

$\frac{-18}{\sqrt{(-18)^2 + (12)^2 + (-4)^2}},$

$\frac{12}{\sqrt{(-18)^2 + (12)^2 + (-4)^2}},$

$\frac{-4}{\sqrt{(-18)^2 + (12)^2 + (-4)^2}}$

$= \frac{-18}{\sqrt{484}}, \frac{12}{\sqrt{484}}, \frac{-4}{\sqrt{484}}$

$= \frac{-18}{22}, \frac{12}{22}, \frac{-4}{22}$

$= \frac{-9}{11}, \frac{6}{11}, \frac{-2}{11}$

4. $x_2 - x_1, y_2 - y_1, z_2 - z_1$

or $x_1 - x_2, y_1 - y_2, z_1 - z_2$

5. $\cos\alpha = \frac{x_2 - x_1}{PQ}, \cos\beta = \frac{y_2 - y_1}{PQ}$

and $\cos\gamma = \frac{z_2 - z_1}{PQ}$

6. (i) The direction cosines of the line segment joining point $P(x_1, y_1, z_1)$ and $Q(x_2, y_2, z_2)$ is

$\cos\alpha = \frac{x_2 - x_1}{PQ}, \cos\beta = \frac{y_2 - y_1}{PQ},$

$\cos\gamma = \frac{z_2 - z_1}{PQ},$

where

$PQ = \sqrt{(x_2 - x_1)^2 + (y_2 - y_1)^2 + (z_2 - z_1)^2}$

So, $PQ = \sqrt{(1+2)^2 + (2-4)^2 + (3+5)^2}$

$= \sqrt{77}$

Therefore, the direction cosines of a line passing through the points $(-2, 4, -5)$ and $(1, 2, 3)$ are

$l = \frac{x_2 - x_1}{PQ}, m = \frac{y_2 - y_1}{PQ},$

$n = \frac{z_2 - z_1}{PQ}$

i.e. $l = \frac{3}{\sqrt{77}}, m = \frac{2}{\sqrt{77}}.$

and $n = \frac{8}{\sqrt{77}}$

So, the direction cosines are

$\frac{3}{\sqrt{77}}, -\frac{2}{\sqrt{77}}, \frac{8}{\sqrt{77}}.$

(ii) The direction cosines of the line segment joining point $(2, -4, 6)$ and $(2, 3, 4)$.

Direction cosines are

$\frac{2-2}{\sqrt{0+49+4}}, \frac{3-(-4)}{\sqrt{0+49+4}},$

$\frac{4-6}{\sqrt{0+49+4}}$

i.e. $\frac{0}{\sqrt{53}}, \frac{7}{\sqrt{53}}, \frac{-2}{\sqrt{53}}.$

7. The X-axis makes angles 0°, 90°, and 90° respectively with X, Y and Z-axes.

Therefore, the direction cosines of X-axis are $\cos 0°, \cos 90°, \cos 90°$ i.e. 1, 0, 0.

Similarly, direction cosines of Y-axis and Z-axis are 0, 1, 0 and 0, 0, 1 respectively.

8. (True)

Direction ratios of line joining A and B are

$1-2, -2-3, 3+4$

i.e. $-1, -5, 7$.

The direction ratios of line joining B and C are

$3-1, 8+2, -11-3$

i.e. $2, 10, -14$.

It is clear that direction ratios of AB and BC are proportional.

Hence, AB is parallel to BC.

Here, point B is common to both AB and BC.

Therefore, A, B, C are collinear points.

9. (c) We have, $\vec{a} = 5\hat{i} + 2\hat{j} - 4\hat{k}$

and $\vec{b} = 3\hat{i} + 2\hat{j} - 8\hat{k}$

Therefore, vector equation of the line is

$\vec{r} = 5\hat{i} + 2\hat{j} - 4\hat{k} + \lambda(3\hat{i} + 2\hat{j} - 8\hat{k})$

The correct equation is

$\vec{r} = 5\hat{i} + 2\hat{j} - 4\hat{k} + \lambda(3\hat{i} + 2\hat{j} - 8\hat{k})$

10. We have, $\vec{a} = \hat{i} + 2\hat{j} - 3\hat{k}$

and $\vec{b} = 3\hat{i} + 2\hat{j} - 2\hat{k}$

Therefore, vector equation of the line is

$\vec{r} = \hat{i} + 2\hat{j} - 3\hat{k} + \lambda(3\hat{i} + 2\hat{j} - 2\hat{k})$

Now, $\vec{r}$ is the position vector of any point $P(x, y, z)$ on the line.

Therefore,

$$x\hat{i} + y\hat{j} + z\hat{k} = \hat{i} + 2\hat{j} - 3\hat{k} + \lambda(3\hat{i} + 2\hat{j} - 2\hat{k})$$

$$\Rightarrow x\hat{i} + y\hat{j} + z\hat{k} = (1+3\lambda)\hat{i} + (2+2\lambda)\hat{j} + (-3-2\lambda)\hat{k}$$

On eliminating λ, we get

$$\frac{x-1}{3} = \frac{y-2}{2} = \frac{z+3}{-2},$$

which is the required equation.

11. (c) A. The direction ratios of line through the points $(1, -1, 2)$, $(3, 4, -2)$ are $2, 5, -4$ and direction ratios of the line through the points $(0, 3, 2)$, $(3, 5, 6)$ are $3, 2, 4$.

Now, $a_1a_2 + b_1b_2 + c_1c_2$

$$= 2\times3 + 5\times2 + (-4\times4)$$
$$= 6+10-16$$
$$= 0$$

B. The direction ratios of the line through the points $(4, 7, 8)$, $(2, 3, 4)$ are $-2, -4, -4$ and direction ratios of the line through the points $(-1, -2, 1)$, $(1, 2, 5)$ are $2, 4, 4$.

Now, two lines are parallel, if

$$\frac{a_1}{a_2} = \frac{b_1}{b_2} = \frac{c_1}{c_2},$$

which satisfies for the above lines.

C. Let (a_1, b_1, c_1), (a_2, b_2, c_2) and (a_3, b_3, c_3) represent the direction cosines of the given lines.

Then, $a_1a_2 + b_1b_2 + c_1c_2$

$$= \frac{12}{13}\left(\frac{4}{13}\right) + \left(\frac{-3}{13}\right)\left(\frac{12}{13}\right) + \left(\frac{-4}{13}\right)\left(\frac{3}{13}\right)$$

$$= \frac{48-36-12}{169} = 0$$

$a_2a_3 + b_2b_3 + c_2c_3$

$$= \frac{4}{13}\left(\frac{3}{13}\right) + \frac{12}{13}\left(-\frac{4}{13}\right) + \frac{3}{13}\left(\frac{12}{13}\right)$$

$$= \frac{12-48+36}{169} = 0$$

$a_3a_1 + b_3b_1 + c_3c_1$

$$= \frac{3}{13}\left(\frac{12}{13}\right) + \left(\frac{-4}{13}\right)\left(\frac{-3}{13}\right) + \frac{12}{13}\left(\frac{-4}{13}\right)$$

$$= \frac{36+12-48}{169} = 0$$

12. (i) We have,

$$\frac{x+3}{2} = \frac{y-5}{4} = \frac{z+6}{2}$$

Compare with

$$\frac{x-x_1}{a} = \frac{y-y_1}{b} = \frac{z-z_1}{c}$$

gives $a = 2, b = 4, c = 2$

and $x_1 = -3, y_1 = 5, z_1 = -6$

Thus, the required line is passing through the point $(-3, 5, -6)$ and is parallel to the vector $2\hat{i} + 4\hat{j} + 2\hat{k}$.

Then, $\vec{r} = -3\hat{i} + 5\hat{j} - 6\hat{k} + \lambda(2\hat{i} + 4\hat{j} + 2\hat{k})$

(ii) The given equation in standard form is $\dfrac{x-5}{-3} = \dfrac{y-(-4)}{7} = \dfrac{z-6}{2}$

So, $a = -3, b = 7, c = 2$

and $\vec{r} = 5\hat{i} - 4\hat{j} + 6\hat{k}$

Vector equation is

$\vec{r} = 5\hat{i} - 4\hat{j} + 6\hat{k} + \lambda(-3\hat{i} + 7\hat{j} + 2\hat{k})$

13. (c) Since, the line passes through $(-2, 4, -5)$ and line is parallel to line $\dfrac{x+3}{3} = \dfrac{y-4}{5} = \dfrac{z+8}{6}$

So, $a = 3, b = 5, c = 6$

Equation of line in the cartesian form is

$$\frac{x-(-2)}{3} = \frac{y-4}{5} = \frac{z-(-5)}{6}$$

$$\frac{x+2}{3} = \frac{y-4}{5} = \frac{z+5}{6}$$

14. (i) Here, $\vec{b_1} = \hat{i} + 2\hat{j} + 2\hat{k}$

and $\vec{b_2} = 3\hat{i} + 2\hat{j} + 6\hat{k}$

The angle is given by

$$\cos\theta = \left|\frac{\vec{b_1}\cdot\vec{b_2}}{|\vec{b_1}||\vec{b_2}|}\right|$$

$$= \left|\frac{(\hat{i} + 2\hat{j} + 2\hat{k})\cdot(3\hat{i} + 2\hat{j} + 6\hat{k})}{\sqrt{1+4+4}\sqrt{9+4+36}}\right|$$

$$\cos\theta = \left|\frac{3+4+12}{3\times7}\right| = \left|\frac{19}{21}\right|$$

$$\Rightarrow \theta = \cos^{-1}\frac{19}{21}$$

(ii) The direction ratios of the first line are 3, 5, 4 and that of second line are 1, 1, 2.

Then,

$$\cos\theta = \left|\frac{3\times1 + 5\times1 + 4\times2}{\sqrt{3^2+5^2+4^2}\sqrt{1^2+1^2+2^2}}\right|$$

$$\cos\theta = \left|\frac{16}{\sqrt{50}\sqrt{6}}\right| = \frac{8\sqrt{3}}{15}$$

$$\Rightarrow \theta = \cos^{-1}\left(\frac{8\sqrt{3}}{15}\right)$$

15. Two lines are perpendicular, if $a_1a_2 + b_1b_2 + c_1c_2 = 0$

The given lines

$$\frac{1-x}{3} = \frac{7y-14}{2p} = \frac{z-3}{2}$$

and $\frac{7-7x}{3p} = \frac{y-5}{1} = \frac{6-z}{5}$

can be written as

$$\frac{x-1}{-3} = \frac{y-2}{2p/7} = \frac{z-3}{2}$$

Here, $a_1 = -3, b_1 = \frac{2p}{7}, c_1 = 2$

$a_2 = \frac{-3p}{7}, b_2 = 1, c_2 = -5$

and $\frac{x-1}{-3p/7} = \frac{y-5}{1} = \frac{z-6}{-5}$

$$\therefore \left\{(-3) \times \frac{(-3p)}{7}\right\} + \left(\frac{2p}{7} \times 1\right) + \{2 \times (-5)\} = 0$$

$$\frac{9p}{7} + \frac{2p}{7} - 10 = 0 \Rightarrow p = \frac{70}{11}$$

16. (i) On comparing given equations with $\vec{r} = \vec{a}_1 + \lambda \vec{b}_1$ and $\vec{r} = \vec{a}_2 + \mu \vec{b}_2$, we get

$$\vec{a}_1 = \hat{i} + \hat{j},\ \vec{b}_1 = 2\hat{i} - \hat{j} + \hat{k}$$

and $\vec{a}_2 = 2\hat{i} + \hat{j} - \hat{k}$,

$$\vec{b}_2 = 3\hat{i} - 5\hat{j} + 2\hat{k}$$

Therefore, $\vec{a}_2 - \vec{a}_1 = \hat{i} - \hat{k}$

and $\vec{b}_1 \times \vec{b}_2 = \begin{vmatrix} \hat{i} & \hat{j} & \hat{k} \\ 2 & -1 & 1 \\ 3 & -5 & 2 \end{vmatrix}$

$$= 3\hat{i} - \hat{j} - 7\hat{k}$$

So, $|\vec{b}_1 \times \vec{b}_2| = \sqrt{9 + 1 + 49} = \sqrt{59}$

Hence, $d = \left|\frac{(\vec{b}_1 \times \vec{b}_2) \cdot (\vec{a}_2 - \vec{a}_1)}{|(\vec{b}_1 \times \vec{b}_2)|}\right|$

$$= \left|\frac{3 - 0 + 7}{\sqrt{59}}\right| = \frac{10}{\sqrt{59}}$$

$$= \frac{10\sqrt{59}}{59} \text{ units}$$

(ii) Given vector equations are

$$\vec{r} = 2\hat{i} - 5\hat{j} + \hat{k} + \lambda (3\hat{i} + 2\hat{j} + 6\hat{k})$$

and $\vec{r} = 7\hat{i} - 6\hat{k} + \mu(\hat{i} + 2\hat{j} + 2\hat{k})$

Here, $\vec{a}_1 = 2\hat{i} - 5\hat{j} + \hat{k}$,

$$\vec{b}_1 = 3\hat{i} + 2\hat{j} + 6\hat{k}$$

and $\vec{a}_2 = 7\hat{i} - 6\hat{k}$

$$\vec{b}_2 = \hat{i} + 2\hat{j} + 2\hat{k}$$

Therefore,

$$\vec{a}_2 - \vec{a}_1 = 5\hat{i} + 5\hat{j} - 7\hat{k}$$

and $\vec{b}_1 \times \vec{b}_2 = \begin{vmatrix} \hat{i} & \hat{j} & \hat{k} \\ 3 & 2 & 6 \\ 1 & 2 & 2 \end{vmatrix}$

$$= -8\hat{i} + 4\hat{k}$$

So, $|\vec{b}_1 \times \vec{b}_2| = \sqrt{64 + 0 + 16} = 4\sqrt{5}$

Hence,

$$d = \left|\frac{(-8\hat{i} + 4\hat{k}) \cdot (5\hat{i} + 5\hat{j} - 7\hat{k})}{4\sqrt{5}}\right|$$

$$= \left|\frac{-40 + 0 - 28}{4\sqrt{5}}\right|$$

$$= \left|\frac{-68}{4\sqrt{5}}\right| = \frac{17\sqrt{5}}{5} \text{ units}$$

17. Here, $\vec{a}_1 = \hat{i} + 2\hat{j} - 4\hat{k}$,

$$\vec{a}_2 = 3\hat{i} + 3\hat{j} - 5\hat{k}$$

and $\vec{b} = 2\hat{i} + 3\hat{j} + 6\hat{k}$

$$\vec{c}_2 - \vec{a}_1 = 2\hat{i} + \hat{j} - \hat{k}$$

Therefore, distance between the parallel lines is

$$d = \left|\frac{\vec{b} \times (\vec{a}_2 - \vec{a}_1)}{|\vec{b}|}\right|$$

$$d = \left|\frac{\begin{vmatrix} \hat{i} & \hat{j} & \hat{k} \\ 2 & 3 & 6 \\ 2 & 1 & -1 \end{vmatrix}}{\sqrt{4 + 9 + 36}}\right|$$

$$= \frac{|-9\hat{i} + 14\hat{j} - 4\hat{k}|}{\sqrt{49}}$$

$$= \frac{\sqrt{293}}{7} \text{ units}$$

18. (i) The shortest distance between the lines is

$$d = \left|\frac{\begin{vmatrix} x_2 - x_1 & y_2 - y_1 & z_2 - z_1 \\ a_1 & b_1 & c_1 \\ a_2 & b_2 & c_2 \end{vmatrix}}{\sqrt{(a_1b_2 - a_2b_1)^2 + (b_1c_2 - b_2c_1)^2 + (c_1a_2 - c_2a_1)^2}}\right|$$

We have, $\frac{x+1}{7} = \frac{y+1}{-6} = \frac{z+1}{1}$

or $\frac{x-(-1)}{7} = \frac{y-(-1)}{-6} = \frac{z-(-1)}{1}$

gives $x_1 = -1, y_1 = -1, z_1 = -1$

$$a_1 = 7, b_1 = 6, c_1 = 1$$

and $\frac{x-3}{1} = \frac{y-5}{-2} = \frac{z-7}{1}$

gives $x_2 = 3, y_2 = 5, z_2 = 7$

$a_2 = 1, b_2 = -2, c_2 = 1$

So, $d = \left|\frac{\begin{vmatrix} 4 & 6 & 8 \\ 7 & -6 & 1 \\ 1 & -2 & 1 \end{vmatrix}}{\sqrt{(-14+6)^2 + (-6+2)^2 + (1-7)^2}}\right|$

$$= \left|\frac{-16 - 36 - 64}{\sqrt{116}}\right|$$

$$d = |-\sqrt{116}| = 2\sqrt{29} \text{ units}$$

(ii) We have,

$$\frac{x-1}{6} = \frac{y-1}{7} = \frac{z-1}{1}$$

$x_1 = 1, y_1 = 1$ and $z_1 = 1$

$a_1 = 6, b_1 = 7, c_1 = 1$

$$\frac{x+3}{1} = \frac{y+5}{2} = \frac{z-7}{1}$$

$x_2 = -3, y_2 = -5$ and $z_2 = 7$

So,

$$d = \left|\frac{\begin{vmatrix} -4 & -6 & 6 \\ 6 & 7 & 1 \\ 1 & 2 & 1 \end{vmatrix}}{\sqrt{(12-7)^2 + (7-2)^2 + (1-6)^2}}\right|$$

$$d = \left|\frac{-4(7-2) + 6(6-1) + 6(12-7)}{\sqrt{25 + 25 + 25}}\right|$$

$$d = \left|\frac{-20 + 30 + 30}{5\sqrt{3}}\right|$$

$$= \frac{40}{5\sqrt{3}} = \frac{8\sqrt{3}}{3} \text{ units}$$

Assertion-Reason

1. (d) Since, direction cosines of a line are the cosines of the angels made by the line with the positive directions of the coordinate axes.

$\therefore$ Assertion is false.

Since, the slope of line $x - 2 = 0$ is ∞.

The slope of line $\sqrt{3}x - y - 2 = 0$ is $\sqrt{3}$.

Let $m_1 = \infty, m_2 = \sqrt{3}$ and the angle between the given lines is θ, then

$\Rightarrow \quad \tan\theta = \left|\dfrac{m_2 - m_1}{1 + m_1 m_2}\right|$

$\Rightarrow \quad \tan\theta = \left|\dfrac{\dfrac{m_2}{m_1} - 1}{\dfrac{1}{m_1} + m_2}\right|$

$\Rightarrow \quad \tan\theta = \dfrac{1}{\sqrt{3}}$

$\Rightarrow \quad \theta = 30°$

$\therefore$ Reason is true.

2. (b) Given points are $A(2, 3, -4)$, $B(1, -2, 3)$ and $C(3, 8, -11)$.

Direction ratios of line joining A and B are

$(1-2, -2-3, 3-(-4))$

i.e. $(-1, -5, 7)$.

Direction ratios of line joining B and C are

$(3-1, 8+2, -11-3)$

i.e. $(2, 10, -14)$.

Now, ratios of direction ratios of AB and BC are

$\dfrac{-1}{2}, \dfrac{-5}{10}, \dfrac{7}{-14}$

i.e. $-\dfrac{1}{2}, -\dfrac{1}{2}, -\dfrac{1}{2}$.

Thus, the direction ratios of AB and BC are proportional. So, AB is parallel to BC. But B is common to both AB and BC.

Hence, A, B and C are collinear points.

Let direction cosines of the line be l, m and n.

Given, $\alpha = 90°$, $\beta = 135°$ and $\gamma = 45°$

Then, $l = \cos\alpha = \cos 90° = 0$

$m = \cos\beta = \cos 135° = \dfrac{-1}{\sqrt{2}}$

and $n = \cos\gamma = \cos 45° = \dfrac{1}{\sqrt{2}}$

Hence, the direction cosines of a line are $0, \dfrac{-1}{\sqrt{2}}$ and $\dfrac{1}{\sqrt{2}}$.

3. (a) Given, direction ratios are $(-2, 1, -2)$ i.e. $a = -2$, $b = 1$ and $c = -2$.

Then, $\sqrt{a^2 + b^2 + c^2}$

$= \sqrt{(-2)^2 + 1^2 + (-2)^2}$

$= \sqrt{9} = 3$

Now, direction cosines are

$\dfrac{a}{\sqrt{a^2+b^2+c^2}} = -\dfrac{2}{3}$

$\dfrac{b}{\sqrt{a^2+b^2+c^2}} = \dfrac{1}{3}$

$\dfrac{b}{\sqrt{a^2+b^2+c^2}} = \dfrac{-2}{3}$

4. (d) We know that the cartesian equation of a line passing through the two points $A(x_1, y_1, z_1)$ and $B(x_2, y_2, z_2)$ is given by

$$\frac{x - x_1}{x_2 - x_1} = \frac{y - y_1}{y_2 - y_1} = \frac{z - z_1}{z_2 - z_1}$$

Here, $x_1 = -1$, $x_2 = 2$, $y_1 = 1$, $y_2 = 4$, $z_1 = 2$ and $z_2 = 5$

$\therefore$ The cartesian equation of the line is

$$\frac{x-(-1)}{2-(-1)} = \frac{y-1}{4-1} = \frac{z-2}{5-2}$$

$\Rightarrow \quad \dfrac{x+1}{3} = \dfrac{y-1}{3} = \dfrac{z-2}{3}$

i.e. $\quad \dfrac{x+1}{1} = \dfrac{y-1}{1} = \dfrac{z-2}{1}$

5. (d) Given equation of lines are

$\vec{r} = -\hat{i} + 4\hat{j} + 3\hat{k} + \lambda(4\hat{i} + \hat{j} + \hat{k})$

and

$\vec{r} = (-4\hat{i} + \hat{j}) + \mu(5\hat{i} + 2\hat{j} + \hat{k})$

On comparing with standard equation $\vec{r} = a + \lambda b$, we get

$\vec{a}_1 = -\hat{i} + 4\hat{j} + 3\hat{k}, \vec{b}_1 = 4\hat{i} + \hat{j} + \hat{k}$

and

$\vec{a}_2 = (-4\hat{i} + \hat{j}), \vec{b}_2 = 5\hat{i} + 2\hat{j} + \hat{k}$

The condition, for the shortest distance between given lines is zero, is

$(\vec{a}_2 - \vec{a}_1)\cdot(\vec{b}_1 \times \vec{b}_2) = 0 \quad \ldots \text{(i)}$

Now, $\vec{a}_2 - \vec{a}_1 = (-4\hat{i} + \hat{j}) - (-\hat{i} + 4\hat{j} + 3\hat{k})$

$= -3\hat{i} - 3\hat{j} - 3\hat{k}$

and $\vec{b}_1 \times \vec{b}_2 = \begin{vmatrix} \hat{i} & \hat{j} & \hat{k} \\ 4 & 1 & 1 \\ 5 & 2 & 1 \end{vmatrix}$

$= \hat{i}(1-2) - \hat{j}(4-5) + \hat{k}(8-5)$

$= \hat{i} + \hat{j} + 3\hat{k} = -\hat{i} + \hat{j} + 3\hat{k}$

From Eq. (i), we get

$(-3\hat{i} - 3\hat{j} - 3\hat{k})\cdot(-\hat{i} + \hat{j} + 3\hat{k}) = 0$

$\Rightarrow \quad 3 - 3 - 9$

$\Rightarrow \quad -9 \neq 0$

A is false.

6. (c) Since. $P = (5, y, z)$

Equation of line joining $(3, 2, -1)$ and $(6, -4, -2)$ is

$$\frac{x-3}{6-3} = \frac{y-2}{-4-2} = \frac{z+1}{-2+1}$$

i.e. $\dfrac{x-3}{3} = \dfrac{y-2}{-6} = \dfrac{z+1}{-1}$

So, if point P lies on the line, then it must satisfy the above equation

$\therefore \dfrac{5-3}{3} = \dfrac{y-2}{-6} = \dfrac{z+1}{-1}$

$\Rightarrow \quad \dfrac{y-2}{-6} = \dfrac{2}{3}$

$\Rightarrow \quad y - 2 = -4$

$\Rightarrow \quad y = -2$

Hence, Assertion is true.

Since, the two lines $x = ay + b$, $z = cy + d$ and $x = a'y + b'$, $z = c'y + d'$ will be perpendicular, iff $aa' + cc' + 1 = 0$.

$\therefore$ Reason is false.

7. (a) Vector equation of a line passing through two points with position vectors $\vec{a}$ and $\vec{b}$ is

$\vec{r} = \vec{a} + \lambda(\vec{b} - \vec{a})$.

Given, two points are $A(-1, 0, 2)$ and $B(3, 4, 6)$.

So, $\vec{a} = -\hat{i} + 2\hat{k}$ and

$\vec{b} = 3\hat{i} + 4\hat{j} + 6\hat{k}$

$\therefore \vec{r} = \vec{a} + \lambda(\vec{b} - \vec{a})$

$= (-\hat{i} + 2\hat{k}) + \lambda[(3\hat{i} + 4\hat{j} + 6\hat{k} - (-\hat{i} + 2\hat{k})]$

$= -\hat{i} + 2\hat{k} + \lambda(4\hat{i} + 4\hat{j} + 4\hat{k})$

8. (b) Given, equation of line

$$\frac{x-2}{3} = \frac{y-1}{2} = \frac{3-z}{-1}$$

Here, $\vec{a} = 2\hat{i} + \hat{j} + 3\hat{k}$ and

$\vec{b} = 3\hat{i} + 2\hat{j} + \hat{k}$

So, the vector equation of the given line is given by $\vec{r} = \vec{a} + \lambda\vec{b}$

i.e.

$\vec{r} = 2\hat{i} + \hat{j} + 3\hat{k} + \lambda(3\hat{i} + 2\hat{j} + \hat{k})$

Given, point $(2, 1, 3)$ and line

$$\frac{x-3}{1} = \frac{y-2}{2} = \frac{z-4}{-2}$$

So, the required cartesian equation of line is

$$\frac{x-2}{1} = \frac{y-1}{2} = \frac{z-3}{-2}$$

i.e. $2x - 4 = y - 1 = 3 - z$.

9. (a) We know that vector equation of a line passing through the point with position vector $\vec{a}$ and parallel to the vector $\vec{b}$ is $\vec{r} = \vec{a} + \lambda\vec{b}$.

Here, point is (1, 1, 0) and vector is $\hat{i} + \hat{j} + \hat{k}$.

So, the required equation is given by $\vec{r} = \vec{a} + \lambda\vec{b}$

i.e. $\vec{r} = (\hat{i} + \hat{j}) + \lambda(\hat{i} + \hat{j} + \hat{k})$.

10. (a) Here, the direction vectors are $\vec{a} = 2\hat{i} - \hat{j} + 3\hat{k}$ and $\vec{b} = 6\hat{i} - 3\hat{j} + 9\hat{k}$

We have,

$$\frac{2}{6} = \frac{-1}{-3} = \frac{3}{9} = \frac{1}{3}$$

$$\text{Now, } \vec{a} \times \vec{b} = \begin{vmatrix} \hat{i} & \hat{j} & \hat{k} \\ 2 & -1 & 3 \\ 6 & -3 & 9 \end{vmatrix}$$

$$= \hat{i}(-9+9) - \hat{j}(18-18) + \hat{k}(-6+6) = 0$$

$\Rightarrow \quad \vec{a} \times \vec{b} = 0$

$\therefore \quad \vec{a} = 0$ or $\vec{b} = 0$

or $\quad \vec{a} \,||\, \vec{b}$

Case Based Questions

1. (i) (b) The lines along which motor cycle A is running is $\vec{r} = \lambda(\hat{i} + 2\hat{j} - \hat{k})$, which can be written as

$$x\hat{i} + y\hat{j} + z\hat{k} = \lambda\hat{i} + 2\lambda\hat{j} - \lambda\hat{k}$$

$$\Rightarrow x = \lambda, y = 2\lambda, z = -\lambda$$

$$\Rightarrow \frac{x}{1} = \lambda, \frac{y}{2} = \lambda, \frac{z}{-1} = \lambda$$

Thus, the required cartesian equation is

$$\frac{x}{1} = \frac{y}{2} = \frac{z}{-1},$$

(ii) (c) Clearly, direction ratios of the required line are <1, 2, −1>.

$\therefore$ Direction cosines are

$$< \frac{1}{\sqrt{1^2 + 2^2 + (-1)^2}}, \frac{2}{\sqrt{1^2 + 2^2 + (-1)^2}}, \frac{-1}{\sqrt{1^2 + 2^2 + (-1)^2}} >$$

$$\text{i. e.} < \frac{1}{\sqrt{6}}, \frac{2}{\sqrt{6}}, \frac{-1}{\sqrt{6}} >$$

(iii) (c) The line along which motorcycle B is running is $\vec{r} = (3\hat{i} + 3\hat{j}) + \mu(2\hat{i} + \hat{j} + \hat{k})$, which is parallel to the vector $2\hat{i} + \hat{j} + \hat{k}$.

$\therefore$ Direction ratios of the line are < 2, 1, 1 >

(iv) (a) Here, $\vec{a}_1 = 0\hat{i} + 0\hat{j} + 0\hat{k}$,

$\vec{a}_2 = 3\hat{i} + 3\hat{j}$,

$\vec{b}_1 = \hat{i} + 2\hat{j} - \hat{k}, \vec{b}_2 = 2\hat{i} + \hat{j} + \hat{k}$

$\therefore \vec{a}_2 - \vec{a}_1 = 3\hat{i} + 3\hat{j}$

$$\text{and } \vec{b}_1 \times \vec{b}_2 = \begin{vmatrix} \hat{i} & \hat{j} & \hat{k} \\ 1 & 2 & -1 \\ 2 & 1 & 1 \end{vmatrix}$$

$$= \hat{i}(2+1) - \hat{j}(1+2) + \hat{k}(1-4)$$

$$= 3\hat{i} - 3\hat{j} - 3\hat{k}$$

$$\text{Now, } (\vec{a}_2 - \vec{a}_1)(\vec{b}_1 \times \vec{b}_2) = (3\hat{i} + 3\hat{j})(3\hat{i} - 3\hat{j} - 3\hat{k})$$

$$= 9 - 9$$

$$= 0$$

Hence, the shortest distance between the given lines is 0 unit.

2. (i) The direction ratios of OA are <1 − 0, 0 − 0, 0 − 0>,

i.e.< 1, 0, 0>

(ii) Equation of diagonal OB' is

$$\frac{x-0}{1} = \frac{y-0}{2} = \frac{z-0}{3}$$

$$\text{i.e. } \frac{x}{1} = \frac{y}{2} = \frac{z}{3}$$

(iii) Direction ratios of AB are <1 − 1, 2 − 0, 0 − 0 >

i.e. < 0, 2, 0 >

$\therefore$ Direction cosines are

$$< \frac{0}{\sqrt{0^2 + 2^2 + 0^2}}, \frac{2}{\sqrt{0^2 + 2^2 + 0^2}}, \frac{0}{\sqrt{0^2 + 2^2 + 0^2}} >$$

$$\text{i.e. } < 0, \frac{1}{2}, 0 >$$

Chapter-12

Linear Programming Problems

1. (a)
2. Problem contains the word maximise, then the dealer gain profit.
3. Objective function
4. Feasible region
5. (False)

Let R be the feasible region and $Z = ax + by$ be the objective function, when x and y are decision variables and a, b are constants, then the optimum value subject to constraints must occur at a corner point of the feasible region.

6. (a)
7. (a) **Statement I** A set of values of decision variables of LPP satisfying the constraints and the non-negative restrictions is called feasible solution. Every point in the feasible region is a feasible solution of the given LPP.

Statement II Any point in feasible region that gives the optimal value (maximum or minimum) of the objective function is called optimal solution.

8. (i) Outside
(ii) Optimal solution
(iii) Infinite
(iv) A corner point of a feasible region is a point in the region, which is the intersection of two boundary lines.
(v) If the feasible region (let R) is unbounded, then a maximum or minimum value of the objective function may not exist or *vice-versa*.

9. (b) The common region determined by the constraints and non-negative restriction is called feasible region.

A feasible region of a system of linear inequalities is said to be bounded feasible region, if it can be enclosed within a circle.

A feasible region of a system of linear inequalities is said to be unbounded feasible region, if it cannot be enclosed within a circle.

10. (b) The shaded region in the following graph is the feasible region determined by the given system of constraints.

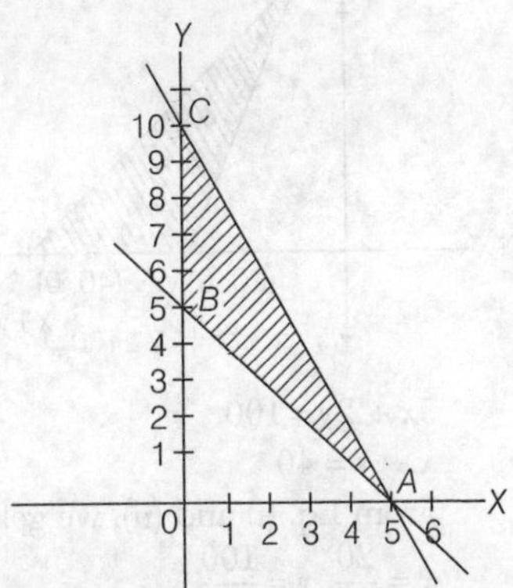

ABC is the bounded feasible region, which is triangular in shape.

11. (c) For any linear function, $Z = ax + by$, x and y are the decision variables and a, b are constants.

12. (i) (True)

The graph shows the feasible region of the given constraints.

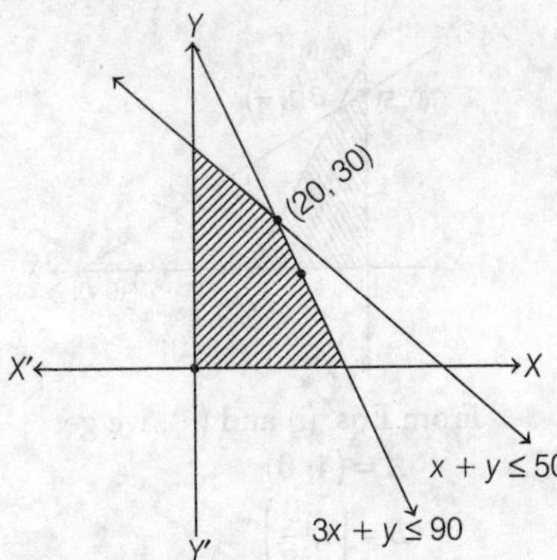

The corner points of the feasible region are (0, 50), (20, 30), (30, 0) and (0, 0).

Corner points	$Z = 4x + y$
(0, 0)	$Z = 4 \times 0 + 0 = 0$
(30, 0)	$Z = 4 \times 30 + 0 = 120$
(0, 50)	$Z = 4 \times 0 + 50 = 50$
(20, 30)	$Z = 4 \times 20 + 30 = 110$

Hence, the maximum value of Z is 120 at (30, 0).

(ii) The shaded portion in the following graph is the feasible region determined by the given system of constraints.

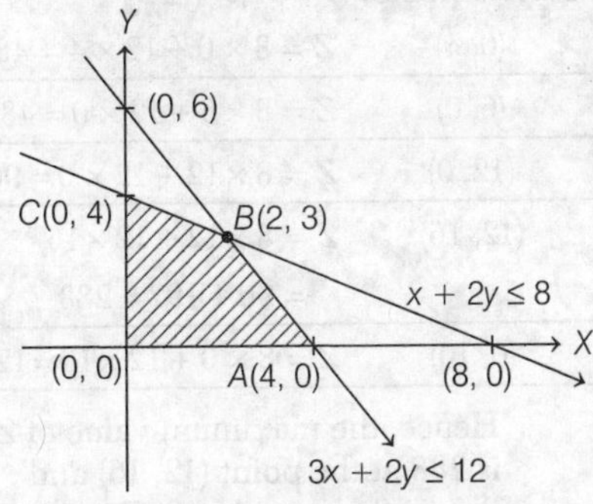

The corner points are (0, 0), (4, 0), (2, 3) and (0, 4).

Table for $Z = 5x + 7y$

Corner points	$Z = 5x + 7y$
(0, 0)	$Z = 0$
(4, 0)	$Z = 5 \times 4 = 20$
(2, 3)	$Z = 5 \times 2 + 7 \times 3 = 31$
(0, 4)	$Z = 5 \times 0 + 7 \times 4 = 28$

Therefore, the minimum value of Z is 0 and the maximum value of Z is 31.

(a) True

(b) True

(iii) (False)

The feasible region determined by the constraints is shown in the figure.

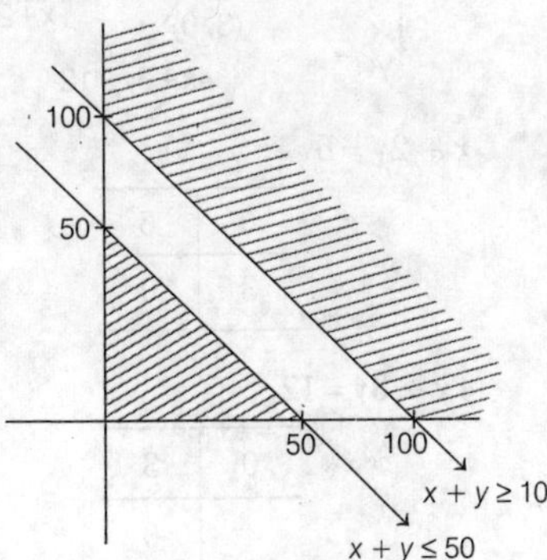

The given area is not bounded. Therefore, there would be no maximum value.

13. (i) The shaded portion in the following graph is the feasible region determined by the given system of constraints.

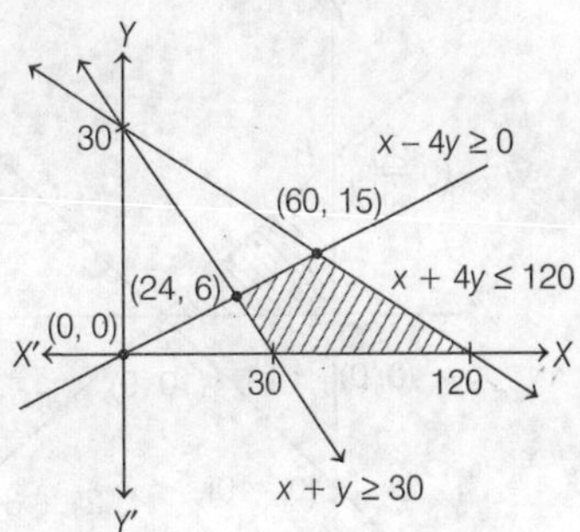

The corner points of the feasible region are (24, 6), (60, 15), (30, 0) and (120, 0).

$Z = 5x + 10y$

Z at $(24, 6) = 5 \times 24 + 10 \times 6$
$= 120 + 60 = 180$

Z at $(60, 15) = 5 \times 60 + 10 \times 15$
$= 300 + 150 = 450$

Z at $(30, 0) = 5 \times 30 = 150$

and Z at $(120, 0) = 5 \times 120 = 600$

Z is maximum at (120, 0) and the maximum value is 600.

(ii) The shaded portion in the following graph is the feasible region determined by the given system of constraints.

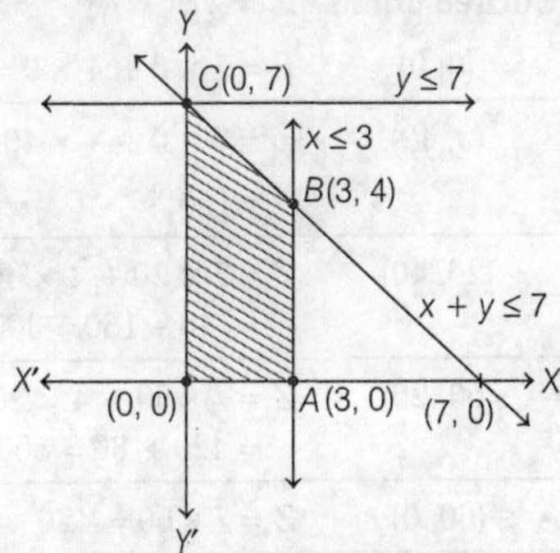

The corner points of the feasible region $OABC$ are (0, 0), (3, 0) (3, 4) and (0, 7).

$Z = 11x + 8y$

Z at $(0, 0) = 11 \times 0 + 8 \times 0 = 0$

Z at $(3, 0) = 11 \times 3 + 8 \times 0 = 33$

Z at $(3, 4) = 11 \times 3 + 8 \times 4$
$= 33 + 32 = 65$

Z at $(0, 7) = 11 \times 0 + 7 \times 8$
$= 56$

Z is maximum at (3, 4) and the maximum value is 65.

(iii) The feasible region determined by the constraints is shown in the figure.

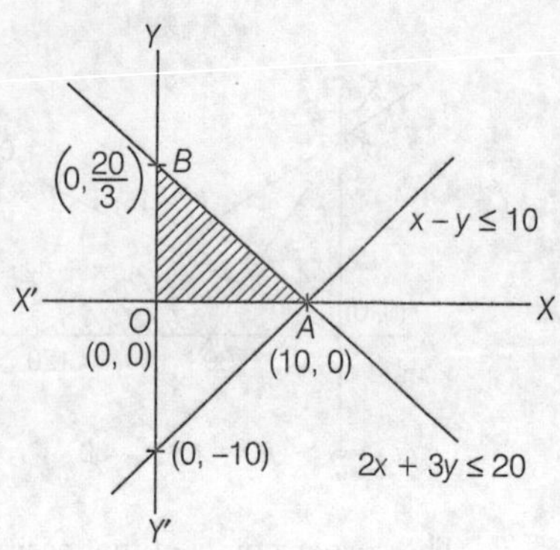

The corner points are (0, 0), (10, 0) and $\left(0, \frac{20}{3}\right)$.

Corner points	$Z = x + 2y$
(0, 0)	$Z = 0 + 0 = 0$
(10, 0)	$Z = 10 + 0 = 10$
$\left(0, \frac{20}{3}\right)$	$Z = 0 + 2 \times \frac{20}{3} = \frac{40}{3}$

Hence, the maximum value of Z is $\frac{40}{3}$ at $\left(0, \frac{20}{3}\right)$.

14. (a)

Corner points	$Z = 7x + 4y$
(0, 0)	$Z = 7 \times 0 + 4 \times 0 = 0$
(0, 40)	$Z = 7 \times 0 + 4 \times 40$ $= 160$
(20, 40)	$Z = 7 \times 20 + 4 \times 40$ $= 140 + 160 = 300$
(60, 20)	$Z = 7 \times 60 + 4 \times 20$ $= 420 + 80 = 500$
(60, 0)	$Z = 7 \times 60 = 420$

Maximum value of Z is 500.

Hence, the quantity in column I is greater.

15. (True)

Corner points	$Z = 3x - 4y$
(0, 0)	$Z = 3 \times 0 - 4 \times 0 = 0$
(0, 8)	$Z = 3 \times 0 - 4 \times 8$ $= -32$ (Minimum)
(4, 10)	$Z = 3 \times 4 - 4 \times 10$ $= 12 - 40 = -28$
(6, 8)	$Z = 3 \times 6 - 4 \times 8$ $= 18 - 32 = -14$
(5, 0)	$Z = 3 \times 5 - 4 \times 0 = 15$

Hence, the minimum value of Z occurs at (0, 8).

16. (a)

Corner points	$Z = 8x + 12y$
(0, 4)	$Z = 8 \times 0 + 12 \times 4 = 48$
(6, 0)	$Z = 8 \times 6 + 12 \times 0 = 48$
(12, 0)	$Z = 8 \times 12 + 12 \times 0 = 96$
(12, 16)	$Z = 8 \times 12 + 12 \times 16$ $= 96 + 192 = 288$
(0, 10)	$Z = 8 \times 0 + 12 \times 10 = 120$

Hence, the maximum value of Z is 288 at the point (12, 16) and the minimum value of Z is 48 at the points (0, 4) and (6, 0).

17. The maximum value occurs at 2 points (4, 5) and (5, 0).

$\Rightarrow a(4) + b(5) = a(5) + b(0)$

$\Rightarrow \quad 4a + 5b = 5a$

$\Rightarrow \quad a = 5b$

Assertion-Reason

1. (a) Given, $x + 2y \le 6$ and $4x + 3y \le 12$

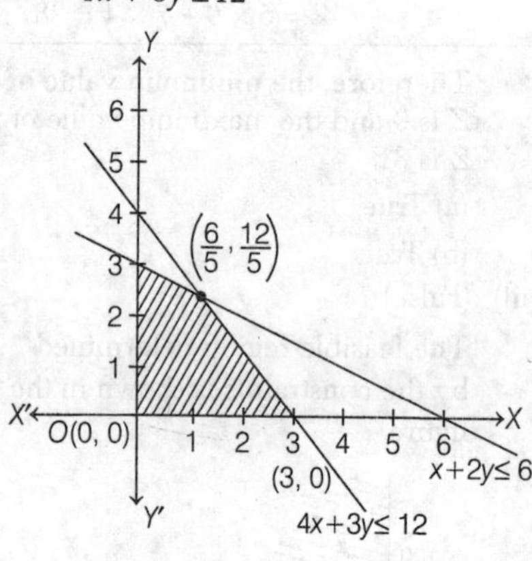

$x + 2y = 6$

x	0	6
y	3	0

$4x + 3y = 12$

x	0	3
y	4	0

$\because$ A solution that satisfies all the constraints of the problem.

$\therefore$ Assertion and Reason are true and Reason the correct explanation of Assertion.

2. (d) Given, $5x + 2y \ge 100$ and $x + y \le 40$

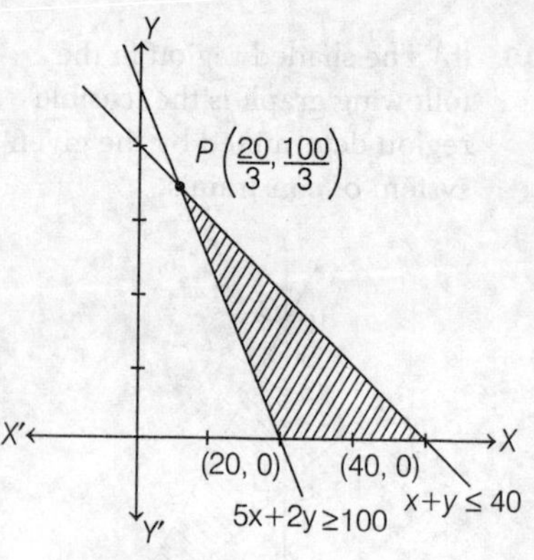

$5x + 2y = 100 \quad \ldots(i)$

$x + y = 40 \quad \ldots(ii)$

From Eq. (i) and (ii), we get

$x = \frac{20}{3}, y = \frac{100}{3}$

Feasible region for the system of inequalities is bounded.

$\therefore$ Assertion is false and Reason is true.

3. (d) Given, $x + 2y \le 10$ and $3x + 2y \le 12$

$x + 2y = 10 \quad \ldots(i)$

$3x + 2y = 12 \quad \ldots(ii)$

From Eqs. (i) and (ii), we get

$A = (4, 0)$

$B = \left(1, \frac{9}{2}\right)$

$C = (0, 5)$

When $x = 1, y = \frac{9}{2}$

$z = 2x + y$

$Z_A = 2 \times 4 + 0$

$\Rightarrow \quad Z_A = 8$

$Z_B = 2 \times 1 + \frac{9}{2}$

$\Rightarrow \quad Z_B = 6.5$

$Z_C = 2 \times 0 + 5$

$\Rightarrow \quad Z_C = 5$

Hence, the maximum value of Z is 8 at (4, 0).

$\therefore$ Assertion is false.

Reason is true.

4. (a) Given, lines $x \geq 1$ and $y \leq 2$
The feasible region for the above lines in 1st and 2nd quadrant.
$\therefore$ Assertion is true.
Reason, graph for the inequalities $x \geq 1$ and $y \leq 2$ is true.
$\therefore$ Reason true and the correct explanation of assertion.

5. (d) Given, $x + y \leq 20$, $x + y \geq 40$, $x \geq 0$, $y \geq 0$

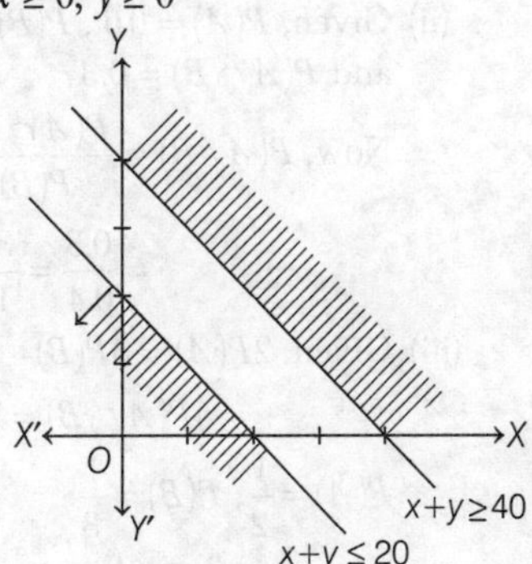

$x + y = 20$ ...(i)
$x + y = 40$ ...(ii)

In this graph, the area of a LPP is unbounded there is no feasible region. Here is the minima and maxima values of Z does not exists.
$\therefore$ Assertion is false and Reason is true.

6. (b) Given, inequalities
$x + y \leq 7$, $x + y \geq 14$, $x \geq 0$, $y \geq 0$

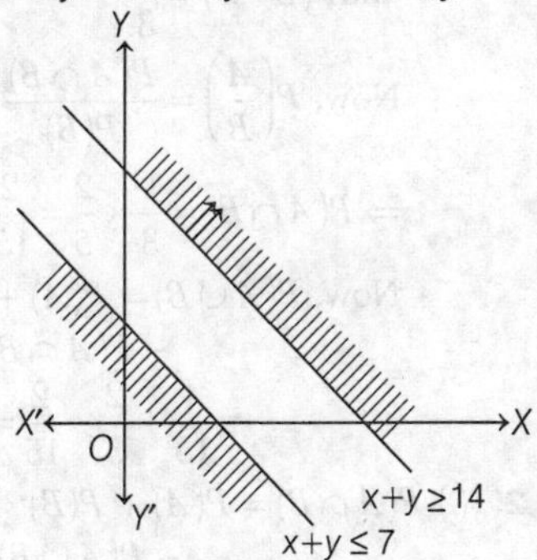

The feasible region determined by the constraints is shown in the figure.
There is no feasible region for the constraints defined in the LPP.
The given area is not bounded.
Therefore, there would be no maximum value.
$\therefore$ Assertion is true.
If the feasible region of a LPP is unbounded, then it may or may not have optional solution.

$\therefore$ Reason is true but not correct explanation of assertion.

7. (a) Given, linear inequalities
$5x + y \leq 100$, $x + y \leq 60$, $x \geq 0$, $y \geq 0$

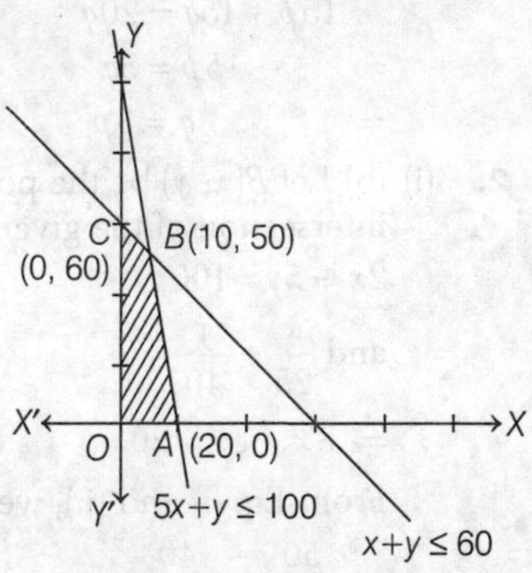

$5x + y = 100$ ...(i)
$x + y = 60$ ...(ii)

From Eqs. (i) and (ii), we get
$x = 10$, $y = 50$
$5x + y = 100$

x	20	0
y	0	100

$x + y = 60$

x	60	0
y	0	60

The shaded region in the above graph is the feasible region determined by the given system of constraints.
And the corner point of the feasible region are (10, 50), (0, 60), (20, 0) and (0, 0).
$\therefore$ Assertion is true.
and Reason is true, it is correct explanation of assertion.

8. (a) Given,
Linear inequalities $5x + 3y \leq 15$, $2x + 3y \leq 6$, $x \geq 0$, $y \geq 0$

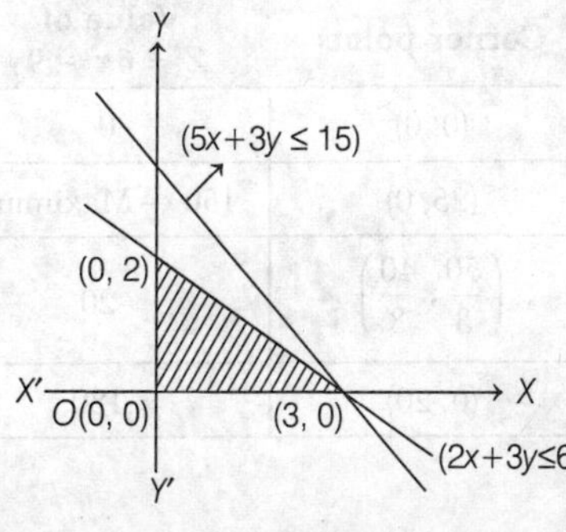

$5x + 3y = 15$

x	3	0
y	0	5

$2x + 3y = 6$

x	3	0
y	0	2

$\because$ The graph shows the feasible region of the given constraints.
$\therefore$ Assertion is true,
and the corner points of the feasible region are (0, 0), (3, 0) and (0, 2).
It is the all vertices of feasible region.
$\therefore$ Reason is true and correct explanation of assertion.

9. (d) Given, $z = x_1 + x_2$
$x_1 + x_2 \leq 1$, $3x_1 + x_2 \geq 1$

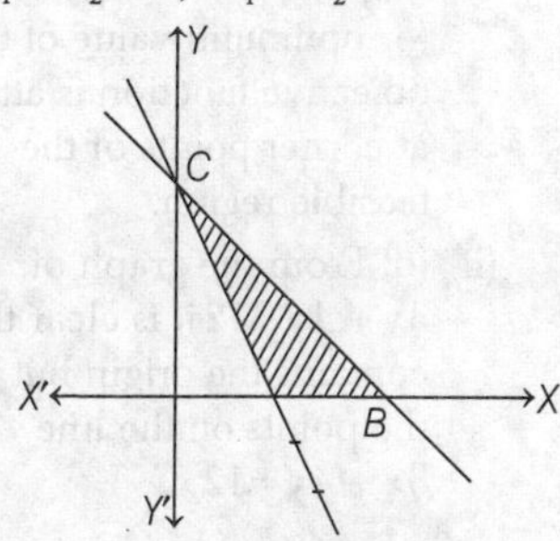

$x_1 + x_2 = 1$

x_1	0	1	–1
x_2	1	0	2

$3x_1 + x_2 = 1$

x_1	0	1	0.33
x_2	1	–2	0

Here is feasible region is ABC
$\therefore$ Assertion is false.
Now, $Z = 7x + y$,
$5x + y \leq 5$, $x + y \geq 3$, $x \geq 0$, $y \geq 0$

Corner points	$Z = 7x + y$
(3, 0)	21
$\left(\frac{1}{2}, \frac{5}{2}\right)$	6
(7, 0)	49
(0, 5)	5

Hence, maximum value of Z is 49 at (7, 0).
$\therefore$ Reason is true.

10. (a) Given, $z = 20x_1 + 20x_2$

$x_1 + 2x_2 \geq 8$

$3x_1 + 2x_2 \geq 15$

$5x_1 + 2x_2 \geq 20$

Corner points	$Z = 20x_1 + 20x_2$
(8, 0)	160
$\left(\frac{5}{2}, \frac{15}{2}\right)$	200
$\left(\frac{7}{2}, \frac{9}{4}\right)$	115
(0, 10)	200

Assertion is true and Reason is true, it is the correct explanation of Assertion.

Case Based Questions

1. (i) (c) When we solve an LPP graphically, the optimal (or optimum) value of the objective function is attained at corner points of the feasible region.

(ii) (d) From the graph of $3x + 4y < 12$ it is clear that it contains the origin but not the points on the line $3x + 4y = 12$.

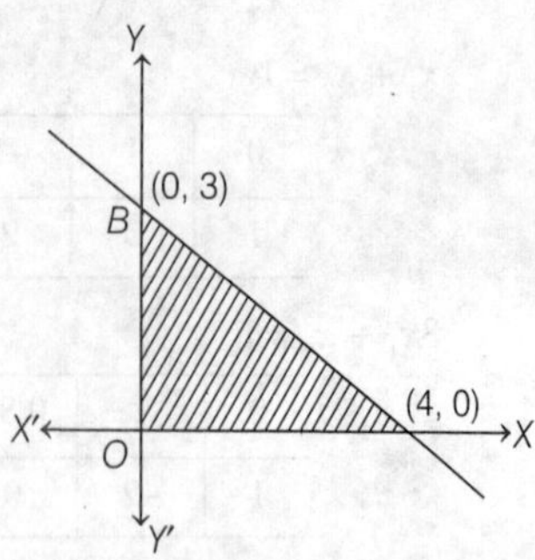

(iii) (d) Maximum of objective function occurs at corner points.

Corner points	Value of $Z = 2x + 5y$
(0, 0)	0
(7, 0)	14
(6, 3)	27
(4, 5)	33 ← Maximum
(0, 6)	30

(iv) (d) Value of $Z = px + qy$ at (15, 15) $= 15p + 15q$ and that (0, 20) $= 20q$.

According to given condition, we have

$$15p + 15q = 20q$$

$$\Rightarrow \quad 15p = 5q$$

$$\Rightarrow \quad q = 3p$$

2. (i) (b) Let $B(x, y)$ be the point of intersection of the given lines

$2x + 5y = 100$ ...(i)

and $\frac{x}{25} + \frac{y}{40} = 1$

$\Rightarrow 8x + 5y = 20$ ...(ii)

From Eq. (i) and (ii), we get

$x = \frac{50}{3}, y = \frac{40}{3}$

$\therefore$ Point of intersection

$$B(x, y) = \left(\frac{50}{3}, \frac{40}{3}\right)$$

(ii) (d) The corner points of the feasible region shown in the given graph are

$O(0, 0)$, $A(25, 0)$, $B\left(\frac{50}{3}, \frac{40}{3}\right)$, $C(0, 20)$

(iii) (a) Here, $z = x + y$

Corner points	Value of $Z = x + y$
(0, 0)	0
(25, 0)	25
$\left(\frac{50}{3}, \frac{40}{3}\right)$	30 ← Maximum
(0, 20)	20

Thus, max $Z = 30$ occurs at point $\left(\frac{50}{3}, \frac{40}{3}\right)$.

(iv) (b)

Corner points	Value of $Z = 6x - 9y$
(0, 0)	0
(25, 0)	150 ← Maximum
$\left(\frac{50}{3}, \frac{40}{3}\right)$	−20
(0, 20)	−180

Chapter-13

Probability

1. (i) $P(A/B) = \frac{P(A \cap B)}{P(B)}$

$= \frac{3/19}{11/19}$

$= \frac{3}{11}$

(ii) Given, $P(A) = 0.6$, $P(B) = 0.4$ and $P(A \cap B) = 0.3$

Now, $P(A/B) = \frac{P(A \cap B)}{P(B)}$

$= \frac{0.3}{0.4} = \frac{3}{4}$

(iii) Given, $2P(A) = 3P(B)$

$= 5P(A \cap B) = 1$

$P(A) = \frac{1}{2}, P(B) = \frac{1}{3}$

and $P(A \cap B) = \frac{1}{5}$

Now, $P(A/B) = \frac{P(A \cap B)}{P(B)}$

$= \frac{\frac{1}{5}}{\frac{1}{3}} = \frac{3}{5}$

(iv) Given, $P(A) = \frac{4}{15}$, $P(B) = \frac{2}{5}$

and $P(A/B) = \frac{1}{3}$

Now, $P\left(\frac{A}{B}\right) = \frac{P(A \cap B)}{P(B)}$

$\Rightarrow P(A \cap B) = \frac{1}{3} \times \frac{2}{5} = \frac{2}{15}$

Now, $P(A \cup B) = P(A) + P(B) - P(A \cap B)$

$= \frac{4}{15} + \frac{2}{5} - \frac{2}{15} = \frac{8}{15}$

2. (i) $P(A \cap B) = P(A) + P(B) - P(A \cup B)$

$= \frac{1}{6} + \frac{1}{2} - \frac{7}{12} = \frac{1}{12}$

(ii) $P(A/B) = \frac{P(A \cap B)}{P(B)} = \frac{1/12}{1/2}$

$= \frac{1}{12} \times 2 = \frac{1}{6}$

(iii) $P(B/A) = \frac{P(B \cap A)}{P(A)} = \frac{1/12}{1/6}$

$= \frac{1}{12} \times 6 = \frac{1}{2}$

3. (i) $E = \{HHH, HHT, THH, THT\}$

$F = \{TTH, TTT\}$

$E \cap F = \phi$

$P(E \cap F) = 0$

and $P(F) = \frac{2}{8} = \frac{1}{4}$

$\therefore P(E/F) = \frac{P(E \cap F)}{P(F)} = \frac{0}{\left(\frac{1}{4}\right)} = 0$

(ii) $E = \{HTT, THT, TTH, TTT\}$

$F = \{HHH, HTH, THH, TTH\}$

$E \cap F = \{TTH\}$

$P(E \cap F) = \frac{1}{8}$

and $P(F) = \frac{4}{8} = \frac{1}{2}$

$\therefore P(E/F) = \frac{P(E \cap F)}{P(F)} = \frac{1/8}{1/2} = \frac{2}{8} = \frac{1}{4}$

(iii) $E = \{HHT, HTH, HTT, THH, THT, TTH, TTT\}$

$F = \{HHT, HTH, HTT, THH, THT, TTH, TTT\}$

$E \cap F = \{HHT, HTH, HTT, THH, THT, TTH, TTT\}$

$P(E \cap F) = \frac{7}{8}$ and $P(F) = \frac{7}{8}$

$\therefore P(E/F) = \frac{P(E \cap F)}{P(F)} = \frac{7/8}{7/8} = 1$

4. (i) $E = \{(1, 3), (2, 3), (3, 3), (4, 3), (5, 3), (6, 3)\}$

$F = \{(2, 1), (2, 2), (2, 3), (2, 4), (2, 5), (2, 6)\}$

$E \cap F = \{(2, 3)\}$

$P(E \cap F) = \frac{1}{36}$

and $P(F) = \frac{6}{36} = \frac{1}{6}$

$\therefore P(E/F) = \frac{P(E \cap F)}{P(F)} = \frac{1/36}{1/6} = \frac{6}{36} = \frac{1}{6}$

(ii) $E = \{(1, 1), (1, 2), (1, 3), (2, 1), (2, 2), (3, 1)\}$

$F = \{(1, 1), (2, 1), (3, 1), (4, 1), (5, 1), (6, 1)\}$

$E \cap F = \{(1,1), (2,1), (3,1)\}$

$P(E \cap F) = \frac{3}{36} = \frac{1}{12}$

and $P(F) = \frac{6}{36} = \frac{1}{6}$

$\therefore P(E/F) = \frac{P(E \cap F)}{P(F)} = \frac{1/12}{1/6} = \frac{6}{12} = \frac{1}{2}$

(iii) $E = \{(1, 6), (2, 3), (3, 2), (6, 1)\}$

$F = \{(1, 6), (2, 6), (3, 6), (4, 6), (5, 6), (6, 1), (6, 2), (6, 3), (6, 4), (6, 5), (6, 6)\}$

$E \cap F = \{(1, 6), (6, 1)\}$

$P(E \cap F) = \frac{2}{36} = \frac{1}{18}$

and $P(F) = \frac{11}{36}$

$\therefore P(E/F) = \frac{P(E \cap F)}{P(F)} = \frac{1/18}{11/36} = \frac{1}{18} \times \frac{36}{11} = \frac{2}{11}$

5. (False)

$P(\bar{A}/\bar{B}) = \frac{P(\bar{A} \cap \bar{B})}{P(\bar{B})} = \frac{1 - P(A \cup B)}{P(\bar{B})}$

6. $P(A \cup B / F) = P(A/F) + P(B/F) - P((A \cap B)/F)$

If A and B are disjoint events, then $P(A \cap B) = 0$

Hence, $P(A \cup B / F) = P(A/F) + P(B/F)$

$\therefore A$ and B are disjoint events.

7. It is given that

$E = \{1, 2, 3\}$, $F = \{3, 5\}$

and $G = \{1, 2, 3, 4, 5\}$

(i) $E \cap F = \{3\}$,

$P(F) = \frac{2}{6} = \frac{1}{3}$

and $P(E \cap F) = \frac{1}{6}$

$\therefore P(E/F) = \frac{P(E \cap F)}{P(F)} = \frac{1/6}{1/3} = \frac{1}{2}$

(ii) $F \cap E = \{3\}$,

$P(E) = \frac{3}{6} = \frac{1}{2}$

and $P(F \cap E) = \frac{1}{6}$

$\therefore P(F/E) = \frac{P(F \cap E)}{P(E)} = \frac{1/6}{1/2} = \frac{1}{3}$

(iii) $E \cap G = \{1, 2, 3\}$,

$P(G) = \frac{5}{6}$

and $P(E \cap G) = \frac{3}{6} = \frac{1}{2}$

$\therefore P(E/G) = \frac{P(E \cap G)}{P(G)} = \frac{1/2}{5/6} = \frac{1}{2} \times \frac{6}{5} = \frac{3}{5}$

(iv) $G \cap E = \{1, 2, 3\}$,

$P(E) = \frac{1}{2}$

and $P(G \cap E) = \frac{1}{2}$

$\therefore P(G/E) = \frac{P(G \cap E)}{P(E)} = \frac{1/2}{1/2} = 1$

(v) $E \cup F = \{1, 2, 3, 5\}$,

$(E \cup F) \cap G = \{1, 2, 3, 5\}$,

$P(G) = \frac{5}{6}$

and $P\{(E \cup F) \cap G\} = \frac{4}{6}$

$\therefore P\{(E \cup F)/G\} = \frac{P\{(E \cup F) \cap G\}}{P(G)} = \frac{4/6}{5/6} = \frac{4}{5}$

8. Let b stand for boy and g for girl. The sample space

$S = \{(b, b), (g, b), (b, g), (g, g)\}$

Let E be the event that the second child is a girl and F be the event that first child is a girl

$P(F) = \frac{2}{4}$, $P(E \cap F) = \frac{1}{4}$

$P(E/F) = \frac{P(E \cap F)}{P(F)} = \frac{\frac{1}{4}}{\frac{2}{4}} = \frac{1}{2}$

9. Let E be the event in which all the three coins show tail and F be the event in which of the coins show tails

$F = \{HHT, HTH, THH, HTT, THT, TTH, TTT\}$

and $E = \{TTT\}$

$\therefore$ Required probability,

$$P(E/F) = \frac{P(E \cap F)}{P(F)} = \frac{1}{7}$$

10. (a) Let A be the event of getting 14 as the sum of three numbers and B be the event of getting 3 in the first throw.

Now, $n(B) = 36$

because first throw is of 3.

So, another throws stop by

$6 \times 6 = 36$ types.

In three times throw, it has only two throws, which starts from 3 and give sum 14

i.e. (3, 5, 6) and (3, 6, 5).

$n(A \cap B) = 2$

$$P(A/B) = \frac{P(A \cap B)}{P(B)} = \frac{2}{36} = \frac{1}{18}$$

11. Number of girls in class XII

$= 20\%$ of $450 = 90$

Let E be the event that a student studies in class XII and F be the event that the chosen student is a girl.

$$P(F) = \frac{450}{1200}$$

$$P(E \cap F) = \frac{90}{1200}$$

$$P(E/F) = \frac{P(E \cap F)}{P(F)}$$

$$= \frac{\frac{90}{1200}}{\frac{450}{1200}} = \frac{90}{450} = \frac{1}{5}$$

12. (c) **Statement I**

$$P(A'/B) = \frac{P(A' \cap B)}{P(B)}$$

$$= \frac{P(B) - P(A \cap B)}{P(B)}$$

$$= 1 - \frac{P(A \cap B)}{P(B)} = 1 - P(A/B)$$

Statement II

$$P(F/F) = \frac{P(F \cap F)}{P(F)}$$

$$= \frac{P(F)}{P(F)} = 1$$

Hence, both Statements are correct.

13. Let S denotes the students who go to swimming and G denotes the students who go to gym.

It is given that

$$P(S) = \frac{40}{100} = \frac{2}{5}$$

$$P(G) = \frac{60}{100} = \frac{3}{5}$$

$$P(S \cap G) = \frac{20}{100} = \frac{1}{5}$$

(i) $P(S \cup G)' = 1 - P(S \cup G)$

$= 1 - \{P(S) + P(G) - P(S \cap G)\}$

$= 1 - \left(\frac{2}{5} + \frac{3}{5} - \frac{1}{5}\right) = 1 - \frac{4}{5} = \frac{1}{5}$

(ii) $P\left(\frac{G}{S}\right) = \frac{P(S \cap G)}{P(S)}$

$= \frac{1/5}{2/5} = \frac{1}{2}$

(iii) $P\left(\frac{S}{G}\right) = \frac{P(S \cap G)}{P(G)}$

$= \frac{1/5}{3/5} = \frac{1}{3}$

14. (False)

$P(A \cap B) = P(A) + P(B) - P(A \cup B)$

$= \frac{2}{7} + \frac{5}{14} - \frac{1}{2}$

$= \frac{4 + 5 - 7}{14} = \frac{2}{14} = \frac{1}{7}$

If A and B are independent events, then

$P(A \cap B) = P(A) \times P(B)$

but $P(A) \times P(B) = \frac{2}{7} \times \frac{5}{14} = \frac{5}{49}$

$P(A \cap B) \neq P(A) \times P(B)$

Hence, A and B are dependent events.

15. Let E and F be the events that the first marble drawn is white and the second marble drawn is black respectively.

$P(E) = P$ (white marble in first draw)

$= \frac{5}{13}$

$P(F/E) = \frac{8}{12} = \frac{2}{3}$

16. (b) Let E be the event that he drinks cold drink and F be the event that he goes to the market.

$P(F) = 0.15$ and $P(E/F) = 0.90$

$P(E \cap F) = P(F)\ P(E/F)$

$= 0.15 \times 0.90 = 0.135$

17. $P(A) = \frac{13}{52} = \frac{1}{4}$

$P(B/A) = \frac{25}{51}$

$P(B \cap A) = P(A) \times P(B/A)$

$= \frac{1}{4} \times \frac{25}{51} = \frac{25}{204}$

18. (a) Let E be the event that mail is spam and F be the event that the spam filter identifies an email as spam.

$P(E) = 20\% = 0.2$

$P(F/E) = 90\% = 0.9$

$P(F/E') = 2\% = 0.02$

$P(E \cap F) = P(E)\ P(F/E)$

$= 0.2 \times 0.9$

$= 0.18$

Hence, there is 18% chance that the mail is a spam and was identified as spam.

19. P (A solve the problem) $= \frac{1}{2}$

P (B solve the problem) $= \frac{2}{3}$

P (A do not solve the problem)

$= 1 - \frac{1}{2} = \frac{1}{2}$

P (B do not solve the problem)

$= 1 - \frac{2}{3} = \frac{1}{3}$

P (A and B do not solve the problem)

$= P(A')P(B')$

$= \frac{1}{2} \times \frac{1}{3} = \frac{1}{6}$

P (Problem is solved) $= 1 - \frac{1}{6} = \frac{5}{6}$

20. (True)

P (Rahul will hit a boundary) $= \frac{2}{3}$

P (Rahul will not hit boundary)

$= 1 - \frac{2}{3} = \frac{1}{3}$

P (Rahul will not hit a boundary in next 3 balls) $= \frac{1}{3} \times \frac{1}{3} \times \frac{1}{3} = \frac{1}{27}$

P (Rahul will hit atleast one boundary in next 3 balls)

$= 1 - \frac{1}{27} = \frac{26}{27}$

21. P (A speaking the truth) $= \frac{70}{100} = \frac{7}{10}$

P (A not speaking the truth)

$= 1 - \frac{7}{10} = \frac{3}{10}$

P (B speaking the truth) $= \frac{60}{100} = \frac{3}{5}$

P (B not speaking the truth)

$= 1 - \frac{3}{5} = \frac{2}{5}$

$\therefore$ Required probability

$= P$ (A speaking the truth) $\times P$ (B not speaking the truth) $+ P$ (B speaking the truth) $\times P$ (A not speaking the truth)

$= \frac{7}{10} \times \frac{2}{5} + \frac{3}{10} \times \frac{3}{5}$

$= \frac{14}{50} + \frac{9}{50} = \frac{23}{50}$

22. (c) If A and B are independent events, then

$P(A \cap B) = P(A) \times P(B)$

$P(A \cup B) = P(A) + P(B) - P(A \cap B)$

$= P(A) + P(B) - P(A)\, P(B)$

$\therefore P(A \cup B)$

$= P(A) + P(B)\,[1 - P(A)]$

$= P(A) + P(B)\, P(A')$

$= 1 - P(A') + P(B)\, P(A')$

$= 1 - P(A')\,[1 - P(B)]$

$= 1 - P(A')\, P(B')$

23. (False)

Given, A and B are independent events

$P(A \cap B) = P(A) \cdot P(B)$

$P(A' \cap B) = P(B) - P(A \cap B)$

$= P(B) - P(A)\, P(B)$

$= P(B)\,(1 - P(A))$

$= P(B) P(A')$

Therefore, A' and B are independent events.

$P(A' \cap B')$

$= P(A \cup B)'$

$= 1 - P(A \cup B)$

$= 1 - P(A) - P(B) + P(A \cap B)$

$= 1 - P(A) - P(B) + P(A)\, P(B)$

$= 1\,(1 - P(A)) - P(B)\,[1 - P(A)]$

$= (1 - P(B))\,(1 - P(A))$

$= P(B')\, P(A')$

Therefore, A' and B' are also independent events.

24. (a) $P(E) = \frac{1}{2}$, $P(F) = \frac{1}{2}$

$P(E \cap F) = P(E) \times P(F)$

$= \frac{1}{2} \times \frac{1}{2} = \frac{1}{4}$

25. (True)

The probability that the ball falls into the basket in a single attempt $= 0.2$

The probability that the ball does not fall into the basket in a single attempt $= 1 - 0.2 = 0.8$

Given that each attempt is independent.

The probability that the ball falls into basket only in the second attempt $= 0.8 \times 0.2 = 0.16$

26. Given, $P(A) = \frac{1}{2}$ and $P(B) = \frac{3}{5}$

(i) $P(A \cap B) = P(A)\, P(B)$

[$\because$ A and B are independent events]

$= \frac{1}{2} \times \frac{3}{5} = \frac{3}{10}$

(ii) $P(A \cup B) = P(A) + P(B) - P(A \cap B)$

$= \frac{1}{2} + \frac{3}{5} - \frac{3}{10} = \frac{4}{5}$

(iii) $P(A / B) = \frac{P(A \cap B)}{P(B)}$

$= \frac{3/10}{3/5} = \frac{1}{2}$

(iv) $P(B / A) = \frac{P(A \cap B)}{P(A)}$

$= \frac{3/10}{1/2} = \frac{3}{5}$

27. (i) P (A and B) $= P(A \cap B)$

$= P(A) \cdot P(B)$

$= \frac{1}{2} \cdot \frac{1}{3} = \frac{1}{6}$

(ii) P (A and not B) $= P(A \cap B')$

$= P(A) - P(A \cap B)$

$= \frac{1}{2} - \frac{1}{6} = \frac{1}{3}$

(iii) P (A or B) $= P(A \cup B)$

$= P(A) + P(B) - P(A \cap B)$

$= \frac{1}{2} + \frac{1}{3} - \frac{1}{6} = \frac{2}{3}$

(iv) P (neither A nor B)

$= P(A' \cap B')$

$= P(A \cup B)'$

$= 1 - P(A \cup B)$

$= 1 - \frac{2}{3} = \frac{1}{3}$

28. Total number of balls $= 16$

Number of white balls $= 9$

Number of red balls $= 7$

(i) Probability of getting both the balls red $= \frac{7}{16} \times \frac{7}{16} = \frac{49}{256}$

(ii) Probability of getting first ball as white and second ball as red $= \frac{9}{16} \times \frac{7}{16} = \frac{63}{256}$

(iii) Probability that one of them is white and other is red

$= \left(\frac{9}{16} \times \frac{7}{16}\right) + \left(\frac{7}{16} \times \frac{9}{16}\right)$

$= \frac{63}{128}$

29. (i) $P(E) = \frac{13}{52} = \frac{1}{4}$

$P(F) = \frac{4}{52} = \frac{1}{13}$

$P(E \cap F) = \frac{1}{52}$

Now, $P(E) \times P(F)$

$= \frac{1}{4} \times \frac{1}{13} = \frac{1}{52}$

$= P(E \cap F)$

$\therefore$ The events E and F are independent.

(ii) $P(E) = \frac{26}{52} = \frac{1}{2}$

$P(F) = \frac{4}{52} = \frac{1}{13}$

$P(E \cap F) = \frac{2}{52} = \frac{1}{26}$

Now,

$P(E) \times P(F) = \frac{1}{2} \times \frac{1}{13} = \frac{1}{26}$

$= P(E \cap F)$

$\therefore$ The events E and F are independent.

(iii) $P(E) = \frac{8}{52} = \frac{2}{13}$

$P(F) = \frac{8}{52} = \frac{2}{13}$

There are 4 cards which are ace or king and king or jack.

$\therefore P(E \cap F) = \frac{4}{52} = \frac{1}{13}$

Now, $P(E) \times P(F) = \frac{2}{13} \times \frac{2}{13}$

$= \frac{4}{169} \neq \frac{1}{13}$

$\therefore$ The events E and F are not independent.

30. Let E_1 and E_2 be the events of selecting boys and girls respectively and A be the event of selecting a Maths student.

$$P(E_1) = P(E_2) = \frac{1}{2}$$

$$P(A/E_1) = \frac{40}{100} = \frac{2}{5}$$

$$P(A/E_2) = \frac{50}{100} = \frac{1}{2}$$

$$P(A) = P(E_1)\,P(A/E_1) + P(E_2)P(A/E_2)$$

$$= \frac{1}{2} \times \frac{2}{5} + \frac{1}{2} \times \frac{1}{2} = \frac{1}{5} + \frac{1}{4} = \frac{9}{20}$$

31. (a) Let E_1, E_2 and E_3 be the events that students P, Q and R are chosen respectively and A be the event that problem is solved.

$$P(E_1) = P(E_2) = P(E_3) = \frac{1}{3}$$

$$P(A/E_1) = \frac{1}{2}$$

$$P(A/E_2) = \frac{1}{3}$$

$$P(A/E_3) = \frac{2}{3}$$

$$P(A) = \sum_{i=1}^{3} P(E_i)P(A/E_i)$$

$$= \frac{1}{3} \times \frac{1}{2} + \frac{1}{3} \times \frac{1}{3} + \frac{1}{3} \times \frac{2}{3}$$

$$= \frac{1}{6} + \frac{1}{9} + \frac{2}{9}$$

$$= \frac{3+2+4}{18} = \frac{1}{2}$$

32. Let E_1 and E_2 be the events of choosing a machine I and II respectively and A be the event that a machine produced a defective item.

$$P(E_1) = \frac{50}{100} = \frac{1}{2}$$

$$P(E_2) = \frac{30}{100} = \frac{3}{10}$$

$$P(A/E_1) = \frac{2}{100} = \frac{1}{50}$$

$$P(A/E_2) = \frac{3}{100}$$

$$P(A) = P(E_1)P(A/E_1) + P(E_2)P(A/E_2)$$

$$= \frac{1}{2} \times \frac{1}{50} + \frac{3}{10} \times \frac{3}{100}$$

$$= \frac{1}{100} + \frac{9}{1000} = \frac{19}{1000}$$

$$= 0.019 \text{ or } 1.9\%$$

33. Let E_1 be the event of choosing bag I and E_2 be the event of choosing bag II and A be the event of choosing white ball

$$P(E_1) = P(E_2) = \frac{1}{2}$$

$$P(A/E_1) = \frac{4}{10},\ P(A/E_2) = \frac{4}{9}$$

$$P(E_1/A) = \frac{P(E_1)\,P(A/E_1)}{P(E_1)\,P(A/E_1) + P(E_2)\,P(A/E_2)}$$

$$= \frac{\frac{1}{2} \times \frac{4}{10}}{\frac{1}{2} \times \frac{4}{10} + \frac{1}{2} \times \frac{4}{9}}$$

$$= \frac{\frac{1}{5}}{\frac{1}{5} + \frac{2}{9}} = \frac{1/5}{19/45} = \frac{9}{19}$$

34. Let E_1 be the event that he gets head, E_2 be the event that he gets tail and A be the event that he reports head after tossing the coins.

$$P(E_1) = P(E_2) = \frac{1}{2}$$

$$P(A/E_1) = \frac{3}{4}$$

$$P(A/E_2) = \frac{1}{4}$$

$$P(E_1/A) = \frac{P(E_1)\,P(A/E_1)}{P(E_1)P(A/E_1) + P(E_2)P(A/E_2)}$$

$$= \frac{\frac{1}{2} \times \frac{3}{4}}{\frac{1}{2} \times \frac{3}{4} + \frac{1}{2} \times \frac{1}{4}}$$

$$= \frac{3}{3+1} = \frac{3}{4}$$

35. (b) Let E_1 be the events that the insured person is a light vehicle driver, E_2 be the event that the insured person is a medium vehicle driver and E_3 be the event that the insured person is a heavy vehicle driver and A be the event that the insured person met with an accident.

$$P(E_1) = \frac{1000}{6000} = \frac{1}{6}$$

$$P(E_2) = \frac{2000}{6000} = \frac{1}{3}$$

$$P(E_3) = \frac{3000}{6000} = \frac{1}{2}$$

$$P(A/E_1) = 0.01$$

$$P(A/E_2) = 0.02$$

$$P(A/E_3) = 0.25$$

$$P(E_3/A) = \frac{P(E_3)\,P(A/E_3)}{P(E_1)\,P(A/E_1) + P(E_2)P(A/E_2) + P(E_3)P(A/E_3)}$$

$$= \frac{\frac{1}{2} \times 0.25}{\frac{1}{6} \times 0.01 + \frac{1}{3} \times 0.02 + \frac{1}{2} \times 0.25}$$

$$= \frac{\frac{25}{2}}{\frac{1}{6} + \frac{2}{3} + \frac{25}{2}} = \frac{25}{\frac{1}{3} + \frac{4}{3} + 25}$$

$$= \frac{25 \times 3}{1+4+75} = \frac{75}{80} = \frac{15}{16}$$

36. Let E_1 be the event that he knows the answer, E_2 be the event that he does not know the answer and A be the event that he gets the correct answer.

$$P(E_1) = 80\% = \frac{80}{100} = \frac{4}{5}$$

$$P(E_2) = 1 - \frac{4}{5} = \frac{1}{5}$$

$$P(A/E_1) = 1$$

$$P(A/E_2) = \frac{1}{4}$$

$$P(E_2/A) = \frac{P(E_2)\,P(A/E_2)}{P(E_1)P(A/E_1) + P(E_2)\,P(A/E_2)}$$

$$= \frac{\frac{1}{5} \times \frac{1}{4}}{\frac{4}{5} \times 1 + \frac{1}{5} \times \frac{1}{4}}$$

$$= \frac{\frac{1}{20}}{\frac{4}{5} + \frac{1}{20}} = \frac{1}{20} \times \frac{20}{17} = \frac{1}{17}$$

37. Let E_1 be the event that both A and B speak truth, E_2 be the event that both A and B speak lie and E_3 be the event that both agrees.

$$P(E_1) = ab$$

$$P(E_2) = (1-a)(1-b)$$

$$P(E_3/E_1) = P(E_3/E_2) = 1$$

$$P(E_1/E_3) = \frac{P(E_1)\,P(E_3/E_1)}{P(E_1)\,P(E_3/E_1) + P(E_2)\,P(E_3/E_2)}$$

$$= \frac{ab}{ab + (1-a)(1-b)}$$

$$= \frac{ab}{2ab + 1 - (a+b)}$$

38. (c) Let E_1, E_2 and E_3 be the respective events of choosing a two-headed coin, fair coin and biased coin and A be the event that shows tail

$$P(E_1) = P(E_2) = P(E_3) = \frac{1}{3}$$

$$P(A/E_1) = 0$$

$$P(A/E_2) = \frac{1}{2}$$

$$P(A/E_3) = \frac{30}{100} = \frac{3}{10}$$

$$P(E_3/A) = \frac{P(E_3)P(A/E_3)}{P(E_1)\,P(A/E_1) + P(E_2)\,P(A/E_2) + P(E_3)P(A/E_3)}$$

$$= \frac{\frac{1}{3}\times\frac{3}{10}}{\frac{1}{3}\times 0 + \frac{1}{3}\times\frac{1}{2} + \frac{1}{3}\times\frac{3}{10}}$$

$$= \frac{\frac{1}{10}}{0 + \frac{1}{6} + \frac{1}{10}}$$

$$= \frac{1/10}{16/60}$$

$$= \frac{6}{16} = \frac{3}{8}$$

39. (True)

Let E_1, E_2 be the events of picking a prime and non-prime number respectively and A be the event that a man reports that it is a prime number.

$$P(E_1) = \frac{4}{10} = \frac{2}{5}$$

$$P(E_2) = \frac{3}{5}$$

$$P(A/E_1) = \frac{2}{3}$$

$$P(A/E_2) = \frac{1}{3}$$

$$P(E_1/A) = \frac{P(A/E_1)P(E_1)}{P(A/E_1)P(E_1) + P(A/E_2)P(E_2)}$$

$$= \frac{\frac{2}{3}\times\frac{2}{5}}{\frac{2}{3}\times\frac{2}{5} + \frac{1}{3}\times\frac{3}{5}}$$

$$= \frac{4}{4+3} = \frac{4}{7}$$

40. Let events E_1, E_2, E_3 be the following

E_1 : The bulb is of type X

E_2 : The bulb is of type Y

E_3 : The bulb is of type Z.

$$P(E_1) = 0.25$$

$$P(E_2) = 0.45$$

$$P(E_3) = 0.30$$

Let A be the event that bulb is defective

$$P(A/E_1) = 0.05$$

$$P(A/E_2) = 0.03$$

$$P(A/E_3) = 0.02$$

$$P(E_3/A) = \frac{P(A/E_3)P(E_3)}{P(E_1)\,P(A/E_1) + P(E_2)\,P(A/E_2) + P(E_3)P(A/E_3)}$$

$$= \frac{0.02\times 0.30}{0.25\times 0.05 + 0.45\times 0.03 + 0.30\times 0.02}$$

$$= \frac{60}{125+135+60}$$

$$= \frac{60}{320} = \frac{6}{32} = \frac{3}{16}$$

Assertion-Reason

1. (a) Assertion and Reason both are correct and reason is the correct explanation of Assertion.

2. (b) Assertion (A) is correct.

$$P(A\,|\,\overline{B}) = \frac{P(A\cap\overline{B})}{P(\overline{B})}$$

$$P(A\,|\,\overline{B}) = \frac{P(A)}{P(\overline{B})}$$

[Since, given A and B are two mutually exclusive events]

$$P\left(\frac{A}{\overline{B}}\right) = \frac{\left(1-\frac{5}{6}\right)}{\left(1-\frac{1}{3}\right)}$$

$$= \frac{\frac{1}{6}}{\frac{2}{3}}$$

$$= \frac{1}{4}$$

Reason is also correct

For independent events,

$$P(A\,|\,\overline{B}) = P(A)$$

$$= 0.2$$

3. (a) Assertion and Reason both are correct and Reason is the correct explanation of Assertion.

4. (c) Assertion is correct.

$A \subset B$ and $B \subset A \Rightarrow A = B$

Hence, $P(A) = P(B)$

But Reason is wrong.

$A \subset B \Rightarrow \overline{B} \subset \overline{A}$

Therefore, $P(\overline{A}) \geq P(\overline{B})$

5. (d) Assertion is wrong.

If the probability of an event is 0, then it is called as an impossible event.

But Reason is correct.

From Basic Theorem of Probability,

$P(B - A) = P(B) - P(A)$, this is true only if the condition given in the question is true.

6. (a) Assertion and Reason both are correct and Reason is the correct explanation of Assertion.

7. (a) Let E_1 = event of choosing bag (i) and E_2 the event of choosing the bag (ii) and A be the event of drawing red ball

$$\therefore P(E_1) = P(E_2) = \frac{1}{2}$$

$$\therefore P\left(\frac{A}{E_1}\right) = \frac{3}{7},\ P\left(\frac{A}{E_2}\right) = \frac{5}{7}$$

$$\therefore P\left(\frac{E_2}{A}\right) = \frac{P(E_2)P\left(\frac{A}{E_2}\right)}{P(A)}$$

$$= \frac{\frac{1}{2}\times\frac{5}{11}}{\frac{1}{2}\times\frac{3}{7} + \frac{1}{2}\times\frac{5}{11}} = \frac{35}{68}$$

8. (a) Two coins are tossed simultaneously. Sample space i.e. possible outcomes are

{HT, TH, HH, TT}

E = Event of getting two heads

F = Event of getting at least one head

$$P(E) = \frac{1}{4},\ P(F) = \frac{3}{4},$$

$$P(E\cap F) = \frac{1}{4}$$

$$P\left(\frac{E}{F}\right) = \frac{P(E\cap F)}{P(F)}$$

$$= \frac{\left(\frac{1}{4}\right)}{\left(\frac{3}{4}\right)}$$

$$= \frac{1}{3}$$

Case Based Questions

1. Here, sample space

$= \{1,2,3,4,5,6\}, A \cap B = \{2\}$

$B \cap C = \{2, 5\}, A \cap C = \{1,2\},$

$A \cap B \cap C = \{2\}$

and $\{A \cup B\} \cap C = \{1,2,5\}$

Also, $P(A) = \frac{2}{6}, P(B) = \frac{3}{6},$

$P(C) = \frac{3}{6}$

$P(A \cap B) = \frac{1}{6}, P(B \cap C) = \frac{2}{6},$

$P(A \cap C) = \frac{2}{6},$

$P(A \cap B \cap C) = \frac{1}{6}$ and

$P((A \cup B) \cap C) = \frac{3}{6}$

(i) (b) : $P(A \mid B) = \frac{P(A \cap B)}{P(B)}$

$= \frac{\frac{1}{6}}{\frac{3}{6}} = \frac{1}{3}$

(ii) (a) : $P(B \mid C) = \frac{P(B \cap C)}{P(C)}$

$= \frac{\frac{2}{6}}{\frac{3}{6}} = \frac{2}{3}$

(iii) (d) :

$P(A \cap B \mid C) = \frac{P(A \cap B \cap C)}{P(C)}$

$= \frac{\frac{1}{6}}{\frac{3}{6}} = \frac{1}{3}$

(iv) (c) : $P(A \mid C) = \frac{P(A \cap C)}{P(C)}$

$= \frac{\frac{2}{6}}{\frac{3}{6}} = \frac{2}{3}$

(v) (d) : $P(A \cup B \mid C)$

$= \frac{P((A \cup B) \cap C)}{P(C)} = \frac{\frac{3}{6}}{\frac{3}{6}} = 1$

2. (i) (b) Required probability

$= \frac{{}^{11}C_2}{{}^{50}C_2}$

$= \frac{11 \times 10}{50 \times 49} = \frac{11}{245}$

(ii) (a) Required probability

$\frac{{}^{13}C_2}{{}^{50}C_2} = \frac{13 \times 12}{50 \times 49} = \frac{78}{245}$

(iii) (b) Clearly,

$P(A \mid E_1) = \frac{{}^{11}C_2}{{}^{50}C_2}$

$= \frac{11 \times 10}{50 \times 49} = \frac{11}{245}$

$P(A \mid E_2) = \frac{78}{245}$

$P(A \mid E_3) = P(A \mid E_4) = \frac{78}{245}$

$\therefore \sum_{i=1}^{4} P(A \mid E_i)$

$= \frac{11}{245} + \frac{78}{245} + \frac{78}{245} + \frac{78}{245} = 1$

(iv) (b) P(getting both king)

$= \frac{{}^{4}C_2}{{}^{52}C_2} = \frac{4 \times 3}{52 \times 51} = \frac{1}{221}$

(v) (a) P(drawing a king)

$= \frac{4}{52} = \frac{1}{13}$

$\therefore P$ (not drawing a king)

$= 1 - \frac{1}{13} = \frac{12}{13}$

$\therefore$ Required probability

$= \frac{12}{13} \times \frac{12}{13} = \frac{144}{169}$

Competition Connect

1. (i) (No)

All the probabilities must be positive.

$\because P(3) = -0.1$

$\therefore$ It is not the probability distribution of a random variable.

(ii) (Yes)

The sum of the probabilities should be 1.

$\because 0.3 + 0.4 + 0.3 = 1$

$\therefore$ It is the probability distribution of a random variable.

(iii) (Yes)

The sum of probabilities should be 1.

$\because 0.3 + 0.2 + 0.2 + 0.3 = 1$

$\therefore$ It is the probability distribution of a random variable.

(iv) (Yes)

The sum of probabilities should be 1.

$\because 0.2 + 0.3 + 0.4 + 0.1 + 0 = 1$

$\therefore$ It is the probability distribution of a random variable.

(v) (No)

The sum of probabilities should be 1.

Now, $0.3 + 0.5 + 0.4 = 1.2 \neq 1$

$\therefore$ It is not the probability distribution of a random variable.

2. (True)

If X denotes the number of days in a month, then

$X = \{28, 29, 30, 31\}$

X takes the finite value so it is a discrete random variable.

3. Let the marbles in the bags be denoted by $\{b_1, g_1, g_2\}$, then the sample space,

$S = \{b_1g_1, b_1g_2, b_1b_1, g_1b_1, g_1g_1, g_1g_2, g_2b_1, g_2g_1, g_2g_2\}$

Here, $W \in S$

$X(W)$ = Number of black marbles

$X(g_1g_1, g_1g_2, g_2g_1, g_2g_2) = 0$

$X(g_1b_1, g_2b_1, b_1g_1, b_1g_2) = 1$

$X(b_1b_2) = 2$

Hence, X is a random variable which takes values 0, 1 or 2.

4. $P(X) = P(X = 0) + P(X = 1) + P(X = 2) + P(X = 3)$

$1 = 0 + \frac{1}{4} + \frac{1}{4} + P(X = 3)$

$P(X = 3) = 1 - \frac{1}{2}$

$= \frac{1}{2}$

5. (c) As the sum of probabilities of all the random variable is 1.

$\therefore P(X = 0) + P(X = 1) + P(X = 2) + P(X = 3) = 1$

$\Rightarrow 0 + K + 2K + 3K = 1$

$\Rightarrow \quad 6K = 1$

$\therefore \quad K = \frac{1}{6}$

6. (i) The number of kings is a random variables. Let it be denoted by X. X can take the value 0, 1 or 2.

$P(X = 0) = P$ (Non-King and Non-King)

$= \frac{48}{52} \times \frac{48}{52}$

$= \frac{12}{13} \times \frac{12}{13}$

$= \frac{144}{169}$

$P(X=1) = P$ (King and Non-King or Non-King and King)

$= P$ (King) P (Non-King) $+ P$ (Non-King) P (King)

$= \frac{4}{52} \times \frac{48}{52} + \frac{48}{52} \times \frac{4}{52}$

$= \frac{1}{13} \times \frac{12}{13} + \frac{12}{13} \times \frac{1}{13} = \frac{24}{169}$

$P(X=2) = P$ (King) P (King)

$= \frac{4}{52} \times \frac{4}{52} = \frac{1}{13} \times \frac{1}{13} = \frac{1}{169}$

X	0	1	2
$P(X)$	$\frac{144}{169}$	$\frac{24}{169}$	$\frac{1}{169}$

(ii) The number of jack is a random variable. Let it be denoted by X. X can take the value 0, 1 or 2.

$P(X=0) = \frac{48}{52} \times \frac{48}{52} = \frac{144}{169}$

$P(X=1) = \left(\frac{1}{13} \times \frac{12}{13}\right) + \left(\frac{12}{13} \times \frac{1}{13}\right)$

$= \frac{24}{169}$

$P(X=2) = \frac{1}{13} \times \frac{1}{13} = \frac{1}{169}$

X	0	1	2
$P(X)$	$\frac{144}{169}$	$\frac{24}{169}$	$\frac{1}{169}$

(iii) The number of spade is a random variable. Let it be denoted by X. X can take the value 0, 1 or 2.

$P(X=0) = \frac{39}{52} \times \frac{39}{52} = \frac{9}{16}$

$P(X=1) = \left(\frac{13}{52} \times \frac{39}{52}\right) + \left(\frac{39}{52} \times \frac{13}{52}\right)$

$= \frac{3}{8}$

$P(X=2) = \frac{13}{52} \times \frac{13}{52} = \frac{1}{16}$

X	0	1	2
$P(X)$	$\frac{9}{16}$	$\frac{3}{8}$	$\frac{1}{16}$

7. (c) Let X be the number of diamond cards

$P(X=0) = P$ (non-diamond and non-diamond)

$= P$ (non-diamond) $\times P$ (non-diamond)

$= \frac{39}{52} \times \frac{39}{52}$

$K_1 = \frac{9}{16}$

$P(X=1) = P$ (diamond and non-diamond or non-diamond and diamond)

$= P$ (diamond) P (non-diamond) $+ P$ (non-diamond) P (diamond)

$= \frac{13}{52} \times \frac{39}{52} + \frac{39}{52} \times \frac{13}{52}$

$K_2 = \frac{3}{8}$

$P(X=2) = P$ (diamond and diamond)

$= P$ (diamond) $\times P$ (diamond)

$K_3 = \frac{13}{52} \times \frac{13}{52} = \frac{1}{16}$

8. (True)

Let X be the random variable which denotes a prime number on atleast one die in two tosses of a die.

X may take value 0, 1 or 2.

$P(X=0) =$ Probability of a non-prime number on both tosses

$= \frac{3}{6} \times \frac{3}{6} = \frac{1}{4}$

$P(X=1) =$ Probability of one prime number on one toss and a non-prime number on another toss

$= \frac{3}{6} \times \frac{3}{6} + \frac{3}{6} \times \frac{3}{6}$

$= \frac{1}{2}$

$P(X=2) =$ Probability of a prime number on both die

$= \frac{3}{6} \times \frac{3}{6} = \frac{1}{4}$

Hence, the probability distribution is

X	0	1	2
$P(X)$	1/4	1/2	1/4

9. (i) It is known that the sum of probabilities of a probability distribution of random variables is one.

$\therefore K + 2K + 3K + 4K^2 + K + 6K^2 + 2K = 1$

$\Rightarrow 10K^2 + 9K - 1 = 0$

$\Rightarrow (10K-1)(K+1) = 0$

$\Rightarrow K = -1, \frac{1}{10}$

$K = -1$ is not possible.

$\therefore K = \frac{1}{10}$

(ii) $P(X<3) = P(X=0) + P(X=1) + P(X=2)$

$= K + 2K + 3K = 6K$

$= \frac{6}{10} = \frac{3}{5}$

(iii) $P(X>3) = P(X=4) + P(X=5) = 6K^2 + 2K$

$= \frac{6}{100} + \frac{2}{10} = \frac{13}{50}$

(iv) $P(0<X<4) = P(X=1) + P(X=2) + P(X=3)$

$= 2K + 3K + 4K^2 + K$

$= 4K^2 + 6K$

$= \frac{4}{100} + \frac{6}{10} = \frac{16}{25}$

10. (True)

Let X denotes a random variable of "number of 6" in three tosses of a die.

Then, $X = 0, 1, 2, 3$

$P(X=0) = P$ (no six)

$= \frac{5}{6} \times \frac{5}{6} \times \frac{5}{6} = \frac{125}{216}$

$P(X=1) = P$ (1 six and 2 non-six)

$= \frac{1}{6} \times \frac{5}{6} \times \frac{5}{6} + \frac{5}{6} \times \frac{1}{6} \times \frac{5}{6} + \frac{5}{6} \times \frac{5}{6} \times \frac{1}{6}$

$= \frac{75}{216}$

$P(X=2) = P$ (2 six and 1 non-six)

$= \frac{1}{6} \times \frac{1}{6} \times \frac{5}{6} + \frac{1}{6} \times \frac{5}{6} \times \frac{1}{6} + \frac{5}{6} \times \frac{1}{6} \times \frac{1}{6}$

$= \frac{15}{216}$

$P(X=3) = P$ (3 sixes)

$= \frac{1}{6} \times \frac{1}{6} \times \frac{1}{6}$

$= \frac{1}{216}$

The probability distribution is

X	0	1	2	3
$P(X)$	$\frac{125}{216}$	$\frac{75}{216}$	$\frac{15}{216}$	$\frac{1}{216}$

Mean $= \Sigma x_i p_i$

$= 0 \times \frac{125}{216} + 1 \times \frac{75}{216} + 2 \times \frac{15}{216} + 3 \times \frac{1}{216}$

$= \frac{1}{2}$

11. (i) Let X be a random variable of 'number of tails', then

$X = 0, 1, 2, 3$

$P(X=0) = P$ (no tail)

$= \frac{1}{2} \times \frac{1}{2} \times \frac{1}{2}$

$= \frac{1}{8}$

$P(X=1) = P$(1 tail and 2 head)

$= P(THH) + P(HTH) + P(HHT)$

$= \frac{1}{2} \times \frac{1}{2} \times \frac{1}{2} + \frac{1}{2} \times \frac{1}{2} \times \frac{1}{2} + \frac{1}{2} \times \frac{1}{2} \times \frac{1}{2}$

$= \frac{3}{8}$

$P(X=2) = P$ (2 tail and 1 head)

$= P(TTH) + P(THT) + P(HTT)$

$= \frac{1}{2} \times \frac{1}{2} \times \frac{1}{2} + \frac{1}{2} \times \frac{1}{2} \times \frac{1}{2} + \frac{1}{2} \times \frac{1}{2} \times \frac{1}{2}$

$= \frac{3}{8}$

$P(X=3) = P$ (all tails)

$= \frac{1}{2} \times \frac{1}{2} \times \frac{1}{2} = \frac{1}{8}$

The probability distribution table is

X	0	1	2	3
$P(X)$	$\frac{1}{8}$	$\frac{3}{8}$	$\frac{3}{8}$	$\frac{1}{8}$

$E(X) = \Sigma x_i p_i$

$= 0 \times \frac{1}{8} + 1 \times \frac{3}{8} + 2 \times \frac{3}{8} + 3 \times \frac{1}{8} = \frac{3}{2}$

$E(X^2) = \Sigma x_i^2 p_i$

$= 0 \times \frac{1}{8} + 1 \times \frac{3}{8} + 4 \times \frac{3}{8} + 9 \times \frac{1}{8} = 3$

$\sigma^2 = E(X^2) - [E(X)]^2$

$= 3 - \left(\frac{3}{2}\right)^2 = \frac{3}{4}$

(ii) Let X be a random variable of a composite number of throwing two dice simultaneously, X can be 0, 1, 2.

$P(X=0) = P$ (Both non-composite number)

$= \frac{4}{6} \times \frac{4}{6}$

$= \frac{4}{9}$

$P(X=1) = P$ (1 composite and 1 non-composite number)

$= \frac{4}{6} \times \frac{2}{6} + \frac{2}{6} \times \frac{4}{6}$

$= \frac{4}{9}$

$P(X=2) = P$ (both composite number)

$= \frac{2}{6} \times \frac{2}{6} = \frac{1}{9}$

$E(X) = \Sigma x_i p_i$

$= 0 \times \frac{4}{9} + 1 \times \frac{4}{9} + 2 \times \frac{1}{9}$

$= \frac{2}{3}$

$E(X^2) = 0 \times \frac{4}{9} + 1 \times \frac{4}{9} + 4 \times \frac{1}{9}$

$= \frac{8}{9}$

$\sigma^2 = E(X^2) - [E(X)]^2$

$= \frac{4}{9}$

12. (True)

$E(X) = \Sigma x_i p_i$

$= 1 \times 0.3 + 2 \times 0.4 + 3 \times 0.3$

$= 0.3 + 0.8 + 0.9$

$= 2$

$E(X^2) = \Sigma x_i^2 p_i$

$= 1 \times 0.3 + 4 \times 0.4 + 9 \times 0.3$

$= 0.3 + 1.6 + 2.7$

$= 4.6$

$\sigma^2 = E(X^2) - [E(X)]^2$

$= 4.6 - (2)^2$

$= 4.6 - 4 = 0.6$

13. (d) The probability distribution table is

X	0	1	2	3
$P(X)$	$\frac{1}{4}$	$\frac{1}{4}$	$\frac{3}{16}$	$\frac{5}{16}$

Mean $= E(X) = \Sigma x_i p_i$

$= 0 \times \frac{1}{4} + 1 \times \frac{1}{4} + 2 \times \frac{3}{16} + 3 \times \frac{5}{16}$

$= \frac{25}{16}$

$E(X^2) = 0 \times \frac{1}{4} + 1 \times \frac{1}{4} + 4 \times \frac{3}{16} + 9 \times \frac{5}{16}$

$= \frac{61}{16}$

Variance $= E(X^2) - [E(X)]^2$

$= \frac{351}{256}$